Contents at a Glance

KU-221-252

Contents

About the Authors

 **Alex Homer** is a computer geek and Web developer with a passion for ASP.NET. Although he has to spend some time doing real work (a bit of consultancy and training and the occasional conference session), most of his days are absorbed in playing with the latest Microsoft Web technology and then writing about it. Living in the picturesque wilderness of the Derbyshire Dales in England, he's well away from the demands of the real world—with only an Internet connection to maintain some distant representation of normality. But, hey, what else could you want from life?

You can contact Alex through his own software company, Stonebroom Limited, at alex@stonebroom.com.

 **Dave Sussman** is a hacker in the traditional sense of the word. That's someone who likes playing with code and figuring out how things work, which is why he spends much of his life working with beta software. Luckily, this coincides with writing about new technologies, giving him an output for his poor English and grammar. He lives in a small village in the Oxfordshire countryside. Like many programmers everywhere, he has an expensive hi-fi, a big TV, and no life.

You can contact Dave through his own company, ipona Limited, at davids@ipona.co.uk.

Introduction

ASP.NET IS A HUGE ADVANCE from previous incarnations of ASP, with one of its goals being pure HTML output that achieves maximum cross-browser compatibility. The server-side event architecture tends to engender this approach, but amid the first flush of excitement it's often forgotten that there's still a place for rich clients and handling data in a multitude of places. Distributed data-driven applications aren't new, but the range of possibilities and ease of development have both increased with the introduction of .NET.

This book approaches data management and data applications from several different points of view:

- Understanding the new .NET data management philosophy for both relational and XML data

- Grasping the different techniques that it encompasses and how they relate to real-world requirements

- Exploring the application architecture and design implications of the .NET data management classes

- Designing distributed data-driven ASP.NET applications that benefit from the new data management techniques

- Examining the rich-client philosophy and how .NET can be used to bring this about

- Demonstrating how easy it is to take advantage of several different types of client device, providing the best user experience possible for each one

Many books describe the basic techniques for working with data in ASP.NET. However, this book goes not just a step further but in fact takes you on a complete journey by exploring how to provide the user with the best possible client-side experience when working with data. It also focuses on the server-side design and development process, such as using the *n*-tier architecture in your applications, and specific techniques such as correctly managing updates to a data store by multiple concurrent users.

In this book, we assume a basic grasp of ASP.NET and the general data access techniques that the .NET Framework makes available (although we do provide some grounding to reinforce the important aspects). Where this book really is different, however, is that it's wholly aimed at seeing how you can actually build useful, interactive, and efficient distributed applications.

What This Book Is

This book is all of the following:

- It's a voyage of exploration through almost all aspects of building ASP.NET applications that handle data and work across the Internet (or other HTTP networks such as an intranet).

- It's a practical approach to building task-specific components, Web pages, and Web applications based on a server running ASP.NET.

- It's a demonstration of what's possible with ASP.NET, without requiring special expertise, long development times, or complex third-party components.

- It's focused on *n*-tier architecture design and the way it can be coded, using SQL Server as a data source and simple Web server hardware.

- It's clearly divided into chapters and sections that cover all the relevant theory and practice for the different parts of the sample application that's developed throughout the entire book.

- It's a source of useful techniques and snippets of code that can be reused in your own applications.

- It's written using mainly Visual Basic .NET (VB .NET) for the code listings. However, C# versions of the samples are available for download as well as VB .NET versions.

- A useful and enjoyable read (we hope).

What This Book Isn't

This book is none of the following:

- It's not an academic text or a theory-oriented book. We describe the workings of the application in down-to-earth language, use technical terms only where necessary, and try to avoid any off-topic discussion and irrelevancies.

- It's not a reference book in the sense that techniques we use are described where they fit into the application rather than as alphabetically organized tables.

- It's not a book about hardware performance, server optimization, or software security. We'll attempt to show how you can get the best performance from your systems when designing applications, but we won't be delving into these other areas.

- It's not a book about SQL programming, data storage theory, or complex back-end systems. The techniques we use are designed to be easily translatable to any back-end system that ASP.NET can access.

- It's not a book for system administrators or database administrators. It's about programming and aimed at developers fluent in ASP.NET.

- It's not a detective story.

What This Book Covers

This book concentrates on using ASP.NET versions 1.0 and 1.1 for building applications for Internet or intranet use and looking at the possibilities that rich clients bring to both application design and a better user experience. There often appears to be confusion over how the .NET data management and page-processing models fit into the overall distributed application architecture, how it changes this, and how it provides exciting new opportunities. So we'll spend some time exploring the whole architecture and design issue, and you'll see how it can be addressed in different ways.

In particular, throughout the whole book, we attempt to provide inspiration through a range of ideas on how data can be used to drive Web applications and how that data can be most effectively utilized at each level of the design. Web applications will usually benefit from the encapsulation of business rules into components, and the .NET Framework provides ways to build several types of components. So we'll show both the construction and use of these.

There's no specific focus in this book on Windows Forms or executable applications or on the client-server environment in which they normally reside. However, to work really well in a distributed Web-based environment, the client can benefit from the use of Windows Forms or other client-side executables that access the server in conjunction with an ASP.NET-based application. Again, we'll demonstrate this in the book.

There are many development environments for ASP.NET applications and components already available and "on the way." The primary one is Visual Studio .NET. Traditionally, ASP pages have been built in a text editor or text-based tool, and because this book concentrates on the code rather than the tool used to create it, we predominantly use just a text editor to develop ASP.NET pages. However, the features of Visual Studio .NET for building components and Windows Forms applications is covered where appropriate.

Most of the code in the book is Visual Basic .NET because this gives the best opportunity for all developers. Even if you prefer to work in C# (or another language), you should be able to follow the VB .NET code quite easily. The alternative of providing listings and descriptions of the code for both languages would have meant we could get a lot less into the book overall, reducing the features we could cover and the techniques we could describe. However, the downloadable samples are provided in both VB .NET and C#. Of course, the client-side code we use in the browser isn't a .NET language. Predominantly we use JavaScript, though one example uses client-side VBScript to demonstrate that it can be done.

We also use a mixture of notations in our code. You'll see Hungarian notation in many places, which is aimed at making it easy to follow the code by clearly showing to which data type each variable refers. However, under .NET, Microsoft suggests that we should all move away from this notation style—but they don't say what we should move to instead. You can send suggestions or comments to the authors (via our usual feedback address feedback@daveandal.net) if you feel strongly about any other issue we've brought up here or throughout the remainder of the book.

Who Is This Book For?

This book is for developers who want to learn ASP.NET for building distributed data-driven applications, especially where they have a requirement for displaying and processing data in a wide range of different ways. In other words, it's for developers who require more than just simple "read and update" scenarios but instead must tackle building truly distributed applications.

What You Need to Use This Book

We'd like to think that you have a passion for ASP.NET, but in reality there may be one or two people who just use it because they have to do so. Either way, ASP.NET is what this book is about, and what we expect you to be familiar with. You'll also need to have some database experience and the appropriate software and hardware available. We summarize all the requirements in the next two sections.

Prerequisite Knowledge and Experience

This book is aimed at developers who have learned about .NET, and in particular ASP.NET, and are probably experienced in Web application development using previous versions of ASP. However, knowledge of Web application fundamentals (perhaps from another environment) and a firm grasp of the basics of ASP.NET will suffice.

Also, knowledge of programming using VB .NET (or at least a reasonable grasp of VB .NET as it relates to the predecessor VBScript) will be useful. If you're fluent in C# and prefer to use that, the techniques we demonstrate can easily be implemented in that (or any other) .NET language. The downloadable samples files are supplied in both VB and C# versions.

You can download the sample files from `http://www.apress.com` or `http://www.daveandal.net/books/4923/`. You can also run most of the samples online on our own server at `http://www.daveandal.net/books/4923/`.

Development Tools and Runtime Environment

Basically, all you need is a text editor and a server running version 1.0 or 1.1 of the .NET Framework. However, you'll also need to obtain and install the Microsoft Mobile Internet Toolkit (MMIT) to be able to run all the examples.

To get the .NET Framework, go to `http://msdn.microsoft.com/net/`.

Get the MIT from `http://msdn.microsoft.com/vstudio/nextgen/device/mitdefault.asp`.

A database server is also required—though it can be on the same server as the .NET Framework. The database used in the book is Microsoft SQL Server, but you can use any database to which you can connect from ASP.NET and within which you can create stored procedures.

You can use Microsoft Visual Studio .NET to create and compile the .NET components, but it's not a requirement because you can compile the class files from the command line instead (we provide simple batch files with the sample code to make this easier). VS .NET isn't our main development environment for ASP.NET pages because we use inline format rather than the code-behind format that VS .NET demands. For the Windows Forms application, we do use Visual Studio .NET although the downloadable code will work without it. However, you won't be able to view the design of the forms.

Information about Visual Studio is available from `http://msdn.microsoft.com/vstudio/`.

To test the pages in different environments, you might want to install several browsers. We tested the code in Opera and Netscape Navigator, as well as the Nokia mobile phone emulator.

Navigator is available from `http://home.netscape.com/computing/download/index.html`.

Opera is available from `http://www.opera.com/`.

The Deck-It emulator is available from `http://www.pyweb.com/tools/`.

The Nokia toolkit is available from `http://forum.nokia.com/`.

The Openwave toolkit is available from `http://openwave.com/`.

CHAPTER 1

The Distributed Application

IF THIS BOOK were a detective novel, then this chapter would probably start something like this: "It was raining so heavily that Cressey could barely make out the dim orange glow filtering through the grubby curtains of the apartment across the road…." Then it would set the scene and start to introduce the characters. As you read further, you'd begin to see how these characters interact with one another, and you'd learn more about their individual personality traits and what part each one plays in the story. Soon, you'd begin to get a mental picture of what the plot was about and how each character fits into it; the picture would grow as you immersed yourself in the story. Finally, as the book progressed toward a climax, you'd see all the various characters interacting to produce that final nail-biting outcome.

Admittedly, a chapter title such as "The Distributed Application" doesn't immediately suggest a gripping work of fiction, and (of course) that isn't what we're here to provide. But, we hope we can follow the well-trodden path of such a story in the .NET world and lead you toward a useful conclusion—even if it's not quite as exciting as that detective novel.

We'll set the scenes and fill you in on the background. We'll introduce the main characters along the way and help you to become familiar with their individual traits and quirks. We'll show you how they all fit together and help you fill out that mental picture of the whole process. Finally, we'll show you how they can interact to produce our own nail-biting result—a distributed application based on a range of .NET and other technologies.

The purpose of first chapter is to show you:

- Just exactly what a distributed application is

- The basics involved in planning, designing, and implementing a distributed application

- The various objects and techniques you can use to implement such an application

- How these objects can interact to provide the features you want or need

- An overview of the ADO.NET relational data access classes

- An overview of the System.Xml document access classes

- How data access fits into the n-tier model

We'll start with the customary background, and we'll try to avoid too many vague references to detective novels. Of course, we're still obliged to include one or two bad puns and off-the-cuff comments, but that's just the geeks in us showing through.

What Are Distributed Data Applications?

The term *distributed application* rolls easily off the tongue in today's Web-centric world, and developers use it to refer to all kinds of applications. This isn't helped by the fact people use the term *application* to refer to so many different things. You can use it in the generic sense to mean "a program that does something useful," and you can also use it in more specific and "technical" ways.

For example, you can refer to an *application root* and a *virtual application* when you configure Internet Information Services (IIS). You can refer to the package of components you install in Windows Component Services as a *COM+ Application*. When you use *Microsoft Application Center* (there's that word again), you refer to the complete set of files, configuration settings, registry entries, and components that make up a Web site as an application.

Sometimes, it's also really hard to understand exactly what the term *distributed* means. For example, when you build a Web site, you're distributing Hypertext Markup Language (HTML) and other resources to clients that load the pages. When you expose ADO Recordset objects through the Remote Data Service (RDS) feature, you're distributing data. And when you package an application on CD and mail it to everyone you know, you're distributing an application.

Our Definition

But none of these are what we really mean by a *distributed application*. In this book, we use this term to mean a program, a Web site, or some other service that involves processing in more than one place. These "places" could be geographically separate, but that's not a necessity—it could be a "logically distributed" application, consisting of a couple of components or programs, hosted on the same machine, that work together by exchanging information.

Of course, in many cases, you'll *want* some degree of geographical separation. For example, the application will need to be able to communicate information to people who aren't sitting in the server room—you'd tend to get quite a limited audience otherwise. Therefore, your distributed application is going to involve some sort of *network*, which transports information from one part of the application to another that's geographically removed.

Of course, this movement of data from one place to another is, in itself, a significant complexity—surely any application would be easier to build if the whole thing just ran on one machine. We'll challenge you to look harder for the reasons behind wanting to build distributed applications.

Why Do You Need to Distribute?

The main reason is obvious: The data is in one place, and the client is in another. We touched on this a moment ago, and it's a perfectly justifiable reason. It's how the first distributed applications came into being. Over the years, the various ages of Information Technology (IT) have encompassed several strategies for distributed computing. Each strategy was driven by the capabilities of the hardware and software available at that time and the requirements of businesses that use the information being processed.

First the Hardware Was King

Early computing revolved around the *central data processing* model, where the hardware was king. Computers were rare, expensive, and unreliable, and they required a staff of engineers as well as programmers to keep them going. We housed them in big air-conditioned rooms and (once we got over the punch card thing) allowed people to use simple dumb terminals to talk to them.

This is great because all the data is in one place, and everyone gets a fair share of it and the processing time available. In many places this model still survives in the form of thin-client computing—though of course with modern hardware and software. It has many advantages, particularly in circumstances where a *specific* set of users need to access and manipulate a *constrained* set of data to perform a predefined set of tasks. Example scenarios include order-entry systems, customer service desks, and so on.

Then the Software Was King

The second age came with *peer-to-peer* and *client-server* computing. As computers became cheap enough for users to have one each, the peer-to-peer model came about as ways were found to connect them together to share information and resources. This model is useful, but it means that information becomes scattered across the organization as each user keeps their own version and manipulates it in their own way.

In many business scenarios, this arbitrary distribution of the data isn't acceptable, and a more structured and controlled data environment is required. Client-server computing went back to the previous model to some extent by storing the data in a central location—on one or more servers. Clients connect to the server(s) and work with the data. However, they do so on their own computer rather than with a dumb terminal—in other words, the client takes over part of the processing work from the server.

From our point of view, this is where the terms *distributed computing* and *distributed applications* really start to come into play. Instead of doing all the work on the server, you can offload some of it to the client. This often provides a more interactive, responsive, and useful environment. However, it does raise other issues, such as managing concurrency. In other words, what happens when two users are working independently with the same set of data on their own machines, and both want to update the original data set? This is one of the things you'll look at throughout the second half of the book.

Now the Network Is King

We're now officially out of the client-server age and into the "third generation" of computing—one based on a *network* that's truly global, all-purpose, and (amazingly) still free. Moreover, although internal corporate networks still run local applications within the business (and, in some cases, private networks to connect to other locations), the one real requirement for all applications now is that they should work over the Internet.

OK, so it's not always an ideal solution. There are issues such as privacy, machine and data security, reliability, speed, and (particularly in some countries) availability. But it's cheaper, more widespread, and more universally compatible than anything else. You can use it to publish information publicly to all or to only specifically selected groups of clients (this concept is referred to as the *extranet*). It's becoming so widely accepted that businesses have even adopted the protocols it uses within internal networks to produce the *intranet*.

However, when you step outside your local network and into the big wide world of the Internet, you lose some of the vital features that were so familiar in the old client-server computing environment. For example, some of the protocols don't have any concept of unique connections for clients—so you have to build applications in a way that can cope with this. Furthermore, if you can't gain some control over the type(s) of device being used by your clients, then you can't assume that the client will be able to carry out part of the processing for you. Finally, the whole concept of "Internet time" (driven by the increasing need of all businesses to be first to market) means faster development is required for applications that are—at the same time—becoming more and more complex to meet the requirements of the user.

How Can You Do "Distributed" on the Internet?

So, effectively we've dug ourselves a hole and obligingly fallen in. In a short time, we've come to depend on a network and protocols that were never designed to handle distributed applications.

But the Internet is a great mechanism for transferring information, particularly because to connect to it you don't *have* to use the same "kit" as everyone else. It's relatively easy to build your own servers and clients (many universities and academic institutions do so, and that's where software such as Apache and some Unix variations came from). You can also take advantage of whichever protocol suits you best—or even adapt them.

Internet Protocols

In its early days, the Internet was used in military and academic circles because it was an effective way to disseminate information, pass electronic mail messages, and provide repositories of data and programs. It uses a set of protocols that doesn't easily allow you to adapt your client-server applications to run over the Internet:

Hypertext Transfer Protocol (HTTP): Using 7-bit American Standard Code for Information Interchange (ASCII) characters only. HTTP has no concept of durable connections. It was originally designed to transmit HTML pages and other resources anonymously between server and client and allow clients to update the server content. Now it's used predominantly in read-only mode for Web sites and Web applications, with Secure Sockets Layer (SSL) added to provide an encrypted transmission capability.

File Transfer Protocol (FTP): Establishes and holds a durable connection and is designed to transfer binary or text data from one place to another on command. FTP is reliable, and servers generally now include a "resume" feature for interrupted transfers.

Simple Mail Transport Protocol (SMTP): Using transient connections to send messages purely as text between suitably equipped servers (in other words, email messages). In recent years, techniques have evolved for including formatting information and attaching files to messages. However, the content is still just text, encoded in a way that allows suitable clients to handle attachments and formatting.

Of course, many other protocols have been used (and in some cases are still in use), but the three listed previously form the core of Internet communication today. They use the underlying Transmission Control Protocol (TCP)/Internet Protocol (IP) network protocol that forms the foundation for data transfer over the Internet, and each is effectively a "layer" that adds specific task-related features to the underlying protocol. Other protocols include Archie and Gopher (menu-driven or command-driven document location systems), Telnet (designed to allow remote clients to log into a server and manipulate it as though working at the local console), Address Resolution Protocol (ARP), Finger (used to get information about remote services) and Point-to-Point Protocol (PPP) for encapsulating transmission between two linked systems.

So, why can't you just add another layer of your own on top of TCP/IP—one specifically designed to give the features you want for your distributed applications? You could, but the whole issue now is compatibility. To be able to make your applications useful to the widest audience, you have to build them in such a way that they work with *existing* standards, as well as new ones. They also have to work with the wide variety of clients that may access them. You'll look in more detail at this topic next.

Internet Clients

One of the biggest strengths of the Internet is its ability to address almost any client using standard techniques and protocols. When you create simple Web pages, you don't have to worry about whether the eventual client will be using a particular operating system or a certain kind of browser or other access software (user agent). You can provide information in a standard format, and you can assume the clients will know how to handle that standard format—they'll be able to display the information on a screen or send it to a printer, and they'll even present it in a specific way to suit the user's requirement (for example, to meet the special requirements of users who have sight- or movement-related disabilities).

You might also decide to take advantage of client-specific techniques on the Web, such as JavaScript or Macromedia Flash animations. In most cases there's a high level of support for these in the various clients used to access the Internet (or, at least, there is at the moment). In general, though, we don't insist on the user running (for example) a particular version of Windows or a specific distribution of Linux—we just send them HTML and text.

Of course, there's a good reason for this. In an Internet scenario, we tend to want to make the information as accessible as possible to get maximum readership. Whether we're selling stuff or giving it away for free, it's generally not a good plan to turn people away at the door by including noncompatible content in your pages.

Clients' Capabilities Are Becoming More Disparate

For a while, a couple of years ago, everything was looking good. Web browsers were becoming much more compatible with one another, and there were quite advanced techniques that would work with 90–95 percent of requests to your site or application. But now, this situation is actually being reversed. Clients are becoming much more disparate in their capabilities, and you have to cope with many more different classes of devices.

For example, small-screen devices and mobile (cellular) phones continue to grow in usage as they gain more features and the communications infrastructure they use provides more bandwidth. But these devices are quite different from the average Web browser: Often they don't support color, sometimes they don't support graphics, and in many cases they don't even understand ordinary HTML.

At the same time, the TV set-top box or complete "Internet television" is growing in popularity. Although often this is intended for browsing activities (rather than for interacting with complex applications), it still adds more variety to the mix. In particular, these clients tend to be used with a simple remote handset, with the user much farther away from the display than they would be if they were using a regular browser, so a contemporary page design containing myriads of tiny hyperlinks doesn't work.

Server Port and Firewall Configurations

Finally, the rising concerns over machine and network security mean that you can't rely on many of the available application protocols to do much for you, and you certainly have little chance of adding new ones except in specific circumstances (such as a controlled client group).

Most Web servers and networks are protected by firewalls that only allow access to a small range of the ports on a machine. For Web-based (HTTP) applications, you can expect port 80 (and usually port 443 for the secured HTTPS/SSL protocol) to be open and possibly port 25 (for the SMTP and associated protocols used by mail servers). But it's unlikely that many others will be accessible. So, whatever you want to do, you really ought to try to achieve it using HTTP alone.

7

The Elements of a Distributed Application

Now that you have at least some idea about the environment in which your distributed application must live, you'll move on and meet the main characters. You already know that you may have up to four areas to deal with:

- The central data store(s) in which the information resides

- Some kind of intermediate processing that manipulates the information

- The client device, which can be any one of myriad types

- The network that connects them

However, there may be many varieties of these basic elements. For example, the data may reside in relational databases, mail servers, a directory service, Extensible Markup Language (XML) documents, "office" documents (such as word-processed documents and spreadsheets), or documents of other types (in plain text or special custom formats).

It's the same with the client element. It could be a desktop computer connected to a fixed network—itself connected to the Internet directly or through an Internet Service Provider (ISP). Or it could be a mobile device, such as a laptop computer or a Pocket PC that's designed to be used both when it's connected to the network and when it's disconnected. Or it might be some kind of phone-based device, which connects to the Internet through a wireless gateway belonging to a telecommunications provider such as the local telephone company. Furthermore, depending on the capabilities of the client device, the actual display of (and interaction with) the information at the client may be through a standard Web browser, some custom device-dependent software, or an executable application tailored to the client and its operating system.

You get the idea. The point is that there are a whole host of possibilities and combinations, as demonstrated in Figure 1-1. We've tried to show several of the different types of client devices (in the left column), intermediate processing (in the middle column), and data stores (in the right column).

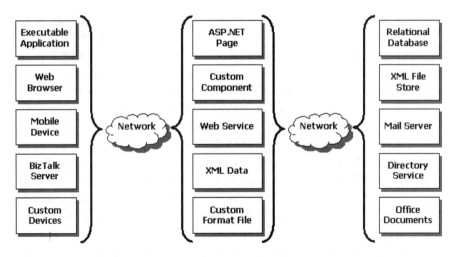

Figure 1-1. Possible elements of a distributed application

You can derive an interesting possibility from this figure. Namely, the client of one application may itself be the data provider for another application. In other ...rmation in a format that a completely ... this application could provide a service ... For example, consider an application ...ht lookup service of an airline's applica-... book seats. In this example, the travel ...f the airline company's application! ...*Web Services*, which can expose data and ...ng standard protocols that work through ...TP via the Web Service implemented by ...w concept, but the increasing standardi-...the Simple Object Access Protocol (SOAP) ...viable way to interact with other servers

...*s for using Web Services as you progress*

9

Although SMTP has proved to be an excellent standard for transporting electronic mail messages, it does suffer from limitations that can make it unsuitable for use directly as a data transport protocol for applications. These limitations include a lack of traceability or guaranteed once-only delivery. There are now several services, each of which wraps SMTP (and other protocols, where available) into an integrated message transportation system that provides the features SMTP can't. Microsoft's BizTalk Server is just one of these.

Although we try to cover many of the various types of device, services, and applications in this book, we obviously can't provide a full reference to them all. Some, such as BizTalk Server, won't be covered in great detail. We'll also concentrate on the features that the .NET Framework makes available. After all, this book is predominantly designed to be about building ASP.NET-based applications that are logically or physically distributed.

So, within that context, let's look a little deeper at the technologies you have available to implement the various parts of a distributed application such as the ones you've just considered.

Client Devices and Client Applications

With so many and such varied types of client devices now coming into use, how can you approach the problem of building useful distributed applications that are available and usable on these devices? This is, of course, the core question for the whole book.

In the past, it has often been the case that an application's design issues, hardware and software choices, and implementation details were controlled by the nature of the data source. The existence of vendor-specific data formats, coupled with a lack of appropriate drivers, data providers, and effective cross-platform transport formats, often made it hard to get at data and build applications that could use this data in a truly distributed fashion. As you'll see, progress in these areas has brought solutions to these issues—particularly through standard formats such as XML and standard protocols such as SOAP.

These days, it's often the nature of the *client* that really dictates how you design and build applications. Choosing how, and where, to perform processing is the hardest part of building responsive and efficient distributed applications.

Working with "Rich" Clients

When you use the term *rich client*, you're really talking about custom applications (or executables) that run on the client machine or the more advanced Web browsers (such as Internet Explorer version 4 and higher, Navigator 6, Mozilla, and Opera 6) whose built-in features allow them to act more like a client application than just a way of displaying HTML. If you have such a rich client, you can use its features (plus features such as client-side scripting, Java applets, or other components and applications) to reduce network round-trips and the consequent delays they introduce. You can cache data on the client, use it locally, and then post changes and updates back to the server as required.

Here are some examples:

You can use RDS to send an ADO disconnected Recordset from the server to the client. The client can process the Recordset (even using data binding as in a program such as Microsoft Access) and then flush changes back to the server. However, RDS suffers from concerns over security and hasn't proved to be a viable solution in the long term. It's also limited to some extent to Internet Explorer 4 and higher (though plug-ins are available for other clients).

You can use an XML parser component (often installed as part of the standard Web browser installation) to read and manipulate XML documents on the client. Internet Explorer uses the MSXML parser (installed automatically with Internet Explorer 5 and higher), and there's a range of parsers available for other platforms. The programming interface for compliant XML parsers is reasonably standardized, so code should work on any client platform and browser.

You can take advantage of new features in the latest browsers that (with the help of a small downloadable component) allow them to interact with Web Services. In the near future, you can expect to see components or Java applets that will do the same for other makes of Web browser.

You can create custom applications that access your server, extract and manipulate the data, and then (if required) post changes back to it. Of course, in this case, you have to tailor the application to suit the intended platform or operating system the client is using—even when using Java, there are compatibility issues. If you can ensure that the .NET Framework is installed on the client (a relatively small redistributable is available and can be downloaded), then you can use the same code and techniques as you do in ASP.NET on the server. The Framework contains plenty of classes specifically designed for adding networking support to applications using a range of protocols.

You can use custom components or ActiveX controls that you create yourself or buy from other suppliers. These can be instantiated from within script in a Web page to carry out the client-side processing you need.

Working with "Down-Level" Clients

Web browsers and other applications that don't provide the kind of features referred to in the previous section are usually termed *down-level clients.* When you can't be sure you're serving to a rich client, you must therefore assume you have a down-level client at the other end of the network. In this case, you need to find other techniques that will allow some client-side processing where this is possible. As long as the client isn't just a "dumb" terminal, or a severely restricted device such as a standard Wireless Application Protocol (WAP)–enabled cellular phone, you really only have two choices:

> As with rich clients, you can create custom applications that access your server, extract and manipulate the data, and then post any changes back to it. If the .NET Framework is installed on the client, then you can again use the same kind of code and techniques as you do in ASP.NET on the server. On some cellular phones and small-screen devices (such as the Pocket PC), it may be possible to write for the Compact Mobile Framework—a cut-down version of the .NET Framework that allows applications to be run on the client.

> You simply rely on the capabilities of the Web browser installed on the device. Unless it's a severely crippled device, it should at least support client-side scripting in JavaScript or WMLScript (depending on the device type). There's a severe limitation as to what you can achieve when only using script code that's active for the duration of the page view, and if the device can't support frames (which you can use to cache information) or instantiate objects from within the script, then you're probably going to have to abandon any attempt at getting it to participate in processing for the application.

Server-Side Data Stores

At the other end of the application, across the network, is the data store. Because we're talking about distributed data applications in this book, you can be pretty sure that we'll always have some kind of data store to deal with. In the majority of the examples in this book, the data store will take the form of a relational database—mainly because it's easily available and the most common in real-world scenarios.

However, Figure 1-1 did suggest some of the other sources of data with which you might have to deal. Because email has become the engine of so many business processes (to the extent that many organizations send more automated email messages than they do "handwritten" ones), this is obviously an important scenario. With Active Directory, most Windows-based applications will also have access to a fully integrated directory service, as has been the case in many organizations using other operating systems in the past. XML is also everywhere you look these days— it's coming out of the woodwork in almost every new application that appears, and the ways it can be used seem to grow by the week.

So, you need a server-based technology that makes it easy to integrate all these types of data and more. Thankfully, the .NET Framework, which will be used on the server within the applications in this book, provides all the tools you need:

- A set of Framework classes that can access and manipulate relational data from a variety of sources, through any of the following:

  - A generic OLE-DB provider for access to data stores that implement a suitable managed code OLE-DB driver

  - A special provider that uses the Tabular Data Stream (TDS) interface to give excellent performance with Microsoft SQL Server (only)

  - A set of classes devoted to accessing Oracle databases (although these are only included in version 1.1 of the .NET Framework)

  - An ODBC driver for access to various data stores using standard ODBC techniques. This is included in the .NET Framework in version 1.1 or available as a separate download from http://www.microsoft.com/data/ for use with version 1.0; there are also specific ODBC drivers for Oracle available from Microsoft or available directly from Oracle at http://otn.oracle.com/software/content.html.

  - A Jet driver for Access-style databases (Microsoft.Jet.OLEDB.4.0) that can be used with the OLE-DB provider

  These classes are referred to as *ADO.NET*, but—as you'll see later in this chapter—ADO.NET is *much more* than just an updated version of traditional ADO.

- A set of Framework classes specially designed to work with XML and its derivatives and extensions, including XML schemas, XSL Transformations (XSLT), and any other XML-formatted documents. These provide W3C-compliant interfaces, as well as plenty of .NET-specific extensions to make all kinds of XML processing requirements easy to achieve.

- A set of classes that provide access to directory services such as Active Directory through the Lightweight Directory Access Protocol (LDAP) and the Active Directory Service Interfaces (ADSI). These allow both reading and writing of directory information, so applications have the opportunity to access information about the organization itself and other company-wide information.

- OLE-DB providers and ODBC drivers for other types of applications, such as mail servers, "office" documents (such as word-processed documents and spreadsheets), and data that may be stored in other types of format—in particular older formats such as dBase or even plain text.

- A set of classes that allow you to expose and consume Web Services using SOAP. This means you can treat a Web Service as a data source if required and read from or write to it using standard techniques.

Processing and Presenting Information

In the pre-.NET Windows Distributed Network Application (DNA) architecture, you were encouraged to follow the *n-tier* design principles for your applications. Basically, this means separating the three main functions of an application into separate layers, or *tiers*. This has been a principle of good application design since developers said goodbye to the traditional client-server model and embraced the Internet with open arms.

In essence, the three tiers representing an application's three main functions are as follows:

- **Data tier**: This contains the data stores and the components or services that interact with it. These components and services are functionally separated (though *not necessarily* physically separated—they can be on the same machine) from the middle tier.

- **Middle tier**: This consists of one or more components and/or services that apply the business rules, implement the application logic, and carry out the processing required for actually making the application work. As part of this process, the middle tier is responsible for processing data that has been retrieved from the data stores and data that's to be sent to the data stores.

- **Presentation tier**: This takes the information from the middle tier and (as you probably guessed) presents it to the user. It's also responsible for interacting with the user, collating the information to return, and sending it back to the middle tier for processing.

Often these three layers are referred to as the *backend, business rules*, and *interface* layers, respectively—you can mix and match the words in these two paragraphs with a fair amount of impunity.

> **NOTE** *The important point to bear in mind is that the tiers of an n-tier application aren't defined by the physical structure (in other words, the hardware) that runs the application. The tiers are a function of the logical way that the application works, and they define the different task stages that the application will execute. You'll see more of the physical distribution of logical tiers in the figures in the next few pages.*

You probably noticed that, at the beginning of this section, we introduced the term *n-tier* as being distinct from classical client-server architecture—and then proceeded to talk about only three tiers. Isn't that strange terminology? What about the other *n*–3 tiers?

In fact, *n*-tier is a generalization of three-tier; the number of tiers really all comes down to the actual distribution of the processing. This is where the story starts to get even more interesting. If you're distributing processing between the client and the server, where do you put each of the tiers just described?

A Simple Three-Tier Design

Figure 1-2 shows probably the simplest design for an *n*-tier application. You have a server and a client, separated by a network. The server contains the data store and the data access components that make up the data tier, and it contains the business logic that makes up the middle tier. The client simply provides the interface to the application as the presentation tier.

NOTE *Don't be distracted by trying to work out where the Web server software (IIS 5.0, or whatever you plan to use) fits in these pictures. It's easier to think of the Web server software as being part of the* network *architecture, not the application architecture. In particular, when considering ASP.NET pages, you should be more interested in whether those individual pages are implementing business logic or presentation logic and less concerned with the fact that they run within the Web server's process space.*

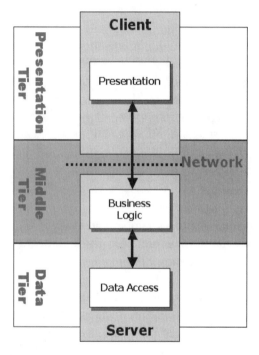

Figure 1-2. A simple three-tier application

In the simplest case, you might have a relational database and a couple of components or stored procedures that access the data. Then you could have an ASP.NET page that accesses the components or stored procedures to extract information, processes and formats it to suit the particular client, and then passes it to the client over the network. The client just has to display the information, collect user input, and send this back to the middle tier.

A More Realistic Three-Tier Design

Although the previous example is a common scenario for small applications (and, of course, for many samples in programming books), it's unlikely you'll meet this in the real world. There, the data store is most often located on specifically chosen and specially adapted hardware. It might be located on a cluster of Windows-based servers running SQL Server, but it's just as likely to be an Oracle or other database server running on a non-Windows platform.

In this case, the separation between the data tier and the middle tier is more obvious—there's a network connection between them. Figure 1-3 shows the basic idea, where the business logic is confined to the server that carries out all the middle-tier processing.

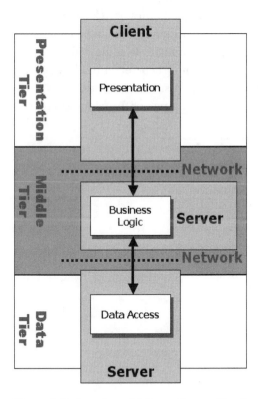

Figure 1-3. A real-world three-tier application

Moving to n-Tier Designs

Both of the previous scenarios assume two things: that the client is a down-level device (and is therefore not taking part in the actual processing required within the application) and that there's only one "set" of business rules (that is, all the business logic processing is carried out in one place, the middle tier).

In fact, neither of these assumptions is likely to be true in many of the real-life applications you build. For example, you can usually expect the business rules to be located in places *other* than the middle tier. It might be appropriate to implement certain business logic early in the process of extracting data, and you could choose to implement this in the components that access the data store. This "pocket" of business logic could therefore live on the same server as the data store or even (in a clustered situation) on another intermediate "routing" server.

Often, you also want to take advantage of the capabilities of rich clients where possible to provide a better user experience and reduce network loading and round-trip delays. So, by a similar argument, you could locate some of the business logic on the client. With these changes, the simple two-server model begins to look something like Figure 1-4, where pockets of business logic have been broken off from the middle tier and located on the data server or the client where they can be more effective.

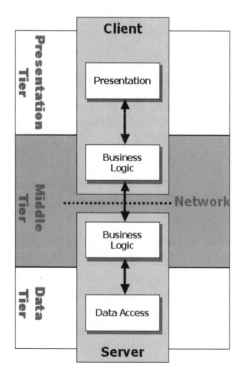

Figure 1-4. A single-server n-tier application

A More Realistic n-Tier Design

We could probably go on for ages producing these architecture figures, but we'll confine ourselves to one more example (don't worry, you'll see plenty more throughout the book). Because we'll generally have one or more separate servers to host the data store(s) we're using, Figure 1-5 shows three machines separated by two networks. However, now the business logic is split into three sections—some will run on the same server(s) as the data store, some on the "middle-tier" server, and some on the client.

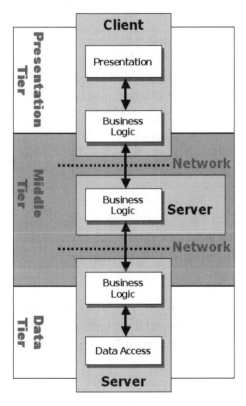

Figure 1-5. A real-world n-*tier application*

What's clear from all this is that trying to define the actual tiers themselves isn't easy. What we really mean by *the middle tier* is the business logic itself (remember that it's often referred to by the term *business rules layer* or similar), and as you've seen in the previously discussion, different elements of the business logic can justifiably exist on different servers.

Framework Resources for the Middle Tier

When it comes to actually processing information in the middle tier on the server(s), you have the whole .NET Framework at your fingertips. You can use the ADO.NET and XML Framework classes described next in this chapter to process data that's passed to the middle tier in a suitable format (either from the server or from the client). You also have access to other useful classes and features:

- The Web and Web.UI classes (and others) that implement ASP.NET itself and allow you to build almost any kind of processing into an application using any of the supported languages such as Visual Basic .NET, C#, and so on.

- The features of the Framework that allow you to build a range of different types of reusable components, such as user controls, custom server controls, business objects, and so on. You can also use existing COM and COM+ components if required by wrapping them up so that they look like .NET components.

- The ability to extend or replace parts of the ASP.NET environment, including building custom modules and HTTP handlers that can process information as it arrives at and leaves the server.

- A set of classes that provide access to the Component Services and Message Queue Services of the Windows operating system, allowing the construction of robust applications that use distributed transactions and guaranteed message delivery.

- Many other useful classes, such as classes for sending email messages from within an application, writing messages to the event log, creating performance counters, reading from (and writing to) the hard disk, and so on.

Data Access Techniques Overview

Having spent the previous sections of this chapter talking about the concepts involved in designing and building a distributed Web-based application, you now need to take off the rose-tinted glasses and dig into some more details about how you might implement the various parts. All this design stuff is incredibly useful and necessary, but at some point you do need to work at the nuts-and-bolts level.

In terms of the detective story (see the chapter introduction if you aren't sure where that came from), you need to meet the characters and find out what they actually do. In fact, in this chapter, you'll analyze the two most common sets of objects used in any data-driven application. However, rather than doing this analysis as if this were a reference book (which it clearly isn't), you'll meet the characters in the context of the part they play in the story.

Our aim in the remainder of this chapter is to present the different ways in which you can, within the .NET Framework and ASP.NET, *extract data* from a data store and *display it.* We'll cover the following:

- An overview of the ADO.NET relational data access classes

- An overview of the System.Xml document access classes

- How data access fits into the *n*-tier model

We start this section with an overview of the new data access technologies provided by the .NET Framework. Most developers who live in the Microsoft world have become familiar with ADO as a data access technology. It has pretty well taken over from the previous technologies that worked fine in connected client-server applications. ADO (so-called because the technology was originally called *ActiveX Data Objects*) evolved from earlier data access technologies and had various features "bolted on" over time to provide the capabilities required as ASP developed and became a prime platform for Web applications.

With .NET, you have a whole new technology for handling relational data—namely ADO.NET. Interestingly, between beta 1 and beta 2 of the product, the term *ADO* disappeared completely from the Framework class names, members, and documentation. All the classes are implemented within the root namespace System.Data, and so the term *ADO.NET* is only a generic term that's applied to this namespace—rather than a concrete and visible name within the Framework.

About "Relational" Data Access

By *relational data*, we mean data that's exposed in the form of *rows* and *columns* (*tuples* and *domains* in database theory parlance) or *tables* of data (note that the previous terminology of *fields*, *records*, and *recordsets* has been abandoned in .NET). However, this doesn't mean we're *just* talking about relational databases—many other data stores expose data this way.

For example, technologies such as Distributed Authoring and Versioning (DAV) and the Windows Indexing Service both provide a row/column format via the appropriate data provider, as does Active Directory and other applications for which OLE-DB providers or ODBC drivers are available. Within .NET, you still have the capability to access data this way, but at the time of this writing the providers and drivers were only just starting to appear for some types of data store.

Classic ADO via Interop

Furthermore, because managed code running under the .NET Common Language Runtime (CLR) can interoperate with COM and COM+ components, you can (if you want) still use previous versions of ADO, rather than ADO.NET. Version 2.7 of ADO, part of the Microsoft Data Access Components 2.7 (MDAC 2.7), is designed to provide maximum interop performance with .NET, and Microsoft recommends you install MDAC 2.7 before installing the .NET Framework if you intend to use classic ADO in this way.

In this book, you'll mainly be using ADO.NET for your relational data access tasks. There are a few exceptions, in places where you work with clients that don't have the Framework installed (such as pages designed for Internet Explorer)—in such cases, of course, you'll be forced to use whatever version of ADO is available on that machine.

Classic ADO Techniques

In classic ADO, there was a single repository for holding and working with data— the Recordset object. Over successive incarnations of ADO, the Recordset evolved to provide both connected and disconnected features. An ADO Recordset can be connected to a data store via a Connection and (optionally) a Command object, and it can be used to extract and manipulate the source data. SQL statements and stored procedures can be executed via Connection or Command. Any that return data will usually do so by exposing it within a Recordset for use as required.

To provide disconnected access to a data store, the ADO Recordset object allows the ActiveConnection to be removed and then replaced later so that changes can be pushed back into the data store. However, the removal and replacement of the connection such as this are conscious actions that the developer must take. In ADO.NET, things are different.

The ADO.NET Data Access Classes

Web applications, and especially distributed applications, often require you to work with data in a disconnected way. ADO.NET has a new object, the DataSet, which provides disconnected access to a data store. It can't be used in a connected fashion, but it does provide an ideal way to handle data when you want to *remote* it (that is, to pass it to another tier or to a client). The DataSet object also provides features that weren't supported by ADO Recordset objects—for example, it can store more than one table and the relationships between these tables.

However, you don't always need to remote your data. In many cases (for example, when you're using data only to create a Web page that displays the data), you can follow the established approach of using a connected object to access the data—closing the connection as soon as the necessary data has been obtained. For this, ADO.NET provides the DataReader object—a fast and efficient way to connect to any relational data store and access the data. To see how you can use these two new ADO.NET objects in your distributed applications, you'll examine them in more depth shortly.

The .NET Data Providers

Before going further, there's one other aspect to using these objects that we should mention. In classic ADO, there were two main techniques for connecting to data stores—ODBC drivers and pure OLE-DB providers. Within the .NET Framework, you need to use providers that are written as managed code (providers that are designed for use with the Framework data access objects).

At the time of writing, the following providers were available, and more are arriving all the time:

A special Tabular Data Stream (TDS)–based provider for Microsoft SQL Server only. The classes for this are in the System.Data.SqlClient namespace.

A generic .NET data provider for OLE-DB data providers, called OleDb. The existence of this provider means that .NET applications can access any data source that could previously be accessed through an OLE-DB data provider (thus allowing legacy ADO code that used OLE-DB data providers to be migrated to .NET). The classes for this are in the System.Data.OleDb namespace.

A generic .NET data provider for ODBC data drivers. Similarly, the existence of this provider means that .NET applications can access any data source that could previously be accessed through an ODBC driver. The classes for this are in the System.Data.Odbc namespace in version 1.1 of the Framework or in the namespace Microsoft.Data.Odbc if you download and install them separately on version 1.0.

A special provider for Oracle databases is included in version 1.1 of the Framework. The classes for this are in the System.Data.OracleClient namespace. Other .NET providers for Oracle are available directly from Oracle as well.

Note that when you're writing code, your choice of .NET data provider dictates which objects you need to use. There are different "sets" of ADO.NET objects (for example, DataAdapter, Command, and Connection) to suit the different data providers:

A set of objects specially designed for use with the SqlClient provider. These take advantage of the efficient and fast TDS interface that SQL Server exposes, and so they can provide performance that's up to 50 percent better than the OLE-DB providers, depending on the operation being performed. The names of these objects are all prefixed with Sql—for example, SqlDataAdapter and SqlCommand.

A set of objects prefixed with OleDb for use with the OleDb data provider; these objects include OleDbDataAdapter and OleDbCommand.

The set of objects prefixed with Odbc for use with the Odbc data provider; these objects include OdbcDataAdapter and OdbcCommand.

In version 1.1, the set of objects prefixed with Oracle for use with the OracleClient data provider; these objects include OracleDataAdapter and OracleCommand.

Connected Data Access—The DataReader

When you simply want to make a connection to a data store and extract data (that is, you want to read from the data store but not write to it), you generally use a DataReader object. The DataReader is best thought of as a "pipe" or "stream" object. It doesn't store the data itself but just provides a channel where you can access the data store.

For example, when you execute a SQL SELECT statement, the data store itself performs the task of collating the appropriate set of rows, sorting and grouping them if required, and then it caches this rowset within the data store as a temporary "table." The DataReader provides a pipe through which you can stream the data back to your application code and work with it.

To use a DataReader, you obviously have to connect it to your data store. In ADO.NET, you use a Command object and a Connection object, which are fairly similar to those found in classic ADO (this technique worked fine there, so why change it?)

The Connection object holds the data store connection details, such as the connection string, provider details, and so on. The Command object uses the connection to pass the query details (SQL statements, stored procedure details, table names, and any required parameters) and exposes the returned parameter values and a count of the number of rows affected.

Figure 1-6 shows the objects in outline. You can see that the overall model is almost identical to the one found in classic ADO, with the DataReader replacing the

`Recordset` object. Just bear in mind that the `DataReader` doesn't actually store the data—it's just a pipe between the data store and the application code.

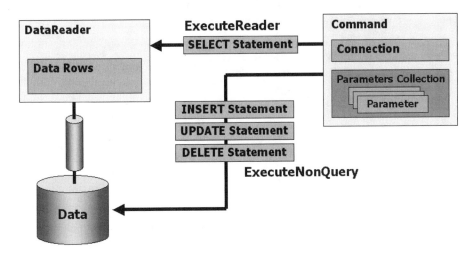

Figure 1-6. Using a DataReader *and* Command

In this figure, `ExecuteReader` and `ExecuteNonQuery` are two `Command` object methods by which you execute different types of SQL command. You'll see this in the example fragments that follow.

Executing a SELECT Command

Using the `DataReader` to extract data is easy. You create a suitable connection string and a SQL statement to use as the command string. Then you create a `Connection` object and a `Command` object, and declare a variable to hold the returned `DataReader` object. After opening the connection you use the `Command` object's `ExecuteReader` method to execute the SQL statement within the data store. This method returns a `DataReader` object that's connected to the resulting rows, and you can use this object to iterate through them or (as you'll see later) present them in other ways.

The following code fragment uses the OleDb data provider to demonstrate this:

```
'specify the connection details
Dim strConnect As String = "provider=SQLOLEDB.1;" _
                    & "data source=servername;" _
                    & "initial catalog=databasename;" _
                    & "uid=username;pwd=password;"
```

```
'specify the SELECT statement to extract the data
Dim strSelect As String = "SELECT * FROM tablename"

'create a new Connection object using the connection string
Dim objConnect As New OleDbConnection(strConnect)

'create a new Command using Connection and SQL statement
Dim objCommand As New OleDbCommand(strSelect, objConnect)

'declare a variable to hold a DataReader object
Dim objDataReader As OleDbDataReader

Try
  'open the connection to the database
  objConnect.Open()

  'execute the SQL statement against the command to get DataReader
  objDataReader = objCommand.ExecuteReader()

  'use the DataReader to iterate through the rows returned
  'the Read method returns False when there are no more rows
  Do While objDataReader.Read()
    Response.Write(objDataReader("columnname"))
  Loop

Catch objError As Exception
  'display error details
  Response.Write("Error while accessing data. " & objError.Message)

Finally
  'close the DataReader and Connection
  objDataReader.Close()
  objConnect.Close()

End Try
```

> **NOTE** *In version 1.1 of the .NET Framework, the* DataReader *class gains a new property named* HasRows *that you can use to check if any rows were returned by the query or stored procedure without having to call the* Read *method.*

Closing the Database Connection

Note that it's important to close the connection to the database when the DataReader is no longer required. You do this by calling the Close methods of both the DataReader and the Connection. Because database connections are a precious resource, you should always release them as soon as you can. Although the .NET Framework does look after "cleaning up" through its integrated garbage collection process, it may not do so immediately. The delightful term applied to the .NET garbage collection service is *nondeterministic finalization*, which basically means you can't rely on the object being removed from memory immediately.

It's worth noting that if you've passed a DataReader object *by reference* to another tier in your application (for example, by returning it as the result of a function), it isn't easy to get at the Connection object directly to close it. One way to make sure the connection is closed at the appropriate time is to specify the value CommandBehavior.CloseConnection as the parameter to the Command object's ExecuteReader method:

```
objDataReader = objCommand.ExecuteReader(CommandBehavior.CloseConnection)
```

This forces the connection to close automatically when the DataReader itself closes. So, when you've finished with the DataReader, you just have to call its Close method, and the connection will be closed and freed up for other applications to use.

Executing a Stored Procedure That Returns a Rowset

If you're using a stored procedure to extract the data, you just need a few minor changes to the code. You specify the stored procedure name when you create the Command object and set the CommandType property to CommandType.StoredProcedure:

```
'specify the connection details
Dim strConnect As String = "provider=SQLOLEDB.1;" _
                        & "data source=servername;" _
                        & "initial catalog=databasename;" _
                        & "uid=username;pwd=password;"

'specify the stored procedure name
Dim strStoredProc As String = "storedprocname"

'create a new Connection object using the connection string
Dim objConnect As New OleDbConnection(strConnect)
```

```
'create a new Command using Connection and command string
Dim objCommand As New OleDbCommand(strStoredProc, objConnect)

'tell the data store it is a stored procedure
objCommand.CommandType = CommandType.StoredProcedure
...
```

> **NOTE** *We omitted the* CommandType *property assignment in the previous fragment because the default value—*CommandType.Text*—was the correct one for that example.*

At this point, you may also need to provide parameters for the stored procedure. This is easy to do—you just have to create each Parameter object and add them to the Parameters collection of the Command object. You'll see this process in detail when you look at the code for the application later in this book.

Executing an INSERT, UPDATE, or DELETE Command

As well as retrieving data, this simple technique of using a Connection and a Command to connect to a data store works when you want to fire off a SQL "action" statement (that is, an INSERT, UPDATE, or DELETE statement) to the data store. It also allows you to use stored procedures that don't return a rowset. In this case, you use the Command object's ExecuteNonQuery method (rather than its ExecuteReader method), and you don't need to provide a DataReader object at all:

```
'specify the connection details
Dim strConnect As String = "provider=SQLOLEDB.1;" _
                          & "data source=servername;" _
                          & "initial catalog=databasename;" _
                          & "uid=username;pwd=password;"

'specify the DELETE statement to delete some data
Dim strSQL As String = "DELETE FROM tablename WHERE columnname='AX142'"

'create a new Connection object using the connection string
Dim objConnect As New OleDbConnection(strConnect)

'create a new Command using connection and SQL statement
Dim objCommand As New OleDbCommand(strSQL, objConnect)
```

```
'declare an Integer variable to hold the number of records affected
Dim intRowsAffected As Integer

Try
  'open the connection to the database
  objConnect.Open()

  'execute the SQL statement against the command
  'ExecuteNonQuery method returns number of rows affected
  intRowsAffected = objCommand.ExecuteNonQuery()
  Response.Write("Deleted " & intRowsAffected.ToString() & " rows.")

Catch objError As Exception
  'display error details
  Response.Write("Error while updating data. " & objError.Message)

Finally
  'just need to close the Connection
  objConnect.Close()

End Try
```

If you wanted to use a stored procedure (instead of a SQL statement) to do this, you'd adopt similar techniques to those used in the previous DataReader example. You'd specify the stored procedure name when you create the Command object and set the CommandType property to CommandType.StoredProcedure. Likewise, you'd add parameters to the Command if required—you'll see how to do this in the code for the sample application later in the book.

Disconnected Data Access—The DataSet

The second main character in the data access story is the DataSet object. This object provides you with a rich, highly automated, and very powerful tool for storing, manipulating, and remoting data. Of course, this means that the DataSet is nowhere near as efficient or lightweight as the DataReader. There's a lot of overhead required for constructing tables, parsing the data into rows, and persisting it to disk or stream on demand. Plus, it contains logic to allow some complex operations to be carried out on the stored data.

However, it's when you require a disconnected "data storage" object that the DataSet really comes into its own. It's used in conjunction with three ancillary objects that load the data, and it can also update the original data source. These are the Connection and Command objects that you've already encountered, plus the

DataAdapter object, which performs most of the magic. Figure 1-7 shows these objects and how they relate to each other.

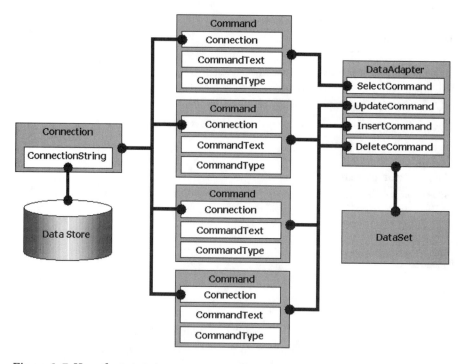

Figure 1-7. How the DataSet *connects to a data store*

Although it looks complicated, the theory behind the process is actually quite simple. The DataAdapter object contains references to between one and four Command objects. To extract data (for example, when using a SQL SELECT statement), you only actually need one Command object—the SelectCommand. The other three are used only when you come to push updates back into the data store and represent the UPDATE, INSERT and DELETE SQL statements or the equivalent stored procedures.

Each Command object contains a reference to a Connection object (the same one can be shared between all four), and the Connection object provides the link to the data store via its connection string.

The DataAdapter Object

The "magic" part of the process comes from the DataAdapter, when you want to extract the data into the DataSet or push changes back into the data store. By calling the DataAdapter object's Fill method, you set in process a chain of events. The DataAdapter instructs the Command object to fetch the data through its Connection object. When the first data row is returned, the DataAdapter figures out the structure required in the DataSet to hold this data, and it instructs the DataSet to build the appropriate tables with the correct data types for each column. It then pulls the rows from the data source and fills the table in the DataSet.

> **NOTE** *You generally know what the structure of the table will be at the time you write the code. Therefore, it's usually possible to create the schema information at design-time and use it at runtime to create a typed* DataSet. *The advantage of this is that it saves the* DataAdapter *from the task of working out the schema information at runtime, resulting in better performance. Visual Studio .NET makes it easy to define a typed* DataSet.

The code required to fill a DataSet is quite simple and compact. Assuming that you already have a SQL SELECT statement in strSelect and a connection string in strConnect, the following code shows how you might fill your DataSet with a single table. Notice that you don't have to create a Command object explicitly this time. When you create the DataAdapter, specifying the SQL statement and the Connection object to use, it automatically creates a Command object behind the scenes (rather like classic ADO does with the Recordset object) and assigns it to the SelectCommand property of the DataAdapter:

```
'create a new Connection object using the connection string
Dim objConnect As New OleDbConnection(strConnect)

'declare a variable to hold a DataSet object
Dim objDataSet As New DataSet()

Try
  'open the connection to the database
  objConnect.Open()

  'create new DataAdapter using connection object and SQL statement
  Dim objDataAdapter As New OleDbDataAdapter(strSelect, objConnect)

  'fill the dataset with data from the DataAdapter object
  objDataAdapter.Fill(objDataSet, "Books")

Catch objError As Exception
  'display error details
  Response.Write("Error while accessing data. " & objError.Message)

End Try
```

However, this is only the simplest scenario. As we mentioned already, the DataSet object can also store more than one table and (if required) the relationships between them. If the data store you're using accepts multiple SQL statements, or stored procedures that can return multiple rowsets, the DataAdapter will automatically create these multiple tables as it fills the DataSet.

The DataAdapter maps each column in the data source to a column in the table within the DataSet. You can also set up custom column mappings to control the column names and the way that the data is mapped. Furthermore, once the data is loaded, you can use methods of the DataSet (and its constituent tables and data rows) to create new tables and columns, add constraints and primary keys to the tables, set default values, add and delete rows, and modify the existing data in almost any way you need. You'll see many of these techniques demonstrated in the sample applications you build throughout the book.

Pushing Changes Back to the Data Store from a DataSet

As you saw in the earlier description of Figure 1-7, you can also push changes made to the data within the DataSet back into the original data store (or into another data store, provided that the table and column mappings are correctly defined). This process uses the other three Command objects—those referenced by the UpdateCommand, InsertCommand, and DeleteCommand properties of the DataAdapter.

The DataSet object's Update method automatically calls the appropriate Command objects in turn, depending on whether the rows in the DataSet table(s) have been modified, inserted, or deleted since the data was loaded (or since the AcceptChanges method was last called). Provided that the Command object contains the correct SQL statement or accesses an appropriate stored procedure, the changes to the rows are then pushed back into the data store. You'll look at the processes for updating data in Chapter 8.

Understanding System.Xml

Even though the XML advance is reaching ever further into applications and data processing, the bulk of today's data is still stored (at least in most corporations) in relational databases. However, XML is clever. Not only can it easily represent "unstructured" information, it can just as easily represent data that you think of as being "relational."

Representing Data and Information

For example, the following XML document is obviously a valid representation of three rows from a database table:

```
<?xml version="1.0" ?>
<BookList>
  <Book>
    <Title>Beginning Active Server Pages 3.0</Title>
    <PublicationDate>1999-12-01</PublicationDate>
    <StockQty>756</StockQty>
  </Book>
  <Book>
    <Title>Professional Visual Basic 6 XML</Title>
    <PublicationDate>2000-03-01</PublicationDate>
    <StockQty>108</StockQty>
  </Book>
  <Book>
    <Title>Professional Outlook 2000 Programming</Title>
    <PublicationDate>1999-12-01</PublicationDate>
    <StockQty>28</StockQty>
  </Book>
</BookList>
```

However, this doesn't tell you everything you'd usually know from examining a database table containing this information. It doesn't tell you what the data types are, what rules there are about null values, which is the row key, and so on.

On the other hand, it does have advantages. The syntax and rules for XML are standardized across all operating systems and platforms, so the data is now useful without depending on a platform-specific object such as a DataSet to store it. Moreover, it's only text and limited to 7-bit characters, which means it can easily be transported across the Internet without resorting to UUencoding or other fancy tricks that binary data requires.

Schemas and DTDs

You can also add an inline *schema* or Document Type Definition (DTD), or provide a separate one, that defines the acceptable structure for the XML content. Although this still can't provide all the "rules" you usually set up in a relational data table or rowset, it does allow quite a strict definition of what's acceptable and what's not.

For example, the following is an XML schema that would work with the XML document you saw a moment ago. It defines which elements can appear where and how they can be repeated. It also specifies how the values of the elements should be interpreted—in other words, what data type they represent:

```
<xs:schema id="BookList" xmlns=""
           xmlns:xs="http://www.w3.org/2001/XMLSchema"
           xmlns:msdata="urn:schemas-microsoft-com:xml-msdata"
           msdata:Locale="en">
  <xs:element name="Book" msdata:Locale="en">
    <xs:complexType>
      <xs:sequence>
        <xs:element name="Title" minOccurs="1" type="xs:string" />
        <xs:element name="PublicationDate" minOccurs="1" type="xs:date" />
        <xs:element name="StockQty" minOccurs="1" type="xs:integer" />
      </xs:sequence>
    </xs:complexType>
  </xs:element>
  <xs:element name="BookList">
    <xs:complexType>
      <xs:choice maxOccurs="unbounded">
        <xs:element ref="Books" />
      </xs:choice>
    </xs:complexType>
  </xs:element>
</xs:schema>
```

NOTE *DTDs provide an alternative way of specifying the structure of an XML document. However, DTDs are much more limited in their capabilities and are generally now superceded by schemas.*

Unstructured Information

One area where XML really comes into its own, and an area where development of XML was probably originally aimed, is that of representing *unstructured information*. Outside the corporate database, most of the information in a company is stored in email messages, word-processed documents, contact manager software, and so on.

This information is, of course, still data—it's part of the knowledge pool of a company or institution. Unfortunately, it's generally really hard to get at and even harder to extract anything useful from. Although documents can be indexed so that you can search for specific words and phrases, it's not easy to perform the same kinds of task that you can with a relational database.

For example, suppose you need to get a list of corporate Word documents that discuss Project X and contain the name of the chief engineer but have the list displayed by date according to when the surveyor last visited the site. In normal circumstances with XML documents, such a task would be practically impossible.

A similar situation already exists when you think about news articles—how do you search for a specific set of articles? You might specify a person's or a company's name, a date, or a location. Now, if all the articles were held in a format along the lines of the following example, it should be easy to locate the correct one:

```
<?xml version="1.0" ?>
<NewsArticle>
  <Headine>
    New operating system invented during lunch break
  </Headline>
  <Story>
    It was revealed today that three students at
    <Location>Cambridge College <State>MI</State></Location>
    invented a new operating system during their lunch break.
    The lead programmer in the team, <Person>Dull Wick</Person>
    said last night that <CorpRef>Microsoft</CorpRef> and
    <Person>Bill Gates</Person> had better watch out. I've seen
    the future and it's Purple, said well-known industry analyst
    <Person>Billy Jilly</Person>.
  </Story>
</NewsArticle>
```

This "information" isn't in a format that could easily be stored in a relational manner. Articles will contain chunks of text—an unspecified number of references to locations, people, corporations, dates, and so on. They could also be nested (and hence related) in a range of ways—as in the `<Location>Cambridge College <State>MI</State></Location>` section of the example document.

So, for this type of information, XML provides a far better representation model. The content of an XML document is often represented graphically as a *tree* structure. The new article then becomes what's shown in Figure 1-8.

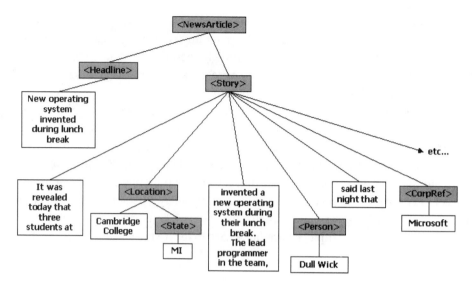

Figure 1-8. Representing unstructured information in XML

The XML nodes (the elements) appear shaded, and you can see how the actual information stands out. Using the nodes to provide navigation, you can "walk" the branches of the tree, extracting, modifying, and generally working with the information. Furthermore, of course, when you want to search for information, it becomes a much more precise operation. You can specify what types of nodes to look for, what relationships they can have with other nodes (for example, whether they're parents or children of other identified nodes), and what information to return from those that do match your search criteria. All these features are provided in the System.Xml classes of the Framework.

The W3C Interface Recommendations

The World Wide Web Consortium (W3C) produces recommendations for a range of XML manipulation techniques, and the core of these are the XML Document Object Model (DOM) and XML Schemas specifications.

The XML DOM recommendations lay out a set of standard interfaces that should be exposed by applications designed to manipulate XML. For example, there are properties and methods that should be exposed by an object that stores XML documents, and there are other properties and methods that should be available for the objects that represent each node within a document.

The recommendations for XML Schemas are more recent, and they provide a standard way to define the structure, the acceptable content, and the rules for an XML document. The schema you saw earlier contains a Microsoft-specific namespace, but it aligns directly with the W3C recommendations. For more information on the W3C recommendations, visit `http://www.w3.org/TR/xmlschema-1/`.

There are also many other recommendations, such as the XSLT specification for performing transformations to XML using style sheets and the XPath specification for defining how applications should be able to locate nodes and search for information in documents.

The `System.Xml` classes (and their subsidiary classes) implement these recommendations and add extra features that make common operations much easier to perform. There are also objects in the class library that provide alternative approaches to accessing and manipulating XML documents. We'll briefly present these various classes next.

The System.Xml Classes

As you've just seen, XML is a rich environment for storing information of all kinds—be it a representation of rowset-style data or the storage of unstructured data. This richness extends to the ways you can handle XML.

The XML Document Objects

There are three document objects you can use to store or access XML documents in the `System.Xml` namespace:

- The `XmlDocument` object provides W3C-compliant interfaces for accessing the document and its content (each node in the document). There are also several Microsoft-specific extensions to the properties and methods.

- The `XmlDataDocument` object is based on the `XmlDocument` object and provides the same interfaces. However, it extends the `XmlDocument` object's capabilities by also providing a way to access the content as though it were relational data—in other words, you can use relational data access techniques to read and modify the content of the XML document it holds.

- The XPathDocument object is a fast, efficient, and highly optimized object for accessing XML documents via XPath queries (although XPath queries can be carried out against any of the document objects). It doesn't support the XML DOM interfaces and is usually used in conjunction with an XPathNavigator object—which you'll look at next.

The XML Navigator Object

The technique for accessing the contents of an XML document using the XML DOM recommendations involves walking the tree that represents the document. Each node exposes properties and methods that can be used to locate parent, sibling, and child nodes. However, this isn't always the most efficient way to get to a specific node or to stream the content from a document into another object.

Instead, in .NET, you can create an XPathNavigator object based on any of the three document types (it isn't limited to using an XPathDocument) and use the interface this exposes to access the document content. The XPathNavigator provides a series of methods that allow you to move to the next node, to move to the next node of a specific type, or to select a node or a range of nodes from the document using an XPath query.

XML and Relational Data Synchronization

One of the most exciting features of the .NET data access classes is the way that XML and relational data have merged to provide a comprehensive environment for working with both types of data. More importantly, however, is the ability to convert data from one format to another.

In fact, this is something of a simplification—within the .NET data access methodology (ADO.NET as well as System.Xml), *all* data is persisted as XML. When you save the data to disk from a DataSet, or persist it to a stream, it's as XML.

So, you can save data from a DataSet as XML, and you can also load XML into a DataSet if required. To make the whole thing more interesting, you can use the special features of the XmlDataDocument object to work with XML documents. The XmlDataDocument has a DataSet property that exposes the XML document as a DataSet. Hence, you can load an XML document and then use relational techniques to modify the content of that document just as you would if the data were extracted directly from a relational database.

The XML Writer and Reader Objects

The System.Xml namespace provides objects you can use to stream XML from one object to another or directly to a disk file. You can use the XmlTextWriter object to build an XML document node by node using code rather than by using the XML DOM methods for inserting nodes into an XmlDocument object. You can also use it as the output for many other objects, allowing the content of these objects to be streamed to another object or to a disk file.

The XmlTextReader and XmlNodeReader objects work along the same principles as the DataReader object that you met earlier in this chapter. They provide a channel or stream through which XML can be read into another object. They also allow you to perform the reading programmatically, node by node, so that you can work with the document if required.

Again demonstrating the interoperability of ADO.NET and the System.Xml classes, there's a special version of the ADO.NET Command object's execute methods that returns an XML reader object. It's used in conjunction with the FOR XML SQL statements supported by Microsoft SQL Server 2000, allowing you to extract rows of data from SQL Server as XML and use the data to build XML documents or pass to other applications.

The XML Validation Objects

If you need to perform validation of XML documents against an inline DTD or schema, you can use the XmlValidatingReader object. This is created from an XML reader object like the ones we've just been discussing and can be used to validate the XML documents you load into any of the document objects or that are read by any of the reader objects. There are also ancillary objects that allow you to validate against external (linked) schemas and DTDs.

The XSL Transformation Object

Finally, to perform XSL transformations on XML documents, you can use the XslTransform object. This provides a range of ways you can present the document; for example, the output can be sent to a stream, another object, or a disk file.

An Overview of the System.Xml Namespace

Figure 1-9 shows the range of objects available in the System.Xml namespace and subsidiary namespaces such as System.Xml.XPath and System.Xml.Xsl.

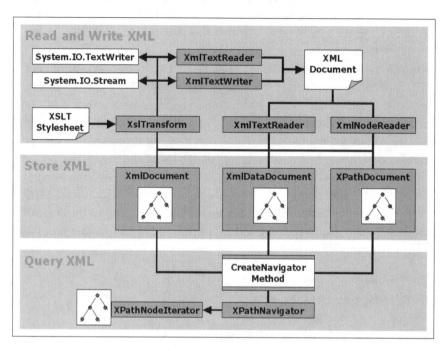

Figure 1-9. A conceptual view of the System.Xml *namespace*

You can see a couple of objects in the figure that we haven't mentioned so far. The TextWriter and Stream objects, from the System.IO namespace, provide access to objects outside the System.Xml namespaces. These objects are useful if you want to pass the XML to or from (for example) the ASP.NET Request and Response objects, which both provide access via a Stream object.

The other object you can see in the figure is the XPathNodeIterator object. This is used when you select sets of nodes using an XPath query, and it allows you to work with those nodes.

Although the common XML manipulation tasks are generally quite easy to accomplish using the objects you've looked at in this section, they do have quite complex interfaces. For this reason, we haven't provided code examples—this would soon fill the chapter, and the information is available in the .NET Software Development Kit (SDK) and other references and resources. You'll be looking in detail at how you use these objects throughout the remainder of this book.

Data Access and the *n*-Tier Model

Having perused the various data access options available under the .NET Framework, the next step is to consider how you can use these objects within the *n*-tier architecture that you're aiming to take advantage of in your applications. In the remainder of this chapter, we'll show you an overview of some of the possibilities.

What Is the Data Being Used For?

The first important point is to consider what you actually want to *do* with the data you extract from your data store. The answer to this question will influence the basic object you use more than anything else, and to some extent it defines the kind of performance you can expect to achieve.

The core issue is that the most efficient way to connect to a data store and extract data is via a reader object. The data comes to you as a stream, and there's no intermediate storage and little intermediate processing required. Examples of this are the ADO.NET `DataReader`, for which you saw some simple example code earlier in this chapter, and the XML readers such as `XmlTextReader` and `XmlNodeReader`.

Do You Need to Remote the Data?

However, there's a problem with this if you need to remote data. These fast and efficient reader objects can only be remoted when they're passed as references. Passing a `DataReader` to a client as a reference means that the `DataReader` would still reside on the server, but it could be used from a client application. You're not actually remoting data in this case, but instead you're using a remote object. This works in many situations, but a `DataReader` isn't the best object with which to do this. That's because it's a connected object—from the moment you open the reader to the moment you close it, you're connected to the data store. To be able to remote data in the way you want, you need an object that can persist the content. In ADO.NET, this is the `DataSet` object, but you can also use a `DataTable` object.

You also have a choice of several objects when using XML. You can remote an `XmlDocument` and an `XmlDataDocument`. Both have the ability to persist the content and can be passed between tiers of an application. Notice, however, that you *can't* remote an `XPathDocument`. This object is designed to operate in many ways like a reader object, and it can't persist the data to allow it to be passed between separate tiers of an application.

So in summary, the choice of objects you'd normally use for remoting data between physically separated tiers of an application basically comes down to these:

- The ADO.NET `DataSet` object

- The ADO.NET `DataTable` object

- The `XmlDocument` object

- The `XmlDataDocument` object

Serialization and the System.Runtime.Remoting Classes

There's another way you can pass data to the client. You can use *serialization* and/or the `System.Runtime.Remoting` classes. Serialization describes the process of an object converting its data into a format that can be copied to another process. For a `DataSet`, the data is the rows and columns for each table, and the persisted format of that data is an XML file. The remotable objects mentioned earlier have the ability to serialize their entire content (all the data and programmatic features such as the methods and properties they expose) so that they can be passed across a *channel*. This channel can be via TCP/IP directly or through HTTP. Also, of course, they can deserialize themselves at the other end. Thus, the client obtains a complete copy of the original object. This is referred to as Marshal By Value (MBV) remoting.

An alternative approach is to use the objects provided by the `System.Runtime.Remoting` namespace to create a *proxy* to the object. In this case, the object stays on the server, and the client just receives a reference to a proxy object, which represents the original server-based object, as shown in Figure 1-10 (this is how you could use a `DataReader` remotely).

To the client, this proxy object looks just like the real thing—it exposes the same methods and properties as the original object. However, when the client interacts with the proxy (for example, by calling one of the methods that the original object exposes), the call is automatically serialized and passed over the channel (the network) to the object on the server. Any response or result is then passed back to the client through the channel. This approach is referred to as Marshal By Reference (MBR) remoting.

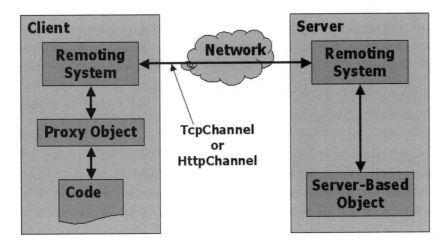

Figure 1-10. Remoting a `DataSet` through a proxy

Both of these remoting techniques allow the client to use objects that were originally created on the server. You can serialize a `DataSet` object or XML document, and you can also serialize other objects such as collections—for example, a `Hashtable` or an `Array`. You'll look in more detail at how you use these remoting techniques in Chapter 4 and in a later sample application.

Are You Just Displaying the Data?

If you're only going to display the data to the end user in a fixed format (for example, as a table in a Web page), there's generally no need to remote the data at all. You don't need to send all the *data* to the client over the wire—you can just send the final presentation information in whatever format the client device can accept.

In this scenario, the reader objects provide an ideal best-performance technique. In addition, in conjunction with server controls that can perform server-side data binding, you get a highly efficient way of displaying data. The only minor issue you need to be aware of is that the `DataReader` object isn't just read-only, but it's also forward-only. You can think of the reader objects as being like a fire-hose cursor in classic ADO. This means that you can only read the data from the `DataReader` once, without closing and reopening it.

> **NOTE** *In classic ADO, you can open a* Recordset *object with different types of cursors; some cursors allow you to move from any record to any other record or to iterate through the entire rowset as many times as you like. Under the .NET Framework, you can't iterate through the data in a* DataReader *more than once, and there are no options available to change this behavior.*

So if you're using server controls or custom controls that need to access the same rowset more than once, using a reader object is probably not going to be an efficient approach. It means multiple trips to the data store to fetch the data. Instead, where you need to access the data more than once, you can load it into an object that can store (or persist) the data. Obvious candidates are the DataSet and XmlDocument objects, both of which allow your code to move freely around the data and read it as many times as required without involving extra trips to the data store.

Some n-Tier Data Access Scenarios

To understand in more detail how you might divide the various tiers in your applications, you'll now look at some possible scenarios. This isn't an exhaustive list but provides the basis for the most common approaches.

Displaying Data

You'll start by looking at some of the possibilities for just displaying data. You'll consider how you might implement the features required to update the data and return the updates to the server shortly.

Doing It All on the Server

The most general scenario for displaying data on the client is to perform all of the processing on the server or on one or more servers clustered together. The data tier and the middle tier are confined to the server(s), and the client simply provides the presentation interface. Of course, as suggested earlier, the data tier and the middle tier can be on different physical servers—one or more clustered machines acting only as the "data store" and the remainder of the processing (such as the ASP.NET pages) executing on one or more other servers.

This type of architecture also suits applications where the data is being remoted in some specific and perhaps custom format for use by another application or service. The actual format of the data depends on what the client requires. For a Web browser, the format will usually be HTML; for a cell phone or similar device, it could be Wireless Markup Language (WML). However, if your client is some kind of remote service such as BizTalk Server, then it'll probably expect a custom format such as XML, SOAP, or perhaps a Comma-Separated Values (CSV) document.

Figure 1-11 demonstrates some of the possibilities. You can use a stored procedure or a SQL statement to extract the data you require and then use ASP.NET to process it, or you can use them to implement a Web Service that exposes the data over the network to the client in a format that it can use directly. A third possibility, also shown in Figure 1-11, is to extract the data as XML fragments from the data store and then process it and expose it to the client. Note that we use the reader objects in this case because they provide the best performance when you only need to deliver the data to the client.

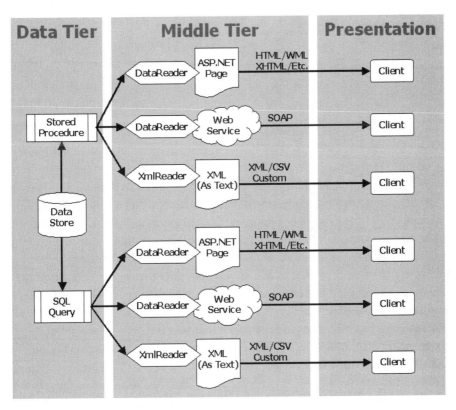

Figure 1-11. Displaying relational data by processing it on the server

Figure 1-11 shows some of the possibilities when the data is stored in a data store such as a relational database. If the data is stored as XML documents, or in a form that'll expose it to the data tier as XML, then you have some other opportunities.

Figure 1-12 shows how you might extract and process XML data to send to the client for use there. Again, the extraction of the data is via a reader object, and you can use various techniques to process it and expose it to the client.

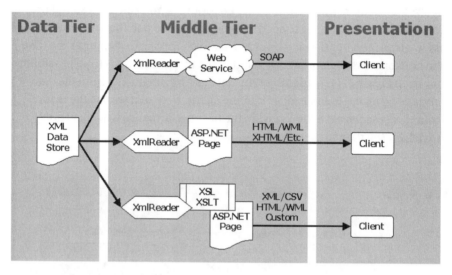

Figure 1-12. Displaying XML data by processing it on the server

Expanding the Middle Tier

Although the extracting and processing of data often takes place in one object, such as an ASP.NET page, you'll regularly need to provide a more granular architecture to take advantage of the benefits provided by using component-based design. You might have business rules that need to be applied to the data before it's displayed or sent to the client. Alternatively, it could be for security reasons, for implementing distributed transactions, or just for providing reusability and easier application maintenance.

For example, you might have many pages that access a data store to extract a list of customers. By building this process into a component that's separate from the ASP.NET page or other objects that expose the data to the client, you can provide a layer of abstraction. Then, if you need to change the data store or the structure of the data at some point in the future, or change the rules for accessing it, you can just replace the component with a new version.

As long as the component's interface remains unchanged, all the applications that use it will see the same output from the component and continue to work as before. However, the methods that the component uses internally to extract and process the data from the data store can be modified as required. This is one of the most common and useful architectures for presenting data and the one that many applications use (see Figure 1-13).

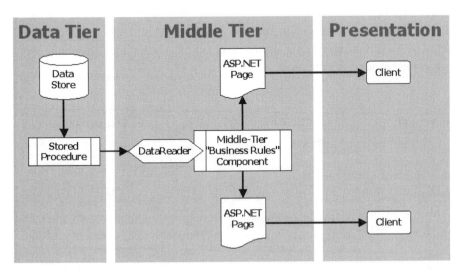

Figure 1-13. Expanding the middle tier when displaying data

Of course, there's no reason why the process can't use more than one component. It may make sense to break down the processing even further (into more component layers) if the data extraction is highly complex or if the same data is used in several places. For example, you could use a component to extract the data as a series of rows containing all the required columns in primary key order. This component could then be the source of data for other components that sorted the data in a different order or that exposed only certain columns from the data.

Moving Processing to the Client

In later chapters, you'll look in detail at some ways you can process data on the client. In the meantime, you'll explore an overall architecture approach that can support this. In earlier sections of this chapter we listed some of the ways that you can provide client-side processing for your data. What we want to do here is show how you might get that data to the client and what kinds of processing they might be able to carry out.

In general, you'll take advantage of client-side scripting (usually JavaScript but perhaps VBScript for Internet Explorer or WMLScript for cell phone–type devices), client-side components written in Java or a platform-specific language, or client-side executable programs written with languages such as Visual Basic 6.0, C++, Delphi, and so on. Of course, all the features you need are also part of the .NET Framework, which can be made available on the client through the user downloading and installing the Framework redistributable.

Therefore, Figure 1-14 shows some of the ways you might implement getting the data to the client and processing it there. Of course, this isn't by any means the full set of possibilities. However, it should give you a flavor for how you might approach the task in different ways.

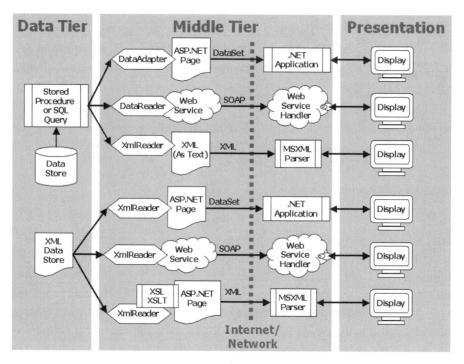

Figure 1-14. Processing relational and XML data on the client

Getting Updates Back to the Server

In many cases, such as the examples shown earlier, your only requirement is to get data to the client in as fast and efficient a manner as possible. However, many applications require the client to send data back, as well. This might be to update the data store or to carry out other specific actions that require data input.

HTML Forms and Query Strings

The usual ways of transmitting simple sets of data from the client to the server used in previous versions of ASP still work fine in ASP.NET. You can invite a user to enter data into an HTML `<form>` on the page and collect that data when the page is submitted to the server. You can also collect values that are appended to the query string when the client requests a page.

In fact, as you'll discover when building `<form>` pages with ASP.NET (or *Web Forms*, to give them their proper name), the postback architecture and the built-in viewstate make it all much easier. Values in HTML controls that are declared with the `runat="server"` attribute (server controls) automatically persist their values between page postbacks. Plus, you can always use the traditional technique of inserting values into `hidden`-type controls and posting the form back to the server.

As far as receiving "commands" from the client, the ASP.NET event-driven architecture (provided by the new postback mechanism) does most of the work for you. An event handler can be connected to any server-side control, and the code in that event handler executes automatically when the user interacts with the control on the client.

Client-Side Components

It's also possible to arrange for rich clients to send data back without submitting the complete page by using a client-side component. An obvious example in Internet Explorer 5 and higher is the XMLHTTP component. This is part of the MSXML parser that's installed with Internet Explorer 5 and higher, and it can perform `GET` or `POST` requests to the server, sending data that appears in the ASP.NET `Request.Form` or `Request.QueryString` collections.

Other client-side components are available, including Java applets that perform the same kind of process. Alternatively, you could create your own ActiveX controls or Java applets and arrange for these to be downloaded and installed when the user first visits the page.

Of course, these techniques will only work on rich clients that can provide the environment to run the appropriate components or applications. There are also issues regarding users' concerns over security. You'd usually need to digitally sign the code to make it acceptable to users—if not, their browser may refuse to accept it at all (depending on the security level they've set up). Nevertheless, this might be a useful technique in an intranet or extranet scenario where you can control the type of client-side device and the user's security settings.

Client-Side Executables, Windows Forms Applications, and Services

The third common scenario for rich clients is where the client is running some kind of executable program or service that communicates with your Web server. Client-side applications can be written in any language that the client can support, as long as that language provides features to access the network, send HTTP requests, and handle the HTTP responses that your server generates.

The languages mentioned a couple of pages ago (in the "Moving Processing to the Client" section)—such as Visual Basic 6.0, C++, Delphi, and others—are suitable for this task. In addition, of course, all the features you need are part of the .NET Framework. As you saw earlier in this chapter, this can be made available on the client through the user downloading and installing the Framework redistributable (approximately 25MB). It can also be installed as a service pack for the operating system through the Windows Update feature in Windows XP, Windows 2000, and Windows Server 2003.

You might therefore have a situation where the client just requires you to deliver some data, and you leave them to do all the processing. Or it might be a collaborative effort where (for example) the selected data is extracted and sorted on the server, and then the client manages the display and can show and hide appropriate rows or columns on demand without requiring any intervention from the server. Alternatively, the client might be a service of some type, which uses the data from your application as its own source data and then submits changes back after its client has processed that data.

Once the client-side data updates are complete, or the new data has been gathered from the user, the client application packages it up (or *marshals* it, to use the correct terminology) in a suitable format and submits it to the server for processing and storage. The *package*, or format, of the submitted data must be suitable for your application to handle. Of course, for a client that's running on the .NET Framework, the same remotable objects discussed earlier—a DataSet, a DataTable, an XML document, and so on—are suitable.

Figure 1-15 shows some of the ways you might implement such architecture with rich clients, where the data is processed on the client and then marshaled back to the server to update the original data store.

Again, this is by no means a comprehensive list of possibilities. The way that data is sent back might not be related to the way it was delivered. Remember that ADO.NET and the System.Xml classes provide a seamless approach to handling data in either relational or XML format. So you might deliver a DataSet and get back an XML update document instead.

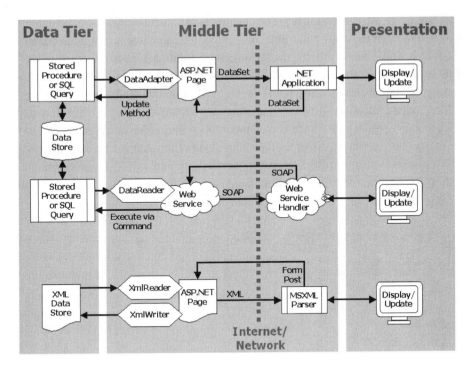

Figure 1-15. Updating relational and XML data by processing it on the client

In fact, this is a distinct possibility if you decide to take advantage of the *diff-gram* capabilities of ADO.NET. A diffgram is just an XML document that describes the contents of a DataSet, including any changes that have been made to the data in that DataSet. You'll look at diffgrams in Chapter 9 while you examine the issue of updating the source data in more detail.

Summary

This chapter was designed to give you a feel for what the book is about, as well as introduce the main characters that will appear within it. We talked about the meaning of the term *distributed application* and how to define the basic architecture for these types of applications. We also presented the possibilities for implementing the different tiers (or layers) of the application using a range of techniques.

Furthermore, we discussed some of the limitations imposed on your application by two parts of the environment in which it must live. We very briefly discussed the protocols available on the Internet and their limitations. We also presented the problems of servicing the increasingly wide range of disparate client devices—from Web browsers and Internet televisions to cellular phones and the Pocket PC.

Then we presented architecture issues in more detail and gave an overview of the capabilities of the new data access techniques available within the .NET Framework. We discussed how you might implement the various features you want to include in your applications and why we think that .NET provides a great development environment for building these kinds of applications.

Overall, the chapter covered the following topics:

- Just exactly what a distributed application is

- The basics involved in planning, designing, and implementing a distributed application

- The various objects and techniques you can use to implement such an application

- How these objects can interact to provide the features you want or need

- An overview of the ADO.NET relational data access classes

- An overview of the System.Xml document access classes

- How data access fits into the *n*-tier model

You'll examine all of these topics in a lot more depth in later chapters as you become more involved in the plot—and you start to form your own opinions of how you can apply the techniques to your own applications. In the next couple of chapters, you'll get down to the details and see some of the different ways you can extract and expose data from both relational and XML-based data sources to the various tiers in your applications.

CHAPTER 2

Components and
Data Access

YOU'VE NOW REACHED a stage in our story where we've covered the background in sufficient depth to be able to start implementing some useful code. You've met all the characters, you know their names and what they look like, and now you need to get them interacting. It's time to start seeing how you can construct your applications to use an *n*-tier architecture, business object components, and the services of the operating system and .NET itself.

In this chapter, you'll look at a range of topics connected with extracting data from a data source—be it a relational database or an Extensible Markup Language (XML) document. When you build applications that are truly distributed (so that all parts of the application don't reside on the same machine), you may need to expose data in a range of different formats. The techniques for doing so are also often extremely useful when you want to include different presentation tier components or serve different types of clients from a common back-end infrastructure.

Therefore, in this chapter, you'll do the following:

- See an overview of the different ways you can build components

- Consider why—and how—you should build data access into components

- Take a more detailed look at the DataSet object

- Look at some examples of returning relational data in different formats

You'll start with a brief review of the different ways you can build and use "components" under .NET. Then you'll move on to see how and why you might decide to build data access components that return data as a range of different object types and different data formats.

Different Types of "Component"

We've been blithely talking about components throughout the previous chapter. What do we mean by *component* in this context? Before going any further, it's worth quickly reviewing the ways you can create separate reusable sections of code for use in your .NET applications. Basically, there are five options:

- **.NET components**: Compiled into a Dynamic Link Library (DLL) and executed within the .NET Framework runtime.

- **COM** or **COM+ components**: Executed via the Component Object Model (COM) interop feature of .NET

- **User controls**: Sections of code that are compiled into the ASP.NET page itself at runtime

- **Include files**: Files containing code that's inserted into the page before it's passed to ASP.NET

- **Server controls**: Predominantly used to provide custom User Interfaces (UIs) in an application

In this book, the first option—.NET components—is the one you'll predominantly be using. However, you'll also take advantage of user controls in some situations. Include files are also useful for inserting sections of standard HTML or text into your pages, as you'll see in the examples later. You'll look at each of these five options in a little more detail here.

.NET Components

Within the .NET Framework, a great deal of effort has been put into providing a robust, secure, and reliable environment in which components can be used to create *n*-tier applications. Although .NET components are compiled into DLLs, they aren't like the DLLs you're used to using in Windows. They don't use COM to communicate with the application and with each other, and they aren't directly callable via a binary interface (they can't be accessed in the same way as `kernel32.dll`, `gdi32.dll`, and other "system" DLLs). Instead, they're compiled into Microsoft Intermediate Language (MSIL), just like ASP.NET pages and other .NET applications. At runtime, the Common Language Runtime (CLR) executes the MSIL.

In fact, the type of component we're talking about here isn't technically a *component* in the .NET sense. With the arrival of the .NET Framework, Microsoft has tightened up the terminology it uses to refer to objects that can be instantiated under the Framework. As you'll see shortly, compiling a file that contains one or more class definitions creates a .NET component of the type you use in this book, and the technically correct term for this is an *assembly*. Only when the class implements the IComponent interface is it really appropriate to use the term *component*.

However, throughout this book, we'll use the terms *object*, *component*, and *assembly* fairly interchangeably when we want to refer to them as part of an application. For example, when we refer to the object or objects that implement the data access tier, we'll generally use the term *data access component*. Bear in mind that the individual compiled .NET objects may in fact be a single, or more than one, assembly.

All .NET assemblies contain a *manifest* that describes the contained modules and types and provides a *versioning system* that allows multiple versions of the same assembly to coexist on the same machine. They can also be installed simply by copying them to a bin directory on the machine—no registration is required (this is often referred to as *XCOPY deployment*). However, if you want the assembly to be *globally* available on the machine in the same way as the .NET Framework classes, rather than just available to the application in which the bin directory resides, you need to do a little more than this. To install the assembly into the Global Assembly Cache (GAC), you must run a special utility on the machine after copying the compiled DLL to it.

> **NOTE** *For details of installing .NET components and assemblies into the GAC, see the "Global Assembly Cache" topic within the "Inside the .NET Framework" section of the .NET documentation or run a search for gacutil.exe.*

It's also possible to create a *wrapper* around a .NET assembly so that it *can* be used as if it were a COM or COM+ component. This provides the opportunity to continue using existing components whose functionality is available neither in the Framework nor from a .NET assembly. The tlbexp utility builds a COM type library for the component, so it can be used just like a .NET assembly, as well as within Component Services in Windows 2000 (to take part in distributed transactions), or as a queued component. It can also be used in other non-.NET applications.

> **NOTE** *For details of using .NET components and assemblies via COM interop, see the "Interoperating with Unmanaged Code" topic within the "Programming with the .NET Framework" section of the .NET documentation.*

Building .NET Components

All .NET assemblies consist of one or more *classes*, optionally within a *namespace* that you specify. You'll see what the code looks like in more detail later in this chapter, but for the meantime the broad outline is much the same as you used to build COM components in Visual Studio 6. In Visual Basic .NET (VB .NET), the outline of the class file looks like this:

```vbnet
'import any framework classes required
Imports System
Imports System.Data
Imports System.Xml

'namespace for the component
Namespace OrderListData

  'main class definition
  Public Class SupplierListXml

    'private internal variable
    Private m_XmlFilePath As String    'path and name of XML file


    '-----------------------------------------------------


    'constructor for component
    Public Sub New()
      MyBase.New() 'call constructor for base class
    End Sub


    '-------------------------------------------------------


    'subroutines, functions and property definitions that
    'provide the working parts of the component
    Public Function MyFunction() As ReturnType
      ...
    End Function

  End Class
End Namespace
```

Obviously, a competent development tool such as Visual Studio .NET makes it easier to build all kinds of components because these tools provide features such as integrated help, debugging, and compilation. The pop-up tips and statement completion are also a bonus. However, there's no reason why you can't write components using a text editor or some other tool and then compile them afterward using the command line compilers provided with the .NET Framework. You certainly don't *need* to go out and buy Visual Studio .NET.

You can compile a class file into an assembly without using any other tool if you want. The VB .NET and C# compilers are installed along with the Framework, so you could compile the previous class from the command line using the following command:

```
vbc /t:library /out:bin\MyDLL.dll vb-components\MyApp\MySourceCode.vb ⏎
/r:system.dll,system.data.dll,system.xml.dll
```

> **NOTE** *This assumes that (a) you've navigated the command prompt to the parent folder of the* bin *and* vb-components *folders, (b) the code shown previously is in the (fictional)* MySourceCode.vb *file specified in the command, and (c) you want the DLL to be compiled into a file called* MyDLL.dll *in the* bin *folder. Note how you have to specify the Framework namespaces you reference in the class file. And if you have multiple version of the Framework installed on your machine, you should specify the full path to the instance of* vbc.exe *you want to use. The default path to* vbc.exe *is:* C:\Winnt\System32\Microsoft.NET\Framework\[*version*]\vbc.exe

Once compiled, however you go about the compilation, the DLL is simply dropped into the bin folder of an ASP.NET application. This bin folder must be placed directly within the application virtual root folder or application directory. An ASP.NET application, or any other component within the application, can locate the component by looking in this folder. Alternatively, as mentioned earlier, you can use the gacutil.exe tool to add the component to the GAC.

> **NOTE** *The samples provided include a batch file named* make.bat *for each class file (in the subfolder containing the source file for the class). This batch file contains the command required to compile the source file and place the resulting DLL in the* bin *folder.*

Using a .NET Component

The simple outline example shown previously produces a component (or, to be more exact in our use of terminology, an *assembly*) that you can use within an ASP.NET page. First, you must import it using the namespace defined in the assembly (in this case OrderListData):

```
<%@Import Namespace="OrderListData" %>
```

Then you can create an instance of it using VB .NET:

```
Dim MyList As New SupplierListXml()
```

Or, you can use it in C#:

```
SupplierListXml MyList = new SupplierListXml();
```

Finally, you can call its methods, read and set any properties it exposes, and generally work with it like you would any other .NET Framework class.

For example, in VB .NET:

```
MyList.MyProperty = sValue
sResult = MyList.MyFunction()
```

Or in C#:

```
MyList.MyProperty = sValue;
sResult = MyList.MyFunction();
```

As you can see, it's easy—certainly no harder than you're used to when building COM or COM+ components. The built-in cross-language debugging features of the Framework and development tools such as Visual Studio .NET are a pleasure to use, and the removal of the requirement for registering components makes it even easier to test and update them.

COM and COM+ Components

Just because Microsoft has invented a new execution platform for your applications (.NET) doesn't mean that you'll immediately throw away all the applications you're using now. If you decide to migrate existing applications, or even when you're building new ones under .NET, you might need to take advantage of the services provided by existing COM or COM+ components.

This is possible; the Framework includes a utility named `tlbimp` that creates a .NET wrapper around a COM or COM+ component. This allows it to be stored in the `bin` directory of an application (or the GAC) and used just like a standard .NET component. Obviously, the process is less efficient than making calls to a native .NET component, but it's an extremely useful option until you can rewrite the components under .NET or replace them with "commercial" .NET versions.

The main factors governing the efficiency of wrapped components are the number of calls that need to be made to the component (does it require several properties to be set each time it's used, or is there one method call that uses parameters?), and the volume of data that's being passed across the managed/unmanaged boundary between .NET and the component itself.

> **NOTE** *For information on using COM and COM+ components within .NET via COM Interop, see the topic Interoperating with Unmanaged Code within the "Programming with the .NET Framework" section of the .NET documentation.*

User Controls

.NET introduces a new way to build modules of reusable code. A *user control* is basically just an "excerpt" or section of an ASP.NET page. It can contain both a UI (for example text, HTML, server controls, and so on) and server-side or client-side executable code. Or it can contain just one of these types of content. Server-side code will usually be in the form of subroutines or functions, and these can be called from within the page that hosts the control—just as if it was a compiled .NET component. User controls are stored on disk with the file extension `.ascx`.

As an example, Figure 2-1 shows a user control that you'll include in one of the example pages in Chapter 12. It renders an HTML table in a page that's used to reconcile data update errors. The point is that the entire table is generated dynamically by the user control each time the page loads. You can use it more than once in the same page and reuse it in other pages as required.

Modified row in **Orders** table. Order ID:**10890**									
Error: Concurrency violation: the UpdateCommand affected 0 records.									
	Required	Shipped	ShipVia	Freight	Name	Address	City	Code	Country
Proposed values:	16/03/1998	18/02/1998	Speedy Express[1]	$10.00	Du monde entier	67, rue des Cinquante Otages	Nantes	44000	France
Existing values:	16/03/1998	18/02/1998	Speedy Express[1]	$20.00	Du monde entier	67, rue des Cinquante Otages	Nantes	442222	France
Replace existing values?	☐	☐	☐	☐	☐	☐	☐	☐	☐

Figure 2-1. An example of a user control provided with the sample applications for this book

User controls don't have to generate output that's visible in the page; in other words, they don't have to create parts of the UI (as demonstrated previously). Instead, you can use them simply to insert some reusable server-side code into a page. The following code shows another user control, which provides a function that might perform some really useful task with numbers. Notice that the source file contains the Control directive instead of the Page directive:

```
<%@Control Language="VB"%>

<script language="VB" runat="server">

Public Function DoSomethingUseful(iInput As Integer) As String
  ' do something really clever here to get value to return
  Dim sResult As String = ....
  Return sResult
End Function

</script>
```

Properties of User Controls

User controls can also expose properties, just as a server control or assembly does. A property that can be read and written (a read/write property) is defined with both a "setter" and a "getter" routine:

```
Public Property MyProperty() As String
  Get
    ' get value from internal variables or calculation
    Dim sInternalValue As String = ....
    Return sInternalValue
  End Get
  Set(ByVal sValue As String)
    sInternalValue = sValue
  End Set
End Property
```

In VB .NET, if a property is read-only or write-only, the declaration must contain ReadOnly or WriteOnly. The following declares a read-only property named AnotherProperty:

```vb
Public ReadOnly Property AnotherProperty() As Integer
  Get
    ' get value from internal variables or calculation
    Dim iInternalValue As Integer = ....
    Return iInternalValue
  End Get
End Property
```

The same thing in C# looks like this:

```csharp
<%@Control Language="C#"%>

<script language="C#" runat="server">

public String DoSomethingUseful(int iInput) {
  // do something really clever here to get value to return
  String sResult = .... ;
  return sResult;
}

public String MyProperty {
  get {
    // get value from internal variables or calculation
    String sInternalValue = .... ;
    return sInternalValue;
  }
  set {
    sInternalValue = value;
  }
}

public int AnotherProperty {
  get {
    // get value from internal variables or calculation
    int iInternalValue = .... ;
    return iInternalValue;
  }
}

</script>
```

A user control like the one you've just seen, which contains no UI elements, isn't actually visible in the page. However, the contents are compiled into the page the first time the page is accessed. (Changes to the user control file also cause the original page to be recompiled with the new version automatically when it's next accessed.) So, unlike a compiled .NET component (which is compiled as a separate object, and so must be instantiated separately each time it executes) there's no runtime performance hit.

However, user controls are generally less flexible than compiled .NET assemblies or components. Furthermore, they can only be used within ASP.NET pages (files with an .aspx file extension), which can produce a serious limitation—for example, they can't be used within a Web Service (.asmx) file.

Implementing a User Control

Any ASP.NET page can take advantage of a user control, such as the one we've just described, by first registering the element that will be used to identify it and then inserting the control. If the control generates any output in the page (in other words, if it contains visible text, HTML, or other content), this output will appear at the location of the user control within the source (.aspx) page. The user control can be in the same language as the page or in a different language. So, for example, you can use a user control written in VB .NET in a C# page, or vice versa.

The following code shows how you might insert the nonvisible control we showed earlier, but the technique is identical irrespective of the content of the user control. You register the control in the page using a Register directive, which specifies the tag prefix and tag name, plus the location of the .ascx file. Then you insert an instance of the control into the page at the required location using this element (tag):

```
<%@ Register TagPrefix="dda" TagName="useful"
             Src="my-user-control.ascx" %>

<%'-- insert user control into the page --%>
<dda:useful id="ctlUseful" runat="server"/>
```

Now it's simply a matter of referencing the control to be able to access the routines it contains. In VB .NET, to call the DoSomethingUseful function, you can use this:

```
Dim sResult As String = ctlUseful.DoSomethingUseful(42)
```

Or, in C#, you can use:

```
String sResult = ctlConnectStrings.DoSomethingUseful(42);
```

Likewise, to set or read properties, it works just like any other server control. In VB .NET, it works like this:

```
Dim sValue As String = ctlUseful.MyProperty
ctlUseful.MyProperty = "A new value"
Dim iValue As Integer = ctlUseful.AnotherProperty
```

Or, in C#, it works like this:

```
String sValue = ctlUseful.MyProperty;
ctlUseful.MyProperty = "A new value";
int iValue = ctlUseful.AnotherProperty;
```

Include Files

One technique that has long been used in ASP to provide some level of encapsulation of reusable content is the Server-Side Include (SSI) feature supported by Internet Information Services (IIS) and most other Web servers. In our example pages, we use the following SSI directive:

```
<!-- #include file="/global/foot.inc" -->
```

You can include this line at the foot of every page—this has the effect of inserting the contents of the file foot.inc into the page. As the filename suggests, foot.inc contains the text and HTML that appears at the bottom of the example pages. If we needed to change the page footer, we'd just edit this file and every page would use the new version.

SSIs are in fact a feature of IIS and aren't implemented by ASP or ASP.NET. The ASP preprocessor sees the #include directive and passes the page to the IIS processor ssinc.dll, which simply fetches the referenced file and replaces the directive with the contents of this file. Once ASP.NET gets to see the page, it appears as though the contents of the include file are just part of the page.

The SSI "include" feature does impose a marginal performance hit when the page is first accessed—but, like user controls, the content is compiled into the page and so subsequent requests aren't affected.

Server Controls

The final type of "component" listed earlier is the *server control*. These aren't really applicable to *n*-tier development and are designed to allow the creation of custom UIs instead. The server controls provided as part of the ASP.NET installation are obvious examples of this technology, and control developers can build their own controls that behave and are used in the same way.

For example, you can inherit from an existing server control and extend it by overriding or adding new methods and properties. Or you can create controls from scratch that implement some specific feature you want in your pages. In theory, you could create server controls that combine the features of fetching and displaying data or performing multiple and complex tasks all at once. However, this generally defeats the whole principle of *n*-tier design and can reduce the reusability and extensibility of an application.

We don't cover building or using custom server controls in this book. However, you'll take advantage of the server controls provided with ASP.NET—including the more complex beasts such as the `DataGrid` and `DataList` controls.

Accessing and Exposing Data

One important advantage you get from using the .NET Framework is seamless integration between relational data (data stored in a relational database such as SQL Server) and XML data stored in documents. This integration means you can choose the format in which you want to expose the data, without having to know beforehand the type of data store with which you'll be interacting.

Delivering Data to Rich Clients

For example, if you're dealing with a rich client that's going to carry out some of the processing work for you, you might find that this client requires you to deliver an ADO.NET-style `DataSet` object to them. If the data store is a relational database, then you can easily fill a `DataSet` from it using ADO.NET techniques. If the data store is an XML document, however, you must use a different technique to load it into a `DataSet`—and then deliver this `DataSet`.

Furthermore, the data may be in a different format; for example, it may be delivered by a Web Service (as an XML document but not necessarily in the correct format for the client to use). It might instead be a Comma-Separated Values (CSV) file, a collection or array of values, or even some application-specific binary or text format. The point is that you can still use a component within your application's data access tier that reads the data in one format and delivers it in another format.

Managing Data for Down-Level Clients

In contrast, the client may be "dumb" and require you to create the complete page including the data on the server and deliver it as HTML—or Wireless Markup Language (WML) for a mobile device. In this case, the intermediate data format depends on the techniques you intend to use to create the data display.

For example, if you're using an ASP.NET `DataGrid` server control, you need the data to be in a suitable format such as a `DataSet`, a `DataView`, or a reference to a `DataReader`. In this case, when the data source is a relational database, the normal ADO.NET methods will work fine. However, if the data source is something different, you might need to perform some translation by using different server-side data access code.

Displaying XML Data

Both the previous scenarios assume you're delivering data or using it server side, as an ADO.NET `DataSet`. Instead, you might decide that the output you want is best created by using an *XSLT stylesheet* to perform a transformation on the source data.

Again, this is easily implemented because you can extract your data from any type of data store and expose it as XML so that the transformation can be carried out. For example, you might simply have to load the XML from a document file on disk. On the other hand, you might have to extract the data from a relational database instead and then assemble it into an XML document.

This second scenario is simple enough to implement using one of several techniques. You can fill a `DataSet` using ADO.NET techniques and then export the content as an XML document. Alternatively, if the data store is Microsoft SQL Server, you can use the SQLXML technology (discussed later in the chapter) that it provides to extract the data as XML elements and then build them into a valid XML document. You could even access the data store using a `DataReader` and then use code to assemble the values into an XML document in much the same way as was common using classic ADO in ASP 3.0 and earlier.

Later in this chapter and in the next one, we'll demonstrate a range of ways that you can extract, transform, and format data so that the output is in the appropriate format for the client or for a business-tier component that lies between the data source and the client.

Working with the DataSet Object

To circumvent the restrictions imposed by the traditional Recordset object that has always been the basic way of handling rowsets in previous versions of ADO, ADO.NET introduces the DataSet object. A DataSet can contain one or more tables (DataTable objects), together with all the metadata required to work with these tables. This includes the data type and size of each column and any constraints and primary keys you want to define for the table and its columns.

It can also hold one or more relationships between the tables. This means that the DataSet can act as a data storage and remoting (data transfer) object, while allowing data to be accessed based on the relationships between the tables, as well as accessed as individual data rows.

The Structure of the DataSet Object

Figure 2-2 shows the basic structure of a DataSet object. The DataSet itself has two collections:

- A Tables collection containing DataTable objects that store the data.

- A Relations collection containing Relation objects representing the relationships between the tables. The developer can create these relationships after the tables have been loaded into the DataSet (or, in the case of a typed DataSet, before the data is loaded).

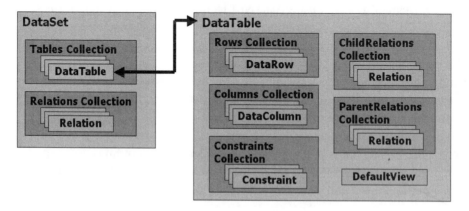

Figure 2-2. The DataSet *object and the subsidiary classes it uses*

The DataTable Object

Each DataTable object has five collections of other objects and a DefaultView. The DefaultView returns a view of the data in the table as a DataView object, which is lighter and doesn't contain all the metadata about the table. It's often used for server-side data binding.

The five collections supported by the DataTable object are as follows:

- A Rows collection containing DataRow objects that store the data for each row in this table.

- A Columns collection containing DataColumn objects that store the metadata about each column in the table.

- A Constraints collection containing Constraint objects, which define the unique properties, default values, primary keys, and so on for this table.

- A ChildRelations collection containing Relation objects that identify relationships where this table is the parent table in that relationship.

- A ParentRelations collection containing Relation objects that identify relationships where this table is the child table in that relationship.

Filling a DataSet with a DataAdapter

Chapter 1 briefly introduced the way you can use a Connection, a Command, and a DataAdapter to connect your DataSet to a data source. Figure 2-3 shows this process.

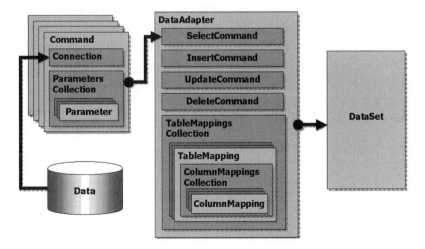

Figure 2-3. The objects involved in connecting a DataSet *to a data source*

The value you define for the SelectCommand controls what data the DataAdapter object extracts. The Command object attached to the DataAdapter's SelectCommand property uses this to fetch the data via the Connection. Usually, the SelectCommand value will be a SQL statement or the name of a stored procedure within the database. However, depending on the data source, you may be able to provide other application-specific commands here, such as just the name of a table in that database.

As you saw in the Chapter 1, the Command object exposes a collection of Parameter objects that define the parameters that will be used with the command. If you're using a stored procedure to update the original data, you'll need to provide these parameters, unless the stored procedure doesn't require any parameters.

Table and Column Mappings

One question that arises is this: How does the DataAdapter know what to do with the data when it comes to fill the DataSet? By default, the table names and column names in the original data store are used to create the new tables in the DataSet.

However (as you can see in Figure 2-3), the DataAdapter also provides a collection of TableMapping objects that define how the original table structure in the data source is mapped to the tables and columns in the DataSet. A TableMapping object specifies the name of the original table in the DataSet and the name of the corresponding table in the DataSet object.

Moreover, each TableMapping object has its own collection of ColumnMapping objects. These objects specify the names of each of the columns that are extracted from the original data source and map them to the names of the corresponding columns used in the tables in the DataSet. Figure 2-4 shows this process.

This feature is extremely useful. It allows you to change (or *alias*) the names of the tables and columns as you fill the DataSet. If you use the DataGrid server control to display the data (as you saw in Chapter 1), it shows the column headings automatically using the column names—so you can display appropriate column names with this technique without having to alias them in the stored procedure or SQL statement. When you come to update the original data, the table and column mappings are even more crucial. You'll look at updating a data source in Chapter 8.

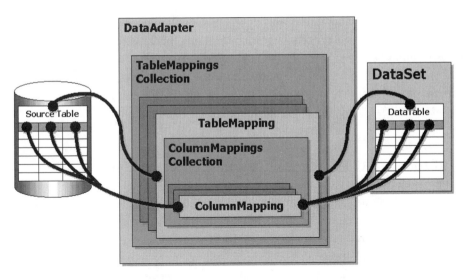

Figure 2-4. Table and column mappings relate the source and destination for data in a DataSet

When Should You Use a DataSet?

You've seen how the DataSet provides a powerful and comprehensive container in which you can store data and remote it to other tiers of an application. The big question is this: Should you always be using a DataSet, or are there better alternatives? In this book, we use a mixture of objects for data access, but you'll see that a great many of our applications depend on the DataSet.

For developers building ASP.NET applications that run on a single machine or a Web farm, there's often no requirement to remote data in the real sense. The data access components, any business logic required, and the code to create the user interface (the presentation tier) can all run on the same machine. The data source itself can, of course, be on a different server—the OLE-DB and SQL Server–specific providers in .NET can easily access a database running on another machine.

Hence, there's no need to use a data structure that can survive being remoted to a different machine. In this scenario, it's quite acceptable to pass a reference to a "connected" data access object such as a DataReader from one tier to the next. In fact, this is positively encouraged because it's far more efficient when just reading data or firing updates back at the data source than it is to create a DataSet object and work via that.

However, most of our "rich client" applications will require disconnected access to the data. This is the whole point of building this kind of application because it allows some or all of the processing to be passed to the client. If the client wants to be able to use the application while disconnected from the server, then disconnected data access support is a necessity. In these situations, for relational data, the DataSet is the obvious choice.

Relational Data Access Component Examples

To demonstrate some of the techniques discussed so far, you'll see a few example data access components that implement some of these features. We'll use these components throughout the book—they'll form the data access tier for some of the applications you'll build later.

The aim here is to demonstrate the various ways you can expose the same data in different formats. In most cases, the format used is independent of the actual source of the data, be it a relational database or an XML document. We'll show how you can transform the data within these data stores into specific output formats to suit different types of client. In the remainder of this chapter, you'll do this with a relational data store as the source, and then you'll look at how you can access XML documents in the following chapter.

We'll also try to provide some feedback on the expected levels of efficiency of these various techniques. Some are certainly less than optimally efficient because of the nature of the processing they carry out.

For example, returning a CSV file or a custom array from an XML document involves some complex processing within the data access components. By contrast, if the result is that a rich client can use the data without continually having to post back to the server and absorb the bandwidth and extra processing this requires, you'll usually end up with a more efficient overall solution. The most significant factor affecting server performance is likely to be the number of rows that have to be processed and returned to the client.

Setting Up the Examples

All the examples described in this book are available for you to download and run on your own server, in both VB .NET and C#, from the Downloads section of the Apress Web site at http://www.apress.com or from http://www.daveandal.net/books/4923/. (You can also view and run most of them from the second of these locations.) The sample download includes a readme.txt file in the root folder, which contains full installation instructions for the sample files and the database. Follow these steps:

1. Unzip the sample files into a folder within your default Web site (we suggest you create a new folder under wwwroot). Make sure you have the Restore Folders or Restore Directories option turned on to ensure that the original folder structure stored in the zip file is maintained.

2. Create a virtual application for the sample files by selecting the folder you just created (and which should now contain the readme.txt file) in Internet Services Manager. Right-click, select Properties, and in the Home Directory tab click the Create button in the Application Settings section.

3. Edit the file web.config in this same root folder of the samples so that the two connection strings defined in the <appSettings> node point to your database server. The user named anon is created by the SQL scripts and automatically given access to the database; if you already have the Northwind database installed, you may need to check and change the username and password in the connection strings.

4. Follow the instructions in the readme.txt file to add the stored procedures used in the example pages to the Northwind database or to install the complete example database. The examples use the sample Northwind database provided with SQL Server 7.0 and above. You'll need to create the stored procedures used in the example pages within this database—you can do this by running the necessary SQL scripts (provided in the database folder of the download) against the database in SQL Server Query Analyzer. We've also provided SQL scripts that will create a suitable database, which you can use if you don't have Northwind installed.

The source files for the components used in these examples are in the folders named vb-components and cs-components. If you're running a different version of the Framework than was used to originally build these component DLLs, you may need to recompile all the DLLs used in the examples. If you receive the error "Cannot find System.Data or one of its dependencies" (or a similar error message), recompile the DLLs by running the make.bat files provided in each of the subfolders of the vb-components and cs-components folders (depending on whether you installed the VB .NET or C# versions of the example files) in a Command window.

> **NOTE** *Note that the path to the folder containing the* vbc.exe *and/or* csc.exe *.NET compilers must be included in your* PATH *command when using the* make.bat *files. Go to Start ➤ Settings ➤ Control Panel ➤ System, and in the Advanced tab click the Environment Variables button. In the System Variables section is an entry for Path, and you should add the path to the Framework version folder you want to use. This is* %SystemRoot%\Microsoft.NET\Framework\[version]\.

Accessing and Returning Relational Data

The main menu page for the data access examples is in the `accessing-data` folder of the samples. It shows the two data sources you'll use—a relational database (SQL Server accessed via the OLE-DB provider) and an XML document stored as a disk file. It also shows the various formats/objects that you're returning that data as, as shown in Figure 2-5.

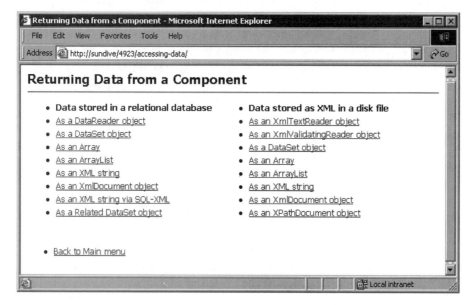

Figure 2-5. The main menu page for the examples in this chapter, showing the two types of data source they use

NOTE *We installed the samples in a folder named* 4923 *on a server named* sundive, *as you can see in the figures. You can use any folder name you like and just navigate to this folder to display the main samples menu. From this main menu, follow the Returning Data with Data Access Components link to see the page shown in Figure 2-5, which is in the* accessing-data *folder—along with all the sample files in this and the next chapter.*

Rather than create separate data access components for each example page, which would quickly become confusing and difficult to manage, we've created just three components that between them expose all the methods required to implement the pages listed in this menu. You'll examine each of these components and their methods in turn as you look at the different example pages.

Returning a DataReader Reference

All the examples in the left column use a relational database for the data source. The first example shows how you can return a reference to a DataReader object and use that object in your ASP.NET page. You can see the result of running the page in Figure 2-6.

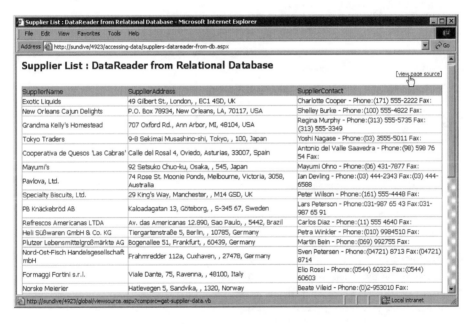

Figure 2-6. Returning a reference to a DataReader

Notice that there's a link at the top-right corner of every page that allows you to view the source code for the page. If you click that link, the resulting page contains another link that allows you to view the source code for the component that the page uses.

The SupplierList Data Access Component

The data access component we've created is in a DLL named `SupplierList.dll`, placed in the `bin` folder of the application. The source code for this component is named `get-supplier-data.vb` and is in the `SupplierListDB` subfolder of the `vb-components` and `cs-components` subfolders. The component contains `Imports` statements for the Framework classes it uses, has its own `Namespace` definition of `SupplierListDB`, and defines a class named `SupplierList` that contains the routines it exposes for use by the ASP.NET pages:

```vb
Imports System
Imports System.Data
Imports System.Data.OleDb
Imports System.Data.SqlClient
Imports System.Xml
Imports System.Collections
Imports Microsoft.VisualBasic

'the namespace for the component
Namespace SupplierListDB

  'the main class definition
  Public Class SupplierList

    'private internal variable to store connection string
    Private m_ConnectString As String


    '-----------------------------------------------------


    'constructor for component - requires the connection
    'string to be provided as the single parameter
    Public Sub New(ByVal ConnectString As String)
      MyBase.New() 'call constructor for base class
      m_ConnectString = ConnectString
    End Sub


    '-----------------------------------------------------


    *** other methods defined here ***


  End Class
End Namespace
```

There's a single `Private` "member" variable that's used by most of the methods within the component—the database connection string. When you come to instantiate the data access component, you must provide a valid connection string in the single parameter to the constructor. The constructor is defined within `Sub New()`, and the parameter value is used to set the internal member variable. Notice that the first action within the constructor is a call to the base class constructor. The ASP.NET page you saw in the previous screenshot, and all the other relational database examples, reference this component by importing it at the top of the page code:

```
<%@Import Namespace="SupplierListDB" %>
```

The GetSuppliersDataReader Method

Following the definition of the constructor function, you'll find the definitions of the functions that implement the other methods of the component. Among these is the method called `GetSuppliersDataReader` used in this first example page. This method simply executes a stored procedure named `GetSupplierList`, which we've created within SQL Server's sample Northwind database. This is what the stored procedure looks like:

```
SELECT
  SupplierName=CompanyName,
  SupplierAddress=ISNULL(Address, '') + ', '
    + ISNULL(City,'') + ', ' + ISNULL(Region,'') + ', '
    + ISNULL(PostalCode,'')+ ', ' + ISNULL(Country,''),
  SupplierContact=ISNULL(ContactName,'') + ' - Phone:'
    + ISNULL(Phone,'') + ' Fax:' + ISNULL(Fax,'')
FROM Suppliers
```

Once the stored procedure has been executed, the method simply returns the reference to the `DataReader` object:

```
Public Function GetSuppliersDataReader() As OleDbDataReader

  'declare a String containing the stored procedure name
  Dim strQuery As String = "GetSupplierList"

  'create a new Connection object using connection string
  Dim objConnect As New OleDbConnection(m_ConnectString)
```

```
'create new Command using stored proc name and Connection
Dim objCommand As New OleDbCommand(strQuery, objConnect)

Try
 'open connection to the database
  objConnect.Open()

  'execute the stored proc to initialize the DataReader
  'connection will be closed when DataReader goes out of scope
  Return objCommand.ExecuteReader(CommandBehavior.CloseConnection)

Catch objErr As Exception
  Throw objErr

End Try
End Function
```

Notice the use of the value `CommandBehavior.CloseConnection` in the `Command` object's `ExecuteReader` method to ensure that the connection is closed automatically as soon as the `DataReader` is closed.

You can also see that we use a `Try...Catch` construct to handle any exception or error that might occur. If this happens, we simply raise the error to the calling routine using the `Throw` statement. This is a big bonus with .NET components in that you can freely pass exception objects back up the call chain to be handled by the calling routine. In COM components, it was always difficult to properly handle errors and notify the caller.

Of course, if all you're doing is throwing the `Exception` back to the calling routine, you can dispense with the `Try...Catch` construct altogether and allow the calling routine to catch the error. This would allow other "details" of the error, such as the stack trace, to be displayed by the calling routine. Alternatively, you'd catch different types of `Exception` here and take an appropriate course of action depending on the type of error that occurred. Because error-handling techniques aren't the focus of this discussion, we leave it to you to consult the Software Development Kit (SDK) or other documentation for a complete description of error handling methods.

Displaying the Results

The ASP.NET example page (`suppliers-datareader-from-db.aspx`) contains an `asp:Label` control where you can display any error message and the declaration of an ASP.NET `DataGrid` control that you use to display the results—the rows returned through the `DataReader`:

```
<asp:Label id="lblMessage" runat="server" />
<asp:DataGrid id="dgrSuppliers" runat="server">
  <HeaderStyle BackColor="#c0c0c0"></HeaderStyle>
  <AlternatingItemStyle BackColor="#eeeeee"></AlternatingItemStyle>
</asp:DataGrid>
```

To use the GetSuppliersDataReader method in our ASP.NET page, we've imported the class (or assembly) into the page using this:

```
<%@Import Namespace="SupplierListDB" %>
```

So now, in the Page_Load event, we can instantiate the component and call the GetSuppliersDataReader method. We catch any error that might be passed back from the component by using a Try...Catch construct here, as well:

```
Sub Page_Load()

  'get connection string from web.config
  Dim strConnect As String
  strConnect = ConfigurationSettings.AppSettings("NorthwindConnectString")

  Try
    'create an instance of the data access component
    Dim objSupplierList As New SupplierList(strConnect)

    'call the method to return the data as a DataReader
    dgrSuppliers.DataSource = objSupplierList.GetSuppliersDataReader()

  Catch objErr As Exception
    'there was an error and no data will be returned
    lblMessage.Text = "ERROR: No data returned. " & objErr.Message

  End Try

  If Not dgrSuppliers.DataSource Is Nothing Then
    'bind the data to display it
    dgrSuppliers.DataBind()
  End If
End Sub
```

So, returning a DataReader is easy, quick, and efficient if you have a relational database as the data source or some other data source that exposes its contents via a suitable OLE-DB provider, ODBC driver, or similar.

Returning a DataSet Object

The second example (suppliers-dataset-from-db.aspx) uses a method in the data access component that returns a DataSet object rather than a reference to a DataReader. The output in the page is identical because you'll use the same ASP.NET DataGrid control to display the data. The only differences in the ASP.NET page code are that you call the GetSuppliersDataSet method this time to get back a DataSet:

```
dgrSuppliers.DataSource = objSupplierList.GetSuppliersDataSet()
```

Because a DataSet can contain more than one table, you also have to specify the DataMember (the name of the table to use) when you bind the DataSet to your ASP.NET DataGrid control:

```
'set data member and bind the data to display it
dgrSuppliers.DataMember = "Suppliers"
dgrSuppliers.DataBind()
```

The GetSuppliersDataSet Method

Of course, the implementation of the GetSuppliersDataSet method within the data access component must this time create, fill, and return a DataSet object containing the results of executing the stored procedure, rather than returning the results via a DataReader. This is easy enough to do using the standard techniques as follows. We've highlighted the code lines that differ from the previous DataReader example:

```
Public Function GetSuppliersDataSet() As DataSet

  'declare a String containing the stored procedure name
  Dim strQuery As String = "GetSupplierList"

  'create a new Connection object using connection string
  Dim objConnect As New OleDbConnection(m_ConnectString)

  'create new DataAdapter using stored proc name and Connection
  Dim objAdapter As New OleDbDataAdapter(strQuery, objConnect)
```

```
'create a new DataSet object to hold the results
Dim objDataSet As New DataSet()

Try
   'get the data into a table named "Suppliers" in the DataSet
   objAdapter.Fill(objDataSet, "Suppliers")

   'return the DataSet object to the calling routine
   Return objDataSet

Catch objErr As Exception
   Throw objErr

End Try
End Function
```

OK, so the final result in the page when you use a DataSet is the same as the previous DataReader example—but that's only because you used the same UI component (an ASP.NET DataGrid) to display the data. The point is that the *data itself* is arriving and being used in a different way underneath when you bind it to the DataGrid control.

The DataReader doesn't actually return any data until the DataGrid control's DataBind method is invoked. Remember that the DataReader is simply a "pipe" that connects your ASP.NET page or component to the results set created by the data store, which is still only cached within the data store. So, if you chose to close the connection to the data store before binding the data to the DataGrid control, you'd get nothing.

In contrast, the DataSet has already extracted the data from the data store and is holding it in memory. It closed the connection itself automatically once it had extracted the data, and so it's *truly* disconnected. This is what makes the DataSet such a powerful tool in a distributed application environment—you can persist the data to disk, pass it around between tiers, and modify it while in memory. And all with no persistent connection to the original data store.

Note that the DataSet will automatically close the database connection when the Fill method completes *only* if it actually opened the connection in the first place. If you open the connection yourself before calling Fill, it'll be left open when the method ends. This is useful if you want to call Fill several times with the same connection—you can do so without closing and reopening the connection each time. Just remember that in this case, you must close the connection yourself once you've finished filling the DataSet with data.

Returning a Custom Array Reference

The next example page returns the rows from the Suppliers table in the Northwind database as a custom Array object. One minor problem here is that you don't know in advance how many rows there will be. You could get round this in a couple of ways. You could execute a SQL statement or stored procedure that returns the number of rows, but that means an extra round-trip to the database. You could create the array with more rows than you'd ever need or just keep dynamically resizing it as you read data, but these aren't exactly efficient approaches either.

We chose to provide an optional parameter to the GetSuppliersArray method, which allows the calling routine to specify the maximum number of rows to return. If omitted, the value defaults to 10 rows. As a bonus, if you changed the stored procedure to return the rows sorted on some specific column, then this technique could provide a simple "top 10" or "top whatever" feature:

```
Public Function GetSuppliersArray( _
            Optional ByVal MaximumRowNumber As Integer = 10) As Array
```

Getting the data from the data store into an array isn't difficult, but it isn't exactly efficient either. The only way to do it is to iterate through the rows returned by a DataReader and a Command object that you create and use to execute your stored procedure against the data store.

The array has to be of the correct data type for the values you extract from the database table. In general, the obvious choice is an array of type String because you can easily convert numeric values into strings to store in the array. Of course, if *all* the values being returned are numeric or some other type, then the array can be declared of this type instead. It all comes down to what you intend to do with the values.

Filling the Array

The component's GetSuppliersArray method first creates a DataReader object (that code isn't reproduced here—it's exactly the same as the code you saw in the GetSuppliersDataReader method earlier). Then you can figure out how big the array needs to be and create it. The next step is to iterate through the rows in the DataReader until either you run out of rows (objReader.Read returns False) or you've filled MaximumRowNumber rows of the array:

```
'get the index of the last column within the data
Dim intLastColIndex As Integer = objReader.FieldCount - 1

'declare a variable to hold the result array
Dim arrValues(intLastColIndex, MaximumRowNumber) As String

Dim intRowCount As Integer = 0    'to hold number of rows returned
Dim intCol As Integer   'to hold the column iterator

'iterate through rows by calling Read method until False
While objReader.Read() And intRowCount < MaximumRowNumber

  'store column values as strings in result array
  For intCol = 0 To intLastColIndex
    arrValues(intCol, intRowCount) = CType(objReader(intCol), String)
  Next

  'increment number of rows found
  intRowCount += 1

End While
objReader = Nothing 'finished with DataReader
```

> **NOTE** *In version 1.1 of the .NET Framework, the* DataReader *class gains a new property named* HasRows *that you can use to check if any rows were returned by the query or stored procedure without having to call the* Read *method.*

The final step is to resize the array to make sure that it doesn't contain empty rows (which will be the case if there were fewer rows in the data than specified in the method parameter for the original size of the array). Then you finish up by returning the array to the calling routine:

```
ReDim Preserve arrValues(intLastColIndex, intRowCount - 1)
Return arrValues    'and return array to the calling routine
```

Displaying the Results

The sample page `suppliers-array-from-db.aspx` uses the `GetSuppliersArray` method just described to fetch an array and then displays the contents, as shown in Figure 2-7.

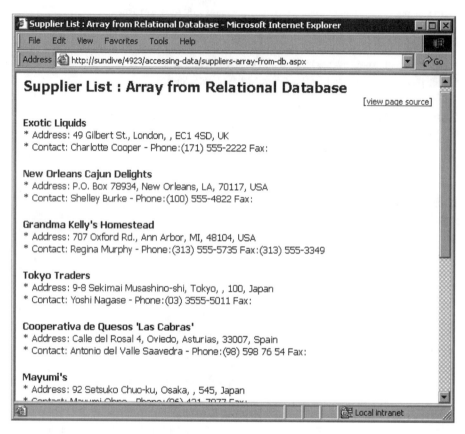

Figure 2-7. Displaying the results from the `GetSuppliersArray` *method*

The code within the `Page_Load` event handler in this page first declares a variable to hold the array returned by the method and then creates the component instance and calls the `GetSuppliersArray` method—specifying that a maximum of 10 rows should be returned:

```
'declare a variable to hold the array returned from the method
Dim arrResult As Array

'create an instance of the data access component
Dim objSupplierList As New SupplierList(strConnect)
```

```
'call the method to return the data as an Array and
'specify we only want a maximum of 10 items
arrResult = objSupplierList.GetSuppliersArray(10)
```

Having done that (and checked for an error—the Try...Catch logic isn't shown here), the code simply iterates through the array placing the values in a string, which is then displayed in an ASP.NET Label control in the page. Notice that you can get the "length" of the array (the number of rows returned) by calling the GetLength method and specifying the index of the "column" you want to get the length of:

```
'iterate through array to display values returned
'get number of rows in the array, may be less than maximum specified
Dim intLastRowIndex As Integer = arrResult.GetLength(1) - 1

Dim strResult As String = ""     'to hold results for display
Dim intRow As Integer            'to hold column iterator

For intRow = 0 To intLastRowIndex
   strResult += "<b>" & arrResult(0, intRow) & "</b><br />"
   strResult += "* Address: " & arrResult(1, intRow) & "<br />"
   strResult += "* Contact: " & arrResult(2, intRow) & "<p />"
Next

lblMessage.Text = strResult   'assign result string to Label control
```

Returning an ArrayList Reference

There are often occasions when you'll want to get just a single set of values from a data source rather than complete rows. For example, you may want to bind a list box to a set of customer names or a check box list to a set of product categories. In this case, the obvious choice of data structure is an ArrayList—a collection-based structure containing only one "column" of values.

This data access component exposes a function named GetSuppliersArrayList, which returns an ArrayList consisting of only a list of supplier names from the Northwind sample database. The technique it uses is similar to the one used in the previous example (which returned an array) but is actually quite a bit simpler. An ArrayList automatically resizes itself as you add items to it, so you don't need to worry about how many rows there are in the data source.

The function creates a DataReader in the same way as the previous example (except it uses a stored procedure named GetSupplierName that returns only the single column you want—there's no point in returning the complete rows when you only want one column). The stored procedure we created in the Northwind database looks like this:

```
CREATE PROCEDURE GetSupplierName AS
  SELECT SupplierName=CompanyName FROM Suppliers
```

Filling the ArrayList

Then the code iterates through the rows adding the values from the single column to the ArrayList. Note that you use the GetString method of the DataReader to ensure that you get a String value for the ArrayList:

```
Public Function GetSuppliersArrayList() As ArrayList

  'declare a String containing the stored procedure name
  Dim strQuery As String = "GetSupplierName"

  '* create the Connection, Command and DataReader objects here
  '* and then execute the stored procedure as before

  'create a new ArrayList object
  Dim arrValues As New ArrayList()

  'iterate through rows by calling Read method until False
  While objReader.Read()
    arrValues.Add(objReader.GetString(0))
  End While

  objReader = Nothing      'finished with DataReader

  Return arrValues         'return ArrayList to the calling routine

End Function
```

Displaying the Results

Because an `ArrayList` is a collection-based structure, you can use it with server-side data binding to populate any ASP.NET list control that supports data binding. In this example, you'll again use an ASP.NET `DataGrid` control. You just create the instance of the data access component as before, call the `GetSuppliersArrayList` method, bind the resulting `ArrayList` to your `DataGrid` control, and then call its `DataBind` method:

```
'create an instance of the data access component
Dim objSupplierList As New SupplierList(strConnect)

'call the method to return the data as an ArrayList and
'bind it to the DataGrid server control
dgrSuppliers.DataSource = objSupplierList.GetSuppliersArrayList()
dgrSuppliers.DataBind()
```

Figure 2-8 shows the results (`suppliers-arraylist-from-db.aspx`). Notice that the column heading is *Item*—this is what you always get from an `ArrayList`. That's because the `ArrayList` doesn't contain any information about the "column" names—each value in the list is referenced via the `Item` property of the list.

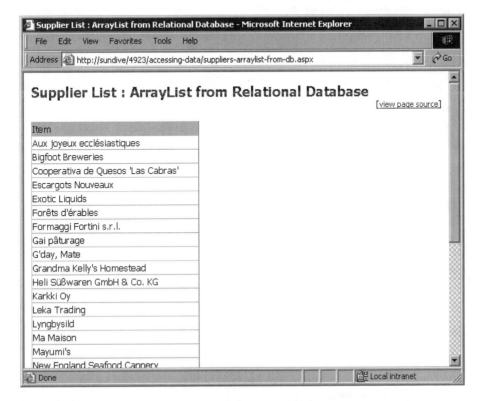

Figure 2-8. The results from the `GetSuppliersArrayList` *method*

Returning an XML String

No matter how hard you try to avoid it, as a developer working with today's technologies (especially .NET), you'll be constantly exposed to XML. So, if you still aren't on the bandwagon, you might as well get used to using it from now on. The next example demonstrates how easy it is to extract data from a relational database and return it as an XML document. In this case, you'll actually return a String that contains the XML (in the next example, you'll see how you can also return the XML as an object).

The GetSuppliersXml method in the data access component takes an optional parameter named IncludeSchema, which is False by default (if no value is provided). In this case, the returned string will contain only the XML document, without a schema. When this parameter is set to True, it forces the method to add the appropriate XML schema to the beginning of the returned document:

```
Public Function GetSuppliersXml( _
            Optional ByVal IncludeSchema As Boolean = False) As String
```

You use the same GetSupplierList stored procedure in this method as you have in most of the other examples. However, instead of accessing it through a DataReader, you use a DataSet in this case:

```
'declare a String containing the stored procedure name
Dim strQuery As String = "GetSupplierList"

'create a new Connection object using connection string
Dim objConnect As New OleDbConnection(m_ConnectString)

'create new DataAdapter using stored proc name and Connection
Dim objAdapter As New OleDbDataAdapter(strQuery, objConnect)

'create a new DataSet object to hold the results
Dim objDataSet As New DataSet()

'get the data into a table named "Suppliers" in the DataSet
objAdapter.Fill(objDataSet, "Suppliers")
```

We've omitted the error handling code here to make it easier to follow, but you can see that you now have a DataSet containing the rows from the data store. Next, you create a suitable string to hold the results. Then, to get the schema (if required) and the XML content from the DataSet, you just need to call the GetXmlSchema and GetXml methods:

```
'declare an empty String to hold the results
Dim strXml As String = ""

'get schema if specified in optional method parameter
If IncludeSchema = True Then
  strXml = objDataSet.GetXmlSchema & vbCrLf & vbCrLf
End If

'get XML data and append to String
strXml &= objDataSet.GetXml

'return the XML string to the calling routine
Return strXml
```

Displaying the Results

Because you now have XML as the output of the data access component, you can't use a DataGrid to display the results. However, you can use another of the fiendishly clever ASP.NET server controls—the asp:Xml control. The sample page suppliers-xml-from-db.aspx demonstrates this. You insert the control into the page like this:

```
<asp:Xml id="xmlResult" runat="server" />
```

If you just want to display the raw XML string, you can specify it as the DocumentContent property of this control. However, this will only show the text content of the document because the elements will not be rendered in the browser page. Instead, we've provided an XSL stylesheet that transforms the XML into an HTML table that resembles the one created by the DataGrid control used in previous examples.

Figure 2-9 shows the results, and you can see that there are links in the page where you can open the original XML document to view it and the XSL stylesheet you used to transform this XML.

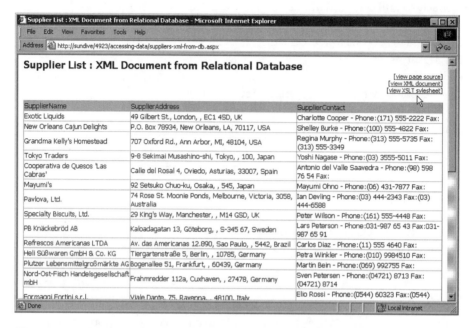

Figure 2-9. Displaying the XML results through a stylesheet, with links to the stylesheet and original data

So, in the Page_Load event, all you need to do is instantiate your data access component, call the GetSuppliersXml method, and assign the result to the DocumentContent property of the asp:Xml control. You can then assign the name of the stylesheet to the TransformSource property and leave it to the control to automatically perform the transformation on the server and send the results to the client for display:

```
'create an instance of the data access component
Dim objSupplierList As New SupplierList(strConnect)


'call the method to return the data as an Xml String and
'assign it to the Xml Server Control
xmlResult.DocumentContent = objSupplierList.GetSuppliersXml()


'specify path to XSLT stylesheet that transforms XML for display
xmlResult.TransformSource = "supplier-list-style.xsl"
```

The Resulting XML and the XSL Stylesheet

For completeness, Figure 2-10 shows a section of the XML generated by the
GetSuppliersXml method.

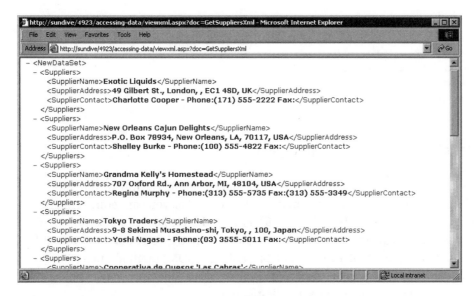

Figure 2-10. The XML generated by the GetSuppliersXml *method*

The following code shows the XSL stylesheet used to generate the output
as a table (supplier-list-style.xsl). This stylesheet uses an older syntax, XSL,
because the Xml control passes the stylesheet to the client in the case of Internet
Explorer 5.0 and above, and we wanted to be sure to avoid using the latest features
of XSLT to ensure that the transformation can take place on the client with all
versions of Internet Explorer from 5.0:

```
<xsl:stylesheet xmlns:xsl="http://www.w3.org/1999/XSL/Transform" version="1.0">

  <xsl:template match="/">
    <table cellspacing="0" rules="all" border="1" id="dgrSuppliers"
          style="border-collapse:collapse;">
      <tr style="background-color:Silver;">
        <td>SupplierName</td>
        <td>SupplierAddress</td>
        <td>SupplierContact</td>
      </tr>
      <xsl:for-each select="//Suppliers">
        <tr>
```

```
            <td><xsl:apply-templates select="SupplierName" /></td>
            <td><xsl:apply-templates select="SupplierAddress" /></td>
            <td><xsl:apply-templates select="SupplierContact" /></td>
          </tr>
        </xsl:for-each>
      </table>
  </xsl:template>

  <xsl:template match="*">
    <xsl:value-of select="." />
  </xsl:template>
</xsl:stylesheet>
```

Returning an XmlDocument Object

In the previous example, you returned the data from the Northwind database as a string containing an XML document. As an alternative, you can return a reference to a .NET XmlDocument object instead. The method GetSuppliersXmlDocument that's exposed by the data access component does just that. If you intend to work with the XML using the XML Document Object Model (DOM) methods, this will save you the effort of having to load the XML string into a "document"-type object when it gets to your client or a middle-tier object.

The method uses identical code to execute the GetSupplierList stored procedure within the database and fills a DataSet with the results. The easiest way to get an XmlDocument object from this DataSet is to first create an XmlDataDocument object from the DataSet.

An XmlDataDocument is a specialized version of the XmlDocument object, which is designed to provide synchronicity between two views of the data it contains—it can be treated as a DataSet object (via the DataSet property of the XmlDataDocument object), or you can use XML DOM methods to manipulate the content directly (you'll look at the XmlDataDocument object in more detail in the next chapter):

```
Public Function GetSuppliersXmlDocument() As XmlDocument

  '* create a DataSet containing the supplier details here, as before

  'create a new XmlDataDocument object based on the DataSet
  Dim objXmlDataDoc As New XmlDataDocument(objDataSet)

  'return it as an XmlDocument object to the calling routine
  Return CType(objXmlDataDoc, XmlDocument)

End Function
```

Once you've got the data as an `XmlDataDocument` object, you can cast it (convert it using `CType` in VB.NET) to an `XmlDocument` object reference; however, it will be converted implicitly to the correct return type for the function in this case if you don't cast it explicitly. Alternatively, you could simply change the method definition and return an `XmlDataDocument` object instead if this is what the client requires.

Displaying the Results

This example page (`suppliers-xmldoc-from-db.aspx`) produces identical output to the previous example—it uses the same data but in the form of an `XmlDocument` object instead of an XML string. The code in the `Page_Load` event that displays the data is therefore almost the same as before. The only difference is that now (because you have a "document" object) you set the `Document` property of the ASP.NET `Xml` control instead of the `DocumentContent` property:

```
'create an instance of the data access component
Dim objSupplierList As New SupplierList(strConnect)

'call the method to return the data as an XmlDocument and
'assign it to the Xml Server Control
xmlResult.Document = objSupplierList.GetSuppliersXmlDocument()

'specify path to XSLT stylesheet that transforms XML for display
xmlResult.TransformSource = "supplier-list-style.xsl"
```

Returning XML via SQLXML from SQL Server

SQL Server 2000 includes the SQLXML technology for reading and writing XML data directly to and from SQL Server. Although this was available as an add-on for SQL Server 6.5 and 7.0, it can only be used under the .NET platform with SQL Server 2000. In all, it's a full and quite complex technology and is well described in the SQL Server Books Online help file (if you installed this with SQL Server) or on the Web at `http://msdn.microsoft.com/library` (select Enterprise Development, then select .NET Enterprise Servers, then look for the section "XML and Internet Support" under the SQL Server 2000 entries). However, to show the basic principle, we've included one method in the data access component that uses it to return an XML document as a `String`.

We created a stored procedure named GetSupplierXml within our sample Northwind database. It's almost the same as the GetSupplierList stored procedure used in previous examples, but with one important difference—it includes the statement FOR XML AUTO:

```
SELECT
  SupplierName=CompanyName,
  SupplierAddress=ISNULL(Address, '') + ', '
    + ISNULL(City,'') + ', ' + ISNULL(Region,'') + ', '
    + ISNULL(PostalCode,'')+ ', ' + ISNULL(Country,''),
  SupplierContact=ISNULL(ContactName,'') + ' - Phone:'
    + ISNULL(Phone,'') + ' Fax:' + ISNULL(Fax,'')
  FROM Suppliers
  FOR XML AUTO
```

This tells SQL Server to send the data back as a series of XML elements. By default, the values in this case appear as attributes rather than as the element values, but you can modify the format by changing the statement if required. Details of all the available options are, however, beyond the scope of this chapter.

When you execute the stored procedure, or any FOR XML SQL statement like this, the result is a series of XML elements. This means you can't expect to be able to use a DataReader to access the results because the DataReader is designed to work with relational data in the form of rows and columns. Instead, you use an XmlTextReader object. You'll learn about the XmlTextReader in more detail in the next chapter. In the meantime, you can think of it as the functional equivalent of the DataReader in the XML world.

The GetSuppliersSqlXml Method

The GetSuppliersSqlXml method implemented within the data access component uses an OleDbConnection and an OleDbCommand object to connect to the database and execute the stored procedure. This happens in the same way as in the earlier examples that use a DataReader:

```
Public Function GetSuppliersSqlXml() As String

  'declare a String containing the SQL-XML stored proc to execute
  Dim strQuery As String = "GetSupplierXml"

  'create a new Connection object using connection string
  Dim objConnect As New SqlConnection(m_ConnectString)
```

```
'create new Command using stored proc name and Connection
Dim objCommand As New SqlCommand(strQuery, objConnect)

'open connection to the database
objConnect.Open()
```

Next, you can define a variable to hold an XmlTextReader object and then call the ExecuteXmlReader method of the Command to execute the stored procedure and return a reference to an XmlTextReader object that's pointing to the results set:

```
'create a variable to hold an XmlTextReader object
Dim objReader As XmlTextReader

'execute the stored proc to initialize the XmlTextReader
objReader = objCommand.ExecuteXmlReader()
```

Now you just have to collect the results and assemble them into an XML document. Remember that the stored procedure only returns a set of XML elements, not a complete document. So you define a String to hold the document you're going to build and another one to contain the double-quote character you'll use for the double-quotes in your XML document. In the first string, you create the XML declaration element and a comment (just to prove that the result is being generated dynamically). You also need to add the opening tag of a root element to make it into a legal XML document.

Then you can call the ReadString method of the XmlTextReader to initialize it, and then you can read all of the results (using the GetRemainder.ReadToEnd method) and append it to the string. You finish the string off with the closing tag for the root element, close the connection and the XmlTextReader, and return the string to the calling routine:

```
Dim strXml As String
Dim QUOT As String = Chr(34)

'create the document prolog
strXml = "<?xml version=" & QUOT & "1.0" & QUOT & "?>" _
       & "<!-- Created: " & Now() & " -->" _
       & "<SupplierList>"

'read the first result row and then read remainder
objReader.ReadString()
strXml &= objReader.GetRemainder().ReadToEnd()
```

```
'add the document epilog
strXml &= "</SupplierList>"

'close connection and destroy reader object
objConnect.Close()
objReader = Nothing

'return the XML document object to the calling routine
Return strXml
```

> **NOTE** *As in previous examples, we've removed the error handling code from this listing to make it easier to follow. The full code is contained in the set of samples that you can download from* http://www.apress.com *or* http://www.daveandal.net/ books/4923/.

Figure 2-11 shows a section of the XML document you get back from the stored procedure. You can see that each supplier is returned as a `<Suppliers>` element, with the column values in attributes within that element.

Figure 2-11. The resulting XML document from the GetSuppliersSqlXml *method*

Displaying the Results

The page that demonstrates the `GetSuppliersSqlXml` method
(`suppliers-sqlxml-from-db.aspx`) is identical in appearance to the two previous
examples, and it contains the same links to the XML document and the XSLT
stylesheet used to transform the XML for display. In fact, the HTML in the page
and the code in the `Page_Load` event are also identical; they use the same `asp:Xml`
server control to create the visible output as a table.

The difference is that, because of the different format of the XML, this time
you need to use a different stylesheet to transform it. In fact, the stylesheet named
`supplier-sqlxml-style.xsl` is much the same as the one you used previously, but
now it specifies that the match for the values is made on the attributes (by prefix-
ing the @ character to the value name):

```
<xsl:template match="/">
  <table cellspacing="0" rules="all" border="1" id="dgrSuppliers"
       style="border-collapse:collapse;">
    <tr style="background-color:Silver;">
      <td>SupplierName</td>
      <td>SupplierAddress</td>
      <td>SupplierContact</td>
    </tr>
    <xsl:for-each select="//Suppliers">
      <tr>
        <td><xsl:apply-templates select="@SupplierName" /></td>
        <td><xsl:apply-templates select="@SupplierAddress" /></td>
        <td><xsl:apply-templates select="@SupplierContact" /></td>
      </tr>
    </xsl:for-each>
  </table>
</xsl:template>
```

Returning Related Tables in a DataSet Object

The final example you'll look at in this chapter shows something a little more useful than the simple lists of suppliers you've been creating so far. It demonstrates
how you can use a `DataSet` to hold data from multiple (OK, just two in this case)
tables and relate these tables together using a primary and foreign key.

The final link in the left column of the menu page allows you to examine the orders in the Northwind sample database that were placed by any customer—by entering a search string that identifies the customer. The first page for this example (`orders-dataset-from-db.aspx`) contains a text box where you enter this search string and an option to display the results as a table or as a list. Figure 2-12 shows the default settings of all orders for Alfreds Futterkiste as two separate tables.

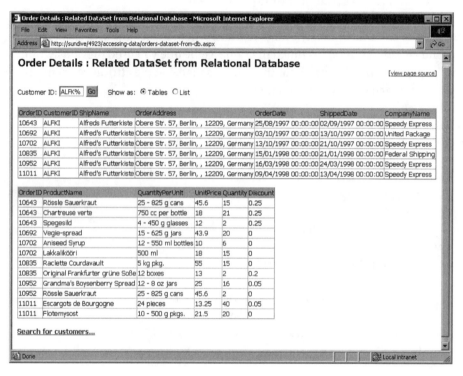

Figure 2-12. The related tables showing orders placed by Alfreds Futterkiste

The Data Access Component and Stored Procedures

This page uses a method in a separate data access component, called `OrderListData.dll`. The source code is included in the `vb-components` folder of the samples, and you can also view it using the link at the top of the page. Click the [view page source] link to see the source for this `.aspx` page, and then click the [view source for component] link in that page to see the component source code.

The method you'll use executes two stored procedures to fill two tables in a `DataSet` object. The first is named `GetOrdersByCustomer` and returns a rowset of details for customers who match the search string supplied as a parameter to the stored procedure:

```
CREATE PROCEDURE GetOrdersByCustomer @CustID nvarchar(5) AS
SELECT
  Orders.OrderID, Orders.CustomerID, Orders.ShipName,
  OrderAddress = ISNULL(Orders.ShipAddress, '') + ', '
    + ISNULL(Orders.ShipCity, ') + ', '
    + ISNULL(Orders.ShipRegion, '') + ', '
    + ISNULL(Orders.ShipPostalCode, '') + ', '
    + ISNULL(Orders.ShipCountry, ''),
  Orders.OrderDate, Orders.ShippedDate, Shippers.CompanyName
FROM Orders JOIN Shippers
  ON Orders.ShipVia=Shippers.ShipperID
WHERE Orders.CustomerID LIKE @CustID
```

This returns rows in the format that you can see in the first table in Figure 2-12. You need to join the Orders and Shippers tables so that you can include the name of the shipping company—it's stored in a separate linked table in the database.

The second stored procedure is named GetOrderLinesByCustomer, and it looks like this:

```
CREATE PROCEDURE GetOrderLinesByCustomer @CustID nvarchar(5) AS
SELECT
  Orders.OrderID, Products.ProductName, Products.QuantityPerUnit,
  [Order Details].UnitPrice, [Order Details].Quantity,
  [Order Details].Discount
FROM ([Order Details] JOIN Orders
  ON [Order Details].OrderID = Orders.OrderID)
JOIN Products
  ON [Order Details].ProductID = Products.ProductID
WHERE Orders.CustomerID LIKE @CustID
```

In this case, you need to join the Orders and Order Details tables to get the order lines given a specific customer ID (which isn't included in the rows in the Order Details table). You also need to join the Products table to get the product names and the quantity because this again is a linked table. You can see the format of the rows returned by this stored procedure in the second table in Figure 2-12.

The GetOrdersByCustomerDataSet Method

These two stored procedures are used in the GetOrdersByCustomerDataSet method within the data access component. You pass the customer ID search string in as a parameter and get back a DataSet containing the results as two separate tables.

The first steps are to specify the stored procedure names and create a new empty DataSet object:

```
Public Function GetOrdersByCustomerDataSet(ByVal strCustID As String) As DataSet

  'specify the stored procedure names
  Dim strGetOrders As String = "GetOrdersByCustomer"
  Dim strGetOrderLines As String = "GetOrderLinesByCustomer"

  'declare a variable to hold a DataSet object
  Dim objDataSet As New DataSet()
```

Now you can create the customary Connection object. You do it outside the Try...Catch construct so that you can access it later. You'll see why shortly. Next, you need a Command object that uses this connection and the first of your stored procedures. Notice that you tell the Command object that the value you've provided for the "query" parameter is the name of a stored procedure—this makes execution a bit faster because the database doesn't have to search for all types of object that might have this name. Then you create a Parameter object to hold the single parameter with the name CustID and the value of the strCustID parameter that was passed to the method:

```
  'create a new Connection object using the connection string
  Dim objConnect As New OleDbConnection(m_ConnectString)

  Try
    'create a new Command object and set the CommandType
    Dim objCommand As New OleDbCommand(strGetOrders, objConnect)
    objCommand.CommandType = CommandType.StoredProcedure

    'create a variable to hold a Parameter object
    Dim objParam As OleDbParameter

    'create a new Parameter object named 'CustID' with correct data
    'type to match a SQL database varchar' field of 5 characters
    objParam = objCommand.Parameters.Add("CustID", OleDbType.VarChar, 5)

    'specify that it's an Input parameter and set the value
    objParam.Direction = ParameterDirection.Input
    objParam.Value = strCustID
```

Filling the Tables

Now you can create a `DataAdapter` object. You'll change the values set in the `Command` object during its lifetime; therefore, you don't provide any parameters to the constructor of the `DataAdapter`. Instead, you assign your `Command` object to its `SelectCommand` property afterward:

```
'create a new DataAdapter object
Dim objDataAdapter As New OleDbDataAdapter()
'and assign the Command object to it
objDataAdapter.SelectCommand = objCommand
```

Then you can call the `Fill` method to get the data into a table named `Orders` in the `DataSet`. Notice that you're opening the connection manually by calling the `Open` method. This makes the routine that bit more efficient. Otherwise, the `Fill` method will open and close the connection each time it's called:

```
'open database connection first for max efficiency
'because we are calling Fill method twice
objConnect.Open()

'get data from stored proc into table named "Orders"
objDataAdapter.Fill(objDataSet, "Orders")
```

Now you change the name of the stored procedure in the `Command` object and call `Fill` again to get the result data from the second stored procedure into a second table named `OrderLines`:

```
'change the stored proc name in the Command object
objCommand.CommandText = strGetOrderLines

'get data from stored proc into table named "OrderLines"
objDataAdapter.Fill(objDataSet, "OrderLines")
```

Creating the Relationship Between the Tables

Having filled your tables with data, the final task before you return it is to create the relationship between these tables. You'll create a new `DataRelation` object, specifying the parent and child tables and the names of the columns that hold the primary and foreign keys for the relationship. Then you can return the populated `DataSet` to the calling routine. As with all of the methods in the components (although not shown in all the other code extracts), you catch any errors and raise them to the calling routine:

```
'declare a variable to hold a DataRelation object
Dim objRelation As DataRelation

'create a Relation object to link Orders and OrderLines
objRelation = New DataRelation("CustOrderLines", _
              objDataSet.Tables("Orders").Columns("OrderID"), _
              objDataSet.Tables("OrderLines").Columns("OrderID"))

'and add it to the DataSet object's Relations collection
objDataSet.Relations.Add(objRelation)

Catch objError As Exception
  Throw objError   'throw error to calling routine

Finally
  'must remember to close connection - we opened it ourselves
  'so the Fill method will not close it automatically
  objConnect.Close()

End Try

Return objDataSet   'return populated DataSet to calling routine
End Function
```

Remember that you opened the connection manually in your code before calling the Fill method the first time. It will therefore remain open afterward, so you must remember to close it. You do this (as you can see in the previous code) in the Finally section of the Try...Catch construct.

You now have a DataSet object that you can pass to your client, to a middle-tier component, or remote to another location. It contains all the order details and all the associated order line details for customers who match the search string you provide when you call the method. Furthermore, if you use a search string that matches more than one customer, as you can verify from trying this, you'll see that the DataSet tables can contain orders and order lines for more than one customer.

Displaying the Results in Tables

Figure 1-12 showed the results from the GetOrdersByCustomerDataSet method as two tables. You achieve this in the same way as most of the earlier examples by using two ASP.NET DataGrid server controls in the page. You can also see in the following code the HTML <form> and other controls you can use to create the text box and option buttons:

```
<form runat="server">
  Customer ID:
  <asp:TextBox id="txtCustID" columns="5" maxlength="5"
               runat="server" text="ALFK%" />
  <asp:Button text="Go" runat="server" />      Show as:
  <asp:RadioButton id="optTables" groupname="ShowAs" text="Tables"
                   autopostback="true" runat="server" checked="true" />
  <asp:RadioButton id="optList" groupname="ShowAs" text="List"
                   autopostback="true" runat="server" />
</form>

<asp:Label id="lblMessage" runat="server" />

<asp:DataGrid id="dgrOrders" runat="server">
<HeaderStyle BackColor="#c0c0c0"></HeaderStyle>
<AlternatingItemStyle BackColor="#eeeeee"></AlternatingItemStyle>
</asp:DataGrid><br />

<asp:DataGrid id="dgrOrderLines" runat="server">
<HeaderStyle BackColor="#c0c0c0"></HeaderStyle>
<AlternatingItemStyle BackColor="#eeeeee"></AlternatingItemStyle>
</asp:DataGrid><br />
```

The Page_Load event then just has to collect the values from these <form> controls, fetch the data using the data access component, and then bind it to the two DataGrid controls. In this case, just to demonstrate the alternatives, we're binding each table to the control directly rather than binding the DataSet to the control and specifying the table name as the DataMember:

```
'get customer ID to use in stored procs from text box
Dim strCustID As String = txtCustID.Text

'declare variable to hold instance of DataSet object
Dim objDataSet As DataSet

'create an instance of the data access component
Dim objOrderList As New OrderList(strConnect)

'call the method to return the data as a DataSet
objDataSet = objOrderList.GetOrdersByCustomerDataSet(strCustID)
```

```
If optTables.Checked Then    'show as separate tables of data

  'assign table named Orders to first DataGrid server control
  dgrOrders.DataSource = objDataSet.Tables("Orders")

  'assign table named OrderLines to second DataGrid server control
  dgrOrderLines.DataSource = objDataSet.Tables("OrderLines")

  'if there are tables in DataSet, bind all server controls on page
  If Not dgrOrders.DataSource Is Nothing Then Page.DataBind()

Else    'show as a nested list
  ...
```

Using the Data Relationship Information

When you display the data as two tables, you aren't making use of the relationship between the tables that you stored in your DataSet object. However, if you change the option in the page to display the data as a list, you can see how the code uses the relationship between the tables to display the appropriate order lines for each order (see Figure 2-13).

In this case, you're building up the results for display row by row by iterating through the tables in the DataSet using code in your Page_Load event. You create a String variable to hold the results and get a reference to the parent table named Orders within your DataSet. You also get a reference to the DataRelation you created within the DataSet and declare a couple of other variables you'll need:

```
...
Else    'show as a nested list

  'create a variable to hold the results for display
  Dim strResult As String = ""

  'create a reference to the Orders (parent) table in the DataSet
  Dim objTable As DataTable = objDataSet.Tables("Orders")

  'create reference to the relationship object in the DataSet
  Dim objRelation As DataRelation = objTable.ChildRelations("CustOrderLines")

  'declare variables to hold row objects and an array of rows
  Dim objRow, objChildRow As DataRow
  Dim colChildRows() As DataRow
```

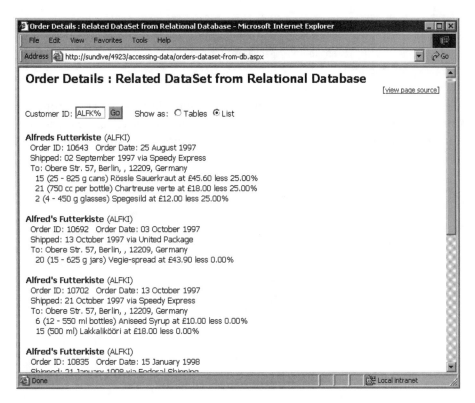

Figure 2-13. Using the relationship between the tables to display the data as nested lists

Now you iterate through each row in the parent table (the Orders table), collecting the values from this row in the "results" string as you go. Notice how you check for null values in a column with the IsDbNull function (you could equally well use the Framework method Convert.IsDBNull instead of the VB-specific method):

```
'iterate through the rows in the Orders table
For Each objRow In objTable.Rows

  'get the order details and append them to the "results" string
  strResult &= "<b>" & objRow("ShipName") & "</b> (" _
          & objRow("CustomerID") & ")<br />  Order ID: " _
          & objRow("OrderID") & "   Order Date: " _
          & FormatDateTime(objRow("OrderDate"), 1) & "<br />  "
  If IsDbNull(objRow("ShippedDate")) Then
    strResult &= "Awaiting shipping"
  Else
```

```
        strResult &= "Shipped:" & FormatDateTime(objRow("ShippedDate"), 1)
      End If
      strResult &= " via " & objRow("CompanyName") & "<br />" _
              & "   To: " & objRow("OrderAddress") & "<br />"
```

For each parent row, you can now use the relationship to get an array from the OrderLines table of all the child rows that are related to the current Orders row. You iterate through this array putting the column values into the "results" string:

```
'get collection (array) of matching OrderLines rows for this row
colChildRows = objRow.GetChildRows(objRelation)

'iterate through matching OrderLines rows adding to the result string
For Each objChildRow In colChildRows
  strResult &= "     " & objChildRow("Quantity") _
          & " (" & objChildRow("QuantityPerUnit") & ") " _
          & objChildRow("ProductName") & " at " _
          & FormatCurrency(objChildRow("UnitPrice")) & " less " _
          & FormatPercent(objChildRow("Discount")) & "<br />"
Next
```

Then you can finish off the string and display it in the page:

```
    strResult += "<br />"
  Next   'and repeat for next row in Orders table

  lblMessage.Text = strResult   'display the results
End If
```

So, the DataSet can provide a really useful package for storing and transporting data that consists of more than one table. As well as creating relationships between the tables in it (you can have several tables and several relationships in one DataSet), you can also create constraints, primary keys, calculated columns, and other rules within the DataSet.

Searching for Customers by Name

At the bottom of the page you've been viewing in this example is a link that allows you to search the Customers table in the Northwind database by customer ID or by any part of the customer's name, as shown in Figure 2-14.

Figure 2-14. The link to search for customers by name

This opens the page shown in Figure 2-15, which shows a search for all customers whose name contains the text *super*:

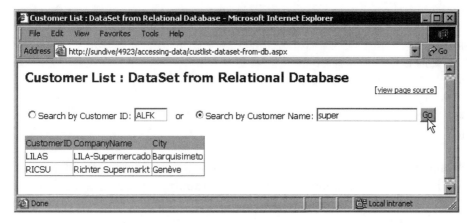

Figure 2-15. Searching for "super" customers by name

This page uses another method of the data access component, GetCustomerByIdOrName, which accepts two parameters—a customer ID and a string that's part of the customer's name:

```
Public Function GetCustomerByIdOrName(ByVal strCustID As String, _
                            ByVal strCustName As String) As DataSet
```

This method uses a stored procedure named `GetCustomerListByIdOrName`. It takes these two parameters and executes a `SELECT` statement that returns the appropriate rows. However, it only searches by customer ID if the value passed in the customer name parameter is an empty string:

```
CREATE PROCEDURE GetCustomerListByIdOrName
  @CustID nvarchar(5), @CustName nvarchar(40)
AS
IF @CustName=''
 BEGIN
  IF LEN(@CustID) < 5 BEGIN SET @CustID = @CustID + '%' END
  SELECT CustomerID, CompanyName, City FROM Customers
  WHERE CustomerID LIKE @CustID ORDER BY CustomerID
 END
ELSE
 BEGIN
  SET @CustName = '%' + @CustName + '%'
  SELECT CustomerID, CompanyName, City
  FROM Customers
  WHERE CompanyName LIKE @CustName ORDER BY CompanyName
 END
```

This allows a single stored procedure and a single data access method (it could be a separate component) to perform both kinds of search. All a client or middle-tier object that uses the component has to do is pass appropriate values for the parameters.

So the `Page_Load` event code in the `custlist-dataset-from-db.aspx` page simply has to extract the values from the controls on the page, instantiate the component, call the `GetCustomerByIdOrName` method with these values, and display the results. Here's that code in full:

```
Sub Page_Load()

  Dim strCustID As String = ""
  Dim strCustName As String = ""

  'get one or other value from text boxes depending on selection
  If optByID.Checked Then
    strCustID = txtCustID.Text
  Else
    strCustName = txtCustName.Text
  End If
```

```
'get connection string from web.config
Dim strConnect As String
strConnect = ConfigurationSettings.AppSettings("NorthwindConnectString")

Try
  'create an instance of the data access component
  Dim objOrderList As New OrderList(strConnect)

  'create a variable to hold a DataSet object
  Dim objDataSet As DataSet

  'call the method to return the data as a DataSet
  objDataSet = objOrderList.GetCustomerByIdOrName(strCustID, strCustName)

  If objDataSet.Tables(0).Rows.Count > 0 Then
    dgrCustomers.DataSource = objDataSet.Tables(0)
    dgrCustomers.DataBind()

  Else
    lblMessage.Text = "No matching customers found in database ..."

  End If

Catch objErr As Exception
  'there was an error and no data will be returned
  lblMessage.Text = "ERROR: No data returned. " & objErr.Message

End Try

End Sub
```

We haven't listed the code for the data access component method here because the code involved is similar to the previous example. You can view it in the same way by using the links at the top of the page if you want.

Summary

This chapter started with a discussion of how you can build components of various types for use in your ASP.NET (and other) applications. Of all the five common types of "component" introduced, you'll concentrate on using .NET-compiled components for the majority of the tasks in this book. However, as you've seen in this chapter, you'll also use user controls and server-side include files.

All three types of component can, to varying degrees, provide the encapsulation, reusability, ease of maintenance, and staged development you want. The standard .NET compiled component generally offers the best of all worlds—especially now that deployment and updates within the .NET managed code runtime environment are so much easier than COM components.

You also spent some time in this chapter examining the DataSet object and when you should consider using it. As you'll see in forthcoming chapters, the features it provides often make up for the extra overhead of using it. Just remember that in the majority of cases when you're just displaying, and not remoting the data, the DataReader will prove faster and more efficient.

This chapter finished with a look at ways you can encapsulate your data access code into components. We showed you how data extracted from a relational database can be returned to a client in a whole range of formats—ideal to suit different client requirements.

This chapter covered the following topics:

- An overview of the different ways you can build "components"

- Building data access into components—why and how?

- A more detailed look at the DataSet object

- Some examples of returning relational data in different formats

In the next chapter, you'll continue looking at data access components by examining the various ways you can extract data from an XML document and return it in different formats. You'll also learn more about the ways you can validate and otherwise work with XML data.

CHAPTER 3

Accessing XML Documents

IN THE PREVIOUS CHAPTER, you learned how to expose data via components in your application's data tier in a range of formats. Depending on the features of your application's middle tier, or the type of client you're serving to, you may have to tailor the data format to suit their requirements. As you saw, this is relatively easy with the .NET data access classes included in the Framework.

However, all the examples in the previous chapter accessed a data source that's a *relational* data store—in this case, a SQL Server database. What if the data source isn't relational but (as is increasingly becoming the case) an XML document? It could be a file stored on disk, a stream of XML delivered by another component, a Web Service, or another service or application such as BizTalk Server. Or it might simply be delivered over HTTP as a POST from a Web page.

In this chapter, you'll continue examining the examples you started looking at in the previous chapter. As well as a series of pages that use data extracted from a relational database, there's an equivalent set of pages that use data stored as an XML document in a disk file. So, the plan for this chapter is to show you the following:

- How you can build components that access XML documents

- How you can convert and return the XML as various object types

- How you can display the XML easily in your ASP.NET pages

You'll start by looking at the data access component you'll use throughout this chapter.

Introducing the XML Data Access Component Examples

All the examples you looked at in the previous chapter accessed data stored in a relational database, predominantly using ADO.NET objects (such as the DataReader and DataSet) to extract the data and return it in various formats—such as an Array and an XML document. However, there are an increasing number of occasions where the data is supplied in XML format. Obvious cases are when it's stored as a disk file, streamed from another component, or delivered to an application via a Web Service using SOAP.

109

The client may require the data in a format suitable for data binding, such as a rowset of some kind. Or, as previously discussed, there are useful possibilities for using data as XML where the client is able to process this XML directly—for example, using an XML parser located on the client machine. We demonstrate this in a range of ways in later chapters. Of course, if the .NET Framework is installed on the client, you can use the .NET System.Xml classes there instead. However, in the remainder of this chapter, you'll see how you can take XML data and expose it to the client or the middle tier in a variety of ways.

> **NOTE** *You can download the samples shown in this chapter to run on your own system. See the section "Setting Up the Examples" in the previous chapter for details of how to install and configure them on your machine.*

Accessing and Returning Relational Data

The example files provided include a set of components whose source code is provided in the vb-components and cs-components folders and include a series of pages stored in the accessing-data folder that use these components. The accessing-data folder also contains the default.htm menu page (originally shown in the previous chapter) for the examples you'll see in this chapter (see Figure 3-1).

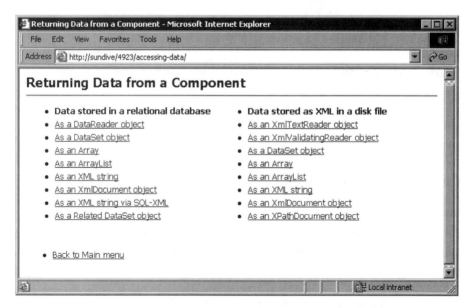

Figure 3-1. The main menu page for the examples in this chapter

Using the SupplierListXml Data Access Component

As in the previous chapter, we've provided one data access component for all the examples in this chapter. The component, SupplierListXml.dll, implements several methods that you can use to expose the XML data in different ways. The source code of the component is the file get-supplier-xml.vb, which you can examine in the vb-components/SupplierListXML folder (or as get-supplier-xml.cs in cs-components/SupplierListXML, depending on your preferred language). Alternatively, you can follow the links at the top of each example page—as demonstrated in the relational data access examples in the previous chapter.

The component imports the .NET classes it requires, in this case, System and the three System.Xml namespaces. You also need the System.Collections namespace for the arrays you use within the component and the System.Data namespace so that you can reference a DataSet. It defines the namespace for the component class as SupplierListXml, and the class itself is named SupplierList. There are also several Private member variables that you'll want to be able to access from more than one function or method within the component:

```
Imports System
Imports System.Xml
Imports System.Xml.XPath
Imports System.Xml.Schema
Imports System.Collections
Imports System.Data

'the namespace for the component
Namespace SupplierListXml

  'the main class definition
  Public Class SupplierList

    'private internal variables
    Private m_XmlFilePath As String  'path and name of XML file
    Private m_SchemaPath As String   'path and name of schema file
    Private m_Validate As Boolean = False  'if validation to be performed

    'variable to hold instance of XmlTextReader object
    'allows it to be accessed by separate functions
    Private m_XTReader As XmlTextReader
```

The constructor for the component comes next. It accepts two parameters—the first is mandatory and specifies the full path to the XML source file on disk that you'll use as the data source. The second optional parameter is the full path to an XML Schema Definition (XSD) file that you'll want the component to use to validate the XML document. If this parameter is omitted, no validation is performed:

```
Public Sub New(ByVal XmlFilePath As String, _
                    Optional ByVal SchemaPath As String = "")
  MyBase.New() 'call constructor for base class
  m_XmlFilePath = XmlFilePath
  m_SchemaPath = SchemaPath
  If m_SchemaPath.Length > 0 Then m_Validate = True
End Sub
```

However, note that three of the functions in the component *require* a schema to be provided, and these methods will raise an error if they're called and the optional second parameter to the constructor wasn't set when the component instance was created. The three methods are GetSuppliersValidatingReader, GetSuppliersDataSet, and GetSuppliersXmlString.

Returning an XmlTextReader Reference

You'll start with a simple example, returning a reference to an open XmlTextReader object. Members of the XmlReader family of objects (XmlTextReader and XmlNodeReader) are the XML equivalent of the DataReader object you used in the previous chapter. They act like a "pipe" between the applications and an XML document (stream or disk file).

However, unlike the DataReader, they return XML elements rather than data rows and columns. You used an XmlTextReader in an example in the previous chapter to return the XML elements that the SQLXML technology built into SQL Server 2000 returns.

All you have to do to implement your GetSuppliersXmlTextReader method is create and initialize an XmlTextReader object from a disk file. You specify the full physical path to the file in the XmlTextReader object's constructor, catch any error (for example, File Not Found), and raise this error to the calling routine. Otherwise, you just pass back a reference to the XmlTextReader:

```
Public Function GetSuppliersXmlTextReader() As XmlTextReader

  Try

    'create new XmlTextReader object and load XML document
    Return New XmlTextReader(m_XmlFilePath)
```

```
Catch objErr As Exception

   Throw objErr    'throw exception to calling routine

  End Try

End Function
```

Displaying the Results

The page suppliers-xtreader-from-xml.aspx uses this function to read the XML source document used in these examples. When you open it, the page displays a list of elements from the XML document (see Figure 3-2).

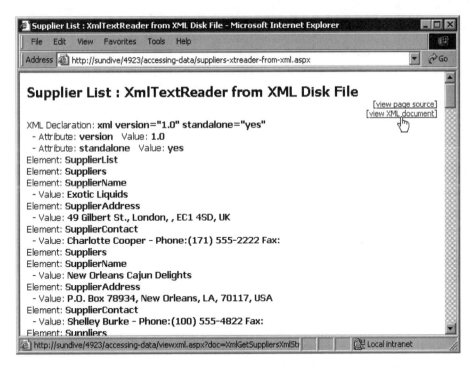

Figure 3-2. Returning an XmlTextReader *that references an XML disk file*

There are links at the top of the page to view the source of the .aspx file (and from that screen, the component source code) and to display the XML document itself. Figure 3-3 shows a section of this XML document—you can see it's the same as the XML you returned from the relational database in some of the examples in the previous chapter.

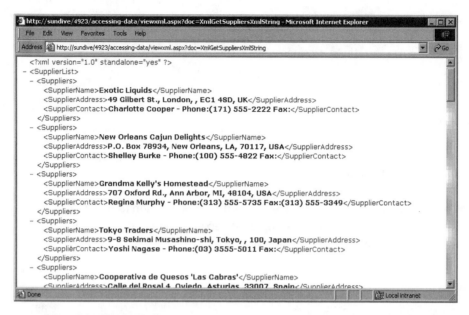

Figure 3-3. Viewing the XML document content

The example page contains an `Import` directive for the component, as well as one for the `System.Xml` classes (you'll use some of the types defined there in the code in the page):

```
<%@Import Namespace="SupplierListXml" %>
<%@Import Namespace="System.Xml" %>
```

It also contains an `asp:Label` control in which you display the results:

```
<asp:Label id="lblMessage" runat="server" />
```

The Page_Load Event Handler

The `Page_Load` event code is responsible for instantiating the component and calling the method that returns an `XmlTextReader`. The first step is to create the physical path to the XML file you're using—this section of code is the same in most of the pages you'll see in this chapter:

```
Sub Page_Load()

  'create physical path to XML file (in same folder as ASPX page)
  Dim strCurrentPath As String = Request.PhysicalPath
```

```
Dim strPathOnly As String = Left(strCurrentPath, _
                          InStrRev(strCurrentPath, "\"))
Dim strXMLPath As String = strPathOnly & "supplier-list.xml"
```

Now you declare a variable to hold the XmlTextReader returned by the method, create the component instance, and call the GetSuppliersXmlTextReader method:

```
'declare variable to hold XmlTextReader object
Dim objReader As XmlTextReader

Try

  'create an instance of the data access component
  Dim objSupplierList As New SupplierList(strXMLPath)

  'call the method to return the data as an XmlTextReader
  objReader = objSupplierList.GetSuppliersXmlTextReader()
```

Now you can use the XmlTextReader in the page. You'll want to display the XML it references, so you create a separate function within this page that reads and parses the XML and returns it as a String. The function ParseXmlContent takes the XmlTextReader and returns the content ready for display, so you can just assign it to the asp:Label control:

```
'if we got a result, display the parsed content
If Not objReader Is Nothing Then
  lblMessage.Text = ParseXmlContent(objReader)
End If
```

You now have two more tasks to take care of. If there was an error using the component, you want to catch this and display it in the page, and finally, you must remember to close the XmlTextReader you used:

```
Catch objErr As Exception

  'there was an error and no data will be returned
  lblMessage.Text = "ERROR: No data returned. " & objErr.Message

Finally

  objReader.Close()    'close the reader to release file

End Try

End Sub
```

This example page uses a custom function named `ParseXmlContent` to read the XML content directly from the `XmlTextReader` and return it as a `String` ready for display. We'll describe that function next—it's also used in the next example in this chapter.

Parsing an XML Document

The `XmlReader` objects provided in the `System.Xml` namespace of the Framework provide a *pull* model for accessing XML documents in much the same way as the `DataReader` does for relational data (unlike a SAX XML parser, which uses the *push* model and requires event handlers to be created to handle events as the document is read).

In many ways, the .NET pull model of accessing data is more intuitive and easier to use. The `XmlReader` objects have methods that allow you to read nodes from a document in a specific format or retrieve them as node objects. As each node is read, you can get information about the node, access the attributes of that node, or skip nodes.

The following `ParseXmlContent` function demonstrates many of these features. It reads nodes in turn from the document and checks to see what types they are—outputting appropriate information for the three common types that you know exist in the document. Then it looks for any attributes and outputs information about these before moving on to the next node:

```
Function ParseXmlContent(objXMLReader As XmlTextReader) As String

  'read or "pull" the nodes of the XML document
  Dim strNodeResult As String = ""
  Dim objNodeType As XmlNodeType

  'read each node in turn - returns False if no more nodes to read
  Do While objXMLReader.Read()

    'select the type of the node (these are only some of the types)
    objNodeType = objXMLReader.NodeType

    Select Case objNodeType

      Case XmlNodeType.XmlDeclaration:
        'get the name and value
        strNodeResult += "XML Declaration: <b>" & objXMLReader.Name _
                    & " " & objXMLReader.Value & "</b><br />"
```

```
   Case XmlNodeType.Element:
     'just get the name, any value will be in next (#text) node
     strNodeResult += "Element: <b>" & objXMLReader.Name & "</b><br />"

   Case XmlNodeType.Text:
     'just display the value, node name is "#text" in this case
     strNodeResult += "  - Value: <b>" & objXMLReader.Value _
                    & "</b><br />"

 End Select

 'see if this node has any attributes
 If objXMLReader.AttributeCount > 0 Then

   'iterate through the attributes by moving to the next one
   'could use MoveToFirstAttribute but MoveToNextAttribute does
   'the same when the current node is an element-type node
   Do While objXMLReader.MoveToNextAttribute()

     'get the attribute name and value
     strNodeResult += "  - Attribute: <b>" & objXMLReader.Name _
                    & "</b>   Value: <b>" & objXMLReader.Value _
                    & "</b><br />"
   Loop

 End If

Loop    'and read the next node

'and return the resulting string
Return strNodeResult

End Function
```

So, returning an `XmlTextReader` object is a useful way to provide your application with access to an XML document that arrives as a stream or is stored as a disk file. However, bear in mind that it exhibits the same pros and cons as the `DataReader` you used in the previous chapter to access relational data.

The `XmlReader` objects are *connected* data sources, so they require their connection (or *reference*) to the source data to be maintained while the XML data is being read. However, they're lightweight, fast, and efficient for situations where the "connected" limitation is acceptable.

On the other hand, when you want to remote data and work with it in a disconnected environment, you need to look for a different object to use. Later in this chapter, you'll see some options—including using a `DataSet` and one of the `XmlDocument` family of objects.

Returning an XmlValidatingReader Reference

One regular requirement when reading XML is to validate it against a specific schema to ensure that the format is suitable for the application that's using it. It makes sense to do this within the data access layer components as you actually read the document from a stream or disk file.

Within the .NET `System.Xml` namespace classes, validation is usually performed through an `XmlValidatingReader`. You "attach" this to an `XmlReader` object in order to perform the validation as the document is read. The example data access component contains a method named `GetSuppliersValidatingReader` that instantiates and returns an `XmlValidatingReader`. The following listing shows this method. You can see that it uses a separate function named `GetValidatingReader` within the data access component to actually get the `XmlValidatingReader` you return to the calling routine:

```
Public Function GetSuppliersValidatingReader() As XmlValidatingReader

  If m_Validate = True Then   'schema must be specified

    Try

      'get instance of validator from separate function
      Dim objValidator As XmlValidatingReader = GetValidatingReader()

      'add the event handler for any validation errors found
      AddHandler objValidator.ValidationEventHandler, _
              AddressOf ValidationError

      Return objValidator   'return it to the calling routine

    Catch objErr As Exception

      Throw objErr            'throw exception to calling routine

    End Try

  Else   'no schema provided
```

```
    'create a new Exception and fill in details
    Dim objSchemaErr As New Exception("You must provide a Schema" _
                    & " when using the GetSuppliersValidatingReader method")
    objSchemaErr.Source = "SupplierListXml"

    Throw objSchemaErr  'throw exception to calling routine

  End If

End Function
```

You can also see how you create a custom exception to return to the calling routine if the path of the XML schema wasn't provided when the component's constructor was originally called. Obviously, you can't perform validation unless you have a schema. It's possible to use an inline schema for validation (one that's part of the XML document), but that feature isn't enabled in the example.

> **NOTE** *In general, when using a "standard" XML document format for data transport on a regular basis (in other words, a document that's of the same structure each time), using an inline schema only adds to the payload sent across the network. It's probably better in this situation for each party to have a copy of the schema locally and validate against that.*

Creating and Initializing an XmlValidatingReader Object

The GetValidatingReader function used in the GetSuppliersValidatingReader method is created by a separate routine, which is listed next. You simply create an XmlTextReader for the document (in this case, a disk file) and then use this in the constructor for an XmlValidatingReader. Next, you set the validation type. In this case, you use Auto so that it'll detect the schema type automatically—it can also handle generic XSD schemas written in the now deprecated Microsoft-specific XML Data Reduced (XDR) format and Document Type Definitions (DTDs):

```
Private Function GetValidatingReader() As XmlValidatingReader

  'create new XmlTextReader object and load XML document
  m_XTReader = New XmlTextReader(m_XmlFilePath)

  'create an XmlValidatingReader for this XmlTextReader
  Dim objValidator As New XmlValidatingReader(m_XTReader)

  'set the validation type to "Auto"
  objValidator.ValidationType = ValidationType.Auto
```

You also need to create an XmlSchemaCollection object that references the schema(s) you want to validate against (there could be more than one if they inherit from each other), add the schema to it, and assign this collection to the Schemas property of the XmlValidatingReader before returning it to the calling routine. The version (overload) of the Add method you're using to add the schema to the XmlSchemaCollection takes two string parameters. This first is the namespace for the schema (use the default by providing an empty string for this parameter), and the second is the path to the schema file:

```
'create a new XmlSchemaCollection
Dim objSchemaCol As New XmlSchemaCollection()

'add our schema to it
objSchemaCol.Add("", m_SchemaPath)

'assign the schema collection to the XmlValidatingReader
objValidator.Schemas.Add(objSchemaCol)

Return objValidator  'return to calling routine

End Function
```

Catching Validation Events

If you just use the XmlValidatingReader as it is now, any validation errors that are detected while reading the XML document will cause an exception. Often you'll want to handle these validation errors separately—or at least get specific information about the error. You can do this by handling the event that the XmlValidatingReader raises when a validation error is encountered.

If you look back at the definition of the GetSuppliersValidatingReader method, you'll see that you assigned an event handler within the data access component to this event:

```
'add the event handler for any validation errors found
AddHandler objValidator.ValidationEventHandler, _
          AddressOf ValidationError
```

The event handler is a separate subroutine that accepts an instance of a ValidationEventArgs object as the second parameter. This object contains several details of the error although you're only using the Message property in this example. You just create a custom exception and raise it to the calling routine:

```
Private Sub ValidationError(ByVal objSender As Object, _
                            ByVal objArgs As ValidationEventArgs)

  'create a new Exception and fill in details
  Dim objValidErr As New Exception("Validation error: " & objArgs.Message)
  objValidErr.Source = "SupplierListXml"

  Throw objValidErr   'throw exception to calling routine

End Sub
```

Displaying the Results of the GetSuppliersValidatingReader Method

The example page, suppliers-validreader-from-xml.aspx, uses the
GetSuppliersValidatingReader method and displays the results of reading
the disk file named supplier-list.xml and validating it against an XML schema
named supplier-list.xsd. The code in the Page_Load event creates the physical
path to the document and the schema files, and then it creates an instance of the
data access component (specifying both of these paths):

```
'create physical path to XML file (in same folder as ASPX page)
Dim strCurrentPath As String = Request.PhysicalPath
Dim strPathOnly As String = Left(strCurrentPath, _
                                InStrRev(strCurrentPath, "\"))
Dim strXMLPath As String = strPathOnly & "supplier-list.xml"
Dim strSchemaPath As String = strPathOnly & "supplier-list.xsd"

'create an instance of the data access component
Dim objSupplierList As New SupplierList(strXMLPath, strSchemaPath)
```

Then it calls the GetSuppliersValidatingReader method to get back the
XmlValidatingReader, and it displays the results using the same ParseXmlContent
method as in the previous example:

```
'declare variable to hold XmlValidatingReader object
Dim objReader As XmlValidatingReader

'call the method to return the data as an XmlValidatingReader
objReader = objSupplierList.GetSuppliersValidatingReader()

'if we got a result, display the parsed content
If Not objReader Is Nothing Then
  lblMessage.Text = ParseXmlContent(objReader)
End If

objReader.Reader.Close()    'close the Reader to release file
```

Because you used the same XML document and the same `ParseXmlContent` method as the previous example, the output is identical to that in Figure 3-2. To see a validation error, all you have to do is edit the XML source file named `supplier-list.xml`; for example, Figure 3-4 shows the result after changing the name of one of the `<SupplierName>` elements.

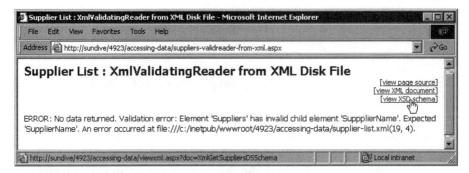

Figure 3-4. An example of the message displayed when the XML document content is invalid

You can also view the schema you're validating against by clicking the links at the top right of the page (see Figure 3-5).

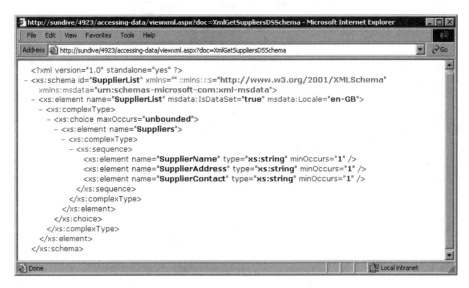

Figure 3-5. Viewing the schema that was used for the validation

Returning a DataSet Object

So far you've returned the XML document through a couple of objects that are part of the XML armory—defined within the System.Xml and its subordinate namespaces. However, you can take advantage of the synchronization between XML and relational data formats discussed in the previous chapter to return the XML document using objects that are normally associated with the relational data world.

The next example demonstrates this by returning an ADO.NET DataSet object that contains a relational representation of the XML document:

```
Public Function GetSuppliersDataSet() As DataSet
```

To "convert" XML into a relational format, you can use an XmlDataDocument object. In Chapter 1 we discussed how this maintains and exposes two synchronized "views" of the data it contains. It exposes the normal XML DOM and XPath-compatible view of the data in the same way as is exposed by an XmlDocument object. It also has a DataSet property that returns an ADO.NET DataSet-compatible view of the data.

So, all you need to do is load the XML document into an XmlDataDocument object and return a reference to its DataSet property. However, to be able to access this, you have to use a schema as well and load this into the XmlDataDocument object before you load the XML document itself.

In this example, you also take advantage of the GetValidatingReader function within the data access component to read the XML document and validate it as you load it into the XmlDataDocument. So, the first step is to get the XmlValidatingReader that references the XML document, and you also have to specify the event handler you want to use for validating it (as in the previous example):

```
'get instance of validator from separate function
Dim objValidator As XmlValidatingReader = GetValidatingReader()

'add the event handler for any validation errors found
AddHandler objValidator.ValidationEventHandler, AddressOf ValidationError
```

Creating the XmlDataDocument

Now you can create the new XmlDataDocument object, load the schema from disk, and then load the XML document via the XmlValidatingReader. Once loaded, you close the XmlTextReader from which you created the XmlValidatingReader (this is why it's declared as a member variable within the component) and return the DataSet reference:

```
'create a new XmlDataDocument object
Dim objDataDoc As New XmlDataDocument()

'load schema into DataSet exposed by XmlDataDocument object
objDataDoc.DataSet.ReadXmlSchema(m_SchemaPath)

'load document - it's validated against schema as it loads
objDataDoc.Load(objValidator)

'close the XmlTextReader
 m_XTReader.Close()

'return the DataSet to the calling routine
Return objDataDoc.DataSet
```

NOTE *We've removed the error-handling code from this listing to make it easier to follow, but it's in the examples you can download and run on your own system.*

Displaying the Results

The example page suppliers-dataset-from-xml.aspx uses the GetSuppliersDataSet method and displays the results. As you get back a DataSet object, you can display the rows in it using a DataGrid control like you did in many examples in the previous chapter (which also helps to prove it's a real DataSet you get back!):

```
<asp:DataGrid id="dgrSuppliers" runat="server">
<HeaderStyle BackColor="#c0c0c0"></HeaderStyle>
<AlternatingItemStyle BackColor="#eeeeee"></AlternatingItemStyle>
</asp:DataGrid>
```

Figure 3-6 shows what the page looks like when you open it in the browser. There are the now-customary links to show the source code, the XML document, and the schema used.

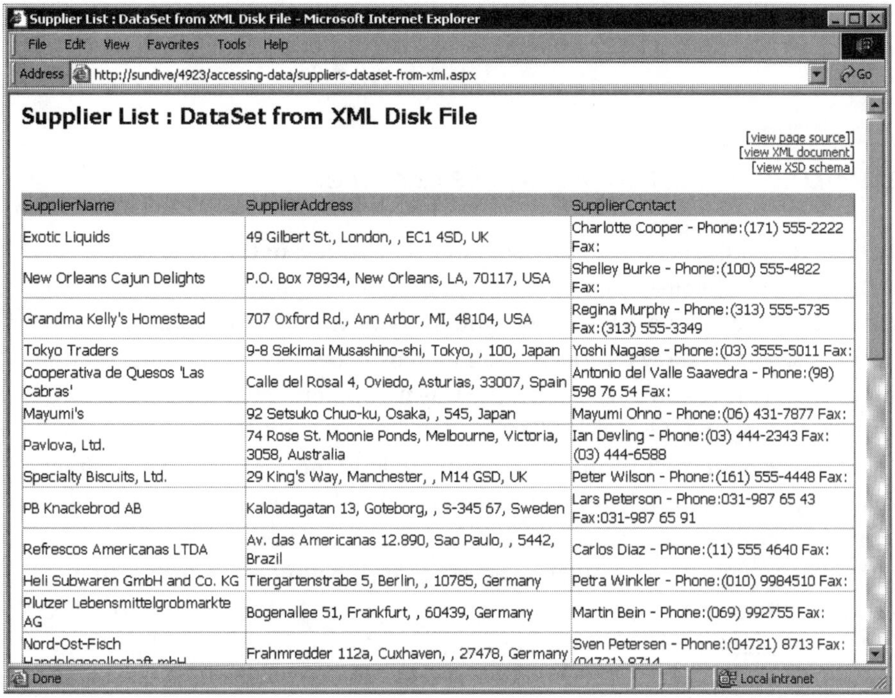

Figure 3-6. Returning a DataSet *object from an XML disk file*

In the Page_Load event, all you need to do is create the physical paths to the XML document and the schema you want to use and then create the data access component instance (as in the previous examples). Then you call the GetSuppliersDataSet method and assign the result to the DataGrid control. Because a DataSet can contain more than one table, you also have to specify the name of the table that you want to act as the data source for the grid and finally call the DataBind method:

```
'create an instance of the data access component
Dim objSupplierList As New SupplierList(strXMLPath, strSchemaPath)

'call the method to return the data as a DataSet and
'assign it to the DataGrid server control for display
dgrSuppliers.DataSource = objSupplierList.GetSuppliersDataSet()
```

```
'check we got a result - will be Nothing if there was an error
If Not dgrSuppliers.DataSource Is Nothing Then

  'set data member and bind the data to display it
  dgrSuppliers.DataMember = "Suppliers"
  dgrSuppliers.DataBind()

End If
```

Returning a Custom Array Reference

One of the examples used with the relational data source in the previous chapter returned the supplier list as an array of strings. You can easily do the same from an XML document if this is the format you need for your application. The method named GetSuppliersArray returns the same set of values as the relational example from the previous chapter. Of course, the way it's implemented within the XML data access component is quite different.

In this method, you use an XPathDocument to hold the XML while you extract the values you want from it. An XPathDocument object is a special version of the document objects provided in the System.Xml (and its related) namespaces. It's designed to provide fast and efficient access to the document contents using "path" definitions from the W3C XPath query language. It doesn't support the XML DOM techniques for accessing the content, and it's consequently "lighter" and more efficient if you only need to use XPath queries.

One of the methods in the data access component, GetSuppliersXPathDocument, returns the data as an XPathDocument to the calling routine. You'll use it in a later example in this chapter, and you'll see it in more detail there. In the meantime, you can use this method from within the GetSuppliersArray method to get an instance of XPathDocument that contains the XML document from the disk file:

```
Public Function GetSuppliersArray() As Array

  'use function in this class to get an XPathDocument
  Dim objXPathDoc As XPathDocument = GetSuppliersXPathDocument()
```

To access an XPathDocument, you can use XPath queries directly. However, a more generally useful technique when you want to iterate through the document content is to create an XPathNavigator object based on the XPathDocument object:

```
'create a new XPathNavigator object using the XPathDocument object
Dim objXPNav As XPathNavigator = objXPathDoc.CreateNavigator()
```

Using the XPathNavigator and XPathNodeIterator Objects

Now you can use the XPathNavigator to access the content of the XML document. You declare a couple of variables to hold XPathNodeIterator objects. These are collection-like objects designed to hold a set of nodes from an XML document, and they support iterating through the nodes contained, as you'll see shortly:

```
'declare variables to hold two XPathNodeIterator objects
Dim objXPRowIter, objXPColIter As XPathNodeIterator
```

You move to the first child element in this document, which will be the root element in this case because you created the XPathNavigator on the document object itself (you could've created it pointing to a specific node if required by calling the CreateNavigator method of that node instead). Then you use the Select method of the XPathNavigator to return an XPathNodeIterator that references all the nodes that match a specified XPath expression. In this case, the XPath expression is child::*, meaning all child nodes (the <Suppliers> nodes in the XML document):

```
'move to document element
objXPNav.MoveToFirstChild()

'select all the child nodes of the document node into an
'XPathNodeIterator object using an XPath expression
objXPRowIter = objXPNav.Select("child::*")
```

You can find out how many nodes you got from the Count property of the XPathNodeIterator and store this away in a variable. Then you move to the first child of this node (the <SupplierName> element in the document) and repeat the process to find out how many child nodes this node has:

```
'get number of "rows" (number of child elements)
Dim intLastRowIndex As Integer = objXPRowIter.Count - 1

'move to first child of first "row" element
objXPNav.MoveToFirstChild()

'select all the child nodes of this node into another
'XPathNodeIterator object using an XPath expression
objXPColIter = objXPNav.Select("child::*")

'get number of "columns" (one per child element)
Dim intLastColIndex As Integer = objXPColIter.Count - 1
```

Building the Array

You now know how large the array needs to be (in other words, the number of "rows" in the data) and how many values there are for each "row" (the number of "columns" in the data, in other words). Hence, you can declare a suitably sized array:

```
'can now create an Array of the appropriate size
Dim arrResult(intLastColIndex, intLastRowIndex) As String
Dim intLoop As Integer    'to hold index into array
```

At last you're in a position to collect the data from the XML into the new array. You iterate through the "rows" of data using the XPathNodeIterator you set to the collection of <Supplier> elements. For each one, you can iterate through the child elements (the <SupplierName>, <SupplierAddress>, and <SupplierContact> elements) and fill in the array as you go. Afterward, you just return the array to the calling routine:

```
'iterate through the "rows"
While objXPRowIter.MoveNext

  'create an XPathNavigator for this "row" element
  objXPNav = objXPRowIter.Current

  'get an XPathNodeIterator containing the child nodes
  objXPColIter = objXPNav.Select("child::*")

  'iterate through these child nodes adding values to array
  For intLoop = 0 To intLastColIndex
    objXPColIter.MoveNext()
    arrResult(intLoop, objXPRowIter.CurrentPosition - 1) _
                        = objXPColIter.Current.Value
  Next

End While

'return the array to the calling routine
Return arrResult

End Function
```

Displaying the Results

The result of calling this method is a simple two-dimensional array of strings, which is the same as you got back from the GetSuppliersArray method of the relational data access component in the previous chapter. The version of the page that uses the XML data source, suppliers-array-from-xml.aspx, is therefore just about identical to the relational version, both in the way it works and the output it produces (see Figure 3-7).

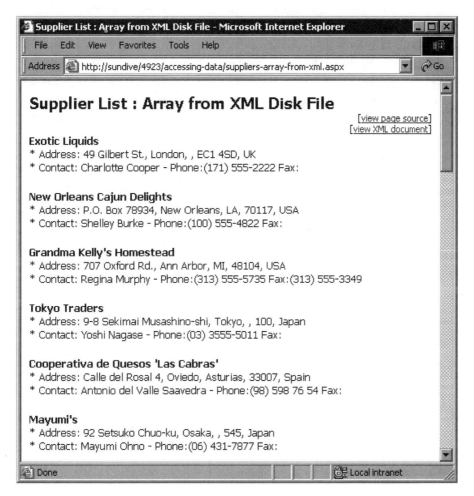

Figure 3-7. Returning the XML data as a two-dimensional String *array*

In fact, the only difference is that you have to create the physical path to the XML document disk file you want to use, as in the previous examples in this chapter. Also, of course, you need to create an instance of the XML data access component this time. We haven't listed the code here, but you can view it using the link at the top of the page.

Returning an ArrayList Reference

The second type of collection object demonstrated in the previous chapter was the ArrayList. We also provide a method in the XML data access component that returns the data from the XML disk file as an ArrayList.

An ArrayList can only hold one "value" in each row. This means the code is actually a lot simpler than the previous example in this chapter, which returned a two-dimensional String array. This method accepts a parameter that you set to the element name (the "column" of the data) that you want to return in your ArrayList.

In the example page (coming later), you'll see that we have specified the SupplierName element, so the ArrayList will just contain the supplier names (as in the previous chapter's ArrayList example). In this method, you use the same approach as the previous example, creating an XPathDocument and an XPathNavigator based on it. You also create a single XPathNodeIterator object:

```
Public Function GetSuppliersArrayList(ByVal strElementName As String) _
                                                        As ArrayList

  'use function in this class to get an XPathDocument
  Dim objXPathDoc As XPathDocument = GetSuppliersXPathDocument()

  'create a new XPathNavigator object using the XPathDocument object
  Dim objXPNav As XPathNavigator = objXPathDoc.CreateNavigator()

  'declare variable to hold an XPathNodeIterator object
  Dim objXPIter As XPathNodeIterator
```

However, now you can just move to the document element and use an XPath query that selects all the required element nodes in the document. You use the XPath predicate descendant rather than child this time because the nodes you want aren't actually direct children of the root node—they're one level deeper than this:

```
'move to document element
objXPNav.MoveToFirstChild()


'select the required descendant nodes of document node into
'an XPathNodeIterator object using an XPath expression
objXPIter = objXPNav.Select("descendant::" & strElementName)
```

Creating the ArrayList

From here, you can now create an ArrayList and iterate through the collection of elements, copying their values into the ArrayList. You finish by passing the ArrayList back to the calling routine:

```
  'create an ArrayList to hold the results
  Dim arrResult As New ArrayList()

  'iterate through the element nodes in the XPathNodeIterator
  'collection adding their values to the ArrayList
  While objXPIter.MoveNext()
    arrResult.Add(objXPIter.Current.Value)
  End While

  Return arrResult    'and return it to the calling routine

End Function
```

Displaying the Results

You won't be the least surprised to know that the page you use to display the contents of the ArrayList returned by the data access component in this example is just about identical to the version you used with an ArrayList in the previous chapter. Figure 3-8 shows the page suppliers-arraylist-from-xml.aspx.

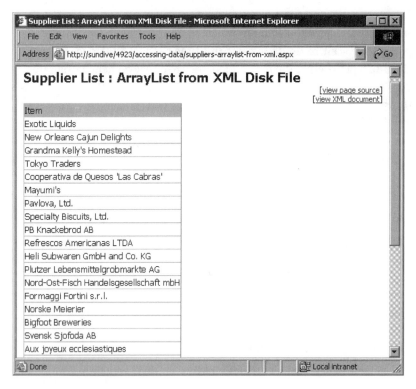

Figure 3-8. Returning an ArrayList *from an XML disk file*

It uses an ASP.NET DataGrid control bound to the ArrayList to display the contents:

```
<asp:DataGrid id="dgrSuppliers" runat="server">
<HeaderStyle BackColor="#c0c0c0"></HeaderStyle>
<AlternatingItemStyle BackColor="#eeeeee"></AlternatingItemStyle>
</asp:DataGrid>
```

In the Page_Load event, you create the physical path to the XML document disk file (as in the previous examples in this chapter). You then create an instance of the XML data access component and call the GetSuppliersArrayList method. Notice that this time you specify the SupplierName element as the one you want to select the values from:

```
dgrSuppliers.DataSource = objSupplierList.GetSuppliersArrayList("SupplierName")
```

You assign the result of the method to the DataGrid (as shown previously) and then call DataBind to display the data. Again, we haven't listed all the code here, but you can view it using the link at the top of the page.

Returning an XML String

The final three methods in the XML data access component show how you can
return an XML document in three document formats—a String, an XmlDocument
object, and an XPathDocument object. If you're simply streaming the XML to a non-
.NET client or object, you'll usually choose to return a string containing the XML.
This can be sent to a client as the HTTP response across the network.

However, if you're dealing with a .NET client or object, you might prefer to
return an XmlDocument or XPathDocument object that it can manipulate directly.
Chapter 4, which introduces the .NET Remoting technology, demonstrates how
you can send objects such as this across an HTTP network such as the Internet.

Therefore, the format you choose for an application depends on how you
intend to remote the data to the client or middle tier and what the client or
middle tier objects will be doing with the data. We'll start by showing you how
you can return an XML string from a component; the following listing of the
GetSuppliersXmlString in the example data access component does just that:

```
Public Function GetSuppliersXmlString() As String

  Try

    'use function in this class to get an XmlValidatingReader
    Dim objValidator As XmlValidatingReader = GetSuppliersValidatingReader()

    'create a new XmlDocument to hold the XML as it is validated
    Dim objXmlDoc As New XmlDocument()
    objXmlDoc.Load(objValidator)

    'return the complete XML content of the document
    Return objXmlDoc.OuterXml

  Catch objErr As Exception

    Throw objErr          'throw exception to calling routine

  Finally

    m_XTReader.Close()    'close the XmlTextReader

  End Try

End Function
```

Validating the XML Content

You can see that you're validating the XML in this example by calling the method within the component named GetSuppliersValidatingReader, which you saw earlier in this chapter. It returns a reference to an initialized XmlValidatingReader for the document, so you can load this into a new XmlDocument object as it stands. The XmlDocument object will automatically call the Read method of the underlying XmlTextReader to get the contents of the document, and any validation errors will be flagged as this process proceeds.

After remembering to close the XmlTextReader, you can then return the OuterXml property of the XmlDocument object. This is one of the useful extensions to the XML DOM that Microsoft implements within the XmlDocument object. It saves you having to iterate through the object yourself, extracting each element in turn. Other similar and useful extension properties are InnerXml, which includes all the XML and text content but without the containing element tags, and InnerText, which includes only the text content of the node and all its descendants.

Displaying the Results

The example page suppliers-xml-from-xml.aspx displays the XML string that the data access component generates. As usual, you can view the source of the page, the XML string itself, the schema you used to validate it, and the XSL Transformations (XSLT) stylesheet through the links at the top of the page (see Figure 3-9).

This page uses the same technique as the examples in the previous chapter that display XML documents. You declare an asp:Xml server control in the page:

```
<asp:Xml id="xmlResult" runat="server" /><br />
```

In the Page_Load event, you create the physical paths to the XML document and the stylesheet and create the data access component instance, as in the previous examples in this chapter. Then you can call the GetSuppliersXmlString method of the component and assign the result to the DocumentContent property of the asp:Xml control. You also assign the path to the XSLT stylesheet to the TransformSource property of the control:

```
'create an instance of the data access component
Dim objSupplierList As New SupplierList(strXMLPath, strSchemaPath)

'call the method to return the data as an Xml string and
'assign it to the XML server control
xmlResult.DocumentContent = objSupplierList.GetSuppliersXmlString()

'specify path to XSLT stylesheet that transforms XML for display
xmlResult.TransformSource = "supplier-list-style.xsl"
```

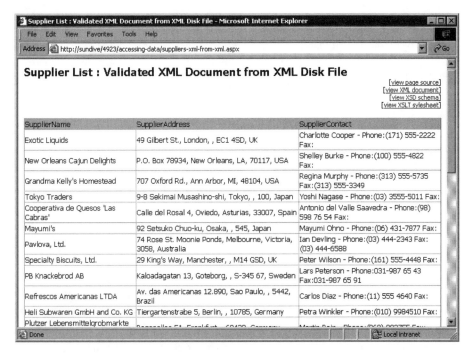

Figure 3-9. Returning an XML string and styling it with XSLT

Returning an XmlDocument Object

If you need an XmlDocument object, rather than just a string that contains the document, you can use the GetSuppliersXmlDocument method of the data access component. In this case, you can instantiate the component with or without specifying an XML schema. The function first creates a new empty XmlDocument object and then checks the member variable m_Validate to see if a schema was specified in the constructor to the component when it was instantiated:

```
Public Function GetSuppliersXmlDocument() As XmlDocument

  'create a new XmlDocument object
  Dim objXmlDoc As New XmlDocument()

  If m_Validate = True Then  'validate against schema

    Try

      'use function in this class to get an XmlValidatingReader
      Dim objValidator As XmlValidatingReader = GetSuppliersValidatingReader()

      'load the XML and validate as it's being loaded
```

```
        objXmlDoc.Load(objValidator)

    Catch objErr As Exception

      Throw objErr    'throw exception to calling routine

    Finally

      m_XTReader.Close()   'close the XmlTextReader

    End Try

  Else  'validation not required
    ....
```

Validating the XML If Required

If there was a schema specified, the code calls the method in the component
you saw earlier to get an XmlValidatingReader that references the XML disk file and
uses this to load the XML into the XmlDocument object (as shown in the previous
code). Any error that's detected when loading the document is raised to the
calling routine.

Alternatively, if there was no schema specified, you simply use the Load
method of the XmlDocument object you created at the beginning of the method to
load the XML from disk directly (as shown in the following code). Again, any error
is raised to the calling routine:

```
    ....
  Else  'validation not required

    Try

      'load the XML from disk without validation
      objXmlDoc.Load(m_XmlFilePath)

    Catch objErr As Exception

      Throw objErr    'throw exception to calling routine

    End Try

  End If

  'return the XmlDocument object
  Return objXmlDoc

End Function
```

Displaying the Results

The example page that uses this method, `suppliers-xmldoc-from-xml.aspx`, is identical to the previous example except that it now assigns the result to the `Document` property of the `asp:Xml` control. This property expects an `XmlDocument` object, whereas the `DocumentSource` property expects a string. You also specify the same XSLT stylesheet, which creates the table in the page:

```
'call the method to return the data as an XmlDocument and
'assign it to the XML server control
xmlResult.Document = objSupplierList.GetSuppliersXmlDocument()

'specify path to XSLT stylesheet that transforms XML for display
xmlResult.TransformSource = "supplier-list-style.xsl"
```

Returning an XPathDocument Object

The final example in this chapter demonstrates how you can return an `XPathDocument` object from an XML disk file. In fact, you used this method a couple of times earlier within other methods discussed. You'll see how it works here.

Fundamentally, the technique is similar to the previous example of creating and returning an `XmlDocument` object. However, an `XPathDocument` object doesn't have a `Load` method, so you can't create an empty one and load the XML afterward like you did with an `XmlDocument` object. Instead, you have to specify the source of the XML document in the constructor for the `XPathDocument`.

So, the method first checks to see if a schema was specified when the component's constructor was called. If so, it uses the `GetSuppliersValidatingReader` method in the component to get an `XmlValidatingReader` that references the XML disk file. Then it calls the constructor for a new `XPathDocument` object, specifying the `XmlValidatingReader` as the source of the document:

```
Public Function GetSuppliersXPathDocument() As XPathDocument

  'declare a variable to hold an XPathDocument object
  'cannot create an "empty" one and load the XML afterward
  Dim objXPathDoc As XPathDocument

  If m_Validate = True Then  'validate against schema

    Try

      'use function in this class to get an XmlValidatingReader
```

```
        Dim objValidator As XmlValidatingReader = _
                          GetSuppliersValidatingReader()

      'load the XML and validate as it's being loaded
      objXPathDoc = New XPathDocument(objValidator)

   Catch objErr As Exception

      Throw objErr     'throw exception to calling routine

   Finally

      m_XTReader.Close()    'close the XmlTextReader

   End Try

 Else   'validation not required
   ...
```

If validation isn't required—in other words, if no schema was specified in the constructor for the component—you simply create the XPathDocument by specifying the physical path to the XML disk file instead:

```
   ...
 Else   'validation not required

   Try

      'load the XML from disk without validation
      objXPathDoc = New XPathDocument(m_XmlFilePath)

   Catch objErr As Exception

      Throw objErr     'throw exception to calling routine

   End Try

 End If

 Return objXPathDoc    'return it to the calling routine

End Function
```

Displaying the Results

The example page that uses the GetSuppliersXPathDocument method is a little different from the earlier examples that displayed XML documents. This page, suppliers-xpathdoc-from-xml.aspx, displays just the supplier names as a list (see Figure 3-10).

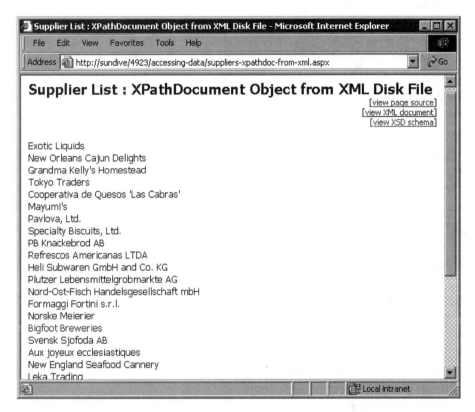

Figure 3-10. Returning an XPathDocument *object from an XML disk file*

To do this, you use an asp:Label control declared in the page:

```
<asp:Label id="lblMessage" runat="server" />
```

In the Page_Load event, you still create the physical paths to the XML document and XML schema disk files, and you create the data access component
instance as before. However, you also declare a variable to hold the XPathDocument
that the method returns so that you can work with it to extract the data you want
to display (we've removed some of the error-handling code for clarity here):

```
'declare a variable to hold an XPathDocument object
Dim objXPDoc As XPathDocument

'create an instance of the data access component
Dim objSupplierList As New SupplierList(strXMLPath, strSchemaPath)

'call the method to return the data as an XPathDocument
objXPDoc = objSupplierList.GetSuppliersXPathDocument()
```

Creating an XPathNavigator

Now you create an XPathNavigator based on the XPathDocument and a variable to
hold an XPathNodeIterator object like you used in the Array and ArrayList examples. You move the XPathNavigator to the root element of the document using the
MoveToFirstChild method and then create a collection in the XPathNodeIterator of
all the SupplierName elements:

```
'create an XPathNavigator object against the XPathDocument
Dim objXPNav As XPathNavigator = objXPDoc.CreateNavigator()

'declare variable to hold an XPathNodeIterator object
Dim objXPIter As XPathNodeIterator

'move to document element
objXPNav.MoveToFirstChild()

'select all the SupplierName nodes of the document node into an
'XPathNodeIterator object using an XPath expression
objXPIter = objXPNav.Select("descendant::SupplierName")
```

Then it's simply a matter of iterating through the collection and building up a
string to display in the asp:Label control on the page:

```
Dim strResult As String    'to hold results for display

'iterate through the element nodes in the XPathNodeIterator
```

```
'collection adding their values to the output string
While objXPIter.MoveNext()
  strResult += objXPIter.Current.Value & "<br />"
End While

lblMessage.Text = strResult
```

Summary

You've spent a lot of time in this and the previous chapter looking at the various types of data access components that the .NET Framework makes so easy to build. The fundamental foundation for any distributed (or, for that matter, nondistributed) data application is its ability to fetch and update data in a way that's efficient but also maintainable, extensible, and flexible.

Having to completely rebuild an application just because the data source has changed isn't a great approach for developers in today's results-oriented world. By separating the data access features into a separate physical or logical "tier," you allow the application to evolve as the data source changes and adapt to new requirements more easily.

What we've attempted to demonstrate in these two chapters is the various ways you can access data in different formats and yet expose it to your applications in the format that best suits them. You aren't shackled with just a relational view or just an XML view as you often were in the past. As you've seen, you can freely mix these to get the output format you want from almost any data source. On top of that, you can choose between a connected approach (such as the DataReader or XmlReader objects) and a disconnected approach (using a DataSet or an XML "document-style" object).

This chapter covered the following topics:

- Building components that access XML documents

- Converting and returning the XML as various different object types

- Displaying the XML easily in your ASP.NET pages

So far, you've only worked with reading data. In later chapters, you'll build data access components to see how you can go about updating the source data from a component and returning information about the success or otherwise of these updates. You'll also see how you can use components such as the ones in this chapter within some example applications.

CHAPTER 4

The Application Plumbing

UP TO NOW, our story has concentrated on the server. We did talk in Chapter 1 about how you might allow the client to take over some of the processing in your application; but mostly you've been busy exploring the server-based techniques you can use to extract the data that powers your dynamic pages. Now the time has come to move over to the client and see what you can achieve there.

There are many ways that the client can perform some of the processing for you, and you'll explore them all in this and the next few chapters. As well as the many techniques you can use, you also need to think about the nature of the data you're going to send to the client. It could be a representation of data you want to handle in a "relational" way (a DataSet, for example), or it could be Extensible Markup Language (XML), plain text, comma-delimited values, or some other format.

As well as deciding what technologies you want to use, you must consider other obvious issues, such as detecting whether the client can take advantage of the chosen technology. You also need to be able to detect situations where the client doesn't support some features that you may take for granted, such as ASP.NET sessions.

So the plan for this chapter is as follows:

- Look at the range of programming features that are available on the client side

- Look at a range of techniques for managing data on the client

- See how you can remote data to the client in different ways

- Look at the issues involved in using ASP.NET sessions

- See how you can detect the client device type and serve appropriate pages

- See an example of client detection and the type of information that's exposed by different types of clients

We'll avoid any detailed examination of handling data on the client until the next chapter. Nevertheless, we'll start here with an overview of the techniques available for working hand in hand with the client to build interactive applications.

Overview of Client-Side Techniques

You know from the first couple of chapters that you generally have a problem trying to build distributed applications that use a Web server and the Internet—or any HTTP–based network such as an intranet—as their communication channel. The fundamentally disconnected nature of HTTP means that you can't create and maintain a permanent connection between the server and the client as you would in a traditional client-server scenario.

You also have the problem that the client may be any number of types of devices, and so the capabilities of that client may not allow the type of distributed communication you want to employ. Because of these limitations, several techniques for enabling communication between the client and server have appeared in the last few years, and yet none are universally compatible with all types of client.

Available Client-Side Programming Techniques

In general, the only thing you can rely on for all (or at least the vast majority) of the browser-type clients that you need to service is support forHTML 3.2, though with browser-specific extensions. For interacting with the user, you're limited to the HTML `<form>` element and the standard HTML controls such as `<input>`.

Most mainstream HTML browsers also provide support for client-side scripting in JavaScript. By staying with "vanilla" JavaScript 1.0, you can rely on support from all Netscape browsers and Opera, and Internet Explorer will just treat it as JScript.

Furthermore, almost all of the current Web browsers will support Java applets. However, here you may find that users have disabled Java or that they choose not to accept a Java applet when prompted (depending on the security settings in their browsers). In fact, some users may also disable client-side scripting, and in this case no client-side user-interaction is possible other than by using the HTML `<form>` controls to submit values from the client to the server.

In small-screen and mobile devices, the situation is often even more restrictive. Cellular phones and similar devices usually accept only a version of Wireless Markup Language (WML) rather than HTML. You probably want to stay with WML 1.0 where possible, to suit as many devices as you can. However (as you'll see in this and later chapters), the server controls provided with the ASP.NET Microsoft Mobile Internet Toolkit (MMIT) can relieve you of many of the problems in this area.

Choosing Client Support

When you try to move processing to the client, you have to make a choice. Either you make it simple and rely on, say, HTML form controls and client-side scripting (and possibly Java applets), or you have to fix your application against a limited set of client devices. To be more specific and take into account mobile (WML) devices, you probably have to make your choice based on Table 4-1 (where a "tick" indicates that a particular technology is supported).

Table 4-1. Technology Support in Different Types of Client

Technology	Any HTML 3.2 Client	Internet Explorer 4	Internet Explorer 5/6	Any WML 1.0 Client
WMLScript 1 scripting				✓
WML <form> and control elements				✓
.NET Web Services			*	
MSXML parser			✓	
Remote Data Service		✓	✓	
Java applets (may be disabled)	✓	✓	✓	
JavaScript 1 (may be disabled)	✓	✓	✓	
HTML <form> and control elements	✓	✓	✓	

NOTE *In Table 4-1, an asterisk (*) means that the browser requires a plug-in. Internet Explorer 5 and Internet Explorer 6 can use a special behavior plug-in (component) to interact with Web Services. We'll discuss this briefly later and demonstrate it in Chapter 6.*

Of course, forcing visitors to use a particular type of client is nothing new—people have been doing it on the Web for a long while now. For example, the latest "limitation" that's being widely applied is support for Macromedia Flash graphics. This is sometimes the only format offered on many sites (and usually with no good reason), causing huge problems for some visitors whose hardware, software, network configuration or physical disabilities may mean that the site is effectively inaccessible.

Providing Alternative Client Support

When you come to build a distributed application where client-side processing is required, you're forced along the same route to some extent because of the wide disparities in support already described. On the other hand, this doesn't mean you can't offer support for other clients as well. You can easily detect the browser/client type within ASP.NET and provide alternatives for devices that don't provide the level of support you require for client-side processing.

In fact, this is what some of the built-in ASP.NET server controls do. For example, the validation controls provided with ASP.NET detect the browser type automatically. If the browser bring used is Internet Explorer 5 or higher, these controls output client-side script that both performs validation client-side and uses Dynamic HTML (DHTML) to modify the display to indicate validation errors. In other clients, the same controls omit this script code and instead depend on postbacks to the server to perform the same actions.

You can always obtain comprehensive details of the current client device from within an ASP.NET page by querying the properties of the Browser object, as you'll see shortly.

In this way you could build into your application a feature that allows clients to select a set of rows (perhaps a list of orders for a particular customer) and then sort and filter the list as they want afterward. If the user's client supports your chosen remoting technique, you could send them all the details of all the orders for the selected customer and then let the client handle sorting, filtering, and displaying data. Otherwise, you'd send a page that offered each filtering and resorting option as a postback to the server, where the page would be rebuilt to suit the user's selections.

This is also a good way to indicate to visitors that you prefer them to use a certain client device or version. Rather than just turning them away, you can explain to users that they'll get better performance and a more responsive interface (especially over a slow Internet link) if they use the client you specify.

Adapting Content for Individual Clients

Providing individualized pages for different clients is an approach that has been common for quite some time. Every client should provide a *user agent string* in the HTTP headers of the request for any resource so that the server can tell what type of client is making the request. In fact, the user agent string often contains other useful items of information such as the operating system of the client (and sometimes even details of the proxy server the client is using). For example, Internet Explorer 6.0 sends the following user agent string:

```
Mozilla/4.0 (compatible; MSIE 6.0; Windows NT 5.0)
```

so you can detect the browser type by examining the user agent string contents. However, this is a messy approach, and you could make it cleaner by using a component that's designed to interpret these strings. In ASP 3.0, the BrowsCap (Browser Capabilities) component is provided as part of the default installation. There are also more feature-rich versions such as CyScape's BrowserHawk (http://www.cyscape.com/).

This means you can detect the browser type being used to make a request and insert the appropriate HTML elements into a page. When using the ASP BrowsCap component, you instantiate it and then query the properties like this:

```
<!-- ASP 3.0 example -->
<%
Set bc = Server.CreateObject("MSWC.BrowserType")
strType = bc.Browser
If strType = "IE" Then
  Response.Write "<marquee>Some Annoying Text Here</marquee>"
ElseIf strType = "Netscape" Then
  Response.Write "<blink>Some Annoying Text Here</blink>"
Else
  Response.Write "<span class="garish-pink">Some Annoying Text Here</span>"
End If
%>
```

In ASP.NET, you can do the same kind of thing. However, when you use the built-in features of the .NET Framework, the technique for detecting the browser type is different. The ASP.NET Request object exposes a property called Browser. This is a reference to a Browser object, which itself exposes properties that are similar to those of the ASP 3.0 BrowsCap object.

You can get details about the current client using this:

```
<!-- ASP.NET example -->
strType = Request.Browser.Type
strVer = Request.Browser.Version
```

Confusingly, the `Browser` object also has a property named `Browser`, which returns the general description of the browser or user agent you're dealing with:

```
strUserAgentName = Request.Browser.Browser
```

Figure 4-1 shows the range of values that are exposed by the `Browser` object when the browser is Internet Explorer 6.0.

Figure 4-1. The values exposed by the `Browser` *object for Internet Explorer 6.0*

Using Client "Categories"

It's fine to adapt the content of a page dynamically for each client for which you want to provide specific support, but over the past year or so this technique has proved to be stretched to its limits. There are many more different types of clients that you really should consider supporting, and the feature sets and capabilities of these clients are becoming ever more varied.

For example, the increasing use of mobile devices means you should certainly consider providing access to visitors using such devices. And what about the promised boom in the use of TV-based Web browsers, games consoles, microwaves, and fridges with Web browsing built in, and other even more esoteric devices? Does your site need to work with these?

The range of capabilities of each of the common client devices that might access a site has grown from being just a matter of a few differences in the HTML they support and the way they render specific HTML to being the requirement for a fundamentally different page design and structure. In the case of mobile devices, it even means a different vocabulary for specifying the page content—WML instead of HTML in most cases.

So instead of trying to build one page that dynamically tailors itself to each browser, it's becoming obvious that the only really viable approach is to build different sets of pages targeted at specific clients or groups of clients. That doesn't mean each set of pages can't be dynamic and adapt to different clients within that group. You'll see what we mean as you look at some possible groups, or *categories*, next.

Our Chosen Categories

Defining the client categories or groups isn't a precise science. A lot depends on what techniques you intend to use within the pages—especially when it comes to remoting data to a client. In the example application, the final choices basically depend on two aspects of the client: the screen size and resolution (which affect the page design and structure) and the support for remoting data (and manipulating and caching it on the client). At the time of writing, you can use the following groups with some success:

- **Internet Explorer 5.0 and higher**: These browsers support XML through the MSXML parser and can use behaviors to work with Web Services.

- **Internet Explorer 4.0**: This supports RDS and client-side data binding, which can provide an extremely interactive and rich client interface.

- **Other HTML-enabled browsers**: You can restrict yourself to features that are available in HTML 3.2 for maximum compatibility with all such clients.

- **Small-screen HTML-enabled devices**: This includes the Pocket PC, for example.

- **Mobile devices and cell phones that support WML**: Again, you can restrict yourself to features available in WML 1.0 for maximum compatibility with all such clients.

At first glance, this set of category choices may seem to be contentious. For example, why isn't there a category for Netscape Navigator 4 or Navigator 6? The reasons we haven't assigned Navigator its own categories are as follows:

- The level of compatibility between the various 4.*x* and 6.*x* releases of Navigator is less than optimal—this makes it difficult to create a page that uses DHTML, Layers, Cascading Style Sheets (CSS), or XML *and* works in all versions. It probably requires plug-ins to be available.

- The actual number of Netscape browsers we expect to serve is low as a proportion of all requests, and so the requirement for several categories for Netscape would mean a disproportionate amount of work for the number of hits. We will, of course, still support Navigator—but as part of the HTML 3.2 category.

- The features we most want in our "specific" client categories (the ones we pull out for special treatment) are the ability to handle data remotely, and the standard features available in Navigator 4.*x* aren't optimized for this. So we'd then be limited to Navigator 6 and possibly the open-source Mozilla browser (though these aren't directly compatible either in some areas).

We also chose to pull out Internet Explorer 4 as a separate category in the examples. In fact, the number of requests from Internet Explorer 4 is likely to be low, and we really only chose this as a separate category so that we could demonstrate some of the useful built-in features it provides for remoting data to and manipulating data on the client. These features are equally supported in the later versions (5.*x* and 6.*x*), so you may prefer to use these features for *all* Internet Explorer 4.*x* and higher clients.

Choosing Categories Based on Actual Client Requests

Of course, a lot depends on the ratio of hits you get from different client types. If you do serve pages to a large proportion of Netscape browsers, you may prefer to build specific sets of pages from these. You can use hidden layers to cache data, and the excellent download and install capabilities for plug-ins means you can build extremely usable solutions.

If you have a narrow set of clients to serve (perhaps on an intranet application), you could decide to support only those specific client types. Alternatively, you may decide to support even more types in applications designed for "general" access. We haven't even considered the issues involved in providing usable pages for clients such as a TV-based browser. In this case, users are likely to be a long way from the screen and using a simple input device—so the way the page is designed must be fundamentally different from that of a normal Web browser (which is viewed close up and provides input via a keyboard and mouse).

Remoting Data to the Client

As well as the display limitations of a client, you also have to design and build applications in such a way that they actually work on all the client platforms and devices you decide to support. More to the point, you'll really want to get the maximum performance from each client if possible—both in speed of operation and perceived "interactiveness." As a bonus, the more of the processing load you can pass to the client (which should provide that highly interactive user experience), the less work your server has to do. You'll see what we mean in the examples coming up in later chapters.

In essence, with a distributed data application, you gain good client interactivity by sending the data to the client so that it can be processed locally, rather than by having all updates to the page done on your server. To understand the choices you have for remoting data to the client, you'll now look at the options in more detail.

Remoting Relational Data to the Client

You'll start with a look at the technologies available for remoting "relational" data to the client. Bear in mind that by *relational* we mean only that it'll be available on the client as a set of rows and columns (what we previously referred to as a *recordset*). The actual data may be in another format during transmission across the network—for example, it'll be XML when remoting a .NET DataSet object. Table 4-2 summarizes the common techniques for remoting relational data.

Table 4-2. Common Data Remoting Techniques

Data Format	Remoting and Client-Side Technologies	Description
MIME-encoded Recordset (ADO)	RDS with ADC object or Java applet	Internet Explorer 4 and higher. Allows automated updates, but there are concerns over security. Windows-based clients only. Also supports client-side data binding.
XML	RDS with ADC object or Java applet	Internet Explorer 4 and higher. Exposes the XML in relational form. Also supports client-side data binding, but automated updating *isn't* available.
CSV or other text-based format	RDS with TDC object	Internet Explorer 4 and higher. Read-only text-based data source control. Also supports client-side data binding.
DataSet, Array, Hashtable, and so on	Using .NET Remoting system	Client must be running the .NET Framework and a custom client-side .NET application.
SOAP (any data structure)	Web Services	Client must be running the .NET Framework or use a plug-in for the browser. Limited to clients supporting the W3C WSDL and SOAP standards.

The Remote Data Service with Relational Data

RDS allows you to send a variety of types of data to the client for processing there. The two client-side ActiveX controls are the Advanced Data Control (ADC) and the Text Data Control (TDC). There are also Java applets available that do much the same as the ADC ActiveX control. You can use these on operating systems other than Windows to achieve the same effect.

The Advanced Data Control

The ADC can create a connection to a data source or business object on the server and extract the data itself. Afterward, it can re-establish this connection and update the original data source. However, exposing the server to clients in this way does raise concerns over security. Microsoft has largely answered this in Windows 2000 by setting up extra controls over how RDS can operate. It requires specific entries in the registry to be able to launch business objects (called `DataFactory` objects) on the server. It's also possible to add security limitations to the default `DataFactory` object by editing a text configuration file named `msdfmap.ini` (found in the `Winnt` folder).

The ADC can also accept an XML document, and it parses it into a rowset so that it can be accessed using relational techniques. Note that you can't perform automated updates using an XML document as the source.

The Text Data Control

The other RDS object, the TDC, accepts delimited text data and exposes it as a rowset on the client. The delimiting character can be any character you like, and the control will cache the data and make it available to other controls or script in the page. This is a useful technique with no security implications because the control doesn't have any facility to update the original data. Of course, if such a facility is a requirement in your application, then you need to build extra code to post updates to the server and update the original data source.

One of the great features of RDS, which often makes it worth considering if you can guarantee the required client device (Internet Explorer 4 and higher), is the support for client-side data binding. It works with both the ADC object and the TDC object, and you'll see how you can use this in Chapter 6.

Client-Side .NET Framework

To allow the best and most seamless techniques to be used, you'll want to be able to write your client-side code using .NET. If the Framework is installed on the client, the native .NET Remoting technology will make it easy to send a collection, an array, a `Hashtable`, or a `DataSet` to the client almost as easily as if it was a process running on the same machine. What's more, of course, you can return the same kinds of data structure to the server in the same way. You'll see how all this works later in this chapter.

Using a Web Service

The final option in Table 4-2 is Web Services. The intention of all the major manufacturers, and the W3C, is to have a standard syntax and format for Web Services that allows any client to connect to any server. In this context, the term *client* refers to either a browser or some executable or other application or service. However, this panacea for all your distributed application problems is still some way away.

At the time of writing, support was just starting to become established, but there are no standard browsers that support Web Services, so using them will still require a conscious choice of which clients you want your application to support. One currently available technique when .NET isn't installed on the client (other than creating a custom application) is to use the `webservices.htc` custom behavior (or plug-in) for Internet Explorer 6. We'll demonstrate this use of a Web Service in Chapter 6.

Remoting XML Data to the Client

In general, remoting XML to a client is much easier than remoting relational data. XML is designed to work across a network using a protocol, such as HTTP, that only offers 7-bit support, so no fancy encoding is required. XML consists of plain text only, so it can simply be streamed to the client and back to the server. Of course, the tough part is deciding how to cache and use it on the client, and the obvious route is to use an XML parser object. In general, all remote caching techniques will use some kind of XML parser on the client, but the environment in which it runs will vary.

Table 4-3 summarizes the common techniques for remoting XML data to the client.

Table 4-3. Techniques for Remoting XML Data

Data Format	Client-Side Technology	Description
XML	MSXML parser and client-side script	Internet Explorer 5 and higher or other custom Microsoft clients running on Windows. Internet Explorer 5 also supports *data islands*, which use the MSXML parser.
Simple Object Access Protocol (SOAP) (any XML structure)	Web Services	Client must be running the .NET Framework or use a plug-in for the browser. Limited to clients supporting the W3C Web Service Description Language (WSDL) and SOAP standards.
XML	Custom application, Java applet, or ActiveX control	Any client and any platform to match the application or component used, for example, .NET Framework, Windows, Java, or any other.

Client-Side XML Parsers

One of the goals of the W3C recommendations for working with XML is to achieve platform and operating system independence. There's nothing in the XML recommendations that specifies what platform, programming language, operating system, application, or other technical variation should form the basis for processing XML documents. So, in theory, you can use any XML parser that's available for the client platform and operating system.

Sounds great. You just have to write code to manipulate the XML document using the W3C-recommended interfaces (the methods and properties listed in the W3C recommendations—see `http://www.w3.org/TR/DOM-Level-2-Core/`).

Unfortunately there is, of course, a catch. This assumes that the client has a suitable XML parser available; otherwise your code must figure out which one is required and install it over the network.

Then comes the next problem. One thing that the W3C recommendations don't do is specify the syntax for the "nonmanipulative" methods. For example, there's no recommendation for how you actually load an XML document into the parser or how you extract and save it afterward. So you always need to establish which client device your application is serving, and which XML parser, and then tailor the code to suit it.

So we still aren't at the point of universality with XML. However, because you've already come to the conclusion that you need to restrict your client-side processing to specific types of client device, you're no worse off either. It just means you have to target specific devices or browsers and create multiple pages if you want to support more than one. You also, of course, need a "down-level" page that doesn't attempt to pass processing to the client and instead does it all on the server.

The MSXML Parser

The Microsoft XML Parser (MSXML) is by far the most common XML parser in use with Microsoft applications. This parser appeared with Internet Explorer 5.0 and is integrated on the client side to the extent that it's automatically used to parse XML files for display in the browser. The original version of this parser supported Microsoft's own implementations of XML XSL and added several useful extensions to the original W3C XML DOM Level 1 specifications.

MSXML is now available both as version 3 and the new version 4. Much of the older and nonstandard syntax compatibility has been removed from the latest version to improve overall performance. However, in the example applications, we'll attempt to provide support for version 2 of MSXML—in particular, version 2.5a (installed by default with Internet Explorer 5.01 and higher).

Although we could demand a higher version, and you might decide to do so in your own applications, there's nothing we really need to achieve that version 2.5a doesn't provide. However, as discussed in later chapters that describe the application you're building, it'd be useful to have version 4 installed in a few specific situations. Version 4 allows you to use extra functionality to get around a few minor limitations with the earlier versions (3 and lower). The problem is that you immediately limit the range of clients you can support—in fact, it usually means forcing the user to download and install the parser first.

You can find the version of MSXML that's currently installed and set as the default by viewing the registry. For example, you can find the path for version 2 at the following location: `HKEY_LOCAL_MACHINE\SOFTWARE\Classes\ Msxml2.DOMDocument\ CurVer`.

MSXML Parser Versions

The installation and filenames of MSXML are a little vague to say the least. Table 4-4 attempts to show which versions are installed with the various versions and Service Packs (SPs) for Internet Explorer and other software. Notice that the filename *doesn't* provide an accurate guide to the actual version number.

Table 4-4. MSXML Versions and Their Common Installation Sources

Version	Filename	Installed with…
1.0	msxml.dll	Internet Explorer 4.0
1.0a	msxml.dll	Internet Explorer 4.0a
2.0	msxml.dll	Internet Explorer 4.01 and 5.0
2.0a	msxml.dll	Office 2000, Internet Explorer 5.0a
2.0b	msxml.dll	Internet Explorer 5.0b
2.5a	msxml.dll	Internet Explorer 5.01
2.5	msxml.dll	Windows 2000
2.5 (SP1)	msxml.dll	Windows 2000 (SP1), Internet Explorer 5.01 (SP1), and Internet Explorer 5.5
2.6	msxml2.dll	SQL Server 2000, BizTalk Server
3.0	msxml3.dll	Internet Explorer 6.0
4.0	msxml4.dll msxml4a.dll msxml4r.dll	Now known as *Microsoft XML Core Services*, version 4 is installed in side-by-side mode rather than replacement mode. This means that, by default, you have to specify the full type when you create an instance of version 4, for example: `Dim oXML As New Msxml2.DOMDocument.4.0.`

> **NOTE** *For more information on the versions of MSXML and how to get the latest version, go to* http://msdn.microsoft.com/xml/. *For information on version 4 and side-by-side mode, see* http://msdn.microsoft.com/library/en-us/xmlsdk/htm/sdk_installregister_4r76.asp.

Running the .NET Framework on the Client

As with remoting relational data, the best way to get a smooth and useable connection between the client and server is by running the .NET Framework on the client. This allows most native .NET data objects to be passed transparently across the network to the client, and back to the server, via HTTP. These objects include XmlDocument and XmlDataDocument, as well as many other objects from the various .NET class namespaces.

In Chapter 7, you'll see a version of the sample application that uses .NET Remoting and consequently depends on the Framework being installed on the client. Of course, until the bulk of the population actually installs the Framework on their machines, this is probably more useful in an intranet environment. However, you could—in other environments—provide a link to a place from which the client can download and install the appropriate version of the Framework (dotnetredist.exe, currently about 20MB in total) for their machine.

Once the Framework is installed, there are other exciting possibilities. For example, you can write executable Windows Forms applications and compile them to Dynamic Link Libraries (DLLs) that the client can progressively download and execute on their machine automatically. This provides an even better level of interactivity and application finesse than browser-based application interfaces. You can also remote data and objects to the .NET client in a variety of ways, as you'll see in the following sections.

Deciding on Your Priorities

Chapter 1 discussed the idea of remoting and marshaling data, and the .NET Framework provides several ways in which you can accomplish this. When writing applications, you need to decide which method is most appropriate for your situation, and there are several issues you need to consider:

- **Scalability**: How scalable does your application need to be? Is it an intranet application, where the number of users is stable and known, or an Internet application, where the user base is unknown?

- **Speed**: Is speed the most critical aspect of your application? Although every-one wants their code to perform as fast as possible, there are sometimes trade-offs that need to be made between speed and ease of programming.

- **Security**: If you're giving your application the ability to remote parts of itself across a network, then security is vitally important. How this security is implemented depends upon how you choose to perform the remoting.

You also have to consider exactly *what* you want to remote. Is it just data that needs to be used by another application, or is it application functionality itself? Throughout the rest of this book you'll see plenty of examples of both of these. Using data locally in clients isn't new, even with browser-based applications, but there are problems with this approach:

- Client-side code is visible to the user, leading to a loss of intellectual property.

- Debugging and testing is more problematic because of the lack of good, integrated debuggers.

- Client-side scripting languages are typeless, so you often have to provide more code than typed languages.

- There are many types of client browsers, so coding becomes increasingly more complex (you'll see how you can solve some of these problems when dealing with browsers as you go through the book).

Having .NET on the client, on the other hand, brings a wealth of opportunity, as we've suggested already:

- You have access to native data types, which makes local manipulation of the data extremely simple.

- The performance of a native .NET application will be better than a scripted application.

- .NET applications are compiled, and thus intellectual property is harder for clients to obtain.

- The user interface can be a Windows Forms application, thus bringing a great user experience.

- You can, if required, use a stateful development methodology (in contrast with the stateless environment of Web applications).

Application Domains and Processes

To understand exactly what .NET Remoting entails, you have to understand what's possible. Although remoting is far simpler in .NET than in previous environments, it still requires thought and careful design. This book isn't specifically about remoting, so we won't cover it in detail. However, we'll explain the basic concepts of remoting in this chapter, and then in later chapters we'll show how you can use remoting when dealing with rich clients.

If you think you might have to provide remoting support in your application (whether now or in a future release), then you really need to consider that in your design. Remoting hinges on the notion of application domains and processes. An *application domain* is an isolated unit of memory in which an application runs. A *process* is similar though not exactly the same—it's also an isolated unit of memory, but it's able to host many applications running simultaneously. It does this by loading the applications into separate application domains. Hence, you can think of a process as being a container for one or more application domains, each of which is running an application.

In many cases, an application will run in an application domain that's contained in a process all of its own, but this isn't always the case. For example, the ASP.NET applications hosted by an Internet Information Services (IIS) installation can be configured to run either all in the same domain or all in their own separate domains. This is known as *IIS Application Protection*—if the configuration is set to high or isolated, the applications run in separate processes; otherwise, they all run in the same process.

Why would you want to run applications in separate processes? The answer lies in the fact that each process is *isolated* from other processes. In particular, this means that if an application in one process fails, it'll bring down that process without affecting the applications running in other processes. This option brings security and stability to your applications.

However, this has its price when you have two applications running in separate processes and you need those applications to communicate with one another. Because the processes are isolated, the only way to provide communication between two such applications is by remoting either the data or the logic.

Of course, if two applications are running on different machines, then they're running in different processes—because a process can't span CPUs. So, if your Web application is to delegate some of its activity from the server to a remote client, then remoting is the way for those two processes to communicate.

We've used the terms *client* and *server* quite a lot in this book already. When it comes to remoting, it's worth reiterating that the client is the one requesting the data and the server is the one supplying the data.

Object Marshaling

You've already met the concept of *marshaling* in Chapter 1—it's the act of transferring something between two application domains (or processes). When you're designing an application that involves remoting, you need to decide what actually gets transferred and how it gets transferred. In particular, you need to decide whether you want to transfer the *data* held by an object or the *logic* of an object.

You've already seen marshaling in effect because you're marshaling data every time you transfer information between the server and the client. A Web Service, for example, often creates a DataSet object containing a set of rows from some database query. It then converts this data into a format suitable for transfer to a remote application—that's *serialization*. This is marshaling in action, and you don't have to do anything special in the Web Service to enable this—you just return the DataSet object from the Web Service method. The DataSet automatically knows how to marshal its data.

Not every object is automatically available to be marshaled. Many of the base classes in the .NET class library aren't designed to be marshaled and therefore specify no method of serialization. For example, objects that deal with the file system don't support marshaling because the file system of the client application may differ from the file system of the server application.

In the discussion of marshaling in Chapter 1, we introduced the following terms:

- **Marshal By Value (MBV)**: An object is copied and the copy is passed between application domains. In this case, the object's data is serialized, and the data is marshaled. This data is then used to define the properties of a new instance of the object.

- **Marshal By Reference (MBR)**: A proxy to the object is created and used to access the object remotely. In this case the data isn't serialized because the object remains with the server application.

To allow objects to be marshaled between application domains, you have to specify how this marshaling takes place. Luckily, Microsoft has made this relatively simple by providing attributes and interfaces for you to implement. We'll discuss the reasons for choosing one option over another shortly, but first we'll show you how it's done.

Automatic MBV

There are two ways to marshal an object by value. The first is to declare the
Serializable attribute on a class. For example, suppose you have a class designed
to hold the details of a category from the Categories table of the Northwind database. The Categories table consists of the columns shown in Table 4-5.

Table 4-5. The Northwind Categories *Table Columns*

Column	Type
CategoryID	Integer
CategoryName	String
Description	String
Picture	Binary

Therefore, the class might look something like this (omitting the implementation, for clarity):

```
Public Class Category

  ' Private member variables
  Private _CategoryID As Integer
  Private _CategoryName As String
  Private _Description As String
  Private _Picture As Byte()
  ' Property implementations
  Public Property CategoryID As Integer
    '...
  End Property

  Public Property CategoryName As String
    '...
  End Property

  Public Property Description As String
    '...
  End Property

  Public Property Picture As Byte()
    '...
  End Property

End Class
```

To allow this class to be marshaled, you decorate the class with the appropriate attribute:

```
<Serializable()> _
Public Class Category

  ' Private member variables
  ...

  ' Property implementations
  ...


End Class
```

That's all you have to do to the class—all public and private fields are automatically serialized.

If you decide that you don't want the Picture property to be serialized (because it may be quite large), you can specify that with the NonSerialized attribute:

```
<NonSerialized()> Private _Picture As Byte()
```

When this class is serialized using the SOAP formatter, you get the following:

```
<SOAP-ENV:Envelope xmlns:xsi="http://www.w3.org/2001/XMLSchema-instance"
        xmlns:xsd="http://www.w3.org/2001/XMLSchema"
        xmlns:SOAP-ENC="http://schemas.xmlsoap.org/soap/encoding/"
        xmlns:SOAP-ENV="http://schemas.xmlsoap.org/soap/envelope/"
        xmlns:clr="http://schemas.microsoft.com/soap/encoding/clr/1.0"
        SOAP-ENV:encodingStyle="http://schemas.xmlsoap.org/soap/encoding/">
  <SOAP-ENV:Body>
    <a1:Category id="ref-1" xmlns:a1= ⤶
              "http://schemas.microsoft.com/clr/nsassem/mynamespace/ ⤶
              mbo%2C%20Version%3D0.0.0.0%2C%20Culture%3Dneutral%2C%20 ⤶
              PublicKeyToken%3Dnull">
      <_CategoryID>1</_CategoryID>
      <_CategoryName id="ref-3">First</_CategoryName>
      <_Description id="ref-4">The first category</_Description>
    </a1:Category>
  </SOAP-ENV:Body>
</SOAP-ENV:Envelope>
```

You can see that the properties have been converted to XML—with the exception of the `Picture` property, which you deliberately don't want to be serialized. This XML document would be marshaled to another process, which would then deserialize it, constructing a new `Category` object.

> **NOTE** *You can apply many other attributes to class members to control serialization. See the "Serializing Objects" topic in the .NET Framework documentation for more details.*

Custom MBV

The other method of marshaling by value is to implement the `ISerializable` interface and perform the serialization yourself. The class still needs to have the `Serializable` attribute set, but implementing the interface gives you more control over how the data is to be serialized, and you no longer need to specify properties as being `NonSerialized`.

Modifying the class, you now have the following:

```
<Serializable()> _
Public Class Category
  Implements ISerializable

  ' Private member variables
  Private _CategoryID As Integer
  Private _CategoryName As String
  Private _Description As String
  Private _Picture As Byte()

  Public Sub New()
  End Sub

  Public Sub New(info As SerializationInfo, context As StreamingContext)
    ...
  End Sub

  Overridable Overloads Sub GetObjectData(info As SerializationInfo, _
                                  context As StreamingContext) _
    Implements ISerializable.GetObjectData
    ...
  End Sub
```

```
    Public Property CategoryID As Integer
      '...
    End Property

    Public Property CategoryName As String
      '...
    End Property

    Public Property Description As String
      '...
    End Property

    Public Property Picture As Byte()
      '...
    End Property

End Class
```

The `ISerializable` interface implementation demands that you add the `GetObjectData` method because this is what the runtime calls when serializing a class. It's there that the custom code serialization will be placed. You also add two constructors in this example. The first is an empty constructor, which is required because you're overloading the constructor with another, which in turn is used for deserialization. You also add the blank constructor because the class didn't have one before.

To serialize, you use the `SerializationInfo` argument of the `GetObjectData` method to add objects to the serialized stream. If you want to add a new element specifying the time serialization took place, you could use the following code:

```
Overridable Overloads Sub GetObjectData(info As SerializationInfo, _
                                        context As StreamingContext) _
  Implements ISerializable.GetObjectData

  info.AddValue("SerializedAt", DateTime.Now)
  info.AddValue("CategoryID", _CategoryID)
  info.AddValue("CategoryName", _CategoryName)
  info.AddValue("Description", _Description)

End Sub
```

This simply stores the current properties of the object, as well as the current time. The SOAP request would then look like this:

```
<SOAP-ENV:Envelope xmlns:xsi="http://www.w3.org/2001/XMLSchema-instance"
        xmlns:xsd="http://www.w3.org/2001/XMLSchema"
        xmlns:SOAP-ENC="http://schemas.xmlsoap.org/soap/encoding/"
        xmlns:SOAP-ENV="http://schemas.xmlsoap.org/soap/envelope/"
        xmlns:clr="http://schemas.microsoft.com/soap/encoding/clr/1.0"
        SOAP-ENV:encodingStyle="http://schemas.xmlsoap.org/soap/encoding/">
  <SOAP-ENV:Body>
    <a1:Category id="ref-1" xmlns:a1= ↵
                "http://schemas.microsoft.com/clr/nsassem/mynamespace/ ↵
                mbo%2C%20Version%3D0.0.0.0%2C%20Culture%3Dneutral%2C%20 ↵
                PublicKeyToken%3Dnull">
      <SerializedAt xsi:type="xsd:dateTime">
        2002-01-29T14:49:22.9936960-00:00
      </SerializedAt>
      <CategoryID>1</CategoryID>
      <CategoryName id="ref-3">First</CategoryName>
      <Description id="ref-4">The first category</Description>
    </a1:Category>
  </SOAP-ENV:Body>
</SOAP-ENV:Envelope>
```

Notice the additional SerializedAt element, which represents the new method in the SOAP document. For the deserialization, you'd add the following to the constructor:

```
Public Sub New(info As SerializationInfo, context As StreamingContext)
  Console.WriteLine("Constructed from object serialized at " & _
                                    info.GetDateTime("SerializedAt"))
  _CategoryID = info.GetInt32("CategoryID")
  _CategoryName = info.GetString("CategoryName")
  _Description = info.GetString("Description")
End Sub
```

Again the SerializationInfo argument comes into play, and you use the appropriate Get methods to retrieve the values from the XML file.

Invoking Serialization

To manually serialize or deserialize an object, you can use either of the following:

- The BinaryFormatter class, which is in the
  System.Runtime.Serialization.Formatters.Binary namespace

- The SoapFormatter class, which is in the
  System.Runtime.Serialization.Formatters.Soap namespace

For example, to serialize the Category object to a SOAP XML document, you could use the following code:

```
Dim stream As Stream = File.Open("cat.xml", FileMode.Create)
Dim formatter As New SoapFormatter()
formatter.Serialize(stream, cat)
stream.Close()
```

And to deserialize, you could use this code:

```
Dim stream As Stream = File.Open("cati.xml", FileMode.Open)
Dim formatter As New SoapFormatter()
cat = CType(formatter.Deserialize(stream), Category)
stream.Close()
```

To use the binary formatting option, you just substitute BinaryFormatter for SoapFormatter. The SOAP formatter formats the object according to the SOAP specification—this is what the previous code used. SOAP provides great interoperability between disparate systems but is quite a verbose format. If you know which client type is being used, then using binary formatting will be quicker because the payload (the XML that represents the request) is smaller.

When implementing remote functionality, you generally don't need to perform the serialization manually—it'll happen when the object is remoted. You'll look at this in more detail later in this chapter and later in the book.

MBR

The second way of marshaling is to marshal by reference, where a reference to a server-side object is passed to the client. The big difference, as already stated, is that the class instance actually remains on the server, with the client using a proxy object to reference the server object. The client proxy has an interface that mimics the server class, so the client can use the same methods and properties. The proxy marshals each request from the client to the server-side object and also marshals responses back to the client.

To use this type of marshaling, the class must inherit `MarshalByObjectRef`, which provides the functionality for a class to be used by a proxy from a remote client. For example:

```
Public Class Category
  Inherits MarshalByObjectRef
  ...
End Class
```

That's all you have to do to the class—it now has the ability to pass a reference to itself to another process.

That's not the end of the story, however, because marshaling (whether by value or by reference) requires more than just a change to the class. You need to decide how the client and server are going to communicate (via TCP or HTTP), who starts the communication process (the client or the server), what sort of security you want, and so on. We'll cover these topics in later chapters, showing how you create both clients and servers for marshaling objects by reference.

Should You Use MBV or MBR?

The answer to this question depends on your application and the objects to be marshaled. This makes it difficult to have any specific rules for which type to use, but there are some guidelines.

You should use MBV in the following situations:

- Your object isn't large. Because the entire object is packaged and transferred to the remote application, it doesn't make sense to marshal very large objects.

- Your application accesses the object regularly. With the entire object available in the remote application, accessing properties or methods happen within the application domain of the calling application. Once the object is marshaled, therefore, access is fast and efficient.

You should use MBR in the following situations:

- You need to maintain state. If the server application needs to know the state of the object, then you have to retain the object on the server and use references to it in client applications.

- When the network is sufficiently resilient to maintain the connection between the two application domains.

Activation and Lifetime

The activation and lifetime of MBR objects determine which participant creates the remotable object and how long it lives. There are two types of activation—*client activation* and *server activation*. In the server activation role, objects are created when the server requires them (such as for a property or method call) and not when the client creates an instance of them. There are two types of server-activated object:

- **Singleton**: In this case, there will only ever be one instance of the object, irrespective of the number of client requests. This means that the object must manage its client base.

- **SingleCall**: In this case, there's an object for each client request.

Client-activated objects are created when the client creates a new instance.

The lifetime of the MBR object depends upon its *lease*, which defines who controls the destruction of the object. By default this is handled by the Framework, and objects whose leases expire are garbage collected. This is the same as the creation and destruction of nonremotable objects, which are garbage collected when they're no longer required. There are a number of techniques for controlling the lease information, but that's outside the scope of this book. You should consult the Framework documentation for more details.

Channels

We use the term *channel* to describe the communication link between a server and a client—you can think of it as a "communication pipe" between the two. HTTP and TCP provide the two default channels that are available to you. These channels provide means by which a Web application can listen for incoming messages and send outgoing messages, formatting the message correctly for the associated protocol. You can write effective remoting applications without having to learn all there is to know about network programming or how the protocols work.

By default, the TCP channel uses a binary format, and the HTTP channel uses SOAP as its message format. It's also possible to configure the HTTP channel to use a binary format: This gives the advantage of improved speed because the message will be more compact. You saw the SOAP message format in effect earlier when you looked at serialization—the MBV object was serialized using the `SoapFormatter` class. Both channels and formatters are, like much of the .NET Framework, completely customizable—so if you like, you can use your own objects in place of the existing ones. The channels live in the `System.Runtime.Remoting.Channels` namespace.

Using the channels is quite easy—in the server code, you simply register the channel required:

```
ChannelServices.RegisterChannel(New HttpChannel(8000))
ChannelServices.RegisterChannel(New TcpChannel(8001))
```

You can use either or both the HTTP and TCP channels—this gives you greater flexibility of communication. For example, you could configure your server to support both channels—you might have an intranet application using the TCP channel and a remote Internet application using the HTTP channel. The single argument to the channel class constructor is the port number upon which the server will listen.

Once the channel is registered, you configure it to expose your remotable object. Let's look at an example. Suppose you have a class called Category, like this:

```
Public Class Category
  Inherits MarshalByObjectRef
  ...
End Class
```

You could configure your channel to allow this class of object to be used with it:

```
RemotingConfiguration.RegisterWellKnownServiceType(GetType(Category), _
                                "Category", WellKnownObjectMode.Singleton)
```

On the client, you use the Activator object:

```
Dim cat As Category
cat = CType(Activator.GetObject(GetType(Category), _
                                "http://localhost:8000/Category"), Category)
```

Or you use this:

```
Dim cat As Category
cat = CType(Activator.GetObject(GetType(Category), _
                                "tcp://localhost:8001/Category"), Category)
```

You'll see this in action in Chapter 7.

Configuration

Instead of hard coding the channel configuration details, you can put that information into a configuration file. For example, the server configuration file would look like this:

```
<configuration>
  <system.runtime.remoting>
    <application>
      <service>
        <wellknown mode="Singleton"
                   objectUri="Category"
                   type="mynamespace, Category"/>
      </service>
      <channels>
        <channel port="8000"
                 type="System.Runtime.Remoting.Channels.Http.HttpChannel,
                       System.Runtime.Remoting" />
      </channels>
    </application>
  </system.runtime.remoting>
</configuration>
```

The server code now becomes this:

```
ChannelServices.RegisterChannel(New HttpChannel(8000))
RemotingConfiguration.Configure("server.exe.config")
```

Likewise, on the client, you could add the following to the configuration file:

```
<configuration>
  <system.runtime.remoting>
    <application>
      <client>
        <wellknown type="mynamespace, Category"
                   url="http://localhost:8000/Category" />
      </client>
    </application>
  </system.runtime.remoting>
</configuration>
```

and change the client code to this:

```
RemotingConfiguration.Configure("client.exe.config")
Dim cat As New Category()
```

The latter is much more intuitive and produces far neater code; it also allows you to make dynamic changes to applications. However, when used on the client, this method does mean that certain server details are exposed in a client-side XML file.

Hosting the Server in IIS

As an alternative to writing a server application, you could host your remotable object within IIS. To use this method, you first create an application, place the remotable object in the application's bin directory, and modify the web.config file:

```
<configuration>
  <system.runtime.remoting>
    <application>
      <service>
        <wellknown mode="SingleCall"
                   objectUri="CatService.rem"
                   type="mynamespace, Category"/>
      </service>
      <channels>
        <channel ref="http"/>
      </channels>
    </application>
  </system.runtime.remoting>
</configuration>
```

You'll look at IIS and remoting servers in more detail in Chapter 7.

Security

The security model of the .NET Framework provides a rich set of features for securing access to remote clients and servers. When choosing what sort of security model you should implement in your remoting application, you should consider these factors:

- How are you hosting your server application? A server application hosted in IIS can take advantage of the authentication and authorization that IIS provides. A custom server model, on the other hand, has to provide its own authentication and authorization.

- Which channel are you using for remoting? The HTTP channel can use IIS as its server, whereas a TCP channel-based system doesn't have a default security model on which it can rely.

Along with the issues of authentication and authorization is *code access security*. When dealing with a remote client, you have to convince the client that your code is safe to run. This is an issue that already exists in the Web browser world where client-side scripting is common and the threat of malicious code accessing machine resources is real. The same is true of remoted objects, and that's where the .NET code access security model comes into effect. It allows the code to determine what permissions it requires and arranges for those permissions to be granted by the user. This allows the user to trust the code depending upon a set of guidelines, such as its author or its function.

You'll look at this topic later in the book, when you start building a rich client based upon the .NET Framework. For the moment, though, you've seen what's involved in the basics of .NET Remoting and have plenty of food for thought. Now it's time to move your focus back to ASP.NET and see some more issues surrounding the server and client detection.

Using ASP.NET Sessions

Before you actually get down to building an application, it's a good idea to decide what features of ASP.NET your application will depend on and to check that these features will be available with the clients you target. One feature that's often taken for granted, but isn't always available, is support for ASP.NET sessions.

Sessions allow you to store values that are specific to an individual client and retrieve these values in any request from that client at any time while that session is active. By default, IIS 5.0 sets each Web site's session support to be on for all clients and sets the timeout (the period that must elapse between requests from that client before a session ends) to 20 minutes. (You can override these in the Internet Services Manager by right-clicking the Web site, selecting Properties, selecting the Home Directory tab, clicking the Configuration button, and then selecting the App Options tab.)

Sessions Configuration in ASP.NET

ASP.NET replaces the sessions feature of ASP 3 with a new system, but the code you use within your ASP.NET pages to interact with sessions is almost identical to earlier versions. However, the configuration settings for supporting and controlling sessions are quite different from ASP 3 and earlier and are independent of the setting in IIS. The settings used for ASP.NET sessions are controlled by two configuration options:

- The web.config files in the application folder, and its parent or ancestor folders, and the machine.config file that controls the whole server

- The Page directive in the individual .aspx pages

In the web.config and machine.config files, the simplest and default format for these options is as follows:

```
<sessionState mode="InProc" cookieless="false" timeout="20" />
```

The mode attribute specifies how the values for the sessions will be maintained by ASP.NET. The four possible values for this attribute are as follows:

Off: ASP.NET sessions won't be supported for any client.

InProc: The session data is stored in memory on the machine from which the client requests the page. This is the same as the session support provided in earlier versions of ASP. It's the fastest and most efficient approach but only works where the same machine answers *every* request from a specific user because the session data is stored *only* on this server. The server must also have sufficient resources and memory available to store the data for the total number of sessions that may be active at any one time.

StateServer: The session data is held in memory by a special service that runs on a specified server (in other words, out of process). This is slower and less efficient because of the need to access the data over the network rather than locally on the same machine, but it allows the data to be shared across several machines that form a cluster or Web farm (we'll cover this in more detail later in the chapter). This also frees individual servers from the need to store the data for each session.

SQLServer: The session data is stored in a special table in a SQL Server database that you specify. This is even slower and less efficient than the StateServer option because of database access latency. However, it allows the data to be persisted even when the Web server is restarted, as well as being available across multiple-server clusters and Web farms. It also allows more sessions to be handled in extreme situations and is limited only by database size rather than available memory (as in the StateServer option).

The cookieless attribute of the sessionState element specifies whether sessions should be managed and maintained by automatically *munging* (or inserting) the session key into the URL of the page and every hyperlink on that page. Values for this attribute are False (the default) and True.

The third attribute, timeout, specifies the timeout value in minutes for all sessions in the application(s).

Disabling Session Support

The default implementation of ASP.NET sessions, using the InProc setting so that they work as they did in ASP 3.0 and earlier, is fine for a single machine that isn't too heavily loaded. However, there are times when you need to review when and how you'll use ASP.NET sessions.For example, if you don't actually need to use sessions, you can turn off support and hence eliminate the work ASP.NET has to do connecting each request with a session or creating a new one. You can turn off ASP.NET session support altogether in web.config:

```
<sessionState mode="Off" />
```

You can also turn off session support for specific pages only. This is useful if you want to hold values in the session on behalf of the application but don't want to access them in this particular page. You can do this through the Page directive:

```
<%@Page EnableSessionState="False" ... %>
```

You can also use the Page directive to specify that session data is read-only for that page. Read-only access to session data is faster than the default read-write access because it removes the requirement for a complete stage in the page execution cycle where the values in the session are updated:

```
<%@Page EnableSessionState="ReadOnly" ... %>
```

Sessions and Web Farms

Another issue with session data is that, by default, it's stored on the machine that started the session—that is, the machine that the client first accessed to run the application. In a Web farm situation, the user's first (session-starting) request might be sent to one server within the farm, and their second request to a different server. If the second server doesn't have access to the session data created by the first, then the second request can't be processed as part of that session.

Some Web farm routing algorithms compensate for this by redirecting clients to the same server machine for as long as their session lasts. However, as mentioned previously, ASP.NET gives you two options for storing the session values independently of any specific machine within a Web farm cluster: You can use the ASP.NET `StateServer` option, or you can store the data in a SQL Server database.

To store the session data in the ASP.NET State Server service, you set the `mode` attribute of the `sessionState` element to `StateServer` and specify connection information in the `sessionState` element's `stateConnectionString` attribute. The connection information required is the TCP/IP address and port number of a server that's running the service:

```
<sessionState mode="StateServer" cookieless="false" timeout="20"
              stateConnectionString="tcpip=192.168.0.1:42424" />
```

The `StateServer` service is then started on the specified server with the `net start` command (it doesn't start automatically unless you change the properties for the service):

```
net start aspnet_state
```

The alternative is to use a SQL Server database to store the session values on one or more clustered SQL Server machines. A script, called `InstallSqlState.sql`, creates the ASPState database needed for holding the session data—this script is provided with ASP.NET, and you can find it in the `\WINNT\Microsoft.NET\Framework\` `[version]\` folder. To configure ASP.NET to use SQL Server for session storage, you set the `mode` attribute to `SQLServer` and specify the connection information in the `sqlConnectionString` attribute. The connection information required is the name or IP address of the SQL Server machine (or a SQL Server cluster) and the login details. For example:

```
<sessionState mode="SQLServer" cookieless="false" timeout="20"
 sqlConnectionString="data source=192.168.0.1;user id=uid;password=pw" />
```

Checking for Session Support

ASP.NET sessions work because each request from the client passes a session identifier to the server as part of the request. This session identifier is stored on the client as a cookie.

If you're going to depend on session support being available in the application (irrespective of the way you store the session values), you should check specifically that the client device supports sessions when a user first accesses the application. There's a simple way to perform this check. At the beginning of the first requested page, you set a value in the user's ASP.NET session. In the second requested page, you can check for that value in the session. If the client doesn't support cookies (or if session data is unavailable for some other reason), then the session value will be unavailable.

For example, suppose the user's first request is `default.aspx`. You can make sure that this page contains the following code:

```
'set a session variable to see if sessions are supported
'by checking if it exists when the next page is loaded
Session("Supported") = "Yes"
Response.Redirect("nextpage.aspx")
```

Now suppose that the user requests (or is redirected to) a second page, `nextpage.aspx`. Here's the code you can use in that page to check for the session data:

```
'see if sessions are supported
If CType(Session("Supported"), String) = "Yes" Then
  '... sessions are supported
Else
  '... sessions are not supported
End If
```

NOTE *Note that this test only works when the second page request is* explicit— *for example, through a hyperlink or* <form> *submission, or through some method of client-side redirection (such as the* Response.Redirect *method, a* <meta http-equiv="refresh"> *element, or client-side script). It won't work when the second page is an* implicit *page call (using the* Server.Transfer *or* Server.Execute *method in your ASP.NET code).*

Munging URLs for Session Support

As we've said, if the client doesn't support cookies, then it can't use the cookie mechanism to remember which session it was using. You can get around this by using munged URLs instead of cookies to support sessions. This is where you write the session identifier into the URL, instead of sending it to them as a cookie. In subsequent requests, the client then passes the same session identifier as part of the query string, rather than passing it up within a cookie. ASP.NET can provide URL munging automatically if you specify this feature in the `web.config` file for the application:

```
<sessionState cookieless="true" />
```

Note that you must do this in the web.config file in an application root, not in a web.config file in a subfolder of the application root.

If ASP.NET session support is a necessity for your application, then this might be a feature worth exploring. You can establish whether your user's client browser or user agent supports cookies, and if not, you can redirect them to a set of pages in a separate virtual directory that uses URL munging. We haven't actually implemented this in the example application coming later—we simply report whether sessions are supported. However, all you need to do if you want to provide session support for browsers that "fail" the sessions test is to redirect them to a version of the application containing a web.config file that specifies cookieless sessions.

Client Detection Example

Throughout this book you'll see several versions of an application that uses the categories of client described earlier in the chapter. However, before you can even start to build such an application, you need to decide how you're going to detect the client device type in the first place and then redirect the request to the correct set of pages.

The following sections describe a simple implementation of client detection and redirection and also show you the values available from the ASP.NET Browser object for each one. You'll also go a little further by detecting a couple of other features on which your application may depend. For example, you'll usually want to know whether the client currently supports client-side scripting in JavaScript and whether their browser is currently set up to accept cookies. Remember that both these features can be disabled by the user; you'll check for both in this section.

> **NOTE** *You must have the MMIT installed or these example pages will fail to work. You can obtain the MMIT from* http://download.microsoft.com/download/ .netframesdk/Install/1.0/NT45XP/EN-US/MobileIT.exe.

Overview of the Process

In principle, the technique for detecting the capabilities of a client isn't difficult. However, it can become complicated when there are several types of device and when there are several features you want to check. This example uses the approach shown in Figure 4-2.

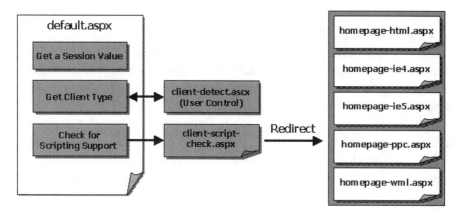

Figure 4-2. Detecting a client's capabilities

The stages shown in Figure 4-2 are as follows:

1. Set a value in the user's session so that you can check for session support in the next page they request. You saw how to do this in the previous section.

2. Detect the client type—in this example, you simply detect which of the groups defined earlier in this chapter the client belongs to. You use a custom user control for this step, instantiated and referenced within the default.aspx page.

3. Redirect the client to the page client-script-check.aspx, specifying the page you want to load next.

4. In the page client-script-check.aspx, redirect the client to the appropriate home page, adding a value to the query string if client-side scripting is enabled.

You'll work through the stages of the process in more detail next.

Detecting the Client Type

To detect the client type in this example, you can use the user control named client-detect.ascx that's described next. This is stored in the global folder of the application (and you'll find it in the global folder of the sample code).

The file `client-detect.ascx` will establish the client type and then perform a redirection. Therefore, this page contains no interface. (Redirection is only possible before the HTTP headers have been written to the client. When the server starts to send the page body, it's implicit that the HTTP headers have been sent—because the body must come after the header. At this stage, it's too late to perform a redirection.)

The user control just contains a function that returns an integer value indicating which of the predefined groups the client fits into. You can see these groups in the `client-detect.ascx` code:

```VB
<%@Control Language="VB" %>

<script language="VB" runat="server">

Function ClientType() As Integer
  'return an integer indicating the type of device
  ' 0 = Not Supported by Application
  ' 1 = HTML 3.2. client
  ' 2 = Internet Explorer 4
  ' 3 = Internet Explorer 5 or above
  ' 4 = Small Screen HTML ( < 50 chars per line or < 400px wide)
  ' 5 = WML Supporting Device (i.e. cell phone)
  ' 9 = Error While Detecting Type
  ...
```

Detecting Non-HTML Client Devices

You need to be aware of one of the main problems concerning mobile devices such as cellular phones and other clients that use WML rather than HTML. You can't send any output to them unless it's the correct format and has the correct Multipurpose Internet Mail Extension (MIME) type. If you try to do that, the client machine will report an error and refuse to load the page.

This means you must use some server-side code to generate a response with the correct MIME type for the output, right from the start. In the case of a WML-supporting device, this MIME type is `text/vnd.wap.wml`; for HTML-supporting clients, the MIME type is `text/html`.

An HTTP header named `CONTENT-TYPE` defines the MIME type of the response, and you can always change this using code in your page before you send any output to the client:

```VB
Response.ContentType = "text/vnd.wap.wml"
```

Using the Mobile Internet Toolkit

So one solution would be to use this code to change the output MIME type. However, there are other issues as well. How do you actually *detect* a cellular phone, never mind capabilities such as screen size, make and model, graphics support, and so on? We've chosen to take advantage of the MMIT because it's a free download for ASP.NET version 1.0, and is part of the default installation in ASP.NET version 1.1. It plugs into the .NET Framework, adding support for mobile and small-screen devices. It also includes a designer that allows you to build applications and pages using the mobile controls in Visual Studio .NET.

Of course, if you don't intend to support non-HTML devices, you don't have to worry about what MIME type you return. However, at this stage it's really worth thinking about detecting WML-enabled devices, even if you don't actually intend to build pages for them in the application. Redirecting them to a WML page containing a phone number, contact address, or other useful information is much better than the client just seeing an error message.

The Client Type Detection Code

So, getting back to the user control, you first declare a variable to hold the result you want to return. Then you can get a reference to the Request.Browser object. This is what exposes the capabilities of the current client. However, when the MMIT is installed on your server, you can cast this to an object of the MobileCapabilities type. This gives you access to extra information about the client that's more specific to small-screen and mobile devices:

```
...
'create integer variable to hold client type
Dim intType As Integer

Try
  'get reference to Browser Capabilities
  Dim objBCaps As System.Web.Mobile.MobileCapabilities = Request.Browser
  ...
```

Determining the Type for WML Clients

The first thing you want to determine is whether this client expects you to serve HTML or WML (or some other format, in which case you'll return a value to indicate that you don't support this device). You check to see whether the PreferredRenderingType property for this client includes the string wml, and if so, you can return a value indicating that it's a mobile device that expects to receive WML content:

```
...
'check the preferred rendering type of the device
Dim strRenderType As String = objBCaps.PreferredRenderingType.ToLower()

If strRenderType.IndexOf("wml") <> -1 Then
  intType = 5      'type is WML device
  ...
```

Determining the Type for HTML Clients

Next, you check to see if the client expects to receive HTML. If so, you first assume that it's a generic HTML 3.2 browser (return value 1). To see if it's a small-screen HTML device (such as a Pocket PC), you check the width of the screen. You can use two properties for this: the width in pixels (which will be set if it's a graphical screen device) or the width in characters. If either are less than the values you notionally chose to indicate that you need to provide different content, you set the return type to 4. Then, if it isn't a small-screen device, you can check if it's Internet Explorer 4.*x*, 5.*x*, or higher. You set the appropriate return value for these types with this code:

```
  ...
ElseIf strRenderType.IndexOf("html") <> -1 Then
  intType = 1      'assume it's an HTML 3.2 device

  'next check the screen size
  If objBCaps.ScreenPixelsWidth < 400 _
  Or objBCaps.ScreenCharactersWidth < 50 Then
    intType = 4      'it's a small screen HTML device

  Else
    'assume it's a normal browser - check if its IE
    If objBCaps.Browser = "IE" Then
        'check the version number
        If objBCaps.MajorVersion >= 5 Then
          intType = 3   'IE 5.x or above

        ElseIf objBCaps.MajorVersion = 4 Then
          intType = 2   'IE 4.x

      End If
    End If
  End If
  ...
```

Dealing with Non-WML, Non-HTML Clients

If the expected rendering type doesn't contain wml or html, then you can't support this client. In this case, you return the value 0 to indicate this. Finally, if you get an error during the process, you return the value 9:

```
    ...
    Else    'not WML or HTML
      intType = 0    'not recognized or supported

    End If

  Catch objErr As Exception
    intType = 9    'error during detection

  End Try

  Return intType
End Function
```

The default.aspx Page

Having seen how the user control (client-detect.ascx) works, you'll look at the page that uses it. The default.aspx page (which you'll find in the detect-client folder) is the page loaded by every client when it first hits the application. You start in that page by registering the user control and then inserting it into the page using the appropriate element you've just defined:

```
<!-- register the user control that contains the detection code -->
<%@Register TagPrefix="dda" TagName="GetClientType"
            Src="../global/client-detect.ascx" %>

<!-- insert user control into the page -->
<dda:GetClientType id="ClientDetect" runat="server" />
```

The only other thing in this page is a Page_Load event handler (remember that there's no visible output generated by this page—you're simply detecting the client type and redirecting based on this type). You set the session variable to check for session support, as described earlier, and then call the ClientType function defined in the user control. You then redirect the client to the page client-script-check.aspx, appending the name of the home page for that client to the query string:

```
Sub Page_Load()

  'set a session variable to see if sessions are supported
  'by checking if it exists when the next page is loaded
  Session("Supported") = "Yes"

  'redirect depending on the client type
  Select Case ClientDetect.ClientType
    Case 2   'IE 4.x
      Response.Clear
      Response.Redirect("client-script-check.aspx?target=homepage-ie4.aspx")
      Response.End
    Case 3   'IE 5.x and above
      Response.Clear
      Response.Redirect("client-script-check.aspx?target=homepage-ie5.aspx")
      Response.End
    Case 4   'small-screen HTML device
      Response.Clear
      Response.Redirect("client-script-check.aspx?target=homepage-ppc.aspx")
      Response.End
    Case 5   'WML-supported mobile phone client
      Response.Clear
      Response.Redirect("homepage-wml.aspx")
      Response.End
    Case Else   'assume HTML 3.2 client
      Response.Clear
      Response.Redirect("client-script-check.aspx?target=homepage-html.aspx")
      Response.End
  End Select
End Sub
```

Notice that you don't redirect WML devices to the client-script-check.aspx page. As you'll see shortly, this page relies on client support for HTML, so it won't work in a WML-enabled client. In fact, you could use the Server.Transfer method instead of the Response.Redirect method, which would be useful if the client didn't support client-side redirection. However, this would prevent the check for session support from working, as described earlier.

Detection Errors and Unsupported Clients

One thing we didn't mention in the previous discussion is what you should do if there's an error during the client detection process or if you find it's a client type your application doesn't support. The first of these cases is easy—you'll just redirect them to the "base" HTML version of the application and hope for the best. You don't know why the detection failed—but you probably have the best chance of supporting the client through the HTML version. This should run fine on rich clients as well as down-level ones. In fact, this situation is already taken care of by the Case Else section of the default.aspx page.

If you detect a client that doesn't support WML or HTML, then there's no point in redirecting them to any version of your application. In this case, you might choose to simply send back some text that the client application may be able to load and display in some way so that the visitor can tell what happened. You may not expect to get many hits from devices that don't support WML or HTML, but dealing with them doesn't actually require much effort. All you need to do is add the appropriate Case section to the Select Case statement:

```
Case 0  'not supported
  Response.Clear
  Response.ContentType = "text/text"
  Response.Write("Sorry, this application does not support " _
            & "your client type: " & Request.UserAgent)
  Response.End
```

You set the MIME type (the ContentType) of the response to text/text, rather than the default of text/html, and write a text message to it. We chose here to include the user agent string, but you could obviously include contact details for your company or organization instead.

Checking for Client-Side Scripting Support

The default.aspx page redirects all recognized clients except WML devices to the page client-script-check.aspx. This is responsible for checking whether the client has JavaScript scripting installed (and not disabled by the user). OK, so you could use the ASP.NET Browser object's JavaScript property to check whether the browser has a JavaScript Active Scripting engine installed; however, many clients have security options in which the user can disable scripting capability, and the JavaScript property doesn't expose those security settings in all browsers.

The `client-script-check.aspx` page gets around that oversight. The principle for detecting whether the JavaScript engine is installed *and enabled* is to present the client with a page that contains both a script-powered redirection and a `<meta>` element redirection that has a built-in slight delay. By seeing which is followed, you can tell whether scripting is enabled.

You first use server-side ASP.NET code to collect the name of the page you previously determined was suitable for the client type. You get that information from the query string and pass it into a string variable named `strClientPage`:

```
<% Dim strClientPage As String = Request.QueryString("target") %>
...
```

Next, you add a `<meta http-equiv>` element to the `<head>` section of the page; this redirects the client to their appropriate home page after a one-second delay:

```
...
<html>
  <head>
    <meta http-equiv="refresh" content="1;url=<% = strClientPage %>" />
    <title>Checking for Active Scripting Support</title>
    ...
```

Redirecting the Client If Scripting Is Enabled

After this, you define a JavaScript function that redirects the client to the same page, but this time with the name/value pair `script=yes` appended to the URL to indicate that scripting is enabled:

```
...
<script language="JavaScript">
<!--
  function jumpScripting() {
    // jump to page using client-side JavaScript - if jump not executed
    // then client does not have scripting available or it is disabled
    window.location.href='<% = strClientPage %>?script=yes';
  }
//-->
</script>
...
```

In the opening `<body>` tag of the page, you can then call this function once the page has loaded:

```
    ...
  </head>
  <body onload="jumpScripting()">
    <font size="2" face="Tahoma,Arial,sans-serif">
      Checking support for Active Scripting...
    </font>
  </body>
</html>
```

If the user has "turned off" active scripting in their browser, then this function will not be called; instead, after a one-second delay, the `<meta>` refresh element will redirect them to the same page but without the query string `script=yes` appended to the URL.

The Device-Specific Home Pages

In the home page that the client is redirected to from the page `client-script-check.aspx`, you can determine whether client-side JavaScript is enabled by looking for the name/value pair `script=yes` in the query string. You can also see if this client supports sessions—you look for the value you stored in this client's session data earlier in the session.

So, the `Page_Load` event handler for each of the home pages (except the one for WML clients) contains the following code. This sets the text in a couple of `asp:Label` controls located elsewhere on the page:

```
Sub Page_Load()

  'see if scripting is supported
  If Request.QueryString("script") = "yes" Then
    lblScripting.Text = "True"
  Else
    lblScripting.Text = "False"
  End If


  'see if sessions are supported
  If CType(Session("Supported"), String) = "Yes" Then
    lblSessions.Text = "True"
  Else
    lblSessions.Text = "False"
  End If


End Sub
```

Displaying the Results

The remainder of the page simply accesses the `Request.Browser` properties directly and displays their values (the actual formatting of the page varies for each client, but the basic technique is as follows):

```
...
User-Agent Name: <b><% = Request.Browser.Browser %></b><br />
Browser Type: <b><% = Request.Browser.Type %></b><br />
Version Number: <b><% = Request.Browser.Version %></b><br />
MajorVersion Part: <b><% = Request.Browser.MajorVersion %></b><br />
MinorVersion Part: <b><% = Request.Browser.MinorVersion %></b><br />
America Online (AOL) browser: <b><% = Request.Browser.AOL %></b><br />
Beta Version: <b><% = Request.Browser.Beta %></b><br />
Web Crawler: <b><% = Request.Browser.Crawler %></b><br />
Supports ECMAScript Version:
    <b><% = Request.Browser.EcmaScriptVersion %></b><br />
Microsoft HTML DOM Version:
    <b><% = Request.Browser.MSDomVersion %></b><br />
W3C XML DOM Version:
    <b><% = Request.Browser.W3CDomVersion %></b><br />
.NET CLR Version:
    <b><% = Request.Browser.ClrVersion %></b><br />
JavaScript Enabled:
    <b><asp:Label id="lblScripting" runat="server" /></b><br />
...
```

In the HTML version, and in both Internet Explorer versions, the previous code is rendered in the left column of the page (refer to Figures 4-3 and 4-4 a little later in the chapter). Notice that the last of these is the `asp:Label` where you indicate whether client-side scripting is currently enabled. The code that produces the right column of values is as follows:

```
...
Supports HTML Tables: <b><% = Request.Browser.Tables %></b><br />
Supports HTML Frames: <b><% = Request.Browser.Frames %></b><br />
Supports Cookies: <b><% = Request.Browser.Cookies %></b><br />
Supports Background Sounds:
    <b><% = Request.Browser.BackgroundSounds %></b><br />
Supports Channel Definition Format (CDF):
    <b><% = Request.Browser.CDF %></b><br />
Supports JavaScript: <b><% = Request.Browser.JavaScript %></b><br />
Supports VBScript: <b><% = Request.Browser.VBScript %></b><br />
Supports ActiveX Controls:
    <b><% = Request.Browser.ActiveXControls %></b><br />
```

```
Supports Java Applets: <b><% = Request.Browser.JavaApplets %></b><br />
O/S Platform: <b><% = Request.Browser.Platform %></b><br />
Is 16-bit Windows: <b><% = Request.Browser.Win16 %></b><br />
Is 32-bit Windows: <b><% = Request.Browser.Win32 %></b><br />
ASP.NET Session Support Enabled:
    <b><asp:Label id="lblSessions" runat="server" /></b><br />
Current Execution Path: <b><% = Request.CurrentExecutionFilePath %></b>
Complete User-Agent String: <b><% = Request.UserAgent %></b><br />
```

This includes the asp:Label where you indicate whether sessions are enabled for this client, followed by a couple of other useful values that you extract directly from the Request object's properties. We chose to show the user agent string to indicate how hard it can be to determine the exact details of the client from just this. However, it may contain specific information (such as the name of a proxy server) that you want to access in a particular application.

The page also shows the value of the Request object's CurrentExecutionFilePath property. If you use the Server.Transfer or Server.Execute method to load a different page without performing a client-side redirection, you'll still see the original path in many of the Request properties. This one does reflect the true current file path and name, which may be useful in some circumstances. Furthermore, if you want to know about the actual request itself (rather than details about the client device), you'll find plenty of information in the many properties of the Request object. There are also some more esoteric values available from the Request.ServerVariables collection, but in ASP.NET most are exposed as Request properties.

The WML-Specific Home Page

If the client turns out to be a WML-based device, you'll redirect them to the page homepage-wml.aspx. You won't check whether JavaScript is enabled because it's extremely unlikely that any WML device will support this. Some devices support scripting in WMLScript, but not all do; furthermore, of those that do support it, they don't all behave in the same way.

For the moment, at least, we don't expect a high proportion of visitors to be using WML-based devices to access the application; therefore, we'll provide just the basic level of support for all these clients from a single set of pages that don't use script at all. If the proportion of WML-based visitors is high, of course, you could use similar techniques to those described for HTML-based devices to redirect clients to the appropriate one of a whole series of WML-enabled sets of pages in your application.

In the WML-enabled home page, you have the two directives that define this
as being a page designed for use with the MMIT classes. You have an `Inherits`
attribute in the `Page` directive to indicate that you want the page itself to be of
object type `MobilePage`. This has special extra capabilities and removes some of the
built-in limitations of the "standard" page designed for use with HTML. You also
register the tag prefix `mobile` to indicate the elements you'll be using from the MIT
`System.Web.UI.MobileControls` classes:

```
<%@Page Inherits="System.Web.UI.MobileControls.MobilePage" Language="VB" %>
<%@Register TagPrefix="mobile" Namespace="System.Web.UI.MobileControls"
            Assembly="System.Web.Mobile"%>
```

Next comes a mobile `<form>` that defines one "page" (or *card*) to display on the
device. You have a page heading indicating that it's a page destined for WML-
enabled devices only, followed by a series of empty `mobile:Label` controls:

```
<mobile:Form runat="server">
  <mobile:Label id="lbl1" Font-Bold="True" runat="server" >
    Page for a WML client only
  </mobile:Label>
  <mobile:Label id="lbl2" runat="server" />
  <mobile:Label id="lbl3" runat="server" />
  <mobile:Label id="lbl4" runat="server" />
  ...
  ...
  <mobile:Label id="lbl16" runat="server" />
  <mobile:Label id="lbl17" runat="server" />
</mobile:Form>
```

Getting the Capabilities Information

Because this page is aimed primarily at mobile devices such as cellular phones,
you need to display a different set of capabilities than the ones in the browser-
based home pages. This example allows you to see some of those available—all
the others used in the HTML and Internet Explorer pages are, of course, available
as well.

In the `Page_Load` event handler of this page, you first get a reference to the `MobileCapabilities` object (as you did in previous sections of this chapter). Then you can set the text values of the various `Label` controls:

```
Sub Page_Load()

    'get a reference to the MobileCapabilities object
    Dim objMobCap As System.Web.Mobile.MobileCapabilities
    objMobCap = CType(Request.Browser, System.Web.Mobile.MobileCapabilities)

    'display values in Label controls on page
    lbl2.Text = "Make: " & objMobCap.MobileDeviceManufacturer
    lbl3.Text = "Model: " & objMobCap.MobileDeviceModel
    lbl4.Text = "MIME Type: " & objMobCap.PreferredRenderingMime
    lbl5.Text = "Rendering Type: " & objMobCap.PreferredRenderingType
    lbl6.Text = "Image MIME Type: " & objMobCap.PreferredImageMime
    lbl7.Text = "Color Screen: " & objMobCap.IsColor
    lbl8.Text = "Screen Height (chars): " & objMobCap.ScreenCharactersHeight
    lbl9.Text = "Screen Width (chars): " & objMobCap.ScreenCharactersWidth
    lbl10.Text = "Screen Height (pixels): " & objMobCap.ScreenPixelsHeight
    lbl11.Text = "Screen Width (pixels): " & objMobCap.ScreenPixelsWidth
    lbl12.Text = "Supports Bold Text: " & objMobCap.SupportsBold
    lbl13.Text = "Supports Italic Text: " & objMobCap.SupportsItalic
    lbl14.Text = "Input Type: " & objMobCap.InputType
    lbl15.Text = "Has Back Button: " & objMobCap.HasBackButton
    lbl16.Text = "Num Soft Keys: " & objMobCap.NumberOfSoftkeys
    If CType(Session("Supported"), String) = "Yes" Then
        lbl17.Text = "ASP.NET Sessions: True"
    Else
        lbl17.Text = "ASP.NET Sessions: False"
    End If
End Sub
```

You can see the `If...Then...Else` construct at the end of the previous code—this is where you detect whether sessions are supported for this device. It's the same as the way you did it in the browser-based pages earlier.

Viewing the Results

Having stepped through the code, let's look at the rewards you can expect from requesting the same URL (in this example, `http://localhost/4923/detect-client/default.aspx`) from a number of different clients.

Viewing Results in a Netscape Navigator Browser

Figure 4-3 shows the results of opening the `default.aspx` page in a Netscape Navigator client. Cookies and client-side scripting are enabled in this figure, but you can turn them off in the Edit ➤ Preferences dialog box and check that the page returns the correct values in this case.

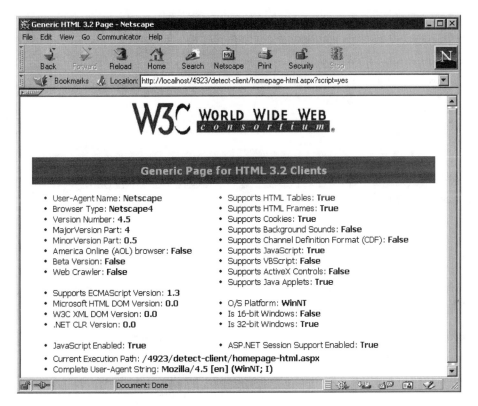

Figure 4-3. Viewing the results in Netscape 4.5

Viewing Results in Internet Explorer 6.0

Figure 4-4 shows the results when the client is Internet Explorer 6.0.

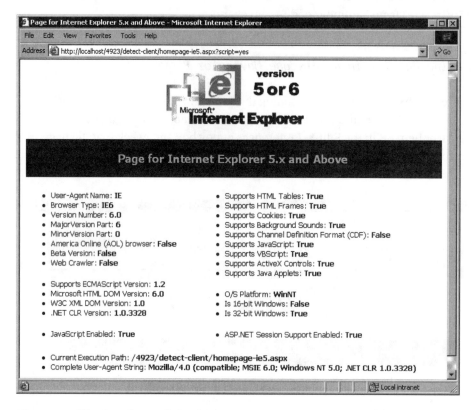

Figure 4-4. Viewing the results in Internet Explorer 6.0

Notice how the properties include the versions that are installed and/or supported for ECMAScript (the nonproprietary version of JavaScript), the Microsoft HTML Document Object Model (DOM), the XML DOM for the currently installed MSXML parser, and the .NET Framework runtime that's installed. These are useful when you build applications that run on the client. You can detect whether the browser has the required version *before* you launch into the application—this gives you the opportunity to redirect the client to a different version of the application if they have old components installed that you know can cause problems with the code in your application.

Viewing Results in WML Devices

We used a phone simulator program to display the WML page from the example. To experiment for yourself, you'll need to obtain a suitable simulator. Some emulators you might like to try are as follows:

- PyWeb Deck-It, available from `http://www.pyweb.com`

- Nokia tools, available from `http://forum.nokia.com`

- Openwave tools, available from `http://www.openwave.com`

We're using the first of these, the Deck-It emulator, here. Figure 4-5 shows part of the home page that's displayed for WML-enabled devices (you can see the limitations these kinds of devices impose when it comes to displaying information!):

Figure 4-5. Viewing the results in the Deck-It WML emulator

The complete display reads like the following—you can see from the last line of the output that the device simulator does not support ASP.NET sessions:

Make: Nokia

Model: Unknown

MIME Type: text/vnd.wap.wml

Rendering Type: wml11

Image MIME Type: image/vnd.wap.wbmp

Color Screen: False

Screen Height (chars): 4

Screen Width (chars): 20

Screen Height (pixels): 40

Screen Width (pixels): 90

Supports Bold Text: False

Supports Italic Text: False

Input Type: telephoneKeypad

Has Back Button: False

Num Soft Keys: 2

ASP.NET Sessions: False

> **NOTE** *Note that this simulator (like most mobile devices) doesn't support cookies and hence doesn't support ASP.NET sessions. There's also a strict limit in most mobile devices on the actual size of the pages they can handle. This second issue means that the controls in the MMIT don't use the normal approach of storing the viewstate for a page within hidden controls in the page. Instead, they store it in the user's session. However, if the client doesn't support cookies, an ASP.NET session can't be maintained for them.*

> **TIP** *To get round this, you'll probably find pages that depend on storing view-state and that use the MMIT controls work properly only within an ASP.NET application that has cookieless session support enabled. As you discovered when you looked at ASP.NET session support earlier in this chapter, this means that the session key will be automatically munged into the URL, obviating the need for cookies to be used to maintain it.*

You can see that you can get a lot of information about the device from the MobileCapabilities object. In fact, we've only scratched the surface—there are many more properties available that indicate all kinds of features, requirements, and limitations for each mobile device. And there's still all the data in the "normal" Request.Browser object available as well.

To finish off this look at client detection and redirection, the following code shows the actual output created by the mobile controls in the MMIT for the home page you saw earlier. It's not very different from HTML, but it's sufficiently different that trying to build single pages that dynamically adapt for all the device types covered in this chapter would be extremely difficult:

```
<?xml version="1.0"?>
<!DOCTYPE wml PUBLIC "-//WAPFORUM//DTD WML 1.1//EN"
 "http://www.wapforum.org/DTD/wml_1.1.xml">
<!-- Source Generated by WML Deck Decoder -->

<wml>
  <head>
    <meta http-equiv="Cache-Control" content="max-age=0"/>
  </head>

  <card>
    <do type="prev" label="Back">
      <prev/>
    </do>
    <p>
      <b>Page for a WML client only</b><br/>
      Make: Nokia<br/>
      Model: Unknown<br/>
      MIME Type: text/vnd.wap.wml<br/>
      Rendering Type: wml11<br/>
      Image MIME Type: image/vnd.wap.wbmp<br/>
      Color Screen: False<br/>
      Screen Height (chars): 4<br/>
```

```
        Screen Width (chars): 20<br/>
        Screen Height (pixels): 40<br/>
        Screen Width (pixels): 90<br/>
        Supports Bold Text: False<br/>
        Supports Italic Text: False<br/>
        Input Type: telephoneKeypad<br/>
        Has Back Button: False<br/>
        Num Soft Keys: 2<br/>
        ASP.NET Sessions: False
    </p>
  </card>
</wml>
```

Summary

This chapter has been a bit of a mixed bag; it covered some of the important issues you need to consider when building useable, interactive, and efficient distributed data applications with ASP.NET and various associated technologies. As you can no doubt see by now, there are a great number of opportunities available for almost every part of such an application.

In this chapter, we tried to fill in the gaps between the client and the server by showing the various types of client you might decide to support, how you can categorize these into a small number of "device groups," and how you can detect into which group each client falls. This is, obviously, the first step to providing interactive and efficient pages that support a wide range of clients.

You also looked at how you can remote data to these different categories of clients, how you can configure and test for ASP.NET session support, and how you can check to see whether client-side scripting is enabled. These are all features that will influence the way you build your application and how you deal with each type of client. In later chapters, you'll see how these decisions come into play in more detail.

This chapter covered the following topics:

- An overview of the range of programming features that are available on the client side

- An overview of a range of techniques for managing data on the client

- How to remote data to the client in different ways

- The issues involved in using ASP.NET sessions

- How to detect the client device type and serve appropriate pages

- An example of client detection, demonstrating the information available for different clients

In the next chapter, you'll look at a distributed data application that supports multiple client types and provides the best level of interactivity and efficiency as possible.

CHAPTER 5

Working with Down-Level Clients

In previous chapters, you learned how to access data sources and create a data tier for your applications. We discussed techniques for remoting data to various types of client and how you can detect the client type when they first hit your application. It's now time to see an application that puts all these techniques into practice.

The application in this chapter is quite compact and tries to not obscure the processes by being too complicated. We tried to make it look attractive and easy to understand and use. You'll have to judge how well we succeeded for yourself, of course, but it does neatly demonstrate some useful techniques for combining ASP.NET, server-side .NET components, and client-side programming to create distributed data applications.

Many of the techniques in this book are primarily aimed at rich clients, such as Internet Explorer and .NET applications, and you'll look at these in the following chapters. However, unless you can be certain that these are the only types of client that'll use the application, you should also provide a version that works on other down-level clients. We described how and why we categorize down-level clients in Chapter 1. The term *down-level* is the one Microsoft prefers to use and is possibly less offensive than some other choices!

This chapter covers these topics:

- What the application looks like

- Some of the design considerations involved

- Specific client detection techniques for the example application

- The version of the application aimed at HTML 3.2 clients

- The version aimed at small-screen and mobile devices

You'll start by briefly looking at the appearance and functionality of the application.

A Multiple-Client Order List Application

In this chapter, you'll build an application that you can use to view and edit the orders placed by customers of a fictional food distribution corporation. You'll use the Northwind database that comes as a sample with SQL Server 7.0 onward. You'll support several different types of client, at the same time taking advantage of several different technological approaches.

You'll build a series of pages that take full advantage of several distinct and different types of down-level and rich-client variations. You'll incorporate some client-detection code, like the code you developed in the previous chapter, and you'll use the associated techniques such as remoting data and using ASP.NET sessions. To give you an idea of the clients and technologies you'll be supporting, Figure 5-1 shows the menu page for the application.

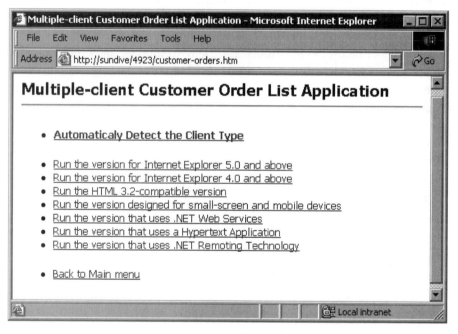

Figure 5-1. The main menu page for the examples in this chapter

> **NOTE** *You can obtain the example source code from* http://www.daveandal.com/books/4923/ *or from* http://www.apress.com/. *For details of how to install and configure the example code and the database that drives the examples, see the section "Setting Up the Examples" in Chapter 2. If you just want to view the results, we've provided the application online at the same URL.*

As well as an option that automatically detects the client type you're using, there are links inviting the user to view the different versions irrespective of the client type. Just bear in mind that some may not work if your client doesn't support the features used by that version of the application. For example, the Internet Explorer 5 and higher version requires the MSXML parser to be installed, so it most likely won't work with previous versions of Internet Explorer or other makes of browser.

The User Interface

With the exception of the pages designed for small-screen and mobile devices and those that use .NET Remoting techniques, the application is designed to provide a similar user interface for all clients. Figures 5-2 and 5-3 show the version designed for use with any Web browser that supports HTML 3.2—you'll see several different browsers in this chapter's figures for this version of the application. The two Internet Explorer–specific versions and the Hypertext Application (which will only work in Internet Explorer 5 and higher) look almost identical.

When the user opens the application, they first specify the customer whose orders they want to view. After entering all or part of the customer ID or name and clicking the Search button, the right section of the page displays a list of matching customers, as shown in Figure 5-2.

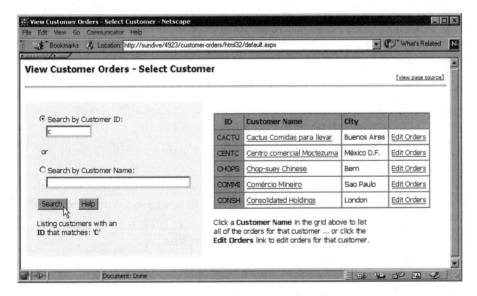

Figure 5-2. The HTML version of the application after selecting a customer's orders

Clicking a customer name in the list opens the second page. The user can then select an order in the left list for this customer, and the details of that order display in the right part of the page, as shown in Figure 5-3.

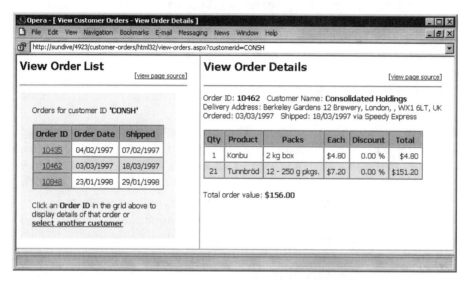

Figure 5-3. Viewing the order details in the HTML version of the application

The application also allows orders to be edited; however, we won't cover this feature just yet. You'll concentrate on how you extract, manipulate, and display the order information in this and the next couple of chapters. You'll come back to look at how you can update the order data later in the book.

Detecting the Client Type

In the menu page you saw in Figure 5-1, the top link (Automatically Detect the Client Type) uses the techniques discussed in Chapter 4 to redirect the client to the appropriate version of the application. It checks for client-side scripting support on the way if this is a requirement in the version designed for the current client. The application uses the `client-detect.ascx` user control developed in Chapter 4 to detect the "group" into which the client falls.

In the `Page_Load` event handler of the `default.aspx` page (`customer-orders/default.aspx`), you can then decide where to redirect the client depending on this group. Notice that the code checks for unsupported clients and sends them a simple text message. It doesn't use client-side scripting for small-screen and mobile devices, so it can transfer them directly to the appropriate version of the application in the mobile subfolder. It redirects all other clients to the page client-script-check.aspx, with the client type appended to the query string

Overall, this is similar to the code you saw for the detect-client/default.aspx page in Chapter 4:

```
Sub Page_Load()
  Select Case ClientDetect.ClientType
    Case 0  'not supported
      Response.Clear
      Response.ContentType = "text/text"
      Response.Write("Sorry, this application does not support " _
                & "your client type: " & Request.UserAgent)
      Response.End
    Case 2  'IE 4.x
      Response.Clear
      Response.Redirect("client-script-check.aspx?client=ie4")
      Response.End
    Case 3  'IE 5.x and above
      Response.Clear
      Response.Redirect("client-script-check.aspx?client=ie5")
      Response.End
    Case 4, 5  'small-screen HTML device or WML client
      Response.Clear
      Server.Transfer("mobile/default.aspx")
    Case Else  'assume HTML 3.2 client
      Response.Clear
      Response.Redirect("client-script-check.aspx?client=html32")
      Response.End
  End Select
End Sub
```

Each client-specific version of the application is stored in a subfolder that's named in the client name/value pair of the query string in this listing. So, for example, Internet Explorer 5 browsers will be redirected to the version in the ie5 folder. And, because you're not checking for session support in this application, you can use Server.Transfer in the case of the version for small-screen and mobile devices.

Checking for Client-Side Scripting Support

This application uses a page named `client-script-check.aspx`, which works in the same way as the example you saw in Chapter 4. If the client has scripting available (*and enabled*), they're redirected to the appropriate version of the application. However, if client-side scripting isn't available (or is disabled), the client is redirected to a page named `no-client-script.aspx`, which displays a message telling the user what options are available to them in this case, as shown in Figure 5-4.

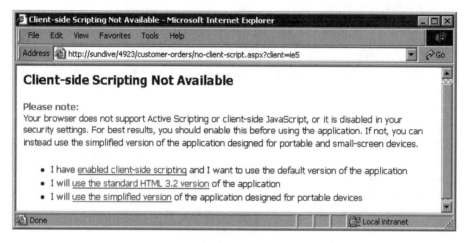

Figure 5-4. The message displayed when client-side scripting isn't available

This page is simple, using ASP.NET code only to set the value in the query string for the first option. If the user enables scripting and then clicks this link, you can take them to the version of the application that your client type detection code originally suggested. Alternatively, they can go directly to the HTML 3.2 or the small-screen and mobile devices version:

```
<% Dim strClientType As String = Request.QueryString("client") %>
...
<ul>
  <li>I have <a href="<% = strClientType %>/default.aspx">
      enabled client-side scripting</a> and I want to use ... </li>
  <li>I will <a href="html32/default.aspx">
      use the standard HTML 3.2 version</a> of the application</li>
  <li>I will <a href="mobile/default.aspx">
      use the simplified version</a> of the application ...</li>
</ul>
...
```

Viewstate and Session Support in Mobile Devices

In this application, you aren't checking for session support for each client. Because you want to do most of the processing on the client, you don't need to use ASP.NET sessions. However, two versions of the application (the HTML 3.2 and the small-screen and mobile devices versions covered in this chapter) will benefit from session support. Nevertheless, it isn't an absolute requirement, even for these. They'll automatically take advantage of sessions to improve performance and reduce the number of data access operations required when supported (or work fine without them otherwise).

Of course, if an application depends on session support, you can use the techniques in Chapter 4 to check that session support exists and redirect users to a version of the application in a different subfolder where you have a web.config file that specifies cookieless sessions (by munging the session ID into the URL itself).

Some cellular phones limit the size of a page, limit the volume of data that can be posted back from a <form>, or require special encoding for the viewstate. All these issues can cause problems if there's a lot of viewstate data. You can use the MobileCapabilities object you saw in Chapter 4 to check these features for devices. The relevant properties are RequiresSpecialViewStateEncoding and MaximumRenderedPageSize.

Another solution you can try when you build pages for mobile devices is to switch off viewstate altogether and manage the values you need to pass between screens with another technique such as a session variable or the query string. The easiest way to see how much viewstate is included in the page is to enable tracing for the page by including the attribute Trace="True" in the Page directive. The trace information shows the size of the viewstate for the page and for each individual control on the page.

> **NOTE** *You may prefer to turn on cookieless session for the application anyway so that mobile devices don't suffer problems with maintaining viewstate. Our tests showed it wasn't a problem in some emulators (such as the Nokia toolkit), but it was required for others such as the Deck-It emulator. Simply change the* <sessionState> *element in the* <system.web> *section of the* web.config *file in the root folder of the application to read* <sessionState cookieless="true" />.

The Data Access Tier

We use the same data access component as in the last couple of examples in Chapter 2 (`OrderListData.OrderList`) for all versions of the application. This is intentional and demonstrates how the separation of data access, business logic, and presentation tiers in your applications allows you to use the *same* data access tier for several versions of the application. If the data store you're using changes in type or structure, or different data access techniques are implemented in the future, you only have to update the single component. As long as it continues to expose the same interface (the same methods with the same parameters, returning the same data types), then all the versions of your application will continue to work with the new component.

As you saw in Chapter 2, the `OrderListData.OrderList` component exposes two methods:

- The `GetCustomerByIdOrName` method accepts two `String` parameters and returns a `DataSet`. The parameters are all or part of the customer ID and all or part of the customer's name. The returned `DataSet` contains a list of customers that matches the ID (if this is provided) or name (if an empty string is used for the ID parameter).

- The `GetOrdersByCustomerDataSet` method accepts a single `String` parameter and returns a `DataSet`. The parameter is the full customer ID, and the returned `DataSet` has two tables that contain all the orders for this customer and all the order lines (details) for these orders.

In some cases, this is a little wasteful because you don't always end up displaying all the information in the `DataSet`. For example, if the user only views one order, then the detail rows you extracted from the database for all the others are never used. In this case, it would be more efficient to fetch the detail rows only when an order is selected, minimizing the volume of data that's extracted from the database. However, if you used this alternative technique when the user wanted to browse order details, it would mean repeated trips to the database to collect the relevant detail rows.

Maximizing Efficiency Through Data Caching

It's generally accepted that the two major bottlenecks in any Web-based application are the data access process and the network bandwidth. As far as server loading goes, data access is usually the worst culprit. So, if you can extract all the data you need in one go, you can minimize server loading and reduce the number of data access hits you get.

OK, so the volume of data you extract is greater, but you're only moving it from the database to the Web server. This will probably be a Local Area Network (LAN) connection where there's plenty of bandwidth; and in the "small site" case where the database and Web server are on the same machine, using Named Pipes for the data transfer, bandwidth is extremely unlikely to be an issue.

What you must do, however, is make sure you cache the data so that you don't need to keep going back to the database each time. In the examples in this chapter, you cache the data in the client's session. Most clients these days do support per-session cookies such as those required for ASP.NET sessions to function correctly. In fact, many modern online applications, such as banking and ecommerce sites, demand per-session cookie support, and users have generally become accustomed to accepting them.

As you'll see later, lack of session support won't break the example applications. If the client doesn't support sessions, you simply hit the data access layer again to fetch a fresh copy of the data. This isn't an ideal situation, but this problem should apply to just a small number of clients, and therefore it isn't worth building special versions of the application. Of course, if your situation is different, and you do have to support a large proportion of clients that don't support cookie-based sessions, you might prefer to build special versions that use cookieless sessions (as mentioned earlier in this chapter and in Chapter 4). Alternatively, you could build a version that uses a DataReader to access the database—thereby reducing the loading that repeated data access hits will produce.

In the versions of the application discussed in later chapters, the data is cached on the client rather than on the server. In most cases this gives the best of both worlds. It limits server loading by avoiding repeated hits on the data access tier, and it avoids the memory and processing overhead required for managing ASP.NET sessions for each user.

The Order List Application: The HTML Version

The figures you looked at earlier are from the HTML version of the application, which is designed to run in any HTML 3.2–compatible browser. The appearance will differ between browsers from different manufacturers and (to some extent) between different versions because it uses Cascading Style Sheets (CSS) and other features to control the display. These might not be supported in full or in the same way in all browsers, but the overall layout and usability should be unaffected. And although you'll use some client-side script in this version of the application, it's only minimal and the pages will still work when client-side scripting isn't supported.

The Outline Process

Figure 5-5 shows the process for the HTML version of the application. The default.aspx page (in the customer-orders\html32 folder) allows users to search for and display a list of customers by ID or name. It uses the GetCustomerByIdOrName method of the data access component. Selecting a customer opens the view-orders.aspx page. This is an HTML frameset, into which the two pages order-list.aspx and order-detail.aspx are loaded.

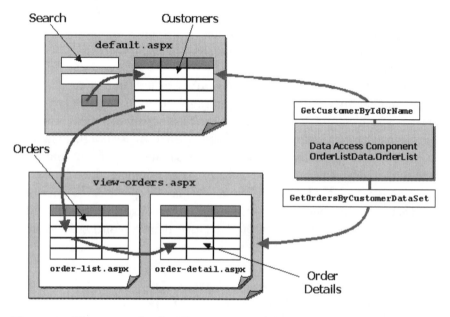

Figure 5-5. The process for the HTML version of the application

> **NOTE** *It's worth noting that the HTML 3.2 specification doesn't include frames—they were introduced into HTML in version 4.0. However, the majority of HTML 3.2–compatible browser clients do support frames—Internet Explorer 3 and Netscape Navigator 2 among them—so you'll assume support for framesets here and provide a simple alternative for the small number of HTML 3.2–compliant clients that don't support frames.*

The left page, order-list.aspx, uses the GetOrdersByCustomerDataSet method of the data access component to get the order data, and it displays a list of all the orders for this customer as soon as this page loads. It also caches the complete DataSet in the user's session. If the page is refreshed for any reason, it uses this cached data automatically. However, if the user elects to go back to the previous page and select another customer, the cached order data for this customer is removed from the session by code in default.aspx. You'll see all this as you step through this code in the coming pages.

Selecting an order in the list in the left frame reloads the page order-details.aspx in the right frame, and it then shows a list of all the detail rows for the selected order. It uses the DataSet that was cached in the user's session by the page order-list.aspx. If this isn't available, it calls the same GetOrdersByCustomerDataSet method to get the data directly from the data store instead.

Searching for Customers

When this version of the application starts, it displays the Select Customer page, as shown in Figure 5-6. As well as some hints on how to search for customers by ID or name, it contains the relevant text boxes and a Search button—plus a Help button that the user can click to redisplay the search hints. In this figure, we're searching for all customers whose ID starts with *c*.

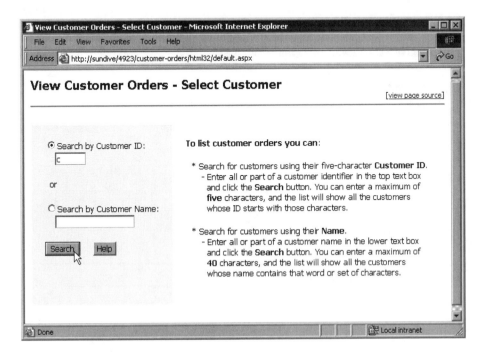

Figure 5-6. The Select Customer page

This page contains the Import directives for the custom data access component OrderListData and for the System.Data namespace. You'll need the default.aspx page to be able to create a DataSet object in your code:

```
<%@Page Language="VB" %>
<%@Import Namespace="OrderListData" %>
<%@Import Namespace="System.Data" %>
```

The HTML Form Controls

The code in the previous listing is followed by the HTML that creates the visible portion of the page. You use a server-side include statement to insert a stylesheet that's common to most of your application versions, and you define the client-side JavaScript function that makes the interface a little more useable by setting the option buttons to the relevant value as the user types in the text boxes. This function is used for the (client-side) onkeypress events of the two text boxes:

```
<html>
  <head>
    <title>View Customer Orders - Select Customer</title>
    <!-- #include file="../../global/style.inc" -->
    <script language="JavaScript">
      <!--
        // client-side script section used to set radio
        // buttons to correct option as text is typed.
        function setCheck(strName) {
          document.forms(0).elements(strName).checked = true;
        }
      //-->
    </script>
  </head>

  <body link="#0000ff" alink="#0000ff" vlink="#0000ff">
  ...
  <form runat="server">
    <table border="0" cellpadding="20">
      <tr><td valign="top" bgcolor="#ffffacd">
```

```
    <!-- controls for specifying the required customer ID or name -->
    <asp:RadioButton id="optByID" groupname="SearchBy" Align="right"
                text="Search by Customer ID: " runat="server"
                checked="true" /><br />
    <asp:TextBox id="txtCustID" columns="5" maxlength="5"
              onkeypress="setCheck('optByID');" runat="server" /><p />
    or<p />
    <asp:RadioButton id="optByName" groupname="SearchBy" Align="right"
                text="Search by Customer Name:" runat="server" /><br />
    <asp:TextBox id="txtCustName" columns="20" maxlength="40"
              onkeypress="setCheck('optByName');" runat="server" /><p />
    <asp:Button id="btnSearch" text="Search" onclick="DoSearch"
              runat="server" />
    <asp:Button id="btnHelp" text="Help" onclick="ShowHelp"
              runat="server" /><p />
    <asp:Label id="lblStatus" runat="server" />

  </td>
  ...
```

Displaying a List of Customers

Before you look at the remainder of the HTML to see how to display a list of
matching customers in the right part of the page, you'll examine the code that
searches for them to see how it actually works. The server-side code section of the
default.aspx page declares two Page-level (global) variables that you need to store
the values that are selected in the two text boxes. In the Page_Load event handler
that comes next, you just display the help text in the right part of the screen by
calling the ShowHelp function:

```
<script language="VB" runat="server">
  'page-level variables accessed from more than one routine
  Dim strCustID As String = ""
  Dim strCustName As String = ""

  Sub Page_Load()
    'show Help when page first loads
    If Not Page.IsPostBack Then ShowHelp(Nothing, Nothing)
  End Sub
```

Showing the Help Text

The ShowHelp function simply displays some text in an ASP.NET Label control located in the right part of the page—you'll see this control in the next part of the HTML listing, when you look at the DataGrid control:

```
Sub ShowHelp(ByVal objSender As Object, ByVal objArgs As EventArgs)'shows help on
using page in the right-hand part of the window

  lblMessage.Text = "<b>To list customer orders you can</b>:<p />" _
    & "  * Search for customers using their five-character " _
    & "<b>Customer ID</b>.<br />" _
    ...
    ... etc ...
    ...
End Sub
```

Calling the Data Access Component

Getting the DataSet that contains matching customers from the data store is relatively easy. You create a separate function that takes the two parameters required by the data access component, instantiates the component with the connection string obtained from the web.config file, and returns the DataSet created by the data access component. You enclose it all in a Try...Catch construct so that you can trap and display details of any error that might occur:

```
Function GetDataSetFromServer(strCustID As String, _
                       strCustName As String) As DataSet
'uses data access component to get DataSet of matching customers

  'get connection string from web.config
  Dim strConnect As String
  strConnect = ConfigurationSettings.AppSettings("NorthwindConnectString")

  Try
    'create an instance of the data access component
    Dim objOrderList As New OrderList(strConnect)

    'call the method to return the data as a DataSet
    Return objOrderList.GetCustomerByIdOrName(strCustID, strCustName)
```

```
Catch objErr As Exception

    'there was an error and no data will be returned
    lblMessage.Text = "ERROR: No data returned. " & objErr.Message

  End Try
End Function
```

Performing the Customer Search

The following code shows the DoSearch event handler, which executes in response to a click of the Search button. It starts by removing any existing DataSet of order details from the user's session. This is required if the user comes back from examining orders for one customer to search for a different customer. You have to destroy the cached DataSet containing the order details for the previous customer or they won't see any orders for the new one:

```
Sub DoSearch(ByVal objSender As Object, ByVal objArgs As EventArgs)
'display the list of matching customers in the DataGrid control

  'remove any existing "Orders" DataSet from the user's Session
  'as we're searching now for a different customer
  Session("4923HTMLOrdersDataSet") = Nothing
```

Next, you can collect the values from the appropriate one of the two text boxes, depending on which option button (Search by Customer ID or Search by Customer Name) is checked. You also convert any ID value that's entered to uppercase (which is how they're stored in the database):

```
'get one or other value from text boxes depending on selection
If optByID.Checked Then
  strCustID = txtCustID.Text.ToUpper()
  lblStatus.Text = "Listing customers with ID ..." & strCustID
Else
  strCustName = txtCustName.Text
  lblStatus.Text = "Listing customers with Name..." & strCustName
End If
```

Fetching and Displaying the Results

Now you can use the GetDataSetFromServer function described earlier to collect the DataSet, and you can see how many matching customers were actually found by checking the number of rows in the single table within the DataSet:

```
'get DataSet using function elsewhere in this page
Dim objDataSet As DataSet = GetDataSetFromServer(strCustID, strCustName)

'check how many matching customers were found
Dim intRowsFound As Integer = objDataSet.Tables(0).Rows.Count
```

If you find any rows at all, you set the CurrentPageIndex of the DataGrid to zero (though this is the default anyway, so you could get away with omitting this) and assign the single table in the DataSet to the DataSource property of the grid. Before you actually bind it, however, you use the number of rows found to see if you need to display the paging controls. Finally, you can bind the grid and display some informative text to the user:

```
If intRowsFound > 0 Then
    'reset DataGrid page index to zero for new rowset
    'and set DataSource of DataGrid control
    dgrCustomers.CurrentPageIndex = 0
    dgrCustomers.DataSource = objDataSet.Tables(0)

    'display the "paging" controls (Previous/Next) only when required
    dgrCustomers.PagerStyle.Visible = (intRowsFound > dgrCustomers.PageSize)

    'bind the DataGrid and display status message
    dgrCustomers.DataBind()
    lblMessage.Text = "Click a <b>Customer Name</b> in the grid above " _
                    ... etc.

Else
    lblMessage.Text = "No matching customers found in database ..."

End If
End Sub
```

If there were no matching customers found, the Else part of the If...Then construct displays a message to this effect.

The DataGrid to Display the Customer List

The controls shown in the earlier HTML are in a table cell on the left of the page. The *right* cell contains an ASP.NET DataGrid control that you use to display a list of matching customers, an ASP.NET Label control for status messages, and other information. Because the DataGrid isn't bound to a data source when the page loads the first time, it isn't actually visible in the page:

```
...
<td valign="top">
  <!-- DataGrid control to display matching customers -->
  <asp:DataGrid id="dgrCustomers" runat="server"
        AutoGenerateColumns="False"
        CellPadding="5"
        GridLines="Vertical"
        HeaderStyle-BackColor="silver"
        PagerStyle-BackColor="silver"
        AlternatingItemStyle-BackColor="#eeeeee"
        AllowPaging="true"
        PageSize="8"
        PagerStyle-Mode="NextPrev"
        PagerStyle-NextPageText="Next"
        PagerStyle-PrevPageText="Previous"
        PagerStyle-HorizontalAlign="Right"
        PagerStyle-Visible="false"
        DataKeyField="CustomerID"
        OnPageIndexChanged="ShowGridPage">

    <Columns>
      <asp:BoundColumn HeaderText="<b>ID</b>"
          HeaderStyle-HorizontalAlign="center"
          DataField="CustomerID" ItemStyle-BackColor="#add8e6"
      />
      <asp:HyperlinkColumn HeaderText="<b>Customer Name</b>"
          DataTextField="CompanyName"
          DataNavigateUrlField="CustomerID"
          DataNavigateUrlFormatString="view-orders.aspx?customerid={0}"
      />
      <asp:BoundColumn HeaderText="<b>City</b>" DataField="City" />
      <asp:HyperlinkColumn Text="Edit Orders"
          DataNavigateUrlField="CustomerID"
          DataNavigateUrlFormatString= ↵
              "../../update-orders/html32/edit-orders.aspx?customerid={0}"
      />
    </Columns>
```

```
        </asp:DataGrid><p />

        <!-- label to display interactive messages -->
        <asp:Label id="lblMessage" runat="server" />

    </td></tr>
  </table>
</form>
```

You can see from this code that several properties of the DataGrid are set to control its appearance. You also set the AllowPaging property to true so that a list of more than eight customers (the PageSize property) will be broken up into "pages" when displayed. The properties that follow the PageSize define the appearance of the paging controls, and you also make them invisible by default. As you saw in the previous code, you show them by dynamically changing this property value to true if the number of matching customers found exceeds the value of PageSize.

You also specify that the CustomerID column in the DataSet should be used as the DataKeyField, giving you an easy way to extract the row key for a selected row if you need to do so later. Finally, you specify an event handler named ShowGridPage, located within the code section of the default.aspx page, which will executes when the grid paging controls are clicked (the event handler is specified by the OnPageIndexChanged attribute).

Defining the Columns in the DataGrid

When you declare the DataGrid element (as shown in the previous listing), you include the attribute AutoGenerateColumns="False" so that the grid won't automatically generate the columns based on the contents of the data source you bind to it. Instead, you define the columns you want yourself within a <Columns> element. You have a column bound to the CustomerID column in the data source, followed by a column that'll display the customer name as a hyperlink. The combination of the DataNavigateUrlField and DataNavigateUrlFormatString attributes you use mean that this hyperlink's href attribute will contain the value view-orders.aspx with a name/value pair indicating the customer ID for that row is appended to the query string:

```
<asp:HyperlinkColumn HeaderText="<b>Customer Name</b>"
     DataTextField="CompanyName"
     DataNavigateUrlField="CustomerID"
     DataNavigateUrlFormatString="view-orders.aspx?customerid={0}"
/>
```

Next comes a simple bound column that displays the City value from the source DataSet, followed by another hyperlink column that displays the text *Edit Orders* for every row (you'll learn more about this in Chapter 8). You use the DataNavigateUrlField and DataNavigateUrlFormatString attributes for this column to specify that the href for the hyperlink will be the page edit-orders.aspx (in a separate folder of your application). Again, a name/value pair indicating the customer ID for that row is appended to the query string:

```
<asp:HyperlinkColumn Text="Edit Orders"
    DataNavigateUrlField="CustomerID"
    DataNavigateUrlFormatString= ⤶
        "../../update-orders/html32/edit-orders.aspx?customerid={0}"
/>
```

In Figure 5-7, you can see the output that the DataGrid creates after searching for customers whose ID starts with the letter *c*. There are only five that match, so the paging controls don't appear (recall that you set the Visible property for the pager row within your code every time you fetch the list of matching customers).

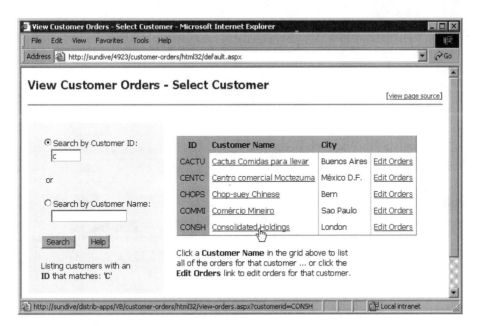

Figure 5-7. The DataGrid *showing the list of matching customers*

You can also see in the status bar the URL that the HyperlinkColumn creates from the values of the DataTextField, DataNavigateUrlField, and DataNavigateUrlFormatString you specified for the Customer Name column when you declared the DataGrid template.

Handling Paging in the DataGrid

However, the paging controls *do* appear when you get more than eight matching customers in the list. To see this, click Search with a blank string for both the ID and name so that the data access component returns all the customers in the database. (In a production environment, you might prefer to limit the number of rows returned by the data access tier to some specific maximum, such as 100 rows, to protect against excessive use of bandwidth and server resources if you have a large number of customers.) In Figure 5-8, we've used the paging controls to go to the second page of results.

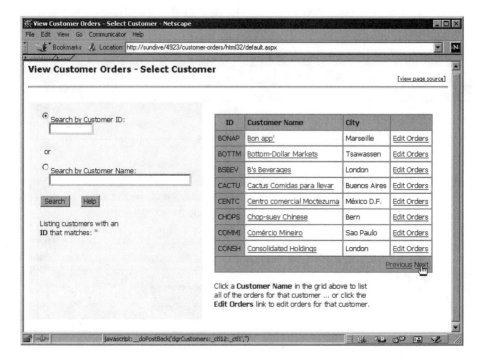

Figure 5-8. Using the paging controls that appear when more than eight matching customers are found

When you define your `DataGrid` control, you specify that the event handler named `ShowGridPage` should execute automatically when the pager controls are clicked:

```
OnPageIndexChanged="ShowGridPage"
```

The `ShowGridPage` routine is remarkably simple. All it has to do is extract the index of the new page (the one that has just been requested) from the `NewPageIndex` property of the arguments to the event handler, set the `CurrentPageIndex` property of the `DataGrid` to this value, collect the customer ID or name from the text boxes on the left side of the page, and rebind the grid control to the original data source:

```
Sub ShowGridPage(ByVal objSender As Object, _
                 ByVal objArgs As DataGridPageChangedEventArgs)
'runs when the paging contols are clicked to display different page

  'set page index of DataGrid control to new value
  dgrCustomers.CurrentPageIndex = objArgs.NewPageIndex

  'get one or other value from text boxes depending on selection
  If optByID.Checked Then
    strCustID = txtCustID.Text.ToUpper()
  Else
    strCustName = txtCustName.Text
  End If

  'get the DataSet to populate the control and bind it
  dgrCustomers.DataSource = GetDataSetFromServer(strCustID, strCustName)
  dgrCustomers.DataBind()

End Sub
```

Notice that this involves another hit on the data access component. You could get around this by caching the original `DataSet` in the user's session (as you do with the order details). However, this may not actually improve performance or reduce server loading. It'll only be of benefit if there are usually more than eight matching customers and the user has to page through the list to find the one they want. If not, you're taking up server resources by caching data in the session that will only rarely be reused. Like so many design decisions, the best choice depends mostly on the nature of the data and how the application will be used!

Displaying a List of Orders

In the list of customers in the page you've just seen, each customer name is a hyperlink pointing to the page view-orders.aspx, with a name/value pair that contains the customer ID appended to the query string—for example, view-orders.aspx?customerid=CONSH.

The Order List Frameset Page

As you saw in the schematic earlier, the page view-orders.aspx is an HTML frameset page that contains other pages. It also includes some ASP.NET code that collects the customer ID from the query string and passes it to the page in the left frame. This is the code you use for view-orders.aspx:

```
<% Dim strCustID As String = Request.QueryString("customerid") %>
```

The next code shows the HTML that creates the frameset. You can see that you use the customer ID in the query string of the URL for the page order-list.aspx that you load into the left frame:

```
<frameset rows="*,60" frameborder="0">
  <frameset cols="320,*" frameborder="0">
    <frame name="left" src="order-list.aspx?customerid=<% = strCustID %>"
           frameborder="0" />
    <frame name="right" src="order-detail.aspx"
           frameborder="0" />
  </frameset>
  <frame src="footer.htm" frameborder="0" scrolling="no"/>
</frameset>
```

The right frame page, order-detail.aspx, doesn't require any query string because it won't display any data until the user makes a selection in the list in the left frame. At the end of the frameset, you can also see the narrow strip where you'll display a standard page footer.

As mentioned earlier, we're assuming that the majority of the HTML 3.2–compliant browsers using this version of the application *also* have support for HTML frames. For those few that don't, you can include the following escape hatch, which will take them to a simpler version of the application:

```
<noframes>
  <font size="2" face="Tahoma,Arial,sans-serif">
    This page requires HTML Frames support.
    As your browser does not support<br />
    frames, you should use the
    <b><a href="../mobile/default.aspx">simplified version</a></b>
    of the application instead.
  </font>
</noframes>
```

Getting the Data from the Session or Server

When the view-orders.aspx frameset page is loaded in response to a click in the list of customers on the previous page, it'll load the page order-list.aspx into the left frame—passing it the ID of the selected customer.

In the page order-list.aspx, you just need to collect the customer ID, use it to look up a list of orders for this customer, and display the list in the page. However, before you build that code, you need to think a little more about how you're going to *use* the data you extract from your database.

You're using a data access component that returns a DataSet containing the two tables required for displaying both the list of orders and the details of each one (the order lines). In this example, you're presenting this information in two DataGrid controls on two separate pages, but there's no reason why you couldn't use it in other ways. For example, you could use the relationship between the tables in the DataSet to display the data hierarchically if required.

But we're straying from the point; what you need to consider is how you cache and use the DataSet that your data access tier exposes in your user's session (something you already decided was a good idea and would usually offer a considerable performance boost). Getting data into the session is easy—you just specify the key you want to refer to it by later:

```
Session("key-name") = MyDataSetObject
```

To get it back out, you use the key and cast (convert) the returned object to the correct data type:

```
MyDataSetObject = CType(Session("key-name"), DataSet)
```

However, in this application you're using this data in two pages concurrently, so you need to be sure that it's appropriate for both of these pages. You only want to fetch and store one copy of it. In fact, the second page (order-detail.aspx, which you'll look at shortly) has an extra requirement for the data. Each detail row contains columns for the product, quantity, price, and discount, but you'll *also* want to display the line total for each row.

You *could* calculate this line total as you display the data, but it makes a lot more sense to make it part of the data itself. This way you only calculate the values once, and it also makes binding the data to the DataGrid control for display much easier. Even better, you can actually do it without having to calculate the totals yourself—you can let the DataSet do it for you.

The GetDataSetFromSessionOrServer Function

In the page order-list.aspx, you have a function GetDataSetFromSessionOrServer that's responsible for returning the order details as a DataSet for a specified customer. It first attempts to fetch the DataSet from the session using a key that's unique for this version of the application. If the DataSet isn't stored in the session at this point, the variable objDataSet will be empty, so you need to go off to your data access tier and fetch it from the database in this case. Here's the code from order-list.aspx:

```
Function GetDataSetFromSessionOrServer(strCustID As String) As DataSet
'gets a DataSet containing all orders for this customer

  Try
    Dim objDataSet As DataSet

    'try and get DataSet from user's Session
    objDataSet = CType(Session("4923HTMLOrdersDataSet"), DataSet)

    If objDataSet Is Nothing Then    'not in Session

      'get connection string from web.config
      Dim strConnect As String
      strConnect = ConfigurationSettings.AppSettings("NorthwindConnectString")

      'create an instance of the data access component
      Dim objOrderList As New OrderList(strConnect)

      'call the method to return the data as a DataSet
      objDataSet = objOrderList.GetOrdersByCustomerDataSet(strCustID)
      ...
```

Now you can manipulate the DataSet to make sure it's compatible with the order-detail.aspx page. You simply add a new column to the OrderLines table in the DataSet and specify an expression for this column that will calculate the line total for each row automatically:

```
...
'add a column containing the total value of each line
Dim objLinesTable As DataTable = objDataSet.Tables("OrderLines")
Dim objColumn As DataColumn
objColumn = objLinesTable.Columns.Add("LineTotal", _
                        System.Type.GetType("System.Double"))
objColumn.Expression = "[Quantity] * ([UnitPrice] - ([UnitPrice]" _
                & " * [Discount]))"
...
```

Having done that, you can store the DataSet in your user's session and then return it to the calling routine. If there's an error, you display a message in the page and return Nothing:

```
    ...
    'save DataSet in Session for next order inquiry
    Session("4923HTMLOrdersDataSet") = objDataSet

  End If

  Return objDataSet

Catch objErr As Exception
  'there was an error and no data will be returned
  lblMessage.Text = "* ERROR: No data returned. " & objErr.Message

  Return Nothing
 End Try
End Function
```

The next time the user submits a request that calls this function the DataSet will be extracted not from the database but from the session. (Of course, this assumes the session hasn't timed out.) The DataSet will already have the extra LineTotal column, so you can just return it "as is."

The DataGrid to Display the Order List

Now that you've got your DataSet, you can think about how you'll display it in the page. You'll use a DataGrid server control for this, specifying a custom column layout as in the previous example page. However, in this page, you'll also turn off viewstate support so that the values in the DataGrid aren't persisted across postbacks:

```
<%@Page Language="VB" EnableViewstate="False" %>
```

This means that there will be no hidden-type control in the page to store the values of the DataGrid (this is how viewstate is persisted by default), so the page will be smaller. You don't need viewstate to be supported because you aren't planning to do postbacks directly from this page.

Note that you couldn't do this in the previous page. There, you enabled paging in your DataGrid, which requires viewstate support in order to work. You aren't using paging in either of the pages that display the order details. Of course, if you potentially have many orders per customer, you may decide to use paging, in which case you'll need to enable viewstate support for the page.

This code also defines a single Page-level (global) variable that you'll use to hold the current customer ID:

```
'page-level variable accessed from more than one routine
Dim strCustID As String = ""
```

So, back to the HTML; the following is the declaration of the DataGrid control and the two Label controls that provide ancillary information for the user:

```
<form runat="server">
  <!-- label to display customer ID -->
  <asp:Label id="lblStatus" runat="server" /><p />

  <!-- DataGrid control to display matching orders -->
  <asp:DataGrid id="dgrOrders" runat="server"
      AutoGenerateColumns="False"
      CellPadding="5"
      GridLines="Vertical"
      HeaderStyle-BackColor="#c0c0c0"
      ItemStyle-BackColor="#ffffff"
      AlternatingItemStyle-BackColor="#eeeeee">

    <Columns>
```

```
        <asp:TemplateColumn HeaderText="<b>Order ID</b>"
                      ItemStyle-BackColor="#add8e6"
                      ItemStyle-HorizontalAlign="center">
    <ItemTemplate>
      <asp:Hyperlink Text='<%# Container.DataItem("OrderID")%>'
           NavigateUrl='<%# DataBinder.Eval(Container.DataItem, "OrderID", _
             "order-detail.aspx?customerid=" & strCustID & "&orderid={0}") %>'
           Target="right" runat="server" />
    </ItemTemplate>
  </asp:TemplateColumn>

        <asp:BoundColumn HeaderText="<b>Order Date</b>"
                      HeaderStyle-HorizontalAlign="center"
                      ItemStyle-HorizontalAlign="center"
                      DataField="OrderDate" DataFormatString="{0:d}" />

        <asp:BoundColumn HeaderText="<b>Shipped</b>"
                      HeaderStyle-HorizontalAlign="center"
                      ItemStyle-HorizontalAlign="center"
                      DataField="ShippedDate" DataFormatString="{0:d}" />
  </Columns>
</asp:DataGrid><p />

<!-- label to display interactive messages -->
<asp:Label id="lblMessage" runat="server" />
</form>
```

Again, you're generating the columns in the grid yourself (you set the
AutoGenerateColumns property to False). The only complicated column is the first
one—an asp:TemplateColumn. You use this because it allows you to implement the
content using a template, and a template allows a more flexible approach to setting the content than any other technique in the previous example.

Using a "Template" Column

The reason you need the extra flexibility is because you want to use a hyperlink
in the column, but you also want to specify the target attribute of this hyperlink so
that the target page is loaded into the other frame of your frameset rather than the
current frame. If you use a standard hyperlink column (as in the previous example), you can't set the target attribute in your declaration of the DataGrid.

The following code shows the template content again. It defines an asp:Hyperlink, which will output an <a> element in the table, and you can see that it specifies the right frame (rather unimaginatively named right in the frameset page) as the Target attribute. The text of the hyperlink is the value of the OrderID column in the DataSet table that's bound to the DataGrid control. The syntax used is that of server-side data binding, and it indicates you want this specific column (DataItem) from the data source that's bound to the control (the Container):

```
<ItemTemplate>
  <asp:Hyperlink Text='<%# Container.DataItem("OrderID")%>'
      NavigateUrl='<%# DataBinder.Eval(Container.DataItem, "OrderID", _
        "order-detail.aspx?customerid=" & strCustID & "&orderid={0}") %>'
      Target="right" runat="server" />
</ItemTemplate>
```

The NavigateUrl attribute of the hyperlink specifies the href attribute that'll be added to the output <a> element. In this you're using the Eval method of the DataBinder object (the object that carries out the binding) to specify the format of the string you want to be used for the href. You can see that the method takes the data source (Container.DataItem) as its first parameter, the column name within the data source as its second parameter, and the format string as the third parameter.

The great thing is that this is a "proper" method call (notice the underscore at the end of the line where the third parameter has wrapped to the next line), and it means you can use code to build the format string. You use the Page-level variable named strCustID and the value of the order ID for the current row, so the href will be something like this:

```
order-detail.aspx?customerid=CONSH&orderid=10462
```

So, in the view-orders.aspx page, you can extract the customer ID from the query string and use it in your code. Figure 5-9 shows what the view-orders.aspx frameset page looks like when it first loads.

Figure 5-9. The list of orders for a selected customer

The Page_Load Event Handler

To display the list of orders shown in Figure 5-9, you execute some code in response to the Page_Load event. If it isn't a postback (this is the first time the page has been loaded), you collect the customer ID from the query string and store it in the Page-level variable named strCustID. If a customer ID wasn't specified (perhaps because the page was loaded directly rather than from the previous default.aspx page), you display an error message—you need the customer ID to be able to look up their orders:

```
Sub Page_Load()

  If Not Page.IsPostBack Then
    strCustID = Request.QueryString("customerid")
    If (strCustID Is Nothing) Or (strCustID = "") Then
      'display error message
      lblMessage.Text = "* ERROR: no Customer ID provided.<br />" _
        & "You must <a href='default.aspx' target='_top'><b>select" _
        & " a customer</b></a> first."
```

```
    Else
       'display all orders for this customer
       ShowOrders()

    End If
  End If
End Sub
```

As long as you received a customer ID, you can call the ShowOrders routine located elsewhere in this page to display the list of orders for the specified customer.

Displaying the Order List

The ShowOrders routine is relatively simple. It just has to fetch the DataSet from the custom GetDataSetFromSessionOrServer function you looked at earlier and bind it to the DataGrid control. However, there are a couple of other issues with which to contend. Recall that you're "sharing" this DataSet with the page in the other frame of the <frameset> (order-detail.aspx). As you'll see when you look at that page, it applies a filter to the Orders table in the DataSet to extract and display details of the shipping address and the carrier that's delivering it.

If the user refreshes this page, the row filter will prevent all the other orders for this customer from being listed, so you take the precaution of removing it by setting the RowFilter property of the table's DefaultView to an empty string:

```
Sub ShowOrders()
'display list of all orders for this customer in DataGrid control

  'get DataSet using function elsewhere in this page
  Dim objDataSet As DataSet = GetDataSetFromSessionOrServer(strCustID)

  'remove any existing filter from table DefaultView
  'otherwise refreshing page in browser shows only one row
  objDataSet.Tables("Orders").DefaultView.RowFilter = ""
  ...
```

The only other issue is to check whether you actually have any orders for this customer to display and show an appropriate message in the Label control on this page:

```
  ...
  'check if any orders were found for this customer
  If objDataSet.Tables("Orders").Rows.Count > 0 Then
    'diplay heading above DataGrid
    lblStatus.Text = "Orders for customer ID <b>'" & strCustID & "'</b>"
```

```
    'set DataSource, bind the DataGrid and display status message
    dgrOrders.DataSource = objDataSet.Tables("Orders")
    dgrOrders.DataBind()
    lblMessage.Text = "Click an <b>Order ID</b> in the grid above to" _
                  & "<br /> display details of that order or "

  Else
    lblMessage.Text = "No orders found for this customer ..."

  End If

  lblMessage.Text &= "<br /><a href='default.aspx' target='_top'>" _
                  & "<b>select another customer</b></a>"
End Sub
```

Displaying the Order Details

The final page in the HTML version of the application (order-detail.aspx) displays in the right frame of the view-orders.aspx page. Most of the techniques are similar to the previous two pages you've seen. The page contains an ASP.NET DataGrid control to display the list of order lines for the selected order, plus a couple of Label controls to display the shipping details for the order and the total value.

Declaring the DataGrid and Labels

The following code shows the HTML for this page. You can see the Label controls and the DataGrid. As in previous pages, you "turn off" the AutoGenerateColumns property of the DataGrid. You just have a series of standard asp:BoundColumn elements in this page—there's one for each column in the OrderLines table of your DataSet (including the calculated column that you added to the DataSet when you stored it in the session). Here's the code for the order-detail.aspx page:

```
<form runat="server">

  <!-- label to display order details -->
  <asp:Label id="lblMessage" runat="server" /><p />

  <!-- DataGrid control to display order lines -->
  <asp:DataGrid id="dgrOrders" runat="server"
      AutoGenerateColumns="False"
      CellPadding="5"
      GridLines="Vertical"
```

```
                HeaderStyle-BackColor="#c0c0c0"
                AlternatingItemStyle-BackColor="#eeeeee">

        <Columns>
          <asp:BoundColumn HeaderText="<b>Qty</b>"
                           HeaderStyle-HorizontalAlign="center"
                           ItemStyle-HorizontalAlign="center"
                           DataField="Quantity" />
          <asp:BoundColumn HeaderText="<b>Product</b>"
                           HeaderStyle-HorizontalAlign="center"
                           DataField="ProductName" />
          <asp:BoundColumn HeaderText="<b>Packs</b>"
                           HeaderStyle-HorizontalAlign="center"
                           DataField="QuantityPerUnit" />
          <asp:BoundColumn HeaderText="<b>Each</b>"
                           HeaderStyle-HorizontalAlign="center"
                           ItemStyle-HorizontalAlign="right"
                           DataField="UnitPrice" DataFormatString="${0:N2}" />
          <asp:BoundColumn HeaderText="<b>Discount</b>"
                           HeaderStyle-HorizontalAlign="center"
                           ItemStyle-HorizontalAlign="right"
                           DataField="Discount" DataFormatString="{0:P}" />
          <asp:BoundColumn HeaderText="<b>Total</b>"
                           HeaderStyle-HorizontalAlign="center"
                           ItemStyle-HorizontalAlign="right"
                           DataField="LineTotal" DataFormatString="${0:N2}" />
        </Columns>

    </asp:DataGrid><p />

    <!-- label to display order total -->
    <asp:Label id="lblTotal" runat="server" /><p />

</form>
```

You'll notice that you specify values for the DataFormatString property of the last three columns to display the content as currency or as a percentage format. You use the standard format specifier P to format the percentage column. For the other two, you use the currency character $ followed by the numeric value formatted to two decimal places (N2). You might be tempted to use the standard currency format specifier, C, here—but this would cause the page to display a currency character that depends on the locale settings of the server. If your database holds the price in U.S. dollars, you probably don't want to display that number with any other currency symbol!

The ASP.NET Code for the Page

The code declares two Page-level variables that'll contain the customer ID and the order ID for the selected order:

```
'page-level variables accessed from more than one routine
Dim strCustID As String = ""
Dim strOrderID As String = ""
```

This page will probably be loaded several times as the user browses through the list of orders displayed in the left frame of the view-orders.aspx page; each time they select an order, the current page (order-detail.aspx) reloads with the customer ID and the order ID in the query string. So, in the Page_Load event, you can extract the customer ID and the order ID from the query string each time the page loads:

```
Sub Page_Load()

  If Not Page.IsPostBack Then
    strCustID = Request.QueryString("customerid")
    strOrderID = Request.QueryString("orderid")
    If (strOrderID Is Nothing) Or (strOrderID = "") _
    Or (strCustID Is Nothing) Or (strCustID = "") Then
      'display help message
      lblMessage.Text = "Select an order from the first column " _
        & "in the list shown on the left to display the order details."

    Else
      'display order details for this order
      ShowOrderLines()

    End If
  End If
End Sub
```

Notice that the code displays a simple help message if there's no customer ID or order ID. When the frameset containing this page loads the first time, there will be no "current order" (you saw this in Figure 5-9).

When the page loads *with* customer ID or order ID values in the query string, you call the ShowOrderLines routine elsewhere in your page to display the details of the selected order.

Getting the DataSet from the Server or Session

You'll need to be able to extract the data for this page from the DataSet created by the data access tier of your application. If the client supports sessions, this will already be in the user's session—placed there by the order-list.aspx page that you loaded into the left frame. This DataSet also has the calculated LineTotal column you need in this page.

However, if the client doesn't support sessions, you have to hit the data access component again to extract it from the database and add the calculated column. In fact, the function you need is the same as the one you used in the order-list.aspx page, so you just include the same function (GetDataSetFromSessionOrServer) in this page as well:

```
Function GetDataSetFromSessionOrServer(strCustID As String) As DataSet
'gets a DataSet containing all orders for this customer
... exactly the same as in order-list.aspx page ...
... and it uses the same session-cached DataSet ...
End Function
```

The ShowOrderLines Routine

The ShowOrderLines routine is a little more complex than the equivalent function you used in previous pages because it has to display data from *both* of the tables in the DataSet. The shipping details come from the Orders table, and the detail line rows come from the OrderLines table.

You start by calling the routine to get the DataSet from the session or directly from the data tier:

```
Sub ShowOrderLines()
'display all the order line details for this order in DataGrid control

  'get DataSet using function elsewhere in this page
  Dim objDataSet As DataSet = GetDataSetFromSessionOrServer(strCustID)
  ...
```

Next, you get a reference to the DefaultView of the Orders table and apply a filter so that the *only* row exposed is the one for the current order. (This is the same filter you have to remove in order-list.aspx so that *all* order rows are shown whenever that page refreshes, discussed earlier in the chapter.) You also get a reference to the DefaultView of the OrderLines table and apply the same filter to that DataView:

```
...
'create filtered DataView from Orders table in DataSet
Dim objOrderView As DataView = objDataSet.Tables("Orders").DefaultView
objOrderView.RowFilter = "OrderID = " & strOrderID

'create filtered DataView from OrderLines table
Dim objLinesView As DataView = objDataSet.Tables("OrderLines").DefaultView
objLinesView.RowFilter = "OrderID = " & strOrderID
...
```

Calculating the Order Total and Displaying the Details

Now you can calculate the total value of the order by summing the values in the LineTotal calculated column that you've already added to the DataSet:

```
...
'calculate total value of order
Dim dblTotal As Double = 0
Dim objDataRowView As DataRowView
For Each objDataRowView In objLinesView
  dblTotal += objDataRowView("LineTotal")
Next
...
```

Next, you check that there's at least one order line for this order (this should always be the case) and display the shipping details—selecting them from the appropriate table as you go. Notice the use of the VB.NET IsDbNull function to test for a null value for the shipping date. As well as providing a more informative output, this prevents an error arising from trying to format a null value:

```
...
'check that there are some matching order lines
If objLinesView.Count > 0 Then

  'display the shipping details in Message Label
  lblMessage.Text = "Order ID:" & strOrderID _
    & "Customer Name:" & objOrderView.Item(0)("ShipName") & "<br />" _
    & "Delivery Address:" & objOrderView.Item(0)("OrderAddress") _
    & "Ordered: " & FormatDateTime(objOrderView.Item(0)("OrderDate"))
  If IsDbNull(objOrderView.Item(0)("ShippedDate")) Then
    lblMessage.Text &= "Awaiting shipping"
  Else
    lblMessage.Text &= "Shipped: " _
      & FormatDateTime(objOrderView.Item(0)("ShippedDate"))
  End If
  lblMessage.Text &= " via " & objOrderView.Item(0)("CompanyName")
  ...
```

The final steps are to bind the `DefaultView` of the `OrderLines` table to your `DataGrid` control and display the total order value. Again, you specify the currency symbol explicitly rather than depending on the local settings of the server. If there happen to be no order lines for this order, you just display a message to this effect instead:

```
...
'set DataSource and bind the DataGrid
dgrOrders.DataSource = objLinesView
dgrOrders.DataBind()

'display the total value of the order
lblTotal.Text = "Total order value:" & dblTotal.ToString("$#,##0.00")

  Else
    lblMessage.Text = "No order lines found for this order..."

  End If
End Sub
```

Figure 5-10 shows the results for order number 10462 for customer Consolidated Holdings:

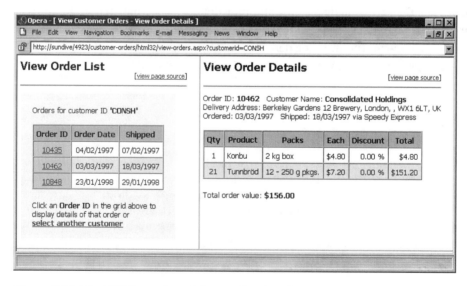

Figure 5-10. The HTML version of the application displaying details of an order

The Order List Application: The Mobile Version

The other down-level client you'll look at in this chapter is the small-screen or mobile device, such as a Personal Digital Assistant (PDA) or a cellular phone. Although you can't offer the same kind of usability for these devices as you can in a standard Web browser, their increasing use for mobile Internet access means that you can benefit from supporting them as best as you possibly can.

The version of the application for mobile devices gives the same functionality as the browser-based equivalents, but it tries to minimize the effects of the small screen and the lack of a keyboard and mouse for input. You'll build it with controls from the Microsoft Mobile Internet Toolkit (MMIT), so it'll also work fine in a PDA or handheld device that supports HTML rather than the more usual Wireless Markup Language (WML) of the cellular phone.

> **NOTE** *Remember that you may have to use a cookieless session for the application in order to view the mobile pages without an error if the emulator or device you're using has problems with maintaining viewstate. Simply change the* <sessionState> *element in the* <system.web> *section of the* web.config *file in the root folder of the application to read* <sessionState cookieless="true" />.

Figure 5-11 shows the opening page of the application in a cellular phone emulator and in an HTML browser (actually a resized Internet Explorer window). For the mobile phone emulator, browse to http://localhost/4923/customer-orders/default.aspx, and the application should redirect you to the http://localhost/4923/customer-orders/mobile/default.aspx page automatically. In a browser, you can use the menu page you saw at the start of this chapter in Figure 5-1 (customer-orders.htm) to navigate specifically to the version of the application designed for mobile devices.

> **NOTE** *The emulator we're using here, and throughout this chapter, is part of the Nokia Mobile Internet Toolkit. Various versions are available, and you can read about these and download them from* http://forum.nokia.com/.

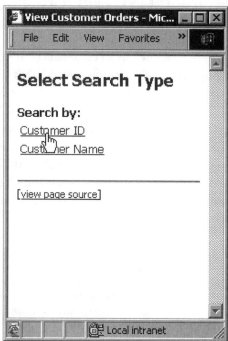

Figure 5-11. Viewing the application on a phone emulator and in Internet Explorer (Emulator images © Nokia Corporation)

The Outline Process

The way you structure pages for use with the MMIT controls is different from the way you do this in a normal HTML-targeted ASP.NET page. Devices that support WML rather than HTML have the concept of multiple "screens" (often called *cards* in WML-speak) for each page. And so, not surprisingly, the page itself is often referred to as a *deck* (there's a huge opportunity for bad puns when developing for mobile devices).

The theory is that devices such as cellular phones have narrow-bandwidth and high-latency connections (at least at the moment), so sending several screens in one go provides a more interactive and responsive user interface. However, if each screen is dynamically generated on the server, it means that a server connection and a postback are still required for each screen—but the principle is there and is useful if you decide to use client-side WMLScript to manipulate the pages.

To implement the requirement for multiple screens in one page, the MMIT provides a subclassed version of the Page object that accepts multiple server-side <form> elements (the standard Page object won't). Each <form> becomes a single screen or card, and you can activate (or display) the appropriate ones within your code as the user interacts with the page.

So, to implement the application requirements, you have a single page, default.aspx (in the mobile subfolder of the application), which contains five <form> elements that implement the five screens, as shown in Figure 5-12.

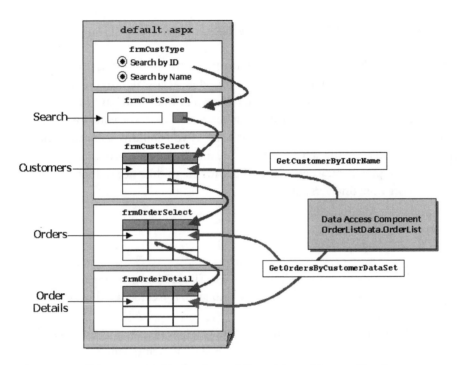

Figure 5-12. The process steps for the mobile version of the application

The first two screens (frmCustType and frmCustSearch) collect the search details from the user, and the third screen displays a list of matching customers using the GetCustomerByIdOrName method of your application's standard data access component. Selecting a customer then displays a list of all their orders in the next screen, using the GetOrdersByCustomerDataSet method of the same component. Finally, the fifth screen displays the details of the order that the user selected in the previous screen—again using the GetOrdersByCustomerDataSet method.

So the data access processes are similar to those you used in the HTML version of the example. You also take advantage of sessions in exactly the same way, and the application still works if sessions aren't supported.

Every screen (except the first) allows the user to jump backward through the process using either the hyperlinks at the bottom of each screen or the "soft keys" that are implemented on most mobile devices. In the final screen, they can return to the previous screen (the list of orders for the selected customer) and select a different order.

Fetching Data from the Server

Before you look at the server controls and the page structure for this example, you'll examine the code that interacts with your data access tier. To provide the kind of compact display you need for small-screen devices, you have to "massage" the data a little in your application's middle tier. In this case, the code for this is actually part of this page, but there's no reason why you couldn't separate it into a component if you need the same functionality for other versions of the application. In later chapters, you'll actually do this with the middle tier so that you can reuse it in more than one version.

Fetching the Customer List

Getting the list of customers is a simple process. The GetCustomerDataSetFromServer function takes care of all this—it's almost identical to the GetDataSetFromServer function found in the HTML version.

As in the HTML version of the application, you first remove any existing DataSet containing order details from the user's session before you fetch the data for the customer they selected this time. The partial or full customer ID or name are passed to this function in the two parameters in the same way as in the earlier examples. Here's the default.aspx page:

```
Function GetCustomerDataSetFromServer(strCustID As String, _
                                      strCustName As String) As DataSet

   'remove any existing "Orders" DataSet from the user's Session
   'as we're searching now for a different customer
   Session("4923MobileShowOrdersDataSet") = Nothing
   ...
```

Now you can collect the connection string from the web.config file, instantiate the data access component, and fetch and return the DataSet it exposes:

```
...
'get connection string from web.config
Dim strConnect As String
strConnect = ConfigurationSettings.AppSettings("NorthwindConnectString")

Try
   'create an instance of the data access component
   Dim objOrderList As New OrderList(strConnect)

   'call the method to return the data as a DataSet
   Return objOrderList.GetCustomerByIdOrName(strCustID, strCustName)

Catch objErr As Exception
   'there was an error and no data will be returned
   Return Nothing

End Try
End Function
```

Fetching the Order Data

Fetching the order data for a specific customer is more complex. It's handled by the GetOrderDataSetFromSessionOrServer method (which is similar to the GetDataSetFromSessionOrServer function in both order pages of the HTML version but, as you'll see here, has some important additional coding).

Here, as in the HTML version, you'll get back a DataSet containing two tables—an Orders table containing the details of every order for this customer and an OrderLines table containing the order rows for all these orders. You also cache this DataSet in the user's session when you first fetch it from the data access component, so you can reuse this on subsequent calls to the function:

```
Function GetOrderDataSetFromSessionOrServer(strCustID As String) As DataSet

  Dim objDataSet As DataSet

  Try
     'try and get DataSet from user's Session
     objDataSet = CType(Session("4923MobileShowOrdersDataSet"), DataSet)

     If objDataSet Is Nothing Then    'not in Session
```

```
'get connection string from web.config
Dim strConnect As String
strConnect = ConfigurationSettings.AppSettings("NorthwindConnectString")

'create an instance of the data access component
Dim objOrderList As New OrderList(strConnect)

'call the method to return the data as a DataSet
objDataSet = objOrderList.GetOrdersByCustomerDataSet(strCustID)
...
```

Massaging the DataSet

At this point in the code, you know that the DataSet wasn't in the session, and you have extracted it from your data access tier. Before you cache it in the session, you need (as in the HTML version) to make some changes to it. You aren't using fancy User Interface (UI) controls such as the DataGrid in this version of the application. Instead, you'll want to provide columns that contain *all* the information in a compact format ready for display.

For the Orders table, you add a column named DisplayCol that contains the concatenated values for the order ID and the order date. This will be used for the list of orders from which the user can choose:

```
...
'get a reference to the "Orders" table in the DataSet
Dim objTable As DataTable = objDataSet.Tables("Orders")

'add column containing order ID and date as one string value
Dim objColumn As DataColumn
objColumn = objTable.Columns.Add("DisplayCol", _
                    System.Type.GetType("System.String"))

'fill column for each row with "#{order number} - {order date}"
Dim objRow As DataRow
Dim objDate As DateTime
For Each objRow In objTable.Rows
  objDate = objRow("OrderDate")
  objRow("DisplayCol") = "#" & objRow("OrderID") & " - " _
                    & objDate.ToString("d")
Next
...
```

For the OrderLines table, you want to provide a column that concatenates the quantity, product name, pack details, unit price, discount (if any), and the line total. You go about this by first adding a calculated column to the table in the same way as you did for the HTML version of the application. Then you can use this and the other columns values to build the content for the new DisplayCol column in this table:

```
...
'get a reference to the "OrderLines" table in the DataSet
objTable = objDataSet.Tables("OrderLines")

'add column containing total value of each line
objColumn = objTable.Columns.Add("LineTotal", _
                    System.Type.GetType("System.Double"))
objColumn.Expression = "[Quantity] * ([UnitPrice] - ([UnitPrice]" _
                    & " * [Discount]))"

'add column containing the order details as one string value
objColumn = objTable.Columns.Add("DisplayCol", _
                    System.Type.GetType("System.String"))

'fill with "qty x product (pack) @ price less discount = total"
Dim strColValue As String
For Each objRow In objTable.Rows
  Dim dblThisPrice as Double = objRow("UnitPrice")
  strColValue = objRow("Quantity").ToString & " x " _
            & objRow("ProductName") & " (" _
            & objRow("QuantityPerUnit") & ") @ " _
            & dblThisPrice.ToString("$#0.00")
  If objRow("Discount") > 0 Then
    dblThisPrice = objRow("Discount")
    strColValue &= " Less " & dblThisPrice.ToString("P")
  End If
  dblThisPrice = objRow("LineTotal")
  objRow("DisplayCol") = strColValue & " = " _
                    & dblThisPrice.ToString("$#0.00")
Next
...
```

Now you can save this "massaged" DataSet in the user's session ready for use in the Order List and Order Details screens of the application. You finish by returning it to the calling routine. Of course, if there's a DataSet already in the session, you simply return this instead of re-creating it:

```
  ...
  'save DataSet in Session for next order inquiry
  Session("4923MobileShowOrdersDataSet") = objDataSet

End If

Return objDataSet    'return DataSet to calling routine

Catch objErr As Exception

  'there was an error and no data will be returned
  Return Nothing

End Try

End Function
```

The Mobile Page Content

Next you'll look at the structure of the page itself and see how you build each screen. The page starts with the special Page directive for the MMIT MobilePage object and a Register directive to register the MMIT controls. You follow this with the Import directives for your custom data access component and the System.Data namespace, which you need to be able to use objects such as the DataSet, DataColumn, and DataRow you saw in the previous code listings:

```
<%@Page Inherits="System.Web.UI.MobileControls.MobilePage" Language="VB"%>
<%@Register TagPrefix="Mobile" Namespace="System.Web.UI.MobileControls"
            Assembly="System.Web.Mobile"%>
<%@Import Namespace="OrderListData" %>
<%@Import Namespace="System.Data" %>
```

Adding Style to the Output

When you serve content to devices such as cellular phones, you don't have much control over the style or appearance of the output. However, you can also use the MMIT controls to create output for devices that support HTML, as you saw in Figure 5-12. It's nice to be able to add at least some basic styling to these, and you do this through the `mobile:Stylesheet` control that's implemented by the MMIT.

This requires you to set up choices using a `web.config` file, which specifies the devices that belong to a specific `<Choice>` filter category in a stylesheet (such as the one you'll examine in a moment). In this sample application, you have a `web.config` file in the root folder of the application that contains the following `<deviceFilters>` section:

```
<configuration>
  ... other settings here ...
  <system.web>
    ... other settings here ...

    <deviceFilters>
      <filter name="IsIE" compare="browser" argument="IE" />
      <filter name="IsHTML32" compare="PreferredRenderingMIME"
              argument="text/html" />
    </deviceFilters>

  </system.web>
</configuration>
```

This sets up two filters. One is named `IsIE` and will only include Internet Explorer browsers. The other filter, named `IsHTML32`, will only include client devices that support HTML. The `compare` attribute is an entry from the list of properties exposed by either the `MobileCapabilities` object or the `BrowserCapabilities` object, and the `argument` attribute is (obviously) the value for the property you want to match.

The Mobile Stylesheet for your Application

The following code shows the `mobile:Stylesheet` you use in this version of the application. You'll find it in `default.aspx`. You can see that it implements three styles in separate `<Style>` elements. The first is the style you'll apply to every screen in the application, and it specifies the content you want to include at the top and bottom of the screen where the current client supports HTML (using the `IsHTML32` filter you defined in `web.config`):

```
<mobile:Stylesheet runat="server">

  <Style name="styPage">
```

```
    <DeviceSpecific>
      <Choice Filter="IsHTML32">
        <HeaderTemplate>
          <body bgcolor="#ffffacd"
                style="font-family:Tahoma, Arial, sans-serif; font-size:10pt">
            <font face="Tahoma,Arial,sans-serif" size="2">
        </HeaderTemplate>
        <FooterTemplate>
          <br /><hr /></font>
          <font face="Tahoma,Arial,sans-serif" size="1">
          <div style="font-family:Tahoma, Arial, sans-serif; font-size:8pt">
          &copy;2003 <a href="http://www.daveandal.com/">
          ... etc ...
          </font></body>
        </FooterTemplate>
      </Choice>
    </DeviceSpecific>
  </Style>
  ...
```

This useful feature means you can easily tailor the output for HTML devices to make the screens attractive and to include extra content. None of this content will be sent to other clients such as cellular phones that expect WML—if this wasn't the case, the client would report an error when it encountered a nonsupported element.

The other two styles you include in the page are also specific to HTML clients. They simply define the style for page headings (large blue text) and lists (small black text):

```
  ...
  <Style name="styHeading">
    <DeviceSpecific>
      <Choice Filter="IsHTML32" Font-Name="Tahoma,Arial,sans-serif"
              ForeColor="blue" Font-Size="large" Font-Bold="true" />
    </DeviceSpecific>
  </Style>

  <Style name="styListAndLink">
    <DeviceSpecific>
      <Choice Filter="IsHTML32" Font-Name="Tahoma,Arial,sans-serif"
              ForeColor="black" Font-Size="small" />
    </DeviceSpecific>
  </Style>

</mobile:Stylesheet>
```

Setting the Search Type

At last you're in a position to see some of the controls that create the visible parts of your application. Figure 5-13 shows the opening screen again, in both the Nokia emulator and an HTML client.

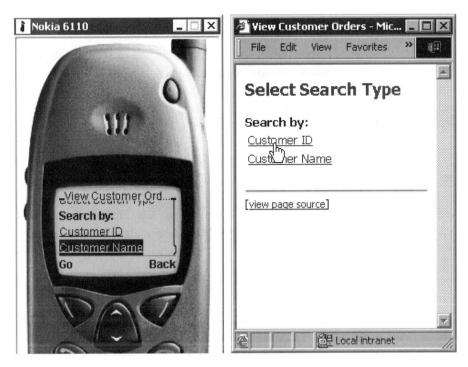

Figure 5-13. The opening screen in a phone emulator and in Internet Explorer

This output is created by the first <form> in your page. It's quite basic, using the MMIT controls to create the text in two Label controls and the two options within a List control. The form itself has the ID value frmCustType and the caption *View Customer Orders*. Notice how you can specify the style to apply to each control—some use a reference to one of the styles in the stylesheet you saw earlier, and some use attributes of the control to set the appearance:

```
<mobile:Form id="frmCustType" title="View Customer Orders"
             styleReference="styPage" runat="server">
  <mobile:Label id="lblMsg1" styleReference="styHeading" runat="server">
    Select Search Type
  </mobile:Label><br /><br />
  <mobile:Label id="lblType" Font-Bold="true" runat="server">
```

```
      Search by:
  </mobile:Label>
  <mobile:List id="lstType" styleReference="styListAndLink"
              OnItemCommand="SetSearchType" runat="server">
    <Item Text="Customer ID" Value="CustID" />
    <Item Text="Customer Name" Value="CustName" />
  </mobile:List>
</mobile:Form>
```

The List control has the OnItemCommand attribute pointing to an event handler named SetSearchType, which is located elsewhere in your page, and executes when the user selects one of the options. As in an HTML <select> list, you can specify values for the visible text of each item (using the Text attribute) and the value that's returned when the item is selected (using the Value attribute).

Specifying the Search String

To understand what the code that runs in response to a selection in the list does, you first need to look at the declaration for the next screen. The following code implements the frmCustSearch form, which contains three Label controls, a TextBox control, a Command control, and a Link control:

```
<mobile:Form id="frmCustSearch" title="Customer Search"
              styleReference="styPage" runat="server">
  <mobile:Label id="lblMsg2" styleReference="styHeading" runat="server">
    Search for Customer
  </mobile:Label><br /><br />
  <mobile:Label id="lblSearchType" Font-Bold="true" runat="server" />
  <mobile:TextBox id="txtSearchString" runat="server" />
  <mobile:Command id="cmdSearch" CommandName="Search" runat="server"
              OnClick="GetCustomers" SoftKeyLabel="Search" Text="Search" />
  <mobile:Label id="lblSearchTips" runat="server" /><br />
  <mobile:Link NavigateUrl="#frmCustType" SoftKeyLabel="Back"
              Text="Change Search Type"
              styleReference="styListAndLink" runat="server" />
</mobile:Form>
```

Notice that the Label controls with the id attributes lblSearchType and lblSearchTips have no text content at the moment. You'll set this text within your code by assigning it to the Text property of these controls. This means that you can change the caption for the text box and the *Hint* text displayed below it, depending on the selection the user made in the previous screen. For example,

Figure 5-14 shows what this screen looks like when the user selects Customer ID on the previous screen.

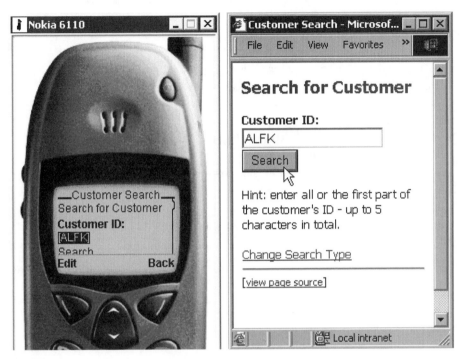

Figure 5-14. Searching for a customer in the mobile version of the application

You can also see from this that the Command control automatically creates a device-specific Search button—a soft key command in a phone and an HTML button in the browser. You can also see (at least in the HTML output) the effect of the Link control you added at the end of the `<form>`. In the phone it creates a second soft key command (Back), and in the browser it creates a hyperlink. The declaration you use for this control is as follows:

```
<mobile:Link NavigateUrl="#frmCustType" SoftKeyLabel="Back"
        Text="Change Search Type"
        styleReference="styListAndLink" runat="server" />
```

The SoftKeyLabel attribute sets the soft key in a phone, and the NavigateUrl attribute you use is the ID of the `<form>` you want to activate when the link is clicked.

The Code in the SetSearchType Event Handler

You're not quite finished with this screen yet. We still need to show how you set the text of the Label controls and how you activate the next screen. When the user makes a selection for the search type in the first screen, as you saw earlier, the event handler named SetSearchType executes:

```
Sub SetSearchType(objSender As Object, objArgs As ListCommandEventArgs)
'set the correct text on page 2 (frmCustSearch) and display it

  'fill in Label text
  If objArgs.ListItem.Value = "CustName" Then
    lblSearchType.Text = "Customer Name:"
    lblSearchTips.Text = "Hint: enter any part of the customer... etc."
  Else
    lblSearchType.Text = "Customer ID:"
    lblSearchTips.Text = "Hint: enter all or the first part...etc."
  End If

  'display screen 2
  ActiveForm = frmCustSearch

End Sub
```

All this code has to do is set the text of the two Label controls in the second screen and then activate it so that it displays. Depending on the user's selection in the first screen, they'll see different text in the two Label controls.

Showing the Customer List

Once the user enters the search string into the text box on the second screen, they use the Command control in that screen (a soft key or a button, depending on the device) to get a list of customers that match their criteria. The declaration of that Command control looks like this:

```
<mobile:Command id="cmdSearch" CommandName="Search" runat="server"
            OnClick="GetCustomers" SoftKeyLabel="Search" Text="Search" />
```

So, your event handler named GetCustomers will execute when this Command is activated, and the user will see the list of customers in the next screen—which has the ID frmCustSelect. The declaration of this screen's <form> contains a heading Label control, an empty Label control with the ID property value lblStatus1, a List control, and a Link control:

```
<mobile:Form id="frmCustSelect" title="Select Customer"
              styleReference="styPage" runat="server">
  <mobile:Label id="lblMsg3" styleReference="styHeading" runat="server">
    Select Customer
  </mobile:Label><br /><br />
  <mobile:Label id="lblStatus1" Font-Bold="true" runat="server" />
  <mobile:List id="lstCustomers" OnItemCommand="GetOrders"
              styleReference="styListAndLink" runat="server" /><br />
  <mobile:Link NavigateUrl="#frmCustType" SoftKeyLabel="Customer"
              Text="Change Search"
              styleReference="styListAndLink" runat="server" />
</mobile:Form>
```

The empty Label control is where you'll insert status information, and the List control will display the matching customers you found. The link you use here is similar to that in the previous screen, allowing the user to go back and enter different search criteria. Figure 5-15 shows what this screen looks like after searching for customers with the ID *ALFK*.

Figure 5-15. Displaying a list of customers who match the search criteria

The Code in the GetCustomers Event Handler

You can get a list of customers that match the search criteria by calling the function named GetCustomerDataSetFromServer, which is located elsewhere in this page. We described this function when you started looking at this version of the application. However, your event handler has a few other things to do as well, and the GetCustomers event handler (comparable to the DoSearch event handler in the HTML 3.2 version) takes care of these.

You hide the List control by setting its Visible property to False while you fetch the data, and you only show it again if you actually find one or more matching customers. You also have to decide what type of search the user specified by collecting the value from the text box in the frmCustSearch screen. Notice how you can reference the values for controls on any <form> in your page directly. All the values are held in the viewstate of the page, as in an ordinary ASP.NET HTML page:

```
Sub GetCustomers(objSender As Object, objArgs As EventArgs)
'create and display list of matching customers in screen 3

  Dim strCustID As String = ""
  Dim strCustName As String = ""

  'hide the list control until we see if we get a result
  lstCustomers.Visible = "False"

  'check customer search type selection
  If Instr(lblSearchType.Text, "Name") > 0 Then
    strCustName = txtSearchString.Text
  Else
    strCustID = txtSearchString.Text.ToUpper()
  End If
  ...
```

Now you can go and fetch the data you need and check that there were no errors. If you don't get a DataSet back (because an error occurred), you set the text of the status label to show this. Otherwise, you can see how many rows were returned by querying the Count property of the Rows collection for the table in the DataSet. If it's greater than zero, you can bind the DataSet table to the List control in this screen, make it visible again, and display a suitable status message:

```
...
'get DataSet using function elsewhere in this page
Dim objDataSet As DataSet = _
              GetCustomerDataSetFromServer(strCustID, strCustName)
```

```
'if there was an error display message
If objDataSet Is Nothing Then
  lblStatus1.Text = "Error accessing database"

Else
  'check how many matching customers were found
  Dim intRowsFound As Integer = objDataSet.Tables(0).Rows.Count

  If intRowsFound > 0 Then

    'bind the DataGrid and display status message
    lstCustomers.DataSource = objDataSet.Tables(0)
    lstCustomers.DataTextField = "CompanyName"
    lstCustomers.DataValueField = "CustomerID"
    lstCustomers.DataBind()
    lstCustomers.Visible = True
    lblStatus1.Text = "Found Customers:"
    ...
```

As you can see, the MMIT List control (and a few other MMIT controls) supports server-side data binding to the same data types as the ordinary ASP.NET list controls. Here you specify the column to be used for the text displayed in the list (the customer name) and a different column (the customer ID) to be used for the value of each list item.

If no matching customers were found, you set the text of the status label to inform the user. Finally, you activate this screen to display the list of any matching customers:

```
    ...
  Else
    lblStatus1.Text = "No matching customers found in database ..."

  End If

End If

'display screen 3 containing the list
ActiveForm = frmCustSelect

End Sub
```

Listing the Orders for the Selected Customer

In the third screen (the Select Customer screen), you now should have a list of customers that match the search criteria the user specified. When you declare the List control, you specify that selecting an item should execute an event handler named GetOrders:

```
<mobile:List id="lstCustomers" OnItemCommand="GetOrders"
            styleReference="styListAndLink" runat="server" /><br />
```

The GetOrders routine will fetch a list of orders for the selected customer and display them, much as the GetCustomer event handler code did to display a list of customers. You'll look at the code shortly. The following code shows the declaration of the screen that will display this list of orders:

```
<mobile:Form id="frmOrderSelect" title="Select Order"
            styleReference="styPage" runat="server">
  <mobile:Label id="lblMsg4" styleReference="styHeading" runat="server">
    Select Order
  </mobile:Label><br /><br />
  <mobile:Label id="lblStatus2" Font-Bold="true" runat="server" />
  <mobile:List id="lstOrders" OnItemCommand="ShowOrderDetail"
            styleReference="styListAndLink" runat="server" /><br />
  <mobile:Link NavigateUrl="#frmCustType" SoftKeyLabel="Customer"
            Text="Select Customer"
            styleReference="styListAndLink" runat="server" />
  <mobile:Link id="lnkEditOrders"
            SoftKeyLabel="Edit Orders" Text="Edit Orders"
            styleReference="styListAndLink" runat="server" />
</mobile:Form>
```

Figure 5-16 shows the output generated by this <form>. The empty Label control with the ID value lblStatus2 has its text set by code in the page as it runs, and the List control is bound to the DataSet of orders returned by your data access tier. The two Link controls provide soft keys or hyperlinks (depending on the client type) so that the user can go back and select a different customer or edit the orders for this customer. (You'll look at the editing feature in a later chapter.)

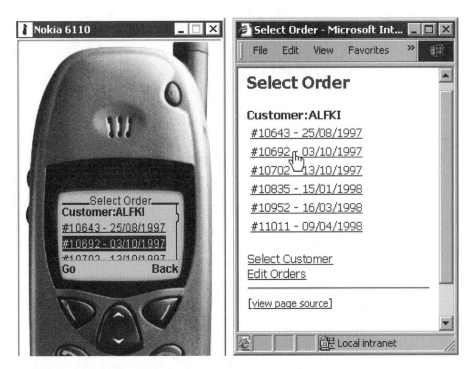

Figure 5-16. Returning a list of orders for the selected customer

The Code in the GetOrders Event Handler

The GetOrders event handler itself is comparable in purpose to the ShowOrders function in the HTML 3.2 version of the application. When the user selects a customer in the Select Customer screen, you retrieve the order ID from the list control in that screen and use it in a call to the GetOrderDataSetFromSessionOrServer you looked at earlier. If you get back a DataSet (there were no errors), you can then check to see if any orders were found and display them by binding the Orders table in the DataSet to the List control in this screen. Notice that you bind to the new column named DisplayCol that you added to the Orders table within your GetOrderDataSetFromSessionOrServer function:

```
Sub GetOrders(objSender As Object, objArgs As ListCommandEventArgs)
'create a list of all orders for this customer on page 4

  'get CustomerID from selection made in List control on page 3
  Dim strCustID As String = objArgs.ListItem.Value
```

```
'get DataSet using function elsewhere in this page
Dim objDataSet As DataSet = GetOrderDataSetFromSessionOrServer(strCustID)

'if there was an error display message
If objDataSet Is Nothing Then
  lblStatus1.Text = "Error accessing database"

Else
  'check if any orders were found for this customer
  If objDataSet.Tables("Orders").Rows.Count > 0 Then
    'diplay heading above List control
    lblStatus2.Text = "Customer '" & strCustID & "'"

    'set DataSource and bind the List control
    lstOrders.DataSource = objDataSet.Tables("Orders")
    lstOrders.DataTextField = "DisplayCol"
    lstOrders.DataValueField = "OrderID"
    lstOrders.DataBind()
    ...
```

You also have to set the href of the Edit Orders Link control at the bottom of the screen so it contains the selected customer ID in the query string. This link opens a page that allows the user to edit the orders of this customer (you'll look at this in Chapter 8). Then you can activate this screen to display it:

```
    ...
    'set URL for editing orders in Link control
    lnkEditOrders.NavigateUrl = _
              "../../update-orders/mobile/edit-orders.aspx" _
              & "?customerid=" & strCustID

  Else
    lblStatus2.Text = "No orders found for this customer ..."

  End If

End If

'display page 4 containing the list
ActiveForm = frmOrderSelect

End Sub
```

Displaying the Order Details

The Order Details screen in this version of the application displays details of the order selected in the Select Customer screen. This screen is activated when the user selects an order in the previous screen, where you have a List control that specifies the event handler named ShowOrderDetail:

```
<mobile:List id="lstOrders" OnItemCommand="ShowOrderDetail"
             styleReference="styListAndLink" runat="server" /><br />
```

The following code shows the declaration of the Order Details screen. This time you have several Label controls that will contain details of the order itself and a List control to which you'll bind the list of order lines. There are also two Link controls at the bottom of the screen that allow the user to select a different customer or a different order:

```
<mobile:Form id="frmOrderDetail" title="Order Details"
             styleReference="styPage" runat="server">
  <mobile:Label id="lblOrderNo" Font-Bold="true" runat="server" />
  <mobile:Label id="lblCustName" runat="server" />
  <mobile:Label id="lblAddress" runat="server" />
  <mobile:Label id="lblOrdered" runat="server" />
  <mobile:Label id="lblShipped" runat="server" />
  <mobile:Label id="lblVia" runat="server" /><br /><br />
  <mobile:List id="lstOrderLines" styleReference="styListAndLink"
               runat="server" /><br />
  <mobile:Label id="lblTotal" Font-Bold="true" runat="server" /><br />
  <mobile:Link NavigateUrl="#frmOrderSelect" SoftKeyLabel="Order"
               Text="Select Order"
               styleReference="styListAndLink" runat="server" />
  <mobile:Link NavigateUrl="#frmCustType" SoftKeyLabel="Customer"
               Text="Select Customer"
               styleReference="styListAndLink" runat="server" />
</mobile:Form>
```

Figure 5-17 shows what this screen looks like when order number 10692 is selected.

Figure 5-17. Viewing the details of the selected order

The Code in the ShowOrderDetail Event Handler

The ShowOrderDetail function in your page runs when the user selects an order from the list in the Order Details screen. It's somewhat more complex than the ShowOrderLines event handler you saw in the HTML version of your application because it has to display values from both of the tables in your DataSet. You first collect the order ID from the arguments passed to this event handler (the value selected in the list) and the customer ID from the "status" label in the previous screen. Then you can collect the DataSet from your GetOrderDataSetFromSessionOrServer function:

```
Sub ShowOrderDetail(objSender As Object, objArgs As ListCommandEventArgs)
'create order line details to display on page 5

  'get OrderID from selection made in List control on page 4
  Dim strOrderID As String = objArgs.ListItem.Value

  'get CustomerID by parsing out of Label control on page 4
  Dim strCustID As String = Mid(lblStatus2.Text, _
                          InStr(lblStatus2.Text, ":") + 1)
  'get DataSet using function elsewhere in this page
  Dim objDataSet As DataSet = GetOrderDataSetFromSessionOrServer(strCustID)
  ...
```

The DataSet will contain details of all orders for this customer, not just the order selected in the previous screen. This might seem an inefficient approach, but in most cases you'll collect this DataSet from the user's session rather than hitting the database again. You use the same DataSet in the previous screen, and you'll also reuse it if the user chooses a different order to view afterward.

You need to apply a filter to both of the tables in the DataSet so that only the details of the selected order display. You filter both tables on the current order ID:

```
...
'create filtered DataView from Orders table in DataSet
Dim objOrderView As DataView = objDataSet.Tables("Orders").DefaultView
objOrderView.RowFilter = "OrderID = " & strOrderID

'create filtered DataView from OrderLines table in DataSet
Dim objLinesView As DataView = objDataSet.Tables("OrderLines").DefaultView
objLinesView.RowFilter = "OrderID = " & strOrderID
...
```

Now you can calculate the order total by summing the values in the LineTotal column that you added to the OrderLines table in your GetOrderDataSetFromSessionOrServer function. Then you extract the shipping details from the single row in the filtered DataView of the Orders table and display these in the Label controls:

```
...
'calculate total value of order
Dim dblTotal As Double = 0
Dim objDataRowView As DataRowView
For Each objDataRowView In objLinesView
  dblTotal += objDataRowView("LineTotal")
Next

'check that there are some matching order lines
If objLinesView.Count > 0 Then

  'display the shipping details in Labels
  lblOrderNo.Text = "Order No: " & strOrderID
  lblCustName.Text = "Customer: " & objOrderView.Item(0)("ShipName")
  Dim datThisDate as DateTime = objOrderView.Item(0)("OrderDate")
  lblOrdered.Text = "Ordered: " & datThisDate.ToString("d")
  If IsDbNull(objOrderView.Item(0)("ShippedDate")) Then
    lblShipped.Text = "Awaiting shipping"
  Else
```

```
    datThisDate = objOrderView.Item(0)("ShippedDate")
    lblShipped.Text = "Shipped: " & datThisDate.ToString("d")
End If
lblVia.Text = "via " & objOrderView.Item(0)("CompanyName")

'display the total value of the order
lblTotal.Text = "Total value: " & dblTotal.ToString("$#,##0.00")
...
```

Finally, you bind the filtered `DataView` of the `OrderLines` table to the `List` control to display the order line details. Again, you bind to the new column named `DisplayCol` that you added to the `OrderLines` table in your `GetOrderDataSetFromSessionOrServer` function. Then you can activate this screen so that the order details are displayed to the user:

```
...
'set DataSource and bind the List control
lstOrderLines.DataSource = objLinesView
lstOrderLines.DataTextField = "DisplayCol"
lstOrderLines.DataBind()

Else

    lblOrderNo.Text = "No order lines found for this order..."

End If

'display page 4 containing the details
ActiveForm = frmOrderDetail

End Sub
```

Summary

In this chapter you've developed two versions of an example application that lists orders for customers of a fictional food distribution corporation. You saw an overview of its capabilities and learned some of the design decisions, such as how you detect the client type when the application first starts.

You also learned how you can provide the data to drive the application, using components developed in Chapters 2 and 3, to create a separate data tier. From there you examined the version of the application designed for down-level HTML clients and the version for small-screen and mobile devices such as PDAs and cellular phones.

This chapter covered the following topics:

- What the application looks like

- Some of the design considerations involved

- Specific client detection techniques for the example application

- The version of the application aimed at HTML 3.2 clients

- The version aimed at small-screen and mobile devices

In the next chapter, you'll continue to develop this application by examining some of the other versions that we've provided as examples. In particular, you'll see how you can work with rich clients, using XML as the data transfer and storage medium.

CHAPTER 6

Working with Rich Clients

THE PREVIOUS CHAPTER was devoted to how you can use the data access tier components created in Chapters 2 and 3 to create interactive applications that work on most HTML browsers and on small-screen and mobile devices such as Personal Digital Assistants (PDAs) and cellular phones.

In this chapter, you'll use the same data access tier, but this time you'll serve more capable types of client. As you've seen in earlier chapters, distributing the data and the processing load in an application requires the support of specific client-side features. Clients that offer these features are generally referred to as *rich clients*.

Rich clients allow you to offload some (or all) of the processing load, reducing the work your server has to do. Basically, in terms of the *n*-tier model, they allow you to move some of the business rules to the client, as well as all the processing required for the presentation tier. They can often cache data client-side and use this to create the display, giving the extra bonus of reduced network round-trips and server connections. In this chapter, you'll look at several rich clients, though there's a lot of commonality between the techniques demonstrated. The topics covered are as follows:

- How you can use XML as your data storage and transfer medium

- How you can use XML with Microsoft Internet Explorer 5 and higher

- How you can use XML via a Web Service

- How you can use XML in a completely disconnected application

- How you can use delimited text as the data storage and transfer medium

You'll start with a more in-depth look at using XML as your "data protocol."

Working with XML

The rich clients you'll look at in this chapter are actually all versions of Internet Explorer. This isn't to say that other clients aren't "rich." In fact you'll see how you can access Web sites without using a browser at all in the next chapter. However, in this chapter, you'll concentrate mainly on using XML as the data storage and transfer medium. XML techniques are reasonably standardized, and most clients should follow the W3C recommendations. So the techniques you'll use are broadly applicable (although with some adaptation when loading the data) to any other browser or client that supports the W3C standards.

We obviously can't provide a full reference to XML and its associated technologies here. However, we'll attempt to explain all the techniques you'll exploit in your application. As well as basic manipulation of the data within an XML parser, this includes using XSL Transformations (XSLT) to transform the XML data for display.

Why XSL and XSLT?

Extensible Stylesheet Language (XSL) is an extremely powerful way of interacting with XML-formatted data. Since its inception, the original XSL working draft has been split into two distinct areas. The transformation section has become XSLT (or XSL-T). The other part of the original draft, an XML-based formatting objects language called XSL-FO, is still undergoing development—it turned out to be a much bigger task than originally anticipated. XSLT allows you to transform XML data into any output format you want. You'll display the data in an HTML-enabled Web browser in this example; so obviously, you'll transform your data into HTML format. To do this, you'll provide XSLT stylesheets that contain the transformation information.

To cache the XML data that's delivered to the client from your server, you'll require a client-side XML parser object. In Windows, the obvious choice is usually Microsoft's MSXML parser. MSXML supports all the XML processing features you'll need for this application, including XSLT, and is automatically installed with Internet Explorer 5 and higher. The latest versions of MSXML (version 3 with Service Pack 2 and version 4) are available from `http://www.microsoft.com`.

Exposing and Delivering XML

The XML data you'll send to the client comes from the same data access tier you used in the previous chapter to power your down-level clients. As you'll recall, the data is exposed as a `DataSet` by both methods of the data access component. That's no problem—you can easily extract the XML data from the `DataSet` and deliver it to the client using the `DataSet`'s `GetXml` or `WriteXml` methods. Then you just pass the XML across the network to the client as plain text, where it's loaded into the client-side XML parser ready for use.

Another technique for exposing XML is via a Web Service. We've already touched on Web Services in earlier chapters. Web Services are a part of a developing industry-wide standard based on two protocols: Web Service Description Language (WSDL) and Simple Object Access Protocol (SOAP). There's also a Universal Description, Discovery, and Integration (UDDI) protocol that allows clients to "discover" Web Services and use them. None of these are Microsoft-specific protocols or standards.

We provide a version of the example application that uses a Web Service as the data source. The content that a Web Service delivers is XML, but the SOAP protocol allows this XML content to be treated as parameters to a function—in other words, as individual "values." In the example, you'll return an XML document from the Web Service so that you can load it into an XML parser on the client and handle it the same way as with the other XML-based versions of the application.

The three versions of the sample application that use XML are as follows:

Internet Explorer 5.0 and higher using XML: This version uses standard ASP.NET pages to create the visible UI. The pages instantiate the MSXML parser on the client to fetch the XML data from a middle tier component (actually a separate ASP.NET page), manipulate it, and display it.

Internet Explorer 5.0 and higher via a Web Service: This version also uses standard ASP.NET pages to create the visible UI. However, the pages use a special Internet Explorer 5 behavior component to connect to the Web Service and fetch the XML data. Then they pass this data to the MSXML parser on the client for manipulation and display.

A **Hypertext Application (HTA) in Internet Explorer 5.0 and higher**: This version uses the special capabilities of Internet Explorer 5 that implement hypertext applications to create the visible UI. These pages can be loaded and run from a remote or a local Web server, and they have access to the local machine outside the "sandbox" within which ordinary Web pages execute. This allows the application to download and store all the data locally so that it can be used without requiring a permanent connection to the original data source. Within the pages, the MSXML parser is used for manipulating and displaying the data.

In the next chapter, you'll examine another version of the application that uses .NET Remoting techniques to connect the server and client—without requiring a browser to be used as the client. Remoting can use XML as the transfer format. However, that's coming later. For now, you'll look at the three XML versions that run in Internet Explorer in more detail.

Using XML in Internet Explorer 5 and Higher

The first example demonstrates how you can consume an XML document delivered over the network as a text stream from the server. Figure 6-1 shows an overview of the process. Two ASP.NET pages make up the "middle tier" in this version of the application, taking their data from the same component that you use as the data access tier for all versions of the application.

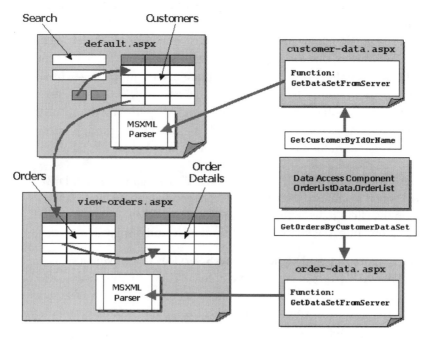

Figure 6-1. The XML-based version of the application

Building the Middle Tier

The first of the middle tier components is the ASP.NET page named customer-data.aspx. It starts with the Import statements for the custom data access component OrderListData and the System.Data namespace you need to be able to instantiate objects such as the DataSet:

```
<%@Page Language="VB"%>
<%@Import Namespace="OrderListData" %>
<%@Import Namespace="System.Data" %>
```

Fetching the Customer List

You get the data from the data access tier by calling the `GetCustomerByIdOrName`
method it exposes, specifying the two parameters for the customer ID and name.
This is the same way as you did it in previous versions of the application:

```
Function GetDataSetFromServer(strCustID As String, _
                             strCustName As String) As DataSet
'use data access component to get DataSet containing matching customers

  'get connection string from web.config
  Dim strConnect As String
  strConnect = ConfigurationSettings.AppSettings("NorthwindConnectString")

  Try
    'create an instance of the data access component
    Dim objOrderList As New OrderList(strConnect)

    'call the method to return the data as a DataSet
    Return objOrderList.GetCustomerByIdOrName(strCustID, strCustName)

  Catch objErr As Exception
    'there was an error so no data is returned

  End Try

End Function
```

The Page_Load Event Handler

The first major difference between the versions of the application for *rich* clients
and the versions for *down-level* clients is visible when you look at the Page_Load
event handler for this version. With down-level clients, you wait for a postback
from the user containing the search string they want to use to look up matching
customers.

However, in the rich-client versions, you'll send the details of *all* the customers in your database to the client as soon as they start the application. This
allows them to search for customers without any further interaction with the
server and thus produces a more responsive and usable interface and better performance generally.

> **NOTE** *Of course, this assumes that the actual number of customers in the* DataSet
> *isn't excessive—you wouldn't want to send an XML document containing the*
> *details of a million customers. If you were dealing with a very large number of*
> *customers, you'd probably try and split them up into groups and deliver only the*
> *appropriate ones. For example, the page could open by prompting the user for a*
> *city name or region and then only deliver the details for customers in that city or*
> *region.*

So in the Page_Load event handler you simply call the GetDataSetFromServer function you just looked at, with two empty string parameters. If you look back at Chapter 2, where you examined the OrderListData component in detail, you'll see that this returns a list of *all* the customers. You also have to set the correct ContentType—the MIME type of the content you're returning—and prefix the XML with the correct declaration:

```
Sub Page_Load()

  Dim objDataSet As DataSet = GetDataSetFromServer("", "")
  Response.ContentType = "text/xml"
  Response.Write("<?xml version='1.0' ?>")
  ...
```

The list comes back from the function as a DataSet, so you could call its GetXml method to get the XML as a String and then write it to the Response. However, a more efficient way to extract the XML content in this case is by using the WriteXml method of the DataSet. This method accepts a Stream object as a parameter, and the XML is sent directly to that stream. So if you specify Response.OutputStream as the parameter, the XML is sent directly to the client without having to be loaded into a String:

```
  ...
  objDataSet.WriteXml(Response.OutputStream)

End Sub
```

Figure 6-2 shows the result of accessing this ASP.NET page directly in Internet Explorer. You can see that the MIME type "text/xml" convinces the browser that it's receiving an XML document rather than a Web page.

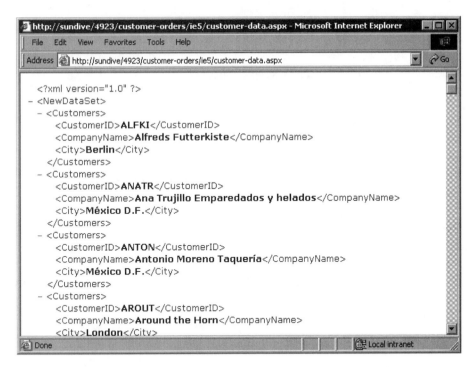

Figure 6-2. Viewing the XML generated by the customer-data.aspx *page*

Fetching the Order List

The second middle tier component for this version of the application is the
ASP.NET page named order-data.aspx. It's similar to the customer-data.aspx page
you just looked at (in fact, you could just as easily combine them both into one
ASP.NET page and use a parameter to specify whether you want customer or order
data). You do, however, have one extra task to perform. You need to add the calculated column for the order line total to the OrderLines table in the DataSet. You do
this in the same way you did it in the down-level versions of the application shown
in the previous chapter. The only difference is that, in this case, you *don't* cache
the resulting DataSet in the user's session on the server:

```
Function GetDataSetFromServer(strCustID As String) As DataSet
'use data access component to get DataSet containing matching orders

  Dim objDataSet As DataSet

  'get connection string from web.config
  Dim strConnect As String
```

```
    strConnect = ConfigurationSettings.AppSettings("NorthwindConnectString")

    Try
      'create an instance of the data access component
      Dim objOrderList As New OrderList(strConnect)

      'call the method to get the data as a DataSet
      objDataSet = objOrderList.GetOrdersByCustomerDataSet(strCustID)

      'add column containing total value of each line in OrderLines table
      Dim objLinesTable As DataTable = objDataSet.Tables("OrderLines")
      Dim objColumn As DataColumn
      objColumn = objLinesTable.Columns.Add("LineTotal", _
                            System.Type.GetType("System.Double"))
      objColumn.Expression = "[Quantity] * ([UnitPrice] - ([UnitPrice]" _
                      & " * [Discount]))"

      'return the DataSet to the calling routine
      Return objDataSet

  Catch objErr As Exception
    'there was an error so no data is returned

  End Try

End Function
```

The Page_Load Event Handler

Although you return a list of all *customers* to your rich clients, you don't want to send them a list of all the *orders* for all customers. Once they've selected a customer, they'll only expect to be able to view the orders for that customer. Selecting a different customer means going back to the first page again—just as in the versions of the application you saw in the previous chapter.

So, in the Page_Load event handler, you extract the selected customer ID from the query string and use this to get the order details for this customer only. You also set the Nested property of the DataRelation within the DataSet before you extract the XML and send it to the client:

```
Sub Page_Load()

  Dim objDataSet As DataSet = _
              GetDataSetFromServer(Request.QueryString("customerid"))
```

```
'set Nested property of relationship between the tables so XML output
'has linked OrderLines elements nested within each Order element
objDataSet.Relations(0).Nested = True

Response.ContentType = "text/xml"
Response.Write("<?xml version='1.0' ?>")
objDataSet.WriteXml(Response.OutputStream)

End Sub
```

Nested XML Output from a DataSet

When you create a relationship (a DataRelation object) that links two tables in a
DataSet, you can use this relationship to navigate from parent row to linked child
rows. You saw this toward the end of Chapter 2 where we discussed the function
GetOrdersByCustomerDataSet within the OrderListData data access component. By
default, the Nested property of a DataRelation is False, and it has no effect when
you're accessing the data in the DataSet using "relational" techniques. However, it
does affect the format of the XML that you expose from the DataSet when you use
the GetXml or WriteXml methods.

For example, with the Orders and OrderLines tables that you have in the
DataSet, the output when the Nested property is False is of this form:

```
<?xml version="1.0" ?>
<NewDataSet>
  <Orders>
    <OrderID>10643</OrderID>
    <CustomerID>ALFKI</CustomerID>
    <ShipName>Alfreds Futterkiste</ShipName>
    <OrderAddress>Obere Str. 57, Berlin, , 12209, Germany</OrderAddress>
    <OrderDate>1997-08-25T00:00:00.0000000+01:00</OrderDate>
    <ShippedDate>1997-09-02T00:00:00.0000000+01:00</ShippedDate>
    <CompanyName>Speedy Express</CompanyName>
  </Orders>
  <Orders>
    ... etc ...
  </Orders>
  <OrderLines>
    <OrderID>10643</OrderID>
    <ProductName>Rössle Sauerkraut</ProductName>
    <QuantityPerUnit>25 - 825 g cans</QuantityPerUnit>
    <UnitPrice>45.6</UnitPrice>
    <Quantity>15</Quantity>
```

```
      <Discount>0.25</Discount>
      <LineTotal>682.28997802734375</LineTotal>
    </OrderLines>
    <OrderLines>
      ... etc ...
    </OrderLines>
</NewDataSet>
```

However, if you set the `Nested` property to `True` before you export the XML, you get the child elements nested *within* the parent elements:

```
<?xml version="1.0" ?>
<NewDataSet>
  <Orders>
    <OrderID>10643</OrderID>
    <CustomerID>ALFKI</CustomerID>
    <ShipName>Alfreds Futterkiste</ShipName>
    <OrderAddress>Obere Str. 57, Berlin, , 12209, Germany</OrderAddress>
    <OrderDate>1997-08-25T00:00:00.0000000+01:00</OrderDate>
    <ShippedDate>1997-09-02T00:00:00.0000000+01:00</ShippedDate>
    <CompanyName>Speedy Express</CompanyName>
    <OrderLines>
      <OrderID>10643</OrderID>
      <ProductName>Rössle Sauerkraut</ProductName>
      <QuantityPerUnit>25 - 825 g cans</QuantityPerUnit>
      <UnitPrice>45.6</UnitPrice>
      <Quantity>15</Quantity>
      <Discount>0.25</Discount>
      <LineTotal>682.28997802734375</LineTotal>
    </OrderLines>
    <OrderLines>
      ... etc ...
    </OrderLines>
  </Orders>
  <Orders>
    ... etc ...
  </Orders>
</NewDataSet>
```

This is generally the format you'll find most useful because it allows your XML parser to navigate from an `Orders` element to the appropriate set of linked `OrderLines` elements without having to use the `OrderID` value to find them. It can just get a collection of child elements for the current `<Orders>` element, safe in the knowledge that these are the order lines for this order.

Selecting a Customer

Now that you've seen how the middle tier works in this version, you'll look at the user interface you generate on the client. The first page that appears when the application opens looks identical to the HTML version you saw in the previous chapter, as shown in Figure 6-3. This is intentional—we tried to make all the versions look the same while exploiting the client's capabilities and reducing server load to the greatest possible extent.

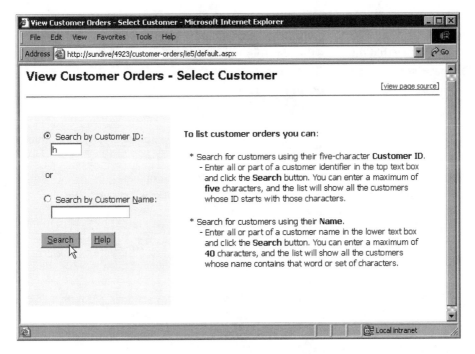

Figure 6-3. The Select Customer page in the XML version

The one difference you'll see is that the Search button is actually disabled (grayed out) when the page first loads, and a "Loading customer list..." message is displayed. This only occurs while the middle tier is fetching the list of all the customers from the data access tier, and the client page is loading this data as an XML document.

The HTML Page Content

The page you see (default.aspx) is created using much the same HTML content as the version demonstrated in the previous chapter. One difference is that you attach a client-side JScript function named loadCustomerList to the <body> element so it runs once the page has been loaded from your server:

```
<body link="#0000ff" alink="#0000ff" vlink="#0000ff"
    onload="loadCustomerList()">
```

The remainder of the page implements a two-column table. The left cell contains the option buttons, text boxes, and a <span> in which status messages display. Notice that this time the controls aren't ASP.NET server controls—there's no runat="server" attribute. You're managing all the processing on the client now, without interacting with or posting back to the server:

```
<form action="">
<table border="0" cellpadding="20">
  <tr><td valign="top" bgcolor="#ffffacd">
    <!-- controls for specifying the required customer ID or name -->
    <input type="radio" id="optByID" name="SearchBy" checked="checked" />
    Search by Customer <u>I</u>D:<br />    
    <input type="text" id="txtCustID" size="5" maxlength="5"
           onkeypress="setCheck('optByID');" accesskey="I" /><p />
      or<p />
    <input type="radio" id="optByName" name="SearchBy" />
    Search by Customer <u>N</u>ame:<br />    
    <input type="text" id="txtCustName" size="20" maxlength="40"
           onkeypress="setCheck('optByName');" accesskey="N" /><p />
    <button id="btnSearch" disabled="true" accesskey="S"
            onclick="doSearch('CustomerID')"><u>S</u>earch</button>
    <button id="btnHelp" accesskey="H"
            onclick="showHelp()"><u>H</u>elp</button><p />
    <span id="lblStatus">Loading customer list - please wait ...</span>
  </td>
    ...
```

In the two text boxes, the onkeypress event handler is just the same as in the HTML version of the application and sets the option buttons to the appropriate values when the user types in the text boxes. The client-side JScript function to implement this is as follows:

```
function setCheck(strName) {
//set radio buttons to correct option as text is typed
  document.forms(0).elements(strName).checked = true;
}
```

Access Keys and Button Captions

You can also see from the HTML listing that you take advantage of some Internet Explorer–specific features to make the page more usable. You specify an accesskey attribute for most of the controls, allowing Alt+*<key>* to be used to switch focus directly to that control. For example, pressing Alt+N moves the input focus to the customer name text box. To make this obvious to the user, you underline the appropriate letter in the caption for this text box:

```
Search by Customer <u>N</u>ame:
<input type="text" id="txtCustName" ... accesskey="N" />
```

You also do the same for the <button> elements, allowing them to be "clicked" with the appropriate Alt+*<key>* combination:

```
<button id="btnSearch" disabled="true" accesskey="S"
        onclick="doSearch('CustomerID')"><u>S</u>earch</button>
```

The Help Text and Results Display Area

The right cell in the table contains only two <div> elements—the first will display the list of matching customers, and the second can display other interactive messages. Both are empty when the page loads, but the second one is used to display the help text once the data has loaded and before a customer search is carried out. You'll see how to do this shortly:

```
  ...
  <td valign="top">
    <div id="divResult"></div><p />

    <!-- label to display interactive messages -->
    <div id="lblMessage"></div>

  </td></tr></table>
</form>
```

Loading the XML Customers List

The first step when the page loads is to fetch the list of all the customers from the middle tier component and then enable the controls on the page. In the client-side script section, you declare a "global" variable to hold an instance of the MSXML parser you'll be using to fetch and cache the data:

```
<script language="JScript">
<!--
var objXMLData;  // to hold reference to XML parser
```

The client-side `loadCustomerList` function runs once the page has been loaded from the server. This function begins by declaring the URL of the middle tier component that exposes the customer data. In this example, this is the ASP.NET page `customer-data.aspx`. Then you can instantiate the MSXML parser object you'll need. You also check that the instantiation succeeded, just in case the client machine doesn't have the correct version of MSXML installed:

```
function loadCustomerList() {
// load a complete list of customers from server

  // create URL and query string to load all customers
  var strURL = 'customer-data.aspx';

  // create a new parser object instance
  try {
    objXMLData = new ActiveXObject('MSXML2.FreeThreadedDOMDocument');
  }
  catch(e) {}

  // check that the parser object is actually available, because
  // appropriate version of MSXML may not be installed on client
  // if not, display error message and exit
  if (objXMLData == null) {
    var strError = '* <b>ERROR: Incorrect XML parser version.</b><br />'
      + 'Sorry, you cannot use this version of the application.';
      document.all('lblStatus').innerHTML = strError;
    return;
  }
  ...
```

You're specifying version 2 of the MSXML parser here, as installed with Internet Explorer 5.01 and higher, and using the free-threaded version. You'll use an XSLT stylesheet that accepts parameters to display the relevant customer data in the page, and for this you must use the free-threaded version. Chapter 4 provides a guide to the different versions of MSXML.

Next, you specify the name of a function (defined elsewhere in the page) as the onreadystatechange property of the parser object. This function will look after checking when the XML has finished loading. You also turn on validation (though in this example you don't have a schema, but you could add one if required) and tell the parser to load the XML asynchronously. This allows the rest of the page rendering to continue, and the user can resize and interact with the page. They can enter the search criteria in the text boxes, but they can't start looking for customers because the Search button is still disabled at this point:

```
...
// connect event with function to check when loading completes
objXMLData.onreadystatechange = changeFunction;

//set properties to validate while loading
objXMLData.validateOnParse = true;
objXMLData.async = true;

// and load the document
objXMLData.load(strURL);
}
```

Checking the ReadyState

The last line of the previous code instructs the parser to start loading the XML document from the middle tier component specified in strURL. As the document loads, the parser raises a series of readystatechange events, indicating that the value of the parser's readyState property has changed. At any point in time this value indicates the loading progress. When the value is 4, either loading is complete or an error occurred while attempting to load the XML. At this point, you can check for an error by examining the properties of the parseError object that's exposed by the parser:

```
function changeFunction() {
// check value of readyState property of XML parser
// value 4 indicates loading complete
```

```
    if (objXMLData.readyState == 4) {
      if (objXMLData.parseError.errorCode != 0)
        // there was an error while loading so display message
        document.all('lblStatus').innerHTML =
          '<b>* ERROR</b> - could not load customer list.';

      else {
        // clear "Loading" message
        document.all('lblStatus').innerHTML = '';

        // enable "Search" button
        document.all('btnSearch').disabled = false;

        // show Help details
        showHelp();
      }
    }
}
```

If you detect an error, you display a suitable message in the `<span>` element
on the page and exit. The Search button will still be disabled, so the user can't continue. If there's no error, you remove the "Loading..." message, enable the Search
button by setting the `disabled` property to `false`, and call the function that displays
the help text.

Displaying the Help Text

The `showHelp` function executes once the XML data has successfully loaded
and also when the user clicks the Help button in the page. All it does is set the
`innerHTML` property of a `<div>` element in the right side of the page:

```
// show help on using page in right part of window
function showHelp() {
  strHelp = '<b>To list customer orders you can</b>:<p />'
    + '  * Search for customers using their five-character "
    +          "<b>Customer ID</b>.<br /> "
    + "      - Enter all or part of a customer identifier in "
    + ... etc ... ;
  document.all('lblMessage').innerHTML = strHelp;
}
```

Finding and Displaying Customer Details

Once the customer data has loaded, you'll immediately see the difference between this and the HTML version of the application. You can use the text boxes to search for customers without a postback to the server occurring—irrespective of how many times you perform a search. It certainly provides a highly responsive and fast user interface. Figure 6-4 shows the result of searching for all customers whose ID starts with *h*.

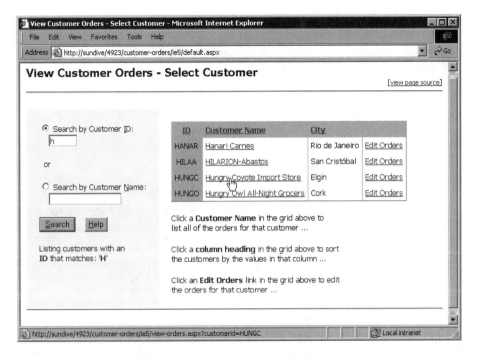

Figure 6-4. Searching for customers whose IDs starts with h

Using an XSLT Stylesheet

Before you look at the function that runs when the Search button is clicked, you'll examine the routine that actually performs the XSLT transformation to generate the list of customers in the right part of the page. Obviously you need an XSLT stylesheet for this, and you'll define this one within the JScript code in the page. You could alternatively load it separately from a disk file on the server, using the same techniques as you did to load the XML document. Although this would make it easier to develop and maintain, and it'd also allow use in more than one application if required, it will require more server connections. In the end, only you can decide which is the most appropriate route to take in your own applications.

This is a section of the XML data document that you'll receive from the server and to which your XSLT stylesheet will be applied:

```
<?xml version="1.0" ?>
<NewDataSet>
  <Customers>
    <CustomerID>ALFKI</CustomerID>
    <CompanyName>Alfreds Futterkiste</CompanyName>
    <City>Berlin</City>
  </Customers>
  <Customers>
    <CustomerID>ANATR</CustomerID>
    <CompanyName>Ana Trujillo Emparedados y helados</CompanyName>
    <City>México D.F.</City>
  </Customers>
  <Customers>
      ... etc ...
  </Customers>
</NewDataSet>
```

The next code listing shows the beginning of the client-side function named getStyledResult. It starts by using the parameters provided to the function to build an XPath string that selects the appropriate customers from the XML document. If all or part of the ID is provided, then it uses that. Otherwise, it uses the partial customer name (users can't specify both). The XPath that's created specifies either of the following:

- All of the descendants of the current node (the root element <NewDataSet> of the document) that are <Customers> elements and that have a child element named <CustomerID> whose value starts with the character string in the custid parameter that you'll provide when you execute the transformation

- All of the descendants of the current node (the root element <NewDataSet> of the document) that are <Customers> elements and that have a child element named <CompanyName> whose value contains the character string in the custname parameter that you'll provide when you execute the transformation

This sounds complicated, but in essence it'll mean that only the <Customers> nodes that match the search criteria will be included in the results to which the stylesheet applies its formatting.

Creating the XPath Statements

So here, as promised, is the code fragment showing the first few lines of the getStyledResult method, in which you express the previous in XPath syntax:

```
function getStyledResult(strCustID, strCustName, strSortOrder) {
// returns the result of applying an XSLT transformation to the
// customer list as a string containing the HTML to display

  // create the XPath required by the style sheet
  if (strCustID.length > 0)
    var strXPath = 'descendant::Customers[starts-with(child::CustomerID,'
              + '$custid)]'
  else
    var strXPath = 'descendant::Customers[contains(child::CompanyName,'
              + '$custname)]';
  ...
```

> **NOTE** *One issue with using the version of the MSXML parser we chose for this application is that you can't easily do case-insensitive searches using the XSLT* contains *function. You could use the* translate *function to convert the XPath arguments to uppercase, but you can't nest this inside the* contains *function. If you confine your code to running on later parser versions, in particular version 3, you can write script functions within the stylesheet to convert values into all uppercase or all lowercase for the comparison. And, in version 4, you can take advantage of the Microsoft-specific* string-compare *function.*

The XSLT Stylesheet

Next comes the code that creates the stylesheet. Notice the `<xsl:param>` elements that define the parameters you'll provide when you execute the transformation. The body of the stylesheet contains a template that matches the root of the document (`<xsl:template match="/">`), and this creates the outline for the HTML table you're building to display the results. After defining the table heading row, you use an `<xsl:for-each>` element with the XPath you created earlier to create each table row, and within this you sort the matching customer elements with an `<xsl:sort>` element that uses the sort order passed to the function in the variable strSortOrder:

```
  ...
  // specify the appropriate stylesheet
  var strStyle = '<?xml version="1.0" ?>\n'
    + '<xsl:stylesheet xmlns:xsl="http://www.w3.org/1999/XSL/Transform"'
```

```
+ '                    version="1.0">\n'
+ ' <xsl:param name="custid" />\n'
+ ' <xsl:param name="custname" />\n'
+ ' <xsl:template match="/">\n'
+ '   <table id="tblCustomers" cellspacing="0" cellpadding="5"\n'
+ '   rules="cols" border="1" style="border-collapse:collapse;">\n'
+ '    <tr style="background-color:silver;">\n'
+ '     <td align="center">\n'
+ '       <a href="javascript:doSearch(\'CustomerID\')"><b>ID</b></a>\n'
+ '     </td>\n'
+ '     <td align="left">\n'
+ '       <a href="javascript:doSearch(\'CompanyName\')"><b>Customer'
+ '         Name</b></a>\n'
+ '     </td>\n'
+ '     <td align="left">\n'
+ '       <a href="javascript:doSearch(\'City\')"><b>City</b></a>\n'
+ '     </td>\n'
+ '     <td></td>\n'
+ '    </tr>\n'
+ '    <xsl:for-each select="' + strXPath + '">\n'
+ '     <xsl:sort select="' + strSortOrder + '" data-type="text"'
+ '               order="ascending" />\n'
+ '     <tr>\n'
+ '      <td align="center" style="background-color:#add8e6;">\n'
+ '       <xsl:value-of select="CustomerID" />\n'
+ '      </td>\n'
+ '      <td align="left">\n'
+ '       <a>\n'
+ '         <xsl:attribute name="href">\n'
+ '          view-orders.aspx?customerid=<xsl:value-of'
+ '                          select="CustomerID" />\n'
+ '         </xsl:attribute>\n'
+ '         <xsl:value-of select="CompanyName" />\n'
+ '       </a>\n'
+ '      </td>\n'
+ '      <td align="left">\n'
+ '       <xsl:value-of select="City" />\n'
+ '      </td>\n'
+ '      <td align="left">\n'
+ '       <a>\n'
+ '         <xsl:attribute name="href">\n'
+ '          ../../update-orders/ie5/edit-orders.aspx?customerid='
+ '                           '<xsl:value-of select="CustomerID" />\n'
+ '         </xsl:attribute>\n'
+ '         Edit Orders\n'
+ '       </a>\n'
+ '      </td>\n'
```

```
      + '        </tr>\n'
      + '      </xsl:for-each>\n'
      + '    </table>\n'
      + '  </xsl:template>\n'
      + '</xsl:stylesheet>';
  ...
```

> **NOTE** *If you aren't familiar with the use of XSLT for transforming XML documents, we recommend learning more about this technology. It's extremely powerful and is increasingly being used in application development today.*

Performing the Transformation

Now that you have a suitable stylesheet in the variable strStyle, you can use it to transform your XML customer list data. For this you need to create a second free-threaded MSXML parser instance and load the stylesheet into it. Because the stylesheet is a string in this case, you use the loadXML method of the parser (instead of the load method you used earlier to fetch the XML from a remote location):

```
...
// create a new parser object instance
var objXMLStyle = new ActiveXObject('MSXML2.FreeThreadedDOMDocument');

// load the stylesheet as a string
objXMLStyle.loadXML(strStyle);
...
```

Next, you create an instance of an MSXML XSLTemplate object and specify the parser instance you just created as its stylesheet property. From this XSLTemplate, you can create an XSLProcessor object by calling the createProcessor method:

```
...
// create a new XSLTemplate object and set stylesheet
var objTemplate = new ActiveXObject('MSXML2.XSLTemplate');
objTemplate.stylesheet = objXMLStyle;

// create a processor to handle the parameters
var objProc = objTemplate.createProcessor();
...
```

It's the `XSLProcessor` that will actually carry out the transformation, and you have to tell it which XML document you want it to process by specifying the original MSXML parser object as the `input` property. Then you can add the two parameters to the processor by specifying their name and value. The values come from the two variables named `strCustID` and `strCustName` that you provided as parameters to the `getStyledResult` function you're looking at:

```
...
// specify the XML parser to use
objProc.input = objXMLData;

// set the parameter values
objProc.addParameter('custid', strCustID);
objProc.addParameter('custname', strCustName);
...
```

Finally, you can perform the transformation and see if it succeeded without error. If it did, you return the result as a string from the `output` property of the processor. If not, you return an empty string:

```
  ...
  // perform transformation and set value of string to return
  if (objProc.transform() == true)
    var strResult = objProc.output
  else
    var strResult = '';
  return strResult;
}
```

The Client-Side doSearch Function

At last you come to the code that runs when the user clicks the Search button in the page. You start by collecting the value of the customer ID or name criteria from the appropriate text box, depending on which option is selected, and display a message indicating the criteria you're using:

```
function doSearch(strSortOrder) {
// display the list of matching customers in the page

  var strCustID = '';
  var strCustName = '';
```

```
// get one or other value from text boxes depending on selection
if (document.all('optByID').checked) {
  strCustID = document.all('txtCustID').value.toUpperCase();
  var msg = "Listing customers with ID that matches: '" + strCustID + "'";
}
else {
  strCustName = document.all('txtCustName').value;
  var msg = "Listing customers whose Name contains: '" + strCustName + "'";
}
document.all('lblStatus').innerHTML = msg;
...
```

Now you can call the getStyledResult function you've just been looking at.
You need to pass in the customer ID and name parameters (one will be an empty
string), as well as the "sort order" parameter. This is obtained from the strSortOrder
parameter to this (doSearch) function. The HTML you used to create the Search
button originally was this:

```
<button ... onclick="doSearch('CustomerID')"><u>S</u>earch</button>
```

So, when the user clicks the Search button, the value of strSortOrder will be
CustomerID, and the output will be sorted by the values in that column of the
results. After calling the getStyledResult function, you can check if there was an
error (the returned string will be empty). If not, you display the resulting string in
the <div> element named divResult on the right side of the page. You also display a
suitable message in the <div> element named lblMessage, which is below this in
the right side of the page:

```
...
// get the result of transforming the XML into a string for display
// uses customer ID or name as a parameter to select matching nodes
var strResult = getStyledResult(strCustID, strCustName, strSortOrder);
if (strResult.length > 0) {
  document.all('divResult').innerHTML = strResult;
  msg = 'Click a <b>Customer Name</b> in the grid above to'
      + '<br /> list all of the orders for that customer ...'
      + '... etc ...';
}
else {
  msg = 'No matching customers found in database ...';
}
document.all('lblMessage').innerHTML = msg;
}
```

And to prove all this stuff works, Figure 6-5 shows the result of searching for customers whose ID starts with *h*.

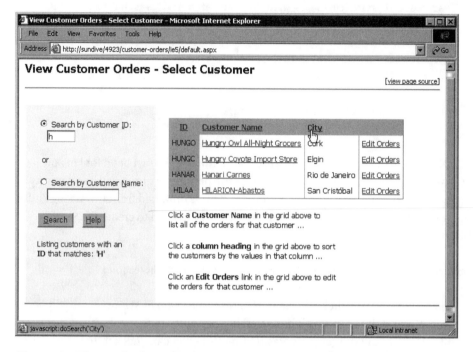

Figure 6-5. The result of searching for customers whose ID starts with h

Sorting and Paging the Customer List

You've already seen how this version of the application adds some useful extra features to the page, such as the use of Alt+*<key>* access keys and the enabling and disabling of buttons. There's one other feature that's useful and that's easy and efficient to provide in a rich-client application such as this.

Each column heading in the list of customers is a hyperlink (as you can see from Figure 6-5), and clicking it sorts the table by the values in that column. You implement this feature within the XSLT stylesheet that creates the table. Each column heading is defined as an `<a>` element, with the `href` attribute defined as a JavaScript function:

```
<a href="javascript:doSearch('CompanyName')"><b>Customer Name</b></a>
```

This simply calls the doSearch function again, with the appropriate sort order specified as the parameter (the backslashes you see in the previous listing of the stylesheet are simply there to escape the apostrophe characters at the start and end of the string value CompanyName).

Of course, you could implement this feature easily in the HTML versions, using the built-in features of the DataGrid server control. If you set the AllowSorting property of a DataGrid control to True and specify an event handler for the OnSortCommand property, the column headings are rendered as hyperlinks. You then use code in the event handler to sort the data source for the grid into the appropriate order. However, this requires a postback to the server every time, whereas the client-side version allows users to search for customers and sort the results without ever having to go back to the server.

One other feature that you haven't implemented is *paging*—splitting the results into several pages as you did in the HTML version of the application. It was easy to do using the built-in features of the DataGrid control, but it requires a lot more work when you're creating the output through XSLT.

Probably an easier technique to implement, if you expect there to be a large number of rows in the resulting tables, is to use CSS absolute positioning and scroll bars. Specify a fixed size for the <div> element that contains the table, and add the overflow=scroll style selector to force scroll bars to appear.

Selecting an Order

The Select Customer page you looked at in the previous section displays the name of each matching customer in the table as a hyperlink. This is created by the XSLT stylesheet you used, which resolves to the following:

```
<a>
  <xsl:attribute name="href">
    view-orders.aspx?customerid=<xsl:value-of select="CustomerID" />
  </xsl:attribute>
  <xsl:value-of select="CompanyName" />
</a>
```

The result is a normal hyperlink <a> element. For example, if the customer ID is ALFKI, then the HTML that the stylesheet creates is this:

```
<a href="view-orders.aspx?customerid=ALFKI">Alfreds Futterkiste</a>
```

This link loads the second page in the application, view-orders.aspx, passing the customer ID to it in the query string. There's also a link with the text Edit Orders in each row of the table, generated in much the same way. For example, the HTML that the stylesheet creates for the same customer is this:

```
<a href="../../update-orders/ie5/edit-orders.aspx?customerid=ALFKI">
  Edit Orders
</a>
```

You'll see how you edit orders in Chapter 11. For the meantime, you'll see how you display orders and order details in the view-orders.aspx page.

The HTML Page Content

The page view-orders.aspx is almost the same in appearance as its equivalent in the HTML version of the application demonstrated in the previous chapter. However, this time you have no need for a frameset because you can easily display both tables of results (the list of orders and the details of the selected order) in one page. Neither do you need to post back to the server every time the user selects a different order because all the data for all the orders for the current customer are contained in the XML document that the middle tier page (order-data.aspx) exposes.

So, the HTML definition for this page contains a simple two-column table with a selection of <span> and <div> elements where you'll display status and information messages, and the results of applying an XSLT stylesheet to the XML document containing the order data:

```
<body link="#0000ff" alink="#0000ff" vlink="#0000ff" onload="loadOrderList()">
  ...
  <table border="0" cellpadding="20">
    <tr><td valign="top" bgcolor="#fffacd">

      <!-- label to display customer ID -->
      <span id="lblStatus">Loading order data, please wait...</span><p />

      <div id="divOrderList"></div><p />

      <!-- label to display interactive messages -->
      <span id="lblMessage"></span>

    </td><td valign="top">

    <!-- controls to display order details -->
    <span id="lblOrderDetail">
      Select an order from the first column in the list
      shown on the left to display the order details.
    </span><p />
    <div id="divOrderLines"></div><p />
    <span id="lblOrderTotal"></span>

    </td></tr>
  </table>
  ...
```

Notice that the first <span> element, in the left part of the page, displays the message "Loading order data…" when the page is first displayed. Once the page itself has finished loading, the onload attribute in the opening <body> tag will cause the client-side function loadOrderList to execute. This loads all the order data for the customer selected by the user in the previous page and displays a list of their orders in the left part of this page. It also removes the "Loading…" message and displays the help text below the order list, as shown in Figure 6-6.

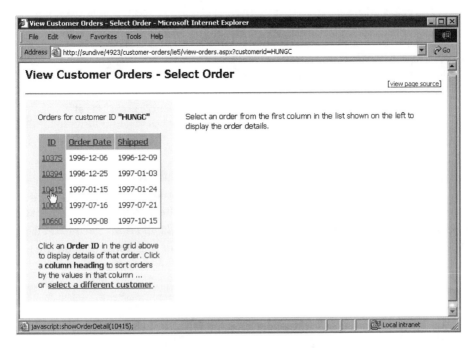

Figure 6-6. Displaying the list of orders and the help text

Loading the XML Orders List

You load the XML data from the middle tier in much the same way as you did the customer data in the previous page. You have two "global" variables to hold a reference to the parser object and the ID of the currently selected customer:

```
var objXMLData;  // to hold reference to XML parser
var strCustID;   // ID of the customer to view orders for
```

When the page has finished loading, the loadOrderList function first collects the customer ID from the query string and checks that one was actually provided.

If not, you can't show any orders and so you just display a suitable message and exit from the function:

```
function loadOrderList() {
// load a list of orders for this customer from server

  // get the customer ID from the query string
  strID = new String(window.location.search);

  strCustID = strID.substring(strID.indexOf('=') + 1, strID.length);

  if (strCustID == '') {
    // display error message
    document.all('lblStatus').innerHTML =
      '* ERROR: no Customer ID provided.<br /> You must '
      + '<a href="default.aspx"><b>select a customer</b></a> first.';
  }
  ...
```

If you did get a customer ID, you create the URL of the middle tier component, adding the customer ID to the query string so that the correct order details are returned, and you create the parser instance. You checked in the previous page that the client has the correct parser version installed, so you don't need to do it again here. Then you can set the properties of the parser as before and load the XML data from the middle tier:

```
  ...
  else {
    // create URL and query string to load all orders for this customer
    var strURL = 'order-data.aspx?customerid=' + strCustID;

    // create a new parser object instance
    objXMLData = new ActiveXObject('MSXML2.FreeThreadedDOMDocument');

    // connect event with function to check when loading completes
    objXMLData.onreadystatechange = changeFunction;

    //set properties to validate while loading
    objXMLData.validateOnParse = true;
    objXMLData.async = true;

    // and load the document
    objXMLData.load(strURL);
  }
}
```

As in the previous page, the check for completion of the XML load process is handled by a function named changeFunction. It displays any error that might have occurred. If all went well, it changes the status message in the page and then calls a function named showOrderList to display the list of orders for this customer:

```
function changeFunction() {
// check value of readyState property of XML parser
// value 4 indicates loading complete

  if (objXMLData.readyState == 4) {
    if (objXMLData.parseError.errorCode != 0) {
      // there was an error while loading so display message
      document.all('lblStatus').innerHTML =
        '<b>* ERROR</b> - could not load order list.';

    }
    else {
      // replace "Loading" message with customer ID
      document.all('lblStatus').innerHTML =
        'Orders for customer ID <b>"' + strCustID + '"</b>';

      // display list of matching orders in left-hand table
      showOrderList('OrderID');
    }
  }
}
```

Finding and Displaying the Order Details

The function showOrderList just has to call another function in the page named getStyledResult and display the results. Notice how, again, the value for the sort order is passed into the function. If nothing is returned from the getStyledResult function, an error has occurred, and a suitable message is displayed instead:

```
function showOrderList(strSortOrder) {
// display the list of orders in the left-hand table

  // get result of transforming XML into a string for display
  var strResult = getStyledResult(false, '', strSortOrder);

  if (strResult.length > 0) {
    document.all('divOrderList').innerHTML = strResult;
    var msg = 'Click an <b>Order ID</b> in the grid above<br />'
            + 'to display details of that order. Click<br />'
```

```
                + ' ... etc ...';
    }
    else
      var msg = 'No orders found for this customer ...<br />'
                + '<a href="default.aspx">Select a different customer</a>';
    document.all('lblMessage').innerHTML = msg;
}
```

Processing the XSLT Stylesheet

You'll recognize the name `getStyledResult` because there was a similar function in the `default.aspx` page earlier. As in that page, the task of this function is to create an XSLT stylesheet and use it to transform the XML data into a string that represents an HTML table—this time containing a list of orders for the current customer. However, you also have to be able to transform the order line details into a separate table (in the right part of the page). But this will require a different stylesheet, so this `getStyledResult` function accepts a couple of extra parameters. The first is set to `true` to get a stylesheet for the order line details or `false` for a stylesheet that creates the list of orders. The second parameter is the order ID, which you pass only if you're creating the order line details table:

```
function getStyledResult(blnOrderDetail, strOrderID, strSortOrder) {
// returns the result of applying an XSLT transformation to the
// orders list as a string containing the HTML to display

  if (blnOrderDetail == false)
    var strStyle = getOrdersStyleSheet(strSortOrder)
  else
    var strStyle = getOrderLinesStyleSheet();
  ...
```

So, depending on the values of the parameters, this function will call either the `getOrdersStyleSheet` function and provide the sort order as the single parameter or the `getOrderLinesStyleSheet`. The stylesheet you use to generate the list of order lines uses an XSLT parameter to specify the order ID (as you'll see later), so no parameters are required in the function call.

Once you've got the appropriate stylesheet back from one of these functions (in the case of the list of orders that you're looking at now, this is the `getOrdersStyleSheet` function), you can use the same code as you did in the previous page to perform the transformation. The only difference is that the order ID parameter will be an empty string when you're just listing the orders, but this doesn't affect the transformation because the stylesheet for the order list doesn't contain the parameter definition:

```
...
... create XSLTemplate and XSLProcessor objects as in default.aspx ...
...

// set the parameter value
objProc.addParameter('orderid', strOrderID);

// perform transformation and set value of string to return
if (objProc.transform() == true)
  var strResult = objProc.output
else
  var strResult = '';
return strResult;
}
```

The XSLT Stylesheet for the Order List

The stylesheet you use to transform the XML for the order list is the same in principle as you used to transform the customer list data. Depending on the value of the sort order parameter, you generate two values to use in the stylesheet for sorting the results:

```
function getOrdersStyleSheet(strSortOrder) {
  // build stylesheet to transform XML document to display orders list

  // decide how to sort the values
  if (strSortOrder == 'OrderID') {
    strDataType = 'number';
    strAscDesc = 'ascending'
  }
  else {
    strDataType = 'text';
    strAscDesc = 'descending';
  }
  ...
```

Then you can simply return a string containing the stylesheet itself. You can see that, like the list of customers, each column heading is a hyperlink that just calls the showOrderList function again with the appropriate column name as the sort order parameter. The sorting of the list is carried out by an <xsl:sort> element, and the three variables (the sort column, sort order, and data type) are used to set the select, order and data-type attributes of this element:

```
...
return '<?xml version="1.0" ?>\n'
  + '<xsl:stylesheet xmlns:xsl="http://www.w3.org/1999/XSL/Transform"'
  + '                version="1.0">\n'
```

```
+ '  <xsl:template match="/">\n'
+ '   <table id="tblOrders" cellspacing="0" cellpadding="5"\n'
+ '          rules="cols" border="1" style="border-collapse:collapse;">\n'
+ '    <tr style="background-color:silver;">\n'
+ '     <td align="center" nowrap="nowrap">\n'
+ '       <a href="javascript:showOrderList(\'OrderID\')">ID</a>\n'
+ '     </td>\n'
+ '     <td align="left" nowrap="nowrap">\n'
+ '       <a href="javascript:showOrderList(\'OrderDate\')">'
+ '         Order Date</a>\n'
+ '     </td>\n'
+ '     <td align="left" nowrap="nowrap">\n'
+ '       <a href="javascript:showOrderList(\'ShippedDate\')">'
+ '         Shipped</b></a>\n'
+ '     </td>\n'
+ '    </tr>\n'
+ '    <xsl:for-each select="//Orders">\n'
+ '    <xsl:sort select="' + strSortOrder + '"'
+ '         order="' + strAscDesc + '" data-type="' + strDataType + '" />\n'
+ '     <tr>\n'
+ '      <td align="center" style="background-color:#add8e6;">\n'
+ '        <a>\n'
+ '         <xsl:attribute name="href">\n'
+ '          javascript:showOrderDetail(<xsl:value-of'
+ '                               select="OrderID" />);\n'
+ '         </xsl:attribute>\n'
+ '         <xsl:value-of select="OrderID" />\n'
+ '        </a>\n'
+ '      </td>\n'
+ '      <td align="left" nowrap="nowrap"\n'
+ '          style="background-color:#ffffff;">\n'
+ '       <xsl:value-of select="substring(OrderDate,1,10)" />\n'
+ '      </td>\n'
+ '      <td align="left" nowrap="nowrap"\n'
+ '          style="background-color:#ffffff;">\n'
+ '       <xsl:value-of select="substring(ShippedDate,1,10)" />\n'
+ '      </td>\n'
+ '     </tr>\n'
+ '    </xsl:for-each>\n'
+ '   </table>\n'
+ '  </xsl:template>\n'
+ '</xsl:stylesheet>';
}
```

Each row in the resulting table contains a hyperlink that points to a client-side function named showOrderDetail and that specifies the order ID for that row. The resolved section of the stylesheet that creates this hyperlink is as follows:

```
<a>
  <xsl:attribute name="href">
    javascript:showOrderDetail(<xsl:value-of select="OrderID" />)
  </xsl:attribute>
  <xsl:value-of select="OrderID" />
</a>
```

So, for order number 10415, this will produce the following HTML <a> element:

```
<a href="javascript:showOrderDetail(10415)>10415</a>
```

Clicking this will then display the details of this order in the right part of the window, as you'll see next.

Viewing Order Details

Figure 6-7 shows the page when order number 10415 has been selected. You can see that you have, in the right section of the page, details of the order, details of each item on the order, and the total value.

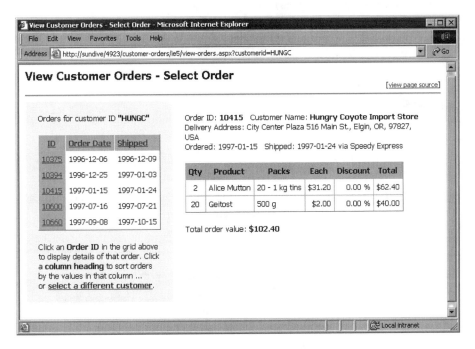

Figure 6-7. Displaying the details for order number 10415

Extracting the Order Details

All this is created by the showOrderDetail function that executes when an order in the left part of the page is selected. The function first gets the shipping details by using XML DOM methods against the instance of the XML parser that's holding the XML orders data. The code declares an XPath query that specifies the selected order and uses this in the selectSingleNode method of the parser object to get a reference to the correct <Orders> node. Then it can extract the details of the order from the child elements of that node:

```
function showOrderDetail(strOrderID) {
// display the list of the order lines in right table

  // get the details of the order to display above table
  // using DOM methods from the current XML parser object
  var strXPath = '//Orders[OrderID="' + strOrderID + '"]'
  var objOrderNode = objXMLData.selectSingleNode(strXPath);
  var strThisOrderID = objOrderNode.childNodes[0].text;
  var strThisCustName = objOrderNode.childNodes[2].text;
  var strThisAddress = objOrderNode.childNodes[3].text;
  var strThisOrdered = objOrderNode.childNodes[4].text;
  // if ShippedDate is null in database, node will not
  // appear in XML so check next node name
  if (objOrderNode.childNodes[5].nodeName == 'ShippedDate') {
    var strThisShipped = objOrderNode.childNodes[5].text;
    var strThisVia = objOrderNode.childNodes[6].text;
  }
  else {
    var strThisShipped = '';
    var strThisVia = objOrderNode.childNodes[5].text;
  }
  ...
```

Now you can build a string containing the details of the order and display it in the first <span> element in the right part of the page:

```
...
var strDetail = 'Order ID: <b>' + strThisOrderID + '</b>'
    + '   Customer Name: <b>' + strThisCustName +  '</b><br />'
    + 'Delivery Address: ' + strThisAddress + '<br />'
    + 'Ordered: ' + strThisOrdered.substring(0, 10) + '   ';
if (strThisShipped == '')
  strDetail += 'Awaiting shipping'
else
  strDetail += 'Shipped: ' + strThisShipped.substring(0, 10);
```

```
strDetail += ' via ' + strThisVia;
document.all('lblOrderDetail').innerHTML = strDetail;
...
```

Next, you call the same getStyledResult function that you used to get the list of orders earlier, but now you pass it the value true to indicate that you want to process the *order line* details, and you also pass in the selected order ID. You assign the result to the <div> element in the right part of the page:

```
...
// get result of transforming XML into a string and display it
var strResult = getStyledResult(true, strOrderID, '');
document.all('divOrderLines').innerHTML = strResult;
...
```

Finally, you can calculate the total order value. You use the selectNodes method to get a reference to all the <OrderLines> element nodes for the current order and iterate through these elements summing the value of the seventh child node (indexed as 6 because the node indices start at zero). Once you've got the total, you convert it to a currency-style string and display it underneath the table of order lines:

```
  ...
  // get the order total by iterating the OrderLines nodes
  var objOrderLines = objOrderNode.selectNodes('OrderLines');
  var dblTotal = new Number(0);
  for (i = 0; i < objOrderLines.length; i++) {
    dblTotal += parseFloat(objOrderLines[i].childNodes[6].text);
  }

  // format it with two decimal places and display it
  var strTotal = dblTotal.toString();
  if (strTotal.indexOf('.') < 0) strTotal += '.';
  strTotal += '00';
  var msg = 'Total order value: <b>$'
    + strTotal.substring(0, strTotal.indexOf('.') + 3) + '</b>';
  document.all('lblOrderTotal').innerHTML = msg;
}
```

The only thing you haven't seen is the stylesheet you use to transform the order line details in the XML data to create the HTML table in the right part of the page. The techniques are, as you'd expect, similar to the previous examples. You create a string that represents the XPath required to select the appropriate order lines first and then build the string containing the stylesheet. You can see the dec-laration of the single parameter named `orderid` that you use with this stylesheet in the `<xsl:param>` element:

```
function getOrderLinesStyleSheet() {
  // build a style sheet that transforms the XML document
  // to display a list of order lines given the OrderID

  // create the XPath required by the style sheet
  var strXPath = 'descendant::OrderLines[descendant::OrderID=$orderid]';

  return '<?xml version="1.0" ?>\n'
    + '<xsl:stylesheet xmlns:xsl="http://www.w3.org/1999/XSL/Transform"'
    + '                version="1.0">\n'
    + '  <xsl:param name="orderid" />\n'
    + '  <xsl:template match="/">\n'
    + '    <table id="tblOrderLines" cellspacing="0" cellpadding="5"\n'
    + '           border="1" style="border-collapse:collapse;">\n'
    + '      <tr style="background-color:silver;">\n'
    + '        <td align="center"><b>Qty</b></td>\n'
    + '        <td align="center"><b>Product</b></td>\n'
    + '        <td align="center"><b>Packs</b></td>\n'
    + '        <td align="center"><b>Each</b></td>\n'
    + '        <td align="center"><b>Discount</b></td>\n'
    + '        <td align="center"><b>Total</b></td>\n'
    + '      </tr>\n'
    + '      <xsl:for-each select="' + strXPath + '">\n'
    + '        <tr>\n'
    + '          <td align="center">\n'
    + '            <xsl:value-of select="Quantity" />\n'
    + '          </td>\n'
    + '          <td align="left">\n'
    + '            <xsl:value-of select="ProductName" />\n'
    + '          </td>\n'
    + '          <td align="left">\n'
    + '            <xsl:value-of select="QuantityPerUnit" />\n'
    + '          </td>\n'
    + '          <td align="right" nowrap="nowrap">\n'
    + '            $<xsl:value-of'
    + '                select="format-number(UnitPrice,\'#,##0.00\')" />\n'
    + '          </td>\n'
    + '          <td align="right" nowrap="nowrap">\n'
    + '            <xsl:value-of'
```

```
+ '                    select="format-number(Discount,\'#0.00\%')" />\n'
+ '            </td>\n'
+ '            <td align="right" nowrap="nowrap">\n'
+ '              $<xsl:value-of'
+ '                    select="format-number(LineTotal,\'#,##0.00\')" />\n'
+ '            </td>\n'
+ '          </tr>\n'
+ '        </xsl:for-each>\n'
+ '      </table>\n'
+ '  </xsl:template>\n'
+ '</xsl:stylesheet>';
}
```

The only other thing to notice here is how you format the contents of the last three columns in the table using the XSLT format-number function within the stylesheet. These columns are the UnitPrice, Discount, and LineTotal columns. And, as in previous examples, you specify the currency symbol you want rather than depending on the locale of the server to generate one for you.

Using Web Services in Internet Explorer 5 and Higher

The second example in which you use XML with rich clients is based on data exposed as a Web Service. Figure 6-8 shows this version of the application in outline—if you compare this with the outline schematic for the previous example, you'll see that the key differences are in the right side of the figure.

You use the same data access component as all the other versions, but this time you have a middle tier that's implemented as a Web Service. It provides two methods, GetCustomers and GetOrders. These methods use the two methods of the data access component to retrieve the data from the database and expose it to the client via HTTP in standard SOAP format.

On the client, other than for the interaction with the Web Service, the code is pretty much the same as the code you used in the previous example. Because the data exposed by the two methods of the Web Service is in the form of XML documents, the same client-side data manipulation techniques will work in this version of the application.

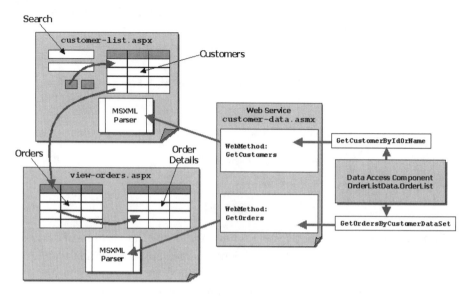

Figure 6-8. The Web Service version of the application

Looking at the Customer Data Web Service

When you first open the application from the main Customer Order List Application menu, a page of information displays before the main application starts, as shown in Figure 6-9.

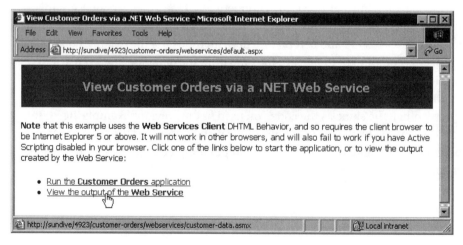

Figure 6-9. The menu page for Web Service version of the application

The first link in this page launches the application proper, but you'll briefly explore the second link first. It points directly to the middle-tier "component" for this version of the application—an ASP.NET Web Service page named `customer-data.asmx`.

When you open a Web Service (`.asmx` page) directly, ASP.NET automatically creates a series of information screens that describe and allow you to interact with the Web Service. In the first page is a link to the Service Description. It's just the same URL as you used to display this page, but with `?WSDL` appended as the query string. You can see this in the status bar shown in Figure 6-10.

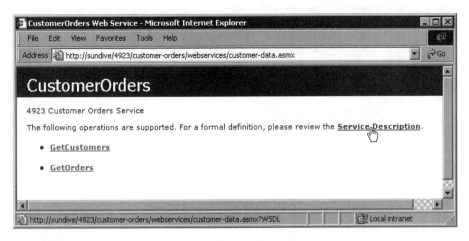

Figure 6-10. The Service Description link showing the query string

This standard technique for retrieving the service description is key to using Web Services. The Web Service's response to this request is an XML document that describes the features provided by the service, the functions it contains, the parameters, the return values, and the data types it uses. This is sometimes referred to as a *SOAP contract* (as with WML clients, Web Services provide plenty of opportunity for really bad puns). We haven't shown the WSDL document here— there's a lot of it and it's fairly predictable, but you can view it by clicking the link shown in Figure 6-10 (if you're running these examples locally) or from the online examples at `http://www.daveandal.com/books/4923/customer-orders/webservices/customer-data.asmx?WSDL`.

Testing a Web Service

You can use the other two links in the page to test the two functions that the Web Service implements. The first, GetCustomers, takes two string parameters and returns a list of customers that match the customer ID or name that you enter, as shown in Figure 6-11.

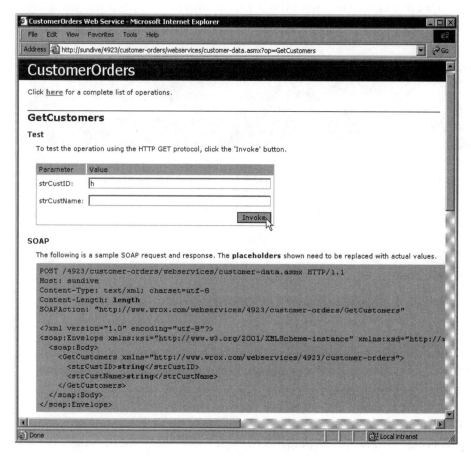

Figure 6-11. Testing the GetCustomers *Web Service method*

In Figure 6-11, you can also see part of the SOAP request and response definition for the Web Service. All this is created automatically by ASP.NET from the Service Description document (the WSDL document). Figure 6-12 shows the response to executing the GetOrders method with the partial customer ID *h* as the first parameter.

Figure 6-12. The result of executing the GetOrders *method*

NOTE *Remember that you have to specify the connection string for your database in the* web.config *file when you run this example on your own machine.*

Notice that the returned XML document contains an inline XML schema. You can also see that the response data type is a DataSet (in the second line) and that the data content (the <NewDataSet> section) is wrapped within a <diffgr:diffgram> element.

You'll look at *diffgrams* in more detail in later chapters, when you update the original data from within your applications. For the time being, it's enough to know that a diffgram is a data format that can contain more than one value for each item—allowing it to include the original and current values of each item after it has been edited.

Building the Middle Tier

Now you'll learn how to use the data from your Web Service to power this version of your application. The main differences are in the middle tier and in the way you access the Web Service and load the data on the client. You'll look at the middle tier first.

As we've said, an ASP.NET "page" named `customer-data.asmx` implements the Web Service you're using in this example. Web Service "pages" are actually class definitions, and they start with a `WebService` directive rather than the ASP.NET `Page` directive. You also have to import all the .NET Framework namespaces you'll need because none are imported by default into a Web Service.

In the following code, you can see the `Imports` statements for the data access component named `OrderListData`, as well as those for the other required classes from the `System`, `System.Data`, and `System.Web` namespaces. You also import the namespace `System.Web.Services` (it contains the classes that actually implement the features of a Web Service) and `System.Configuration` (which allows you to access configuration data in `web.config`):

```
<%@WebService Language="VB" Class="CustomerOrders"%>

Imports OrderListData
Imports System
Imports System.Data
Imports System.Web
Imports System.Web.Services
Imports System.Configuration
...
```

You can now start to define the class that'll implement the Web Service and declare the two methods you need to power your application. You start with the `Class` definition. Notice that you have to *decorate it* (this is the correct technical term!) by adding a `WebService` attribute. You can optionally specify a description for the service—you saw this description earlier in Figure 6-10 where you accessed the Web Service directly. And you should also *always* provide a unique namespace for the service if it'll be exposed publicly on the Internet. A unique namespace allows UDDI and other techniques to identify the methods unambiguously in cases where other Web Services expose methods with the same name:

```
<WebService(Description:="4923 Customer Orders Service", _
 Namespace:="http://www.daveandal.com/webservices/customer-orders" _
 )> Public Class CustomerOrders
...
```

> **NOTE** *Note the unusual syntax of these attributes in Visual Basic .NET, with a colon before the equals sign. In C# you use a different syntax for the attributes— they're enclosed in square brackets rather than the < and > that VB.NET uses and omit the colon before the equals sign.*

The GetCustomers Method

Inside the class, you define the two methods you'll be exposing. The first returns a list of customers from the database, depending on the values provided for the customer ID and customer name parameters. In effect, it's identical to the function you used in earlier examples. Note, however, that you have to decorate the Function statement with the <WebMethod> attribute to indicate that this method is to be made available through the Web Service:

```
...
<WebMethod> Public Function GetCustomers(strCustID As String, _
                                  strCustName As String) As DataSet
'use data access component to get DataSet containing matching customers

  Try
    'get connection string from web.config <appSettings> section
    Dim strConnect As String
    strConnect = ConfigurationSettings.AppSettings("NorthwindConnectString")

    'create an instance of the data access component
    Dim objOrderList As New OrderList(strConnect)

    'call the method to return the data as a DataSet
    Return objOrderList.GetCustomerByIdOrName(strCustID, strCustName)

  Catch objErr As Exception
    'there was an error so no data is returned
    Return Nothing

  End Try

End Function
...
```

> **NOTE** *Public functions that you declare without the* <WebMethod> *attribute will not be available to clients through the Web Service. You can also add a description for each Web Service method if required, using the same syntax as in the* Class *declaration you saw earlier.*

Notice that you don't need to access the DataSet and extract the XML content as you did in the previous example. Of course, there's no reason why you can't extract and return the XML as a string, but you might as well take advantage of the features of Web Services that allow you to return the object as the appropriate data type—in this case, a DataSet. If you were using a different type of client (for example, a .NET Windows Forms application), it would be able to make use of the data as a DataSet object.

The GetOrders Method

The GetOrders method of the Web Service is also extremely similar to that of the other application versions you've looked at so far. In fact, the only difference is that you decorate the method with the <WebMethod> attribute. We've highlighted this difference in bold from the corresponding function in order-data.aspx here, but in fact you've seen all this code before:

```
...
<WebMethod> Public Function GetOrders(strCustID As String) As DataSet
'use data access component to get DataSet containing matching orders

  Dim objDataSet As DataSet

  Try
    'get connection string from web.config <appSettings> section
    Dim strConnect As String
    strConnect = ConfigurationSettings.AppSettings("NorthwindConnectString")

    'create an instance of the data access component
    Dim objOrderList As New OrderList(strConnect)

    'call the method to get the data as a DataSet
    objDataSet = objOrderList.GetOrdersByCustomerDataSet(strCustID)

    'add column containing total value of each line in OrderLines table
    Dim objLinesTable As DataTable = objDataSet.Tables("OrderLines")
```

```
  Dim objColumn As DataColumn
  objColumn = objLinesTable.Columns.Add("LineTotal", _
                          System.Type.GetType("System.Double"))
  objColumn.Expression = "[Quantity] * ([UnitPrice] - ([UnitPrice]" _
                    & " * [Discount]))"


  'set Nested property of relationship between tables so XML output
  'has appropriate linked OrderLines nested within each Order
  objDataSet.Relations(0).Nested = True


  'return the DataSet to the calling routine
  Return objDataSet

 Catch objErr As Exception
  'there was an error so no data is returned
  Return Nothing

 End Try

End Function
End Class
```

The Internet Explorer 5 WebService Behavior

Although Web Services are becoming an industry-accepted standard, Web
browsers have yet to catch up and include features that allow you to interact with
them easily—without having to handcraft special code each time. However, at the
time of writing, the Internet Explorer team at Microsoft is working on a behavior
component named webservice.htc that you can use in Internet Explorer to work
with Web Services.

This behavior component is included in the examples you can download for
this book. Note that this is a beta product at the moment, and you should be pre-
pared for possible changes in the interface and operation. For more details of what
Internet Explorer 5 behaviors actually are, how you use them, and how you can
build your own, refer to http://msdn.microsoft.com/workshop/author/behaviors/
behaviors_node_entry.asp.

The Web Service behavior component locates and caches the WSDL service
description so that the Web Service can be accessed repeatedly without re-retrieving
the WSDL service description each time. It also saves you from having to parse the
SOAP document that's returned from a Web Service. You insert the behavior component into your pages in the same way as you would any other Internet Explorer 5

behavior. In this example, we specify it as the style for an element in the page—we chose (for no particular reason) to use the heading <div> element:

```
<!-- attach Web Service behavior to element in page to get it loaded -->
<!-- also defines ID used to refer to it in script section of page.  -->
<div class="heading" style="behavior:url(../../global/webservice.htc)"
     id="htcWService">
  View Customer Orders - Select Customer
</div>
```

Opening and Using a Web Service

Once you've inserted the webservice.htc behavior into your page, you can use it to access Web Services. The start page for this version of the example application specifies that a function named openWebService will execute when the page is first displayed:

```
<body link="#0000ff" alink="#0000ff" vlink="#0000ff"
     onload="openWebService()">
```

This function first uses the useService method of the behavior to open (connect to) your Web Service. It does this by loading the WSDL document (the SOAP contract) from your server—you can see that you specify this by appending ?WSDL to the query string. You also provide a friendly name, CustData, which you'll use to refer to the Web Service in the code:

```
function openWebService() {
// runs when the page is first opened to load the customer list

  // establish the "friendly name" for the Web Service
  htcWService.useService("customer-data.asmx?WSDL","CustData");
```

Now you can call the Web Service method to get the data. You specify the necessary parameters to the callService method: the name of an event handler that will execute once the response from the Web Service has been received, the name of the method you want to call, and the parameters this method requires. To get a list of all customers (as in the previous example), you use two empty strings for the parameters:

```
  // call the Web Service to get the data. At the same time set up
  // the callback handler named "dataLoaded" to handle the results
```

```
// we want a list of all customers, so empty strings are provided
// for the parameters CustID and CustName parameters in this case
var iCallID = htcWService.CustData.callService(dataLoaded,
                                "GetCustomers", "", "");
}
```

The HTML you use to create the page in this version of the application is identical to the previous version you saw in this chapter, except for the "Loading..." message you display. In this case, you indicate that you're locating the Web Service, as shown in Figure 6-13.

Figure 6-13. The message that's displayed while the customer data is loading

Accessing the Response from the Web Service

The dataLoaded function in the page executes once the response from the Web Service has been received. In it, you can check if there was an error by examining the properties of the result object (here named objResult) that's passed to the function. You can extract details of any error from the properties of its errorDetail object and display them:

```
function dataLoaded(objResult) {
// runs once the Web Service has loaded the data from the server

  // see if there was an error
  if(objResult.error) {
    // get error details from errorDetail properties
```

```
   // of the objResult object passed to the function
   var strErrorCode = objResult.errorDetail.code;
   var strErrorMsg = objResult.errorDetail.string;
   var strErrorRaw = objResult.errorDetail.raw;

   // and display it
   document.all('lblStatus').innerHTML = '<b>* ERROR -</b> '
     + 'could not load customer list.<br />' + strErrorMsg;
 }
 ...
```

If all went well (that is, there was no error), you can transfer the returned data into an instance of the MSXML parser. You change the status message, instantiate the parser object, check that it's available, and set the properties as in earlier examples:

```
 ...
 else {
   document.all('lblStatus').innerHTML = 'Loading customer data '
     + 'from<br />Web Service  - please wait ...';

   // there was no error so create a new parser object instance
   try {
     objXMLData = new ActiveXObject('MSXML2.FreeThreadedDOMDocument');
   }
   catch(e) {}

   // check that the parser object is actually available, because
   // appropriate version of MSXML may not be installed on client
   // if not, display error message and exit
   if (objXMLData == null) {
     var strError = '* <b>ERROR: Incorrect XML parser version.</b><br />'
       + 'Sorry, you cannot use this version of the application.';
     document.all('lblStatus').innerHTML = strError;
     return;
   }

   // connect event with function to check when loading completes
   objXMLData.onreadystatechange = changeFunction;

   //set properties to validate while loading
   objXMLData.validateOnParse = true;
   objXMLData.async = true;
   ...
```

The Web Service behavior is clever—it exposes the result of the call to the Web Service method in different formats, depending on the data type of the result. If it's a simple type, such as a String or an Integer, you can access it through the value property of the result object. Alternatively, you can get the raw XML content from the result object's own raw object. In this case, the XML document is available as a string from the xml property of the raw object:

```
...
// load SOAP document (the results) from the Web Service
objXMLData.loadXML(objResult.raw.xml);
  }
}
```

Using the XML Data in Our Application

The Web Service middle tier in this version of the application exposes the XML data in much the same format as the middle tier of the Internet Explorer 5 example you looked at earlier in the chapter. Furthermore, you load the XML directly into an instance of the MSXML parser as before. However, in fact, the format isn't *exactly* the same here. As you saw earlier, a Web Service exposes XML data from a DataSet as a diffgram. It has an extra element that "wraps" the result. This isn't a problem because the code you use to access the XML can cope with this. You use XPath expressions to select the nodes you want in the XSLT stylesheets, and when you use the XML DOM methods, and these expressions don't depend on the absolute hierarchy of the elements. They just select descendants with the specified element name.

So, the remainder of the code and the results it produces are just the same as in the Internet Explorer 5 version you examined earlier in this chapter. The second page of the Web Service version is also just about identical to the corresponding page in the Internet Explorer 5 version. Obviously, it uses the same techniques to insert and use the Web Service behavior as the Select Customer page you've just been looking at, but otherwise everything works just the same. Figure 6-14 shows the result when you select an order for one of the customers.

One thing you'll notice is that providing the data via a Web Service is quite a bit slower than simply squirting the XML to the client from the middle tier component. The Web Service behavior has quite a lot of work to do initially in contacting the Web Service, fetching and parsing the WSDL document, and then managing the SOAP packets that are returned. However, the advantages of using a Web Service, such as discoverability, open architecture, and global availability, can make up for this. It all comes down to your business and application requirements.

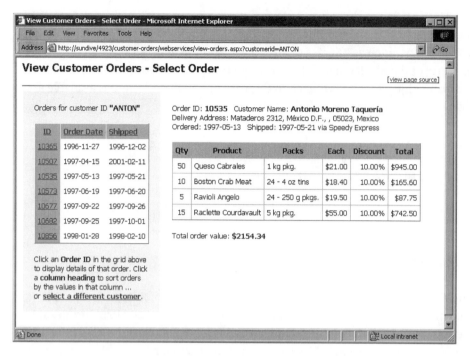

Figure 6-14. Displaying the details of a selected order

Building the Hypertext Application Example

The third version of the example application that uses XML is implemented as an HTML (or Hypertext) Application. Although this may not be a familiar term, it's likely that you've used Hypertext Applications (HTAs) several times before. Many Microsoft products use HTAs during the setup process to display and collect information required by the process.

HTAs run like Web pages in a browser but have the ability to step outside the "sandbox" in which all other Web pages have to play. In the case of the example application, this gives a huge additional opportunity to build a distributed *and fully disconnected* application. You can fetch data from the server and store it as a file on the client's local hard disk. This means that they can start up and use the application without having to be connected to the original server. Figure 6-15 outlines the process.

One concern with persisting data to a client machine like this is that it can rapidly become out-of-date as other users update the original data. This is quite true and certainly an issue you need to consider. One approach would be to set a time limit on the age of the locally persisted data and force a refresh from the server after a specified interval. Adding code to the client that checks the date and time that the file was written to the local disk each time the application starts would be an obvious approach.

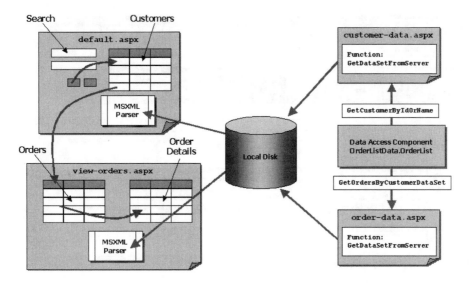

Figure 6-15. The Hypertext Application (HTA) version of the application

However, you need to think about *why* you're persisting the data locally. It's likely to be because the user won't be connected to the server all the time. For example, a salesperson using a laptop or PDA might only connect in the evenings from home or from a hotel room. They might only connect once a week, before leaving the office for a business trip. Does this mean you should stop them being able to access the data after, say, a couple of hours just in case some values have been changed? Of course not!

In general, this approach is best suited to situations where the data doesn't change often. For example, it's ideal for examining data such as details of orders that have been completed, work schedules for the week ahead, or even the canteen menu. It's certainly a lot better than the common alternative of an inch-thick computer printout that arrives by post once a month. Remember, technology isn't the only ruling factor in building applications—you must consider business requirements and mode of operation as well!

Running the Example Hypertext Application

When you select the HTA version from the main Multiple-client Customer Order List Application menu (http://localhost/4923/customer-orders.htm), a page of information displays before the main application starts, as shown in Figure 6-16.

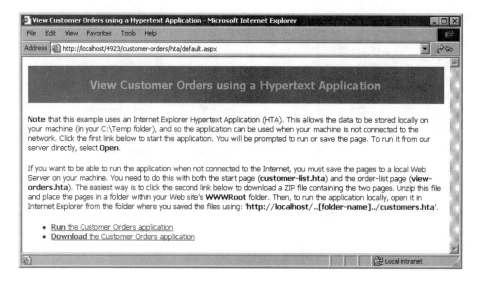

Figure 6-16. The menu page for the HTA version of the application

Notice that you still need a Web server to run the application—HTAs can only be loaded into a browser this way. The big difference here is that you can place the HTA pages on your `localhost` Web server, or a Web server on your local network, and run them from there. You can fetch the data from anywhere on the Internet—it doesn't have to be on the same machine.

Obviously, there are security concerns when using HTAs because they have a great deal of freedom to access your machine and your own local network. So, when you click the link to start the application, a dialog box warns you that you're going to run an HTA—and gives the choice to open or download it. Select Open to run it, as shown in Figure 6-17.

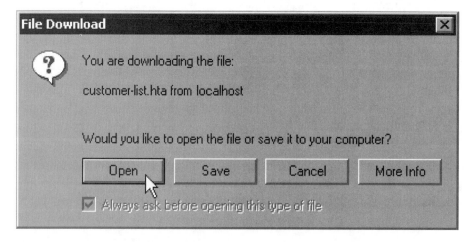

Figure 6-17. Choosing to open the HTA

Loading the XML Data

As the page loads, when you run it for the first time, another dialog box appears. This asks if you want to download the orders data required by the application, as shown in Figure 6-18. In the version supplied, the data downloads from `http://daveandal.com`, but you can change the URL to point to your own server by editing the application code, as shown later. After you click OK, and the data has been downloaded, another dialog box prompts you to download the customers data.

Figure 6-18. Choosing to download the orders data

Providing that you have a `C:\Temp` folder on your local hard disk, the data will be downloaded and stored there as two XML documents named `all-orders.xml` and `all-customers.xml`. The first of these is quite large, and may take a minute or two to download. We're being optimistic here, and it may well take longer than this; however, we've enabled HTTP compression on our server and specified that this should include application documents as well as static ones. So there should be some saving in download time from this when using Internet Explorer (it supports HTTP 1.1, which is required for compression to work).

> **NOTE** *For details of how to enable HTTP 1.1 compression, see the help files installed with Windows 2000 Server (*`http://localhost/iishelp/`*) or the Microsoft Web site at* `http://www.microsoft.com/WINDOWS2000/en/datacenter/iis/htm/core/iihttpc.htm`.

Once the data has loaded, the first page of the application displays. After you've downloaded the data once, this page displays immediately without going out for the data again. However, you can refresh the data from the server at any time using the link below the Search button in the page. Figure 6-19 shows the initial page after searching for customers whose ID starts with *w*:

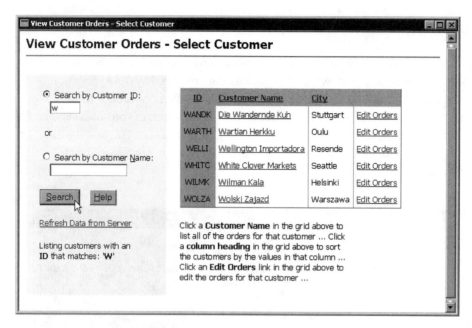

Figure 6-19. Displaying the customers whose ID starts with w

Notice the different appearance of the browser window. There's no status bar or address bar or toolbar, and many options in the right-click shortcut menu (including Back) are unavailable. You can control the appearance, behavior, and size of the browser window very closely when using HTAs to provide an interface that's much more like a traditional executable application than a Web page.

However, the way you code HTA pages is fundamentally similar to the way you build ordinary HTML pages, but they must have the file extension .hta to be recognized by Internet Explorer as being hypertext applications. Inside the page you can use ordinary HTML and client-side scripting in JScript/JavaScript or (because HTAs only work in Internet Explorer) in VBScript.

We'll briefly describe the differences between this version of the application and the previous Internet Explorer 5 and higher version next—starting with the middle tier.

Building the Middle Tier

Because the techniques you're using within the HTA pages for manipulating and displaying the data are the same as in the Internet Explorer 5 version, you won't be surprised to know that the middle tier you use for this version is almost identical as well. To get the list of all the customers, you use *exactly* the same middle tier ASP.NET page customer-data.aspx as before.

However, there's a minor difference in the way you get the order data. In the Internet Explorer 5 version (and in the Web Service version), you only collect the order data when you display the View Orders page. You specify the ID of the selected customer, and the middle tier returns only the orders for that customer. In this version, you want to collect all the order data for *all* of the customers' orders as soon as the application starts. The user can then disconnect from the data server and work locally with the data.

> **NOTE** *Of course, in this situation, you end up loading more data than you would when you first open the Internet Explorer 5 or Web Service example. However, to be able to disconnect from the server, you need to grab all the necessary data at the start. If you're building an application that demands a large data download at the beginning, you might consider whether it's suitable to make just a subset of the data available, rather than all of it. Again, it's a business decision, based on the actual requirements of the users.*

The middle tier ASP.NET page named `order-data.aspx` uses the same `GetOrdersByCustomerDataSet` method of the data access component as the other versions, but this time it specifies just the wildcard character % for the order ID parameter so that all the orders are returned:

```
'call the method to get the data as a DataSet
objDataSet = objOrderList.GetOrdersByCustomerDataSet("%")
```

The other difference is that you return the order data to the client as a diffgram rather than a "normal" XML document. To do this, you specify an extra optional parameter to the `WriteXml` method when you extract the data from the DataSet:

```
'stream the contents of the DataSet to the output as a diffgram
objDataSet.WriteXml(Response.OutputStream, XmlWriteMode.DiffGram)
```

This gives you the same format for the XML as you got from the Web Service, as shown in the previous example. We'll talk more about using a diffgram to update the data source in Chapter 9.

> **NOTE** *Persisting the data client-side as a diffgram allows you to store changes that the user makes to the data when they edit it (while disconnected from the data server) in such a way that you could use it to perform a controlled update to the source data later. You won't actually do this in the example application, but we'll demonstrate how you can edit a diffgram on the client side in Chapter 11.*

The HTA Page Content

There are a few differences between the pages you use in this version of the application and the Internet Explorer 5 version you looked at earlier in this chapter. They're mainly concerned with the way you define the appearance of the HTA page and the way you load the data from your server.

In the `customer-list.hta` page, where the user selects a customer, you have to include the mandatory `hta:application` element that defines the behavior and appearance of the page. Without this, it isn't an HTA page. The code you use is shown next. It specifies the ID and name of the application, the border, caption and window settings, whether the "system menu" buttons appear (the minimize, restore and close buttons), and whether hyperlinks can be used to load other pages:

```
<hta:application id="testapp"
                 applicationname="testapplication"
                 border="thick"
                 caption="View Customer Orders - Select Customer"
                 showintaskbar="yes"
                 singleinstance="no"
                 sysmenu="yes"
                 windowstate="normal"
                 navigable="yes"
/>
```

> **NOTE** *You can find a full reference to HTAs and the elements they use at* `http://msdn.microsoft.com/workshop/author/hta/hta_node_entry.asp`.

Downloading the Data

To load the XML data from the middle tier, you also use a slightly different approach because you want to save it onto the client's hard disk as well as use it in the page. The page contains several "global" variables that define the paths and URLs you'll be using—you can edit these if you want to load the data from a different location or store it in a different folder on your hard disk:

```
// define location of local disk files for persisting XML data
var strCustomersLocalXMLPath = 'c:\\temp\\all-customers.xml';
var strOrdersLocalXMLPath = 'c:\\temp\\all-orders.xml';

// define location of remote server apps providing the data
var strRemoteCustomersXML =
  'http://daveandal.com/books/4923/customer-orders/hta/customer-data.aspx';
var strRemoteOrdersXML =
  'http://daveandal.com/books/4923/customer-orders/hta/order-data.aspx';

var objXMLData;   // to hold reference to XML parser
```

In the opening <body> tag of the page, you specify that a function named pageLoadEvent will execute once the page is loaded. This function first attempts to load the data from the local disk using a function named loadXMLDocument (which is located elsewhere in this page). It passes in the path to the local data file and sets the second parameter to false to indicate that this isn't a remote request but a local one. The third parameter indicates which set of data is required. If the data can't be loaded locally, the function then attempts to load it from the remote location, using the same function but with different parameters:

```
function pageLoadEvent() {
// runs when the page is first opened to fetch the data

  // try and load Orders data from local disk
  if (loadXMLDocument(strOrdersLocalXMLPath, false, "Orders") == false) {

    // try and load Orders data from remote server
    if (loadXMLDocument(strRemoteOrdersXML, true, "Orders") == true) {
    ...
```

If the remote load succeeds, it then calls the saveLocalXML function to save the data fetched from the remote location locally. If the data can't be found at either location, it just exits:

```
...
    // try and save Orders data to local disk
    if (saveLocalXML(strOrdersLocalXMLPath) == false) return;

  }
  else return;
}
...
```

Next, the function attempts to load the customer data using the same technique. If this succeeds, it can update the status message, enable the Search button, and display the help text (just as in the Internet Explorer 5 version):

```
...
  // try and load Customers data from local disk
  if (loadXMLDocument(strCustomersLocalXMLPath, false, "Customers") == false) {

    // try and load Customers data from remote server
    if (loadXMLDocument(strRemoteCustomersXML, true, "Customers") == true) {

      // try and save Customers data to local disk
      if (saveLocalXML(strCustomersLocalXMLPath) == false) return;
    }
  }

  // clear "Loading" message
  document.all('lblStatus').innerHTML = '';

  // enable "Search" button
  document.all('btnSearch').disabled = false;

  // show Help details
  showHelp();
}
```

The loadXMLDocument Function

Next, you'll look at the two functions used in the previous code to download and save the data. The `loadXMLDocument` function loads an XML document from a local disk file or a remote URL in much the same way as in previous examples. However, this time you *aren't* loading it asynchronously. You need to get both the customer and order data loaded, and saved to disk if they aren't already stored there, as quickly as possible while catching any errors immediately.

So, after creating the parser instance and displaying some status information, you set the parser's `async` property to `false` this time. Then you can decide if it's a local or remote download by examining the `blnRemote` parameter that you pass to the function each time you call it. For a remote download you prompt the user before starting so that they can connect to the network if required or cancel the download:

```
function loadXMLDocument(strURL, blnRemote, strDisplay) {
// load an XML document and return any error message

  // create a new parser object instance
  objXMLData = new ActiveXObject('MSXML2.FreeThreadedDOMDocument');

  // set properties to validate while loading
  objXMLData.validateOnParse = false;
  objXMLData.async = false;

  // clear results list and show "Loading" message
  document.all('lblStatus').innerHTML = 'Loading ' + strDisplay + ' data...';
  document.all('divResult').innerHTML = '';
  document.all('lblMessage').innerHTML = '';

  if (blnRemote == true) {
    // prompt for remote download of data
    var strPrompt = 'Download ' + strDisplay
                    + ' data from remote server:\n' + strURL
    if (confirm(strPrompt) == false)
      return false;   //exit from function
  }
  ...
```

Now you can call the `load` method to get the XML document. If you get an error, you display a message with details of the error and return the value `false`. Otherwise, you update the status message and return `true` to show that you're ready to go:

```
...
// load customer list from local or remote server
objXMLData.load(strURL);

if (objXMLData.parseError.errorCode != 0) {
  // there was an error while loading
  // so display message
  document.all('lblStatus').innerHTML =
    '<b>* ERROR</b> - could not load data.<br />'
    + objXMLData.parseError.reason;
  return false;
}
else {
  // show "Loaded OK" message
  document.all('lblStatus').innerHTML = 'Data loaded OK.';
  return true;
}
}
```

The saveLocalXML Function

The other function you used earlier saves the XML that you've downloaded from a remote location onto the local hard disk. This is easy—you just call the `save` method of the parser, specifying the local file path and name, and return the value `true`. If it fails, you display an error message and return `false`:

```
function saveLocalXML(strPath) {
// saves the loaded document to the local disk

  try {
    // save the data to a local folder
    objXMLData.save(strPath);
    return true;

  }
  catch (objError) {
    // can't save locally - display message
    document.all('lblStatus').innerHTML = '<b>* WARNING</b> '
```

```
      + '- could not save data to<br />local disk. You must have a '
      + 'folder<br />named <b>temp</b> on your local hard disk<br />for '
      + 'the data to be stored.';
  }
  return false;
}
```

If the function completes without failing, then the next time the user opens the application, the two XML documents you've saved to the disk will be reloaded, and there will be no need to go out to the data server.

As already discussed, when the user is working with a local copy of the data, there's a potential concurrency issue—the local copy might be out of sync with the version of the server. So this is a good time to see how the concurrency-aware user can refresh the local copy of the data from the server.

The refreshData Function

There will be regular occasions where the user wants to update or refresh the data that's stored locally on their hard disk. The Refresh Data from Server link (which you saw in Figure 6-19) executes a function named refreshData, which does just that:

```
function refreshData() {
// runs when the link to refresh the data is clicked

  // disable "Search" button
  document.all('btnSearch').disabled = true;

  var blnLoaded = false;

  // try and load Orders data from remote server
  blnLoaded = loadXMLDocument(strRemoteOrdersXML, true, "Orders");

  if (blnLoaded == true)
    // try and save Orders data to local disk
    blnLoaded = saveLocalXML(strOrdersLocalXMLPath)
  else
    return;

  // try and load Customers data from remote server
  blnLoaded = loadXMLDocument(strRemoteCustomersXML, true, "Customers");
```

```
  if (blnLoaded == true)
    // try and save Customers data to local disk
    blnLoaded = saveLocalXML(strCustomersLocalXMLPath);

  if (blnLoaded == true)
    // enable "Search" button
    document.all('btnSearch').disabled = false;
}
```

Implementing Hyperlinks in HTA Pages

One thing that works differently in an HTA application, when compared to a normal Web page, is navigation from one page to another. Unless you set the navigable attribute of the opening <hta:application> element to yes, you won't be able to use <a> elements to navigate from one page to another. In this application, you've enabled this feature so that the hyperlinks in the page footer work.

However, it's always possible to open another page by changing the href property of the page's location object with client-side script code. For example, the XSLT stylesheets you use to create the lists of customers and orders contain the following to create the customer ID column values as links that load the View Orders page:

```
<span style="text-decoration:underline;color:blue;cursor:hand">
  <xsl:attribute name="onclick">
    window.location.href="view-orders.hta?customerid=<xsl:value-of
                      select="CustomerID" />";
  </xsl:attribute>
  <xsl:value-of select="CompanyName" />
</span>
```

After transformation, the result is an ordinary <span> element that has style properties added so that the text within it will look like a hyperlink. You even change the cursor to the familiar "hand" shape that's usual for hyperlinks:

```
<span style="text-decoration:underline;color:blue;cursor:hand"
      onclick="window.location.href="view-orders.hta?customerid=WOLZA;">
  Wolski Zajazd
</span>
```

Selecting an Order

The second page in this version of the example application is again just about identical to the equivalent in the Internet Explorer 5 version of the application. You can see what it looks like in Figure 6-20.

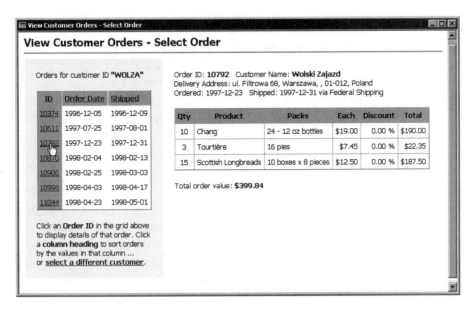

Figure 6-20. Viewing details of an order in the HTA version of the application

This page contains the same code for manipulating and displaying the XML data for each customer's orders as the Internet Explorer 5 version you saw at the start of the chapter. Of course, in this version, all of the order details for all of customers are available—but the techniques and code you use to select and display these details are the same.

You also use the same code as in the previous page of this version of the application to load the XML data from the user's local disk. In this page, you have no need to go out to the server to fetch it because it'll have been fetched if required, and stored locally, by the previous Select Customer page.

Working with Delimited Text Data

All the examples so far in this chapter have used XML as the data transfer and storage protocol. They used different techniques and different technologies to fetch and cache the XML but fundamentally the same techniques for manipulating and displaying it. To finish off this chapter on programming rich clients, you'll briefly look at one other version of the example application. Only, this time, you aren't using XML at all.

In fact, you're digging out your trendy old flared trousers and paisley ties and going back in time. You're going back to delimited text data and the cutting-edge techniques that were first made available in Internet Explorer 4. You can run this version of the application, which is in the `customer-orders/ie4` subfolder of the samples, by selecting the Internet Explorer 4 and higher option from the main menu for the Customer Orders application (`http://localhost/4923/customer-orders.htm`).

Why Use Delimited Text Data?

You're probably wondering why on earth anyone would want to use delimited text as a data transfer (and even storage) format. In fact, there are several reasons. Many legacy services, applications, and database systems have no concept of XML, but they can output data in delimited text format. For this reason, new services such as Microsoft BizTalk Server are designed to interface with and handle delimited text as both an input and output format.

So delimited text data is still around, and it's surviving. It's also more compact than XML—which is useful if bandwidth is a problem. Finally, with Internet Explorer 4 and higher, using it directly on the client side, without having to transform it into another format, is an extremely easy and efficient solution.

Remember the TDC?

As part of the Remote Data Services (RDS) introduced with Internet Explorer 4 came an extremely useful ActiveX object called the Tabular Data Control (TDC)—or Text Data Control (the name varied over time). All you have to do is point the TDC at a local or remote source of delimited text data, and it'll load it and expose it as an ADO-style disconnected `Recordset` object. It even supports client-side data binding, making it extremely easy to create tables of data dynamically in the browser.

OK, so the TDC is no longer "state of the art." But then neither is HTML or CSS, and you still use them where they're appropriate. So, why not take advantage of the TDC where you know the client is Internet Explorer 4 or higher? It's so easy to use that falling off a log looks like a major undertaking in comparison.

But that's enough gushing enthusiasm for the moment. You'll first look at how you can provide the necessary delimited text data in your middle tier.

Building the Middle Tier

In this example, just for a change, we've written the client-side code using VBScript. You know that the TDC and client-side data binding will only work in Internet Explorer 4 and higher, and so VBScript will be available in all cases where these are supported. Moreover, to make up for this travesty, this time you'll look at the version of the application whose middle tier components are written in C#.

The middle tier you use for this version of the application uses similar techniques to those you looked at earlier with other versions. However, you have to modify the techniques slightly to return the data in the appropriate format for the TDC control this time. You'll also, as an example, build a single ASP.NET page that acts as the middle tier and that exposes all three methods you'll need to provide the data to power your pages.

Figure 6-21 shows an outline view of this version of the application.

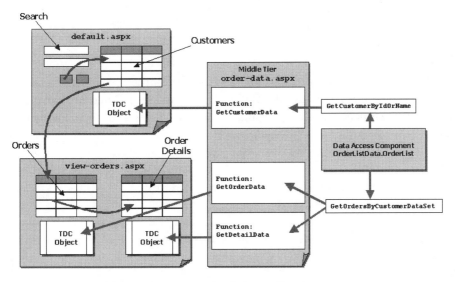

Figure 6-21. The delimited text version of the application

The Component to Generate Delimited Text

The code within the middle-tier component, order-data.aspx, declares a "global" variable named TAB that holds a tab character, making it easier to insert it in the large number of places you'll need to in your code:

```
<script language="C#" runat="server">
char TAB = (char)9;    // TAB character
```

We use a tab delimiter in this example, but the default for the TDC is actually a comma. It just means you have to remember to tell the TDC that you're using a tab delimiter, instead of a comma delimiter, when you instantiate the control in your page. You could use a comma as the delimiter and wrap each value in double quotes in case it contained a comma. However, using a tab (which you know won't appear in the values) is easier in the long run.

In the Page_Load event of the middle tier component you first collect the two parameters that you'll expect to find in the query string. These indicate the type of data you require (a customer list, an order list, or a list of order details), and the selected customer ID when you're extracting an order list or the details of orders for the specified customer:

```
void Page_Load(Object objSender, EventArgs objArgs) {

  // get values from query string
  String strType = Request.QueryString["type"];
  String strCustID = Request.QueryString["customerid"];
  ...
```

Next, you must set the correct MIME type for the returned data—in this case, it's text/text. If you don't do this, the TDC will refuse to load it. Then you can call one of the three functions in this page that create the data as a string and write it to the Response:

```
  ...
  // set content-type to return a tab-delimited text file
  Response.ContentType = "text/text";

  // call function to create output and write to response
  switch (strType)
  {
    case "customerlist":
      Response.Write(GetCustomerDataFromServer());
      break;
```

```
    case "orderlist":
      Response.Write(GetOrderDataFromServer(strCustID));
      break;
    case "orderdetail":
      Response.Write(GetDetailDataFromServer(strCustID));
      break;
  }
}
```

Creating the Customer List Delimited String

Each of the three functions calls the respective method (see Figure 6-21) of the data access component OrderListData.dll that you've used in all of your applications. However, it's important to remember that you can't easily manipulate the data on the client when you use client-side data binding with the TDC. You have to send it rows of text data separated by the delimiter character, with each row terminated by a carriage return. You also have to carry out any formatting you require as you build the text string to return from your function.

In the GetCustomerDataFromServer function, you call the GetCustomerByIdOrName method of the data access component with empty strings for both parameters so that you get a list of all the customers. You create the column headings in the first "row" of the result string and then iterate through the Customers table in the DataSet that this method returns—creating your delimited text string as you go:

```
// call the method to get the data as a DataSet
objDataSet = objOrderList.GetCustomerByIdOrName("", "");

// iterate through each row in the table building the output
String strResult = "CustomerID" + TAB + "CompanyName" + TAB
                 + "City" + TAB + "ViewOrderHref\n";
DataTable objTable = objDataSet.Tables["Customers"];
foreach(DataRow objRow in objTable.Rows){
  strResult += objRow["CustomerID"].ToString() + TAB
             + objRow["CompanyName"].ToString() + TAB
             + objRow["City"].ToString() + TAB
             + "view-orders.aspx?customerid="
             + objRow["CustomerID"].ToString() + "\n";
}
return strResult;
```

If you don't include the column names in the first row of the results, the TDC will allocate names such as Column1, Column2, and so on when it loads the data.

Using the column names will make it easier to manipulate the data later. The other issue is how you'll create the hyperlinks you need in the table of customers. You don't have luxuries such as a "hyperlink column" in the TDC like you do in the ASP.NET DataGrid server control. So you create an extra column in each row. You can see, in the statement where you create the column headings, that this is named ViewOrderHref. This column contains the href values you'll need to open the appropriate list of orders for this customer. The value is the URL of the view-orders.aspx page, with the customer ID appended as the query string. For example, you'll get the following for this item where the customer ID is ALFKI:

```
view-orders.aspx?customerid=ALFKI
```

Creating the Order List Delimited String

For the GetOrderDataFromServer function, you call the GetOrdersByCustomerDataSet function of the data access component, providing the customer ID as the single parameter. Then you create the column headings row and iterate through the rows in the Orders table, building your string. Notice how you format the dates as you go, checking for any null ShippedDate values by comparing the column value to DBNull.Value:

```
// call the method to get the data as a DataSet
objDataSet = objOrderList.GetOrdersByCustomerDataSet(strCustID);

// create the headings row for the output string
String strResult = "OrderID" + TAB + "ShipName" + TAB
                 + "OrderAddress" + TAB + "OrderDate" + TAB
                 + "ShippedDate" + TAB + "CompanyName" + TAB
                 + "OrderDetailHref\n";

// iterate through each row in the table building the output
DataTable objTable = objDataSet.Tables["Orders"];
foreach(DataRow objRow in objTable.Rows){

  // get values from columns as correct data types
  DateTime datOrderDate = (DateTime)objRow["OrderDate"];

  // create the result string for this row
  strResult += objRow["OrderID"].ToString() + TAB
             + objRow["ShipName"].ToString() + TAB
             + objRow["OrderAddress"].ToString() + TAB
             + datOrderDate.ToString("yyyy-MM-dd") + TAB;
```

```
  if (objRow["ShippedDate"] == DBNull.Value) {
    strResult += TAB;    // no "shipped date" value
  }
  else {
    DateTime datShippedDate = (DateTime)objRow["ShippedDate"];
    strResult += datShippedDate.ToString("yyyy-MM-dd") + TAB;
  }
  strResult += objRow["CompanyName"].ToString() + TAB
          + "javascript:ShowOrderDetail('"
          + objRow["OrderID"].ToString() + "')\n";
}
return strResult;
```

Again, you need to include a hyperlink—this time to display the details of the selected order. The value is a javascript: function that calls a client-side VBScript function named ShowOrderDetail, and you include the order ID in each row as the parameter. For example, you'll get the following for the row where the order ID is 10496:

```
javascript:ShowOrderDetail('10496')
```

Creating the Customer List Delimited String

The final function is GetDetailDataFromServer, which returns delimited text data suitable for displaying the details of a selected order (the order lines). In previous versions of the application, you didn't need this because you could use the same XML document that contained all the order details for both the list of orders and the list of order lines. You can't do this with the TDC control—you must provide the input as a separate "file."

You call the GetOrdersByCustomerDataSet function of the data access component, providing the customer ID as the single parameter in the same way as in the previous function. Then you create the column headings row, but this time with headings appropriate for the order line details table. After that, you can iterate through the rows in the OrderLines table building your string. Again, you format the values as you go, and you calculate the total line value and place this in the last column:

```
// call the method to get the data as a DataSet
objDataSet = objOrderList.GetOrdersByCustomerDataSet(strCustID);

// create the headings row for the output string
String strResult = "OrderID" + TAB + "ProductName" + TAB
```

```
                      + "QuantityPerUnit" + TAB + "UnitPrice" + TAB
                      + "Quantity" + TAB + "Discount" + TAB + "LineTotal\n";

// iterate through each row in the table building the output
DataTable objTable = objDataSet.Tables["OrderLines"];
foreach(DataRow objRow in objTable.Rows){

  // get values from columns as correct data types
  decimal dPrice = (decimal)objRow["UnitPrice"];
  short iQty = (short)objRow["Quantity"];
  float fDiscount = (float)objRow["Discount"];

  // calculate total value of this order line
  decimal dTotal = iQty * (dPrice - (dPrice * (decimal)fDiscount));

  // create the result string for this row
  strResult += objRow["OrderID"].ToString() + TAB
             + objRow["ProductName"].ToString() + TAB
             + objRow["QuantityPerUnit"].ToString() + TAB
             + dPrice.ToString("N2") + TAB
             + iQty.ToString() + TAB
             + fDiscount.ToString("p") + TAB
             + dTotal.ToString("N2") + "\n";;
}
return strResult;
```

Of course, you could've used the same technique for the line total as you did in previous versions—by adding a calculated column to the table in the DataSet and then just extracting the values from this column for your output string. However, the previous code demonstrates an alternative technique that would be useful if the calculation was too complex to carry out in an expression for a calculated column. You could create a separate function in your page that calculates the value and call that with the other row values to get the calculated result for the extra column in the output.

Iterate or Transform?

You built up the output string in your middle tier component by iterating through the rows in each table of the DataSet. This is going to reduce the efficiency of the middle tier to some extent, though the gain in efficiency from caching the data on the client should counteract this. However, you aren't forced to do it this way. For example, you could export the data from the DataSet as XML and then apply an XSL transformation to it to get the delimited text (though this will involve extra resource use on the server). Remember that XSL and XSLT can transform an XML document into *any* format. What comes out is only governed by the content of the templates within the stylesheet.

Selecting a Customer

As you'll expect by now, this version of the application looks almost identical to the previous versions you've seen. Once the data has been loaded, the "Loading..." message displayed below the disabled Search button disappears, and the Search button becomes available. In Figure 6-22, we've entered the search criteria *s* and clicked Search to display a list of matching customers.

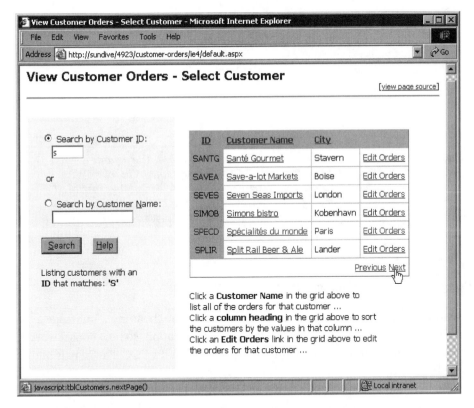

Figure 6-22. Searching for customers whose IDs start with s

Notice that this time you've got paging back again, just like in the HTML version of the application. You didn't implement it in any of the versions that use XML and XSLT, but it's trivially easy to do when you use client-side data binding—as you'll see shortly.

Declaring the Tabular Data Control

Like most ActiveX controls, the TDC object can be inserted into the page using an HTML `<object>` element. This allows you to set the properties using `<param>` elements. You set the field delimiter character to a tab, you set the URL of the middle tier component (the ASP.NET page named `order-data.aspx`) that supplies the data, and you tell the control that the first row of the data is the columns headings. You also turn off case sensitivity for filters (so you won't have the same problem as you did with the XSLT stylesheets in the other versions in this chapter) and specify the character set that your data uses:

```
<object id="tdcCustomers" width="0" height="0"
        classid="CLSID:333c7bc4-460f-11d0-bc04-0080c7055a83">
  <param name="FieldDelim" value="&#09;">
  <param name="DataURL" value="order-data.aspx?type=customerlist">
  <param name="UseHeader" value="true">
  <param name="CaseSensitive" value="false">
  <param name="CharSet" value="utf-8">
</object>
```

> **NOTE** *This last property setting,* CharSet, *is very important. The default is* windows-1252, *which uses Codepage 1252 (Western Alphabet/Windows). With the sample database, this failed to recognize the accented and other special characters in the table. You'll find a full reference to the TDC and its properties and methods at* http://msdn.microsoft.com/workshop/database/tdc/ tabular_data_control_node_entry.asp.

Using the ReadyStateChange Event

You don't use the `onload` event of the page to remove the "Loading..." message or enable your Search button in this version of the application, so how does it work? There's no asynchronous load feature with callbacks in the TDC like there is in the MSXML parser.

However, in Internet Explorer, the `Document` object (the page itself) exposes a `ReadyState` property and an `OnReadyStateChange` event, much like the MSXML parser. If you create an event handler for the `OnReadyStateChange` event, you can check to see when the entire page and all of its content (including the data for the TDC) has finished loading:

```
Sub Document_OnReadyStateChange()
'runs once page and all content (including TDC data) is loaded
'enable the Search button and show the Help details
```

```
  If Document.ReadyState = "complete" Then
    document.all("btnSearch").disabled = false
    document.all("lblStatus").InnerHTML = ""
    ShowHelp()
  End If

End Sub
```

The Data-Bound Table

A core part of the page is the HTML you use to declare the table that'll display the list of matching customers. It's populated through client-side data binding when the DoSearch routine (declared elsewhere in this page) executes. In the following listing, you can see the special data-binding attributes that attach the <table> element to the data source (the ID of the TDC), and each <td> element in the body of the table to a "data field" (column) within the data source, and (in some cases) specify the way that the data should be formatted.

You can also see that the column headings are hyperlinks that call the DoSearch routine again with that column name as a parameter. Notice also that the table is hidden when the page first displays because the opening <table> tag contains the style selector display:none:

```
<table id="tblCustomers" datasrc="#tdcCustomers" datapagesize="6"
       cellspacing="0" cellpadding="5" border="1"
       style="border-collapse:collapse;display:none;">
  <thead>
    <tr style="background-color:silver;">
      <td align="center">
        <a href="javascript:DoSearch('CustomerID')">ID</a>
      </td>
      <td align="left">
        <a href="javascript:DoSearch('CompanyName')">Customer Name</a>
      </td>
      <td align="left">
        <a href="javascript:DoSearch('City')">City</a>
      </td>
    </tr>
  </thead>
  <tbody>
    <tr>
      <td align="center" style="background-color:#add8e6;">
        <span datafld="CustomerID" dataformatas="html"></span>
```

```
          </td>
          <td align="left">
            <a datafld="ViewOrderHref">
              <span datafld="CompanyName" dataformatas="html"></span>
            </a>
          </td>
          <td align="left">
            <span datafld="City" dataformatas="html"></span>
          </td>
        </tr>
      </tbody>
      <tfoot id="tblNavControls" style="display:none;">
        <tr><td colspan="4" align="right">
          <a href="javascript:tblCustomers.previousPage()">Previous</a>
          <a href="javascript:tblCustomers.nextPage()">Next</a>
        </td></tr>
      </tfoot>
    </table>
```

When you declare a table for use with client-side data binding, it's important to use the HTML elements <thead>, <tbody>, and <tfoot> to indicate which rows form the head, body, and footer of the table, respectively. This is how the data-binding feature knows which rows should be repeated for each row in the data source (obviously only the rows in the <tbody> section).

To create the hyperlinks for the Customer Name column, you use the data-binding feature to build the appropriate HTML:

```
<a datafld="ViewOrderHref">
  <span datafld="CompanyName" dataformatas="html"></span>
</a>
```

The <a> element is bound to the column in the TDC data source named ViewOrderHref. This sets the href attribute. Inside the <a> element is a <span> element bound to the CompanyName column in the TDC. So, the resulting HTML that'll be generated by the data binding process for the row containing the customer Alfreds Futterkiste will be this:

```
<a href="view-orders.aspx?customerid=ALFKI">
  <span>Alfreds Futterkiste</span>
</a>
```

This will load the view-orders.aspx page with the appropriate customer ID appended to the query string.

Paging the Table Rows

In the footer section of the preceding table listing, you can see that there's a row containing two hyperlinks, Previous and Next. These are the paging controls. Of course, you don't want them to be visible if there are no more rows to display, so you hide them by adding the style attribute `display:none` to the enclosing `<tfoot>` element.

In the opening `<table>` tag, you specified the attribute `datapagesize="6"`, so the table will only show the first six rows of data exposed by the TDC data source. If there are more than six rows after binding, you'll display these controls in your code by removing the style selector `display:none` from the `<tfoot>` element (this line is in the `DoSearch` event handler, which you'll examine in more detail in a moment):

```
document.all("tblNavControls").style.display = ""
```

When the `<tfoot>` section is visible, users can click the Previous and Next hyperlinks to navigate through the pages. The data-binding feature almost handles this automatically for you as well. As you can see in the following code (repeated from the previous listing), all you have to do in response to a click of one of the links is call the `previousPage` or `nextPage` method of the `<table>` control using its ID `tblCustomers`. It's as easy as this:

```
<a href="javascript:tblCustomers.previousPage()">Previous</a>
<a href="javascript:tblCustomers.nextPage()">Next</a>
```

The DoSearch Subroutine

You have a couple of "global" variables in the client-side script section of your page, which you use to store a reference to the TDC object and the double-quote character you'll need in various places in your code:

```
Dim objCustData   'to hold reference to TDC control
QUOT = Chr(34)    'double-quote character
```

When the Search button is clicked, you want to search for matching customers and display the results in the data-bound table. The declaration of the Search button in the HTML for the page includes the attribute `onclick="DoSearch('CustomerID')"`, so it'll execute the routine named `DoSearch` and pass it the string value `CustomerID`. In the `DoSearch` routine you first get a reference to the TDC and then set its `Sort` property using the value passed to the function as a parameter. This is just a column name, and is all that's required to sort the rows that will be displayed in the table:

```
Sub DoSearch(strSortOrder)
'display the list of matching customers in the table

  'get a reference to the TDC control
  Set objCustData = document.all("tdcCustomers")

  'set the sorting order
  objCustData.Sort = strSortOrder
  ...
```

Filtering the Data

Next you collect the value from the appropriate one of the two text boxes on your page, just like you did in the previous versions of the application, and display a status message. Then you set the Filter property of the TDC so that it only shows matching rows:

```
  ...
  'get one or other value from text boxes depending on selection
  If document.all("optByID").checked Then
    strCustID = UCase(document.all("txtCustID").value)
    strMsg = "Listing customers with an<br /><b>ID</b> that matches: <b>'" _
          & strCustID + "'</b>"

    'set the Filter for the TDC to show matching customers only
    objCustData.Filter = "CustomerID = " & QUOT & strCustID & "*" & QUOT

  Else
    strCustName = document.all("txtCustName").value
    strMsg = "Listing customers whose<br /><b>Name</b> contains: <b>'" _
          & strCustName & "'</b>"

    'set the Filter for the TDC to show matching customers only
    objCustData.Filter = "CompanyName = " & QUOT & "*" & strCustName _
                      & "*" & QUOT

  End If
  ...
```

Displaying the Results

Now you force the TDC to refresh the binding to the table, and the rows are filtered and sorted into the desired order automatically. You also display the message that you just created, indicating what criteria you used:

```
...
'force TDC to rebind the data
objCustData.Reset

'show the results table and display message
document.all("lblStatus").InnerHTML = strMsg
...
```

Next, you need to see if you actually found any matching customers. You get a reference to the Recordset object that's exposed by the TDC and query the RecordCount property. This is the number of rows currently available for binding, taking into account the filter you applied to it earlier. If you get more than zero, you know that you found at least one matching customer, so you can show the table (by removing the display:none style selector that you placed in the opening <table> tag in the HTML declaration) and create a suitable status message:

```
...
'get a reference to the TDC control's Recordset
'there will be an error if the data was not loaded
On Error Resume Next
intRecs = objCustData.Recordset.RecordCount
On Error Goto 0

'see if we found any records for this search
If intRecs > 0 Then
    'show the "results" table and create message
    document.all("tblCustomers").style.display = ""
    strMsg = "Click a <b>Customer Name</b> in the grid above to" _
            & "<br /> list all of the orders for that customer ..." _
            & "... etc ..."
...
```

Now you can check if you found more than the value of `DataPageSize` customers. If you did, you need to display the paging controls in the footer section of the table:

```
'show or hide the Next/Prev links depending on rows found
If intRecs > document.all("tblCustomers").DataPageSize Then
  document.all("tblNavControls").style.display = ""
Else
  document.all("tblNavControls").style.display = "none"
End If
```

If you didn't get any matching customers, you instead hide the table and create a status message that indicates this. Finally, you display the status message (whichever one you created):

```
  ...
Else
  'hide the "results" table and create message
  document.all("tblCustomers").style.display = "none"
  strMsg = "No matching customers found ..."

End If
document.all("lblMessage").InnerHTML = strMsg

End Sub
```

Selecting and Viewing an Order

As in the other versions of the application, the user will select a customer in the page you've just been examining by clicking a hyperlink in the data-bound table. This opens the `view-orders.aspx` page, and you can get the selected customer ID from the query string and display a list of their orders as soon as the page loads. The user then clicks the order ID in this (left) order list, and the details of that order are displayed in the right table, as shown in Figure 6-23.

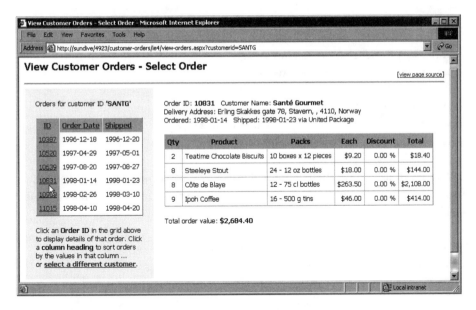

Figure 6-23. Displaying the details of a selected order

Fetching the Data from the Server

Obviously, a lot of the techniques you used in the previous page are used again in this page. However, there are some interesting points to pull out for examination. You have *two* TDC objects in this page—one for the list of orders and one for the order line details. As the page loads, these two TDC objects fetch their data from the server, using the customer ID passed from the previous page in the query string.

So how do you set the DataURL properties of these TDC objects dynamically? In this case, you set them on the server side using ASP.NET code. The value attribute for the two DataURL <param> elements is set using the values of two ASP.NET server-side variables named strOrdersURL and strDetailURL:

```
<object id="tdcOrders" width="0" height="0"
        classid="CLSID:333c7bc4-460f-11d0-bc04-0080c7055a83">
  <param name="FieldDelim" value="&#09;">
  <param name="UseHeader" value="true">
  <param name="CaseSensitive" value="false">
  <param name="CharSet" value="utf-8">
  <param name="DataURL" value="<% = strOrdersURL %>" />
</object>
```

```
<object id="tdcDetail" width="0" height="0"
        classid="CLSID:333c7bc4-460f-11d0-bc04-0080c7055a83">
  <param name="FieldDelim" value="&#09;">
  <param name="UseHeader" value="true">
  <param name="CaseSensitive" value="false">
  <param name="CharSet" value="utf-8">
  <param name="DataURL" value="<% = strDetailURL %>" />
</object>
```

These variables have their values set during the server-side `Page_Load` event. You also save the value of the customer ID passed in the query string in a variable named strCustID:

```
<!-------------- Server-side Script Section ---------------->
<script language="C#" runat="server">

String strCustID, strOrdersURL, strDetailURL;

void Page_Load() {

  // get the customer ID from the query string
  strCustID = Request.QueryString["customerid"];

  if (strCustID != "") {
    // create URLs and query strings to load order details for this customer
    strOrdersURL = "order-data.aspx?type=orderlist&customerid=" + strCustID;
    strDetailURL = "order-data.aspx?type=orderdetail&customerid=" + strCustID;
  }
}
</script>
```

All this code runs and completes before the page is sent to the client. When it arrives there, the ASP.NET value placeholders have been replaced by the actual values, so the TDC <param> elements will now look like this:

```
<param name="DataURL"
       value="order-data.aspx?type=orderlist&customerid=FAMIA" />
```

and this:

```
<param name="DataURL"
       value="order-data.aspx?type=orderdetail&customerid=FAMIA" />
```

Hence, the TDCs will load the appropriate set of rows from the middle tier automatically as the page loads into the browser.

Setting the Customer ID on the Client Side

You also need to be able to get at the customer ID from within your client-side code. You could extract it from the query string, but this is harder than doing it with ASP.NET. Instead, inside the client-side script section of your, page you declare a variable to hold it on the client:

```
<!-------------- Client-side Script Section ---------------->
<script language="VBScript">
<!--
Dim strCustID          'ID of the customer to view orders for
```

Then, in the OnReadyStateChange event handler that runs when the document has finished loading, you can set the value of this client-side variable to the value held in the server-side variable:

```
Sub Document_OnReadyStateChange()
'runs once page and all content (including TDC data) is loaded

  If Document.ReadyState = "complete" Then
    strCustID = "<% = strCustID %>"
    ShowOrderList()
  End If

End Sub
```

The ASP.NET placeholder <% = strCustID %> is replaced by the value of the strCustID variable on the server, so the client just sees the following:

```
strCustID = "FAMIA"
```

The Data-Bound Tables

As well as two TDC controls, you have two data-bound tables—both hidden when the page loads. As in the previous page, you handle the OnReadyStateChange event of the Document object to discover when all the data has finished loading. When it has, you call the ShowOrderDetail routine to bind the list of orders to the left table and display it. There are a couple of points of interest in the HTML section of the page here. You can set reverse sort order for a column just by prepending a minus sign to the column name. This is the definition of one of the column headings in the table you see on the left in Figure 6-23:

```
<a href="javascript:SortOrderList('-OrderDate')"><b>Order Date</b></a>
```

The `SortOrderList` routine referenced inthe `href` property here just sets the `Sort` property of the TDC to the specified value and calls the `Reset` method of the TDC to rebind the table with the row sorted in the specified order.

You also create the hyperlink in each row of this table like you did in the previous example. In this case, the hyperlinks are `javascript:` function calls, as you saw when you looked at the middle tier component for this version for the application earlier. This is the declaration of the bound column in the HTML:

```
<a datafld="OrderDetailHref" dataformatas="text">
  <span datafld="OrderID"></span>
</a>
```

This creates the following elements when the binding takes place for the table:

```
<a href="javascript:ShowOrderDetail('10496')">
  <span>10496</span>
</a>
```

So clicking an order ID in the left table will execute the `ShowOrderDetail` routine in this page, passing in the order ID as a parameter.

The ShowOrderDetail Subroutine

The `ShowOrderDetail` routine is somewhat more complex than the `DoSearch` routine you looked at in the previous page because it has to access and display data from both TDC objects in this page and calculate the order total. You first apply a filter to the TDC that contains the order detail lines to display just the rows for this order and call the `Reset` method so that the bound table is updated:

```
Sub ShowOrderDetail(strOrderID)
'show the list of order lines in the right-hand table

  'set the reference to the right-hand TDC object
  Set objDetailData = document.all("tdcDetail")
```

```
'set the Filter property to display just the selected order
objDetailData.Filter = "OrderID = " & QUOT & strOrderID & QUOT
objDetailData.Reset
...
```

Next you need to select the row in the TDC containing the list of orders so that you can display the shipping details. However, you can't apply a filter because this will hide all the other orders for this customer. Instead, you treat the data as an ADO `Recordset` and iterate through the rows to find the matching one. Once you do, you can extract the values from the columns in this row and build up the string to display this:

```
...
'get references to the two TDC Recordsets
Set objOrdersRecs = objOrdersData.Recordset
Set objDetailRecs = objDetailData.Recordset

'scroll through Orders records to find the selected one
objOrdersRecs.MoveFirst()
Do While objOrdersRecs("OrderID") <> objDetailRecs("OrderID")
  objOrdersRecs.MoveNext()
Loop

'display the shipping details of the order
strDetail = "Order ID: " & objDetailRecs("OrderID") _
  & "  Customer Name: " & objOrdersRecs("ShipName") & "<br />" _
  & "Delivery Address: " & objOrdersRecs("OrderAddress") & "<br />" _
  & "Ordered: " & objOrdersRecs("OrderDate") & "   "
If objOrdersRecs("ShippedDate") = "" Then
  strDetail = strDetail & "Awaiting shipping"
Else
  strDetail = strDetail & "Shipped: " & objOrdersRecs("ShippedDate")
End If
strDetail = strDetail & " via " & objOrdersRecs("CompanyName")
document.all("lblOrderDetail").InnerHTML = strDetail
...
```

You might recall that you checked for `null` values in the table and output an empty string for these, when you were building the delimited text data for the TDC to use (in your middle tier). So, when you come across a `ShippedDate` value that's empty in the previous code, you can display the "Awaiting shipping" message.

The final part of this routine calculates the order total and displays it in the page. You iterate through the ADO Recordset object that you created a reference to earlier in the code, summing the LineTotal value from each one. These values are actually stored in the data as text (after all, the data source is a text file), but the combination of the ADO Recordset capabilities and VBScript's implicit data type conversion mean that you actually do get a calculated total, not just a long string:

```
...
'calculate and display the total value of the order
dblTotal = 0
Do While Not objDetailRecs.EOF
   dblTotal = dblTotal + objDetailRecs("LineTotal")
   objDetailRecs.MoveNext()
Loop
document.all("lblOrderTotal").InnerHTML = "Total order value: <b>$" _
  & FormatNumber(dblTotal, 2) & "</b>"
...
```

All the data-bound tables in the application are hidden when the page first loads. So you need to finish off by making this table visible again:

```
  ...
  'make the table visible
  document.all("tblDetail").style.display = ""

End Sub
```

Specifying Currency and Percentage Formats

In the various versions of the application, you made sure that the locale of the server or client didn't affect the way the data is displayed such that it actually changes the data values. For example, if the database contains prices in U.S. dollars (as in the example), you definitely don't want them to be displayed with a different currency symbol.

In the middle tier component (the relevant code is repeated next), you formatted the data for the order detail lines, which you display in the right table of this page. You specified fixed numeric format with two decimal places, rather than using a conversion to currency. However, you did use the conversion to a percentage format, which might vary based on locale, but a percentage value doesn't change for different localized "percent" symbols:

```
// * this code is in our middle-tier component *
// create the result string for this row
strResult += objRow["OrderID"].ToString() + TAB
        + objRow["ProductName"].ToString() + TAB
        + objRow["QuantityPerUnit"].ToString() + TAB
        + dPrice.ToString("N2") + TAB
        + iQty.ToString() + TAB
        + fDiscount.ToString("p") + TAB
        + dTotal.ToString("N2") + "\n";
```

In the page itself, you then need to add the "dollar" currency symbol to each row in the order detail lines table. You do this by including it in the data-bound table, outside the element that's actually bound to the column in the data source. You can insert any fixed content into the table cells like this—even combining more that one bound element if required:

```
<td align="right" nowrap="nowrap">
$<span datafld="LineTotal" dataformatas="html"></span>
</td>
```

Client-Side Data Binding with XML Anyone?

If this example of RDS and client-side data binding has tempted you to investigate further, you might like to look at the other ActiveX objects (and Java applets) that are available to take advantage of this technique. The Advanced Data Control (ADC) is also installed as part of RDS in Internet Explorer 4 and higher. This control can accept an XML document as its data source and expose it as an ADO-style disconnected Recordset object—as well as supporting client-side data binding. For more details, see http://msdn.microsoft.com/library/en-us/ado270/htm/ mdmscsection2_rds.asp.

The ADC is quite fussy about the format and structure of the XML, but it could prove useful because it too makes dynamically generating tables very easy. And it brings us back to XML formatted data, which was the main topic of the chapter. Could we have planned it better?

Summary

This chapter continued to explore client-specific versions of the Customer Order List application. Chapter 5 was devoted to down-level clients, and this chapter presented various techniques that are available for rich Web browser clients.

Although you concentrated predominantly on using XML as the data transfer and client-side storage protocol, you did wander off in the last example to look at how you can use delimited text-format data as well.

The aim of showing you this rather mixed bag of techniques is to further reinforce the concept that—under .NET—you no longer have to worry about the format of your data. You can take advantage of different types of clients that, between them, can consume data in almost any format. As you saw in earlier chapters, you can also easily convert your data from one format to another.

The use of middle tier components gives you segregation between the client and the data access tier, with only a minor performance hit in most cases. This performance hit is often completely negated by the improvements in performance, efficiency, and usability that you can get from using a rich client.

In this chapter, you looked at the following:

- How you can use XML as your data storage and transfer medium

- How you can use XML with Microsoft Internet Explorer 5 and higher

- How you can use XML via a Web Service

- How you can use XML in a completely disconnected application

- How you can use delimited text as the data storage and transfer medium

In the next chapter, you'll continue your exploration of rich clients, but this time you won't be using a Web browser at all. You'll see how .NET Remoting to a client that has the Framework installed can provide really interactive and high-performance applications.

CHAPTER 7

Remoting to
.NET Clients

IN THE PREVIOUS CHAPTER, you looked at rich clients and examined ways of dealing with data in a Web browser. Dynamic HTML (DHTML) is extremely powerful, and you can build some great user interfaces and applications with it, but ultimately it's restricted by its design. Web browsers weren't designed to be an application platform—additions such as Cascading Style Sheets (CSS), scripting, plug-ins, and so on are all an attempt to make Web applications richer than plain Hypertext Markup Language (HTML). Granted, you can achieve a lot with these features, as you've already seen, but there's so much more you can achieve if you have the option of another platform.

It'll be a fair while before the .NET Framework is available on every machine, but until then there are still many occasions when you know that it'll be there. Corporate applications, for example, are a great case. If you have the option of using the rich environment that .NET provides, is it sensible to use a browser as your user interface? Why not use the richness that a Windows application can provide? You can still take advantage of ASP.NET on the back end and still use the business logic you've developed, but you get the ability to improve the user experience.

So, in this chapter, you'll look at the following:

- The practicalities of remoting to Windows clients

- How data can be used in a Windows interface

- The security implications of running code from a remote location

- How to deploy code to remote locations

Although in this chapter you'll target a Windows Forms application, you can use some of the existing business logic you've already created. This shows that even if you do have to integrate a Windows application into your existing architecture, you can do so without losing the investment you've already made.

What you'll do is build a version of the same application you've been using in the earlier chapters, but using Windows Forms. To start with, you won't deal with updating the data (that'll come in a later chapter), which will allow you to concentrate on the design issues and how to resolve them.

Remoting Refresher

It's worth quickly looking at the topics discussed in Chapter 4 because it's now that you come to the practicalities of using remoting:

- **Serialization**: This is the term given to saving the state of an object so that it can be transferred to another process. Web Services, for example, often serialize data into Extensible Markup Language (XML) to be returned over Hypertext Transfer Protocol (HTTP).

- **Marshal By Value (MBV)**: This is the act of transferring serialized data between processes. It involves the same class on the client and the server, with an instance of the class on the server being serialized and a new instance being created on the client from that serialized data (or serialized from client to server if marshaling in the opposite direction).

- **Marshal By Reference (MBR)**: This is the use of a server-side object on the client. The client requests an instance of an object and receives a reference to it, and the actual instance remains on the server.

As in the rest of the book, you'll concentrate on MBV because that's all that the application requires, but it's important to look at object remoting to see how easy it is, what uses it has, and ultimately why you don't require it.

Remoting Objects

Chapter 4 briefly showed how you can remote objects by inheriting the object from `MarhsalByRefObject`. Let's look at a real-world example to see how easy this is to perform. To get across the point that the object is still running on the server, you'll build a simple logging application that allows the client to log progress. For simplicity, you'll just write these log details to the screen.

The Remotable Object Class

Let's first look at the logging component—this is the one that'll be marshaled:

```
Imports System

Namespace DDA.Remoting.Log

    Public Class Logger
      Inherits MarshalByRefObject

        Public Sub Log(Message As String)

            Console.WriteLine(Message)

        End Sub

    End Class

End Namespace
```

The code for this component is extremely simple but illustrates the point. You define a class that inherits from `MarshalByRef` with one method call, `Log`, which simply writes a string to the console.

The Remote Server

That's all you have to do to this class to allow it to be marshaled by reference, but you also need a server to perform the marshaling. You can use Internet Information Services (IIS) to do this for you, or you can create a server object:

```
Imports System
Imports System.Runtime.Remoting
Imports System.Runtime.Remoting.Channels
Imports System.Runtime.Remoting.Channels.Http
Imports System.Runtime.Remoting.Channels.Tcp
Imports DDA.Remoting.Log

Namespace DDA.Remoting

    Public Class logServer
```

```
    Public Shared Sub Main()

        ChannelServices.RegisterChannel(New HttpChannel(8000))
        ChannelServices.RegisterChannel(New TcpChannel(8001))

    RemotingConfiguration.RegisterWellKnownServiceType(GetType(Logger), _
            "Log", WellKnownObjectMode.Singleton)

        Console.WriteLine("Log server listening...")
        Console.WriteLine("Press enter to stop the server...")
        Console.ReadLine()

    End Sub

  End Class

End Namespace
```

This example is a console application, but it could equally be a Windows service. There are really only two lines of actual code required for the server implementation. The first is creating and registering a channel to listen on, and the second is registering the class to be used on that channel. You'll now look at the code in more detail. At the top there are the references to the remoting namespaces you need:

```
Imports System.Runtime.Remoting
Imports System.Runtime.Remoting.Channels
Imports System.Runtime.Remoting.Channels.Http
Imports System.Runtime.Remoting.Channels.Tcp
```

There are references to both the HTTP and Transmission Channel Protocol (TCP) channels, just to show that the process is the same for both, but you only actually need one channel. The choice of HTTP or TCP depends upon your network really—if you're remoting objects through a firewall, then you need to persuade your system administrator to open the required port. Alternatively, you can let IIS host your server objects, in which case port 80 is used and would need to be open on the firewall to allow the Web site to be accessed.

For this procedure, you instantiate instances of the HttpChannel and TcpChannel classes, passing in port numbers to use. You pass these instances into the RegisterChannel method of the ChannelServices class, which registers the channel as "in use." This is required because port numbers can only be used by one application at a time, so registering them ensures than no one else can use the same port for a different purpose (on the same machine).

Once the channel is registered, it needs to be configured for your particular remotable object. You need to do this so that clients can request your object. The RegisterWellKnownServiceType takes three arguments:

- The type of the remotable object.

- The Uniform Resource Indicator (URI) to provide a unique name for the remotable object.

- The activation mode, which is either SingleCall or Singleton. Using SingleCall means that each request for the object generates a new instance of the object, and Singleton uses the same instances for each request.

Once the service is registered, there's nothing more to do—the listeners will sit and wait for incoming requests. You can add a ReadLine to the code to stop it from exiting—this keeps the server process running and waiting for requests until the return key is pressed. If you just exited straight away, then the listeners would also stop, and there would be no server process for the client to connect to.

IIS Hosted Servers

As an alternative to writing a custom server object that requires a separate application, you can let IIS host the remotable object for you. This involves creating a virtual directory, placing the component in the bin directory of this root, and then creating a web.config file:

```
<configuration>
 <system.runtime.remoting>
  <application>
   <service>
    <activated type="DDA.Remoting.Log.Logger, DDA.Remoting.Log "/>
   </service>
  </application>
 </system.runtime.remoting>
</configuration>
```

IIS now does the listening, and you don't need a server at all. Obviously, your simple component now has a problem because it's writing to the console, and an IIS hosted component doesn't have a console. However, in real life it's unlikely this is all your component will do, and if it does need to log messages, then a log file is much more appropriate than the console.

One good reason for using IIS is that you automatically get the benefits of IIS, such as scalability, resource usage, and security. With your own server, you have to provide these for yourself.

Running the Server

You can now run the server, as shown in Figure 7-1.

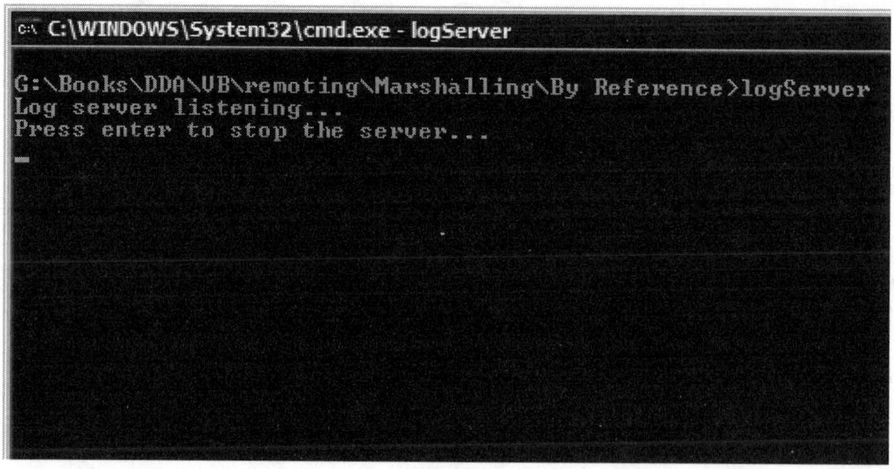

```
C:\WINDOWS\System32\cmd.exe - logServer

G:\Books\DDA\VB\remoting\Marshalling\By Reference>logServer
Log server listening...
Press enter to stop the server...
```

Figure 7-1. Running the server from the command line

Nothing happens yet because you haven't run the client, so you'll now look at that.

The Remote Client

For the client, you use the `Activator` class to create an instance of the remote class. As mentioned earlier, what you actually get is a proxy to that class, but because the proxy has the same methods and properties as the requested class, its operation is the same. Here's the complete code:

```
Imports System
Imports System.Runtime.Remoting
Imports DDA.Remoting.Log
```

```
Namespace DDA.Remoting

    Public Class logClient

        Public Shared Sub Main()

            Dim httpLogger As Logger
            Dim tcpLogger  As Logger

            httpLogger = CType(Activator.GetObject(GetType(Logger), _
                            "http://localhost:8000/Log"), Logger)
            tcpLogger = CType(Activator.GetObject(GetType(Logger), _
                            "tcp://localhost:8001/Log"), Logger)

            httpLogger.Log("HTTP Client Request")
            tcpLogger.Log("TCP Client Request")

        End Sub

    End Class

End Namespace
```

If you look in detail, you can see there are really only three lines of code required to use the object—there are six lines because you're using both the HTTP and TCP channels. The complex line is where you instantiate your object:

```
tcpLogger = CType(Activator.GetObject(GetType(Logger), _
                "tcp://localhost:8001/Log"), Logger)
```

The Activator class allows you to create instances of objects using the type of the object and the Uniform Resource Locator (URL) of its location. The GetObject method returns an object so you have to cast it to your Logger type. As an alternative to this, you could register the class as a well-known client type, allowing you to use New to instantiate the object:

```
RemotingConfiguration.RegisterWellKnownClientType(GetType(Logger), _
                                        "tcp://localhost:8001/Log")


Dim tcpLogger As New Logger()
```

Both methods ultimately produce the same response. The latter is preferable if you're going to instantiate the object several times because it's easier to read. Whichever you use, at this point you have a reference to your server object and can call its methods and properties. You'll run the client to see what happens, as shown in Figure 7-2.

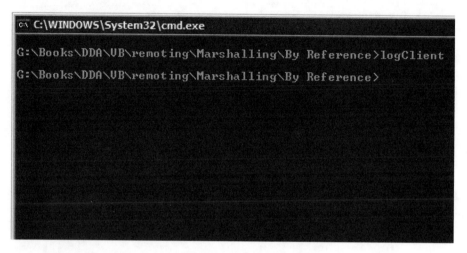

Figure 7-2. Running the client from the command line

Notice that nothing seems to happen—that's because the client doesn't display anything to the screen itself. It calls the Log method of the remotable object, but because this is a server-based object, the output appears on the server, as shown in Figure 7-3.

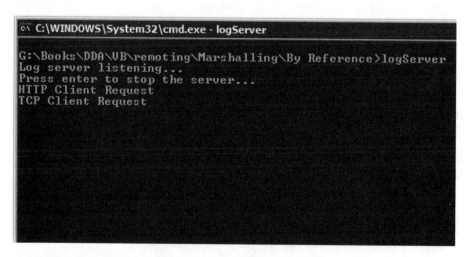

Figure 7-3. The server showing client connections

You haven't done anything to the server but because it's handling your `Logger` object, the output shows here. The server continues to listen until you press Return.

Using IIS-Hosted Servers

When using IIS-hosted servers, you can only use the HTTP channel, and you don't have to provide port details. In this case, your activator code would look like this:

```
httpLogger = CType(Activator.GetObject(GetType(Logger), _
                 "http://localhost/VirtualDirectory"), Logger)
```

Using Configuration Files

Adding a configuration file to the client means that the code doesn't have to contain any of the configuration and also allows the use of the `New` keyword when instantiating components. The configuration file would look like this:

```
<configuration>
 <system.runtime.remoting>
  <application name="Client">

   <client url="http://localhost/DDA/remoting/By Reference/">
    <activated type="DDA.Remoting.Log.Logger, DDA.Remoting.Log" />
   </client>

   <channels>
    <channel ref="http" />
   </channels>

  </application>
 </system.runtime.remoting>
</configuration>
```

The code could now become this:

```
RemotingConfiguration.Configure("logClientIIS.exe.config")

Dim httpLogger As New Logger()

httpLogger.Log("HTTP Client Request")
```

Deploying the Objects

With the previous example, you have three parts—the remotable object, the client, and the server. It's obvious that the client executable goes to the client machine and the server executable goes to the server machine, but what about the remotable object? Both the client and server require it even though it's a server-based object. You can clearly see this by looking at the commands used to compile the example:

```
vbc /rSystem.dll /t:library Logger.vb
vbc /r:System.Runtime.Remoting.dll /r:System.dll /r:Logger.dll logServer.vb
vbc /r:System.Runtime.Remoting.dll /r:System.dll /r:Logger.dll logClient.vb
```

Notice that you have to reference the logging component (Logger.dll) in the compile for both the client and the server. That's because both the client and the server need to know the type of the object with which they're dealing. This might not seem a problem, until you realize that the component is required at runtime as well as compile time. OK, you think, just copy it to the two locations. This is fine if people you trust only use your application, but because the component contains application logic, do you really want it available to all clients? The object logic doesn't need to be on the client because it'll be run from the server. There are a couple of ways around this problem:

- Use the soapsuds tool to generate a proxy of the component and distribute this to the client.

- Use an interface and then implement the interface in the component. The interface should be in a separate assembly, and because it contains no logic can easily be distributed to clients.

Both of these topics are really outside the scope of what you're doing in this book, so for more details, you should consult the help files.

The Windows Application

You've spent the first part of this chapter examining some basic remoting ideas and seeing how easy it is to use remotable objects. What you now need to do is consider what you're trying to achieve—creating a Windows application in the same vein as your Web-based interfaces. Figure 7-4 shows a simple example of what this application might look like.

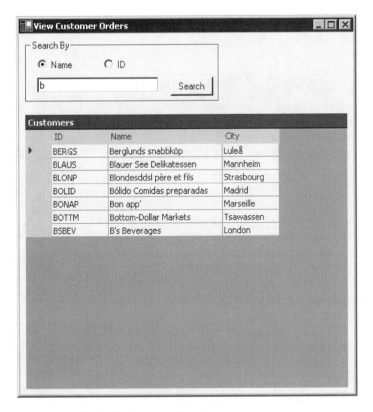

Figure 7-4. The Windows application

Here you have the opportunity to search for customers, either by customer ID or by name. Selecting a customer then shows the orders for them in a separate form, as shown in Figure 7-5.

This uses the standard grid supplied with Visual Studio .NET, and Figure 7-6 shows the page after selecting the link for the order lines.

You could easily have included the order details on the same form as the customers, utilizing a second grid, but there are a number of reasons not to do this:

- Future enhancements are easier because all of the order code is encapsulated.

- Multiple copies of this form can be opened by selecting a different (or the same) customer from the main form.

- It opens the way to easily distribute the application in stages. You'll look at this later in the chapter.

You won't include any update functionality at this stage—you'll come back to that in a later chapter.

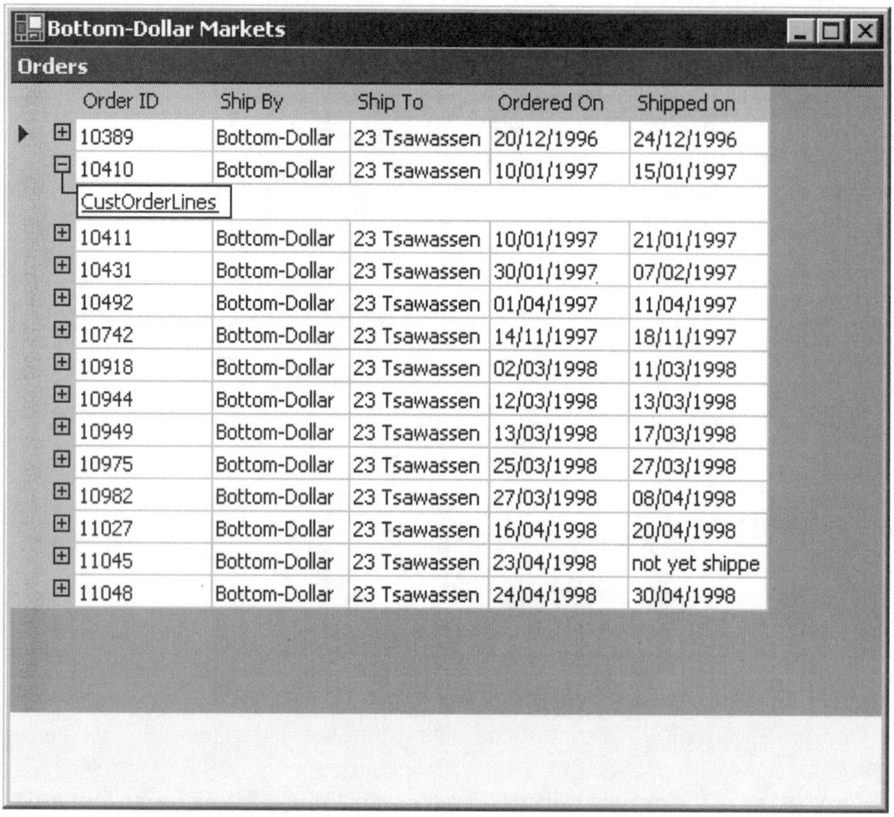

Figure 7-5. Displaying the orders

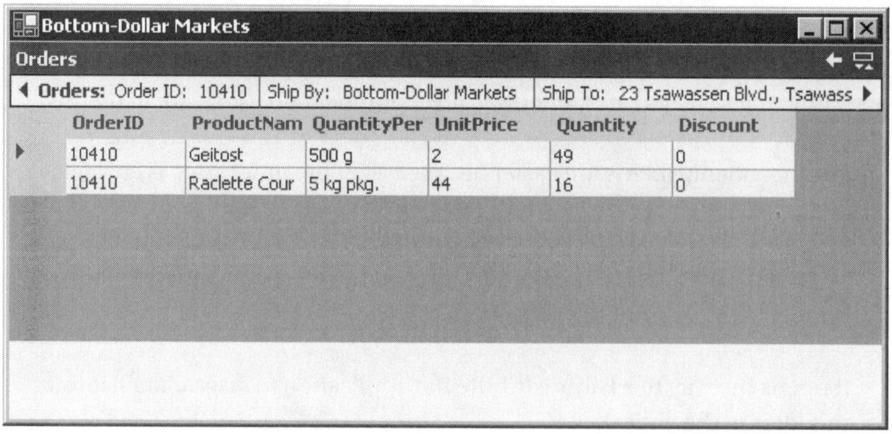

Figure 7-6. Viewing the order details

The Design Choices

At the moment this is a simple application, just allowing you to browse customers and their associated orders. However, even if this is all you want to achieve, you have to decide how to architect the application. With the Web clients you have a multitude of ways of dealing with the data, and that choice increases when you think about .NET clients. Just because you have more choices doesn't mean that you have to use everything that's allowed. Designing an application is about using what's appropriate and not what's available.

So, let's consider what you want to achieve. You need to have the data available locally for processing—that's the prime concern. Is there anything else you need yet? Not yet—all you're doing is displaying data—you don't need any other functionality. So what's the reason for the lengthy discussion of remoting? Well, when making a decision you need as much information as possible. OK, you're not using remoting specifically in this application, but when you come to build applications that require distributed processing and data, you may well need these techniques. Back in Chapter 4 we identified two areas where you should use remoting:

- When you need to maintain state on the server

- When the network is resilient enough to maintain the connection between the two application domains

The application clearly doesn't need server state for its objects, and although you're using it on machines connected to the same network, there's no reason why it can't be used over lesser connections, such as dial-up. At this stage, you'll leave behind the remoting of objects and move back into data.

Remoting Data to Windows Applications

In the previous chapter, you looked at how much code had to be written to handle the data on the client. Now that you've got .NET on the client, you don't have to worry about any esoteric techniques because you can use the native .NET data handling features. The .NET standard for offline storage is the DataSet, so the sensible thing for you to do is use the DataSet locally. Once you've decided upon this, you then have to work out how you get the data from the server to the client. There are several options:

- Directly access the data store from your application. This isn't a sensible solution for several reasons. First, it means you can't use any code you've already written, which fundamentally goes against good design principles. It also means you're bypassing the idea of a middle tier for data access, which is also poor design.

- Build some components to abstract the business and data logic. This is a step in the right direction but still leaves you with too much happening on the client.

- Have all of the data handled on the server and just reuse the data in your client application.

The last one of these is the obvious choice. You may be dealing with a rich client, but rich shouldn't mean fat. There's no reason to have anything in the client that isn't required, so you'll leave the data and business logic on the server. You can reuse some of the components and services that have already been built and add any extra ones you require.

Building the Windows Application

You'll now look at the steps to build this application. The first thing to do is to add references to the existing assemblies, as shown in Figure 7-7.

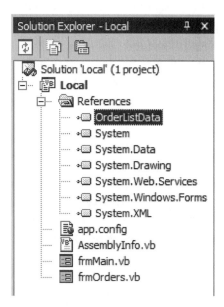

Figure 7-7. Adding references

This uses the `OrderListData` assembly created in previous chapters. You also use `app.config` to store the connection string details. In the Web application, you use the `web.config` to store the details, but this is a Windows application and therefore can't use the same configuration file. However, `app.config` is the Windows Forms equivalent, so yours contains the following:

```
<?xml version="1.0" encoding="utf-8"?>
<configuration>
<appSettings>
    <add key="NW"
          value="provider=SQLOLEDB.1;data source=localhost; ⏎
                   initial catalog=Northwind;uid=anon;pwd=;"/>
</appSettings>
</configuration>
```

The design of the first form is simple—it has a couple of radio buttons, a text box to allow selection of the search items, and a button to run the search. The results are placed directly in a data grid. In the code you first add an `Imports` statement:

```
Imports System.Configuration
```

This will allow you to access the configuration file to extract the connection string details.

Next you define a global variable to hold the set of customer records:

```
Private m_dsCustomers  As DataSet
```

When the user searches, you create an instance of the component, passing in the connection string details extracted from the configuration file:

```
Dim objCustOrder As OrderListData.OrderList

objCustOrder = New _
    OrderListData.OrderList(ConfigurationSettings.AppSettings("NW"))
```

Now you can use the `GetCustomerByIdOrName` method to return a `DataSet` containing the required customers:

```
If rdID.Checked Then
  m_dsCustomers = objCustOrder.GetCustomerByIdOrName(txtSearch.Text, "")
Else
  m_dsCustomers = objCustOrder.GetCustomerByIdOrName("", txtSearch.Text)
End If
```

And finally you bind that DataSet to the grid:

```
dgCustomers.DataSource = m_dsCustomers
```

You set the properties of the grid in design mode so that only the customer ID, name, and city display.

Compared to the Web clients (even the rich ones), you can already see how much less code you have to write. You have the ability to natively handle DataSets, so you don't have to worry about converting the data to XML and all of the complexities that involves.

Showing the Orders

To show order details for a particular customer, you can use the Click event of the grid:

```
Private Sub dgCustomers_Click(ByVal sender As Object, _
                              ByVal e As System.EventArgs) _
                                        Handles dgCustomers.Click
```

The first thing you do is link to the selected row using the CurrentRowIndex property of the grid. You use this to index into the Rows collection of the Table (you've only got one table in this DataSet):

```
Dim CurrentRow As DataRow = _
            m_dsCustomers.Tables(0).Rows(dgCustomers.CurrentRowIndex)
```

Then you extract the ID of the customer from that row:

```
 Dim CustID As String = CurrentRow.Item("CustomerID")
```

Next you instantiate a new instance of the order form (frmOrders), passing the customer ID into the constructor. You'll look at this form in a little while:

```
Dim fOrders As New frmOrders(CustID)
```

Now you set the title of the form to the customer name and show the form:

```
 fOrders.Text = CurrentRow.Item("CompanyName")

 fOrders.Show()

End Sub
```

That's all there is to this form. It's obvious that having the rich controls as well as using the data types on the client makes development much easier. You'll also see this in the orders form.

The Orders Form

For this form you also add the `Imports` statement to allow access to the connection string:

```
Imports System.Configuration
```

You then create a new constructor with the customer ID as its argument:

```
Public Sub New(ByVal CustID As String)
```

The first thing to do is call the default constructor to ensure that the form is initialized correctly:

```
Me.New()
```

Then you perform the connection and object instantiation:

```
Dim objOrderList As OrderListData.OrderList

objOrderList = New _
    OrderListData.OrderList(ConfigurationSettings.AppSettings("NW"))
```

Once the component is instantiated, you use the results of the `GetOrdersByCustomerDataSet` method (which returns a `DataSet`) as the data source for a grid:

```
dgOrders.DataSource = objOrderList.GetOrdersByCustomerDataSet(CustID)
```

```
End Sub
```

That's all the code for this form. The great thing about this is that the orders and order lines are handled by the grid. The `DataSet` returned by `GetOrdersByCus-tomerDataSet` contains two tables, with the appropriate links between them. Because at design time you set the grid to show both the parent and children, you automatically get the relationship preserved.

All in all you've used just over a dozen lines of code to perform what the Web application had to use…err…well, many more. I won't bother counting them. The important thing is to remember that coding for a Windows application often requires less code because there are so many more facilities available.

Creating the Web Services

At this stage, the application is still rather bound to the local machine because you're using local assemblies for data access. To make this work on a remote system, you need a way to get the data, and Web Services are the sensible solution. It'd be quite possible for you to build a remoting server dedicated to serving data for your application, but Web Services already provide that functionality. We've also already got some written, so you can reuse those. You have the `customer-data.asmx` service (from the `customer-orders/webservices` directory) that you can use to return the customer details. You could also use this to return the order details, but you'll create a new Web Service for that.

Why create a new one after we've been promoting reuse? Well, some of the existing services are written specifically with the Web clients in mind—in effect they're the business logic layer for the Web interface. This means that some of them have to do things because of the way the Web interface handles data. Because you have access to `DataSets`, you can do less work in the Web Service. So you create a Web Service called `RemotingOrders` (in `webservices\order-details.asmx`) with the following method:

```
<WebMethod> _
Public Function Orders(strCustID As String) As DataSet

  Dim objDataSet As DataSet

  Try

    Dim strConnect As String = _
            ConfigurationSettings.AppSettings("NorthwindConnectString")

    ' create an instance of the data access component
    Dim objOrderUpdate As New UpdateDataSet(strConnect)

    ' call component to get DataSet containing order details for customer
    objDataSet = objOrderUpdate.GetOrderDetails(strCustID)

    ' add column containing total value of each line in OrderLines table
    Dim objLinesTable As DataTable = objDataSet.Tables("Order Details")
    Dim objColumn As DataColumn = objLinesTable.Columns.Add("LineTotal", _
                              System.Type.GetType("System.Double"))
    objColumn.Expression = _
                "[Quantity] * ([UnitPrice] - ([UnitPrice] * [Discount]))"

    ' set the Nested property of the relationship between the tables so they
    ' are appropriately linked (OrderLines nested within each Order)
```

```
        objDataSet.Relations(0).Nested = True

        ' return the DataSet to the calling routine
        Return objDataSet

    Catch objErr As Exception

        ' there was an error so no data is returned

    End Try

End Function
```

This code is similar to that provided by the other service, but you'll add more methods in a later chapter.

Using the Web Services

To modify the application to use Web Services, you first remove the references to the local components. Next you add a Web reference, as shown in Figure 7-8.

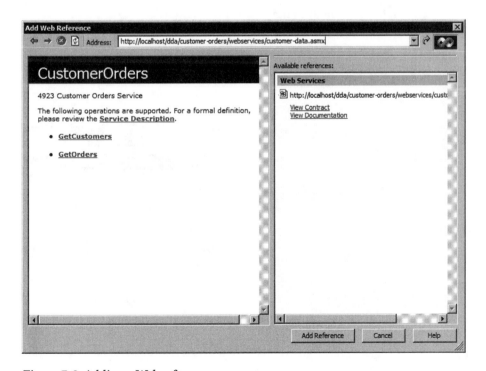

Figure 7-8. Adding a Web reference

In this example, the Web Service is running on the local machine, but it works the same for any machine.

This Visual Studio .NET tool automatically creates the client Web proxy for you and adds the references to the solution, as shown in Figure 7-9.

One useful thing to do once the Web reference has been added is to set the URL Behavior property to Dynamic, as shown in Figure 7-10.

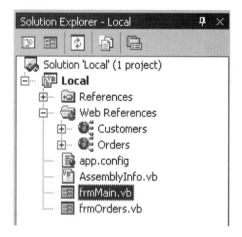

Figure 7-9. The references added to the solution

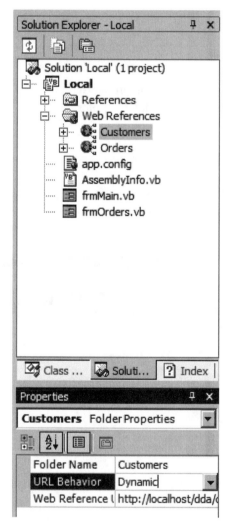

Figure 7-10. Setting the URL Behavior property

This takes the URL and adds it to the configuration file:

```
<?xml version="1.0" encoding="Windows-1252"?>
<configuration>
  <appSettings>
    <add key="Local.Customers.CustomerOrders"
         value="http://localhost/dda/
                customer-orders/webservices/customer-data.asmx"/>
    <add key="Local.Orders.RemotingOrders"
         value="http://localhost/dda/remoting/webservices/order-details.asmx"/>
  </appSettings>
</configuration>
```

Having the URL in the configuration file means that it's read at runtime so is easily configurable.

Now that the service is referenced, all you have to do is use the service as though it were a component. To do that, you modify the search button code:

```
Dim wsCustomers As New Customers.CustomerOrders()

If rdID.Checked Then
  m_dsCustomers = wsCustomers.GetCustomers(txtSearch.Text, "")
Else
  m_dsCustomers = wsCustomers.GetCustomers("", txtSearch.Text)
End If

dgCustomers.DataSource = m_dsCustomers
```

Notice how much simpler this is—just one call to instantiate the Web Service and one call to fetch the data. Now you have no local component usage, and the data is fetched from a remote server. You don't have to change the grid code because that uses the same DataSet—it's only the way you fetched the data that has changed.

The same applies to the constructor for the orders form, which now looks like this:

```
Public Sub New(ByVal CustID As String)

Me.New()

  Dim wsOrders As New Orders.RemotingOrders()

  dgOrders.DataSource = wsOrders.Orders(CustID)

End Sub
```

This simply instantiates the new Web Service you created and uses the data for the source of the grid.

At this stage, the application can now be used on a remote machine because the data is obtained remotely. There are no local components, and it's a simple executable file that can be run on any machine with .NET installed.

Incremental Downloads

Although you've built a simple example, you can imagine how a more complex application could get quite large. One of the problems with monolithic applications is that updating them is cumbersome. How many applications have you had to uninstall and reinstall to get a new version? How many times have you been asked to download large executables because a new version of your favorite tool is available?

What .NET brings to this arena is the ability to perform incremental downloads. In the sample application, you can do the following:

```
Dim fOrders As New frmOrders(CustID)
```

This loads a new copy of a form stored within the application. However, what you can do is load a form from a remote location. In fact, this doesn't just apply to forms but to any assembly, so you have the option of making your application very dynamic.

Creating a Downloadable Form

For a form to be downloaded dynamically, it has to be in a separate assembly. Each form doesn't have to be a separate assembly—you can have multiple forms, perhaps grouped by function, because it's the assembly that's loaded on demand. You'll convert the orders form to be used dynamically.

To do this, you pick the Windows Control Library project type when creating a new project. This gives you a user control. You want a form, so you first change the Inherits statement from this:

```
Public Class OrdersForm
    Inherits System.Windows.Forms.UserControl
```

to this:

```
Public Class OrdersForm
    Inherits System.Windows.Forms.Form
```

Because this form is just a normal Windows form, and you want it to behave exactly the same as the orders form, you add a Web reference to point to the orders Web Service. This time you don't use the dynamic URL behavior because you want the assembly to be completely self-contained, without any configuration files.

Next you want to display the order details as you did previously, so you add a new constructor:

```
Public Sub New(ByVal CustID As String)

    Me.New()

    ' create an instance of the orders Web Service
    Dim wsOrders As New OrdersService.RemotingOrders()

    ' and bind the orders grid to the orders for that customer
    Me.dgOrders.DataSource = wsOrders.Orders(CustID)

End Sub
```

That's all there is to it. Building the solution gives you an assembly containing this form.

Loading the Form Dynamically

Now you have the form in an assembly you need to load that on demand. You can obviously remove the orders form from the main application, and when the user selects a form, you need to find out where that assembly is stored and load it. To perform this action, you first need a reference to the System.Reflection namespace—this contains the classes that allow you to deal with code dynamically:

```
Imports System.Reflection
```

Now you'll see the routine where you select a customer. In the previous version of the application, you had this:

```
Dim fOrders As New frmOrders(CustID)
```

Now you'll create a function called LoadForm, so your code becomes this:

```
Dim fOrders As New Form = LoadForm(CustID)
```

The `LoadForm` function consists of the following code:

```
Private Function LoadForm(ByVal CustID As String) As Form

    Dim FormLocation As String = _
                    ConfigurationSettings.AppSettings("FormsURL") _
                    & "Orders.dll"
    Dim asm As [Assembly] = [Assembly].LoadFrom(FormLocation)
    Dim typ As Type = asm.GetType("Orders.OrdersForm", True, True)
    Dim obj As Object
    Dim args As Object() = {CustID}

    obj = Activator.CreateInstance(typ, args)

    Dim frmOrders As Form = CType(obj, Form)

    Return frmOrders

End Function
```

You'll now look at this in a detail. The first line obtains the location of the form. You've used the configuration file to store this:

```
<?xml version="1.0" encoding="Windows-1252"?>
<configuration>
  <appSettings>
    <add key="FormsURL" value="http://localhost/dda/remoting/Forms/"/>
  </appSettings>
</configuration>
```

This would also contain the details of the Web Service to obtain the customer details—we've left that out here just so you can see this line more easily. This is just a URL pointing to the location where the assembly resides. Here it's a local URL, but because it's HTTP, it can be anywhere. In the downloadable code, the URL points to http://www.daveandal.com.

To read this information, you use the same method as in ASP.NET pages, using the `ConfigurationSettings` class to read the `AppSettings` details. This returns the URL as a string, onto which you add `Orders.dll`, which is the name of the assembly.

Next you need to load the assembly:

```
Dim asm As [Assembly] = [Assembly].LoadFrom(FormLocation)
```

The `Assembly` class is used, unsurprisingly, to deal with assemblies. One of its methods is `LoadFrom`, which loads an assembly from a given location.

Next you need to determine the framework type of the `OrdersForm` object within the assembly:

```
Dim typ As Type = asm.GetType("Orders.OrdersForm", True, True)
```

The `GetType` method is overloaded and can take one, two, or three arguments, which are as follows:

- The full name of the type

- A Boolean, which if set to `True`, ensures that an exception is thrown if the type isn't found

- A Boolean, which if set to `True`, ignores the case of the type name

You want an exception thrown if the type isn't found; otherwise, some of the later code fails.

Once the type is identified, you create a variable to hold the instance of the form and an array of `Objects` to be used as arguments for the constructor. Remember that the orders form has a constructor that takes the Customer ID to load the orders for:

```
Dim obj As Object
Dim args As Object() = {CustID}
```

Now you can actually create an instance of the form:

```
obj = Activator.CreateInstance(typ, args)
```

The `Activator` class has several methods to handle the creation of new objects. The `CreateInstance` method has several forms, and the one you use takes the type to create and the `Object` array of arguments for the constructor.

At this stage you have an `Object`, so you need to cast it to a form before returning from the function:

```
Dim frmOrders As Form = CType(obj, Form)

Return frmOrders
```

The Download Cache

Running the application is no different from the stand-alone application. The only difference is that you may experience a slight delay the first time you load the orders form because this is when the form is downloaded. It'll be a slight delay, though, because this form is less than 20 kilobytes (KB). Once downloaded, it's placed in the download cache and on subsequent loads is retrieved from the cache. You can view the contents of the download cache either by using the `gacutil` tool with the `/ldl` command switch or by navigating to the directory, which is `WINNT/assembly/Download`, as shown in Figure 7-11.

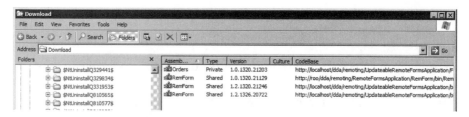

Figure 7-11. Viewing the download cache

Here you can see that there are several copies of the `RemForm` object because they've been downloaded from different locations and have different version numbers. Because you haven't strongly named the assembly (more on this later), a new assembly is downloaded based upon a date/time comparison of the cached assembly compared to the remote assembly. If the remote assembly is new, a new copy is downloaded. This means you can dynamically update remote applications simply by providing a new assembly.

You can clear the download cache by using `gacutil /cdl`.

A *strong name* is how you can uniquely identify an assembly, and it consists of a name, a version number, a public key, and a digital signature. There are several advantages to strong naming:

- You guarantee uniqueness because the key pair is part of the unique name.

- You guarantee the versioning of the assembly because no one else can produce subsequent versions.

- You guarantee that the assembly hasn't changed since it was compiled.

You can sign an assembly either by a public/private key pair or by a digital certificate. The latter is the most secure (because it guarantees the publisher), but you may not have access to certificates, so you'll see the key pair more often. To generate this, you use the sn utility—this has many options, but for your needs you can just use the -k option to generate a key pair:

```
sn -k RemForm.snk
```

The file is where the keys will be stored, and by convention it has an .snk extension. To attach the keys to your assembly, you add the AssemblyKeyFile attribute—this is generally added to the AssemblyInfo source file but can be added to any source file:

```
<Assembly: AssemblyKeyFile("RemForm.snk")>
```

When compiled, you can see that the public key has been attached to the assembly manifest in Figure 7-12.

```
MANIFEST                                                                   _ □ ×
{
  .custom instance void [mscorlib]System.Reflection.AssemblyDescriptionAttribute::.ctor(str
  // --- The following custom attribute is added automatically, do not uncomment -------
  //    .custom instance void [mscorlib]System.Diagnostics.DebuggableAttribute::.ctor(bool,
  //                                                                            bool) =
  .custom instance void [mscorlib]System.Reflection.AssemblyCompanyAttribute::.ctor(string)
  .custom instance void [mscorlib]System.Reflection.AssemblyTitleAttribute::.ctor(string) =
  .custom instance void [mscorlib]System.Reflection.AssemblyKeyFileAttribute::.ctor(string)
  .custom instance void [mscorlib]System.CLSCompliantAttribute::.ctor(bool) = ( 01 00 01 00
  .custom instance void [mscorlib]System.Reflection.AssemblyProductAttribute::.ctor(string)
  .custom instance void [mscorlib]System.Runtime.InteropServices.GuidAttribute::.ctor(strin


  .custom instance void [mscorlib]System.Reflection.AssemblyTrademarkAttribute::.ctor(strin
  .custom instance void [mscorlib]System.Reflection.AssemblyCopyrightAttribute::.ctor(strin
  .publickey = (00 24 00 00 04 80 00 00 94 00 00 00 06 02 00 00   // .$..............
                00 24 00 00 52 53 41 31 00 04 00 00 01 00 01 00   // .$..RSA1........
                AB F4 07 9C 53 6C 8E 92 52 E8 33 F8 9F D7 0D 51   // ....Sl..R.3....Q
                15 DD AD 6B D6 AE 06 F2 D2 55 E4 19 73 51 E8 66   // ...k.....U..sQ.f
                49 33 15 76 A5 DA 66 06 E3 97 2A E9 DE C6 67 6A   // I3.v..f...*...gj
                DE CB 4A BB 63 38 58 42 36 FB B6 44 0F 11 DD 1D   // ..J.c8XB6..D....
                7E 3B 89 91 66 A3 25 C1 47 07 7A 1F C3 20 C6 61   // ~;..f.%.G.z.. .a
                34 11 39 BD C3 FE F6 41 00 D7 18 ED 2E 91 33 87   // 4.9....A......3.
                3E 1E C8 7D 49 A2 24 6E FF CD 45 B6 07 D1 B3 8A   // >..}I.$n..E.....
                01 AC BA A1 51 E3 67 AF E1 17 BF 14 F6 AC 30 BE ) // ....Q.g........0.
  .hash algorithm 0x00008004
  .ver 1:2:773:28715
}
.mresource public RemForm.frmMain.resources
{
}
.module RemForm.exe
// MVID: {C69C64D5-DFE7-4938-80C6-4708DDB95466}
.imagebase 0x11000000
.subsystem 0x00000002
.file alignment 512
.corflags 0x00000009
// Image base: 0x03030000
```

Figure 7-12. Viewing the public key attached to an assembly

Strong Named Assemblies and the Download Cache

Another advantage of strong named assemblies is that assemblies referenced from remote locations will only be downloaded if a specific version is required and that version isn't in the download cache. This means that if you recompile assemblies, and you reference those assemblies with the strong name, you'll need to recompile the main application to include the new version number. If you don't reference the assemblies by their strong name, then the data/time comparison is used.

Deployment

All of this remote loading of forms and remote data is great, but you now have to consider how to deploy your application. With Web applications, it's easy because you just point people at a URL, but with a Windows application, it has to be downloaded. Fortunately, you can take the same approach by simply providing a link to the executable from within a Web page:

```
<html>
<head>
<title>Customers Download Page</title>
</head>

<body>

<h1>Customers Download Page</h1>
<p>This page allows you to download the Customers Application.
Just click on the link to run it</p>
<br/>
<a href="http://www.alanddave.com/books/dda/remoting/ ⤸
        RemoteFormsApplication/bin/RemForm.exe">Run Application</a>

</body>
</html>
```

Here you have a hyperlink reference pointing to RemForm.exe. What you see when you click this link depends on your browser—you're probably used to the typical Open/Save screen when downloading in Internet Explorer, but this is a managed executable and runs within the security context of the .NET Framework. When you install .NET on a client, it modifies Internet Explorer so that it sniffs the executable type. What then happens depends on what version of Internet Explorer you have, which patches you have applied, and which zone your remote form application is stored in. You may see the Open/Save dialog box, or the application may run directly without any dialog box. By default the localhost is a trusted domain and therefore opens directly. However, when accessing a zone that isn't trusted, you may see the warning shown in Figure 7-13.

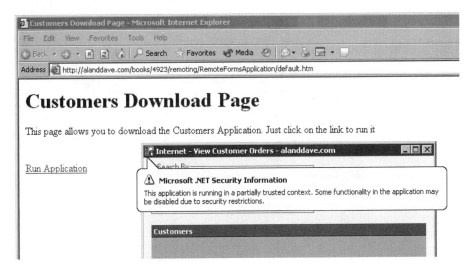

Figure 7-13. Security warning

The pop-up message shows that you retrieved the application from a site in the Internet Zone, which has limited trust for applications and just warns you that some of the functionality in your application may not work. It doesn't examine the application to check this but just warns you that you have fewer permissions than usual. One real disadvantage of this pop-up message is that is appears on subsequently downloaded forms, even if served from the download cache, which could be irritating to the user.

Security

There are many security considerations you have to deal with when providing applications to remote .NET clients. How you install the application has a big impact. For example, consider the previous download page running on a browser that doesn't automatically run applications. Selecting the link for the application will display the dialog box shown in Figure 7-14.

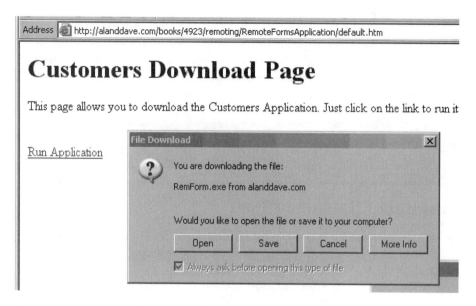

Figure 7-14. Downloading the application

If you open the file directly, you get the behavior as in Figure 7-14. However, if you save the application to your local disk and run it from there, you get a different behavior. For starters, you don't get this dialog box. This is because when running applications from your hard disk, it's assumed that the application is safe, and the level of permissions is dramatically different. What permissions you get depend on a variety of factors and are based around permission sets, code groups, and evidence.

We'll get the definitions out of the way before you look at how they're used—these might seem a bit abstract as you read through them, but they'll all click into place when you see how you use them.

A *permission set* is a set of permissions that an application has—this defines the rights that the application has to access certain resources. There are six named permission sets, which can't be altered:

- **Nothing**: The application has no permission, and code can't be run.

- **Execution**: The application has permission to run but not to access protected resources.

- **Internet**: The permissions of the application are those from an unknown origin, with restricted access to resources.

- **LocalIntranet**: There's restricted access to resources, but it's less restricted than the Internet permission.

- **SkipVerification**: All local resources are available, but code verification can't be skipped.

- **FullTrust**: This has full access to all resources.

The named permission sets correspond to the Internet zones used by Internet Explorer.

A *code group* defines a logical grouping of permissions into a membership. If an assembly meets the set of permissions, then it's a member of the code group.

Evidence is the identity of the assembly, including its strong name and its location. Thus, the same assembly loaded from two locations (one from the hard disk and one from the Internet) has different evidence.

You'll now look at how these terms affect the running of an application. When an assembly is loaded by the Common Language Runtime (CLR), the first thing that's examined is its evidence. This evidence is used to map the assembly into a code group. The assembly then runs within the permissions (identified by permission sets) specified by the code group. What permissions are actually in effect are determined by the security policy on your machine.

Security Policy

The security policy combines the evidence, code groups, and permissions sets to decide what code has permission to what resources. There are several ways in which the code groups and permission sets can be combined. By default the machine policy is as follows:

- The FullTrust permission set is associated with the My Computer Zone, Microsoft Strong Name, and ECMA Strong Name code groups. This allows unrestricted access to all resources.

- The Nothing permission set is associated with the All Code and Restricted Code groups. This allows no access to resources.

- The LocalIntranet permission set is associated with the Local Intranet code group.

- The Internet permission set is associated with the Internet and Trusted Zone code groups.

The first two are easy to understand. If the assembly is loaded from the My Computer Zone (which is the local computer), or the Microsoft or ECMA Strong Names groups identify it, then it has full trust and can do anything. If the assembly matches the All Code or Restricted Code groups, then it can't do anything. It's the latter two that are interesting because the permission sets for these restrict what the assembly is allowed (see Table 7-1).

Table 7-1. Permissions Set for the Local Intranet, Intranet, and Trusted Zones

Permission	Permission Description	Local Intranet Permission Set / Local Intranet Code Group	Internet Permission Internet Code Group / Trusted Zone Code Group
DnsPermission	Access to DNS servers	Unrestricted.	None.
EnvironmentPermission	Access to system and user environment variables	Username and Temp.	None.
EventLogPermission	Access to the event log	Can read and write to existing event logs and can create new event logs.	None.
FileDialogPermission	Access to the file dialog boxes	Unrestricted.	Open (in other words, read-only access to a file).
FileIOPermission	Access to files and folders	Read (but only from the share of origin).	None.
IsolatedStoragePermission	Access to generic isolated storage	Storage is isolated first by user and then by code assembly, with an unrestricted quota.	Storage is isolated first by user and then by domain and assembly, but with a quota of 10KB and expiring after 365 days.
PrintingPermission	Access to printers	Allows printing programmatically to the default printer and through a restricted dialog box.	Printing only from a restricted dialog box.
ReflectionPermission	Access to metadata via the `System.Reflection` classes	Use of `Reflection.Emit` is allowed.	None.
RegistryPermission	Access to the registry	None.	None.
SecurityPermission	Access to the security permissions applied to code.	Allows the code to run, to check that the code's callers have permission, and to configure remote channels and types.	Allows code to run.

(Continued)

Table 7-1. Permissions Set for the Local Intranet, Intranet, and Trusted Zones

Permission	Permission Description	Local Intranet Permission Set Local Intranet Code Group	Internet Permission Internet Code Group Trusted Zone Code Group
SocketPermission	Access to network sockets	None.	None.
UIPermission	Access to the user interface and Clipboard	Unrestricted	Can use safe top-level and subwindows. Can cut and copy to the Clipboard and can read from Clipboard via the Paste function, but not programmatically.
WebPermission	Access to HTTP resources	Allowed to connect to the site of origin.	Allowed to connect to the site of origin.

Here you can see that code running from an Internet or Intranet Zone has reduced permissions. For example, the WebPermission only allows a connection to the place from where the assembly was loaded. This means that the forms you loaded can only load assemblies from the same location, as well as call Web Services from the same location. However, if you save the main application to your hard disk and run it from there, you're running in the My Computer zone and have unrestricted permissions. This impacts the design of the application, too. For example, if you load an assembly that contains a user control and you embed this into your current form, the user control also inherits the permission set. So, as far as UIPermission goes, it can access safe windows, but not the parent window (because that's not deemed safe).

Modifying the Security Policy

Table 7-1 sets out the default permissions for remotely loaded assemblies, but you can modify these if required. You can do this in a variety of ways, the simplest of which is to just move the site you're downloading from into a less restrictive zone. However, that means that the entire site is then trusted. For example, you may want to fully trust RefForm.exe if it comes from www.alanddave.com, but trust nothing else from that site (we're a dubious pair, let's be honest!).

To change the policy, you use the .NET Framework Configuration tool, which is installed into the Administrative Tools folder (see Figure 7-15). Alternatively, you can run this Microsoft Management Console (MMC) snap-in directly by running `mscorcfg.msc`.

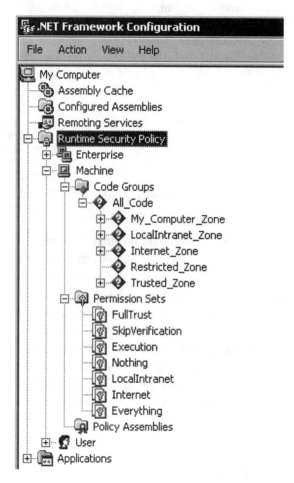

Figure 7-15. The .NET Framework Configuration tool

You can see that configuration can be applied on three levels—to the enterprise, to an individual machine, or to a user. Permissions can get more restrictive, but they can't be increased. So, if your administrator has set a level of permissions for the enterprise, you can't increase those permissions. However, you can add more restrictive permissions for certain users if necessary.

In Figure 7-15, we've expanded the code groups and permission sets for the current machine. You can see how the code groups map to the zones and can modify these according to your needs. For example, consider the case of giving added permissions to an application. Assume that you want your downloaded application to access HTTP resources other than its origin. Without extended permission, you'll get the dialog box shown in Figure 7-16 when trying to access other Web resources.

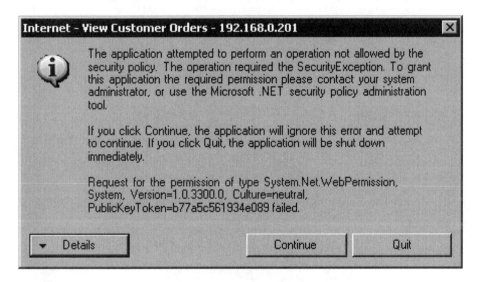

Figure 7-16. Accessing a resource for which permisions are denied

You've tried to access an assembly from an untrusted location, which the policy doesn't allow.

To allow this assembly to be loaded, you must change the WebPermission permission set. To do this, you need a new permission set. Rather than create one from scratch, you can duplicate the Internet one and then change the permissions. So, for the machine, you select the Permission Sets node, then select Internet, and from the content menu select Duplicate. You have to duplicate the permission set because you're not allowed to modify the default permissions. Once duplicated, rename it and then select Change Permissions from the content menu, as shown in Figure 7-17.

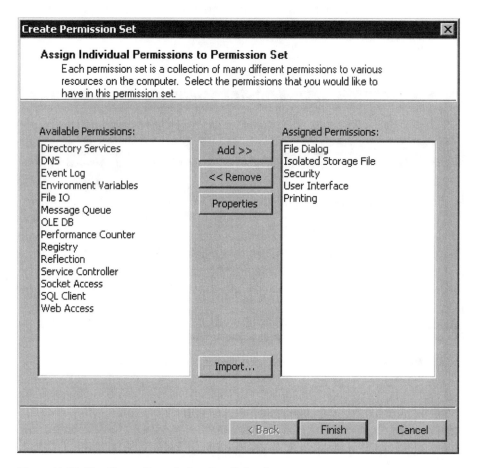

Figure 7-17. The Create Permission Set dialog box

You can see that you have no Web access, so select this permission and click Add to get a dialog box that allows you to enter which sites are permissible, as shown in Figure 7-18.

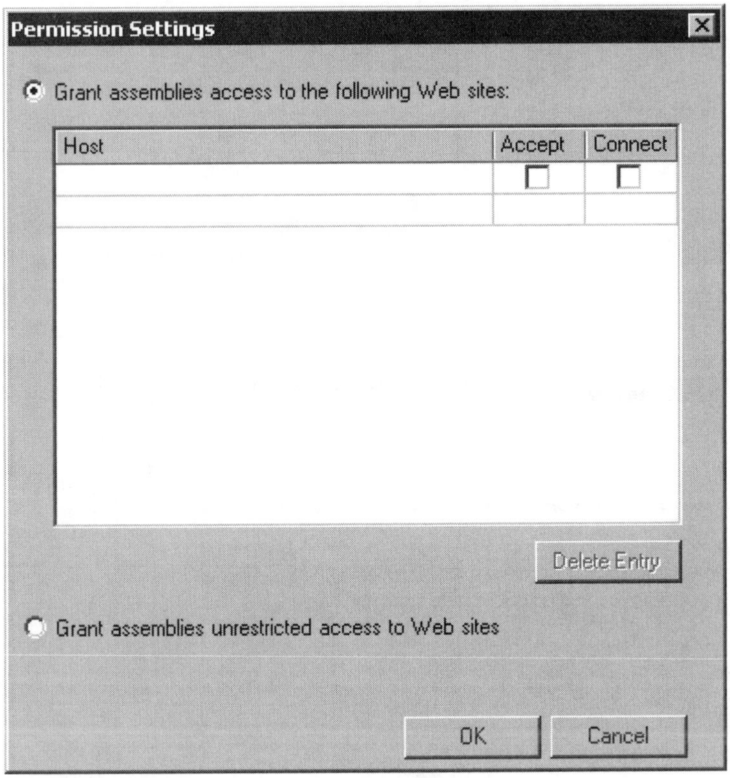

Figure 7-18. The Permission Settings dialog box

Here you can either add a specific site or grant full access to all sites.

Next, you define a new code group. Because this is an Internet application, you select the Internet_Zone option and then select Add a Child Node from the right pane. Give the code group a name, and then you have the option to choose the conditions that apply to the code group, as shown in Figure 7-19.

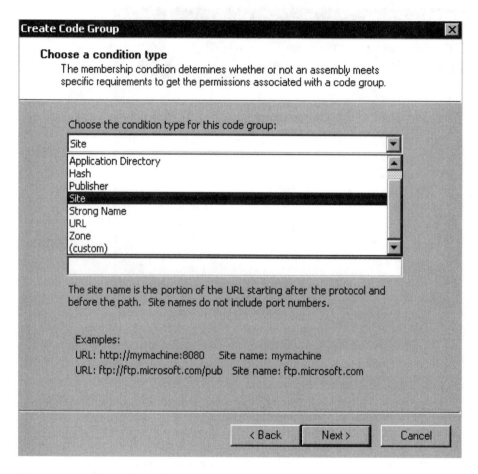

Figure 7-19. The Create Code Group dialog box

You can be precise here, selecting how membership of the code group is applied:

- A URL, so any assembly from the URL

- A Publisher, using a digital certificate to identify the assembly

- A Strong Name, limiting you to a single assembly

And so on. Once you've picked how you want the assembly identified, you can pick what permission sets are applied to the assembly, as shown in Figure 7-20.

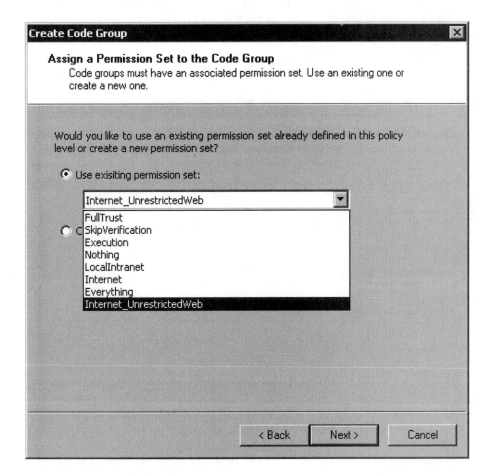

Figure 7-20. Applying permission sets

You can give this code group any of the available permission sets, but picking the one you've just set up ensures that you only get the Internet permissions, plus the addition of Web Access.

Checking Permissions

At this stage you've created the new code group and permission sets, so it's a good idea to check that you've got your permissions right. Select the Runtime Security Policy entry, and from the right pane select Evaluate Assembly, as shown in Figure 7-21.

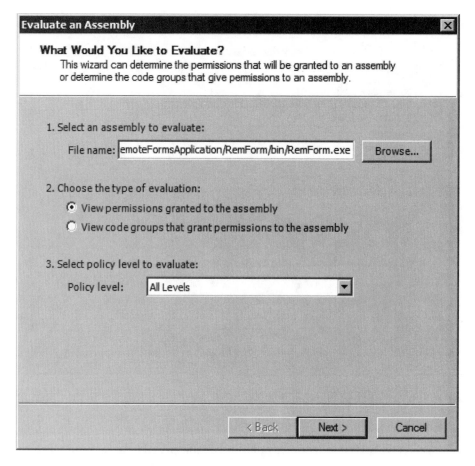

Figure 7-21. The Evaluate an Assembly dialog box

In this dialog box, you get a chance to enter the assembly location and the evaluation that's to take place. Clicking the Next button shows you what permissions will be applied to the assembly, as shown in Figure 7-22.

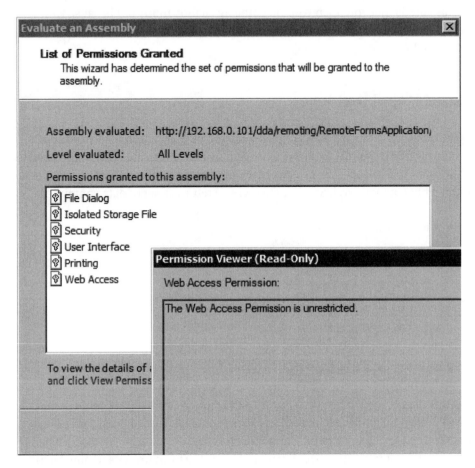

Figure 7-22. Permissions granted

If you view the permissions for Web Access, you'll see that it's unrestricted.

Now when you run the application and it tries to access resources from other Web sites, there will be no security dialog box. You can use this method to add (or remove) a variety of permissions, including extending the printing rights, file Input/Output (I/O) permission, and so on. Of course, the danger in adding more permissions is that you open your machine up slightly more, but because you have such fine control over what can be loaded and from where it can be loaded, you shouldn't worry.

Dynamic Applications

If you look back at the Windows application, you've used a simple technique to load forms from a remote location. Once you realize how simple this is, the possibilities start to flood in. For example, consider a simple stub application that does nothing but contact a Web Service. This service returns a set of data containing:

- A form name

- Its description

- Its data type

- The assembly it's in

- The URL of its location

This data is used to bind to a grid or a list. Or perhaps the data could contain the URL of an image for each form, and these could be used to build a graphical toolbar. The application then sits and waits for a user to click one of these images, at which point it takes the form details and loads the form from its remote location. These forms could then load further forms if required.

It doesn't take long to realize that you could have quite a large application that's loaded on demand. So no huge download—only a succession of quick downloads, as required. Further access to these downloaded forms comes from the download cache, unless a new version of the form is available on the Web server. It's dynamic loading and dynamic updating in a simple manner.

Summary

This chapter has covered quite a lot, looking at remoting from a variety of different viewpoints. You first looked at remoting objects and how you can have server objects running from clients. This is a technique that many people first jump on when they hear about remoting, but it wasn't suitable for the example application. That's an important point because throughout this book you'll see a lot of different techniques to build applications that require some form of remote processing, however small. Knowing which technique to use is extremely important.

You then looked at a Windows Forms version of the application you built in previous chapters. We've left the application very simple because this isn't a book about developing Windows applications—we wanted you to concentrate on how you'd remote the data and how you could deploy the application. The data can be remote in several ways, but the simplest is by use of a Web Service to allow you to use the existing infrastructure that these support, such as security and scalability.

Finally, you looked at the security implications of running remote applications and examined the policies that are in place and how these can be changed.

Overall, you've seen how easy it is to build a Windows version of your application. Later in the book you'll take this one step further and make the application more usable by allowing the data to be modified. In this scenario, you'll look at passing data back to the server, as well as just receiving it.

CHAPTER 8

Updating Data in Down-Level Clients

So FAR, despite being more than halfway through the book, we've still only covered *some* of the issues involved in building distributed data applications with ASP.NET. It's as if you were at page 200 of that detective novel and still hadn't been introduced to the moody, dark, and unpredictable master sleuth who will ultimately solve the case. And although we're probably unlikely to provide much spine-chilling suspense or an adrenalin-inspired conclusion in this book, you do need to move on apace and look at the second major aspect of working with data in all kinds of distributed applications.

Most of the data applications you build are likely to predominantly involve extracting and displaying data, rather than updating the original data source. A quick trip around the Web will soon confirm this assertion. Read-only data access is by far the most common scenario, and we've already covered most of the approaches you can use with ASP.NET. However, that's really only half the story. Yes, it'd be nice to spend the rest of the year on some sun-soaked paradise island beach, but instead you need to look at the second major requirement—updating the source data in a disconnected environment.

In this chapter, you'll begin that process with the customary introduction and background to the topic and then look at the various options. You'll see the following:

- The issues involved in pushing updates back to the data source

- How you cope with multiple concurrent users updating the data

- The tools and technologies that .NET provides to make this easier

- An example of a down-level (Web browser) client data update application

- An example of a data update application for small-screen and mobile devices

We'll start with an overview of the tasks involved in updating a data source in a disconnected environment.

Updating Data Stores: An Overview

As you saw in earlier chapters, getting data out of a data store in all kinds of formats is easy with .NET. However, putting it back is harder. There are several useful objects and techniques built into .NET that you can use, some of which will be familiar to traditional ADO programmers. They help to take the strain and (in most cases) make it easier than it ever was before. But they can't work miracles.

Fundamental issues are involved in updating a data source, which you'll look at in more detail next. To summarize, you need to consider the following:

- The efficiency of the process and the minimization of resource usage

- Monitoring success or failure of the process and providing feedback to the user

- The permissions you grant to users that allow them to access and change the data

- Controlling concurrent data updates made by more than one user simultaneously

You'll look at each of these topics next—starting with the issues to consider for minimizing the load you place on your server.

Making the Process As Efficient As Possible

When you looked at extracting and displaying data in the previous chapters, you spent quite some time concentrating on how you can take advantage of the capabilities of the client to minimize the load on your server and to provide a more responsive user interface. You can do this by remoting the data to the client and caching and manipulating it there. Your server's responsibility in many of the previous examples is limited to just delivering the page and the data to go with it.

Of course, in down-level clients, this generally isn't feasible. You can, however, take advantage of ASP.NET sessions where it's possible to limit the load on your back-end database and the data access tier of your applications.

Caching Data Updates

When you come to update data, you have the same two-level situation. With rich clients, you can allow the user to perform multiple edits on the data and then send all the changes back in one go to your server. You'll look at some examples of this approach in Chapter 11.

However, with down-level clients, this type of process isn't usually an option. Instead, you'll generally need to flush data updates back into your data source one at a time, through your data access tier. You could implement a system where the updates were cached on your server, probably in the ASP.NET session, but this won't work with clients that don't support sessions.

To achieve maximum compatibility with down-level clients, you'd have to build logic into the application that cached the data where possible but flushed it to the database otherwise. This adds a whole level of extra complexity, which may well not be worth the effort. If you expect that most of your clients will support sessions, then the "graceful fallback" model where the application takes advantage of session support but works without it is probably the best approach.

In the examples you'll see in this chapter, we've followed this principle. You'll cache the data to be edited in the session (if the client supports this) and reuse this cached data wherever possible. Although users are browsing the data to find the items that they want to edit, it comes from the session each time. In the (few, you hope) cases where the client doesn't support sessions, the code automatically fetches a fresh copy of the data from the data access tier each time. However, after the user commits any updates (including inserting a new row or deleting an existing row), you destroy the cached data in the session and fetch a fresh copy from the data access tier.

Maintaining a Separate Cached Copy of the Data

You could, of course, apply the updates to the cached copy of the data in the session as well as updating the data source, instead of reloading the data into the session each time. But this poses other problems. Again, it means two versions of the code—one for clients that support sessions and one for clients that don't. It also means that you have to track whether updates actually succeed in the database in case the cached and back-end data get out of sync.

Furthermore, if you have to wait for the database to perform the update and then check if it succeeded, you don't gain much in performance. The code won't run any faster, so the loading on the server is unlikely to be reduced by much at all. If the database is on a separate server from the Web server (as will generally be the case), fetching a fresh copy of the data is unlikely to affect performance to any great extent.

All this depends, however, on the size of the data set with which you're working. In general, when serving data to a down-level client, you'll try and avoid extracting more than the minimum number of rows required each time. Because you're unlikely to send the client hundreds of rows in a page, you'll automatically be using small data sets. With a rich client, you'll tend to use larger data sets to avoid regular server round-trips. But although you deliver more data in this case, you do it less often.

The other issue is that of coping with concurrent updates. You'll look at this topic in mode detail shortly, but it's clear that you're less likely to be working with "stale" data if you regularly refresh your cached copy. Of course, when you take advantage of rich clients by remoting data to them, you increase the chance of their copy of the data and the back-end data getting out of sync as other users update it. You'll consider this issue when you look at these types of clients later.

Measuring the Results and Providing Feedback

Displaying data is a process that generally succeeds irrespective of what other users are doing with the data. Provided there are no bugs in your code, the user gets a page full of information delivered, and you forget about them until they ask for more. If there's a problem with the server or the database, they probably won't get anything at all, but at least the error message you'll provide if this happens ensures that they can see what went wrong.

In contrast, when you're updating data, there are a lot more opportunities for the process to fail. For example, unless the interface you provide prevents it, the user might try to insert a row with an out-of-range value or one that conflicts with an existing unique key. They might try to insert a child row into a table where there's no matching parent row in a related table or try to delete a row that has related child rows when a "cascade deletes" rule isn't enabled (both of which will cause a foreign key violation). Or they might try to perform other updates that conflict with the database schema or the business rules for the application.Users will expect to get some feedback on whether their updates were actually applied. So, in a data update situation, you need to be able to detect update failures and provide status messages to the client. All this makes the process more complex than simply extracting data rows and displaying them.

Controlling Access to Protect the Data

When you build applications that allow users to read data, you can often set up simple permissions to control access in various ways. As long as you don't allow them to compose their own SQL statements (a highly risky approach in any situation), you can control what they can see through the stored procedures and SQL statements you use. You can also create "data views" within the database and specify access permissions on tables and on these views.

When you're updating data, you need to be more careful what you expose to users and how you allow them to modify it. You might allow users to view all the columns in a table but only update some of them. You might allow them to insert new rows but not update or delete existing rows, or in fact any combination of these actions.

There are various ways you can protect your data at this granular level, often involving quite complex logic that uses a combination of user, column, and database permissions. Another common technique is to execute all updates via stored procedures within the database, rather than by executing SQL statements directly. Stored procedures allow you to hide the database structure from view, and they're also more efficient because they can be compiled. The database may also fine-tune and optimize the execution plan depending on the data itself.

Controlling Concurrent Data Updates

The big headache when updating data is the topic we saved until now. Any application that allows data to be updated, and that has more than one concurrent user performing updates, can suffer from concurrency violations. These occur when a user changes data that's being edited by another user at the same time.

Concurrency errors in a database aren't a technical problem, in that the database itself can handle concurrent operations. It actually queues them and applies the updates in turn to the data. The problem has more to do with users' expectations. If one user opens a page to update the data in a row from the database, and then another user changes the same row while the first user is typing in their new values, the result may not be consistent with both users' expectations.

Why Concurrency Errors Arise

The reason that concurrency errors arise is that both users have their own "view" of the data while they're editing it, and neither is aware of any changes made by the other. If they both edit the same column(s) in the row, only the changes made by the user that saved their changes last are persisted in the database. The changes made by the user who saved the row back to the database first are overwritten and lost—but (unless you take the relevant precautions) they won't see any indication of this.

The other problem with concurrency errors is that there's no easy or automatic way of figuring out which changes should be persisted—even if you can detect the problem in the first place. Depending on your business rules, it could be the user in the most senior position, the user in a specific department of the corporation, the user who edited it most recently, or the user who made the most changes to the data. It's impossible to apply any general rule.

The most useful approach is to trap any such errors and report them back to the user who's updates will cause the error to arise—the user who saves the data last. This way they know they're overwriting another user's data. In the example application, this is the approach you'll take.

Concurrency Issues in a Disconnected Application

Concurrency errors are rarer when you're working with connected applications; in fact, some traditional applications employ record locking to prevent more than one user from accessing a row in "edit mode." This is called *pessimistic locking*, and some database systems can even implement it at field (column) level, rather than just at row (or page) level. However, in a disconnected environment, as is the situation with all ASP.NET Web applications, the process uses *optimistic locking* by default (although some environments can still enforce a more aggressive locking scheme). In other words, more than one user can open a row in edit mode, so generally you have to implement the detection and management of concurrency errors yourself.

As mentioned earlier, flushing updates back to the database immediately tends to reduce concurrency errors. Each user has a relatively fresh and recent view of the data. But when you start to cache data to improve your application performance and to allow fully disconnected processing on the client, the risks of a concurrency error arising increase.

All of the example applications detect concurrency errors whenever updates are made to the data. In some cases, the applications take advantage of features of the .NET data access classes (predominantly the ADO.NET DataSet for fully disconnected versions). You'll see how this is implemented as you look at the examples.

Are You Connected, Disconnected, or Fully Disconnected?

It's important to understand the concept of connected and disconnected data access versus disconnected applications. In Chapter 1, we discussed the nature of HTTP and disconnected applications. As far as the Web pages and Web applications you build are concerned, you're *never* working in a connected environment. HTTP doesn't allow that, and it doesn't make sense either if you're going to support a large number of clients. Your server is only connected to the client for the duration of time it takes to deliver the page or resource requested.

When it comes to data access, however, you can work in a connected or a disconnected way. You saw in earlier chapters how the DataReader is a connected data access object, and it maintains a live, open connection to the database all the time that you're using it to extract data. If you want to go back and look at the data again, you have to reconnect it to the database. The same applies with the various other reader objects, such as the XmlReader, TextReader, and so on.

On the other hand, the DataSet object and the XML document objects are fundamentally disconnected data repositories. They connect to the data source to fetch or persist the data and then disconnect again. Once disconnected, you can access the data they contain as often as you need.

So, when we talk about *rich* clients and *down-level* clients, we're *not* suggesting that one is a disconnected client and the other is a connected client. They're all disconnected—it's just that some are "more disconnected" than others. The rich client may be able to persist the data locally and not have to connect again to perform updates until the user decides to persist all the updates back to the server. The down-level client is more likely to connect and disconnect each time an edit to the data takes place. It's not usually able to cache the data and then flush all the edits to it back to the server later.

The conclusion is that all your applications are disconnected, but the "remoteness" of the data that they're using varies depending on the capabilities of the client and the way that the user chooses to work with the application.

Data Update Techniques in .NET

Before you look at the example applications, we'll briefly review the features in ADO.NET that allow you to update a relational data store (such as a database). This involves two different techniques and two different objects. You used both of them to read data in earlier chapters, so you'll concentrate on their update features here.

Executing Updates with a Command Object

The simplest and most efficient way to perform one-off updates to a data store is by executing a SQL statement or (preferably) a stored procedure via a Command object. It works much like the traditional (pre-.NET) ADO Command object. You specify a connection to the data store through a Connection object and call one of the execute methods of the Command object. You can use the Command object's Parameters collection to apply any parameters that a stored procedure requires. Figure 8-1 shows the process. You can execute SQL statements directly against the data or execute a stored procedure.

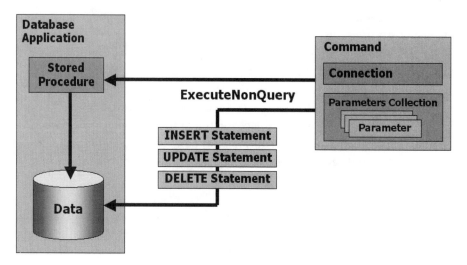

Figure 8-1. Using a Command to update a data store

The ExecuteNonQuery Method

As long as you don't expect to get back a rowset, you use the ExecuteNonQuery method. This avoids the overhead required to build and connect to a cached rowset within the database. It returns an Integer result that indicates how many rows were affected by the process:

```
'specify the stored procedure name
Dim strProcName As String = "MyUpdateProcedure"

'create Connection object using suitable connection string
Dim objConnect As New OleDbConnection(ConnectionString)

Try

   'create Command using Connection and Stored Proc name
   Dim objCommand As New OleDbCommand(strProcName, objConnect)

   'tell the database that it is a stored procedure
   'if not it won't properly recognize any parameters we provide
   objCommand.CommandType = CommandType.StoredProcedure

   'add any required input parameters
   objCommand.Parameters.Add("ParameterName", ParameterValue)

   objConnect.Open()   'open connection
```

```
'execute stored procedure and return number of rows affected
Return objCommand.ExecuteNonQuery()

Catch objError As Exception

    Throw objError       'throw error to calling routine

Finally

    objConnect.Close()    'close connection

End Try
```

Returning Single Values from a Stored Procedure

In some cases, you may want to execute a stored procedure that updates the data *and* returns a rowset. For this, you simply use the same techniques as in Chapters 2 and 3 by calling the Command object's ExecuteReader method. It returns a DataReader (or one of the other types of reader object).

If you just need to get back a single value, you can use the ExecuteScalar method instead, which is faster and more efficient than ExecuteReader for this task. Effectively it returns just the first column of the first row of any resulting rowset. Any other columns and rows are discarded.

However, if you just need one or two specific values, an even better way is to return them as output parameters from the stored procedure. For example, the following code (taken from the UpdateOrders component in the example application) calls a stored procedure that inserts a new row into the Orders table. This table has an OrderID column that's of type Identity, so the new order number will be set automatically when the row is inserted into the database table. The stored procedure extracts this value and returns it as an output parameter:

```
Public Function InsertNewOrder(ByVal CustomerID As String) As Integer
  Dim strProcName As String = "InsertNewOrder"
  Dim objConnect As New OleDbConnection(m_ConnectString)

  Try

    Dim objCommand As New OleDbCommand(strProcName, objConnect)
    objCommand.CommandType = CommandType.StoredProcedure

    'add required parameters for input and output
    objCommand.Parameters.Add("@CustID", OleDbType.VarChar, 5)
```

```
        objCommand.Parameters("@CustID").Value = CustomerID
        objCommand.Parameters.Add("@OrderID", OleDbType.Integer)
        objCommand.Parameters("@OrderID").Direction = ParameterDirection.Output

        objConnect.Open()    'open connection

        objCommand.ExecuteNonQuery()
        Return objCommand.Parameters("@OrderId").Value

    Catch objError As Exception

      Throw objError       'throw error to calling routine

    Finally

      objConnect.Close()    'close connection

    End Try

End Function
```

You can see that you create and initialize a `Command` object and add the `@CustID` parameter (here you use the more verbose syntax rather than the shortcut technique you did in the previous code example). Then you add the parameter `@OrderID` and specify the direction as `ParameterDirection.Output` (the default if you don't specify this, as with the `@CustID` parameter, is `ParameterDirection.Input`). After executing the stored procedure, you return the value of the output parameter.

The DataSet Update Feature

The second technique for updating a data store is through the built-in capabilities of the `DataSet` and `DataAdapter` objects. You'll use these in later chapters to push updates into a database, but we'll briefly outline the process here for completeness.

When you extract data from a database and push it into a `DataSet`, you use a `DataAdapter` as the interface between the `DataSet` and the database. The `DataAdapter` contains the mappings between the tables and columns in the `DataSet` and the corresponding tables and columns in the data source, allowing different names to be used for tables and columns if required.

The `DataAdapter` also references four `Command` objects via its properties. The `SelectCommand` (as you saw in earlier chapters) is used to extract the data when the

Fill method of the DataAdapter executes. The other three, the InsertCommand, the UpdateCommand, and the DeleteCommand properties, reference the Command objects that push edits to the data back into the data source. These Command objects each use a Connection object (generally they share the same one) and a Parameters collection to execute the SQL statements or stored procedures that do the work, as shown in Figure 8-2.

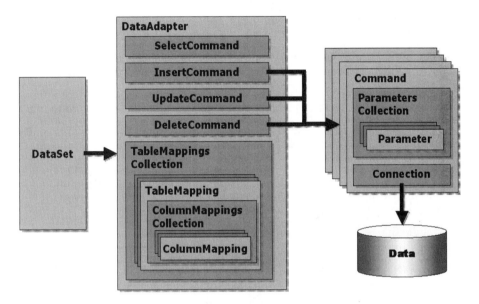

Figure 8-2. Updating a data source with a DataAdapter *and* DataSet

There's a feature of ADO.NET called the CommandBuilder that you can use (in certain specific circumstances) to build SQL statements and create the appropriate Command objects automatically. You'll examine this process shortly. However, you'll generally be looking to create stored procedures rather than use autogenerated SQL statements because this gives you better performance, more control over the update process, and allows more complex updates to be performed efficiently.

Once you've assembled the objects required, as shown in Figure 8-2, you just call the Update method of the DataSet to flush all the changes to the data back into the data store. It sounds easy, and most of the time it works fine. However, you still need to look out for concurrency problems. In fact, they're more likely to arise here because you generally use a DataSet as a data cache for fully disconnected applications—so the data will be less "fresh" and up-to-date than if you flushed every update back immediately by using one of the execute methods of the Command object directly. You'll revisit this issue in detail in Chapter 9.

Using a CommandBuilder to Create Command Objects

A CommandBuilder object is used in ADO.NET to make it easy to create SQL statements for updating a data store. However, there are some quite severe limitations to using a CommandBuilder:

- The rows in the table in the DataSet must have originally come from a single table and can be used only to update a table of the same format (generally the same source table).

- The source table must have a primary key defined (it can be a multiple-column primary key), or it must have at least one column that contains unique values so that the SQL statements generated by the CommandBuilder can locate the correct rows when performing the updates. This column (or columns) must be included in the rows that are returned by the SELECT statement or query that's used for the SelectCommand.

- Table names that include special characters such as spaces, periods, quotation marks, or other nonalphanumeric characters can't be used (even if delimited by square brackets). However, fully qualified table names that do include the period character (such as dbo.BookList) can be used.

It's for these reasons, and for security and efficiency, that you generally use stored procedures with the DataAdapter instead of the SQL statements that the CommandBuilder creates. However, if the previously mentioned criteria can be met and you're happy to use SQL statements rather than stored procedures, the CommandBuilder can provide a viable solution.

The CommandBuilder exposes three methods that automatically create new instances of suitable Command objects for use with the InsertCommand, DeleteCommand, and SelectCommand properties of a DataAdapter, and these methods also populate the properties of the Command objects. This includes creating the correct INSERT, DELETE, or UPDATE SQL statement that'll perform the update process. Another useful feature of the CommandBuilder is the DeriveParameters method. This works rather like the Refresh method of the ADO Recordset object, automatically creating the appropriate set of Parameter objects for the Command when it's being used to execute a stored procedure.

> **NOTE** *Note that* DeriveParameters *(like the ADO* Refresh *method) requires an extra round-trip to collect the information from the database. Therefore, you should only use it during development to discover the parameter types and details, not in production code. You can find full details of this method, and the* CommandBuilder *object itself, in the Framework Software Development Kit (SDK). Look for "OleDb-CommandBuilder" or "SqlCommandBuilder" in the index or search for them.*

You create an instance of a CommandBuilder object using an existing DataAdapter object. This is because the CommandBuilder needs to know how the DataSet and the original data store table are related in terms of the table and column names and any specific mappings that might exist. It can get this information from the DataAdapter but only if at least the SelectCommand property is set—which happens automatically when you provide a SQL statement as a parameter to the constructor (as shown next):

```
Dim strSelect As String = "SELECT * FROM MyTable"
Dim objConnect As New OleDbConnection(ConnectionString)
Dim objDataAdapter As New OleDbDataAdapter(strSelect, objConnect)
Dim objDataSet As New DataSet()

... fill the DataSet and edit row(s) here ...

Try

  'create a CommandBuilder object from the DataAdapter
  Dim objCommandBuilder As New OleDbCommandBuilder(objDataAdapter)
```

Once the CommandBuilder has been created, you can use its methods to get the other Command objects you need to perform the update (although you can omit this, and it'll set them automatically anyway—but it makes it easier to see what's going on in the example):

```
'set the update, insert and delete commands for the DataAdapter
objDataAdapter.DeleteCommand = objCommandBuilder.GetDeleteCommand()
objDataAdapter.InsertCommand = objCommandBuilder.GetInsertCommand()
objDataAdapter.UpdateCommand = objCommandBuilder.GetUpdateCommand()

'perform the update on the original data
objDataAdapter.Update(objDataSet, "MyTable")
```

```
Catch objError As Exception

  Throw objError      'throw error to calling routine

End Try
```

Using Custom Stored Procedures to Update Data

Using stored procedures with a DataAdapter is, admittedly, more work than using the CommandBuilder. However, creating parameters with the correct data type and properties in ADO.NET is much easier than it was in traditional ADO. Also, in general, the stored procedures aren't complex if you're just dealing with single tables or simple database schemas. If the process of updating the data is more complex than this, the autogenerated commands won't work anyway.

However, the CommandBuilder can still help out when you use stored procedures. The DeriveParameters method it exposes returns a populated Parameters collection where you just need to fill in the actual parameter values. Just remember that it's a big performance hit, however, so you should only use it during development to figure out what parameters are required.

To use stored procedures with a DataAdapter, you just create the appropriate Command objects, as in the previous examples, and assign these to the DataAdapter object's InsertCommand, UpdateCommand, and DeleteCommand properties before calling the Update method of the DataSet. There's more detail about this coming up in Chapter 10.

Using Transactions While Updating Data

When updating data, you can use *transactions* to protect the integrity of your data when appropriate. All the changes to the data in your data store within a transaction are applied successfully, or they're all rolled back so that the data is returned to its original state. You can apply transactions in three ways under .NET:

- Database transactions within stored procedures (where the database you use supports these)

- Connection-based ADO.NET transactions (with any data store, via the managed provider)

- Distributed COM+ Application transactions (using Windows 2000 Component Services)

Database Transactions in Stored Procedures

You'll use the SQL Server Transact-SQL (T-SQL) database transaction statements in some of the examples later. This is the type of transaction used with traditional ADO and, in fact, any other type of data access methodology. The transactions are instantiated, maintained, and managed by the database itself. As an example, the following is an extract from a stored procedure used in the example application to delete an order from the database:

```
BEGIN TRANSACTION
  DELETE FROM [Order Details] WHERE OrderID = @OrderID
  DELETE FROM Orders WHERE OrderID = @OrderID
  IF @@ERROR <> 0 GOTO on_error
COMMIT TRANSACTION
RETURN
on_error:
ROLLBACK TRANSACTION
RETURN
```

To delete an order, you have to remove all related child rows from the Order Details table first and then remove the Orders table row. If there's an error, you roll back both the delete processes, leaving both tables in their original states.

Connection-Based Transactions

The second type of transaction is one that ADO.NET is responsible for implementing. You can start one or more transactions against an open Connection object and use them to ensure that all the processes within that transaction complete successfully, or all of them are rolled back. You attach your Command object(s) to the appropriate transaction before calling whichever execute method you're using. This causes all the update processes carried out by the command to be *enrolled* in that transaction.

We've extended the code from an earlier example to show a simple scenario with a single transaction and one Command object:

```
Dim strProcName As String = "MyUpdateProcedure"
Dim objConnect As New OleDbConnection(ConnectionString)

'declare a variable to hold a Transaction object
Dim objTransaction As OleDbTransaction
```

```
Try

  Dim objCommand As New OleDbCommand(strProcName, objConnect)
  objCommand.CommandType = CommandType.StoredProcedure
  objCommand.Parameters.Add("ParameterName", ParameterValue)

  'start a transaction so that we can roll back the changes
  'must do this on an open Connection object
  objConnect.Open()
  objTransaction = objConnect.BeginTransaction()

  'enroll Command object into this transaction
  objCommand.Transaction = objTransaction

  objCommand.ExecuteNonQuery()

  'commit the transaction to persist all updates
  objTransaction.Commit()

Catch objError As Exception

  'rollback the transaction undoing any updates
  objTransaction.Rollback()

  Throw objError
Finally
  objConnect.Close()
End Try
```

Connection-Based Transactions with a DataSet Update

If you're using a DataSet and DataAdapter to perform the update, you need to enroll the three Command objects that the DataAdapter uses into your transaction. The following code shows how you do this in conjunction with a CommandBuilder that's creating the Command objects for you:

```
Dim strSelect As String = "SELECT * FROM MyTable"
Dim objConnect As New OleDbConnection(ConnectionString)
Dim objDataAdapter As New OleDbDataAdapter(strSelect, objConnect)
Dim objDataSet As New DataSet()
... fill the DataSet and edit row(s) here ...
Dim objTransaction As OleDbTransaction
Try
```

```
      Dim objCommandBuilder As New OleDbCommandBuilder(objDataAdapter)
      objDataAdapter.DeleteCommand = objCommandBuilder.GetDeleteCommand()
      objDataAdapter.InsertCommand = objCommandBuilder.GetInsertCommand()
      objDataAdapter.UpdateCommand = objCommandBuilder.GetUpdateCommand()
      objConnect.Open()
      objTransaction = objConnect.BeginTransaction()

      'attach the current transaction to all the Command objects
      objDataAdapter.DeleteCommand.Transaction = objTransaction
      objDataAdapter.InsertCommand.Transaction = objTransaction
      objDataAdapter.UpdateCommand.Transaction = objTransaction

      objDataAdapter.Update(objDataSet, "MyTable")
      objTransaction.Commit()  'commit the transaction
Catch objError As Exception
   objTransaction.Rollback()  'rollback the transaction
   Throw objError
Finally
   objConnect.Close()
End Try
```

If you create your own Command objects for the Update method of the DataAdapter, using stored procedures instead of SQL statements, you do much the same thing. This time, however, you can set the Transaction property of each Command object directly:

```
...
'create three Command objects and set properties here
...
Dim objTransaction As OleDbTransaction
Try
   objConnect.Open()
   objTransaction = objConnect.BeginTransaction()

   'attach the current transaction to all the Command objects
   objMyDeleteCommand.Transaction = objTransaction
   objMyInsertCommand.Transaction = objTransaction
   objMyUpdateCommand.Transaction = objTransaction

   objDataAdapter.DeleteCommand = objMyDeleteCommand
   objDataAdapter.InsertCommand = objMyInsertCommand
   objDataAdapter.UpdateCommand = objMyUpdateCommand
```

```
    objDataAdapter.Update(objDataSet, "MyTable")

    objTransaction.Commit()  'commit the transaction

Catch objError As Exception

    objTransaction.Rollback()  'rollback the transaction

    Throw objError
Finally
    objConnect.Close()
End Try
```

Distributed COM+ Application Transactions

The third type of transaction, Distributed COM+ Application transactions, was discussed briefly in Chapter 1. However, the topic as a whole is outside the scope of this book.

Managing Concurrency While Updating

The final topic you need to understand a little more about before you look at the examples is how you can avoid the data inconsistencies that occur when multiple concurrent users are updating the same data. The only real way to deal with this is to ensure that users can only persist their changes to a data row back into the original data source if that row hasn't been changed by another user concurrently.

In other words, every page (or "screen" or "form") that allows data to be modified must retain two "versions" of the data: the original values in the database when that page was first opened and the new values that the user has entered. Then, when you come to apply that user's modifications, you can check to see if the values in the data source are the same as they were when the user first opened the row to edit it. If they are, you can persist the user's changes. If not, you know that another user has concurrently changed the row.

Three sets of values are important if you want to be able to manage concurrency errors:

- The current values that the user entered—the intended modifications to the data

- The original values in the data store when the user opened the page or form

- The underlying values in the data store when the user comes to commit their changes

So, for any update, you should guard against concurrency errors by comparing the original and underlying values. Only if they're the same should you commit and persist the current values into the data store. However, there are some things you can do to minimize and avoid concurrency errors.

Minimizing Concurrency Errors

Depending on how "disconnected" you want your application to be, you might choose to refresh your cached data more regularly. That way, the original values you're storing are more likely to be up-to-date (the same as the underlying values). In general, the number of users updating data will be only a fraction of the number who use applications to read and display data. So, although you still want to build applications that are efficient and responsive, you can usually accept the need for more server interaction in applications that update rather than just read data.

If updates to the data are predominantly the insertion of new rows, rather than the modification of existing rows, you should try to find a way of minimizing clashes when the rows require some kind of unique row identifier. For example, if your application generates a new order number on the client before you actually insert the row into the database, you need to ensure that every user concurrently filling in the details of an order will get a different order number. Otherwise, one or more of them won't be able to save the order to the database because it'll overwrite any order with the same order number that was saved previously.

If users are predominantly and regularly making changes to existing data, especially if they only tend to change one or a few of the columns in each row, it might make sense to build the data access code so that it only applies updates to the data store for columns that have been changed. This way, two users can successfully edit the same row concurrently as long as they don't change the same columns.

Of course, it may be that the editing process doesn't make sense in this last scenario. For example, if the values that one user decides to enter in a row take into account the values of columns that they can see (but that don't themselves change), and another user then changes these columns , data inconsistencies might still arise. One way around this is to make sure users can only see the values that they're expected to edit, not values that may be changing concurrently (unless these values are inconsequential as far as the user's decision process is concerned).

Detecting Concurrency Errors

You've seen that the usual way of preventing concurrency errors from arising is to check that the underlying values in the data store are still the same as the original values before you persist the current values (the changes) to a row.

You'll usually do this within your stored procedure or within a SQL statement that you execute directly as part of the WHERE clause:

```
UPDATE TableName
SET Col1=CurrentValue1, Col2=CurrentValue2
WHERE KeyCol=KeyValue AND Col1=OriginalValue1 AND Col2=OriginalValue2
```

There's no reason why you can't do it differently; for example, you could execute a SELECT statement first to see if a row with all the original values still exists for a specific primary key value. This might be a useful technique if the update involves several tables because you can check for a concurrency error first. For example, you might use the following stored procedure to delete a parent row and all its related child rows from the database:

```
SELECT OrderID FROM Orders
WHERE OrderID=@OrderID AND Freight=@FreightWas AND ShipVia=@ShipViaWas
  AND ShipName=@NameWas AND ShipAddress=@AddressWas
IF @@ROWCOUNT = 1
BEGIN
  BEGIN TRANSACTION
    DELETE FROM [Order Details] WHERE OrderID = @OrderID
    DELETE FROM Orders WHERE OrderID = @OrderID
    IF @@ERROR <> 0 GOTO on_error
  COMMIT TRANSACTION
  RETURN
on_error:
  ROLLBACK TRANSACTION
  RETURN
END
```

Checking the Number of Rows Affected

Preventing the update being persisted if it'll cause a concurrency error is the important part of the process, but you also need to provide feedback to users if such an error does arise. Their modifications to the data won't be persisted, and (unless you subscribe to the school of hiding bad news until it causes a real problem), you really should detect this and tell them.

In fact, it's easy because almost all databases (and many other types of data store) will return a value indicating the number of rows affected by the execution of a stored procedure or a SQL statement. If the values in the data store have changed concurrently, the WHERE clause will prevent the update (or delete process) from being applied, and the procedure will return zero. If there's no concurrency error and the update succeeds, it should return one.

You'll generally expect an update, delete, or insert process to only affect one row. In some cases, however, your stored procedure may affect more than one row. In the previous code, more than one row will be affected. You'll get one for the SELECT statement, zero or more for the first DELETE statement (depending on how many related child rows exist), and one for the final DELETE statement.

However, you can control the value returned for the number of rows affected in a stored procedure with the NOCOUNT statement. When you turn it on, it resets the value for the number of rows affected to zero and stops counting affected rows until you turn it off again. So, if you turn NOCOUNT on before executing the second DELETE statement, the database will only return the number of rows affected by the statement that executes after you turn it off again:

```
SET NOCOUNT ON
DELETE FROM [Order Details] WHERE OrderID = @OrderID
SET NOCOUNT OFF
DELETE FROM Orders WHERE OrderID = @OrderID
```

Concurrency Management in a DataSet Object

One of the features making your life easier when using a DataSet to cache and transport data is that it automatically maintains the two values you need to detect concurrency errors. Every column in every row maintains an *original* and *current* value, based on the same principles we've been discussing so far. When the DataSet is filled with data through the Fill method of a DataAdapter, the original values are those that are taken from the data source.

As edits are made on the data, these are persisted as the current values of the columns in each row. You can use methods such as AcceptChanges to move the current values to the original values if required, allowing you to control the content of the DataSet as you need. The important part is that, when you come to call the Update method to update the original data, you can detect any concurrency errors that might occur.

When you use the CommandBuilder to create SQL statements for the Update process, these SQL statements automatically include the original values for all the columns in the WHERE clause, so the updates will fail if the row has been changed concurrently. If you provide custom stored procedures for the DataAdapter object's InsertCommand, DeleteCommand, and UpdateCommand properties, however, you need to ensure both that you perform the relevant concurrency checks and that you return the appropriate "rows affected" value. It's only through the "rows affected" value that the Update method can tell whether or not there was a concurrency error.

You'll look in more detail at how you use a `DataSet` and the `DataAdapter` object's `Update` method in the next chapter, where you'll see some example applications that use this feature. However, in all the example applications, you'll apply the "standard" approach to concurrency detection and error prevention. You'll compare all the underlying values in a row in the data store, before you update or delete it, to the original values when you extracted the data that the user edits. You'll see how you do this in the examples in this and the following chapters.

> **NOTE** *An alternative and extremely efficient approach that's often used is to add a "time stamp" column to the table. Many database systems can implement this kind of column type automatically. Whenever the row is edited, even only if a single column value is changed, the time stamp is updated. In this scenario, your code only needs to compare the time stamp values for the row in the database (the underlying value) and the original value in remote rowset. You can achieve the same kind of effect using custom GUIDs for each row, but in this case your code will itself have to manage updating the GUID when any column value in changed.*

Data Update Example for HTML 3.2 Clients

You'll recall, when you worked through the examples in Chapters 5 and 6, that several of the versions of the customer orders application display an Edit Orders link for each customer when you search for customers. The version designed for HTML 3.2 clients is one of those that displays this link, as shown in Figure 8-3.

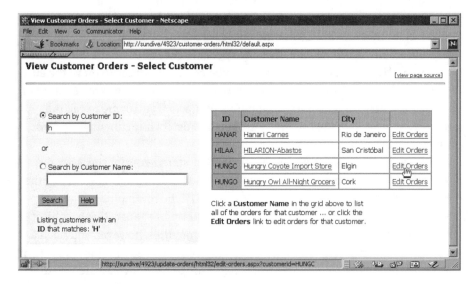

Figure 8-3. The Edit Orders link in the HTML version of the application

An Overview of the Application

As the text of this link implies, it opens a page where the order data for that customer can be viewed and edited. Figure 8-4 shows the first view of this part of the application. All the orders for this customer are listed, along with some basic shipping information for each order.

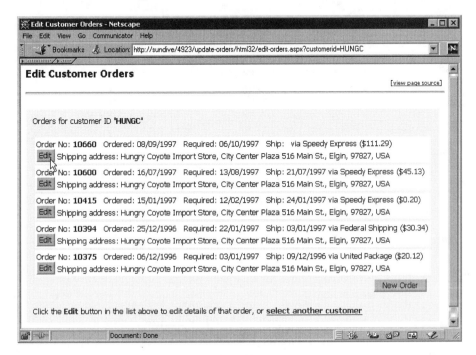

Figure 8-4. The list of orders ready to be edited

At the bottom of the screen is a New Order button. This has nothing to do with the establishment of a fresh worldwide political system (or the 1980's alternative rock band) but is used to add a new order for this customer. You'll see this in action later.

The application also allows you to edit the details of an order and the individual order lines. Click the Edit button for an order that hasn't yet shipped (in other words, one that has an empty Ship date value, such as order number 10660 for Hungry Coyote Import Store) to put that order into edit mode, as shown in Figure 8-5.

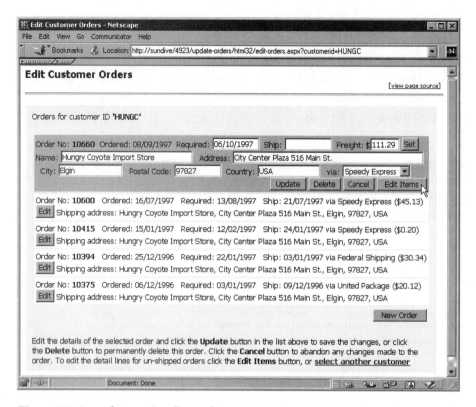

Figure 8-5. An order row in edit mode

To view or edit the order lines, click the Edit Items button in the row that's in edit mode in the Edit Customer Orders page (as shown in Figure 8-5). This opens another page that shows the individual items on this order and allows them to be edited. This page also appears automatically when the New Order button is clicked, as shown in Figure 8-6.

Below the list of order items is a drop-down list where the user can select a product and add it to the order, plus links to go back and select another order or to go back to the original Select Customer page.

Figure 8-6. Editing the detail item rows for an order

Displaying the Order Details

Figure 8-7 shows the basic design for these processes within the example application. You use a data access component named DDA4923OrderUpdate (in the assembly UpdateOrders.dll), which exposes three methods for extracting data about a customer's orders. These three methods are used by functions within your ASP.NET pages (edit-orders.aspx and edit-order-lines.aspx). The functions automatically cache the data they retrieve in the user's session if possible and collect it from there the next time they're called. If the client doesn't support sessions, the functions just hit the data access tier again.

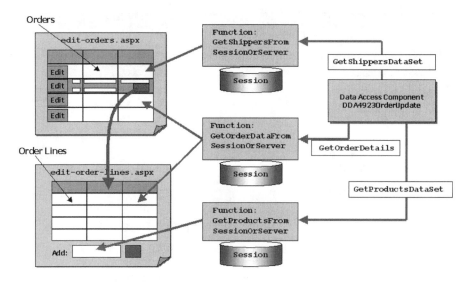

Figure 8-7. The editing process in the HTML version of the application

Within the edit-orders.aspx page, you use an ASP.NET DataList control to display the shipping details of each order, and this control is also used to provide inline editing for individual rows. The page edit-order-lines.aspx uses an ASP.NET DataGrid control to display the items on a selected order, and it also can be switched into edit mode so that the data can be edited inline.

Editing the Order Details

When one of the Edit buttons in the list of orders is clicked, that row switches into edit mode, and most of the values in the row (the ones that can be changed by the user) are displayed in text boxes or a drop-down list. The Set button in the top right of the row can be used to calculate the freight charge for this order if the order contents have been modified. After editing any of the values in the row, the user clicks the Update button to commit the changes to the database. There's also a Delete button to remove this order altogether, a Cancel button to abandon any changes made in the row, and (providing that the order has not yet shipped) an Edit Items button, as shown in Figure 8-8.

The Edit Items button opens the second page, as you saw earlier, and each row of the order can be edited in much the same way as the shipping details in the previous page. Note that only three values in a row can be changed, or the row can be deleted, as shown in Figure 8-9.

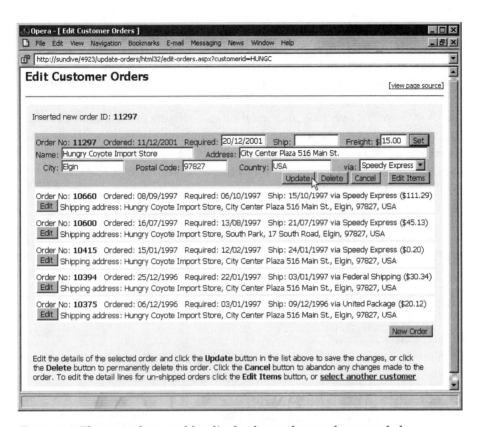

Figure 8-8. The controls to enable edited values to be saved or canceled

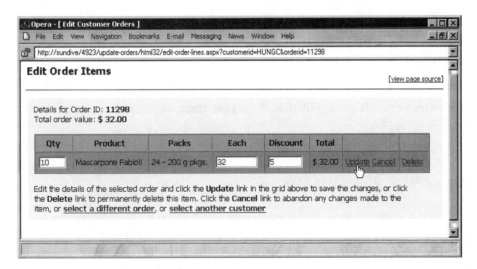

Figure 8-9. An order details row in edit mode

When the user clicks the Update, Cancel, or Delete link in the order details page, the grid goes out of edit mode, and the controls you saw in Figure 8-6 for adding new rows to the order are displayed again.

Figure 8-10 shows the processes involved in editing and updating the data for each order. The data access tier that you use to extract data also exposes a series of methods for inserting new rows and updating and deleting existing rows, in both the Orders and Order Details tables within your database. The methods in the data access component use stored procedures in the database to perform these actions, which also check for concurrency errors every time they're called.

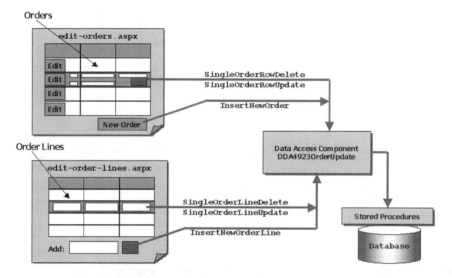

Figure 8-10. The process for updating order and order detail rows in the database

So, having seen an overview of what the application does and what lies beneath that smooth and sophisticated user interface, you'll now look at the code that actually makes it work.

Displaying and Editing Orders

To see how this application works, you'll look at the edit-orders.aspx page in detail. The second page, edit-order-lines.aspx, is similar in concept, and we'll describe the differences between them toward the end of this chapter. Both rely on the data access tier shown in the previous figures, so you'll also investigate how this works.

The Data Access Tier

The first step in the application is to get a list of orders and the related order lines from the server, cache them in the user's session, and return this DataSet to the calling routine. Within the database you have two stored procedures, which only require the customer ID to be specified. They select the specific columns you'll display, including all those that the user can edit. You need to join the Orders and Shippers tables to extract the name of the shipping company:

```
CREATE PROCEDURE OrdersForEditByCustID @CustID nvarchar(5)
AS SELECT
  OrderID, CustomerID, OrderDate, RequiredDate, ShippedDate, ShipVia,
  Freight, ShipName, ShipAddress, ShipCity, ShipPostalCode,
  ShipCountry, ShipperName = CompanyName
FROM Orders JOIN Shippers ON Shippers.ShipperID = Orders.ShipVia
WHERE CustomerID = @CustID ORDER BY CustomerID, OrderID DESC
```

For the order details, you have to join the Orders and Order Details tables so that you can select rows based on the customer ID (it's not in the Order Details table). And, because you need the product name as well as the product ID, you also have to join the Products table:

```
CREATE PROCEDURE OrderLinesForEditByCustID @CustID nvarchar(5)
AS SELECT
  [Order Details].*, Products.ProductName,
  QtyPerUnit = Products.QuantityPerUnit
FROM (Orders JOIN [Order Details]
    ON Orders.OrderID = [Order Details].OrderID)
  JOIN Products ON [Order Details].ProductID = Products.ProductID
WHERE Orders.CustomerID = @CustID ORDER BY Orders.OrderID
```

The GetOrderDetails Function

Using these two stored procedures, you can write a function within your data access tier component (DDA49230rderUpdate) to build and return the DataSet you need for your application. The technique is identical to the several examples of this process you looked at earlier. The variable m_ConnectString is a module-level variable that's set to the correct connection string for the database when the component instance is created:

```
Public Function GetOrderDetails(ByVal CustomerID As String) As DataSet
  Dim strSelectOrders As String = "OrdersForEditByCustID"
```

```
    Dim strSelectOrderLines As String = "OrderLinesForEditByCustID"
    Dim objDataSet As New DataSet()
    Dim objConnect As New OleDbConnection(m_ConnectString)
    Try
      Dim objCommand As New OleDbCommand(strSelectOrders, objConnect)
      objCommand.CommandType = CommandType.StoredProcedure
      objCommand.Parameters.Add("@CustID", CustomerID)
      Dim objDataAdapter As New OleDbDataAdapter(objCommand)
      objDataAdapter.Fill(objDataSet, "Orders")
      objCommand.CommandText = strSelectOrderLines
      objDataAdapter.Fill(objDataSet, "Order Details")
    Catch objError As Exception
      Throw objError
    End Try
    objDataSet.AcceptChanges()
    Return objDataSet
End Function
```

The HTML Page Declaration

The first page you see when you select the Edit Orders link in the list of customers within the original Select Customer page is implemented by edit-orders.aspx. It starts off with an Import statement for the data access component you're using (as well as one for the System.Data namespace):

```
<%@Page Language="VB" %>
<%@Import Namespace="DDA4923OrderUpdate" %>
<%@Import Namespace="System.Data" %>
```

Next comes the declaration of the controls and the HTML page content that creates the visible interface. A server-side <form> contains a hidden-type input control that you use to persist the customer ID between page postbacks, a label to display status information, and an asp:DataList control. There's also a label at the bottom of the page to display help text:

```
<form runat="server">

<!-- hidden control to hold customer id -->
<input id="customerid" type="hidden" runat="server" />

<!-- label to display customer ID -->
<asp:Label id="lblStatus" runat="server" EnableViewState="false" /><p />
```

```
<!-- DataList control to display/edit matching orders -->
<asp:DataList id="lstOrders" runat="server"
     HeaderStyle-BackColor="#c0c0c0"
     ItemStyle-BackColor="#ffffff"
     SelectedItemStyle-BackColor="#ffe4e1"
     EditItemStyle-BackColor="#dcdcdc"
     FooterStyle-HorizontalAlign="Right"
     CellPadding="3" CellSpacing="3"
     DataKeyField="OrderID"
     OnItemCommand="DoItemCommand"
     OnEditCommand="DoItemEdit"
     OnUpdateCommand="DoItemUpdate"
     OnDeleteCommand="DoItemDelete"
     OnCancelCommand="DoItemCancel"
     OnItemDataBound="SetRowVariations">

     ... DataList templates go here ...

  </asp:DataList><p />

<!-- label to display interactive messages -->
<asp:Label id="lblMessage" runat="server" EnableViewState="false" />

</form>
```

We've omitted the declaration of the templates that define the output generated by the DataList from the previous code (you'll see them shortly). What you can see from the previous listing is that you have a series of attributes that define the appearance of the DataList contents, followed by several that control the behavior. You set the DataKeyField to the OrderID column in the DataSet that you'll bind to the DataList and specify the event handlers that'll execute when several events occur.

The events you're handling include OnItemCommand, which occurs when the user clicks any control that causes a postback to the server (such as a button or link). The next four event attributes shown in the DataList define the event handlers that execute when one of the Edit, Update, Delete, or Cancel buttons is clicked. By using ASP.NET Command controls to create these buttons, and by setting the specific values for their CommandName property, you ensure that they raise the appropriate event when clicked. You'll see these in the next listing when you look at the templates for your DataList. The final event you want to handle is the OnItemDataBound event. This occurs once for each row while the binding of the DataList to the data source takes place. At the point when your event handler is called, the data that will be placed in the row is known, but the output to generate the row in the browser hasn't been created. This means you can interact with and change this output. As you'll see, you use this event to show or hide the Edit Items button and to populate the drop-down list of shippers (the Via list) for each row.

The ItemTemplate for the DataList

When the page is first opened, the DataList control has all rows in "normal" mode. Each row is rendered using the content of the ItemTemplate defined within the DataList control. The next code shows the content specified to display the shipping details in each of these rows, using values that come from the DataSet you generate and cache (if possible) in the user's session:

```
<ItemTemplate>
  Order No: <b><%# Container.DataItem("OrderID") %></b>  
  Ordered: <%# DataBinder.Eval(Container.DataItem, _
                       "OrderDate", "{0:d}") %>  
  Required: <%# DataBinder.Eval(Container.DataItem, _
                       "RequiredDate", "{0:d}") %>  
  Ship: <%# DataBinder.Eval(Container.DataItem, _
                       "ShippedDate", "{0:d}") %>
  via <%# Container.DataItem("ShipperName") %>
  ($<%# DataBinder.Eval(Container.DataItem, "Freight", "{0:F2}") %>)
  <br />
  <asp:Button CommandName="Edit" Text="Edit" runat="server" />
  Shipping address: <%# Container.DataItem("ShipName") %>,
  <%# Container.DataItem("ShipAddress") %>,
  <%# Container.DataItem("ShipCity") %>,
  <%# Container.DataItem("ShipPostalCode") %>,
  <%# Container.DataItem("ShipCountry") %>
</ItemTemplate>
```

You can see that you display all the data directly in the page—you don't put it into individual controls. By default the DataList control displays each data item (each row in the Orders table of your DataSet) in a cell within a row of the HTML <table> that it automatically generates, as shown in Figure 8-11. Formatting within each cell (each row) is done with just nonbreaking spaces and <br /> elements. You could use other elements as well, such as <span>, <div>, <asp:Label>, and so on, but there's no requirement to do so. 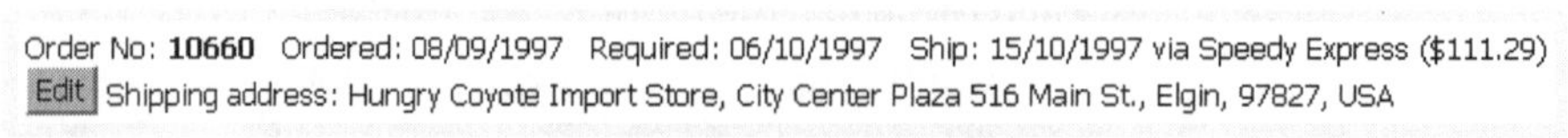

Order No: **10660** Ordered: 08/09/1997 Required: 06/10/1997 Ship: 15/10/1997 via Speedy Express ($111.29)
Edit Shipping address: Hungry Coyote Import Store, City Center Plaza 516 Main St., Elgin, 97827, USA

Figure 8-11. A row in the Edit Orders page in normal mode

> **NOTE** *Note that if you include a definition of a* <table> *and the corresponding* <tr> *and* <td> *elements within a* DataList *control template, the contents of this table are ignored. To display the content for each data item in a nested table, you must set the* ExtractTemplateRows *attribute to* True *for the* DataList *control and use the* <ASP:Table>, <ASP:TableRow>, *and* <ASP:TableCell> *server controls within the templates to create the nested table.*

As mentioned earlier, the name you give to CommandButton controls in a list template affects their behavior. The Edit button in your grid has the CommandName of Edit, and just doing this is enough to cause it to raise the OnEditCommand event when clicked. You'll examine the event handler for this button shortly:

```
<asp:Button CommandName="Edit" Text="Edit" runat="server" />
```

The EditItemTemplate for the DataList

When you set the EditItemIndex of a DataList (or other ASP.NET list control) to a value other than its default of -1, the row at that index is rendered using the content of the EditItemTemplate instead of the ItemTemplate. In this page, you use the following declaration for the EditItemTemplate. You can see how the two columns that can't be edited (the order ID and "required" date) are still displayed in Label controls. However, all the other column values are displayed using a TextBox control or (in the case of the shipper name) a DropDownList control:

```
<EditItemTemplate>
  Order No: <b><asp:Label id="lblOrderID" runat="server"
      Text='<%# Container.DataItem("OrderID") %>' /></b> 
  Ordered: <%# DataBinder.Eval(Container.DataItem, _
                            "OrderDate", "{0:d}") %> 
  Required: <asp:TextBox id="txtRequired" size="11"
      MaxLength="10" runat="server"
      Text='<%# DataBinder.Eval(Container.DataItem, _
                            "RequiredDate", "{0:d}") %>' /> 
  Ship: <asp:TextBox id="txtShipped" size="11"
      MaxLength="10" runat="server"
      Text='<%# DataBinder.Eval(Container.DataItem, _
                            "ShippedDate", "{0:d}") %>' /> 
  Freight: $<asp:TextBox id="txtFreight" size="5"
      MaxLength="6" runat="server"
      Text='<%# DataBinder.Eval(Container.DataItem, _
                            "Freight", "{0:F2}") %>' />
```

```
<asp:Button id="cmdSetFreight" CommandName="SetFreight"
    Text="Set" runat="server" /><br />
Name: <asp:TextBox id="txtShipName" size="40"
    MaxLength="40" runat="server"
    Text='<%# Container.DataItem("ShipName") %>' />  
Address: <asp:TextBox id="txtAddress" size="59"
    MaxLength="60" runat="server"
    Text='<%# Container.DataItem("ShipAddress") %>' /><br /> 
City: <asp:TextBox id="txtCity" size="17"
    MaxLength="15" runat="server"
    Text='<%# Container.DataItem("ShipCity") %>' />  
Postal Code: <asp:TextBox id="txtPostalCode" size="11"
    MaxLength="10" runat="server"
    Text='<%# Container.DataItem("ShipPostalCode") %>' /> 
Country: <asp:TextBox id="txtCountry" size="16"
    MaxLength="15" runat="server"
    Text='<%# Container.DataItem("ShipCountry") %>' />  
via: <asp:DropDownList id="lstShipper" runat="server" />
  <div align="right">
    <asp:Button CommandName="Update" Text="Update" runat="server" />
    <asp:Button CommandName="Delete" Text="Delete" runat="server" />
    <asp:Button CommandName="Cancel" Text="Cancel" runat="server" />
    <asp:Button CommandName="EditItems" id="cmdEditItems"
        Text="Edit Items" Visible="False" runat="server" />
  </div>
```

For each control, you use the same syntax as in the `ItemTemplate` to insert the column values into the controls—formatting some of them using the `DataBinder.Eval` method as you go. At the end of the listing are the four `Button` controls that create the Update, Delete, Cancel, and Edit Items buttons, as shown in Figure 8-12. The first three are automatically "wired up" to the appropriate event handlers because you use the special command name values for them. Notice that the fourth Edit Items button won't be visible by default—you want to show it only when the order hasn't already shipped.

Figure 8-12. A row in the Edit Orders page in edit mode

Storing the Original Values for the Columns

The code in the previous section creates the visible output, as shown in Figure 8-12, but this isn't the end of your EditItemTemplate declaration. If you're going to detect and prevent concurrency errors, you need to have access to the original values of the columns for which the user will edit values. Their newly edited values will be the current values for the columns when you come to perform the update.

So, the EditItemTemplate declaration also includes a series of hidden-type <input> controls that have the original column values as their values. This means that, irrespective of any changes the user makes to the data in the visible controls for the row, you'll still be able to access the original values:

```
<input id="hidRequiredWas" type="hidden" runat="server"
        value='<%# DataBinder.Eval(Container.DataItem, _
                            "RequiredDate", "{0:d}") %>' />
<input id="hidShippedWas" type="hidden" runat="server"
        value='<%# DataBinder.Eval(Container.DataItem, _
                            "ShippedDate", "{0:d}") %>' />
<input id="hidShipNameWas" type="hidden" runat="server"
        value='<%# Container.DataItem("ShipName") %>' />
<input id="hidAddressWas" type="hidden" runat="server"
        value='<%# Container.DataItem("ShipAddress") %>' />
<input id="hidCityWas" type="hidden" runat="server"
        value='<%# Container.DataItem("ShipCity") %>' />
<input id="hidPostalCodeWas" type="hidden" runat="server"
        value='<%# Container.DataItem("ShipPostalCode") %>' />
<input id="hidCountryWas" type="hidden" runat="server"
        value='<%# Container.DataItem("ShipCountry") %>' />
<input id="hidFreightWas" type="hidden" runat="server"
        value='<%# DataBinder.Eval(Container.DataItem, _
                            "Freight", "{0:F2}") %>' />
<input id="hidShipViaWas" type="hidden" runat="server"
        value='<%# Container.DataItem("ShipVia") %>' />
</EditItemTemplate>
```

Instead of using hidden controls for the original values, you could dig around inside the DataSet that your page uses to get these values. If it's cached in the session, then the performance hit will be low, maybe even less than the processing involved in rendering and populating hidden controls each time. However, if the client doesn't support sessions, it'll mean an extra back-end database hit. Overall, the hidden controls probably provide a better solution.

The FooterTemplate for the DataList

Finally comes the `FooterTempate` declaration for your `DataList`. All you need is a `Button` control to add new orders:

```
<FooterTemplate>
  <asp:Button CommandName="NewOrder" Text="New Order" runat="server" />
</FooterTemplate>
```

Because you included the attribute `FooterStyle-HorizontalAlign="Right"` in your `DataList` declaration, the button is displayed at the right end of the footer, as shown in Figure 8-13.

Figure 8-13. The button for creating a new order

Notice that you haven't provided a `SelectedItemTemplate` in your `DataList`, even though you'll be switching one row at a time into "selected mode" on occasion. All you want to do for a "selected" row is change the background color (to indicate which row was just edited), so you just added the following attribute to the `DataList` declaration:

```
SelectedItemStyle-BackColor="#ffe4e1"
```

Because there's no `SelectedItemTemplate` section, the control will use the contents of the "normal" `ItemTemplate` to render the selected row, but with the background color you've specified.

Displaying a List of Orders

Inside the `edit-orders.aspx` page, you declare a page-level "global" variable to hold the current customer ID, followed by the code for the `Page_Load` event handler. This collects the customer ID from the query string when the page loads the first time and afterward from a hidden `<input>` control you declared earlier in the page.

If this is a postback, and you've got a customer ID, it then calls the ShowOrders routine elsewhere in this page to show the orders for this customer:

```
<script language="VB" runat="server">

'page-level variable accessed from more than one routine
Dim strCustID As String = ""

Sub Page_Load()

  If Page.IsPostBack Then  'collect customer ID from hidden control
    strCustID = customerid.Value
  Else
    strCustID = Request.QueryString("customerid")
    If (strCustID Is Nothing) Or (strCustID = "") Then
      lblMessage.Text = "* ERROR: no Customer ID provided."
    Else
      customerid.Value = strCustID  'put customer ID in hidden control
      ShowOrders()   'display all orders for this customer
      lblStatus.Text = "Orders for customer ID '" & strCustID & "'"
    End If
  End If

End Sub
```

The ShowOrders Routine

To display details of the orders for the current customer, you just have to fetch your DataSet from the user's session (or directly from the data access tier if it isn't in the session), bind it to the DataList, and call the DataBind method. You first remove any RowFilter that might have been applied by the Edit Order Lines page so that all the orders for this customer are visible:

```
Sub ShowOrders()

  'get Orders DataSet using function elsewhere in this page
  Dim objDataSet As DataSet = GetOrdersFromSessionOrServer(strCustID)

  'remove filter applied by "Edit Order Lines" page
  Dim objLinesView As DataView = _
                  objDataSet.Tables("Order Details").DefaultView
  objLinesView.RowFilter = ""

  'set DataSource, bind the DataList and display status message
```

```
lstOrders.DataSource = objDataSet.Tables("Orders")
lstOrders.DataBind()

If lstOrders.EditItemIndex > -1 Then   'currently in "edit mode"
  lblMessage.Text = "Edit the details of the selected order ..etc.."
Else
  lblMessage.Text = "Click the Edit button in the list ..etc.."
End If

End Sub
```

The DataSet you're using comes from the function GetOrdersFromSessionOrServer located elsewhere in this page. It's identical to the functions you used in the examples in Chapters 5 and 6, simply checking the session first for a cached copy of the DataSet and going back to the data access tier only if there's no cached copy. We haven't listed the function here, but you can use the View Source link in any page to view the ASP.NET source code for that page.

The OnItemDataBound Event Handler

When you declared your DataList control, you included the following attribute:

```
OnItemDataBound="SetRowVariations"
```

So the ItemDataBound event, which occurs for each row in the DataList while it's being bound to the corresponding row in the data source, will execute your SetRowVariations event handler. In it, you have a couple of things to do. First, you want to only display the Edit Items button if the order hasn't yet shipped (probably a fairly common business rule). Second, you still have some work to do with your shipper name drop-down list. You begin by making sure that your routine only executes when the event is raised for the row that's in edit mode and not for any other row (which would cause an error because the other rows don't contain the controls you'll be referencing). To do this, you get a reference to the row type from the event parameters, cast it to a ListItemType object, and compare it to the enumeration value ListItemType.EditItem:

```
Sub SetRowVariations(objSender As Object, objArgs As DataListItemEventArgs)

  'get type of row that caused event, only set variations for EditItem
  Dim objItemType As ListItemType = _
                        CType(objArgs.Item.ItemType, ListItemType)

  If objItemType = ListItemType.EditItem Then
    ...
```

Showing and Hiding Controls

Now you know that the current row is one created by your <EditItemTemplate>, so you can get a reference to the TextBox control holding the shipped date, and a reference to the Edit Items Button control. Then you apply your business rule by comparing the value in the text box to today's date and setting the Visible property for the Button depending on the outcome:

```
...
'get a reference to the ShippedDate TextBox control in this row
Dim objTextBox As TextBox = _
     CType(objArgs.Item.FindControl("txtShipped"), TextBox)

'get a reference to the "Edit Items" Button control in this row
Dim objButton As Button = _
     CType(objArgs.Item.FindControl("cmdEditItems"), Button)

'business rule: can only edit lines on order if not yet shipped
objButton.Visible = False
If objTextBox.Text.Length = 0 Then
  objButton.Visible = True    'no ship date specified
Else
  Try
    'see if ship date is in the future
    Dim datShip As DateTime = DateTime.Parse(objTextBox.Text)
    If DateTime.Compare(DateTime.Now(), datShip) < 0 Then
      objButton.Visible = True
    End If
  Catch
  End Try
End If
...
```

Filling and Selecting Items in a DropDownList Control

When you declared the <EditItemTemplate> content, you used a DropDownList control for the shipper names. However, you didn't provide any values for the list:

```
via: <asp:DropDownList id="lstShipper" runat="server" />
```

You want the values to come from your database, rather than being hardcoded into the page. That way, as new shippers are added, they'll appear in your list automatically. You also want to set the list so that the current shipper name value for the row you're editing is selected in the list when the page displays. If you don't do this and leave it set to the first item in the list (the default), it'll change the value in the database when the user submits their changes unless they reselect the correct shipper every time.

To fill the list control, you get a reference to it, get a DataSet containing a list of shippers from the database, and bind the DataSet to the list control in the usual way. You use a separate function in this page named GetShippersFromSessionOrServer, which itself uses a simple function in the data access tier and a stored procedure to extract a list of shipper ID values (the primary key in the Shippers table) and their names. This function caches the DataSet in the user's session if possible or fetches it afresh from the database if sessions aren't supported:

```
...
'get a reference to the asp:DropDownList control in this row
Dim objList As DropDownList = _
      CType(objArgs.Item.FindControl("lstShipper"), DropDownList)

Try

  'get Shippers DataSet using function elsewhere in this page
  Dim objShipDataSet As DataSet = GetShippersFromSessionOrServer()

  objList.DataSource = objShipDataSet
  objList.DataTextField = "ShipperName"
  objList.DataValueField = "ShipperID"
  objList.DataBind()
  ...
```

Figure 8-14 shows the list control.

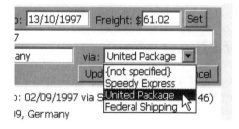

Figure 8-14. The drop-down list of shipper names

> **NOTE** *We chose to cache the list of shippers (and, as you'll see later, the list of products) in the user's session. This means that each user will store a separate copy. You could minimize the server resources required by instead caching this data, which is common to all users, in the ASP.NET* Application *object instead of in the* Session *object. However, then you'd have to add special code to update this when the data in the* Shippers *(and* Products*) tables changes. Unlike* Session *values, which are destroyed when the user's session ends, values cached in the* Application *remain there until the complete application is restarted. Alternatives would be to use the ASP.NET* Cache *object, specifying a timeout after which the value will automatically be destroyed, or to implement your own custom caching method.*

Next you need to set the appropriate SelectedIndex value for this list so that the correct shipper name is selected. You start by getting a reference to the row in the data source that contains the data for this row in your DataList control. The second parameter to your event handler is a DataListItemEventArgs object, which exposes the data as the DataItem property of the current Item. You cast it to a DataRowView object, and you can then access the columns by column name or index.

The value for the selected shipper in the current data source row is an integer—the ShipperID value that's the primary key in the Shippers table for that shipper. You used these values to set the Value property for each item in your drop-down list. So, to select the correct one, you can iterate through the ListItem objects that make up the list in the DropDownList control and select the one that matches the ShipperID value for the current row:

```
...
'objArgs.Item.DataItem returns the data for this row of items
Dim objRowVals As DataRowView = _
     CType(objArgs.Item.DataItem, DataRowView)

'get the Shipping Company ID of the item in the DataRowView
Dim intShipperID As Integer = objRowVals("ShipVia")

Dim objItem As ListItem
For Each objItem In objList.Items
  If objItem.Value = intShipperID Then
    objItem.Selected = True
  End If
Next
```

```
    Catch objErr As Exception

      'display warning if you get an error - wrong one will be selected
      lblMessage.Text = "* ERROR: Shipper details not located."
      objList.SelectedIndex = 0

    End Try

  End If

End Sub
```

Switching to and from Edit Mode

When the rows in your `DataList` are in normal mode, they display the content declared in your `<ItemTemplate>`. This includes the Edit button, which has as its `CommandName` property the value `Edit`. When this button is clicked, it raises both the `ItemCommand` and the `EditCommand` events (rather than just the `ItemCommand` event that all controls raise if and when they initiate a postback).

You handle the `EditCommand` event in a routine named `DoItemEdit`. In it, all you have to do is switch the corresponding row into edit mode by setting the `DataList` controls `EditItemIndex` property to the index of the row containing the Edit button that was clicked. You can obtain this value from the `ItemIndex` property of the current `Item` passed to your event in the `DataListCommandEventArgs` parameter:

```
Sub DoItemEdit(objSource As Object, objArgs As DataListCommandEventArgs)
'runs when the EditCommand button in the Datalist is clicked
'switches DataList into "Edit" mode to show edit controls

  'reset any Selected row
  lstOrders.SelectedIndex = -1

  'set the EditItemIndex property of the list to this item's index
  lstOrders.EditItemIndex = objArgs.Item.ItemIndex

  lblStatus.Text = "Orders for customer ID <b>'" & strCustID & "'</b>"
  ShowOrders()  'bind the data and display it

End Sub
```

Notice that you set the SelectedIndex property of the DataList to -1 when you put any row into edit mode. You use the SelectedIndex to display one row with a different background color to indicate that it has been edited (you'll see how and why shortly). After changing the EditItemIndex, you rebind the control to the data source to display the contents of the <EditItemTemplate> for this row.

When a row in the DataList is in edit mode, the Cancel button displays. This button has its CommandName value set to Cancel, so it's automatically wired up to the CancelCommand event. The attributes you added to your DataList declaration define the event handler for this event to be the routine DoItemCancel. In it, you just have to set the EditItemIndex back to -1 and rebind the DataList control to update the display:

```
Sub DoItemCancel(objSource As Object, objArgs As DataListCommandEventArgs)
'runs when the "Cancel" button in the Datalist is clicked

  'set EditItemIndex property of grid to -1 to switch out of Edit mode
  lstOrders.EditItemIndex = -1
  ShowOrders()  'bind the data and display it
  lblStatus.Text = "Changes to the order were abandoned."

End Sub
```

Handling ItemCommand Events

As noted earlier, the ItemCommand event is raised when any control in the grid causes a postback to the server. So, in the handler for this event, you have to check the CommandName of the control that caused the event to occur before deciding what actions to take. The DataList has the attribute OnItemCommand="DoItemCommand", so the event will execute the event handler named DoItemCommand.

You have three different tasks to perform in this event handler, depending on which control was clicked. You need to carry out specific tasks for the Edit Items button and the Set button (next to the Freight text box) in any row that's in edit mode and for the New Order button in the footer section of the DataList control. Remember that the Edit, Delete, and Cancel buttons will also raise this event, as well as their own "specific" event, so you should always check the CommandName within the event handler to make sure you only execute the code when appropriate.

If it was the Edit Items button that raised the event, you just need to load the second page in this part of the application where the user can edit the contents of an order. You collect the order ID from the Label control named lblOrderID in the current row and use it and the customer ID to build the URL and query string that'll load the `edit-order-items.aspx` page with the correct order displayed. Then you redirect the client to that page:

```
Sub DoItemCommand(objSource As Object, objArgs As DataListCommandEventArgs)
'runs when any Command button in the Datalist is clicked

  'see if it was the "Edit Items" button that was clicked
  If objArgs.CommandName = "EditItems" Then

    'get a reference to the Order ID Label control
    Dim objOrderIDCtrl As Label
    objOrderIDCtrl = CType(objArgs.Item.FindControl("lblOrderID"), Label)

    'create Query String for edit-order-lines page
    Dim strQuery As String = "?customerid=" & strCustID _
                        & "&orderid=" & objOrderIDCtrl.Text

    'open page for editing detail lines for this order
    Response.Clear()
    Response.Redirect("edit-order-lines.aspx" & strQuery)
    Response.End

  End If
  ...
```

Handling the New Order Button

If it was the New Order button that raised the event, you call a separate function within this page named `InsertNewOrder` to insert a new order. You need to make sure no rows are in selected mode first and then create a variable named `intOrderID` to hold the `ByRef` parameter you'll pass to and get back from this function:

```
...
'see if it was the "New Order" button that was clicked
If objArgs.CommandName = "NewOrder" Then

  'reset any Selected row
  lstOrders.SelectedIndex = -1

  'create variable for ByRef function parameter
  Dim intOrderID As Integer = -1

  'call function to insert a new Order row in database for the
```

```
'current customer. Sets OrderID and returns True/False
If InsertNewOrder(intOrderID) = True Then

  'show this row ready for editing
  lstOrders.EditItemIndex = 0
  ShowOrders()

End If

End If
...
```

On return from the `InsertNewOrder` function, you have the ID of the new order in your `intOrderID` variable. You want to put the new row into edit mode in the grid so that the user can change the default values for the order as required. In this example, you just switch to the first row in the list, which works because the list of orders is sorted by descending order number. So the new order will appear in the first row.

A more elegant solution that's less likely to fail if there are concurrent users, and (more importantly) works when the list isn't sorted in descending order, is to use the `OrderID` to iterate through the `DataList` control to find the appropriate row. You can use the `DataKeys` collection for this because you specified the `OrderID` column in the data source as the `DataKeyField` attribute of the `DataList`:

```
'alternative approach to selecting or editing an item
For intIndex = 0 To lstOrders.DataKeys.Count - 1
   If lstOrders.DataKeys(intIndex) = intOrderID Then
     lstOrders.EditItemIndex = intIndex
   End If
Next
```

Setting the Freight Cost

The third task for your routine that handles the `ItemCommand` event is to see if it was the Set (freight charge) button that raised the event. To set the freight charge, you use a simple stored procedure that takes into account the number of items on the order and the chosen shipper. Of course, in a "real" application you'll probably have some lookup tables of freight charges or even use a Web Service or custom request that goes out to the shipper's own site to calculate the charge in real time:

```
CREATE PROCEDURE SetFreightCost @OrderID int
AS DECLARE @ItemCount int, @Shipper int
```

```
SELECT @ItemCount = COUNT(Quantity) FROM [Order Details]
  WHERE OrderID = @OrderID
SELECT @Shipper = ShipVia FROM Orders WHERE OrderID = @OrderID
UPDATE Orders
  SET Freight = (@ItemCount * (1.75 + (ISNULL(@Shipper, 1) * 0.23)) + 15)
WHERE OrderID = @OrderID
```

You call this stored procedure from a simple method (function) named
SetFreightCost within the data access tier of your application (in the component
implemented by updateorders.vb). It uses standard techniques you've already seen
several times to create an ADO.NET Command object, execute the stored procedure,
and return True if it updates one row or False if not:

```
Public Function SetFreightCost(ByVal OrderID As Integer) As Boolean
  Dim strProcName As String = "SetFreightCost"
  Dim objConnect As New OleDbConnection(m_ConnectString)
  Try
    Dim objCommand As New OleDbCommand(strProcName, objConnect)
    objCommand.CommandType = CommandType.StoredProcedure
    objCommand.Parameters.Add("@OrderID", OrderID)
    objConnect.Open()
    Return (objCommand.ExecuteNonQuery() = 1)
  Catch objError As Exception
    Return False
  Finally
    'close connection (occurs before Return is executed)
    objConnect.Close()
  End Try
End Function
```

You call this function in your data access tier from the ASP.NET page
edit-orders.aspx. You have to extract the order ID from the Label control in the
DataList first and convert it to an Integer value. After collecting the connection
string from the web.config file, you can instantiate the data access component
and call your SetFreightCost method with the current order ID. Depending on the
result, you display the appropriate message in the page. You also have to call
the ShowOrders routine to rebind the list and display the new value from the Orders
table. This means you must remove any cached DataSet from the current user's
session first so that the database itself (rather than any cached and now out-of-
date data) is accessed this time:

```
...
'see if it was the "Set Freight" button that was clicked
If objArgs.CommandName = "SetFreight" Then

  'get a reference to and value of OrderID Label control
  Dim objOrderIDCtrl As Label
  objOrderIDCtrl = CType(objArgs.Item.FindControl("lblOrderID"), Label)
  Dim intOrderID As Integer = Integer.Parse(objOrderIDCtrl.Text)

  'get connection string from web.config
  Dim strConnect As String
  strConnect = ConfigurationSettings.AppSettings("NorthwindConnectString")

  'create an instance of the data access component
  Dim objOrderList As New UpdateOrders(strConnect)

  'call routine in data access component to calculate/update
  'freight cost in Orders table and display message
  If objOrderList.SetFreightCost(intOrderID) Then
    lblStatus.Text = "Freight cost recalculated for Order ID: " _
                   & intOrderID.ToString()
  Else
    lblStatus.Text = "* ERROR: Could not calculate freight cost."
  End If

  'remove any cached DataSet from Session and update list
  Session("4923HTMLOrdersDataSet") = Nothing
  ShowOrders()

End If

End Sub
```

Inserting a New Order

There are a couple of ways you could insert a new order into your database. You could use a separate page, or some custom control on the current page, to collect all the values for the new order from the user (and even the contents—a list of order "lines") and then insert all this into the database. However, often a more useful technique is to insert a "blank" order first and then allow the user to fill in the details and add the order lines afterward.

This second approach has a couple of advantages: You can prefill some of the values for them—for example, the shipping address—and you can get the new order number that's automatically generated by the Identity column in the database table when an order is inserted. It also allows you to easily provide "inline" editing within the DataList control using your existing code, and we chose this second approach in the example application. The only downside is if the user decides to cancel the process of inserting the new order, in which case they have to delete the new order row (or you have to do it automatically within your code).

The stored procedure you use takes two parameters—the customer ID and an OUTPUT parameter that returns the ID (order number) for the new order. In the stored procedure, you select the values for the customer's name and address from the Customers table into variables, then insert a new row into the Orders table using these values for the "ship to" name and address. You also specify the default shipper ID (1) and set the default freight cost to $15.00:

```
CREATE PROCEDURE InsertNewOrder @CustID varchar(5), @OrderID int OUTPUT
AS
DECLARE @CompanyName varchar(40)
DECLARE @Address varchar(60)
DECLARE @City varchar(15)
DECLARE @Region varchar(15)
DECLARE @PostalCode varchar(10)
DECLARE @Country varchar(15)

SELECT @CompanyName = CompanyName, @Address = Address,
       @City = City, @Region = Region, @PostalCode = PostalCode,
       @Country = Country
FROM Customers WHERE CustomerID = @CustID

INSERT INTO Orders (CustomerID, OrderDate, ShipName, ShipAddress,
  ShipCity, ShipRegion, ShipPostalCode, ShipCountry, ShipVia, Freight)
VALUES (@CustID, GETDATE(), @CompanyName, @Address, @City, @Region,
  @PostalCode, @Country, 1, 15)

SELECT @OrderID = @@IDENTITY
```

The `OrderID` column in the table is of type `Identity` and will contain the new order ID after the row has been inserted. You can retrieve this using the special built-in `@@IDENTITY` variable, which is automatically set to the most recently inserted value in the `Identity` column of a table during the current connection. This will, of course, be the order ID for the order you just inserted. Therefore, the last line of the procedure can select and return this value.

The Data Access Tier InsertNewOrder Method

You call this stored procedure from the method (function) named `InsertNewOrder` within your data access component. It only requires one `INPUT` parameter— the customer ID. The second parameter for the stored procedure, `@OrderID`, is the `OUTPUT` parameter. After executing the stored procedure, you can return the order number as the value of the `@OrderID` parameter:

```
Public Function InsertNewOrder(ByVal CustomerID As String) As Integer
  Dim strProcName As String = "InsertNewOrder"
  Dim objConnect As New OleDbConnection(m_ConnectString)
  Try
    Dim objCommand As New OleDbCommand(strProcName, objConnect)
    objCommand.CommandType = CommandType.StoredProcedure

    'add required parameters for input and output
    objCommand.Parameters.Add("@CustID", OleDbType.VarChar, 5)
    objCommand.Parameters("@CustID").Value = CustomerID
    objCommand.Parameters.Add("@OrderID", OleDbType.Integer)
    objCommand.Parameters("@OrderID").Direction = _
                                    ParameterDirection.Output

    objConnect.Open()
    objCommand.ExecuteNonQuery()
    Return objCommand.Parameters("@OrderId").Value

  Catch objError As Exception
    Throw objError
  Finally
    objConnect.Close()
  End Try

End Function
```

The ASP.NET Page InsertNewOrder Method

In your `edit-orders.apx` page, you use the method just described within the routine named `InsertNewOrder`, which is executed by the `ItemCommand` event handler when the New Order button is clicked. In this routine you need to remove any cached `DataSet` from the user's session and then execute the data access tier method. It returns the new order number, which you can display in the page:

```
Function InsertNewOrder(ByRef intOrderID As Integer) As Boolean

  Session("4923HTMLOrdersDataSet") = Nothing
  Dim strConnect As String
  strConnect = ctlConnectStrings.OLEDBConnectionString
  Dim objOrderList As New UpdateOrders(strConnect)
  Try

    'call the method to return the data as a DataSet
    intOrderID = objOrderList.InsertNewOrder(strCustID)
    lblStatus.Text = "Inserted new order ID: <b>" _
                & intOrderID.ToString() & "</b>"
    Return True

  Catch objErr As Exception

    lblStatus.Text = "* ERROR: Cannot insert new order.<br />" _
                & objErr.Message
    Return False

  End Try

End Function
```

Once the new order is inserted, the code you saw previously in the `DoItemCommand` routine (which originally called the `InsertNewOrder` routine shown previously) sets the `EditItemIndex` to the new order row and rebinds the `DataList` so that the new row appears in edit mode. The user can edit any values they want to change and click Update to commit these changes as shown in Figure 8-15. And, of course, they can click the Edit Items button to add products to the new order.

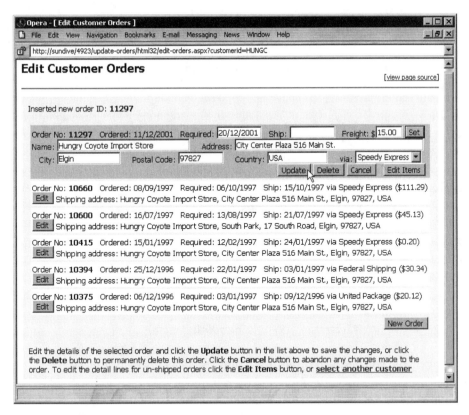

Figure 8-15. Inserting and updating a new order

Updating the Order Details

When the Update button is clicked (after editing an existing order), the
UpdateCommand event is raised. You specified that this will execute your event handler named DoItemUpdate by adding the attribute OnUpdateCommand="DoItemUpdate"
to the DataList declaration.

The stored procedure listed next is in the database and named
UpdateExistingOrder. It updates an order using a series of values supplied as
parameters. Because you want to check for and prevent concurrency errors while
updating the data source, you have to pass into the procedure both the original
and the current values for the columns that the user can edit. You also, obviously,
need to pass in the value of the primary key column OrderID for the row:

```
CREATE PROCEDURE UpdateExistingOrder
  @OrderID varchar(5), @Required datetime,    @Shipped datetime,
  @Freight money,      @ShipName varchar(40),  @Address varchar(60),
```

```
  @City varchar(15),   @PostalCode varchar(10), @Country varchar(15),
  @ShipVia int,        @RequiredWas datetime,   @ShippedWas datetime,
  @FreightWas money,   @NameWas varchar(40),    @AddressWas varchar(60),
  @CityWas varchar(15),    @PostalCodeWas varchar(10),
  @CountryWas varchar(15), @ShipViaWas int
AS
UPDATE Orders SET
  RequiredDate=@Required, ShippedDate=@Shipped, Freight=@Freight,
  ShipVia=@ShipVia, ShipName=@ShipName, ShipAddress=@Address,
  ShipCity=@City, ShipPostalCode=@PostalCode, ShipCountry=@Country
WHERE
  OrderID=@OrderID AND Freight=@FreightWas AND ShipVia=@ShipViaWas
  AND ShipName=@NameWas AND ShipAddress=@AddressWas
  AND ShipCity=@CityWas AND ShipPostalCode=@PostalCodeWas
  AND ShipCountry=@CountryWas
  AND CONVERT(varchar, ISNULL(RequiredDate, 1), 0)
            = CONVERT(varchar, ISNULL(@RequiredWas, 1), 0)
  AND CONVERT(varchar, ISNULL(ShippedDate,1), 0)
            = CONVERT(varchar, ISNULL(@ShippedWas, 1), 0)
```

Notice that you perform some quite complex comparison for the date columns. If the column in the table and the parameter value are both NULL, the comparison will fail unless you use database-specific instructions such as SET ANSI_NULLS=OFF. Instead, using the ISNULL function, you convert NULL values into the value 1 before you compare them. There might also be an issue regarding the format of the date that you provide as a parameter, and an easy way to be sure of an accurate comparison is to convert both values into a standard string (varchar) format first.

The Data Access Tier SingleRowOrderUpdate Method

The method SingleRowOrderUpdate works the same way as most of the other data access functions you've looked at. OK, so it takes a lot more parameters, but the execution of the stored procedure is the same, and you return the number of rows that were affected. However, because of the date values in this procedure, you have to take a few error-prevention actions.

In particular, you must check the values passed to your routine from the ASP.NET page code for dates to see if they're NULL. Your stored procedure expects a SQL Server/OLE-DB datetime parameter, and it'll complain if you try to pass it a .NET DateTime object with the value NULL (Nothing in Visual Basic) instead. So you have to replace these with the "proper" value DBNull.Value. To avoid unnecessary repetition, just the relevant code from the SingleRowOrderUpdate method is shown:

```
...
'add parameters for current values
objCommand.Parameters.Add("@OrderID", UpdateOrderID)
If RequiredDate = Nothing Then
  objCommand.Parameters.Add("@Required", DBNull.Value)
Else
  objCommand.Parameters.Add("@Required", RequiredDate)
End If
If ShippedDate = Nothing Then
  objCommand.Parameters.Add("@Shipped", DBNull.Value)
Else
  objCommand.Parameters.Add("@Shipped", ShippedDate)
End If
objCommand.Parameters.Add("@Freight", Freight)
objCommand.Parameters.Add("@ShipName", ShipName)
objCommand.Parameters.Add("@Address", ShipAddress)
objCommand.Parameters.Add("@City", ShipCity)
objCommand.Parameters.Add("@PostalCode", ShipPostalCode)
objCommand.Parameters.Add("@Country", ShipCountry)
objCommand.Parameters.Add("@ShipVia", ShipVia)
...
'add parameters for original (Was) values here
...
```

NOTE *Remember that you can view the source code for the data access component from within any page by clicking the View Source link and then clicking View Component Source link.*

The ASP.NET Page DoItemUpdate Method

To execute the `SingleRowOrderUpdate` method, you first have to collect all the values you need from the current row in the `DataList` control. You can get the order ID from the `DataKeys` collection of the `DataList`, specifying the index of the current row. This is available from the `ItemIndex` passed to your event handler in the `DataListCommandEventArgs` parameter. For the other current values, you use the `FindControl` method of the `Item` object for this row, casting the result to a `TextBox` object and then accessing its `Text` property:

```
Sub DoItemUpdate(objSource As Object, objArgs As DataListCommandEventArgs)

  'get OrderID for current row from the DataList's DataKeys collection
  Dim intUpdateID As Integer = lstOrders.DataKeys(objArgs.Item.ItemIndex)

  'get current (updated) values from visible controls in DataList
  Dim strRequired As String = _
      CType(objArgs.Item.FindControl("txtRequired"), TextBox).Text
  Dim strShipped As String = _
      CType(objArgs.Item.FindControl("txtShipped"), TextBox).Text
  ...
  ... same for other TextBox controls
  ...
  Dim objList As DropDownList = _
      CType(objArgs.Item.FindControl("lstShipper"), DropDownList)
  Dim strShipVia As String = objList.Items(objList.SelectedIndex).Value
  ...
```

In the last two lines of the previous code, you can see how you get the selected `ShipperID` value from the shipper name drop-down list. You get a reference to the `DropDownList` object and query the `Value` property of the currently selected option item in the list.

Next you collect the original values from the HTML hidden-type `<input>` controls in the row. In this case, because they're not ASP.NET `TextBox` controls, you have to query the `Value` property rather than the `Text` property. Also, because you store the `ShipperID` value in the hidden control named `hidShipViaWas`, you can extract this directly:

```
...
'get the original values from the hidden-type controls in the DataList
Dim strRequiredWas As String = _
    CType(objArgs.Item.FindControl("hidRequiredWas"), _
                              HtmlInputHidden).Value
```

```
Dim strShippedWas As String = _
    CType(objArgs.Item.FindControl("hidShippedWas"), _
                          HtmlInputHidden).Value

...
Dim strShipViaWas As String = _
    CType(objArgs.Item.FindControl("hidShipViaWas"), _
                          HtmlInputHidden).Value

...
```

Parsing the User's Values

Now you can check that the values are all of valid types. You could've used the
ASP.NET validation controls in the rows for the editable items, instead of normal
ASP.NET controls, but this adds another level of complexity that we tried to avoid
in this example so that you could concentrate on the data access process.

To confirm that the entries are valid data types, you parse the strings you collect from the controls, converting them into the appropriate data type for the data
access tier method that you're using to update the row. By doing this within a
Try...Catch construct, you can trap any conversion errors and display a message:

```
...
'declare variables to hold converted data types
Dim dblFreight, dblFreightWas As Double
Dim intShipVia, intShipViaWas As Integer
Dim datRequired, datRequiredWas As DateTime
Dim datShipped, datShippedWas As DateTime

Try

  'convert String values into correct data types
  'leave Date vales as Null (Nothing) to delete them
  dblFreight = Double.Parse(strFreight)
  intShipVia = Integer.Parse(strShipVia)
  dblFreightWas = Double.Parse(strFreightWas)
  intShipViaWas = Integer.Parse(strShipViaWas)
  If strRequired.Length > 0 Then
    datRequired = DateTime.Parse(strRequired)
  End If
  If strRequiredWas.Length > 0 Then
    datRequiredWas = DateTime.Parse(strRequiredWas)
  End If
  If strShipped.Length > 0 Then
    datShipped = DateTime.Parse(strShipped)
```

```
    End If
    If strShippedWas.Length > 0 Then
      datShippedWas = DateTime.Parse(strShippedWas)
    End If

Catch objErr As Exception

  lblStatus.Text = "* ERROR: Incorrect value entered.<br />" _
                  & objErr.Message
  Exit Sub

End Try
...
```

Notice that you leave any empty date values as Nothing. Blank or empty values are perfectly valid in your database table rows for the required and shipped columns, and you've already made sure that your data access tier method and the stored procedure can cope with NULL values. The technique you used to trap errors isn't terribly informative, however, but it does work. You might prefer to use the validation controls to achieve a more complete error-reporting interface or put each Parse statement into a separate Try...Catch construct and display more helpful messages instead.

Calling the Data Access Tier Method

At last you're ready to call the data access tier SingleRowOrderUpdate method. As usual, you collect the connection string for the database from web.config, create the data access component instance, and call the method. Depending on the number of rows affected, you can display a suitable message:

```
...
'get connection string from web.config
Dim strConnect As String
strConnect = ConfigurationSettings.AppSettings("NorthwindConnectString")

Dim objOrderList As New UpdateOrders(strConnect)

Try
  Dim intRows As Integer
  intRows = objOrderList.SingleRowOrderUpdate(intUpdateID, _
            datRequired, datShipped, dblFreight, strShipName, _
            strAddress, strCity, strPostalCode, strCountry, _
```

```
                intShipVia, datRequiredWas, datShippedWas, _
                dblFreightWas, strShipNameWas, strAddressWas, _
                strCityWas, strPostalCodeWas, strCountryWas, _
                intShipViaWas)
  If intRows = 1 Then  'OK - you got one row updated
    lblStatus.Text = "Updated Order ID: " & intUpdateID.ToString()
  Else
    lblStatus.Text = "* ERROR: Could not update Order ...etc..."
  End If
Catch objErr As Exception
  lblStatus.Text = "* ERROR: Failed to Update Order.<br />"
End Try
...
```

Finally, you remove any existing DataSet from the session so that the user sees the updated data, take the row out of edit mode by setting the EditItemIndex to -1, and select the row so that it displays with a different background color. Because the rows take up a different amount of vertical space when in edit mode, this makes it easier for the user to see which row they just updated. And, to reflect the changes to the EditItemIndex and SelectedIndex, you have to call the ShowOrders routine to rebind the grid. Because your code has removed the cached DataSet from the session, the updated values will automatically be fetched from the database and displayed:

```
  ...
  'remove any cached DataSet from the Session
  Session("4923HTMLOrdersDataSet") = Nothing

  'set EditItemIndex property of grid to -1 to switch out of Edit mode
  lstOrders.EditItemIndex = -1

  'set SelectedIndex to indicate row that was updated
  lstOrders.SelectedIndex = objArgs.Item.ItemIndex
  ShowOrders()  'bind the data and display it


End Sub
```

The Result of a Concurrency Violation

In the next pair of figures, you can see an update being performed on an order. However, in this case there's a concurrency violation. Figure 8-16 shows order number 11298 being edited, and the only change you made was to the Freight value—you changed it from the existing value of $27.50 to $15.00.

Orders for customer ID **'HUNGC'**

Order No: **11298** Ordered: 11/12/2001 Required: Ship: via Speedy Express ($16.98)
[Edit] Shipping address: Hungry Coyote Import Store, City Center Plaza 516 Main St., Elgin, 97827, USA

Order No: **11297** Ordered: 11/12/2001 Required: [20/12/2001] Ship: [17/01/2001] Freight: $[15.00] [Set]
Name: [Hungry Coyote Import Store]   Address: [City Center Plaza 516 Main St.]
City: [Elgin]   Postal Code: [97827]   Country: [USA]   via: [Speedy Express ▼]
                                                    [Update] [Delete] [Cancel]

Order No: **10660** Ordered: 08/09/1997 Required: 06/10/1997 Ship: via Speedy Express ($111.29)

Figure 8-16. Changing the Freight value for an order

However, unbeknown to you, another user is editing the same row, and they have saved their edits to the database while you still have the page open (you can demonstrate this effect yourself by starting a second instance of the browser, which will use a separate session from the first one). The other user changed the Address and Shipper values for the same order. So, when you come to update the row (in the first browser instance), you get the message indicating a concurrency error. The row is also displayed with the "new" values for the address and shipping company that were persisted by the update process in the other browser instance, and your updated freight value is lost, as shown in Figure 8-17.

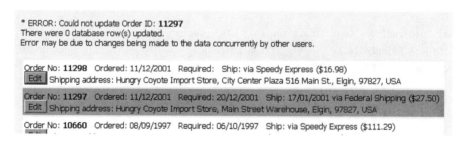

* ERROR: Could not update Order ID: **11297**
There were 0 database row(s) updated.
Error may be due to changes being made to the data concurrently by other users.

Order No: **11298** Ordered: 11/12/2001 Required: Ship: via Speedy Express ($16.98)
[Edit] Shipping address: Hungry Coyote Import Store, City Center Plaza 516 Main St., Elgin, 97827, USA

Order No: **11297** Ordered: 11/12/2001 Required: 20/12/2001 Ship: 17/01/2001 via Federal Shipping ($27.50)
[Edit] Shipping address: Hungry Coyote Import Store, Main Street Warehouse, Elgin, 97827, USA

Order No: **10660** Ordered: 08/09/1997 Required: 06/10/1997 Ship: via Speedy Express ($111.29)

Figure 8-17. The error message displayed when concurrent updates are applied

The code has automatically abandoned the changes you made and kept the values set by the other user. This way, both users know what's happening. The values entered by the user who saved their changes first have been persisted, and are still there, while the user who attempted to save their edited values afterward has been warned about the changes to the underlying values after they finished editing their "copy" of these values and tried to save them.

Of course, the user who has lost all their edits may be upset that all their efforts were in vain, and they have to start all over again. A nice touch is to display the differences between the underlying values and the user's original values and then allow them to make a decision as to what to do. This might be to abandon the changes, overwrite the underlying values, or edit the values in some of the columns to encompass both users' changes. You'll see an example of this when you look at data updates in rich clients in Chapters 11 and 12.

Deleting an Order

The final feature of the edit-orders.aspx page is the ability to delete an existing order from the Orders table. This process also has to delete any/all related child rows in the Order Details table to maintain referential integrity in the data store. You specified in the declaration of the DataList that the DeleteCommand event raised by your Delete button should execute the DoItemDelete event handler by using this attribute:

```
OnDeleteCommand="DoItemDelete"
```

The DoItemDelete routine uses the stored procedure named DeleteExistingOrder. It takes as parameters all the original values of the row to be deleted and prevents any concurrency errors by checking first that a row with these values exists. Then it deletes all related child rows before finally deleting the specified parent row:

```
CREATE PROCEDURE DeleteExistingOrder
@OrderID varchar(5),  @RequiredWas datetime,  @ShippedWas datetime,
@FreightWas money,    @NameWas varchar(40),   @AddressWas varchar(60),
@CityWas varchar(15), @CountryWas varchar(15),
@ShipViaWas int,      @PostalCodeWas varchar(10)
AS
SELECT OrderID
FROM Orders
WHERE
  OrderID = @OrderID AND Freight = @FreightWas
```

```
    AND ShipVia = @ShipViaWas AND ShipName = @NameWas
    AND ShipAddress = @AddressWas AND ShipCity = @CityWas
    AND ShipPostalCode = @PostalCodeWas AND ShipCountry = @CountryWas
    AND CONVERT(varchar, ISNULL(RequiredDate, 1), 0)
            = CONVERT(varchar, ISNULL(@RequiredWas, 1), 0) AND
    CONVERT(varchar, ISNULL(ShippedDate,1), 0)
            = CONVERT(varchar, ISNULL(@ShippedWas, 1), 0)IF @@ROWCOUNT = 1
    BEGIN
      BEGIN TRANSACTION
      SET NOCOUNT ON
      DELETE FROM [Order Details] WHERE OrderID = @OrderID
      SET NOCOUNT OFF
      DELETE FROM Orders WHERE
        OrderID = @OrderID AND
        Freight = @FreightWas AND
        ShipVia = @ShipViaWas AND
        ShipName = @NameWas AND
        ShipAddress = @AddressWas AND
        ShipCity = @CityWas AND
        ShipPostalCode = @PostalCodeWas AND
        ShipCountry = @CountryWas AND
        CONVERT(varchar, ISNULL(RequiredDate, 1), 0)
            = CONVERT(varchar, ISNULL(@RequiredWas, 1), 0) AND
        CONVERT(varchar, ISNULL(ShippedDate,1), 0)
            = CONVERT(varchar, ISNULL(@ShippedWas, 1), 0)
      COMMIT TRANSACTION
    END
```

You can see that this procedure exhibits "paranoid mode" programming, rechecking for a concurrency error by specifying all the original values again in the second DELETE statement. Neither of the delete processes will execute if the first SELECT statement fails to locate the row (if any of the columns have been changed concurrently), so you could just use the OrderID in the WHERE clause of the second DELETE statement and generally be perfectly safe. It's probably only on a clustered or a multiprocessor system that there's any chance of the row changing between the SELECT and DELETE statements being executed.

> **NOTE** *There's one import point to note here. Although the stored procedure you use to delete an order from the* Orders *table in the database does check for concurrency errors in the* Orders *row, by comparing the original and underlying (database) values, it doesn't do this for the related child rows in the* Order Details *table. The current values of these rows aren't available to the stored procedure, so it can't perform a comparison of the values for each one. If you require concurrency checking to be carried out on the child rows before a parent order row is deleted, the best approach would be to enable a rule in the presentation tier (the ASP.NET page) that prevents an order from being deleted unless the user has deleted all the child rows first (concurrency checks* are *carried out when individual* Order Details *child rows are deleted).*

The Data Access Tier SingleRowOrderDelete Method

In the data access tier component, you execute this stored procedure within a method (function) named SingleRowOrderDelete. This is identical to the SingleRowOrderUpdate method code you looked at in the previous sections of this chapter except that it requires (and passes to the stored procedure) fewer parameters. You only need the original values (to check for concurrency errors) when you're deleting a row.

Of course, you still have to handle the date parameter values with the same care as you did in the previous example—checking for empty (Nothing or NULL) values and replacing these with DBNull.Value. We haven't listed the code here, but you can examine it in the samples provided.

The ASP.NET Page DoItemDelete Method

As you may expect, much of the code you use in the edit-orders.aspx page to call the data access tier SingleRowOrderDelete method is the same as for the SingleRowOrderUpdate method. You get the order ID from the DataKeys collection of the DataList and the original values from the hidden-type controls in the current DataList row.

As before, you parse these into the correct data types for your method call. In this case, you shouldn't get any conversion errors because the values aren't coming from visible controls that the user can edit. After calling the data access tier method to delete the row in the database, you then switch the DataList out of edit mode, display a message, remove any cached DataSet from the session, and rebind the DataList to display the result, as shown in Figure 8-18.

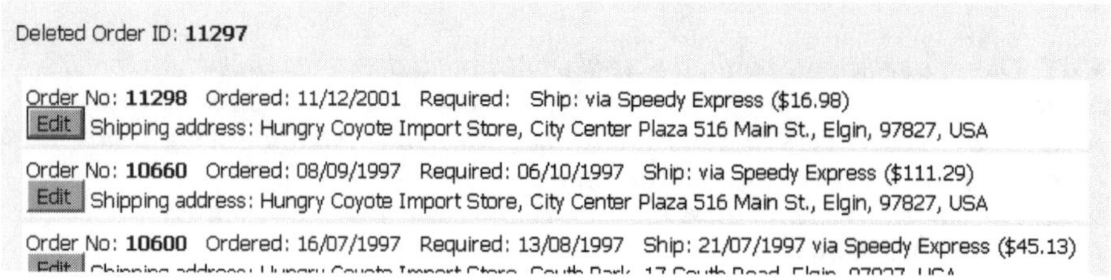

Deleted Order ID: **11297**

Order No: **11298** Ordered: 11/12/2001 Required: Ship: via Speedy Express ($16.98)
 Edit Shipping address: Hungry Coyote Import Store, City Center Plaza 516 Main St., Elgin, 97827, USA

Order No: **10660** Ordered: 08/09/1997 Required: 06/10/1997 Ship: via Speedy Express ($111.29)
 Edit Shipping address: Hungry Coyote Import Store, City Center Plaza 516 Main St., Elgin, 97827, USA

Order No: **10600** Ordered: 16/07/1997 Required: 13/08/1997 Ship: 21/07/1997 via Speedy Express ($45.13)
 Edit Chipping address: Hungry Coyote Import Store, South Park, 17 South Road, Elgin, 97827, USA

Figure 8-18. The result of deleting an order row

Displaying and Editing the Order Contents

Up to now, you've seen how the example application displays and allows the user
to edit orders. The second page, and the second part of the process, is to be able to
view and edit the contents of an order—the order lines. As shown in Figure 8-19,
the page edit-order-lines.aspx provides this feature.

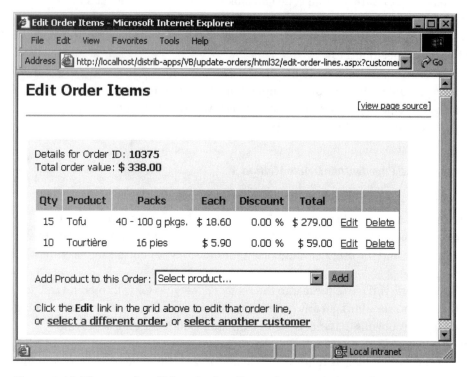

Figure 8-19. The page for editing the detail rows for an existing order

As you saw earlier, you open this page from the previous `edit-orders.aspx` page using the Edit Items button in any unshipped row that's in edit mode. You pass to it (in the query string) the customer ID and the ID of the order containing the Edit Items button.

Much of the code in this page is the same as the previous `edit-orders.aspx` page. The actual techniques are identical; you use some of the same stored procedures and data access methods, and the same `GetDataSetFromSessionOrServer` function provides the data to display in the page. So, in the following sections, we'll point out the differences between the two pages and show any new techniques that you haven't seen so far.

The HTML Page Declaration

To demonstrate some of the differences between the ASP.NET list controls, you'll use a `DataGrid` in this page rather than the `DataList` you used in the previous page. You get less control over the layout of the content, but for the purposes of this page the grid approach suits the data better—you can create a more intuitive interface and give the appearance of a list of items (each row displays only a few "short" column values). You also have a couple of `hidden`-type controls to persist the customer ID and order ID across postbacks and some labels to display information and status messages.

The following code shows the `<form>` section of the page. As before, we've removed the declarations that create the visible output from the `DataGrid`—you'll examine these later:

```
<form runat="server">

<input id="customerid" type="hidden" runat="server" />
<input id="orderid" type="hidden" runat="server" />

<!-- label to display customer ID -->
<asp:Label id="lblStatus" EnableViewState="false" runat="server" /><br />

<!-- label to display order total value -->
<asp:Label id="lblTotalValue" EnableViewState="false" runat="server" />

<!-- DataGrid control to display/edit order lines -->
<asp:DataGrid id="dgrOrderLines" runat="server"
    HeaderStyle-BackColor="#c0c0c0"
    HeaderStyle-HorizontalAlign="Center"
    ItemStyle-BackColor="#ffffff"
```

```
          AlternatingItemStyle-BackColor="#eeeeee"
          SelectedItemStyle-BackColor="#ffe4e1"
          EditItemStyle-BackColor="#dcdcdc"
          CellPadding="5"
          GridLines="Vertical"
          DataKeyField="ProductID"
          OnItemCommand="DoItemCommand"
          OnEditCommand="DoItemEdit"
          OnUpdateCommand="DoItemUpdate"
          OnCancelCommand="DoItemCancel"
          AutoGenerateColumns="False">

  ...
  ... column declarations go here ...
  ...
</asp:DataGrid><p />

<div id="divAddNewLine" style="display:none" runat="server">
  Add Product to this Order:
  <asp:DropDownList id="lstAddProduct" runat="server" />
  <asp:Button OnClick="AddNewLine" Text="Add" runat="server" /><p />
</div>

<!-- label to display interactive messages -->
<asp:Label id="lblMessage" EnableViewState="false" runat="server" />

</form>
```

At the end of the <form> is a <div>, containing the controls to add a new product to the order. You set the style attribute so that this won't be visible by default. You only want to show it when there are no order lines in edit mode. You also turn off viewstate for the Label controls because you don't need them to persist their content across postbacks.

The Columns for the DataGrid Control

A DataGrid control is quite capable of automatically figuring out the structure of the data in a data source and displaying it. You used DataGrid controls in this way in the examples in Chapter 2. Here, however, you want to exert more control over the appearance of the output. So, in the previous declaration of the DataGrid, you add the attribute `AutoGenerateColumns="False"`. You'll generate all the columns you need by declaring them within a `<Columns>` element inside the declaration of the `DataGrid` control.

Within the `Columns` element, you first declare the column for the quantity of products on this order line. You use a `TemplateColumn` element to define this column because it allows you to provide individual templates—just like you did for the `DataList` control in the previous page. You can provide any of the standard template types, but in this example you'll only use an `ItemTemplate` and an `EditItemTemplate`:

```
<Columns>

<asp:TemplateColumn HeaderStyle-HorizontalAlign="center"
     ItemStyle-HorizontalAlign="center" HeaderText="<b>Qty</b>" >

  <ItemTemplate>
    <asp:Label id="lblQuantity" runat="server"
        Text='<%# Container.DataItem("Quantity") %>' />
  </ItemTemplate>

  <EditItemTemplate>
    <asp:TextBox id="txtQuantity" Columns="2" MaxLength="4"
        Text='<%# Container.DataItem("Quantity") %>' runat="server" />
  </EditItemTemplate>

</asp:TemplateColumn>
```

This template gives you a `Label` when the row is in normal mode. In edit mode, it generates a `TextBox` with the size and `MaxLength` that you specify. The next column, for the product name, also uses a `TemplateColumn`. However, this isn't available for edit (the combination of the `OrderID` and `ProductID` make up the primary key for each row in the `Order Details` table), so you don't need an `EditItemTemplate`:

```
<asp:TemplateColumn HeaderText="<b>Product</b>"
     ItemStyle-HorizontalAlign="left">
  <ItemTemplate>
    <asp:Label id="lblProductName" runat="server"
        Text='<%# Container.DataItem("ProductName") %>'/>
  </ItemTemplate>
</asp:TemplateColumn>
```

Using Bound Columns

The other way to specify the columns for a DataGrid is to use a BoundColumn element. This is easier than specifying the template content and layout for normal and edit modes. Instead, you just specify the column in the data source that this column in the table should be bound to and optionally the format for the output. You can also (as in this case for the QtyPerUnit column) specify that the column is read-only:

```
<asp:BoundColumn DataField="QtyPerUnit" HeaderText="<b>Packs</b>"
    HeaderStyle-HorizontalAlign="center"
    ItemStyle-HorizontalAlign="center" ReadOnly="True" />
```

A BoundColumn normally displays its content as text within the output just as though you declared it using a Label control. When a row in the DataGrid is switched into edit mode, a BoundColumn displays its value in a TextBox control. However, if the column is read-only, the value is displayed in a Label control when in edit mode, instead of a TextBox. And you don't have to do anything—all this happens automatically.

Formatting the Price and Discount

Next come the two TemplateColumn declarations for the price and the discount. Both can be edited, so you have an ItemTemplate and an EditItemTemplate for each one. The price column, with the heading Each, uses the DataBinder.Eval method to format the value for display. Notice that, as when displaying price data in the earlier examples, you specify the currency character you want rather than relying on the locale of the server to choose one for you:

```
<asp:TemplateColumn HeaderText="<b>Each</b>"
    ItemStyle-HorizontalAlign="right" >
  <ItemTemplate>
    $ <asp:Label id="lblUnitPrice" runat="server"
          Text='<%# DataBinder.Eval(Container.DataItem, _
                              "UnitPrice", "{0:N2}") %>'/>
  </ItemTemplate>
  <EditItemTemplate>
    <asp:TextBox id="txtUnitPrice" Columns="4" MaxLength="6"
        Text='<%# Container.DataItem("UnitPrice") %>' runat="server" />
  </EditItemTemplate>
</asp:TemplateColumn>
```

The discount column uses the `DataBinder.Eval` method to format the value as a percentage in the `<ItemTemplate>`. However, when the value is presented for editing, you want to remove the % character to make this easier and less error-prone. This means you have to multiply the value by 100 for display; otherwise it'll display as a decimal fraction. Users will probably expect to see something like 5.00 for five percent, not 0.05:

```
<asp:TemplateColumn HeaderText="<b>Discount</b>"
     ItemStyle-HorizontalAlign="right" >
  <ItemTemplate>
    <asp:Label id="lblDiscount" runat="server"
        Text='<%# DataBinder.Eval(Container.DataItem, _
                             "Discount", "{0:P}") %>'/>
  </ItemTemplate>
  <EditItemTemplate>
    <asp:TextBox id="txtDiscount" Columns="3" MaxLength="5" runat="server"
        Text='<%# Container.DataItem("Discount") * 100 %>' />
  </EditItemTemplate>
</asp:TemplateColumn>
```

Each row in the `Order Details` table in the `DataSet` has a calculated column that you generate in your `GetDataFromSessionOrServer` function, as you saw in previous examples. You display this using a `BoundColumn` and include the `DataFormatString` attribute to control the appearance, and the `ReadOnly` attribute to prevent it being shown in a `TextBox` when in edit mode:

```
<asp:BoundColumn HeaderText="<b>Total</b>"
     ItemStyle-HorizontalAlign="right"
     DataField="LineTotal" DataFormatString="${0:N2}" ReadOnly="True" />
```

Using Command Columns

The `DataGrid` control provides a simple but extremely useful feature for switching modes. You can declare an `EditCommandColumn` that'll automatically generate the appropriate Edit, Update, and Cancel links for each row. You can even specify the text you want for these links:

```
<asp:EditCommandColumn EditText="Edit" CancelText="Cancel"
                       UpdateText="Update" />
```

In conjunction with the attributes you included in the declaration of the DataGrid itself, these are automatically wired up to the event handlers you specify:

```
OnEditCommand="DoItemEdit"
OnUpdateCommand="DoItemUpdate"
OnCancelCommand="DoItemCancel"
```

Figure 8-20 shows the links.

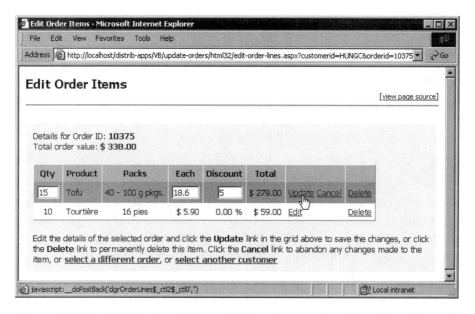

Figure 8-20. The links in the EditCommandColumn *for a row in edit mode and a row in normal mode*

Finally, you have a TemplateColumn that defines a Delete link for each row. You use a LinkButton control and set the CommandName to Delete. In conjunction with the attribute that you include in the declaration of the DataGrid (OnItemCommand="DoItemCommand"), this automatically wires up the event to your event handler named DoItemCommand:

```
<asp:TemplateColumn>
  <ItemTemplate>
    <asp:LinkButton Text="Delete" CommandName="Delete" runat="server" />
    <input id="hidQuantityWas" type="hidden" runat="server"
        value='<%# Container.DataItem("Quantity") %>' />
    <input id="hidUnitPriceWas" type="hidden" runat="server"
```

```
              value='<%# Container.DataItem("UnitPrice") %>' />
        <input id="hidDiscountWas" type="hidden" runat="server"
               value='<%# Container.DataItem("Discount") %>' />
    </ItemTemplate>
  </asp:TemplateColumn>

  </Columns>
```

Notice how you also use this column to store the original values for the three
columns in the row that can be edited. You'll need these values when you come to
perform an update to the original data source. You simply define three hidden-type
controls within the ItemTemplate for this column.

You may be wondering why you placed the hidden-type controls for the
original values in *every* row. In the edit-orders.aspx page you only put the
original values in a row that's in edit mode, not in every row. However, in that
page, the user can only modify (update or delete) the order that's in edit mode.
In the edit-order-lines.aspx page, the Delete link displays for every row, and not
just the one that's in edit mode, so you need the original values for every row to
be available.

Displaying a List of Order Lines

When the edit-order-lines.aspx page first loads, you check that there's a customer
ID and order ID in the query string—if not, you can't display anything. Providing
all is well, you can call the ShowOrderLines routine to display the order contents:

```
Sub Page_Load()

  If Page.IsPostBack Then

    'collect customer ID and Order ID from hidden controls
    strCustID = customerid.Value
    strOrderID = orderid.Value

  Else

    strCustID = Request.QueryString("customerid")
    strOrderID = Request.QueryString("orderid")

    If (strOrderID Is Nothing) Or (strOrderID = "") _
    Or (strCustID Is Nothing) Or (strCustID = "") Then
```

```
      'display error message
      lblMessage.Text = "* ERROR: no Customer or Order ID provided."

   Else

      'put customer ID and Order ID into hidden controls
      customerid.Value = strCustID
      orderid.Value = strOrderID

      'display all orders for this customer
      ShowOrderlines()

   End If

  End If

End Sub
```

The ShowOrderLines Routine

To display the list of order lines, you call the GetOrdersFromSessionOrServer function (identical to the one in the edit-orders.aspx page). You also have to apply a
filter to the DataSet it returns. Now you're displaying rows from the Order Details
table, and this contains all the rows for all the orders for this customer. You also
sort the DataView you create for the table by product name. This makes it easier for
the user to see what products are already on the order:

```
Sub ShowOrderLines()

  'get Orders DataSet using function elsewhere in this page
  Dim objDataSet As DataSet = GetOrdersFromSessionOrServer(strCustID)

  'create sorted and filtered DataView from Order Details table
  Dim objLinesView As DataView = _
                    objDataSet.Tables("Order Details").DefaultView
  objLinesView.RowFilter = "OrderID = " & strOrderID
  objLinesView.Sort = "ProductName"

  'diplay heading above DataList
  lblStatus.Text = "Details for Order ID: <b>" & strOrderID & "</b>"
  ...
```

Displaying the Add Product Controls

The next point is that you only want to display the Add Product controls below the `DataGrid` if there are no existing rows being edited. You check the `EditItemIndex` property of the `DataGrid`, which will be greater than `-1` if there's a row in edit mode. In this case, you hide the Add Product controls by setting the `display` style attribute. If there are no rows in edit mode, you can show the Add Product controls and bind the drop-down list of products to the appropriate data source:

```
...
'see if a line is in "Edit mode"
If dgrOrderLines.EditItemIndex > -1 Then

  'hide list of products and display "Help" message
  divAddNewLine.Style("display") = "none"
  lblMessage.Text = "Edit the details of the selected order ...etc..."

Else

  'show list of products and display "Help" message
  divAddNewLine.Style("display") = ""    'show list of products
  lblMessage.Text = "Click the <b>Edit</b> link in the grid ...etc..."

  'bind list of products to data source to fill in values
  lstAddProduct.DataSource = GetProductsFromSessionOrServer()
  lstAddProduct.DataMember = "Products"
  lstAddProduct.DataTextField = "ProductName"
  lstAddProduct.DataValueField = "ProductID"
  lstAddProduct.DataBind()

  'add extra row at top of list for "Select product ..."
  Dim objItem As New ListItem ("Select product...", "-1")
  lstAddProduct.Items.Insert(0, objItem)

End If
...
```

The data source for the `lstAddProduct` drop-down list is just a `DataSet` containing a single table named `Products`, which contains the `ProductID` and `ProductName` of all products in the database. You generate it with a simple stored procedure and call it through a method of the data access tier in the same way as you did with the list of shippers for the previous page. You even cache this `DataSet` in the user's session just like you did with the list of orders. Finally, in the previous code, you add an extra item, `"Select product..."` (using a product ID value of `-1`), to the top of the drop-down list, as shown in Figure 8-21.

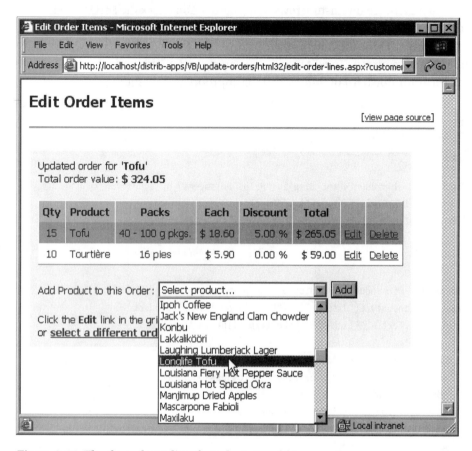

Figure 8-21. The drop-down list of products to add to an order

Displaying the DataGrid and Order Total

The final stage is to see if the order actually has any order lines on it. If not, you want to hide the DataGrid control and display a helpful message to the user. You can tell if there are any rows on the order by querying the Count property of the DataView. If it's zero, you hide the DataGrid. If not, you bind it to the data source, calculate the order total by iterating through the rows in the filtered DataView, and display this in the page:

```
...
'see if there are any order detail lines on this order
If objLinesView.Count = 0 Then
```

```
       lblMessage.Text = "There are no lines on this order ...etc..."
       dgrOrderLines.Visible = False    'hide DataGrid control

   Else

      'set DataSource and bind the DataGrid to show order lines
      dgrOrderLines.DataSource = objDataSet.Tables("Order Details")
      dgrOrderLines.DataBind()
      dgrOrderLines.Visible = True   'make DataGrid visible

      'show order Total Value by iterating rows in DataView
      Dim dblTotal As Double = 0
      Dim objRow As DataRowView
      For Each objRow In objLinesView
        dblTotal += objRow("LineTotal")
      Next
      lblTotalValue.Text = "Total order value: <b>$ " _
                        & dblTotal.ToString("N2") & "</b>"
   End If

End Sub
```

Editing the Order Lines

The DataGrid behaves in much the same way as the DataList when it comes to switching modes. You've already arranged for the Edit and Cancel links in the EditCommandColumn to execute a couple of routines named DoItemEdit and DoItemCancel. In these routines you just need to set the appropriate values for the SelectedIndex and EditItemIndex properties of the DataGrid and call the ShowOrderLines routine in your page to rebind the grid to the data source:

```
Sub DoItemEdit(objSource As Object, objArgs As DataGridCommandEventArgs)
'runs when the "Edit" link in the DataGrid is clicked
'switches DataList into "Edit" mode to show edit controls

  'set the EditItemIndex property of the list to this item's index
  dgrOrderLines.EditItemIndex = objArgs.Item.ItemIndex

  'set the SelectedIndex property to "unselect" all rows
  dgrOrderLines.SelectedIndex = -1

  ShowOrderLines()  'bind the data and display it
```

```
End Sub

Sub DoItemCancel(objSource As Object, objArgs As DataGridCommandEventArgs)
'runs when the "Cancel" link in the Datalist is clicked

  'set EditItemIndex property of grid to -1 to switch out of Edit mode
  dgrOrderLines.EditItemIndex = -1

  ShowOrderLines()  'bind the data and display it
  lblStatus.Text = "Changes to the order were abandoned."

End Sub
```

Adding a New Order Line

To add a new product to the order, the user selects it in the drop-down list and clicks the Add button. This executes the AddNewLine event handler in your page, which collects the selected product ID from the drop-down list and checks that the list isn't still set to the extra "Select product..." row you added to the top of the list (and that has the product ID value -1):

```
Sub AddNewLine(objSource As Object, objArgs As EventArgs)
'runs when the "Add" (product) button below the grid is clicked

  Dim strMessage As String    'to hold status message

  'get selected item index from "Add Product" drop-down list
  Dim intListIndex As Integer = lstAddProduct.SelectedIndex

  'get selected product ID and product name
  Dim intProductID As Integer = _
      CType(lstAddProduct.Items(intListIndex).Value, Integer)
  Dim strProductName As String = lstAddProduct.Items(intListIndex).Text

  If intProductID < 0 Then

    'user did not make a selection in the list
    lblStatus.Text = "*ERROR: You must select a product ...etc..."
    Exit Sub

  End If
  ...
```

Then you can create an instance of the data access component and call the InsertNewOrderLine method that it exposes. This method is fundamentally similar to the one you saw for the previous edit-orders.aspx page, using a stored procedure to add the new line to the Order Details table, so we haven't listed it here. You also remove any cached DataSet from the user's session so that the changes to the data source table display in your DataGrid.

You want to highlight the new row after it's been inserted so that the user can easily see it and edit the quantity, price, or discount as required. Alternatively, you could switch that row into edit mode like you did in the edit-orders.aspx page when a new order is inserted. However, to do either of these, you need to be able to determine the index of the newly inserted row within the DataGrid.

Selecting the New Order Line Row in the DataGrid

In the edit-order.aspx page, the rows are sorted by descending order ID, so the new row always appears at the top of the list—at index zero. In your DataGrid of order lines, the rows are sorted by product name. So, to find the product you just added, you have a bit more work to do. We've included a simple function named GetGridIndexForProduct in this page, which uses the technique hinted at in the description of the edit-orders.aspx page to find a row by searching through the DataKeys collection of the DataGrid for a specified product ID:

```
Function GetGridIndexForProduct(ByVal intProductID As Integer) As Integer

  Dim intResult As Integer = -1
  Dim intIndex As Integer

  'check ProductID for each row in DataGrid's DataKeys collection
  For intIndex = 0 To dgrOrderLines.DataKeys.Count - 1
    If dgrOrderLines.DataKeys(intIndex) = intProductID Then
      intResult = intIndex
      Exit For
    End If
  Next
  Return intResult

End Function
```

However, to use this function, you first have to add the new row to the DataGrid control by calling the ShowOrderLines method to rebind the grid to the data source. Then you can use the GetGridIndexForProduct function to set the SelectedIndex of the DataGrid (or the EditItemIndex if you want to put the row into edit mode). But then, to actually display the row in the new mode, you have to rebind the grid again:

```
...
'to be able to find new row in DataGrid you have to bind it
'to the data source first and then search for it in the grid
ShowOrderLines()  'bind the data and display it

'function in this page can then return index in DataGrid
'for the item with the specified ProductID. This will be
'displayed when grid is bound again before display
dgrOrderLines.SelectedIndex = GetGridIndexForProduct(intProductID)

ShowOrderLines()  'bind the data and display it
...
```

So this is somewhat heavy going as far as server-side processing is concerned. As long as the DataSet is cached in the session after the first call to ShowOrderLines, you'll only hit the data access tier and the database once, but it's still a lot of processing. However, without it, the user will have to scan the order lines to find the new row themselves.

Updating and Deleting Existing Order Lines

As you probably expect, the techniques for handling the updates and deletes you use in this page are fundamentally the same as you used in the previous edit-orders.aspx page. We won't list all the code again, but you can see it using the View Source and View Component Source links in the example pages.

The DoItemUpdate and DoItemDelete event handlers use methods in the data access tier to execute stored procedures that actually do the work—checking for concurrency errors in the same way as you've done previously. In the case of the delete process, of course, you don't have to worry about deleting child rows as well as the parent row like you did when you deleted an order. The Order Details table is the child table, and you can freely delete individual rows from it.

Hence, as in the edit-orders.aspx page, the code in the DoItemUpdate and DoItemDelete event handlers extracts the current values from the visible controls in the row and the original values from the hidden-type controls in the row, and it converts these to the correct data types for the parameters of the data access tier methods. Then they can call the appropriate method in the data access tier and report the result using the status Label controls in your page.

When you update a row, you also want to select it so that the user can easily see the row that they just changed. Although this involves a roundabout process when adding a row, it's easy when you're updating a row. The index of the current row being edited is held in the `EditItemIndex` property of the `DataGrid`, so you just assign this to the `SelectedIndex` property and set the `EditItemIndex` property to -1:

```
'set SelectedIndex of grid to current EditItemIndex to indicate
'updated row, and set EditItemIndex to -1 to switch off Edit mode
dgrOrderLines.SelectedIndex = dgrOrderLines.EditItemIndex
dgrOrderLines.EditItemIndex = -1
```

Data Update Example for Mobile Devices

To finish this look at down-level clients, you'll see how you build a second version of the order update application that's designed to work in small-screen and mobile devices such as PDAs and cellular phones. The great thing with the *n*-tier design approach we've followed is that you can reuse the data access tier methods already created for the HTML version of the application without modification. On top of that, most of the business logic that resides in the ASP.NET code can be reused almost as it stands.

OK, so there's some work involved in designing and building the user interface. The issues of limited screen size and minimal support for manual data entry in these types of devices mean that a different layout and navigation model is required. However, the controls provided in the Microsoft Mobile Internet Toolkit (MMIT), which you saw in Chapters 4 and 5, make it easy. In fact, we built the application you see here on top of our existing data access tier, reusing our existing business logic, in around a day and a half!

We don't intend to list all the code for this application here because much is fundamentally identical to the HTML version. What we'll show you is the approach to the design, the structure of the application, and the result.

The Application Design

In the version of the customer orders application for small-screen devices that you built in Chapter 5, you created an Edit Orders link. Figure 8-22 shows it in our "PDA emulator" (actually a resized Internet Explorer window). The right screen shows the opening page of the Update Orders application that opens from the Edit Orders link.

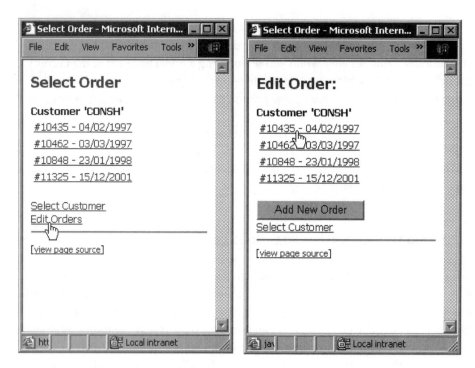

Figure 8-22. Editing an order in a PDA with the mobile version of the application

Obviously you can't use the same kinds of controls and design approach in this application as you did in the HTML version. The DataList and DataGrid don't work with devices that require Wireless Markup Language (WML), and there are no equivalents in the MMIT. Instead, you have much simpler controls available, but they do include a List control and a SelectionList control, which you can use to display data and provide sets of options from which the user can select.

This version of the application uses a series of eight <form> sections in the page to create the separate "screens" or "cards" that the user sees. There's also one <form> that the user never gets to see. Figure 8-23 shows all the screens, the processes, and the navigation paths between them.

But why is there a <form> that the user never sees? The reason is that the MMIT has no concept of a hidden-type control, such as the HTML <input type="hidden"> control you used in the HTML version of the application to store the original values when editing a row. Instead, you use a couple of routines that copy the original values of each row that you're going to edit into Label controls on the hidden <form>.

One advantage of the special MobilePage object that the MMIT provides is that (unlike the normal ASP.NET Page object) it can contain multiple <form>

elements—as you saw in Chapter 5. However, when you post the page back to the server, the viewstate maintains the values in all the controls in all the <form> sections. So you can get at the value of any control on any <form>, irrespective of which one was displayed when the postback occurred and which one you are activating to display next.

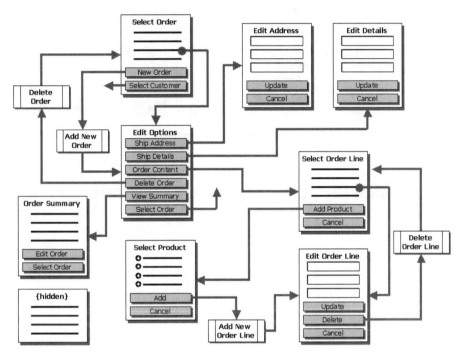

Figure 8-23. The cards and navigation paths in the mobile version of the application

Viewing the Application

So what does this application look like? It's easier to see the actual output in the "PDA emulator," as shown in the following figures. After selecting the order you want to edit, you specify the section of the order you're interested in and then edit the values. Figure 8-24 shows how you can edit the address and the shipping details.

You can also delete and add orders and modify the lines on an order. Figure 8-25 shows how you can add a new order and then edit the order contents (there are none, of course, for a new order).

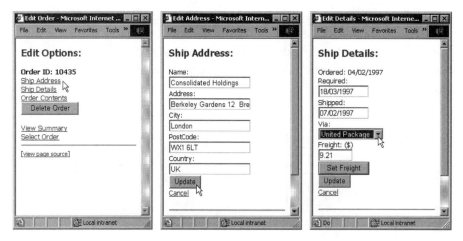

Figure 8-24. Editing the shipping address and shipping details

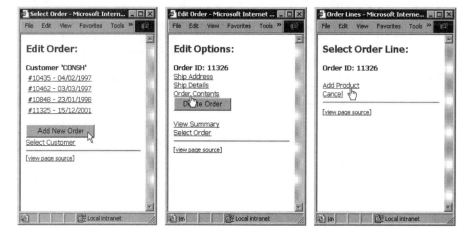

Figure 8-25. Adding an order and editing the order detail rows

However, you can add products to an order and then change the quantity, price, and discount, as shown in Figure 8-26. The Order Summary screen displays the new order.

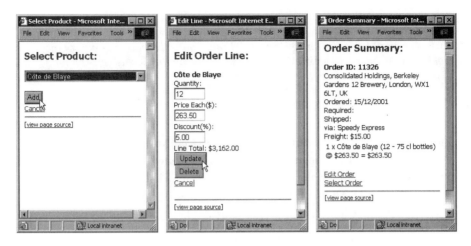

Figure 8-26. Adding new order detail rows and viewing the order summary

Viewing the Application in a Cellular Phone Emulator

Of course, the real reason for using the MMIT controls is usually so that you can output WML rather than HTML for a mobile device such as a cellular phone. Figure 8-27 show the application as viewed in a cell phone emulator. This is the Nokia emulator described in Chapter 5. After selecting the order and the section you're interested in, you can edit the values. You can also edit address details and the shipping details. You can see how the SelectionList control creates a set of option buttons in the phone, whereas it created a drop-down list in the "PDA emulator."

Figure 8-27. Editing the order details in a cell phone emulator
(emulator images © Nokia Corporation)

> **NOTE** *The emulator we're using here, and throughout this chapter, is part of the Nokia Mobile Internet Toolkit. Various versions are available, and you can read about these and download them from* http://forum.nokia.com/.

Adding a new order follows the same process as in your "PDA emulator." After adding it in the first screen, the second screen allows you to edit it. You can add new lines to the order, selecting the product from a list created by another SelectionList control. After editing the order line details, you can view the order summary to see the results, as shown in Figure 8-28.

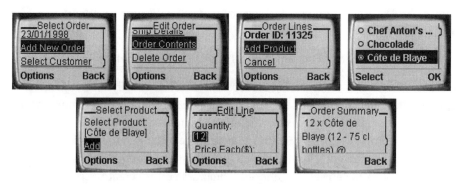

Figure 8-28. Adding a new order and new order detail rows

But is there any real point in building data update applications for small-screen devices such as cellular phones, with the considerable interface, display size, and performance limitations they force on you? Only you can decide that, but it's certainly not a difficult process once you have the back-end and data access tier in place. And it's even less arduous if you can reuse the business logic and other processes from an existing HTML or other down-level client versions.

Look at it another way: If your corporation's salespeople can clinch new and profitable contracts that they'd otherwise miss, just by having access to the application from their phone, you could actually be funding your significant next salary increase.

Summary

This chapter started with a look at the whole issue of updating data sources in a distributed and fundamentally disconnected environment. You examined the four main problem areas—the efficiency of the process, monitoring it and providing user feedback, controlling access permissions, and managing concurrent updates. Of these, the regular "thorn in the side" is detecting and managing concurrency errors.

You also looked in overview at the features provided in ADO.NET that make it easy to manage data update processes. We discussed the use of transactions, the `CommandBuilder` to create update SQL statements, and how the `DataSet` object's `Update` method makes it all easy to do.

Unfortunately, when you build applications for down-level clients (that are generally unable to cache and manage data on the client), the appropriate technique for updating a data store is usually through executing SQL statements or stored procedures individually for each update, insert, or delete action that's required.

To demonstrate this, we devoted the majority of this chapter to investigating a simple down-level application for HTML 3.2–compatible clients that can be used to view and update data in two related tables in a database. Although there wasn't room to itemize and discuss every line of code, you should now have a good understanding of the way you can build these kinds of applications quickly and easily using ASP.NET.

Finally, you used the same data access tier and business logic to build a separate version of the application that offers the same facilities (though probably not the same level of usability!) for small-screen and mobile devices such as PDAs and cellular phones. Other than the different structure and design required to cope with the different interface that these types of clients require, this proved to be an amazingly simple task—reinforcing the benefits provided by ASP.NET, the MMIT, and *n*-tier design principles in general.

In summary, this chapter covered the following topics:

- The issues involved in pushing updates back to the data source

- How you cope with multiple concurrent users updating the data

- The tools and technologies .NET provides to make this easier

- An example of a down-level (Web browser) client data update application

- An example of a data update application for small-screen and mobile devices

In the next chapter, you'll begin to explore how you can provide a better remote interface using an "even more disconnected" design with rich clients.

CHAPTER 9

Updating Remote Cached Data

THE PLOT SO FAR: You've looked in depth at how you can extract data in various formats, irrespective of the way the data is actually stored—be it in a relational database, an XML document, or almost any other type of persisted data. You also built applications that extract and display data in various types of clients, including both down-level clients and a range of rich clients. Then, in the previous chapter, you saw some of the issues involved in updating the original data and how you can do this with a couple of different types of down-level client.

The next obvious step is to learn how you can adopt the *n*-tier design principles and remote data caching techniques you used to display data in the rich clients but extend this to update the original data from a remote client. In other words, you need to consider how you cope with pushing updates made to the remotely cached data back into the data store, so you can update the original data with these changes.

It might seem like a simple extension to the existing techniques you've used, but unfortunately life is never that easy. When the client can make multiple updates to the data, and do so using a data structure that's usually not a standard .NET data type (with a couple of exceptions), the whole process becomes somewhat more complex. In this chapter, you'll see why, and discover how you can get around the problems that arise. The examples you'll see aren't part of the customer orders applications (you'll go back to that in the next chapter), but they demonstrate the foundations upon which you'll be building later.

So, the topics for this chapter are as follows:

- Transferring data and managing updates in rich clients

- Loading different types of data into a DataSet

- Understanding how the DataSet stores original and current values

- Detecting concurrency violations and other errors when updating data

- Providing feedback when such issues are detected

You'll start with an overview of the whole process and see where you have to solve problems that you haven't come across so far.

Reviewing the Architecture

In the previous chapter, we talked about how "disconnected" the different versions of the customer orders application you've built so far actually are. The down-level client versions you looked at in the previous chapter, for HTML 3.2–compatible browsers and for small-screen and mobile devices, are only disconnected in the fact that the user interface (the presentation tier) is the other side of the network. The data access tier and the business rules tier are located on the server.

OK, so the data access tier may be on a separate server from the Web server, but remember that the definition of the *n*-tier architecture doesn't describe the actual physical location of the tiers. It just describes the way you separate and modularize the processes to allow a choice of location, together with all the benefits of abstracting the design and providing component and logic reuse.

What's most important in this application, in terms of the functionality and efficiency it provides, is where you store the data that the user interacts with and how you persist any changes to that data back into the original data store. For example, in the versions that provide a data update feature in down-level clients, you cached the data—where possible—in the user's session on the Web server. When the user makes any changes to the data, you immediately persist these into the back-end data store—effectively updating one row at a time, as shown in Figure 9-1.

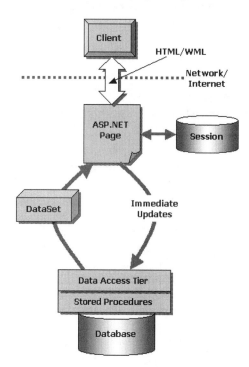

Figure 9-1. The data handling process for down-level clients

Caching Updates on the Client

However, if you're going to take advantage of the ability of rich clients to cache the data (on the client machine), it often doesn't make sense to persist every change to that data immediately. In the previous chapter, where you looked at down-level clients that can't cache the data client-side, you saw that you had to make multiple postbacks to the server to update the data. Then, after the update is complete or if it fails, you have to send both feedback (a status message) and the newly updated data (with the updates included in it) back to the client again for display.

Instead, you can allow the client to perform all the updates they require on the cached data and then post back to the server just these changes when they're ready—where they can be applied to the original data as one operation. And, as you'll see in Chapter 11, you can even send updates back to the server asynchronously, giving a really clean and polished user experience in the client, as shown in Figure 9-2.

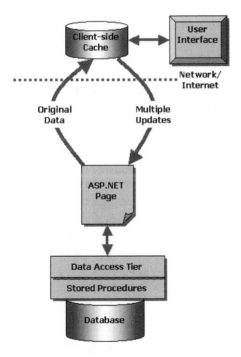

Figure 9-2. The data handling process for up-level (rich) clients

Of course, there may be situations where you actually require the client's changes to be persisted immediately. If other users need to see the changes as soon as possible, or if the security or integrity of the application depends on updates being applied immediately, then you have no choice but to follow the same principles as with the down-level client versions. There's no reason why you can't "mix" the techniques, however, using remote caching when viewing the data but immediately posting any updates back to the server.

Getting Updates Back to the Server

When you're pushing every update back to the data store as it occurs on the client, you have no need to store the changes on the client. However, if you're going to allow multiple updates to be performed on the client and then push them all back into the data store in one operation, you have to find some way to store the changes on the client.

The simplest situation is where the client has the .NET Framework installed, and you're storing the data locally (on the client) within a .NET data type such as a DataSet. The DataSet object stores both the original and the current values for all the columns in every row as the values in it are being edited and updated. When you come to apply the updates to the data store, it looks after all the things that would otherwise require you to write code for. It automatically executes the appropriate SQL statement or stored procedure for each modified row, checks for concurrency and other runtime update errors, and allows you to detect which rows these occurred in and the reason why the error occurred.

So, all you have to do is remote the DataSet to the client, allow it to be modified there, send it back to the server, and apply the updates to the original data store. You can transport the DataSet across the network using native .NET Remoting techniques, and the process is reasonably automatic. Likewise, if you use a Web Service to remote the data as a DataSet, you can pass it back to the server as a DataSet object from any client machine that's running on .NET, as shown in Figure 9-3.

But what happens if the client doesn't have .NET installed? In this case, you can't cache and update the data on the client in a DataSet object. Neither can you instantiate a DataSet to send back to the server. And although you can use Web Services to transfer data when .NET isn't installed on the client (as you saw in Chapter 6), the transfer format and client-side data storage format are as XML documents, not as a DataSet object. On the client, you cache the data inside an instance of the MSXML parser, which has no knowledge at all of what .NET is about, as shown in Figure 9-4.

So, if you want to build applications that cache and manipulate data on a remote client that doesn't have the .NET Framework installed, you have to find some alternative technique. Or, at least, you have to find some way of passing the data back from the client in such a format that it can be translated (or loaded) into a .NET DataSet object on the server.

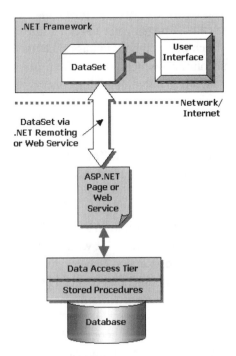

Figure 9-3. Handling updates by remoting a DataSet

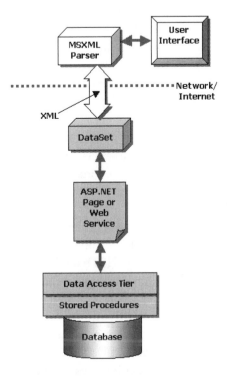

Figure 9-4. Caching data client-side in an XML parser

Why use a DataSet on the server in this case? Well, it comes back to the original intention of building applications so that the data access and business logic tiers are (wherever possible) common to all versions. It means that you maintain all the benefits you've already seen in the *n*-tier design scenario: easier and faster development, reuse of existing components and logic, simpler maintenance, and fewer errors during development and testing. Thankfully, the DataSet provides a raft of ways that you can coerce your data into the appropriate format and then use the DataSet object's automated update features and other useful techniques.

Loading a DataSet

As you saw in earlier chapters, you can load XML data into a DataSet, or you can insert values into the tables it contains directly using code. So, you have at least three options:

- If you can assemble a suitable XML document as a String and post it back to a middle tier component (probably an ASP.NET page), you can read it into the DataSet directly. However, this approach makes it hard to pass back the original and the current values for each column—which you need to protect against concurrency errors. If you're not worried about detecting concurrency errors, it's a simple and useful approach.

- Alternatively, and generally more useful, is to take advantage of the diffgram feature of a DataSet that was briefly discussed in Chapter 6. This allows you to fill in the original and current values in one go, using a suitably formatted XML diffgram document.

- You can also, probably as a last resort if you can't assemble an XML document, use code on the server to create and populate a DataSet with a series of values posted back from the client. You can populate both the original and current values by calling the AcceptChanges method after inserting the original values and then inserting the modified values afterward.

Of these three approaches, the second is the most useful in general. However, you'll also look briefly at how you can apply the other two techniques. None of these techniques involves features of .NET that you haven't—at least in outline—seen before. It's more about the way you actually use these features.

Reading an XML Document into a DataSet

The DataSet object provides the ReadXml method that you can use to populate the tables in the DataSet with data from an XML document. This document can be accessed as a Stream object by accessing the Request.InputStream property of the request from a client that posts the document to the server:

```
objDataSet.ReadXml(Request.InputStream)
```

Alternatively, it can be a String, collected from the request by accessing the appropriate member of the Request.Form collection using the name of the name/value pair containing the XML string:

```
objDataSet.ReadXml(Request.Form("name"\))
```

Another option is to create an XmlTextReader for the XML document that you want to load into the DataSet and pass this to the ReadXml method. Although it's a bit of a roundabout route, it allows you (as shown in a later example) to create an XmlValidatingReader based on the XmlTextReader and validate the incoming XML if required:

```
objDataSet.ReadXml(objXmlTextReader)
```

You can also load a schema into the DataSet first. This is useful if you want to ensure that the structure of the DataSet (the table and column names, data types, and so on) agrees with your database schema. If you don't load a schema first, the structure of the DataSet is inferred automatically from the structure of the XML document.

The ReadXmlSchema method takes as input the same types of objects as the ReadXml method. However, you're most likely to use a schema stored on your server to validate the XML. In this case, you use another overload of the ReadXmlSchema method (which is also supported for the ReadXml method) that reads the schema from a disk file using a physical path and filename:

```
objDataSet.ReadXmlSchema(strPhysicalPath)
```

The default.htm menu page provided with the samples for this book contains a link to the examples for this chapter. You can download all the samples for this book from http://www.daveandal.net/books/4923/ or http://www.apress.com. You can also run most of them online at http://www.daveandal.net/books/4923/. In the examples that follow, we've installed the sample pages on a machine named sundive in a folder named 4923—as you'll see in the figures in this chapter (see Figure 9-5).

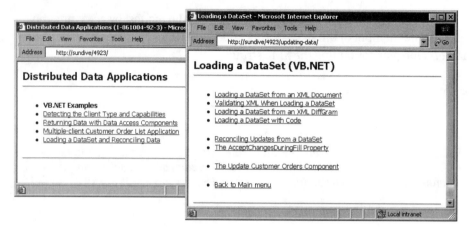

Figure 9-5. The menu pages for the samples used in this chapter

An Example of Reading an XML Document and Schema

The first example (load-dataset-xml.aspx) shows how you can read an XML document into a DataSet and use it to set the original and current values for the columns in the DataSet. Once these have been set to the appropriate values, you can use the DataSet to update the original data store, using the techniques described in the previous chapter. This example doesn't update the database but simply demonstrates the techniques for achieving the appropriate values in each column ready to perform the update.

In these example pages, which you can find in the updating-data subfolder of the code download, you're reading the XML and schema from disk files on the server rather than complicating things unnecessarily by posting them from another page. You first load the schema into the DataSet using the ReadXmlSchema method, which creates the correct structure of tables and columns within the DataSet. Then you load the XML into the DataSet using the ReadXml method:

```
Sub Page_Load()

  'create a new DataSet object
  Dim objDataSet As New DataSet()

  Try

    'specify the XML and schema files to use
    Dim strVirtualPath As String = "somebooks.xml"
    Dim strVSchemaPath As String = "somebooks.xsd"
```

```
  'read schema and data into DataSet from XML documents on disk
  'must use the Physical path to the file not the Virtual path
  objDataSet.ReadXmlSchema(Request.MapPath(strVSchemaPath))
  outMessage.InnerHTML = "Loaded file ...etc..."

  objDataSet.ReadXml(Request.MapPath(strVirtualPath))
  outMessage.InnerHTML += "Loaded file ...etc..."
Catch objError As Exception

  'display error details
  outMessage.InnerHTML = "* Error while reading disk file.<br />" _
        & objError.Message & " " & objError.Source
  Exit Sub  ' and stop execution

End Try
...
```

Notice that you have to provide a physical path to the files, obtained by applying the MapPath method to the virtual path (the files are in the same folder as the ASP.NET page). The ReadXml method has an optional second parameter that defines what to do if a schema is included (inline) within the XML document or linked to it. You can use this parameter to tell the DataSet to ignore any schema it finds and instead infer the structure only from the content of the XML document. You can also specify what type of document it is, as you'll see in the diffgram example coming shortly.

> **NOTE** *The default behavior if this parameter is omitted is* Auto, *which means that an inline schema will be used if one exists. The actual values for this parameter come from the* XmlReadMode *enumeration, which is fully documented in the .NET SDK.*

Displaying Current and Original Column Values

To allow you to see the effect on the original and current values of the rows in a table when loading an XML document into a DataSet, we've created a simple user control that displays these values for every row in a specified table. You can find this file (show-dataset.ascx) in the global folder of the samples, and it contains two <div> elements that are used to output a caption and the list of values:

```
<b><div id="divCaption" runat="server" /></b>
<div id="divValues" runat="server" /><p />
```

The <script> section of the user control implements a single routine named ShowValues that takes as parameters a reference to a DataTable object and a String to use for the caption. All the routine has to do is iterate through the rows in the table extracting the values from each column. You can get the original and current values from any column by specifying the optional extra parameter when you access the column value. This parameter is a value from the DataRowVersion enumeration.

So, to get the current values, you access each column using the value DataRowVersion.Current for this extra parameter:

```
Public Sub ShowValues(objTable As DataTable, strCaption As String)

  Dim intRow, intCol As Integer
  Dim objRow As DataRow
  Dim strColName, strResult As String

  'iterate through all the rows in the Table
  For intRow = 0 To objTable.Rows.Count - 1

    'get a reference to this row
    objRow = objTable.Rows(intRow)

    'show row state and row number
    strResult &= "<b>" & objRow.RowState.ToString() & "</b> row [" _
            & intRow & "]   <b>Current</b>: "

    'iterate through all the columns in this row
    For intCol = 0 To objTable.Columns.Count - 1

      Try

        'get the name of this column and the Current value
        strColName = objTable.Columns(intCol).ColumnName
        strResult &= strColName & "=" _
                & objRow(strColName, DataRowVersion.Current) & " "

      Catch

        strResult &= "{n/a}, "     'no Current value available

      End Try

    Next
    ...
```

Note that you have to protect the code from a runtime error when a value you access hasn't been set. In this case, the value *doesn't* contain NULL or Nothing—it doesn't actually exist at all. If there's no value, you output the string {n/a} instead. Then, having done the current values, the code continues by extracting the original values:

```
...
strResult &= "   <b>Original</b>: "

'iterate through the columns in the same row again
For intCol = 0 To objTable.Columns.Count - 1
  Try
    strColName = objTable.Columns(intCol).ColumnName
    strResult &= strColName & "=" _
            & objRow(strColName, DataRowVersion.Original) & " "
  Catch
    strResult &= "{n/a}, "      'no Original value available
  End Try
Next
strResult &= "<br />"
...
```

Next you examine the RowError property of the row to see if there's any text error message there. You can set this property using code if you want to flag an error in a row, and it's also set automatically when an error occurs during the Update process of a DataSet. If there's any text in this property, you display it beneath the row values. Finally, you can put the text string containing the values, and the caption supplied in the second parameter of this routine, into the <div> elements of the user control:

```
  ...
  'get any RowError value and display this
  If objRow.RowError.Length > 0 Then
    strResult &= " * Row Error: " & objRow.RowError & "<br />"
  End If

Next

'put text into <div> controls on page
divValues.InnerHtml = strResult
divCaption.InnerHtml = strCaption & ":"

End Sub
```

Displaying the DataSet Contents

So, getting back to the `load-dataset-xml.aspx` page, you'll use the user control just described. You register the control using a `Register` directive and then insert it into the page. You're using three copies of the control to display the `DataSet` contents at three different stages of the page's code:

```
<%@Register TagPrefix="dda" TagName="showdataset"
            Src="..\global\show-dataset.ascx" %>


<!-- insert custom controls to display values -->
<dda:showdataset id="ctlShow1" runat="server" />
<dda:showdataset id="ctlShow2" runat="server" />
<dda:showdataset id="ctlShow3" runat="server" />
```

Continuing the `Page_Load` event, you can now get a reference to the single table within the `DataSet` and use the control to display the values it contains:

```
...
Dim objTable As DataTable = objDataSet.Tables(0)

'display current and original values after loading
ctlShow1.ShowValues(objTable, "Row values after loading XML")
...
```

The first set of values in Figure 9-6 show the result. You can see that loading the XML document has set the current values of the columns, but the original values are undefined.

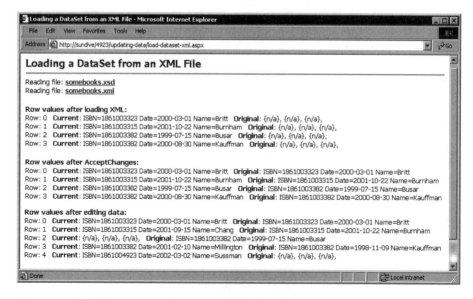

Figure 9-6. Loading a DataSet *from an XML disk file*

You can use the links in the page to view the XML document and the schema used. The following listing shows the XML document, and it's pretty clear where each of the current column values has come from:

```
<?xml version="1.0" standalone="yes" ?>
<NewDataSet>
  <Books>
    <ISBN>1861003323</ISBN>
    <Date>2000-03-01</Date>
    <Name>Britt</Name>
  </Books>
  <Books>
    <ISBN>1861003315</ISBN>
    <Date>2001-10-22</Date>
    <Name>Burnham</Name>
  </Books>
  <Books>
    <ISBN>1861003382</ISBN>
    <Date>1999-07-15</Date>
    <Name>Busar</Name>
  </Books>
  <Books>
    <ISBN>1861003382</ISBN>
    <Date>1998-11-09</Date>
    <Name>Kauffman</Name>
  </Books>
</NewDataSet>
```

Populating the Original Values

As you've just seen, loading an XML document only sets the current values of the rows and columns in the DataSet. However, when you call the AcceptChanges method of the DataSet, the current values are copied to the original values. You can see this in the second set of values in the page, and the code used is simply as follows:

```
...
'call AcceptChanges and display current and original values again
objDataSet.AcceptChanges()
ctlShow2.ShowValues(objTable, "Row values after AcceptChanges")
...
```

You used the AcceptChanges method of the DataSet object here. AcceptChanges is also available for individual tables (DataTable objects) or for individual rows (DataRow objects) within a table—allowing you to accept the changes and populate the original values for specific tables or rows if required.

The next step is to edit some of the values in the table. We've done this using code in the example page, but loading another XML document will achieve much the same result:

```
...
'edit rows and display current and original values again
objTable.Rows(1)("Date") = "2001-09-15"
objTable.Rows(1)("Name") = "Chang"
objTable.Rows(3)("Date") = "2001-02-10"
objTable.Rows(3)("Name") = "Millington"
Dim objDataRow As DataRow
objDataRow = objTable.NewRow()
objDataRow("ISBN") = "1861004923"
objDataRow("Date") = "2002-03-02"
objDataRow("Name") = "Sussman"
objTable.Rows.Add(objDataRow)
objTable.Rows(2).Delete()
ctlShow3.ShowValues(objTable, "Row values after editing data")


End Sub
```

Both these techniques set the current values only, leaving the original values unchanged. At the end of the previous code listing you can see that you call the ShowValues routine in the user control for the third time to display the table contents again, as shown in Figure 9-7.

Row values after editing data:
Row: 0 **Current**: ISBN=1861003323 Date=2000-03-01 Name=Britt **Original**: ISBN=1861003323 Date=2000-03-01 Name=Britt
Row: 1 **Current**: ISBN=1861003315 Date=2001-09-15 Name=Chang **Original**: ISBN=1861003315 Date=2001-10-22 Name=Burnham
Row: 2 **Current**: {n/a}, {n/a}, {n/a}, **Original**: ISBN=1861003382 Date=1999-07-15 Name=Busar
Row: 3 **Current**: ISBN=1861003382 Date=2001-02-10 Name=Millington **Original**: ISBN=1861003382 Date=1998-11-09 Name=Kauffman
Row: 4 **Current**: ISBN=1861004923 Date=2002-03-02 Name=Sussman **Original**: {n/a}, {n/a}, {n/a},

Figure 9-7. The row contents after editing some values

As you can see, this DataSet is now ready for use in updating a database table. It contains a combination of current and original values that would allow concurrency errors to be detected. For rows that have been edited (updated rows), the original values should match those in the data source (in this case they came from the XML document) at the point when the DataSet was first loaded. The current values reflect any changes that the user has made to the columns. When a row has been deleted, the current values have been removed from that row in the table. Where a row has been inserted into the table, there are no original values for the columns.

Validating XML While Reading into a DataSet

If your application is using XML files to update the data source, you'll most likely want to ensure that these documents are valid for the data source. If you load a schema into a DataSet, it just creates the structure of tables and columns specified by the schema. If you then load an XML document that doesn't match the schema, the DataSet will by default allocate any elements it can to the existing columns and leave any other column values as NULL.

You can change this behavior by using the values from the XmlReadMode enumeration, but it's still not a fully controlled process. You can still load invalid XML documents without the DataSet complaining (it only complains if the XML isn't well-formed). Instead, it's safer to validate the incoming XML against the schema and reject it if it's not valid. The next example (load-dataset-validate.aspx) demonstrates how you can do this.

To use an XmlTextReader object you must import the System.Xml namespace into your page. You also need the System.Xml.Schema namespace in this example because it contains the XmlSchemaCollection object you're using to load the schema:

```
<%@Import Namespace="System.Xml" %>
<%@Import Namespace="System.Xml.Schema" %>
```

You saw how you can validate XML documents way back in Chapter 3. Here, in the Page_Load event handler, you create a DataSet object and declare a variable to hold a reference to an XmlTextReader. Then you can open the XmlTextReader against your disk file and create a new XmlValidatingReader object from it:

```
'create a new DataSet object
Dim objDataSet As New DataSet()

'create variable to hold a reference to an XmlTextReader
Dim objXTReader As XmlTextReader

Try
```

```
'specify the XML and schema files to use
Dim strVSchemaPath As String = "somebooks.xsd"
Dim strVirtualPath As String = "errorbooks.xml"
If Request.QueryString("xmlfile") <> "" Then
  strVirtualPath = Request.QueryString("xmlfile")
End If


'create the new XmlTextReader object and load the XML document
objXTReader = New XmlTextReader(Server.MapPath(strVirtualPath))


'create an XMLValidatingReader for this XmlTextReader
Dim objValidator As New XmlValidatingReader(objXTReader)
```

Next you specify the type of schema you're using (you could leave it at the default Auto, but setting it makes the process a little more efficient at runtime). You also create an XmlSchemaCollection and add your schema to it—again using the complete physical path and filename. Then you can specify this collection as the Schemas property of your XmlValidatingReader:

```
'set the validation type to use an XSD schema
objValidator.ValidationType = ValidationType.Schema

'create a new XmlSchemaCollection
Dim objSchemaCol As New XmlSchemaCollection()

'add the booklist-schema.xsd schema to it
objSchemaCol.Add("", Server.MapPath(strVSchemaPath))

'assign the schema collection to the XmlValidatingReader
objValidator.Schemas.Add(objSchemaCol)
```

That's everything set up and ready, and you can now use the XmlValidatingReader to read the XML document into the DataSet. Any validation error will be trapped by the Try...Catch construct and displayed. You also have to remember to close the XmlTextReader after use:

```
'use XmlTextReader to load DataSet
objDataSet.ReadXml(objValidator)

Catch objError As Exception

'display error details
outError.InnerHTML = "* Error while reading disk file.<br />" _
```

```
        & objError.Message & " " & objError.Source
Exit Sub  ' and stop execution

Finally

  'must remember to always close the XmlTextReader after use
  objXTReader.Close()

End Try
```

Figure 9-8 shows the result when you attempt to load an XML document that's invalid for this schema.

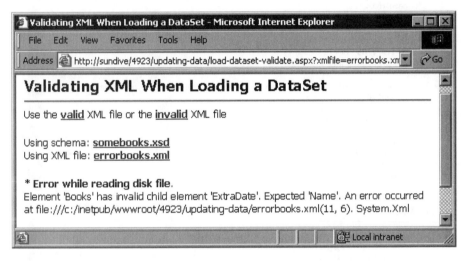

Figure 9-8. The result when trying to load an invalid XML document

There are also links at the top of the page where you can load a valid document to prove that validation does work and view the XML documents and the schema. Once a valid XML document is loaded, the remainder of the code in the page (which is identical to the previous example) edits and displays the values of the columns in the DataSet.

Reading an XML Diffgram into a DataSet

When you looked at the output of a Web Service in Chapter 6, you saw that this is a *diffgram* rather than a "generic" XML document. A diffgram contains extra attributes that identify each row, specify where it's located in the rowset, and what "state" it's in. There's also a section that contains the original values of any rows that have been changed. Figure 9-9 shows the diffgram you'll use in the following example.

Figure 9-9. The diffgram used in these examples

The great thing with the diffgram format is that you can store within it the original and the current values for every row in the data. When you load a diffgram into a DataSet, the original and the current values are populated using the values in the diffgram. This means you can effectively re-create the same DataSet as you receive if you use .NET Remoting or a Web Service to interact with a client that has the .NET Framework installed (and which allows you to create and/or manipulate a DataSet object on the client).

The diffgram shown earlier represents the same data and the same edits that you carried out in the previous examples of loading an XML document into a DataSet. The code you used in those examples is repeated here so that you can compare the effects with the contents of the diffgram:

```
objTable.Rows(1)("Date") = "2001-09-15"
objTable.Rows(1)("Name") = "Chang"
objTable.Rows(3)("Date") = "2001-02-10"
objTable.Rows(3)("Name") = "Millington"
Dim objDataRow As DataRow
objDataRow = objTable.NewRow()
objDataRow("ISBN") = "1861004923"
objDataRow("Date") = "2002-03-02"
objDataRow("Name") = "Sussman"
objTable.Rows.Add(objDataRow)
objTable.Rows(2).Delete()
```

Of course, a diffgram is more complicated to create when you don't have the ability to work with a DataSet on the client. It takes more work to produce the extra elements from the data that you cache (in whatever format) on the client. The great thing is that, when the server receives the diffgram, it can treat it the same way it would when dealing with a .NET client that returns a DataSet object. The middle tier and data access tier will be identical.

An Example of Reading an XML Diffgram

This example (load-dataset-diffgram.aspx) uses the diffgram you saw earlier to populate a DataSet, automatically setting the current and original values of each column in each row. To work properly, it requires a schema that defines the structure of the tables and columns in the DataSet to be loaded first. You use the same code to load the schema and the diffgram file into the DataSet as in the previous examples:

```
Dim strVirtualPath As String = "booksdiffgram.xml"
Dim strVSchemaPath As String = "somebooks.xsd"

'read the schema into the DataSet from file on disk
```

```
objDataSet.ReadXmlSchema(Request.MapPath(strVSchemaPath))
outMessage.InnerHTML += "Reading file ...etc..."

'read the diffgram into the DataSet from file on disk
objDataSet.ReadXml(Request.MapPath(strVirtualPath))
outMessage.InnerHTML += "Reading file ...etc..."
...
```

However, this depends on the default "read mode" for the ReadXml method of the DataSet being set to Auto. In this mode, the DataSet automatically detects if the XML document is a diffgram and changes the "read behavior" so that the values are correctly allocated to the columns in the DataSet. To be sure that the DataSet does use the appropriate behavior, and to save a little processing effort within the method, you could instead specify the XmlWriteMode to indicate that your file is a diffgram:

```
objDataSet.ReadXml(Request.MapPath(strVirtualPath), XmlReadMode.DiffGram)
```

Once you've loaded the schema and the diffgram, you display the contents of the DataSet as before, using the custom user control:

```
...
Dim objTable As DataTable = objDataSet.Tables(0)

'display current and original values after loading
ctlShow1.ShowValues(objTable, "Row values after editing data")
```

Figure 9-10 shows the results. You can see that you've ended up with the same DataSet as you did from loading an XML document and performing the edits afterward using code.

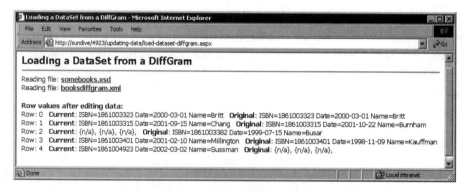

Figure 9-10. Loading a DataSet *from a diffgram*

A diffgram can even hold details of errors that occurred during the Update process of a DataSet object—the RowError property of each row. These values are stored in an optional <diffgr:errors> element that's located after the <diffgr:before> element and before the closing </diffgr:diffgram> element. For example:

```
<diffgr:errors>
  <Books diffgr:id="Books1"
         diffgr:Error="The statement has been terminated..." />
  <Books diffgr:id="Books2"
         diffgr:Error="Concurrency violation: the UpdateCommand..." />
</diffgr:errors>
```

Loading a DataSet Using Code

The final one of the three techniques listed earlier is probably only useful if it isn't possible to create an XML document (or a diffgram) on the client. However, there are other situations where it might be useful. If there are only a few values to update, the effort involved in creating the complex diffgram document on the client is avoided. The extra server-side processing that this technique requires for creating and populating the DataSet will produce only a minimal performance hit.

It might also be useful if the values happen to arrive in some nonstandard format anyway. For example, you might be dealing with data sent by another process or service (such as BizTalk Server) or a legacy application that uses some other industry-standard data transfer format. And, of course, there's nothing to stop you loading a schema into the DataSet first (using the ReadXmlSchema method) to create the correct structure in the DataSet rather than building the DataSet, tables, and columns individually in your code.

An Example of Building a DataSet Using Code

The page load-dataset-code.aspx demonstrates how you can build a DataSet and populate the current and original values using code. Much of it is identical to the previous examples—the only real difference is in the way you actually create the DataSet. You start by creating a new empty DataSet object:

```
Dim objDataSet As New DataSet("TestDataSet")
...
```

Then you create a new DataTable object, create the columns you need within it, and add it to the DataSet object's Tables collection:

```
...
'create a new empty Table object with three columns
Dim objTable As New DataTable("Books")
objTable.Columns.Add("ISBN", System.Type.GetType("System.String"))
objTable.Columns.Add("Date", System.Type.GetType("System.String"))
objTable.Columns.Add("Name", System.Type.GetType("System.String"))
objDataSet.Tables.Add(objTable)  'add to DataSet
...
```

Now you can add rows to the table. You create a new DataRow object, fill in the values, and add it to the DataTable object's Rows collection:

```
...
'create new DataRows in table and fill in values
Dim objDataRow As DataRow
objDataRow = objTable.NewRow()
objDataRow("ISBN") = "1861003323"
objDataRow("Date") = "2000-03-01"
objDataRow("Name") = "Britt"
objTable.Rows.Add(objDataRow)
...
```

Then you repeat the same technique for the other three rows:

```
...
objDataRow = objTable.NewRow()
objDataRow("ISBN") = "1861003315"
objDataRow("Date") = "2001-10-22"
objDataRow("Name") = "Burnham"
objTable.Rows.Add(objDataRow)
objDataRow = objTable.NewRow()
objDataRow("ISBN") = "1861003382"
objDataRow("Date") = "1999-07-15"
objDataRow("Name") = "Busar"
objTable.Rows.Add(objDataRow)
objDataRow = objTable.NewRow()
objDataRow("ISBN") = "1861003401"
objDataRow("Date") = "1998-11-09"
objDataRow("Name") = "Kauffman"
objTable.Rows.Add(objDataRow)
...
```

After this you display the values, accept the changes, display the values again, edit some rows, and finally display the values for the third time. The code you use to edit the rows is identical to the earlier examples where you loaded an XML document into a DataSet. The result is also the same, as shown in Figure 9-11.

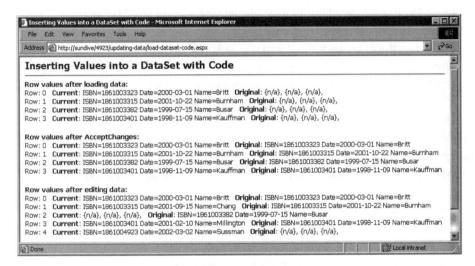

Figure 9-11. Inserting values into a DataSet *using code*

Reading Nonstandard Data Formats

The technique you've just seen provides a way to cope with nonstandard data formats. If values arrive in separate name/value pairs in the query string of a request, for example, you can use them to populate the columns in your table individually. Alternatively, you can parse data streams or disk files and extract the values one at a time and put them into your DataSet.

This would provide a way to handle formats such as tab-delimited text data, such as that you used for one of the customer orders application versions in Chapter 6. If the file contains all the original and current (edited) values, you can parse them out and use them to populate the DataSet table. You would extract the original values first and put them into the columns (where they would actually become the current values) and then call AcceptChanges on the DataSet or the table itself. This would copy them from the current into the original values in each column. Then you would just extract the current values from the data file and apply these to the table rows to set the current values. After that, you could use the Update method to push the changes back into the original data store.

Loading a DataSet Using the Fill Method

You've seen how you can use a DataSet to store the original and current values for each column of every row in a table. Remember that the DataSet object can hold multiple tables, and each can contain the current and original values for its data. You looked at three ways of populating the DataSet—using an XML document, an XML diffgram, and directly in code.

Of course, the other technique you regularly use to populate a DataSet is the Fill method of a DataAdapter object that's connected to a data store. This is what you used in most of the pages and components of the example application versions in previous chapters, and we won't describe the techniques again here.

However, one interesting point is that the Fill method—by default—automatically calls AcceptChanges on every row after inserting the values from the data source into it. This means that, after executing Fill, both the current and the original values in the columns of each row will be set to the values extracted from the data store.

You can change this behavior by setting the AcceptChangesDuringFill property of the DataAdapter to False, but there are probably few situations where this could be useful. You'll see it briefly demonstrated later in this chapter. Next, however, you'll look at what you're going to do with the newly populated DataSet.

Executing the Update Process

As you saw in the previous chapter, you can push changes to the data back into the data store using the Update method of the DataAdapter object. When using a CommandBuilder object to create the appropriate SQL statements for the DataAdapter object's InsertCommand, UpdateCommand, and DeleteCommand, this automatically performs an update of the values in the data store using the current values in each row in the DataSet tables. It also detects concurrency errors by using the original values in the DataSet tables to check that the underlying values in the data store haven't been changed since you loaded the DataSet. If you use stored procedures to perform the updates to the data store rather than the CommandBuilder object's SQL statements, you should create them in such a way that they detect concurrency errors. You did this with the stored procedures you used in the previous chapter by including all the original values in the WHERE clause of the SQL statement inside the stored procedure.

In the next chapter, you'll see an example of how you can create appropriate stored procedures for use with the Update method and how you specify and populate the parameters that you pass to these stored procedures. You'll build a data access tier for the rich client applications to use when they come to update the customer orders data you were viewing in Chapter 6.

In the meantime, though, you'll look at another part of the process. How do you provide feedback to users about what happened when the Update process was executed?

Providing Feedback from the Update Process

It's pretty obvious that you should tell a user if updates they apply to the data are rejected for any reason. You should also, of course, tell them if the process succeeds. If they click an Update button and get no response, they'll probably just keep pressing it—like some manic postman will do to your doorbell when you've decide to have a few minutes extra in bed that morning. It's that human tendency (especially heightened in computer programmers) to try it again and see if it works the next time!

In the applications in Chapter 6, you displayed a simple message indicating success or failure. In the case of an error, you assumed that the most likely cause was a concurrency error and provided a helpful message, as shown in Figure 9-12.

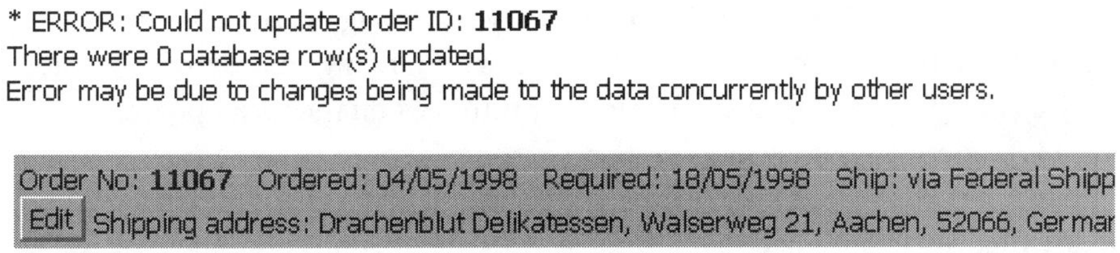

```
* ERROR: Could not update Order ID: 11067
There were 0 database row(s) updated.
Error may be due to changes being made to the data concurrently by other users.
```

```
Order No: 11067   Ordered: 04/05/1998   Required: 18/05/1998   Ship: via Federal Shipp
 Edit | Shipping address: Drachenblut Delikatessen, Walserweg 21, Aachen, 52066, Germar
```

Figure 9-12. The update error message in the HTML version of the application

However, if the user has spent the last hour updating remotely cached data in a rich client, they certainly won't appreciate an error message that basically says "sorry—failed—do it all again." When you're dealing with rich clients, you need to find ways to handle updates in a more sensitive and sensible manner.

What Do You Want from the Process?

Ideally, you want to apply all the updates in one operation and then check which (if any) failed—and why. Then you can tell the user what went wrong with individual row updates and allow them to take corrective action. This means you need to return some data structure that contains the error details to them. What would also be nice is if it contains the values entered so that they can correct the error without having to type them all again.

When you think about how you expect a form on a Web page to work, this is obvious. If you fill in your name and address when placing an order and forget your ZIP code, you probably won't be surprised to get an error message. However, if the form is just redisplayed with all the text boxes empty, you're likely to end up going elsewhere. There should never be any need to force the user to retype everything just because one thing was missing.

> **NOTE** *Unfortunately, this is exactly what happens in the application versions in the previous chapter. You display the existing values for a row in the edit controls when the data is loaded, allowing the user to change these values. However, if an update should fail, you just redisplay the original values rather than showing the values as edited by the user. Of course, when an application is predominantly designed for editing data, rather than entering new data (such as placing an order through a Web site store), then redisplaying the original values may be the better solution—especially if another concurrent user might have updated them.*

So, you know that you want to send back details of any errors that occurred, and the values that the user entered, so that they can try again. And, if they're going to try again, then you also need to have the underlying values from the data store available to protect against concurrency errors when the next update attempt is made.

Taking the process one step further, it'd be useful if you could return a data structure that can be handled in the same way as the previous one, allowing use of the same client-side code to perform the next edit and update on this data.

A formidable list of requirements, but ADO.NET does provide all these features. You can use a `DataSet` object to store all the values you need, in the same format as when you attempted the updates the first time. You'll explore this in more depth in the next section.

Before then, however, you'll briefly consider how the ADO.NET data update features map to those you may have used in traditional (pre-.NET) ADO. It also provides a chance for you to decide if what ADO.NET offers actually is sufficient for your requirements.

Can the ADO.NET DataSet Do What You Want?

In previous versions of ADO, the `Recordset` object provides many of the features of the ADO.NET `DataSet` object, with the exception of the ability to store multiple tables and the relationships between them. However, the ADO `Recordset` can store and expose three values for each column in each row, rather than the two values that are available within the tables of a `DataSet` object. In addition, the

Update method of the ADO Recordset can automatically collect the underlying (existing) values from the data store where an update fails and use these to populate the third set of column values. In other words, the ADO Recordset can support the current, original, and the underlying values of a row if required, but the DataSet can only provide the current and original values. Of course, there's nothing to prevent you from adding a table to the DataSet that contains these values, but there's no facility to populate them automatically during an Update.

So, do you need to abandon ADO.NET in this situation and use COM interop (mentioned briefly in Chapter 1) and the native ADO.NET methods that allow you to interact with an ADO Recordset object? There's no reason why not, if you prefer this route. There are performance hits, but they're generally not that significant. If you need features that are only provided by the ADO Recordset, then COM interop is likely to be just as efficient as the code that you'll have to write to add these features to the ADO.NET DataSet.

> **NOTE** *For details of using ADO and non-.NET components via COM interop, see the topics "Interoperating with Unmanaged Code" and "Using ADO Recordsets in .NET" within the section "Programming with the .NET Framework" of the .NET documentation.*

However, as you'll see in the next section, you usually only need to store two sets of values. So, in fact, the DataSet will do what you need.

What Are the Original Values?

OK, so you can't store all three values for a row (the current, original, and the underlying values) in the tables of the DataSet. Is this actually important? What do you actually need to perform the process, and what do users actually expect to see? Can you make do with just two values instead of three (and don't you hate books that keep asking questions)?

When you remote the data to the client, you know that you need to keep a copy of the value of each editable column in each row so that you can detect changes made to the original data by other concurrent users. You refer to these as the original values. After the user makes changes to the remote data, you store the new values in the DataSet as the current values of the columns.

If the update to the original data source fails, what values are required both to ensure that you can provide the user with the information they need and to be able to apply their subsequent edit to the data source again later? Technically, you only need to store the values that are in the data store (the underlying values) at the point when the update failed. These will become the original values for the next update attempt.

From the user's point of view, they'll expect you to also provide the values that they entered—the current values in the DataSet when the update was attempted. So, these need to be the current values for the next attempt at updating the data as well, though you'll often allow the user to edit these values before the subsequent update attempt.

That leaves the third set of values, the values that were the original values when the first update was attempted. These values reflect what was in the data source when the user first opened the application (when the data was first remoted to the client and cached there ready for editing). If other users have been concurrently editing the rows, these values *don't* indicate the current values in the data store.

If you do have all three values available, you can present the user with a "reconciliation" page or screen that shows them the values they entered (the current values), the actual values in the database (the underlying values), and the values that were in the database when they started editing the data last time (the original values). Of course, in terms of the coming update that they'll carry out to reconcile the data, the underlying values will actually become the original values (the values when the data was sent back to the client after the first update failed). Figure 9-13, which shows the process, should make this clearer.

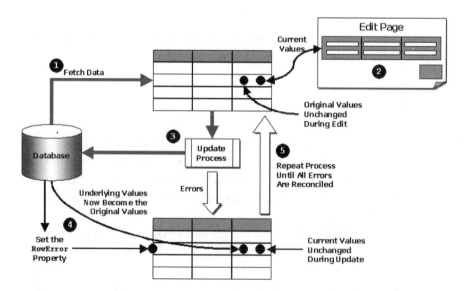

Figure 9-13. The outline process for managing errors during an update to the data store rows

What you can see from this is that both the user and the update process have enough information to be able to sensibly reconcile any errors and make a subsequent update attempt. For each column in each row, you can display to the user the value entered and the value that's currently in the data store. They can decide which ones to "keep" when the update is applied the next time. You can also provide an error message in the RowError property of each row where an error is encountered.

The only advantage you get from the ADO Recordset object's ability to store three values is that you could show the user what the values were when they first opened the application or page. In fact, this is probably more likely to confuse the user than make their decision on what to do easier. What's generally most important is the value that's in the database *now*, and providing a third option for the user to choose from could actually result in a greater chance of an incorrect value being selected, with the subsequent loss of data integrity.

So, after all this, it should be clear that the ADO.NET DataSet object is quite capable of holding the values you need to perform safe managed updates to a data store, as well as informing the user of what's going on if an error should occur. But, more than that, the DataSet also provides all the methods and properties you need to be able carry out safe controlled updates to a data store—as you'll see in the next section.

The Update Process in Detail

To understand exactly what goes on when you apply the process just described, and how you can adopt the techniques in your own applications, you'll walk through the theory next. Then, later, you'll look at an example that follows these steps so that you can see the whole process in action. Here are the individual process steps:

1. **Fill the DataSet**: You load the DataSet with the data you want to make available for editing by the client. You can use the Fill method or one of the techniques you saw earlier in this chapter. You can also fill more than one table if required. The Fill method automatically (by default) sets the original values to the same as the current values by calling AcceptChanges as it loads each row into the tables in the DataSet. If you fill the DataSet using a different technique, you need to call AcceptChanges to make sure that the current and original values are the same.

2. **Edit the data**: The DataSet is then remoted to the client, where some of the rows are edited. This changes the current values but leaves the original values the same as the values in the data store when the DataSet was originally filled (remember *not* to call AcceptChanges after editing rows, which would cause the original values to be "lost"). The DataSet is then sent back to the server for updating.

3. **Marshal the changed rows into a new DataSet**: You'd normally do this on the client before sending the DataSet back across the network to save bandwidth. Either way, you must still do this on the server as well because you need to keep a copy of the changed rows locally for use later in the process.

4. **Use the Update method to push the changes into the data store**: This will raise errors when any updates fail, and you have to make sure that the process doesn't stop when the first error occurs (the default behavior). You do this by setting the DataAdapter object's ContinueUpdateOnError property to True or by handling the RowError event and setting the UpdateStatus flag. We'll discuss these options later.

5. **Use the Fill method to get the current row values from the data store**: After the update has completed, the underlying values in the data store are extracted and placed into the same DataSet as you used to apply the update. This sets both the current and original values of each column in each row to the values that are in the data store.

6. **Merge the newly filled DataSet into the original DataSet sent from the client**: You specify that changes to the original data should be preserved by setting the optional second parameter of the Merge method to True. This means that the current values in the original DataSet aren't replaced by the current values in the new DataSet. In other words, the values entered by the user (still the current values within this original DataSet) are preserved. The original values in the DataSet are, however, replaced with the original values from the new DataSet. These are the values that have just been extracted from the data store (the underlying values).

> **NOTE** *In fact, you can achieve the same result without requiring the second call to the* Fill *method. This is because the* Update *method that precedes it can be persuaded to return the underlying values from the database and insert them into the* DataSet. *You'll see how in the next chapter when you investigate the whole process further, and you'll also come back to see how you can actually implement this in Chapter 13.*

The Result

The result is that you now have a DataSet containing the values that the user entered as the current values and the values that are in the data store now as the original values. This is exactly what you wanted. More to the point, if you use the ContinueUpdateOnError property to prevent any update error from halting the process, it automatically copies the error message generated for each row where an error occurred into the RowError property of that row. When you merge the new DataSet with the original one, these errors are copied across as well.

There is, however, another step you might want to take if you only need to use this DataSet for reconciliation of errors. It still contains rows that the user edited where the update was successful, as well as rows where it failed. You can examine the DataSet, the tables, and the individual rows to see which ones failed the update process. Any that didn't can be removed from the DataSet if you only want to send back a list of errors for the user to reconcile.

However, if you're allowing the user to push updates back and then carry on editing the data, it's probably more appropriate to leave all the rows in the DataSet. That way, you can send back the same set of data they started with—including the details of the updates that still require reconciliation.

All this seems like a complex process, so we'll demonstrate it using a simple example page next. In an application, you'll normally wrap all this processing in your data access tier component(s) and reuse it for several applications. In the next chapter, we'll demonstrate this.

A Data Update Process Example

To demonstrate the update process you've been examining in this chapter, we've provided an example page named reconcile-dataset-fill.aspx. It carries out each of the steps described in the previous sections and displays the intermediate results as each step is carried out.

The example only updates one table and uses a CommandBuilder to avoid the need to create and interact with stored procedures. This makes the individual steps in the process easier to follow. In the next chapter, you'll see the same techniques applied when the data access tier contains stored procedures to carry out the updates to the data store.

Figure 9-14 shows the example page in action. It uses the custom user control you built earlier in this chapter to display the current and original values of each column in each row of the table in the DataSet, together with the value of the RowError property for each row.

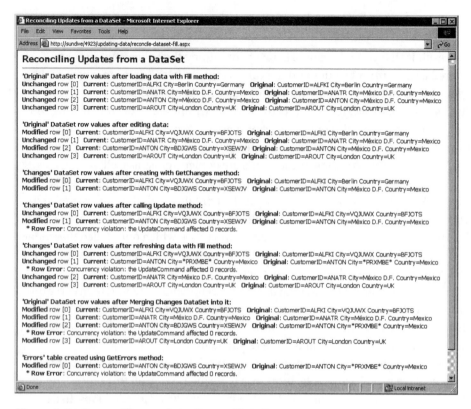

Figure 9-14. Reconciling updates from a DataSet

How It Works

At the start of the page you import the namespaces you'll need and register the custom showdataset user control that the page uses to display the DataSet contents:

```
<%@Import Namespace="System.Data"%>
<%@Import Namespace="System.Data.OleDb"%>

<%@Register TagPrefix="dda" TagName="showdataset"
            Src="..\global\show-dataset.ascx" %>
```

Next you insert seven instances of the showdataset control into the page—one for each stage of the process. There's also a <div> element where you display any error message should the code fail:

```
<!-- insert custom controls to display values -->
<dda:showdataset id="ctlShow1" runat="server" />
<dda:showdataset id="ctlShow2" runat="server" />
```

```
<dda:showdataset id="ctlShow3" runat="server" />
<dda:showdataset id="ctlShow4" runat="server" />
<dda:showdataset id="ctlShow5" runat="server" />
<dda:showdataset id="ctlShow6" runat="server" />
<dda:showdataset id="ctlShow7" runat="server" /><p />

<div id="outError" runat="server" />
```

The remainder of the page consists of the Page_Load event handler and a simple function named GetRandomString that you use to create random String values. You need to simulate a user editing the existing values, so this function provides a value that won't have already been used to update a column. To be able to rerun the page, the edited value must be different each time:

```
Function GetRandomString()
  'create a random string to simulate user editing the values
  Dim strResult As String = ""
  Dim intLoop As Integer
  Randomize
  For intLoop = 1 To 6
    strResult &= Chr(CInt(Rnd() * 25) + 65)
  Next
  Return strResult
End Function
```

The Page_Load Event Handler

In the Page_Load event handler you start by collecting the connection string for the database from the web.config file and create a SQL SELECT statement that will extract a few rows from the Customers table in the sample Northwind database. Then you can create a new DataSet object that you'll fill with values and send to the client for editing:

```
Sub Page_Load()

  'get connection string from web.config
  Dim strConnect As String
  strConnect = ConfigurationSettings.AppSettings("NorthwindConnectString")

  'specify the SELECT statement to extract the data
  Dim strSelect As String
  strSelect = "SELECT CustomerID, City, Country FROM [Customers] " _
          & "WHERE CustomerID LIKE 'A%'"
```

```
'declare a variable to hold a DataSet object
Dim objDataSet As New DataSet()
...
```

You've seen plenty of examples of loading a DataSet from a relational database in previous chapters. So you won't be surprised to see the following code used to execute the Fill method:

```
...
Dim objConnect As New OleDbConnection(strConnect)
Dim objDataAdapter As New OleDbDataAdapter(strSelect, objConnect)
Try
  objDataAdapter.Fill(objDataSet, "Customers")
Catch objError As Exception
  outError.innerHTML = "* Error while accessing data.<br />" _
          & objError.Message & " " & objError.Source
  Exit Sub  ' and stop execution
End Try
...
```

Specifying the Primary Key for the Table

When you execute the Fill method, metadata provided by the data store is used to create the correct structure for the table and its columns within the DataSet. However, this doesn't extend to setting some properties on the individual columns, such as the primary key or whether it accepts unique values, for example. For the update process you're using to work properly, you need to specify a primary key for the table.

This is because the behavior of the process, in particular when you come to refresh the DataSet from the database to get the underlying values and when you merge the new DataSet into the existing one, depends on being able to uniquely identify each row in the table. If one or more columns are defined as the primary key for the table (and so this column or combination of columns contains unique and non-NULL values), the process can use the values to match incoming rows with existing rows.

To specify the primary key for a table, you use an array of DataColumn object references that point to the columns that'll become the primary key. Remember that a table can have more than one column as the primary key—in the Order Details table in the Northwind database, the primary key is the combination of the OrderID and ProductID columns. In the current example, you just have a single column (CustomerID) as the primary key:

```
...
'get a reference to the new Customers Table in DataSet
Dim objTable As DataTable = objDataSet.Tables(0)

'set primary key in DataSet to allow Merge to work
Dim arrKey(1) As DataColumn
arrKey(0) = objTable.Columns("CustomerID")
objTable.PrimaryKey = arrKey

'show values in DataSet
ctlShow1.ShowValues(objTable, _
        "'Original' row values after loading data with Fill method")
...
```

Editing Some of the Row Values

At the end of this code, you can see that you display the contents of the Customers table with the custom user control. The next step is to change some of the values in the table to simulate the remote user editing the data. You use the GetRandomString function you saw earlier to generate random values for the City and Country columns in two of the rows and then display the values again:

```
...
'edit some of the values
objTable.Rows(0)("City") = GetRandomString()
objTable.Rows(0)("Country") = GetRandomString()
objTable.Rows(2)("City") = GetRandomString()
objTable.Rows(2)("Country") = GetRandomString()

'show values in DataSet
ctlShow2.ShowValues(objTable, _
        "'Original' DataSet row values after editing data")
...
```

Figure 9-15 shows the result so far. You can see that the Fill method sets the current and original values of the columns, and you can also see the edits you've made in the second set of values (we don't know about you, but we really fancy living in a city named *Vqjuwx*).

'Original' DataSet row values after loading data with Fill method:
Unchanged row [0] **Current**: CustomerID=ALFKI City=Berlin Country=Germany **Original**: CustomerID=ALFKI City=Berlin Country=Germany
Unchanged row [1] **Current**: CustomerID=ANATR City=México D.F. Country=Mexico **Original**: CustomerID=ANATR City=México D.F. Country=Mexico
Unchanged row [2] **Current**: CustomerID=ANTON City=México D.F. Country=Mexico **Original**: CustomerID=ANTON City=México D.F. Country=Mexico
Unchanged row [3] **Current**: CustomerID=AROUT City=London Country=UK **Original**: CustomerID=AROUT City=London Country=UK

'Original' DataSet row values after editing data:
Modified row [0] **Current**: CustomerID=ALFKI City=VQJUWX Country=BFJOTS **Original**: CustomerID=ALFKI City=Berlin Country=Germany
Unchanged row [1] **Current**: CustomerID=ANATR City=México D.F. Country=Mexico **Original**: CustomerID=ANATR City=México D.F. Country=Mexico
Modified row [2] **Current**: CustomerID=ANTON City=BDJGWS Country=XSEWJV **Original**: CustomerID=ANTON City=México D.F. Country=Mexico
Unchanged row [3] **Current**: CustomerID=AROUT City=London Country=UK **Original**: CustomerID=AROUT City=London Country=UK

Figure 9-15. The updates to the `City` *and* `Country` *column values*

Simulating a Concurrent Edit

Because we want to demonstrate the capability of the update technique to handle concurrency errors, you'll next change one of the values in the database separately from the `DataSet` that's holding the edited values. This ensures that the original value for one of the columns in the table will be different from the underlying value in the database when you come to push the edits back into the data store.

To do this, you use a separate `Connection` and `Command` object from the ones you used to fill the `DataSet`. You generate a random value (this time wrapped in asterisks to make it easier to spot later) and insert it into the `City` column in one of the rows that you've just edited within the `DataSet`:

```
...
'change a value in the original table while the DataSet is holding
'a disconnected copy of the data to force a concurrency error
Dim strUpdate As String
strUpdate = "UPDATE Customers SET City = '*" & GetRandomString() _
        & "*' WHERE CustomerID = 'ANTON'"
Dim objNewConnect As New OleDbConnection(strConnect)
Dim objNewCommand As New OleDbCommand(strUpdate, objNewConnect)

Try

  'open the connection to the database
  objNewConnect.Open()

  'execute the SQL statement
  objNewCommand.ExecuteNonQuery()

Catch objError As Exception

  'display error details
  outError.InnerHtml = "* Error updating original data.<br />" _
        & objError.Message & "<br />" & objError.Source
```

```
    Exit Sub ' and stop execution

  Finally

    objNewConnect.Close()

  End Try
  ...
```

Marshaling the Changes into a New DataSet

Once the DataSet comes back from the client (in this example you simulated the user editing the data within the ASP.NET page), you can marshal the changes that the user made into a new DataSet object. The process of marshaling changes to data in this scenario simply means removing from the data structure any rows that haven't been changed and hence don't need to be passed back to the update process.

It's usual to perform this marshaling on the client because it can considerably reduce the amount of data that's sent back across the network. For example, in terms of the customer orders application described in Chapter 11, the saving is likely to be impressive. You'd probably send on average ten rows from the Orders table and 40 or more rows from the Order Details table to rich clients. If the user only edits three or four rows, marshaling just the changed rows will reduce the size of the data sent back by at least 90 percent.

However, even if this process takes place on the client, you still need to repeat it on the server. As part of the steps you must carry out to perform the overall update process, you need a copy of the original DataSet that contains all the changes made by the user. This is where the current values will come from for the DataSet that you'll send back to the client if reconciliation of concurrency errors is required.

The GetChanges Method

To marshal rows from all the tables in an existing DataSet into a new DataSet, you can use the GetChanges method. With no parameters, this copies all the rows that have been changed in any way (updated, inserted, or deleted) into the new DataSet:

```
NewDataSet = ExistingDataSet.GetChanges()
```

You can alternatively provide a value from the `DataRowState` enumeration if you want just the modified (updated) rows, just the deleted rows, or just the added (inserted) rows:

```
NewDataSet = ExistingDataSet.GetChanges(DataRowState.Modified)
NewDataSet = ExistingDataSet.GetChanges(DataRowState.Deleted)
NewDataSet = ExistingDataSet.GetChanges(DataRowState.Added)
```

You can even create a new `DataSet` that contains only the rows that haven't been changed:

```
NewDataSet = ExistingDataSet.GetChanges(DataRowState.Unchanged)
```

The ability to separately marshal rows that have been modified, added, or deleted is useful when you have relationships between the tables in the data store that might cause updates to fail. For example, if you have added rows to a child table and a parent table in a `DataSet`, you need to make sure you call the `Update` method for the parent table first so that related child rows can be inserted afterward.

However, if the same `DataSet` also specifies rows that have been deleted from both these tables, you need to update the child table first followed by the parent table. This impasse can be circumnavigated by marshaling the deleted rows into a separate `DataSet` from the added rows, allowing each `DataSet` to be used to update the tables in the appropriate order. Another point to bear in mind is that the `Update` method of the `DataAdapter` object processes the rows in each table it updates in their "natural order." This may be the order they were added to the table, the order specified by a primary key, or the `Sort` property of a `DataView` based on the table. So it'll perform the updates, deletes, and inserts in row order. It *doesn't* perform all the updates first, for example, followed by all the deletes, and so on. If you actually want this kind of process ordering, you can do it by creating separate `DataSet` objects for each process.

But we digress. In the example page, you just need to call the `GetChanges` method to create a new `DataSet` containing all the changed rows. Then you can display the contents of this new `DataSet`:

```
...
'marshal just the changed rows into a new DataSet
Dim objChangesDS As DataSet = objDataSet.GetChanges()

'show values in DataSet
Dim objChangeTable As DataTable = objChangesDS.Tables(0)
ctlShow3.ShowValues(objChangeTable, _
        "'Changes' row values after creating with GetChanges method")
...
```

Figure 9-16 shows the result after this stage of the process. Notice that the original and current values are unchanged—the GetChanges method duplicates the rows exactly, including the complete column definitions and properties such as the primary key, unique columns, and so on.

'Changes' DataSet row values after creating with GetChanges method:
Modified row [0] **Current**: CustomerID=ALFKI City=VQJUWX Country=BFJOTS **Original**: CustomerID=ALFKI City=Berlin Country=Germany
Modified row [1] **Current**: CustomerID=ANTON City=BDJGWS Country=XSEWJV **Original**: CustomerID=ANTON City=México D.F. Country=Mexico

Figure 9-16. The contents of the changes DataSet *after calling the* GetChanges *method*

Updating the Data Store

Now you can use the new DataSet to update the database with the values that the user entered. You're taking advantage of the CommandBuilder object here, allowing it to create the appropriate SQL statements for you:

```
...
Try

    'create an auto-generated command builder to create the commands
    'to update, insert and delete the data
    Dim objCommandBuilder As New OleDbCommandBuilder(objDataAdapter)
    ...
```

You'll recall from the earlier description of the process that you must prevent execution of the Update method from halting when a concurrency error occurs. In fact, you can prevent it from being halted by any type of runtime error by setting the ContinueUpdateOnError property of the DataAdapter to True first. When an error is detected by the Update method, it just copies the error message into the RowError property of the row where the error occurred:

```
...
'prevent exceptions being thrown due to concurrency errors
'error details obtained from the RowError property afterwards
objDataAdapter.ContinueUpdateOnError = True
...
```

Handling the RowUpdated Event

Alternatively, another technique you can use to prevent errors from halting the Update process is to handle the RowUpdated event. This fires after the updates to each row have been pushed into the data source, and the RowUpdatedEventArgs object that's passed to the RowUpdated event handler contains details of the process—including any error message.

You can specify the event handler that will execute when the RowUpdated event occurs in Visual Basic .NET using the AddHandler statement. For the seond parameter you provide a reference to the routine that implements the handler (here named OnRowUpdated):

```
AddHandler objDataAdapter.RowUpdated, _
          New OleDbRowUpdatedEventHandler(AddressOf OnRowUpdated)
```

In C#, you simply add an event handler to the DataAdapter, specifying the name of the function that implements the handler:

```
objDataAdapter.RowUpdated += new OleDbRowUpdatedEventHandler(OnRowUpdated);
```

Within this event handler, you can access the parameters to find out what type of update was attempted (Update, Insert, or Delete), the number of rows that were updated (zero if the update failed), and references to any exception objects and their messages and other properties. What's important is that, within the event handler, you have to tell the Update process what to do next if there was an error during the update for this row. By default the process will halt, so you must set the Status property of the RowUpdatedEventArgs object passed in the event handler parameters. To continue processing with the next row, you use this:

```
EventRowArgsObject.Status = UpdateStatus.SkipCurrentRow
```

Pushing the Changes into the Data Store

Whichever technique you adopt, the next thing is to call the Update method to push the changes into the data store. Afterward, in this example, you display the contents of the new DataSet again:

```
...
'perform the update on the original data
objDataAdapter.Update(objChangesDS, "Customers")

Catch objError As Exception

outError.innerHTML = "* Error updating original data.<br />" _
                  & objError.Message & " " & objError.Source
Exit Sub  'and stop

End Try
```

```
'show values in DataSet
ctlShow4.ShowValues(objChangeTable, _
        "'Changes' DataSet row values after calling Update method")
...
```

Figure 9-17 shows the section of results for this part of the process in the example page. Notice that the Update process set the RowError property of the second row. The update failed for this row because the "concurrent" code changed the underlying value for the City column in the database after you filled the DataSet.

'Changes' DataSet row values after calling Update method:
Unchanged row [0] **Current**: CustomerID=ALFKI City=VQJUWX Country=BFJOTS **Original**: CustomerID=ALFKI City=VQJUWX Country=BFJOTS
Modified row [1] **Current**: CustomerID=ANTON City=BDJGWS Country=XSEWJV **Original**: CustomerID=ANTON City=México D.F. Country=Mexico
 * **Row Error**: Concurrency violation: the UpdateCommand affected 0 records.

Figure 9-17. The contents of the changes DataSet *after calling the* Update *method*

Fetching the Underlying Values from the Database

The next step is to collect the underlying values from the data store. For this you use the Fill method again, exactly as you did to fill the original DataSet. But this time you're filling the new DataSet (the one you just used to apply the updates to the database). Afterward you display the contents of this DataSet again:

```
...
Try

  'refresh "changes" dataset from database table
  objDataAdapter.Fill(objChangesDS, "Customers")

Catch objError As Exception

  outError.innerHTML = "* Error while accessing data.<br />" _
      & objError.Message & " " & objError.Source
  Exit Sub   'and stop

End Try

'show values in DataSet
ctlShow5.ShowValues(objChangeTable, _
    "'Changes' row values after refreshing data with Fill method")
...
```

You can call the Fill method directly here only because the DataAdapter you're using is the same instance you used at the start of the page. It already references a Command object through its SelectCommand property that contains the appropriate SQL SELECT statement—the one you specified when you originally created this DataAdapter instance.

When you remote the DataSet to the client (as in a "real" application) and then receive it back from them, you have to create the DataAdapter afresh and specify the SQL statement or details of the stored procedure that'll be used in this stage of the process. The important point is that the SQL statement or stored procedure should return the same rowset as the one that was originally used to fill the DataSet (at the least it must include all the rows that the original one returned). It's most likely, of course, to be the same SQL statement or stored procedure.

Figure 9-18 shows the set of values after you edit them and the results of the Fill method. You can see that the update you made to the first row succeeded because your new edited values have been extracted from the database. However, the second row shows the change to the data made by the SQL statement you separately and directly executed against the database table. This is what caused the concurrency error during the Update process.

'Original' DataSet row values after editing data:
Modified row [0] **Current**: CustomerID=ALFKI City=VQJUWX Country=BFJOTS **Original**: CustomerID=ALFKI City=Berlin Country=Germany
Unchanged row [1] **Current**: CustomerID=ANATR City=México D.F. Country=Mexico **Original**: CustomerID=ANATR City=México D.F. Country=Mexico
Modified row [2] **Current**: CustomerID=ANTON City=BDJGWS Country=XSEWJV **Original**: CustomerID=ANTON City=México D.F. Country=Mexico
Unchanged row [3] **Current**: CustomerID=AROUT City=London Country=UK **Original**: CustomerID=AROUT City=London Country=UK

'Changes' DataSet row values after refreshing data with Fill method:
Unchanged row [0] **Current**: CustomerID=ALFKI City=VQJUWX Country=BFJOTS **Original**: CustomerID=ALFKI City=VQJUWX Country=BFJOTS
Unchanged row [1] **Current**: CustomerID=ANTON City=*PRXMBE* Country=Mexico **Original**: CustomerID=ANTON City=*PRXMBE* Country=Mexico
  * Row Error: Concurrency violation: the UpdateCommand affected 0 records.
Unchanged row [2] **Current**: CustomerID=ANATR City=México D.F. Country=Mexico **Original**: CustomerID=ANATR City=México D.F. Country=Mexico
Unchanged row [3] **Current**: CustomerID=AROUT City=London Country=UK **Original**: CustomerID=AROUT City=London Country=UK

Figure 9-18. The edited values and the result of calling the Update *method*

Looking at Figure 9-18, you can see that you've lost the original values from the new "changes" DataSet. Nevertheless, they're still in the original DataSet, so you can now go about assembling the correct combination of current and original values you want. Before then, however, you need to come back and look at the way that the primary key in the DataSet table affects the behavior of the Fill method.

Are You Refreshing or Filling?

The Fill method can be used in two ways. You can use it to create a new table and the structure for that table and then load the new table with rows from the data source. This is what you did at the beginning of this whole process by creating a new empty DataSet object and then using the Fill method to load four rows from the Customers table. When you called Fill and specified the name of the table that you wanted to use, this table was created within the DataSet.

However, you can also use the Fill method to refresh the data in an existing table in a DataSet. If you specify the name of a table that already exists in the DataSet, the Fill method will attempt to add the rows that are extracted from the data store to this table. The clever part is that, provided you've specified a primary key for the table, new rows are matched with existing rows using the values of the primary key column(s), and the data then overwrites the existing values in the original rows.

Effectively, you've refreshed the table content so that it now contains the underlying values currently in the database. If you think about it, there's actually no other course of action that the Fill method could take if the table contains a primary key. Adding new rows that have the same primary key value wouldn't be possible. One point to watch, however, is that if the table has a column of unique values (a column with its Unique property set to True) but this column isn't specified as the primary key, the Fill method will fail if you try to refresh an existing table.

> **NOTE** *If the structure of the rows (the number and type of columns) in the new data is different from the structure of the table in the* DataSet, *the table structure (the schema) is automatically changed to suit the new data where possible. If constraints such as unique columns or relationships between tables prevent the schema being modified, an error is raised instead. Note that in most cases the table name is case-sensitive.*

You can see the distinction between refreshing a table that contains a primary key and one that doesn't by comparing the last set of values in Figure 9-18 with Figure 9-19. When you created the table in the original DataSet (early in the Page_Load event handler code you're examining), you specified a primary key for the table. So, in Figure 9-18, the rows extracted from the database are used to refresh the existing rows.

However, in Figure 9-19, you see what happens if you don't specify the primary key for the table (we just removed the code that creates the primary key and ran the example page with the original data to get this result). You can see that the four rows retrieved from the database are simply added to the table. In general this isn't a very useful approach—though there may possibly be occasions in your applications where you actually want this behavior.

'Changes' DataSet row values after refreshing data with Fill method:
Unchanged row [0] **Current**: CustomerID=ALFKI City=WLMEDS Country=LDBSEF **Original**: CustomerID=ALFKI City=WLMEDS Country=LDBSEF
Modified row [1] **Current**: CustomerID=ANTON City=SDPGLW Country=XVXSBR **Original**: CustomerID=ANTON City=México D.F. Country=Mexico
  * Row Error: Concurrency violation: the UpdateCommand affected 0 records.
Unchanged row [2] **Current**: CustomerID=ALFKI City=WLMEDS Country=LDBSEF **Original**: CustomerID=ALFKI City=WLMEDS Country=LDBSEF
Unchanged row [3] **Current**: CustomerID=ANATR City=México D.F. Country=Mexico **Original**: CustomerID=ANATR City=México D.F. Country=Mexico
Unchanged row [4] **Current**: CustomerID=ANTON City=*QMCVIZ* Country=Mexico **Original**: CustomerID=ANTON City=*QMCVIZ* Country=Mexico
Unchanged row [5] **Current**: CustomerID=AROUT City=London Country=UK **Original**: CustomerID=AROUT City=London Country=UK

Figure 9-19. The result of the `Fill` *process when the primary key isn't defined*

Merging the Two DataSets

At this point, you have two `DataSet` objects containing data. The first (original) `DataSet` contains the user's edited values as the current values and the values when the `DataSet` was filled as the original values. The second (new) `DataSet` you created with the `GetChanges` method earlier (after the `Update` and subsequent `Fill` operations you just carried out) contains the underlying values that are in the database now for both its current and original values.

The clever part is that you can now call the `Merge` method of the first `DataSet` to merge the contents of the second "changes" `DataSet` into it. The `Merge` method supports an optional second parameter that defines if any changes within the first `DataSet` will be preserved. What this actually means is that, if you set it to `True`, only the original values will be merged into the first `DataSet`, overwriting the original values that were stored there. The current values aren't merged, so the current values in the first `DataSet` are unchanged.

> **NOTE** *If you don't specify* `True` *for this parameter (the default is* `False`*), both the current and original values are merged into the first* `DataSet`*. Hence, you'd lose the user's edited values.*

The `Merge` method behaves just like the `Fill` method in that it requires a primary key to be present in the table(s) if the row values are to be refreshed (replaced with values from the second `DataSet`). Without a primary key, the `Merge` method can't match new rows with existing rows, so it'll attempt to add the new rows to the tables in the `DataSet`.

So, in this example, you call the `Merge` method of the original `DataSet`—passing to it the new `DataSet` and the value `True` for the second "preserve changes" parameter. Then you display the contents of this (the original) `DataSet`:

```
...
'now merge "changes" DataSet back into original DataSet
objDataSet.Merge(objChangesDS, True)

'show values in original (now merged) DataSet
ctlShow6.ShowValues(objTable, _
    "'Original' row values after Merging Changes DataSet into it")
...
```

Figure 9-20 shows the result. You can see that you still have four rows in this original `DataSet`. Two of them (row 0 and row 2) are rows that were edited by the user, and the other two weren't. In fact, these two rows could have been removed from the original `DataSet` before it was sent back to the server if the client had marshaled only the changed rows. They appear again now because you used the `Fill` method to refresh the new "changes" `DataSet` before merging it into this one, so all the original rows are extracted from the database again.

'Original' DataSet row values after Merging Changes DataSet into it:
Modified row [0]   **Current**: CustomerID=ALFKI City=VQJUWX Country=BFJOTS   **Original**: CustomerID=ALFKI City=VQJUWX Country=BFJOTS
Modified row [1]   **Current**: CustomerID=ANATR City=México D.F. Country=Mexico   **Original**: CustomerID=ANATR City=México D.F. Country=Mexico
Modified row [2]   **Current**: CustomerID=ANTON City=BDJGWS Country=XSEWJV   **Original**: CustomerID=ANTON City=*PRXMBE* Country=Mexico
  * **Row Error**: Concurrency violation: the UpdateCommand affected 0 records.
Modified row [3]   **Current**: CustomerID=AROUT City=London Country=UK   **Original**: CustomerID=AROUT City=London Country=UK

Figure 9-20. The original `DataSet` after merging the changes `DataSet` into it

What's exciting here (OK, so we get excited easily) is that you've now got exactly what you need to be able to reconcile the concurrency error that occurred for the third row (at row index 2). The current values are the ones the user entered when they were editing the row, and the original values are those that are in the database now. I've highlighted the value that caused the concurrency error in Figure 9-20 (recall that the code wrapped this in asterisks so that you could easily identify it). On top of that, you can see the error message in the `RowError` property of this row.

Extracting Just the Error Rows

If you intend to allow the user to continue editing the same set of data as before (maybe they have an option to flush their changes to the server on demand or it's done at regular intervals automatically), you can send back the DataSet you've just created. It contains the same rows as the original DataSet but with the appropriate reconciliation information included where any updates failed.

However, you might prefer to use a separate page or screen to allow the user to "fix" all the errors from this update before they go off and do something else. In this case, there's no point in wasting bandwidth by sending them all the original rows again. You need to extract and send back just the rows that have errors and that still require their attention.

You can extract just the rows that contain an error (rows that have a nonempty RowError property) using the GetErrors method of the DataTable object. In this example, we provide a section of generic code that can handle a DataSet containing more than one table—even though there's only a single table here. The GetErrors method returns an array of all the rows (DataRow objects) in the table that contain an error.

However, you can't easily manipulate the existing table rows because, every time you remove one, the row indices change for the remaining rows. Instead, we chose to create a new table and copy the rows with errors into it. To make sure that the new table has the same structure and properties as the existing one, use the Clone method to create the new table. It'll have the same name as the existing table, but this doesn't matter as long as you remove the existing table from the Tables collection of the DataSet before you add the new one to the Tables collection.

The following listing demonstrates the technique. You iterate through the Tables collection of the DataSet using a For...Next construct (you can't use For Each because adding and removing tables will cause the Tables collection to change):

...

```
'finally, build a table containing just the rows with errors

Dim arrRows(), objRow As DataRow
Dim objNewTable As DataTable

'get number of tables in DataSet
Dim intTableCount As Integer = objDataSet.Tables.Count
Dim intTableIndex As Integer = 0

'iterate through existing tables in DataSet
For intTableIndex = 0 To intTableCount - 1
...
```

However, the addition and removal of tables also means that you have to access the table at index zero every time. Existing tables "shuffle up" through the Tables collection as you remove the first one (at index zero) and replace it with the new table (which is added to the end of the Tables collection):

```
...
'get a reference to this table in DataSet
'always use index 0 as tables are added to end of
'the Tables collection so remove/add process shown
'later means new tables are never at index 0
objTable = objDataSet.Tables(0)
...
```

For each table you find, you clone it and then use the GetErrors method of the existing table to get an array of rows with errors. Then you can iterate through the array importing each row into the new table:

```
...
'make a copy of the table
 objNewTable = objTable.Clone

'get reference to rows with errors into array
arrRows = objTable.GetErrors()

'copy these rows into the new table
For Each objRow In arrRows
  objNewTable.ImportRow(objRow)
Next
...
```

All you have to do then is remove the existing table from the DataSet object's Tables collection and add the new one. You finish up by displaying the values in the new table:

```
    ...
    'replace old table with the new one
    objDataSet.Tables.Remove(objTable)
    objDataSet.Tables.Add(objNewTable)

  Next

  ctlShow7.ShowValues(objDataSet.Tables(0), _
          "'Errors' table created using GetErrors method")

End Sub
```

Figure 9-21 shows the final result—the single row that contains a concurrency error ready to send back to the client so that the user can reconcile the error.

```
'Errors' table created using GetErrors method:
Modified row [0]  Current: CustomerID=ANTON City=BDJGWS Country=XSEWJV  Original: CustomerID=ANTON City=*PRXMBE* Country=Mexico
  * Row Error: Concurrency violation: the UpdateCommand affected 0 records.
```

Figure 9-21. The contents of the errors table after searching for errors

Using the HasErrors Property

If no errors are encountered during the Update process, the code you just used will still produce a DataSet containing the same tables as were in the original DataSet. They will just be empty (have no rows). So, on the client, you can detect if an error occurred by checking the Count property of each table's Rows collection. The point is that the client-side code will still have a DataSet containing the same tables to work with, even if these tables are empty. Server-side and client-side data binding and other display techniques will not "break."

An alternative is to send back the value Nothing (null in C#) if there are no errors, instead of an empty DataSet. Or you could only include a table in the DataSet if that table contained an error. The easiest way to do this is to take advantage of the HasErrors property that's exposed by the DataSet, DataTable, and DataRow objects.

You could check the HasErrors property of the DataSet first. If it returned True, you'd then check the HasErrors property of each table in the DataSet. For each one that returned True, you could then use the same technique shown in the previous listing (the GetErrors method) to build the table of rows with errors.

Summarizing the Process

So, as you've seen in this example, it's not difficult to perform detection of concurrency errors and build the appropriate data structure to return to the user for reconciliation of the errors. Yes, it's a little long-winded, but it does provide flexibility and allows you to interact with the process to tailor it for specific requirements.

You'll use the same techniques as you've seen so far in this chapter to perform multiple updates from a rich client in the example customer orders application. However, there, you do so within a data access component and by using stored procedures instead of SQL statements. This makes it harder to see what the actual process involves, so instead we chose to show a separate simplified version as the ASP.NET page you've seen here.

However, bear in mind that the principles of the process are a basic data management technique that you'll use in all kinds of disconnected applications, in many different scenarios and various types of client environment. The process as a whole involves six steps, which were listed earlier in this chapter and which you worked through in the previous example:

- **F**ill the original `DataSet`.

- **E**dit the data in this `DataSet`.

- **G**etChanges to create a new `DataSet`.

- **U**pdate the new `DataSet`.

- **R**efresh the new `DataSet`.

- **M**erge with the original `DataSet`.

Or, if you're into mnemonics, FEGURM—possibly the name of a city used in the example? No doubt you can come up with a memorable phrase to help imprint this onto your brain for good. Perhaps "Feeling Extremely Good Using Reliable Methods"?

The `AcceptChangesDuringFill` Property

Moving on from the schoolboy humor of the previous section, you have one more topic to briefly examine before the bell sounds for the end of the chapter. We mentioned several times earlier in this chapter that the `Fill` method exposes a property that allows you to control how the original and current values are affected by the process.

When you call the `Fill` method, it loads each row from the data store into the matching table within the target `DataSet`. This sets the current value of each column in the row. After loading each row, it calls the `AcceptChanges` method to copy the current value into the original value for every column in that row.

However, if you set the `AcceptChangesDuringFill` property to `False` (the default is, of course, `True`), the original values in each row are unchanged—they won't exist if this is a new `DataSet` or a new table, or will still contain the same values as before if you're refreshing an existing table. Does this help to create a useful data structure when you're updating data?

In fact, it doesn't really help at all. You can see why in the next short example. We took the page you've just been looking at in this chapter and modified it so that you can to see what happens. The new page, reconcile-dataset-noaccept.aspx, contains the following code at the point where you're refreshing the values in the new "changes" DataSet using the Fill method:

```
...
Try

    'prevent AcceptChanges being called after each row has been loaded
    objDataAdapter.AcceptChangesDuringFill = False

    'refresh DataSet from database table
    objDataAdapter.Fill(objDataSet, "Customers")

Catch objError As Exception

    outError.innerHTML = "* Error while accessing data.<br />" _
            & objError.Message & " " & objError.Source
    Exit Sub  'and stop

End Try

'show values in DataSet
ctlShow4.ShowValues(objTable, _
        "Row values after calling Fill without AcceptChanges")
```

Figure 9-22 shows the result. The last set of values are those created by the last line of the previous code and show the contents of the new "changes" DataSet after refreshing the data with the AcceptChangesDuringFill property set to False. You can see that the current value of the third row (highlighted) contains the value that was changed concurrently while the user was working with the DataSet. However, the original value is still the value that was in the database when the DataSet was originally created and filled. So this DataSet is no use for reconciling errors.

If you were now to merge this with the original DataSet, you'd get the underlying value from the database placed into the current row version of the DataSet you originally created and filled, but you really want it to be placed in the original row version. More to the point, you'd then lose the edited values that the user entered, which you previously decided was a major requirement for the process as a whole.

So, although you might find a use for the AcceptChangesDuringFill property in other scenarios, it doesn't provide any useful techniques for updating and reconciling data.

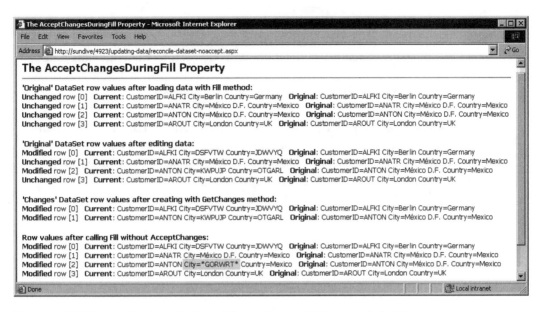

Figure 9-22. The result when the `AcceptChangesDuringFill` *property is* `False`

Summary

This has been a tightly focused chapter, concentrating on one specific set of issues: How do you handle multiple updates to a data store and at the same time detect and reconcile concurrency errors that might arise from multiple users updating your data? It's certainly not a trivial task, as you can see from the discussion and examples in this chapter.

The process we demonstrated may at first seem to be a roundabout way of doing things and complicated compared to previous versions of ADO and the `Recordset` object. However, bear in mind the many useful features you've already discovered with the `DataSet` object in ADO.NET throughout this book. The benefits you get in many situations from using a `DataSet` outweigh the disadvantage of a more complex update process.

In fact, although updating a single table with an ADO `Recordset` might be easier, updating multiple related tables certainly adds an extra level of complexity that probably exceeds that encountered when using a `DataSet` in ADO.NET. Remember that you can still use the ADO `Recordset` in ADO.NET via COM interop if you want.

This chapter covered the following topics:

- Transferring data and managing updates in rich clients

- Loading different types of data into a `DataSet`

- Understanding how the `DataSet` stores original and current values

- Detecting concurrency violations and other errors when updating data

- Providing feedback when such issues are detected

As promised in several places in this chapter, you'll put much of this theory into action in the next chapter. Specifically, you'll build a data access tier for the customer orders application that provides a robust and efficient process for updating the order data and reconciling concurrency errors.

Components for Updating Data

IN THE PREVIOUS CHAPTER, you saw how we can use the features of ADO.NET to update a data source using a `DataSet` object and collect information in this `DataSet` about concurrency or other errors that might arise during the update process. This technique provides an extremely useful foundation for building distributed applications that perform data updates.

For example, you can create a separate data tier using the update methods described in the previous chapter and then take advantage of a "business logic" middle tier to communicate the `DataSet` to and from the client. This means you can build almost any kind of interface and allow it to interact with the data tier—in much the same way as you did when building applications to view the customer orders data in earlier chapters of this book.

You'll look at an example of this kind of application in the next chapter. In the meantime, in this chapter, you'll focus on the following topics:

- Building a data access tier for multiple remote updates

- Using tracing in a component within an ASP.NET page

- Handling IDENTITY columns for multiple row inserts

- Testing the component in an ASP.NET page

You'll start with a look at how you adapt the techniques used in the previous chapter to build a component-based data access tier for your applications.

The UpdateDataSet Component

The data access component you'll build does a similar job to that in Chapter 8 (UpdateOrders.dll). After all, many of the tasks you perform to update data from a down-level client are the same as those in a rich client. For example, you still need to be able to get a list of orders to display in the client, as well as lists of products and shipping companies. The major difference is when you come to perform the update.

In the down-level clients examined in Chapter 8, each update to the data is persisted immediately to the data store during a postback to the server. In a rich client, as discussed in earlier chapters, you want to allow multiple updates to be made to the remotely cached data and then apply all of them to the data store on demand, as one operation.

So, the real difference between the Chapter 8 data access component (UpateOrders.dll) and the component you'll build here (UpdateDataSet.dll) is only down to the method(s) that perform the data update. Instead of the six separate methods that were required in the Chapter 8 examples (a DELETE, INSERT, and UPDATE method for each of the two tables Orders and Order Details), you have just one method for updating the database. This takes a DataSet containing all the changes to the data and returns a DataSet containing errors and reconciliation information such as described in the previous chapter.

Nevertheless, this change does allow you to simplify the code quite considerably. You'll see how you avoid the multiple sets of parameter declarations that were required for the methods described in Chapter 8. We've also equipped the component to support *tracing*, making it easier to follow what's going on when the update method is used. Because the process of updating a data store from a DataSet and reconciling errors is somewhat more complicated than simply executing a single stored procedure, this feature is useful while debugging and when building new applications that use the component.

Enabling Tracing from Within a Component

Before you dive into the component itself, you'll see how you can add tracing to a component that's used from within an ASP.NET page. The page exposes an Http-Context object (the page context), and you can get a reference to this from within a component that's instantiated in the page. The context object itself allows you to access the Trace object that's used for tracing in an ASP.NET page. You can therefore write to this Trace object from within your component, and it'll be visible just like any other trace information.

To use the HttpContext object, you have to import the System.Web namespace into your component (along with the other namespaces you need to access from the code). We've highlighted the relevant lines in bold in the following code:

```
Imports System
Imports System.Data
Imports System.Data.OleDb
'to perform tracing in the ASP.NET page from within the
'component requires the System.Web namespace as well
Imports System.Web
```

You also have to get a reference to the current page context before you can access the Trace object. The easiest way is to do this when you instantiate the component, but you could do it separately within each method if required. If you call methods of the component more than once from within a page, it's probably more efficient to keep a reference to values that aren't specific to each method throughout the life of the component.

So, you declare a "global" (class-level) variable within the component's class to hold the context reference. You also need a Boolean variable that you'll set to indicate if tracing is available for the component in its current environment. If it's instantiated from outside an ASP.NET page (for example, in a Windows Forms application), the HttpContext will probably not be available, so accessing it will result in a runtime error:

```
Namespace DataSetUpdate
  Public Class UpdateDataSet

    'declare variable to hold reference to current page context
    Private m_Context As HttpContext

    'declare variable to indicate if HttpContext is available
    Private m_CanTrace As Boolean = False

    'declare variable to hold the connection string
    Private m_ConnectString As String

    'declare variable to hold Order ID of inserted order rows
    'used by event handlers for UpdateAllOrderDetails method
    Private m_InsertOrderID As Integer

    'declare variable to hold reference to DataSets during update process
    'these are used by event handlers for UpdateAllOrderDetails method
    Private m_ModifiedDataSet As DataSet
    Private m_MarshaledDataSet As DataSet
```

You can also see in the previous listing that you declare several other class-level variables. The m_ConnectString variable is the same as you used in the UpdateOrders component in Chapter 8 to hold the connection string for the database server. The other three are used when you come to insert new rows into the database. You'll look at this topic, and see how these variables are used, later in this chapter.

Next, within the component's constructor, you can attempt to set the m_Context variable to the current page context. If it works (meaning that the HttpContext is available), you switch the m_CanTrace variable to True to indicate that tracing is possible:

```
Public Sub New(ByVal ConnectString As String)

  'constructor for component - requires the connection
  'string to be provided as the single parameter
  MyBase.New() 'call constructor for base class
  m_ConnectString = ConnectString

  'for tracing variables and execution in ASP.NET page require
  'reference to current Context object if available
  Try
    m_Context = HttpContext.Current
    If Not m_Context Is Nothing Then m_CanTrace = True
  Catch
  End Try

End Sub
```

Writing to the Trace Object

Once you've established a reference to the page context, it's easy to write trace messages—just like you do from ASP.NET code within the page itself. You call the Write method of the Trace object and pass in one or two string values. If you use two values, the first is the "category" of the message (an arbitrary name to help locate the entry in the trace list) and the second is the value to display. If you only provide one string parameter to the Write method, it's used as the value to be displayed. To write status or progress information, you can use a simple text string such as this:

```
'write message to Trace object for display in ASP.NET page
If m_CanTrace Then
  m_Context.Trace.Write("UpdateDataSet", "Starting Update Order Rows")
End If
```

If you want to examine values being used by the process within the component, you can simply cast the values to a string and output these. The following code shows the value of the variable named intRowsAffected:

```
'write number of rows updated to Trace object
If m_CanTrace Then
  m_Context.Trace.Write("UpdateDataSet", "Refreshed " _
                        & intRowsAffected.ToString() & " row(s)")
End If
```

When you instantiate the component in an ASP.NET page, the data you write to the Trace object isn't visible by default. However, if you add the Trace directive to the page, the usual trace information is displayed in the page:

```
<%@Page Language="VB" Trace="True"%>
```

Now the output from the component is visible within this trace information, as shown in Figure 10-1.

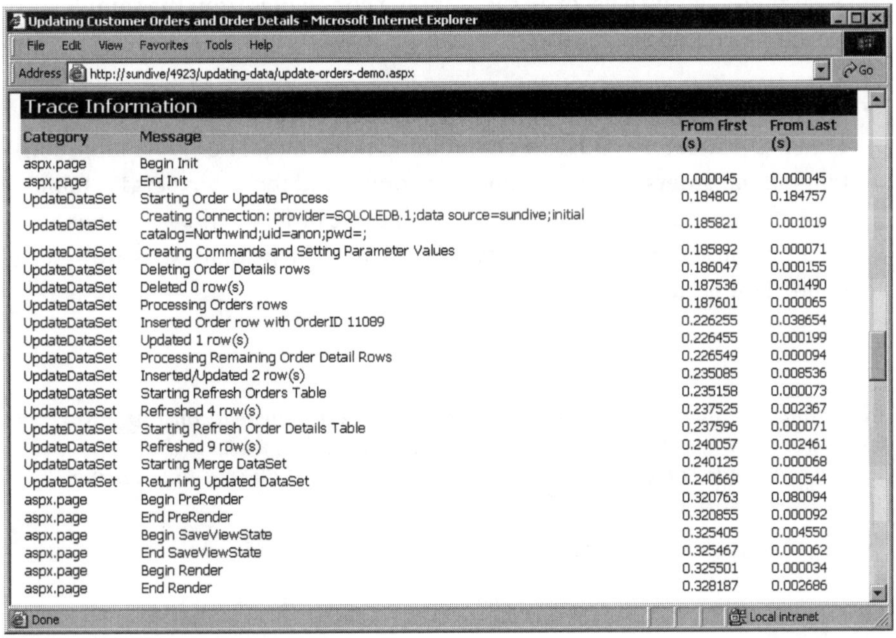

Figure 10-1. Output from the UpdateDataSet *component in the ASP.NET trace list*

Figure 10-1 shows the output from the ASP.NET page demonstrated later in this chapter, which calls the method in the component to persist some changes in a DataSet to the data store. You'll see the Trace.Write statements within the code when you examine this in detail shortly.

The Common Methods in the Component

We mentioned that the UpdateDataSet component you're building here is similar to the UpdateOrders component you used in Chapter 8. In fact, the UpdateDataSet component contains the same three methods for returning data from the data store as the UpdateOrders component (so we won't describe them in this chapter). The three common methods are as follows:

- **GetProductsDataSet**: This method takes no parameters and returns a DataSet containing a list of all the products in the sample Northwind database in the back-end data store.

- **GetShippersDataSet**: This method also takes no parameters, and it returns a DataSet containing a list of all the shipping companies from the sample Northwind database.

- **GetOrderDetails**: This method takes a single String parameter that's a customer ID and returns a DataSet containing two tables. The Orders table contains all the orders for the specified customer, and the Order Details table contains the details (order lines) for all of these orders. The DataSet has a relationship set up between the two tables, and the primary keys are defined for both of the tables as well.

> **NOTE** *You'll see shortly why it's important that you set up the relationship between the tables and define the primary keys. This affects the way the DataSet manages cascaded deletes and updates and the way it handles the rows during the Update and Merge processes.*

Managing IDENTITY Columns for Inserted Rows

Before you start to look at the code for the method that performs the data updates, you need to consider one crucial issue. It's common for database tables to use an IDENTITY or AutoNumber column for values that form the primary key of a table. Examples are product IDs and customer IDs. In the case of the sample database, you have such a situation in the Orders table, where the primary key is the column named OrderID. It's an IDENTITY column, so as new order rows are added, the next available IDENTITY value is automatically assigned to the OrderID column for the new row, as shown in Figure 10-2.

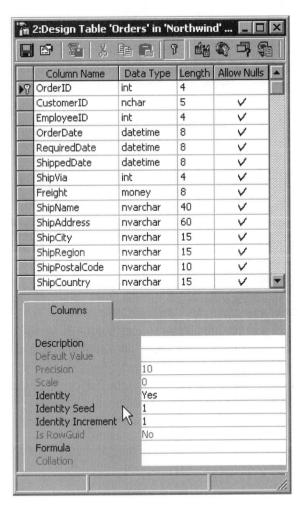

Figure 10-2. The Orders *table in the Northwind sample database*

No doubt you can see the problem. How are you going to manage multiple inserts into the Orders table and the related Order Details table? By default, you can't insert values into the OrderID IDENTITY column of the Orders table. OK, so you can insert values into the OrderID column of the Order Details table because this isn't an IDENTITY column. It's simply a foreign key that links each order line to its parent order. But even if you can insert an OrderID value here, how do you know what the value should be if it's only created when a row is added to the Orders table?

In the down-level client examples in Chapter 8, you don't have this problem. When the user inserts a new Order row, you add it to the Orders table in the database immediately (during the postback), filling in default values based on the current date and using name and address details extracted from the Customers table. The stored procedure you used there to perform the row insert also returns the new OrderID value from the IDENTITY column in the table, so the ASP.NET code can display this to the user after the row has been inserted. Once the new order has been inserted, you allow the user to insert new order lines, which will contain the OrderID that was returned.

However, this isn't a feasible approach when you allow users to insert new Orders and Order Details rows into a remote DataSet for one-touch updates to the data store later. Instead, there are at least a couple of techniques you can use to get around the problem. You can generate your own unique OrderID values and use these in the database tables, or you can intercept the updates as they're being applied to the database and "massage" the data to suit the autogenerated OrderID value as the updates are being performed. You'll look at both techniques here.

Using GUIDs or Random Values for the Primary Key

One way to get around the problem of remotely updating autogenerated row key values, such as an IDENTITY or AutoNumber column, is to generate the values when the row is added to the remote DataSet instead. This sounds like a simple solution, but in fact there are issues that need to be addressed. The most important issue is whether you actually can generate a unique value for the column. An IDENTITY column always uses the next number in sequence (depending on the Identity Seed and Identity Increment settings in the database), so it's guaranteed to be unique for that table.

If you generate the value on the client, while the data is disconnected and remote from the database, you don't know what the "current" identity value is. Even if you did, you wouldn't be able to prevent another client instance using the same value unless you actually insert the row immediately (as in the examples in the previous chapter). The only solution is to make sure that the value you use is random or unique enough for the chances of another client choosing the same value to be extremely unlikely—or even impossible.

The most obvious candidate for a unique value is a Globally Unique IDentifier (GUID). Windows and the .NET Framework both include functions to create GUIDs. It's generally accepted that it's just about impossible for the same GUID to occur more that once—they're 128-bit values that include things such as an encoding of the MAC address of the network card and other machine-specific features, as well as a generous proportion of randomness.

The problem is that the primary key column in the table must be able to accept 128-bit (16 byte) values to use a GUID. This generally means that the table design will need to be changed, together with the related tables and the code that accesses the data. It also prevents the column from actually being an IDENTITY column at all—a feature that other applications using the data might be expecting.

Of course, you could always stay with the 32-bit (4 byte) Integer column type and still create random values for the key. A 32-bit integer can contain any of more than 4 billion different values, so the chances of a collision are reasonably slim if you take care with the generation of the random value. If you have a limited and known subset of clients to service with the application, you could even allocate each client a separate subset of values to use for their key values.

Inserting IDENTITY Values

The other point with this technique is that you may need to insert the random value you create into the IDENTITY column of a table. By default, you can't insert values into IDENTITY or AutoNumber columns in a database table. However, you can get around this by using extra instructions within a stored procedure. For example, in SQL Server, you can use the following:

```
SET IDENTITY_INSERT ON
INSERT INTO Orders (OrderID, OrderDate, RequiredDate, ...etc...)
        VALUES (483526783, '4/3/2001', '7/10/2001', ...etc...)
SET IDENTITY_INSERT OFF
```

The other solution, of course, is to use an ordinary column of the appropriate data type and size for the primary key and not use an IDENTITY column at all. This allows the column to be defined to accept GUIDs if required; or even text so as to allow a combination of letters and numbers to be used as the row key. The problem with this is that all other applications using the data will probably need to be changed—in particular, every application will now have to generate the unique key values.

Reading the IDENTITY Value and Updating the Columns

Creating your own row keys while disconnected provides a way to connect the new rows in the Orders and Order Details tables in the remote DataSet. No matter how you end up actually persisting the data to the data store, you must generate these keys on the client—remote from the database. The previous technique requires that these keys be globally unique for all rows that are in the data store and for all rows that are in the process of being added by all other clients.

The technique you'll look at next avoids this requirement by allowing the database to create the appropriate value for the IDENTITY column when the data is persisted. It's also the generally favored approach because it'll always provide a unique key for the row once it has been persisted into the database.

To use this technique, you still have to generate row keys on the client, remote from the database. However, although the previous technique requires the keys to be globally unique for all rows everywhere, the next technique only requires them to be unique for the current DataSet. They can be the same as existing keys in the database and the same as the keys used in other instances of remote DataSets that are being edited by other clients. In effect, the keys you generate on the client are simply temporary or "dummy" key values. The only reason they're there is to relate the parent and child rows together in the remote DataSet.

Does the DataSet Contain a Relationship?

Before you get too involved in the process used in the example application, we should just expand on the way that the whole update process is affected by the presence or absence of a relationship between the tables in a DataSet. As you saw in earlier examples, it's possible to establish a relationship (a DataRelation object) within a DataSet that links two tables, using a primary key in the parent table and a foreign key in the child table. You did this in Chapter 2 in the OrderListData component, and you use the same technique in the GetOrderDetails method of the UpdateDataSet component described in this chapter:

```
...
'create a relationship between the two tables
Dim objParentCol, objChildCol As DataColumn
objParentCol = objDataSet.Tables("Orders").Columns("OrderID")
objChildCol = objDataSet.Tables("Order Details").Columns("OrderID")
Dim objRelation As New DataRelation("CustOrders", objParentCol, objChildCol)
objDataSet.Relations.Add(objRelation)
...
```

This creates a `UniqueConstraint` for the `OrderID` column of the parent `Orders` table and a `ForeignKeyConstraint` for the `OrderID` column of the child `Order Details` table. It prevents you from adding, deleting, or modifying rows that would break the referential integrity (and hence create orphan child rows in the `DataSet`).

Cascaded Deletes and Updates

By default, creating this relationship also implements automatic *cascading* of row deletes and updates to the primary key of a parent row. If you delete a parent row from the `Orders` table, all related child rows in the `Order Details` table are automatically deleted as well. If you change the value of the primary key (`OrderID`) for a parent row in the `Orders` table, the foreign key in all related child table rows (the `OrderID` values in the `Order Details` table) are automatically updated to the new value.

You can change this behavior by setting the `DeleteRule` and `UpdateRule` properties of the `ForeignKeyConstraint` object that was created when the relationship was added to the `DataSet`. Possible values for these properties come from the `Rule` enumeration:

- `Cascade`: (The default) related child rows are deleted, or the foreign key value is updated automatically.

- `None`: Related child rows aren't deleted or updated. Results in a runtime error when a row is deleted or a primary key value is changed unless the `EnforceConstraints` property of the `DataSet` is set to `False` first.

- `SetDefault`: The foreign key in related child rows is set to its default value or `null` if there's no value specified for the `DefaultValue` property of that column.

- `SetNull`: The foreign key in related child rows is set to `null`.

So, for example, you can disable all cascaded deletes and updates using this:

```
'get a reference to the ForeignKeyConstraint for the relationship
objConstraint = objDataSet.Relations("CustOrders").ChildKeyConstraint

'turn off cascaded deletes and updates
objConstraint.DeleteRule = Rule.None
objConstraint.UpdateRule = Rule.None
```

> **NOTE** *One important point that this raises is that you should* never *use triggers in the database, or any other database-specific events, to change or delete related rows when you have a relationship defined within the* DataSet *unless you disable cascaded deletes and/or updates for that relationship. Otherwise, the* Update *method of the* DataSet *will fail because it'll try to apply the cascaded deletes and/or updates to the child rows, which will already have been deleted or updated by the triggers.*

Accessing the IDENTITY Column Value

The next point to consider is how you might be able to access the value of an IDENTITY column in a row after you insert it into your database. You need to do this to make the technique hinted at earlier (reading the new IDENTITY value and updating the rows) work.

One of the lesser-known features of the Update method of the DataAdapter object is that it'll accept return values from a stored procedure and automatically persist these as the current values for that row in the table (within the DataSet) that was used to update the data store.

The UpdatedRowSource property of the Command object that the DataAdapter is using to push the changes into the data store (the Command object specified as the InsertCommand property) defines how any returned values are used. The default value for this property is UpdateRowSource.Both, which means that any return values from output parameters, or from a SELECT statement within the stored procedure, will be mapped to the current row in the table within the DataSet.

Other values that can be used for the UpdatedRowSource property are as follows: FirstReturnedRecord, where only data in the first row returned from the stored procedure is mapped and inserted into the row in the DataSet table; OutputParameters, where only data in the output parameters of the stored procedure is inserted into the row in the DataSet table; and None, where any returned data is ignored.

> **NOTE** *If you use* Command *objects that are autogenerated by a* CommandBuilder *object, the default value for the* UpdatedRowSource *property is* None. *In this case, the* Command *is using only a single SQL statement, so there can be no returned value.*

So, if you arrange for your stored procedure to return the OrderID value of the newly inserted row (the correct autogenerated primary key from the IDENTITY column), it'll replace the temporary key value in that row of the Orders table within your DataSet.

Interacting with the Update Method

Even though you can return the new value for the IDENTITY column and have it inserted into the table in the DataSet, using the features of the Update method just discussed, you may still need to interact with the DataAdapter object's Update method. It all depends on whether there's a relationship defined within the DataSet.

The Update process automatically sets the correct value for the primary key in the parent table. If there's a relationship defined within the DataSet, and cascaded updates are enabled, this value will also cascade to the foreign keys in all related child rows in the child table. Therefore, when the Update method is called subsequently for the child table in the DataSet, any inserted rows will already have the correct values for this column. You don't have to do anything special. Note, however, that this means you must apply the Update method to the parent table first and then the child table afterward.

However, if there's no relationship defined in the DataSet, you'll have to interact with the Update process to "manually cascade" the updates to the parent row's primary key into the related child rows. If not, the child rows will no longer be linked to the parent row—they will still have the original "dummy" primary key values and will become orphan rows. Because it's most likely that there will be a foreign key constraint defined within the database itself (to prevent loss of referential integrity), this means that the Update process will fail to insert them into the database.

And, unfortunately, things aren't just as simple as they appear so far. You'll recall from the previous chapter that to perform the now-famous FEGURM update process (Fill, Edit, GetChanges, Update, Refresh, and Merge), you use two DataSet objects. One holds the values that you apply to the data store to update the original data, and the other holds the user's edited values so that you can create the correct combination of current and original values in a DataSet to feed back to them afterward should any of the updates fail.

So, as part of the FEGURM process, you *will* need to interact with the DataAdapter object's Update method every time because you'll need to update the primary key and foreign key values for the inserted row in this second DataSet. Of course, if there's a relationship in this DataSet, you only need to update the row in the parent table because the update will then automatically cascade to the related child rows.

Using the Events of the DataAdapter Object

To be able to interact with the Update method of the DataAdapter object, you need to catch each INSERT process for the parent row before it's actually applied to the data store. At this point you can extract the temporary or "dummy" key value from the row. Then you apply the INSERT to the data store *without specifying the value for the primary key IDENTITY column*, allowing the database to set the value for this column automatically.

Once the new row has been inserted, you extract the value from the IDENTITY column of that row. If there's no relationship in the DataSet (meaning that updates aren't cascaded automatically), you can use the new value to update the foreign key column in the child rows within the current DataSet (replacing the temporary "dummy" values) before the Update method is called on this table. Of course, if there's a relationship between the tables, this step isn't required. Either way, when you subsequently call Update for the child table, the correct values for the foreign key columns will be inserted into the data store.

Next you must update the rows in the second DataSet that's holding the edited values sent from the client. Again, the presence or absence of a relationship governs whether the changes will cascade automatically or if you need to update the related child rows in this DataSet yourself.

So, you have to interact with the processing that takes place in the Update method in several ways:

You need to detect an INSERT *before* it's processed during execution of the Update method and access the row's values. You can do this by handling the RowUpdating event of the DataAdapter object. The values in the row that's about to be processed are available from the parameters (arguments) passed to the event handler.

You need to detect an INSERT *after* it's processed during execution of the Update method and access the row's values. You can do this by handling the RowUpdated event of the DataAdapter object. Again, the values of the row that has just been processed are available from the parameters (arguments) passed to the event handler.

You need to retrieve the "real" primary key value that was created in the IDENTITY column after the INSERT process has completed. You can do this by returning it from a stored procedure.

If there's a relationship set up between the tables in the DataSet, changes to the primary key value will by default cascade into the related child rows and update the foreign key automatically. However, if there's no relationship within the DataSet, you must apply the new primary key value to the matching foreign key column in all the related rows in any child tables. You can do this by accessing the DataSet that contains the new rows.

If you have a separate DataSet that was created by calling GetChanges on this DataSet, and you intend to Merge the two DataSet objects later (as part of the FEGURM process), you must update the value of the primary key in the same row of the parent table in that DataSet. Plus, if there's no relationship present in that DataSet, you must also update the value of the foreign key in all related child table rows as well. You can do all this by accessing the separate DataSet that contains these tables.

The DataAdapter object's Update method processes each changed row in a table within a DataSet in the order that the rows occur within that table. It may therefore process a deleted row followed by an inserted row followed by a modified row—it doesn't process all the deleted rows first, all the modified rows first, or all the inserted rows first. However, the RowUpdating and RowUpdated event parameters contain information about the process that's being executed at that point.

The Class-Level Variables

To be able to access objects and values within both the custom component method and the event handler routines, you need to use class-level variables to store references to these objects. In particular, you need to be able to store the temporary key value for a row while it's being processed, as well as references to the two DataSet objects that you use in the FEGURM update process. You can see these Private "member" variables declared at the start of the class file:

```
'declare variable to hold Order ID of inserted order rows
'used by event handlers for UpdateAllOrderDetails method
Private m_InsertOrderID As Integer

'declare variable to hold reference to DataSets during update process
'these are used by event handlers for UpdateAllOrderDetails method
Private m_ModifiedDataSet As DataSet
Private m_MarshaledDataSet As DataSet
```

Handling the RowUpdating Event

As you'll see later, the FEGURM update process in the component calls the Update method of the DataAdapter three times—but you configure the event handlers so that they're only called during the single Update process that pushes the changes to the Orders table into the data store.

Now the Update process will raise the RowUpdating event and call the event handler for each row it updates, just before it pushes the values into the data store. In the event handler (named OnRowUpdating), you can check what type of update process is about to be performed by examining the StatementType property of the RowUpdatingEventArgs object that's passed as a parameter to the event handler.

The value for this property comes from the StatementType enumeration (possible values are Insert, Delete, Update, and Select).

So, if it's an INSERT process, you can access the row and save the temporary "dummy" key value from the OrderID column in the class-level variable:

```
Sub OnRowUpdating(ByVal objSender As Object, _
                  ByVal objArgs As OleDbRowUpdatingEventArgs)

  'see if it's an INSERT statement. If so you need to save the
  'temporary order ID allocated on the client while disconnected

  If objArgs.StatementType = StatementType.Insert Then

    'save the temporary order ID in the class-level variable
    m_InsertOrderID = objArgs.Row("OrderID", DataRowVersion.Current)

  End If

End Sub
```

The Update process will now apply the INSERT to the data store, persisting the values to the Orders table. The value of the IDENTITY column will be created automatically (assuming that the UPDATE process succeeds, of course). The next step is to arrange for this value to be returned from the data store to the Update method so that the row in the DataSet is updated with the new IDENTITY value.

The OrdersInsert Stored Procedure

You need to extract and return the value of the IDENTITY column named OrderID from the Orders table in the database after inserting the new row. Rather than use an output parameter (which would mean treating the Command object for the InsertCommand property of the DataAdapter as a special case—you'll see what we mean later), the choice here is to return it from a SELECT statement within the stored procedure. The default value of the UpdatedRowSource property of the Command object (UpdateRowSource.Both) means that it'll still be used to populate the row in the DataSet table.

The following listing shows the complete OrdersInsert stored procedure that you use with the Update method to insert a new row into the Orders table:

```
CREATE PROCEDURE OrdersInsert
  @OrderID int, @NewCustomerID nvarchar(5), @NewOrderDate datetime,
  @NewRequiredDate datetime, @NewShippedDate datetime, @NewShipVia int,
```

```
@NewFreight money, @NewShipName nvarchar(40),
@NewShipAddress nvarchar(60), @NewShipCity nvarchar(15),
@NewShipPostalCode nvarchar(10), @NewShipCountry nvarchar(15)
AS
INSERT INTO Orders
 (CustomerID, OrderDate, RequiredDate, ShippedDate, ShipVia, Freight,
  ShipName, ShipAddress, ShipCity, ShipPostalCode, ShipCountry)
VALUES
 (@NewCustomerID, @NewOrderDate, @NewRequiredDate, @NewShippedDate,
  @NewShipVia, @NewFreight, @NewShipName, @NewShipAddress,
  @NewShipCity, @NewShipPostalCode, @NewShipCountry)
SELECT OrderID = @@IDENTITY
```

In the last line of the procedure, you get the "real" (autogenerated) value of the OrderID column from the internal @@IDENTITY variable that's automatically set to the value of the Identity column in the most recently inserted row during the current connection. This will be the new order row you just inserted. This doesn't affect the value of the ROWCOUNT either, so the stored procedure will still indicate to the Update method that it only affected one row, which is what you want.

> **NOTE** *Note that simply using* SELECT @@IDENTITY *will not result in the value being correctly returned and recognized by the* DataSet *object's* Update *process. It maps the rowset returned from the stored procedure to the original row in the table in the* DataSet, *so you must alias the* IDENTITY *value with the correct column name—in this case,* OrderID.

Handling the RowUpdated Event

After the InsertOrders stored procedure has been executed, the row in the DataSet table will contain the new and "proper" autogenerated OrderID value. Next, the Update method raises the RowUpdated event, and the event handler named OnRowUpdated executes. In it, as in the RowUpdating event handler, you first check that this event is for an inserted row. Remember that both the RowUpdating and RowUpdated events are raised for every changed row—not just inserted rows. Then you check if the number of rows affected by the process is one (1). If it is, you know that the insert succeeded, and you have a valid OrderID for the new row:

```
Sub OnRowUpdated(ByVal objSender As Object, _
                 ByVal objArgs As OleDbRowUpdatedEventArgs)
```

```
'see if its an INSERT statement
If objArgs.StatementType = StatementType.Insert Then

  'see if the insert was successful
  'expect 1 in success, zero or -1 on failure
  If objArgs.RecordsAffected = 1 Then
    ...
```

So now you can extract the new OrderID from the row that has just been inserted into the data store. A reference to the row being processed is passed to the event handler in the RowUpdatedEventArgs parameter, and you can access the OrderID column to get the value you want:

```
...
'get new order ID from IDENTITY column in this row
Dim intNewOrderID As Integer = objArgs.Row("OrderID", _
                                          DataRowVersion.Current)
...
```

In this example, and the ones provided in the samples for this book, there's a relationship in the DataSet between the Orders and Order Details tables. This relationship is created within the GetOrderDetails method of the UpdateDataSet component. So you don't have to worry about updating the OrderID foreign key column in the Order Details table. The new value will have cascaded automatically when the OrderID primary key value in the Orders table was updated with the value returned from the stored procedure.

If There's No Relationship...

However, if there's no relationship in the DataSet, you'd now have to use the OrderID value to update the foreign key values in all related child rows to preserve relational integrity and ensure that the rows are properly linked in the DataSet. You get a reference to all (any) related child rows in the DataSet by creating a reference to the Order Details table, and you also need an array to hold the related row references. Then you use the Select method of the table to select all rows that have the temporary OrderID that you saved in the class-level variable named m_InsertOrderID:

```
...
'* if there is no relationship, also need to update all matching
'rows in Order Details table of DataSet with new order ID
Dim objTable As DataTable = m_MarshaledDataSet.Tables("Order Details")
Dim arrRows() As DataRow
```

```
'use Select method to find all rows with the temporary order ID
arrRows = objTable.Select("OrderID = '" & m_InsertOrderID & "'")
...
```

Then it's simply a matter of iterating through the array updating each row that it references with the new (permanent) OrderID value:

```
...
'* iterate through these rows updating the order ID
Dim objRow As DataRow
For Each objRow In arrRows
  objRow("OrderID") = intNewOrderID
Next
...
```

> **NOTE** *These two sections of code aren't part of the sample component but are shown to demonstrate the process that would be required if there were no relationship in the* DataSet.

Updating the OrderID in the Second DataSet

Even if there is a relationship in the DataSet (as in this example), you haven't quite finished yet. The next two stages of the FEGURM process will extract (refresh) the values in the DataSet from the data store and then Merge them into the original DataSet. However, the original DataSet still contains the temporary "dummy" value for the OrderID. So you need to repeat the process for the original DataSet as well. You get a reference to the Orders table row with the original "dummy" value for its OrderID column using the Select method (as shown earlier) and then insert the new OrderID value:

```
...
'repeat process with the original DataSet, otherwise the
'rows will not be matched when the Merge method is used later
Dim objTable As DataTable = m_ModifiedDataSet.Tables("Orders")
Dim arrRows(), objRow As DataRow
arrRows = objTable.Select("OrderID = '" & m_InsertOrderID & "'")
For Each objRow In arrRows
  objRow("OrderID") = intNewOrderID
Next
```

As before, the update to the parent table row will automatically cascade to the related child rows because the DataSet does contain a relationship. Of course, if this DataSet didn't contain a relationship, you'd also need to update any child rows with the new permanent OrderID value—because it'll not have cascaded automatically in that case:

```
...
'* if there is no relationship, also need to update all matching
'rows in Order Details table of DataSet with new order ID
objTable = m_ModifiedDataSet.Tables("Order Details")
arrRows = objTable.Select("OrderID = '" & m_InsertOrderID & "'")
For Each objRow In arrRows
  objRow("OrderID") = intNewOrderID
Next
...
```

> **NOTE** *Again, this section of code isn't part of the sample component but is shown to demonstrate the process that would be required if there wasn't a relationship in the DataSet. You might consider testing for the presence of the relationship and conditionally executing the code to update the child table if you want the component to be able to handle both situations.*

Finally, you can write a Trace message and exit from the event handler:

```
    'write message to Trace object
    If m_CanTrace Then
      m_Context.Trace.Write("UpdateDataSet", _
                            "Inserted Order row with OrderID " _
                            & intNewOrderID.ToString())
    End If
   End If
  End If
End Sub
```

By updating the original DataSet as well as the one created by the GetChanges method of the FEGURM process, you ensure that the rows match when the Merge method is used, and the resulting DataSet returned from the process will contain only one row for the inserted row. If you fail to update both DataSet objects, you'll get one row with the temporary OrderID value and one with the permanent OrderID value that was created by the IDENTITY column in the database.

Using the Status Property

One point to note is that you haven't set any "return status" for the RowUpdated event in this example. The Status property of the RowUpdatedEventArgs object passed to the event handler indicates if there was an error and is also used to tell the Update method what to do next. If an error occurred during the update process for the current row, the Status property will have the value UpdateStatus.ErrorsOccurred. Within the event handler, you can set this property to one of three other values from the UpdateStatus enumeration:

- The default value is Continue, which indicates that the Update process should just carry on. However, if there was an error processing the current row, the Update process will stop and report an error. Recall that the default behavior for the Update method is to stop processing rows when the first update error is encountered.

- The second possible value is SkipCurrentRow, which is useful if there was an error in this row. The Update process will continue the updates with the next row.

- The third value you can use is SkipAllRemainingRows, which tells the Update process to stop but not report an error.

In the event handler, you didn't set the Status property at all—yet the process continues even if there's an error. This is because, as you'll recall from the previous chapter, you set the DataAdapter object's ContinueUpdateOnError property to True before you call the Update method:

```
'prevent exceptions being thrown due to concurrency errors
objDataAdapter.ContinueUpdateOnError = True
```

This causes the Update method to store the error messages from any rows that can't be updated in the RowError property of that row and continue execution with the next row. Effectively, it sets the Status property to SkipCurrentRow automatically if there's an error.

Remote Row Inserts Summary

OK, so all this might seem like a long-winded process compared to the much simpler solution of just creating random unique GUIDs or row keys and inserting these into the tables—as described earlier. However, the solution you've just seen is much more elegant, much more reliable, and solves the problem of having to create globally unique values. As long as the row keys are unique just within the current remote DataSet, the process will work and produce the correct result.

Avoiding the FEGURM Refresh

At this point, it's time to look around the room to see how many hands are once again waving furiously in the air. In the previous section, you saw how the DataAdapter object's Update method inserts the OrderID you extract from the IDENTITY column in the data source table into the current row of the DataSet table. This happens solely because you return a row from the stored procedure that contains just a single column—the new OrderID value.

So the question is: What would happen if the stored procedure returned the complete row from the data source table? As you've probably already guessed, it'll update all the columns in the DataSet with the current database values—the underlying values. This is just what you need as part of the FEGURM process so that—when you Merge this DataSet with the original one you created with the GetChanges method—you'll get the correct combination of current and original values in the final DataSet.

This means that you could avoid one step of the FEGURM process—the "refresh" step that uses the Fill method to fetch the underlying values from the data store and update the DataSet (you end up with a FEGUM process instead). In fact, this is the technique that the Visual Studio.NET Data Form Wizard uses when it builds a Windows Form for handling data updates. You'll see more of this in Chapter 13, when you look at the version of the customer orders application that uses the .NET Framework on the client.

Performance and Other Considerations: FEGUM vs. FEGURM

There's a performance penalty with using the FEGUM approach. Every individual update to the data in the DataSet will result in two operations within the stored procedure (or two SQL statements in the case of the Data Form Wizard's default approach). The appropriate UPDATE, DELETE, or INSERT statement will execute, as you saw in the previous chapter, followed by a SELECT statement that builds the rowset to return to the Update method.

When you use the FEGURM process you investigated and saw demonstrated in the previous chapter, you only execute the appropriate UPDATE, DELETE, or INSERT statement that updates the data store (the OrderID value returned from the INSERT stored procedure is obtained from the @@IDENTITY internal variable and doesn't require a separate data access operation). After all the updates have been applied, you execute the Fill method to refresh all the changed rows with the underlying values. This involves only a single SELECT statement (the one that was originally used to extract the data from the data store).

Of course, if you're only performing one or two updates each time, the difference will be negligible. However, the whole purpose of using an architecture that allows multiple remote updates to be performed is to allow several rows to be updated in one go.

The other important point concerns the number of rows for which the original values in the final DataSet are refreshed. The FEGUM approach only refreshes the rows that are updated—the ones that have been changed by the user and for which an INSERT or UPDATE stored procedure has been called. However, the FEGURM process refreshes all the rows in the DataSet. This means that the client will see the values that are in the database now for all the rows in the returned DataSet, reducing the chance of concurrency errors occurring for subsequent updates.

As you keep discovering, there's no "correct" approach for all situations, and you need to design your applications and components to best suit the tasks that they have to accomplish.

So, after the detour to look at both tracing from within a component and solving the problem of handling remotely inserted rows, you can get back to looking at the method in the data access component that performs the updates to the data store.

The UpdateAllOrderDetails Method

There's one public method in the UpdateDataSet data access component that you use to push all the updates back into the data store. This method, named UpdateAllOrderDetails, does all the work of managing multiple changes within a DataSet as one operation, persisting these changes into the database and detecting concurrency or other errors. It uses exactly the same techniques as you used in the ASP.NET page code at the end of the previous chapter—implementing the final four stages of the FEGURM (Fill, Edit, GetChanges, Update, Refresh, and Merge) process. The first two stages are, of course, completed before the DataSet is passed to the component's method.

As well as the DataSet containing the changes to the data, this method accepts one other parameter. To be able to refresh the DataSet and obtain the underlying row values from the data store, you need the customer ID so that you can extract only the appropriate matching rows. So, the declaration of the UpdateAllOrderDetails method looks like this:

```
Public Function UpdateAllOrderDetails(ByVal CustomerID As String, _
          ByRef ModifiedDataSet As DataSet) As DataSet
```

Starting the Process

Once you receive the DataSet from the client, you can call the GetChanges method
to obtain a new DataSet containing only the changed rows. The first step in the
code is to set the class-level variable m_ModifiedDataSet to the DataSet sent from
the client, which will allow you to access it in the RowUpdated event handler later,
and you also write a message to the Trace object:

```
'save reference to original DataSet in class-level variable
'for use in event handlers while updating
m_ModifiedDataSet = ModifiedDataSet

'write message to Trace object for display in ASP.NET page
If m_CanTrace Then
  m_Context.Trace.Write("UpdateDataSet", "Starting Order Update Process")
End If
```

The Merge process absolutely requires the primary keys of the tables you'll
be updating to have been previously set. The Orders table uses only the OrderID
column as the primary key, and the Order Details table requires the OrderID and
ProductID columns to create the primary key. However, the DataSet returned from
the GetOrderDetails method within the component specifies the primary keys for
the Orders and Order Details tables.

And, because you haven't included code in the event handlers for the
RowUpdating and RowUpdated events to handle the situation where there's no relationship between the tables, you also demand that this relationship must already
exist in the DataSet sent to the method. Again, the GetOrderDetails method defines
this relationship in the DataSet, so you don't have to do anything more.

Differences Between the DataSet in Versions 1.0 and 1.1

Version 1.1 of the .NET Framework is in reality a "fix" and "extend" release, adding
a few useful extra features to some of the existing version 1.0 classes (such as the
HasRows property for the DataReader). It also fixes many of the issues and minor
bugs that have been detected since the final release of version 1.0. In particular,
this affects the DataSet. Although the external interface of the DataSet hasn't
changed between versions 1.0 and 1.1 (which provides backward and forward
compatibility), the internal workings have changed to solve some of the problems
that were discovered.

In the next chapter, you'll see two examples of "issues" with the DataSet that
we discovered in the first few weeks after the release of version 1.0—both involving

the reading and parsing of an XML diffgram (see the "Working Around the Empty Diffgram Issue" and "Working Around the Extra Rows Issue" sections in that chapter). However, there's one other change that can affect your existing version 1.0 code when running under version 1.1, and this isn't clearly documented elsewhere.

It's permissible to define the primary key(s) of tables within a DataSet that are already filled (in other words, tables that contain existing data rows). In theory, this isn't best practice, and you should really specify all the schema details (such as primary keys) before filling the table. However, when using the Fill method, where the schema of the database table is automatically used to define the schema of the DataTable objects within the DataSet, you have no choice but to set the primary keys while the tables contain rows.

However, if the DataSet has been filled from a diffgram that contains deleted rows, setting the primary keys afterward is only possible in version 1.0 of the DataSet. In version 1.1, attempting to do so produces a DeletedRowInaccessibleException with the message "Deleted row information cannot be accessed through the row."

For this reason, you can't include code in the component that sets the primary keys of the table because this would prevent it working with some versions of the application that use diffgrams (see Chapters 11 and 12). This is why you make sure that the DataSet you generate in the GetOrderDetails method sets the primary keys for the tables when it creates the DataSet. If you don't intend to use diffgrams, you might be able to get away with setting the primary keys afterward. A good plan would be to check for the presence of the primary key in each table first and then set it only if required. Alternatively, you could add a parameter to the method that indicates if it should attempt to add primary keys to the table.

The GetChanges Stage

After a detour discussing the DataSet class, you can now return to the UpdateAllOrderDetails method. You call the GetChanges method to create the separate DataSet that you'll be using to perform the updates and store this reference in the class-level variable m_MarshaledDataSet:

```
'marshal changed rows only into new DataSet
'require class-level reference for use in event handlers
m_MarshaledDataSet = m_ModifiedDataSet.GetChanges()
```

Note that the GetChanges method is intelligent. If there's more than one table in a DataSet and the tables are related through a DataRelation object (which establishes a foreign key constraint between the related tables), child rows can't exist if there's no matching parent row. This would violate referential integrity within the

DataSet. In the case of the DataSet, every Order Details row must have a matching Orders row.

As an example, imagine a DataSet that contains added, modified, or deleted child rows but where the parent rows for these child rows are unchanged (not marked as added, modified, or deleted). You can use the GetChanges method to create a new DataSet from this original DataSet. The new DataSet will contain only changed (added, modified, or deleted) rows from the parent and child tables, plus any unchanged parent rows that are required to maintain referential integrity.

Which Table Should You Update First?

Before you look at the next stage in the component, which is responsible for applying the changes in the DataSet to the back-end data store, you need to take another short detour to consider a rather thorny issue that raises its head at this point. In the example you looked at in the previous chapter, you only had one table to update. Here, you have two related tables: Orders and Order Details. The big question is: In what order should you apply the updates to the data store?

If you update the Orders table rows first, you'll allow any inserted orders to be persisted to the data store before you try and insert any related order line rows into the Order Details table. This fits in nicely with the earlier discussions about how (and why) you retrieve the "real" value for the OrderID from the Orders table in the database and then cascade it into the related rows in the Order Details child table of the DataSet.

Besides, if you did it the other way round, the foreign key constraints in the database would prevent the Order Details rows from being inserted because there would be no matching parent Orders row in the database. Plus, the event handlers wouldn't work because the correct OrderID value can only be obtained after inserting the parent row into the Orders table in the database.

> **NOTE** *Notice that when you updated the tables in the down-level client examples in Chapter 8, you didn't have this problem. The client interface forces the user to insert a new order row first, before they can add any order line rows to it. When you allow multiple remote changes to be made to the data, you have to consider how you handle new rows in related tables.*

The issue you now have to resolve is that when you come to delete an order row from the Orders table, you have to delete all the order lines for this order from the Order Details table first. The database itself is most likely to contain a foreign key constraint to prevent a parent row that has existing related child rows from being deleted in order to maintain referential integrity. However, you've just seen that you can't process the Order Details child table first. You have to process the Orders table first to allow new rows to be inserted.

Deleting Related Child Rows

This dilemma has no simple "one-click" solution. One approach is to use a stored procedure (for the DeleteCommand of the DataAdapter that updates the Orders table) that automatically deletes all the related child rows from the Order Details table before it deletes the parent row. This will maintain referential integrity and avoid foreign key constraint conflicts. An alternative approach is for the database itself to contain rules or triggers that specify a "cascade deletes" action so that child rows are automatically deleted when the parent row is deleted.

The only problem with this approach is that when you delete a parent row within a DataSet that's remote from the database (during the editing process in the rich client), the child rows will remain in that DataSet. Of course, if you have a relationship between the tables in the DataSet, this will cascade the delete to any related child rows. And if there's no relationship, you'll expect to have to perform this cascade process yourself anyway.

The point is that the child rows will still be there in the DataSet, marked as deleted (they'll have the value DataRowState.Deleted from their RowState property). But the stored procedure (or the database rules and/or triggers) has to remove them from the table in the database first in order to delete the parent row. When you subsequently call the Update method for the Order Details table, it'll also attempt to delete these rows from the database—so will report an error for each one.

To prevent this, you'd have to make sure that all the related child rows have already been removed from the DataSet. Notice we said *removed*, not deleted. As long as the child rows don't appear in the child table (rather than just being marked as deleted), the Update method will succeed without reporting errors.

Unfortunately, this process has another side-affect (as mentioned in Chapter 8) that might not be acceptable. The stored procedure is unlikely to have access to all the current child row values from the client, so it can't perform concurrency checks when it deletes all the related child rows. It'd be possible to add lots of extra parameters to the stored procedure to pass these values into it as well, but the process is extremely complicated (for example, you don't know how many child rows there would be), and it'd soon get completely out of hand. Thankfully, there's a better way—as you'll see next.

A Better Solution: Select and Update Arrays of Rows

A far better approach to the problem of handling related child rows when the parent row is deleted is to perform the update process for the child table in two separate stages. The GetChanges method you use to create a DataSet containing only changed rows can also be used to get just the inserted rows or just the deleted rows (see the section "The GetChanges Method" in the previous chapter for details). So you could perform the updates to the tables in the correct order for both inserted and deleted rows by splitting the process into two separate operations and then merging the rows into a single DataSet again afterward. In this case, the stored procedure would only have to delete the parent row because a separate one would have already deleted all the related child rows.

Even better, and the solution for the component in this chapter, is to take advantage of the DataAdapter object's Update method overload that accepts an array of rows, rather than a DataSet object. Using this, you can apply the Update method with just the deleted child rows from the Order Details table first, then update the parent Orders table, and finally update the inserted and modified rows from the Order Details table. So everything happens in the correct order to avoid foreign key constraint errors, and you get full concurrency checking on the deleted child rows as well.

To get an array of rows from a DataSet table, you can use the Select method. If you use Nothing (null in C#) for the first two parameters (the filter expression and sort order parameters), you'll get an array of all the rows in the table. However, if you add the third parameter for the row state (a value from the DataViewRowState enumeration), you'll only get rows that have the specified value for their RowState property. So, the process in overview is as follows:

```
'apply updates for deleted rows from child table
DataAdapter.Update(child-table.Select(Nothing, Nothing, _
                                      DataViewRowState.Deleted))


'apply updates for all rows from parent table
DataAdapter.Update(DataSet, "parent-table")


'apply updates for inserted and modified rows from child table
DataAdapter.Update(child-table.Select(Nothing, Nothing, _
                                      DataViewRowState.CurrentRows))
```

NOTE *The value* CurrentRows *includes unchanged rows, added rows, and modified rows. Of course, the* Update *method ignores unchanged rows, so only inserted and modified rows will actually be processed in the final line of the previous code.*

The Update Stage

Now that you've seen the theoretical side of the process, you can look at the code in the component. You start by creating a Connection to the data store and displaying the connection string along with the other Trace messages. Next, you create two DataAdapter objects—one for each table you're going to update—and set the ContinueUpdateOnError property to True for both (as in the discussion and example in the previous chapter):

```
'write message to Trace object for display in ASP.NET page
If m_CanTrace Then
  m_Context.Trace.Write("UpdateDataSet", "Creating Connection: " _
                        & m_ConnectString)
End If


'create a Connection object using the connection string
Dim objConnect As New OleDbConnection(m_ConnectString)


'create two new DataAdapter objects, one to update each table
Dim objDAOrders As New OleDbDataAdapter()
Dim objDAOrderDetails As New OleDbDataAdapter()


'prevent exceptions being thrown due to concurrency errors
objDAOrders.ContinueUpdateOnError = True
objDAOrderDetails.ContinueUpdateOnError = True
```

In the previous chapter you used SQL statements to demonstrate the update and reconciliation process. However, in this component you want to use stored procedures instead, so you need to create three appropriately configured Command objects that the DataAdapter will use to persist the updates to the data store.

We've written a couple of functions (GetOrdersCommand and GetOrderLinesCommand) that create the appropriate Command objects for each of the tables you'll be updating, and you'll examine these functions later. To use them, all you need to do is specify the name of the stored procedure, pass in a reference to the Connection object you previously created, and indicate whether the Command object you want is to be used for an INSERT, UPDATE, or DELETE operation:

```
'write message to Trace object for display in ASP.NET page
If m_CanTrace Then
  m_Context.Trace.Write("UpdateDataSet", _
                        "Creating Commands and Setting Parameter Values")
End If
```

```
'specify Command objects using separate custom functions that
'take name of stored procedure, connection object and action
'first for DataAdapter that updates Orders table
objDAOrders.UpdateCommand = GetOrdersCommand("OrdersUpdate", _
                                        objConnect, "UPDATE")
objDAOrders.InsertCommand = GetOrdersCommand("OrdersInsert", _
                                        objConnect, "INSERT")
objDAOrders.DeleteCommand = GetOrdersCommand("OrdersDelete", _
                                        objConnect, "DELETE")

'then for DataAdapter that updates Order Details table
objDAOrderDetails.UpdateCommand = GetOrderLinesCommand("OrderLinesUpdate", _
                                        objConnect, "UPDATE")
objDAOrderDetails.InsertCommand = GetOrderLinesCommand("OrderLinesInsert", _
                                        objConnect, "INSERT")
objDAOrderDetails.DeleteCommand = GetOrderLinesCommand("OrderLinesDelete", _
                                        objConnect, "DELETE")
```

Updating the Deleted Child Rows in the Order Details Table

You're now ready to start updating the data store, and the first step is to apply the updates for only the deleted rows in the Order Details child table. You declare a variable to hold the number of rows updated (for use in the Trace messages), get a reference to the Order Details table in the DataSet, and perform the update for the deleted rows only:

```
'local variable to hold number of rows affected for Tracing
Dim intRowsAffected As Integer

'get reference to Order Details table
Dim objTable As DataTable
objTable = m_MarshaledDataSet.Tables("Order Details")

'write message to Trace object for display in ASP.NET page
If m_CanTrace Then
  m_Context.Trace.Write("UpdateDataSet", "Deleting Order Details rows")
End If

Try

  'delete child rows in Order Details table
  intRowsAffected = objDAOrderDetails.Update(objTable.Select(Nothing, _
                            Nothing, DataViewRowState.Deleted))
```

```
'write number of rows updated to Trace object
If m_CanTrace Then
  m_Context.Trace.Write("UpdateDataSet", "Deleted " _
                        & intRowsAffected.ToString() & " row(s)")
End If

Catch objError As Exception

  'raise the error to the calling routine
  Throw objError

End Try
```

As you saw earlier, the Select method of the table returns an array of DataRow objects, and you can pass this array directly to the Update method. Internally, this method references the parent table for the DataRow object, and it can obtain all the information it requires for the update from this.

> **NOTE** *As an aside, this provides a useful reminder about object-oriented programming principles in general. The array of* DataRow *objects is, of course, just an array of references to the* DataRow *objects in the original table that meet the criteria you specified—those with a* RowState *property value of* Deleted. *If you modify a row through the array of* DataRow *objects, you're actually modifying the row in the original table.*

Setting the Update Event Handlers and Updating the Orders Table

We spent some time earlier in this chapter discussing the problems of inserting new rows into a remote DataSet and then persisting these new rows into the data store where the parent row contains an IDENTITY column. You saw the solution and the event handlers you can use to implement this solution. So, before you execute the Update method for the Orders table, you must configure the DataAdapter to call the event handlers when the RowUpdating and RowUpdated events are raised. The two event handlers are elsewhere in this class file and are named OnRowUpdating and OnRowUpdated:

```
'add event handlers for RowUpdating and RowUpdated events
AddHandler objDAOrders.RowUpdating, _
        New OleDbRowUpdatingEventHandler(AddressOf OnRowUpdating)
AddHandler objDAOrders.RowUpdated, _
        New OleDbRowUpdatedEventHandler(AddressOf OnRowUpdated)
```

Now you can create a variable to hold the number of rows that each update process actually affects (to use in our trace messages) and call the Update method to push the changes from the Orders table into the data store. Any error is raised to the calling routine:

```
'write message to Trace object for display in ASP.NET page
If m_CanTrace Then
  m_Context.Trace.Write("UpdateDataSet", "Processing Orders rows")
End If

Try

  'perform the updates on the original data
  intRowsAffected = objDAOrders.Update(m_MarshaledDataSet, "Orders")

  'write number of rows updated to Trace object
  If m_CanTrace Then
    m_Context.Trace.Write("UpdateDataSet", "Updated " _
                         & intRowsAffected.ToString() & " row(s)")
  End If

Catch objError As Exception

  'raise the error to the calling routine
  Throw objError

End Try
```

You only want your custom event handlers to execute while updating the Orders table. Once this table has been updated, any related rows in the child Order Details table, and the matching rows in the original DataSet referenced by the variable m_ModifiedDataSet, will have the correct values for the OrderID primary key and foreign key columns. So the next step is to remove the event handlers from the DataAdapter object:

```
'remove the event handlers for RowUpdating and RowUpdated events
RemoveHandler objDAOrders.RowUpdating, AddressOf OnRowUpdating
RemoveHandler objDAOrders.RowUpdated, AddressOf OnRowUpdated
```

> **NOTE** *In fact, because you don't use this* DataAdapter *again, you don't have to remove the event handlers. However, it's good practice and will prevent the possibility of an error arising at some later stage if you modified the code and did reuse the* DataAdapter.

Updating the Order Details Rows

The final part of the update stage is to process the inserted and modified rows in the Order Details table in the DataSet. The only difference between the code here and the previous update to the Order Details table is the DataViewRowState value you use in the Select method:

```
'write message to Trace object for display in ASP.NET page
If m_CanTrace Then
  m_Context.Trace.Write("UpdateDataSet", _
                        "Processing Remaining Order Detail Rows")
End If

Try

  'insert new child rows and update modified ones in Order Details table
  intRowsAffected = objDAOrderDetails.Update(objTable.Select(Nothing, _
                                   Nothing, DataViewRowState.CurrentRows))

  'write number of rows updated to Trace object
  If m_CanTrace Then
    m_Context.Trace.Write("UpdateDataSet", "Inserted/Updated " _
                        & intRowsAffected.ToString() & " row(s)")
  End If

Catch objError As Exception

  'raise the error to the calling routine
  Throw objError

End Try
```

The Refresh Stage

The next step is to refresh the DataSet contents with the values in the data store. This is where the underlying values will be placed into the DataSet rows, ready for any update failures to be reconciled by the user later. You use the same two stored procedures as you did in the GetOrderDetails method in this component (and in the UpdateOrders component) to extract the order and order line rows from the data store. Both of these require only the customer ID (passed to the method as a parameter) as the single stored procedure parameter:

```
'specify the stored procedures to extract the original data
Dim strSelectOrders As String = "OrdersForEditByCustID"
Dim strSelectOrderLines As String = "OrderLinesForEditByCustID"
```

Refreshing the Orders Rows

You start by creating a new Command object to refresh rows from the Orders table in the data store, add the CustID parameter, and assign the Command to the DataAdapter you used to update the Orders table earlier. Then you can execute the Fill method to update the DataSet, and write a Trace message showing the result:

```
Try

  'write message to Trace object for display in ASP.NET page
  If m_CanTrace Then
    m_Context.Trace.Write("UpdateDataSet", _
                          "Starting Refresh Orders Table")
  End If

  'create a new Command object
  Dim objCommand As New OleDbCommand(strSelectOrders, objConnect)
  objCommand.CommandType = CommandType.StoredProcedure

  'add the required parameter
  objCommand.Parameters.Add("CustID", CustomerID)

  'assign to SelectCommand of Orders DataAdapter object
  objDAOrders.SelectCommand = objCommand

  'refresh the Orders table from the stored procedure
  intRowsAffected = objDAOrders.Fill(m_MarshaledDataSet, "Orders")
```

```
'write number of rows updated to Trace object
If m_CanTrace Then
  m_Context.Trace.Write("UpdateDataSet", "Refreshed " _
                        & intRowsAffected.ToString() & " row(s)")
End If
```

Refreshing the Order Details Rows

To refresh the Order Details table, you just have to change the stored procedure name in the existing Command object and assign it to the DataAdapter you previously used to update the Order Details table. Then you call Fill to update the DataSet and write another Trace message showing the outcome:

```
'change the stored procedure name in the Command
objCommand.CommandText = strSelectOrderLines

'assign to SelectCommand of Order Details DataAdapter object
objDAOrderDetails.SelectCommand = objCommand

'write message to Trace object for display in ASP.NET page
If m_CanTrace Then
  m_Context.Trace.Write("UpdateDataSet", _
                        "Starting Refresh Order Details Table")
End If

'refresh the Order Details table from the stored procedure
intRowsAffected = objDAOrderDetails.Fill(m_MarshaledDataSet, "Order Details")

'write number of rows updated to Trace object
If m_CanTrace Then
  m_Context.Trace.Write("UpdateDataSet", "Refreshed " _
                        & intRowsAffected.ToString() & " row(s)")
End If

Catch objError As Exception

  Throw objError

End Try
```

Because the tables in the DataSet have a primary key defined, the rows extracted from the data store are matched to the existing rows in the DataSet automatically. Again, this is the same process as you used in the example in the previous chapter.

The Merge Stage

To get the underlying values that are now in the new DataSet into the original DataSet, you use the Merge method. By setting the optional second parameter to True, you indicate that only the original values for each column should be updated, leaving the current values intact. As you saw in the previous chapter, this results in each row containing the value that the user entered as the current value and the underlying data store value as the original value:

```
'write message to Trace object for display in ASP.NET page
If m_CanTrace Then
  m_Context.Trace.Write("UpdateDataSet", "Starting Merge DataSet")
End If


'use parameter to preserve changes
m_ModifiedDataSet.Merge(m_MarshaledDataSet, True)
```

Returning the Updated DataSet

The final step in the component is to return the updated DataSet. You also write a Trace message to indicate that the method of the component has completed successfully:

```
If m_CanTrace Then
  m_Context.Trace.Write("UpdateDataSet", "Returning Updated DataSet")
End If

'return all rows including successful updates
Return m_ModifiedDataSet

End Function
```

So, as you can see, the outline process you use in the data access component is identical to that you used in the example of the previous chapter. The only real differences are that you're working with two tables here (rather than just one), and you're using stored procedures to perform the updates. You also included the extra code to correctly handle inserted rows and to write progress and status information to the ASP.NET Trace object throughout the method.

Creating the Parameterized Command Objects

The one aspect of the UpdateAllOrderDetails method we skipped in the previous sections is how you create the parameterized Command objects to use for the DataAdapter object's InsertCommand, DeleteCommand, and UpdateCommand properties.

One of the issues with using parameterized stored procedures is the repetitive code that's required to populate the Parameters collection of each Command object. The three Command objects you have to provide for the DataAdapter to use with the Update method require similar sets of parameters, and it makes sense to create separate routines that can build the Parameters collections and then reuse these routines wherever possible. This is what we've done in our component.

The Stored Procedures for the Orders Table

To update the Orders table in the data store, you provide three stored procedures within the database—named OrdersUpdate, OrdersInsert, and OrdersDelete. As you can see from the following listings of these stored procedures, the set of parameters they require are similar. The first listing shows the OrdersUpdate stored procedure:

```
CREATE PROCEDURE OrdersUpdate
    @OrderID int, @NewCustomerID nvarchar(5), @NewOrderDate datetime,
    @NewRequiredDate datetime, @NewShippedDate datetime,
    @NewShipVia int, @NewFreight money, @NewShipName nvarchar(40),
    @NewShipAddress nvarchar(60), @NewShipCity nvarchar(15),
    @NewShipPostalCode nvarchar(10), @NewShipCountry nvarchar(15),
    @OldCustomerID nvarchar(5), @OldOrderDate datetime,
    @OldRequiredDate datetime, @OldShippedDate datetime,
    @OldShipVia int, @OldFreight money, @OldShipName  nvarchar(40),
    @OldShipAddress nvarchar(60), @OldShipCity nvarchar(15),
    @OldShipPostalCode nvarchar(10), @OldShipCountry nvarchar(15)
AS UPDATE Orders SET
    CustomerID = @NewCustomerID, OrderDate = @NewOrderDate,
    RequiredDate = @NewRequiredDate, ShippedDate = @NewShippedDate,
    ShipVia = @NewShipVia, Freight = @NewFreight, ShipName = @NewShipName,
    ShipAddress = @NewShipAddress, ShipCity = @NewShipCity,
    ShipPostalCode = @NewShipPostalCode, ShipCountry = @NewShipCountry
```

```
WHERE
  CustomerID = @OldCustomerID AND OrderDate = @OldOrderDate AND
  RequiredDate = @OldRequiredDate AND ShippedDate = @OldShippedDate AND
  ShipVia = @OldShipVia AND Freight = @OldFreight AND
  ShipName = @OldShipName AND ShipAddress = @OldShipAddress AND
  ShipCity = @OldShipCity AND ShipPostalCode = @OldShipPostalCode AND
  ShipCountry = @OldShipCountry
```

One important point to bear in mind is that, when using the OleDb data access objects, parameters are mapped by position, not by name. In other words, the order of the parameters in the Parameters collection of the Command object must be identical to the order of the parameter declarations within the stored procedure.

If they're not, and the data types are different, you'll get an error when the code runs. However, in an UPDATE stored procedure, it's common to have two "sets" of parameters that are the same as far as data type and size go, but that contain different values. This is how you pass the "old" (original) and "new" (current) values into the stored procedure to perform concurrency checking within the WHERE clause. If you get the old and new values reversed there will be no error, but the update will fail because you'll then be using the wrong set of values in the WHERE clause.

You'll also notice here that you provide the facility to update all of the columns except the primary key (OrderID). In fact, in this application, you won't allow users to update some of the columns—in the case of the Orders table, for example, you won't allow them to change the OrderDate column values for existing orders. However, this is a business rules decision. The data access tier could well prove to be more flexible for use in future applications if you keep the business rules separate from the data access process. And, of course, this is one of the principles of the *n*-tier design strategy anyway.

The OrdersDelete Stored Procedure

The stored procedure that deletes rows from the Orders table needs only the "old" values to ensure that another user hasn't changed the row while the client was editing the data remotely:

```
CREATE PROCEDURE OrdersDelete
  @OrderID int, @OldCustomerID nvarchar(5), @OldOrderDate datetime,
  @OldRequiredDate datetime, @OldShippedDate datetime, @OldShipVia int,
  @OldFreight money, @OldShipName  nvarchar(40),
  @OldShipAddress nvarchar(60), @OldShipCity nvarchar(15),
  @OldShipPostalCode nvarchar(10), @OldShipCountry nvarchar(15)
AS
```

```
DELETE FROM Orders WHERE
   OrderID = @OrderID AND CustomerID = @OldCustomerID AND
   OrderDate = @OldOrderDate AND RequiredDate = @OldRequiredDate AND
   ShippedDate = @OldShippedDate AND ShipVia = @OldShipVia AND
   Freight = @OldFreight AND ShipName = @OldShipName AND
   ShipAddress = @OldShipAddress AND ShipCity = @OldShipCity AND
   ShipPostalCode = @OldShipPostalCode AND ShipCountry = @OldShipCountry
```

The OrdersInsert Stored Procedure

As you've seen earlier in this chapter, inserting new rows into the Orders table is more complex for remotely edited data because of the requirement to properly handle IDENTITY column values. The OrderID column is an IDENTITY column, so the new order ID will be created automatically. You saw in the previous sections of this chapter how you handle this, and the stored procedure you use is as follows:

```
CREATE PROCEDURE OrdersInsert
   @OrderID int, @NewCustomerID nvarchar(5), @NewOrderDate datetime,
   @NewRequiredDate datetime, @NewShippedDate datetime, @NewShipVia int,
   @NewFreight money, @NewShipName nvarchar(40),
   @NewShipAddress nvarchar(60), @NewShipCity nvarchar(15),
   @NewShipPostalCode nvarchar(10), @NewShipCountry nvarchar(15)
AS
INSERT INTO Orders
 (CustomerID, OrderDate, RequiredDate, ShippedDate, ShipVia, Freight,
  ShipName, ShipAddress, ShipCity, ShipPostalCode, ShipCountry)
VALUES
 (@NewCustomerID, @NewOrderDate, @NewRequiredDate, @NewShippedDate,
  @NewShipVia, @NewFreight, @NewShipName, @NewShipAddress,
  @NewShipCity, @NewShipPostalCode, @NewShipCountry)
SELECT OrderID = @@IDENTITY
```

To understand why you need to return the value of the OrderID, look back at the section "Managing IDENTITY Columns for Inserted Rows" earlier in this chapter.

The GetOrdersCommand Function

The next function creates the Command objects for updating the Orders table. It starts by creating a new Command object, using the stored procedure name and the Connection object passed in as parameters to this function:

```
Private Function GetOrdersCommand(ByVal strStoredProcName As String, _
                                  ByRef objConnect As OleDbConnection, _
                                  ByVal strCommandType As String) _
                                  As OleDbCommand

  'creates a new Command object and adds parameters, specifying the
  'column name and version from which values will be taken

  Dim objCommand As New OleDbCommand(strStoredProcName, objConnect)
  objCommand.CommandType = CommandType.StoredProcedure
```

Next you get a reference to the Parameters collection of the Command object and add the one parameter that's common to all the Command objects—the order ID. Even though you won't allow the user to edit this value (it's the row key, and doing so would break referential integrity in the database), you specify that the value for this parameter should be the original value of the OrderID for each row:

```
Dim colParams As OleDbParameterCollection = objCommand.Parameters
Dim objParam As OleDbParameter

objParam = colParams.Add("OrderID", OleDbType.Integer, 4, "OrderID")
objParam.SourceVersion = DataRowVersion.Original
```

Now you can add the remaining parameters, depending on what type of Command object you want. If it's to be used in the InsertCommand property of the DataAdapter, you don't want to add the set of parameters for the old values. However, for the DeleteCommand and UpdateCommand, you do need the old values to use in the WHERE clause in the stored procedures. Note that you use the original values of the columns in each row as the parameter values:

```
If strCommandType <> "INSERT" Then
  'add "Original" parameter values for Delete and Update actions
  objParam = colParams.Add("OldCustomerID", OleDbType.Char, _
                                          5, "CustomerID")
  objParam.SourceVersion = DataRowVersion.Original
  objParam = colParams.Add("OldOrderDate", OleDbType.DBDate, _
```

```
                                      4, "OrderDate")
   ...
   ... other parameter declarations removed for clarity
   ...

   objParam = colParams.Add("OldShipCountry", OleDbType.VarChar, _
                                      15, "ShipCountry")
   objParam.SourceVersion = DataRowVersion.Original
End If
```

To prevent unnecessary repetition, we've removed the code for some of the parameters from the listing to allow you to more easily see the process. Remember that you can view the complete code using the View Page Source and View Component Source links in the example pages.

Next, if the Command object you're creating is to be used in the DeleteCommand property of the DataAdapter, you don't want to add the set of parameters for the new values. However, for the InsertCommand and UpdateCommand you do need the new values to set or update the column values in the database. For the new values, you use the current values of the columns in each row as the parameter values:

```
If strCommandType <> "DELETE" Then
    'add "Current" parameter values for Update and Insert actions
    objParam = colParams.Add("NewCustomerID", OleDbType.Char, _
                                       5, "CustomerID")
    objParam.SourceVersion = DataRowVersion.Current
    objParam = colParams.Add("NewOrderDate", OleDbType.DBDate, _
                                       4, "OrderDate")
    ...
    ... other parameter declarations removed for clarity
    ...

    objParam = colParams.Add("NewShipCountry", OleDbType.VarChar, _
                                       15, "ShipCountry")
    objParam.SourceVersion = DataRowVersion.Current
End If

Return objCommand

End Function
```

At the end of the preceding code, once you've populated the Parameters collection, you simply return the new Command object to the method in the component.

The Stored Procedures for the Order Details Table

Updating the Order Details table rows is a similar process to that you've just seen for the Orders table. However, there are fewer columns to deal with, so the stored procedures and function code are simpler. The OrderLinesUpdate stored procedure is as follows:

```
CREATE PROCEDURE OrderLinesUpdate
  @OrderID int, @ProductID int, @OldUnitPrice money,
  @OldQuantity smallint, @OldDiscount real, @NewUnitPrice money,
  @NewQuantity smallint, @NewDiscount real
AS UPDATE [Order Details] SET
  UnitPrice = @NewUnitPrice, Quantity = @NewQuantity,
  Discount = @NewDiscount
WHERE
  OrderID = @OrderID AND ProductID = @ProductID AND
  UnitPrice = @OldUnitPrice AND Quantity = @OldQuantity AND
  Discount = @OldDiscount
```

The OrderLinesInsert Stored Procedure

Inserting a new order line is also trivially simple. The primary key of the table is the combination of the OrderID (which was set to the correct value by the event handler earlier) and the ProductID. This is the stored procedure you use:

```
CREATE PROCEDURE OrderLinesInsert
  @OrderID int, @ProductID int, @NewUnitPrice money,
  @NewQuantity smallint, @NewDiscount real
AS INSERT INTO [Order Details]
  (OrderID, ProductID, UnitPrice, Quantity, Discount)
VALUES
  (@OrderID, @ProductID, @NewUnitPrice, @NewQuantity, @NewDiscount)
```

The OrderLinesDelete Stored Procedure

Finally, the stored procedure to delete an existing order line is as follows:

```
CREATE PROCEDURE OrderLinesDelete
  @OrderID int, @ProductID int, @OldUnitPrice money,
  @OldQuantity smallint, @OldDiscount real
AS DELETE FROM [Order Details] WHERE
  OrderID = @OrderID AND ProductID = @ProductID AND
  UnitPrice = @OldUnitPrice AND Quantity = @OldQuantity AND
  Discount = @OldDiscount
```

The GetOrderLinesCommand Function

The GetOrderLinesCommand function is much the same as the GetOrdersCommand function you just looked at. It creates the appropriate Command objects to execute the three stored procedures you've just examined. Again, you add the parameters that are common to all three Command objects first (the two columns that form the primary key):

```
Private Function GetOrderLinesCommand(ByVal strStoredProcName As String, _
                              ByRef objConnect As OleDbConnection, _
                              ByVal strCommandType As String) _
                              As OleDbCommand

  'creates a new Command object and adds parameters, specifying the
  'column name and version from which values will be taken

  Dim objCommand As New OleDbCommand(strStoredProcName, objConnect)
  objCommand.CommandType = CommandType.StoredProcedure

  Dim colParams As OleDbParameterCollection = objCommand.Parameters
  Dim objParam As OleDbParameter

  objParam = colParams.Add("OrderID", OleDbType.Integer, 4, "OrderID")
  objParam.SourceVersion = DataRowVersion.Original
  objParam = colParams.Add("ProductID", OleDbType.Integer, 4, "ProductID")
  objParam.SourceVersion = DataRowVersion.Original
```

Next, you can add the set of old values if it's a Delete or Update process and the set of new values if it's an Insert or Update process:

```
If strCommandType <> "INSERT" Then
  'add "Original" parameter values for Delete and Update actions
  objParam = colParams.Add("OldUnitPrice", OleDbType.Decimal, _
                                      4, "UnitPrice")
  objParam.SourceVersion = DataRowVersion.Original
  objParam = colParams.Add("OldQuantity", OleDbType.SmallInt, _
                                      2, "Quantity")
  objParam.SourceVersion = DataRowVersion.Original
  objParam = colParams.Add("OldDiscount", OleDbType.Double, _
                                      2, "Discount")
  objParam.SourceVersion = DataRowVersion.Original
End If
```

```
    If strCommandType <> "DELETE" Then
      'add "Current" parameter values for Update and Insert actions
      objParam = colParams.Add("NewUnitPrice", OleDbType.Decimal, _
                                              4, "UnitPrice")
      objParam.SourceVersion = DataRowVersion.Current
      objParam = colParams.Add("NewQuantity", OleDbType.SmallInt, _
                                              2, "Quantity")
      objParam.SourceVersion = DataRowVersion.Current
      objParam = colParams.Add("NewDiscount", OleDbType.Double, _
                                              2, "Discount")
      objParam.SourceVersion = DataRowVersion.Current
    End If


    Return objCommand

  End Function
```

You finish off by returning the new Command object, complete with its populated Parameters collection, to the calling routine.

Using the UpdateDataSet Component

You've now got a shiny new component that will act as the complete data access tier for rich client applications and allow users to update the Orders and Order Details tables in the sample Northwind database. The next step is to put it to use. Before you build a rich client application, however, you'll look at a simple ASP.NET page that uses the component and demonstrates its functionality.

The page you're using is included in the updating-data subfolder of the examples. You can download all the samples for this book from http://www.daveandal.net/books/4923/ or http://www.apress.com. You can also run most of them online at http://www.daveandal.net/books/4923/. From the main menu page for the samples, select the Loading a DataSet and Reconciling Data link to open the Loading a DataSet page you used in the previous chapter. In that page, select the Update Customer Orders Component link, as shown in Figure 10-3.

The example page update-orders-demo.aspx uses the data access component (UpdateDataSet.dll) previously described in this chapter. To allow you to run the page more than once, without having to keep entering and editing values, it creates random values for the rows that you're updating. For the same reason, the page doesn't delete any existing rows. However, it does insert new rows into the Orders and Order Details tables but then deletes them again afterward.

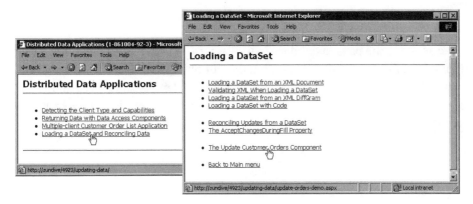

Figure 10-3. The menu pages to locate the example page

The page contains the Import statements for the namespaces you'll need, including the component UpdateDataSet. You also register the user control that you created in the previous chapter to display the contents of a DataSet object:

```
<%@Import Namespace="System.Data" %>
<%@Import Namespace="System.Data.OleDb" %>
<%@Import Namespace="DataSetUpdate" %>

<%@Register TagPrefix="dda" TagName="showdataset"
            Src="../global/show-dataset.ascx" %>
```

Then you can insert the user controls and the other HTML controls you need into the page. You use four instances of the showdataset control to display the contents of the two tables in the DataSet at two different stages of the process:

```
<!-- insert custom controls to display values -->
<dda:showdataset id="ctlShow1" runat="server" />
<dda:showdataset id="ctlShow2" runat="server" />

<div id="outConcurrent" runat="server"></div><p />

<!-- insert custom controls to display values -->
<dda:showdataset id="ctlShow3" runat="server" />
<dda:showdataset id="ctlShow4" runat="server" />

<div id="outError" runat="server"> </div><p />
```

Filling the DataSet

All the action in the page takes place in the Page_Load event handler. You start by instantiating the UpdateDataSet component—supplying the connection string you obtain from the web.config file—and then calling the GetOrderDetails method to retrieve all the order details for the customer whose ID is THECR. If there's an error, you display the details in the <div> element named outError in the page:

```
Sub Page_Load()

  'get connection string from web.config
  Dim strConnect As String
  strConnect = ConfigurationSettings.AppSettings("NorthwindConnectString")

  'create an instance of the data access component
  Dim objOrderUpdate As New UpdateDataSet(strConnect)

  'declare variable to hold a DataSet from the server
  Dim objDataSet As DataSet

  Try

    'call component to get DataSet containing order details for customer
    objDataSet = objOrderUpdate.GetOrderDetails("THECR")

  Catch objError As Exception

    'display error details
    outError.InnerHtml = "Error while fetching order details. " _
        & objError.Message & " Source: " & objError.Source
    Exit Sub  ' and stop execution

  End Try
```

Editing Some Row Values

Now you can edit some of the rows in the tables within the DataSet. In the Orders table you change the ShipCity in the first row (indexed zero) and the ShipCountry in the second row, using the same simple function that generates a string of random characters as you did in the previous chapter example. Then you change the ShipVia value (an integer foreign key to a row in the Shippers table) to some random value:

```
'get a reference to the Orders table
Dim objTable As DataTable = objDataSet.Tables("Orders")

'now modify the values held in this table
objTable.Rows(0)("ShipCity") = GetRandomString()
objTable.Rows(1)("ShipCountry") = GetRandomString()
Randomize      'get random value between 0 and 9
Dim intRand As Single = Int(9 * Rnd())
objTable.Rows(2)("ShipVia") = CInt(intRand / 2)
```

You also want to add a new row to demonstrate the way that the component handles inserted rows during the update process. Notice that you use a "dummy" value for the OrderID—in this case, 999999. After adding the new row to the Orders table in the DataSet, you display the contents of this table using the custom user control created in the previous chapter:

```
'add a new row to the Orders table
Dim objDataRow As DataRow
objDataRow = objTable.NewRow()
objDataRow("OrderID") = 999999
objDataRow("CustomerID") = "THECR"
objDataRow("OrderDate") = "06/01/2002"
objDataRow("RequiredDate") = "06/01/2002"
objDataRow("ShippedDate") = "06/01/2002"
objDataRow("ShipVia") = 2
objDataRow("Freight") = 10.50
objDataRow("ShipName") = "*new row*"
objDataRow("ShipCity") = "*new row*"
objDataRow("ShipPostalCode") = "*new row*"
objDataRow("ShipCountry") = "*new row*"
objTable.Rows.Add(objDataRow)

'display contents after changing the data
ctlShow1.ShowValues(objTable, _
    "Contents of the Orders table after editing locally")
```

Now you edit some rows in the Order Details table within the DataSet. You change the Quantity for the first three rows and add a new row that's related to the row you previously added to the Orders table (you use the same dummy OrderID value). Then you can display the contents of this table in the second instance of the user control:

```
'get a reference to the Order Details table
objTable = objDataSet.Tables("Order Details")

'now modify the values held in this table
objTable.Rows(0)("Quantity") = intRand + 7
objTable.Rows(1)("Quantity") = intRand + 3
objTable.Rows(2)("Quantity") = intRand - 1

'add a new row to the Order Details table
objDataRow = objTable.NewRow()
objDataRow("OrderID") = 999999
objDataRow("ProductID") = 40
objDataRow("UnitPrice") = 25
objDataRow("Quantity") = 10
objDataRow("Discount") = 0.07
objTable.Rows.Add(objDataRow)

'display contents after changing the data
ctlShow2.ShowValues(objTable, _
    "Contents of the Order Details table after editing locally")
```

Viewing the result in the page so far, as shown in Figure 10-4, you can see the values you changed and the new rows you added. We've highlighted these to make it easier to pick them out of the rather crowded output that the user control creates. The original values are, of course, those that were in the database when you filled the DataSet. You can also see the new row with the dummy OrderID value in each table.

Notice that the random number generation has set the ShipVia value for the row at index 2 in the Orders table to the value 4. The Shippers table only contains three rows, and the primary keys for these are numbered 1 to 3, so you can expect to get an update error when you try and push the changes to this row into the database later because there will be no matching row in the Shippers table.

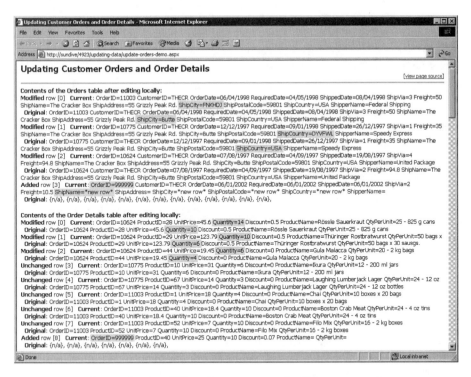

Figure 10-4. The result after filling the DataSet *and editing some values*

Changing the Underlying Database Values Concurrently

Now you can simulate another client concurrently editing the data, using the
same technique as in the previous chapter. You create and open a new connection
to the database and execute four SQL statements that change the underlying values in some of the same rows as you've just edited in the remote disconnected
DataSet:

```
'change some values in the original table while DataSet is holding
'a disconnected copy of the data to force a concurrency error

Dim strConcurrent, strUpdate As String
Dim intRowsAffected As Integer

'need a new (separate) Connection and Command object
Dim objNewConnect As New OleDbConnection(strConnect)
Dim objNewCommand As New OleDbCommand()
objNewCommand.Connection = objNewConnect

Try
```

```
    objNewConnect.Open()

    'modify rows to force concurrency errors
    strConcurrent += "<b>Concurrently executed</b>:<br />"

    strUpdate = "UPDATE Orders SET Freight = " _
            & CStr(intRand * 10) & " WHERE OrderID = 11003"
    objNewCommand.CommandText = strUpdate
    intRowsAffected = objNewCommand.ExecuteNonQuery()
    strConcurrent += strUpdate & " ... <b>" _
        & CStr(intRowsAffected) & "</b> row(s) affected<br />"

    strUpdate = "UPDATE Orders SET Freight = " _
            & CStr(intRand * 7) & " WHERE OrderID = 10775"
    objNewCommand.CommandText = strUpdate
    intRowsAffected = objNewCommand.ExecuteNonQuery()
    strConcurrent += strUpdate & " ... <b>" _
            & CStr(intRowsAffected) & "</b> row(s) affected<br />"

    intRand = intRand / 10

    strUpdate = "UPDATE [Order Details] SET Discount = " _
            & intRand & " WHERE OrderID = 10624 AND ProductID = 28"
    objNewCommand.CommandText = strUpdate
    intRowsAffected = objNewCommand.ExecuteNonQuery()
    strConcurrent += strUpdate & " ... <b>" _
        & CStr(intRowsAffected) & "</b> row(s) affected<br />"

    strUpdate = "UPDATE [Order Details] SET Discount = " _
            & intRand & " WHERE OrderID = 10624 AND ProductID = 29"
    objNewCommand.CommandText = strUpdate
    intRowsAffected = objNewCommand.ExecuteNonQuery()
    strConcurrent += strUpdate & " ... <b>" _
        & CStr(intRowsAffected) & "</b> row(s) affected<br />"

Catch objError As Exception

    'display error details
    outError.InnerHtml = "Error during concurrent updates. " _
        & objError.Message & " Source: " & objError.Source
    Exit Sub  ' and stop execution

Finally

    objNewConnect.Close()

End Try

outConcurrent.InnerHtml = strConcurrent
```

Figure 10-5 shows the results from this part of the code. The "concurrent user" has decided to be extremely generous to this customer, giving them 70 percent discount on two products!

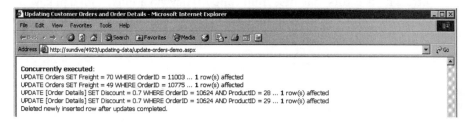

Figure 10-5. The concurrent updates to the database tables

Performing the Update

The next step is to push the changes you made to the rows in the DataSet back into the database. The data access component will do all of the work, so you just need to call the UpdateAllOrderDetails method and pass it the customer ID you're editing orders for and the DataSet you've just been editing:

```
'now ready to perform updates using modified DataSet object
'create a DataSet variable to hold the results
Dim objReturnedDS As DataSet

Try

  'call function to do updates - pass in changed DataSet
  objReturnedDS = objOrderUpdate.UpdateAllOrderDetails("THECR", objDataSet)

Catch objError As Exception

  'display error details
  outError.InnerHtml = "Error during updates to original data. " _
      & objError.Message & " Source: " & objError.Source
  Exit Sub  ' and stop execution

End Try
```

Displaying the Update Errors

If you get an error within the component itself (for example, it can't connect to the database) it'll return Nothing. Note that we *aren't* talking about database update errors here. Errors that arise from concurrency violations or foreign key constraint violations will be flagged up within the DataSet itself, So, once the UpdateAllOrderDetails method has completed, you can check if you got back a DataSet or Nothing:

```
'see if we got a component error, method returns Nothing in this case
If objReturnedDS Is Nothing Then

  'component failed
  outError.InnerHtml = "There was an error within the component."

Else
  ...
```

Providing that the component worked, you'll get back the same set of rows as you passed into the method. In this case, you display the contents of the two tables in the returned DataSet to see the results of the update process:

```
  ...
  'show values within the DataSet tables
  ctlShow3.ShowValues(objReturnedDS.Tables("Orders"), _
      "Contents of Orders table in the DataSet after updating")
  ctlShow4.ShowValues(objReturnedDS.Tables("Order Details"), _
      "Contents of Order Details table in the DataSet after updating")

End If
```

Figure 10-6 shows the results of the updates made in the DataSet after they've been pushed into the database. You can see the updated values in the Orders and Order Details tables on return from the call to the UpdateAllOrderDetails method. We've highlighted the four row errors that the concurrent SQL statements caused in the two tables during the update process.

Figure 10-6. The results after the database has been updated

As you probably expected, the update to the third row in the Orders table also failed. You didn't change this row concurrently, but the value for the ShipVia field prevents the update being persisted into the database. Notice also that the OrderID for the new rows in the Orders and Order Details tables has been changed to the correct value, as created automatically by the IDENTITY column in the Orders table of the database.

> **NOTE** *You'll get different results when you run this page each time because the new values are randomly generated. You may get more or fewer errors, depending on the values that are actually generated, the values in related tables such as the* Shippers *table, and the constraints on column values (for example, the* Quantity *must be greater than or equal to zero).*

Deleting the New Rows You Added

The final section of code in the page just has to delete the new rows you've inserted into the Orders and Order Details tables so that you can run the page repeatedly without the number of rows growing and obscuring the details (this isn't part of the process of demonstrating the component, it's simply there to clean up the database afterward). All you have to do is find the Orders table row that has the value *new row* for the ShipName column and use the OrderID of this row to locate and delete the parent and child row:

```
'delete new rows we added to the Orders and Order Details table
  Try

    objNewConnect.Open()

    'get order ID of newly inserted row
    strUpdate = "SELECT OrderID FROM Orders WHERE ShipName='*new row*'"
    objNewCommand.CommandText = strUpdate
    Dim objReader As OleDbDataReader = objNewCommand.ExecuteReader()
    objReader.Read()
    Dim intOrderID As Integer = objReader("OrderID")
    objReader.Close()

    'delete new child row(s) from Order Details table
    strUpdate = "DELETE FROM [Order Details] WHERE OrderID=" _
            & intOrderID.ToString()
    objNewCommand.CommandText = strUpdate
    objNewCommand.ExecuteNonQuery()

    'delete new row from Orders table
    strUpdate = "DELETE FROM Orders WHERE OrderID=" _
            & intOrderID.ToString()
    objNewCommand.CommandText = strUpdate
    objNewCommand.ExecuteNonQuery()

    outConcurrent.InnerHtml &= "Deleted newly inserted row after " _
                        & "updates completed."

  Catch objError As Exception

    'display error details
    outError.InnerHtml = "Error deleting inserted row. " _
      & objError.Message & " Source: " & objError.Source

  Finally
```

```
    objNewConnect.Close()

  End Try

End Sub
```

Viewing the Trace Information

The example page has tracing enabled in the `Page` directive, so the output includes the customary ASP.NET trace information at the end of the page. Within this you can see the values you write to the `Trace` object from within the component, as shown in Figure 10-7.

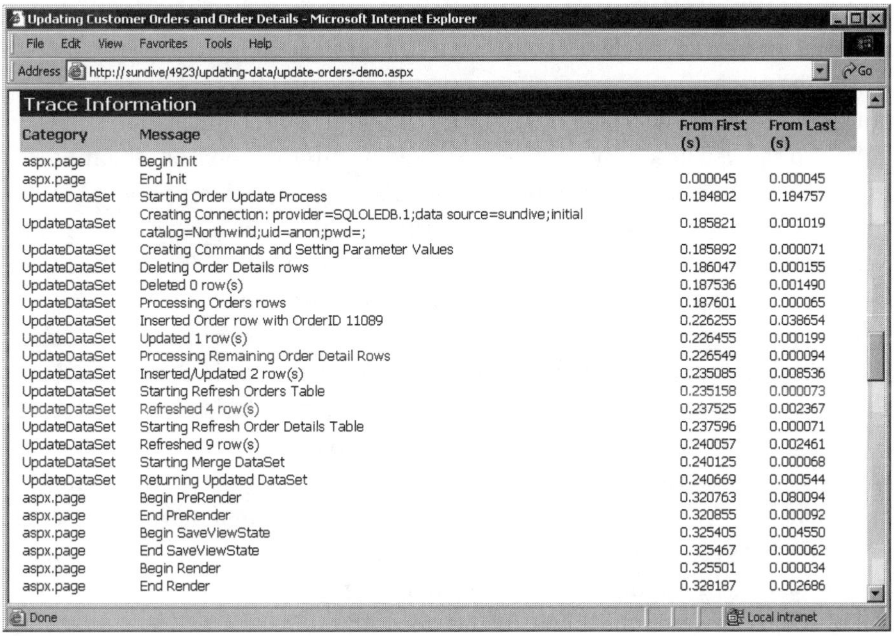

Category	Message	From First (s)	From Last (s)
aspx.page	Begin Init		
aspx.page	End Init	0.000045	0.000045
UpdateDataSet	Starting Order Update Process	0.184802	0.184757
UpdateDataSet	Creating Connection: provider=SQLOLEDB.1;data source=sundive;initial catalog=Northwind;uid=anon;pwd=;	0.185821	0.001019
UpdateDataSet	Creating Commands and Setting Parameter Values	0.185892	0.000071
UpdateDataSet	Deleting Order Details rows	0.186047	0.000155
UpdateDataSet	Deleted 0 row(s)	0.187536	0.001490
UpdateDataSet	Processing Orders rows	0.187601	0.000065
UpdateDataSet	Inserted Order row with OrderID 11089	0.226255	0.038654
UpdateDataSet	Updated 1 row(s)	0.226455	0.000199
UpdateDataSet	Processing Remaining Order Detail Rows	0.226549	0.000094
UpdateDataSet	Inserted/Updated 2 row(s)	0.235085	0.008536
UpdateDataSet	Starting Refresh Orders Table	0.235158	0.000073
UpdateDataSet	Refreshed 4 row(s)	0.237525	0.002367
UpdateDataSet	Starting Refresh Order Details Table	0.237596	0.000071
UpdateDataSet	Refreshed 9 row(s)	0.240057	0.002461
UpdateDataSet	Starting Merge DataSet	0.240125	0.000068
UpdateDataSet	Returning Updated DataSet	0.240669	0.000544
aspx.page	Begin PreRender	0.320763	0.080094
aspx.page	End PreRender	0.320855	0.000092
aspx.page	Begin SaveViewState	0.325405	0.004550
aspx.page	End SaveViewState	0.325467	0.000062
aspx.page	Begin Render	0.325501	0.000034
aspx.page	End Render	0.328187	0.002686

Figure 10-7. The trace information generated by the component as it performs the update

You can see that the method in the component inserted the new row into the `Orders` table with the `OrderID` value `11089`—as shown in the previous figures. However, out of the four changed rows in the `Orders` table (three that were edited and the new one you added), only one was updated in the database. This was the new row because the other three rows produced an error when the update was attempted.

For the Order Details table, you successfully updated two rows. These were the third row in the table, which you edited in the DataSet but didn't change concurrently and the new row you added to the DataSet. The next few lines of trace information show the component refreshing the marshaled DataSet by extracting the same set of rows from the database, merging them into the original DataSet, and then returning the DataSet.

So, the component works and does what you need to build rich client applications that perform edits on remotely cached data. In the remaining chapters, you'll have a go at building such applications using different clients and different data transport protocols.

Summary

This chapter followed on from the previous one by extending the techniques it introduced for updating a data store using a DataSet containing multiple changes. You used the same FEGURM technique as in the previous chapter but packaged it into a component that you can reuse in your distributed data applications.

We also showed how easy it is to expose tracing information from a component, which can be extremely useful not only in debugging the component but also when building applications that use it. Although the trace information is only available in an ASP.NET page, this is a common scenario for a middle tier business rules layer in applications—or when developing and testing new applications.

One topic we spent some time discussing is the thorny problem of inserting new rows into a locally cached copy of the data while disconnected from the database. You looked at two possible solutions and adopted within the component the one that's the most elegant, most portable, and the most reliable.

Finally, after looking at the code in the component, you examined an ASP.NET page that uses the component. It demonstrates the features and makes it easier to appreciate what's going on inside the component. As a useful byproduct, the page also indicates that the component actually does work as expected!

This chapter covered the following topics:

- Building a data access tier for multiple remote updates

- Using tracing in a component within an ASP.NET page

- Handling IDENTITY columns for multiple row inserts

- Testing the component in an ASP.NET page

In the next chapter, you'll start building some applications that use the component and that allow users to edit the order data in the sample database.

CHAPTER 11

Rich Client Update Applications

IN THE PREVIOUS two chapters, you examined the concepts and issues involved in updating data that's cached remotely on a rich client. By exposing the data as a .NET DataSet object, you can serialize it and send it to the client in a range of formats, exactly as you did in the earlier chapter examples where you remoted customer order data to rich clients for viewing only.

However, as you've seen in the previous chapters, managing multiple updates to this remote data and applying them to the data store afterward is a more complex task. After discussing the possible scenarios and solutions in Chapter 9, you built a data access component that can perform these updates in Chapter 10. The next stage, of course, is to use this component in a rich client application.

You'll build this kind of rich client application in this chapter, designed to run in Internet Explorer 5 and higher. This pulls together many of the useful new techniques you discussed in previous chapters, as well as reusing some of the existing techniques (and code) you used in the versions you built to read and display data from the sample Northwind database.

So, the topics for this chapter are as follows:

- Understanding what's required from the rich client application

- Building routines that manipulate a diffgram to reflect updates to the data

- Building a remote data update client interface for Internet Explorer 5 and higher

After a more detailed look at what this chapter covers, we'll give you an overview of the processes required for the application to be able to update the remotely cached data and send it back to the server where the updates can be applied to the data store.

How This Chapter Is Organized

If you just flick quickly through this chapter, you'll see that there's a lot of code. The example page (edit-orders.aspx) runs to around 350 lines of client-side JScript code in total, excluding comments, but we don't attempt to explain every line of every function. A lot of the code that displays the customer's orders is the same as, or very similar to, the read-only version of the application demonstrated in Chapter 6.

What we've attempted to do in this chapter is show you how the application requirements differ from the read-only version—what you need to do to effectively convert the application to a provide read-write access to the data. Of course, there's quite a lot of new code required to handle these requirements. In particular, you'll see a fair amount of emphasis on how you work with an XML diffgram that has been exported from a DataSet object. However, there are several other topics that you also need to explore to provide a complete picture:

> You'll get an overview of the application so that you can see what it looks like and what it aims to achieve. This includes a look at the process steps and the data access tier you use to power the application.

> You look at what the middle tier ASP.NET page (order-data.aspx) that connects the application's presentation tier (the ASP.NET page edit-orders.aspx) with the data access tier component does and how it works.

> You see how you load diffgrams on the client and use them to populate the list controls that you need in order for users to insert and edit orders.

> You focus on the issues involved in manipulating a diffgram. Where the .NET Framework isn't available (as with the client for this version of the application), you can't use a DataSet, so you have to work with the raw XML diffgram directly. You'll see a couple of generic routines for working with diffgrams, as well as exploring what you actually have to do to so that the diffgram can be loaded back into a DataSet afterward (when it is posted back to the server).

> The remainder of the chapter is devoted to the specific functions you use in the edit-orders.aspx presentation tier page that provides the user interface. As well as showing how you display the order data and allow it to be edited, you'll see how you can post it back to the server once editing is complete. However, the bulk of this section is devoted to looking at specific functions that interact with the diffgram. Although it's not difficult to do, it can get a little complex; we cover this in detail so that you can understand and adapt the techniques for your own applications.

An Overview of the Application

We previously discussed the requirements for allowing the client to perform multiple updates to remotely cached data. However, now that you have a suitable data access component to perform all the updates to the data store, you can use this as the foundation for rich client applications of all kinds—without having to concern yourself with how you handle the updates.

In fact, all that's required is to pass a DataSet object containing all the updates to the data access tier's UpdateAllOrderDetails method. This performs the updates, checking for concurrency or other errors as it does so, and returns a DataSet containing the results. Before you look at the process and client application in more detail, Figure 11-1 shows what it looks like when you run it.

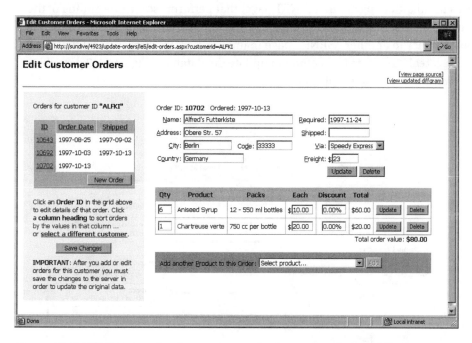

Figure 11-1. Editing an order for a customer in the version designed for Internet Explorer 5 and higher

> **NOTE** *To run this page, open the Internet Explorer 5.0 version of the customer orders application from the main samples menu and select a customer by specifying part of their customer ID or name (as described in Chapter 6). Then select the Edit Orders link for one of the customers to open the page* (edit-orders.aspx *in the* update-orders/ie5/ *subfolder) shown in Figure 11-1.*

The Process in Outline

The application you'll build is based on Internet Explorer 5 and higher and uses the MSXML parser to cache the data on the client while the edits are being performed. The data is obtained from three methods exposed by the data access tier, via a middle-tier object (an ASP.NET page) that performs some fine-tuning of the data before sending it to the client as a diffgram. After editing the data, the client posts it back to another ASP.NET page (named reconcile-changes.aspx) that uses the UpdateAllOrderDetails method to update the database. Figure 11-2 describes the complete process graphically.

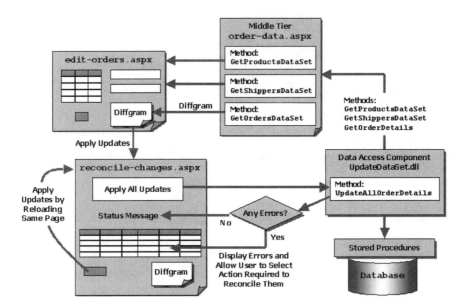

Figure 11-2. The data handling process for the Internet Explorer 5 version of the application

By default, the DataSet containing the update errors that's returned from the UpdateAllOrderDetails method has the same set of rows from the database as when you originally filled it (using another method in the data access tier).

Checking for Concurrency Errors

After the updates are applied to the database, you can check if the UpdateAllOrderDetails method returned any error rows. If not, you just display a message to this effect in the reconcile-changes.aspx page, plus some links where the user can continue to edit orders for this customer or select a different customer.

If there were update errors, you instead display the contents of the correspon-ding rows in the returned DataSet and allow the user to specify what they want to do to reconcile the errors. They might decide to overwrite the existing rows, replace individual column values, or abandon their changes. After making their selections, the Apply Updates button in this page simply reloads the reconcile-changes.aspx page.

However, this time, after it loads the DataSet containing the update errors, code in the page modifies the rows in the DataSet so that the user's reconciliation instructions are carried out before the changes are applied to the data store via the UpdateAllOrderDetails method. The process is repeated until there are no more errors in the DataSet to be reconciled.

You'll see each stage of the process in more detail throughout this chapter and the next one. In this chapter, you'll concentrate on the edit-orders.aspx page that the client uses to edit the data and the order-data.aspx middle tier "compo-nent" that links the client page to the data access tier. In the next chapter, you'll examine the reconciliation process and see how the example page reconcile-changes.aspx works.

The Middle Tier ASP.NET Page

The middle tier component (the ASP.NET page named order-data.aspx) exposes all the data required by the rich client as three XML diffgrams. One contains the list of products in the database (GetProductsDataSet), and one contains the list of shipping companies (GetShippersDataSet). The third DataSet, exposed by the GetOrdersDataSet method, contains two related tables named Orders and Order Details.

Getting the Data from the Data Access Tier

The first two of these methods just calls the similarly named method in the data access component to get the relevant DataSet. The third method, GetOrdersDataSet, calls the GetOrderDetails method of the data access component, supplying as a parameter the ID of the customer whose orders you want to edit. The customer ID is obtained from the query string that the client page uses to load the order-data.aspx middle tier ASP.NET page. Before returning the DataSet to the client, the GetProductsDataSet method also adds a calculated column containing the total for each order line in the Order Details table of the DataSet—in the same way as in the earlier Internet Explorer 5 example applications:

```
Function GetOrdersDataSet (strCustID As String) As DataSet
  ...
  ...
  'create an instance of the data access component
  Dim objOrderUpdate As New UpdateDataSet(strConnect)
  objDataSet = objOrderUpdate.GetOrderDetails(strCustID)

  'add column containing total value of each line in OrderLines table
  Dim objLinesTable As DataTable = objDataSet.Tables("Order Details")
  Dim objColumn As DataColumn
  objColumn = objLinesTable.Columns.Add("LineTotal", _
                          System.Type.GetType("System.Double"))
  objColumn.Expression = "[Quantity] * ([UnitPrice] - ([UnitPrice]" _
                  & " * [Discount]))"
  Return objDataSet
  ...
  ...
End Function
```

Exposing the Data to the Client

The middle tier now has all the data required for the edit-orders.aspx page to use to update the orders for the specified customer. However, these are in the form of DataSet objects. Because the target client (Internet Explorer 5 and higher) doesn't know anything about .NET, you can't send it a DataSet directly. As in the previous IE5 applications, you have to expose the data in an alternative format. The obvious choice is XML. However, because you need to be able to update the data and put it back into a DataSet to use with the data access component, you have to use XML in the format of a diffgram. This contains all the information required to set the current and original values of a DataSet, plus the other properties such as the relationships between the tables, the row state, and any row error details.

You looked at diffgrams in Chapter 9, but you'll learn more about the structure later in this chapter when you come to see how you edit them to get the results you want. In the meantime, in the middle tier order-data.aspx page, you need to convert the DataSet into a diffgram to send to the client.

As you'll discover in this chapter, accessing row data in a diffgram using XML DOM techniques is almost as easy as accessing a "normal" XML document (you'll see what we mean when you look at the edit-orders.aspx page later). In the middle tier, you'll expose the data from all three DataSet objects that you need on the client as diffgrams. Therefore, the Page_Load event of the order-data.aspx page looks like this:

```
Sub Page_Load()

  Dim objDataSet As DataSet

  Select Case Request.QueryString("list")
    Case "customers"
      objDataSet = GetOrdersDataSet(Request.QueryString("customerid"))
    Case "shippers"
      objDataSet = GetShippersDataSet()
    Case "products"
      objDataSet = GetProductsDataSet()
  End Select

  Response.ContentType = "text/xml"
  Response.Write("<?xml version='1.0' ?>")
  objDataSet.WriteXml(Response.OutputStream, XmlWriteMode.DiffGram)

End Sub
```

You can see that the WriteXml method of the DataSet is used with the second parameter set to the value DiffGram from the XmlWriteMode enumeration.

Loading the Diffgrams on the Client

Although based on a special schema that allows it to contain all the information required to rebuild a DataSet object, a diffgram is just ordinary XML. So you can load, save, and manipulate it using normal XML DOM techniques, just like you would with a normal XML document. Internet Explorer 5 loads the three diffgrams exposed by the middle tier into three instances of the MSXML parser.

Loading the Orders Data

You load the list of orders in the same way as in the Internet Explorer 5 application where you were just viewing the customer's orders. After extracting the customer ID from the query string (remember that the edit orders pages are loaded from the view orders application described in Chapter 6), you create the URL for the middle tier ASP.NET page you've just been examining. Then you can create the parser instance, set the properties, and call the load method:

```
function loadOrderList() {

  // get the customer ID from the query string
  strID = new String(window.location.search);
  strCustID = strID.substring(strID.indexOf('=') + 1, strID.length);

  // create URL and query string and load all orders for this customer
  var strURL = 'order-data.aspx?list=customers&customerid=' + strCustID;
  objXMLData = new ActiveXObject('MSXML2.FreeThreadedDOMDocument');
  objXMLData.onreadystatechange = changeFunction;
  objXMLData.validateOnParse = true;
  objXMLData.async = true;
  objXMLData.load(strURL);
}
```

When the XML document (the diffgram) has finished loading, the readyState property returns the value 4, and you can check for errors as you did in previous examples. If there was no error, the next steps are to load the shippers and products diffgrams. You do this by calling two separate functions named loadShippersList and loadProductsList in the page:

```
function changeFunction() {

  if (objXMLData.readyState == 4) {
    if (objXMLData.parseError.errorCode != 0) {
      document.all('lblStatus').innerHTML =
        '<b>* ERROR</b> - could not load order list.';
    }
    else {

      //load list of shippers from server
      if (loadShippersList()) {
```

```
        //load list of products from server
        if (loadProductsList()) {

          // replace "Loading" message with customer ID
          document.all('lblStatus').innerHTML =
            'Orders for customer ID <b>"' + strCustID + '"</b>';

          // display list of matching orders in left table
          showOrderList('OrderID');
        }
        else
          document.all('lblStatus').innerHTML =
            '<b>* ERROR</b> - could not load product details.';
      }
      else
        document.all('lblStatus').innerHTML =
          '<b>* ERROR</b> - could not load shipper details.';
    }
  }
}
```

Loading the Shippers Data

You use two of the sets of data to populate drop-down list boxes from which the user can select the values for the rows as they edit them. You have a list of shipping companies where the user specifies the shipper to use for each order and a list of products from which they can select when adding new lines to an existing order.

After the orders data has been loaded, the loadShippersList function is called. It uses the data it fetches from the middle tier to populate the drop-down list named selShipName, which is declared within the HTML at the end of the page. Notice that it already contains one <option> element that acts as the default selection. Figure 11-3 shows the populated list.

```
<select size="1" id="selShipName" accesskey="V" tabindex="17">
  <option value="0">Select...</option>
</select>
```

Figure 11-3. The drop-down list for the shipper values

The function itself is shown next. We haven't used asynchronous loading this time because the volume of data is small. After loading the diffgram into a new instance of MSXML, you use the selectNodes method of the parser to get a NodeList containing all the <Shippers> nodes (the rows in the original Shippers table in the DataSet). Then you can iterate through this NodeList using the values from the first and second child nodes (the <ShipperID> and <ShipperName> elements) to create the <option> elements and add them to the options collection of the drop-down list:

```
function loadShippersList() {

  // create a new parser object instance and load data
  objXMLShippers = new ActiveXObject('MSXML2.FreeThreadedDOMDocument');
  objXMLShippers.async = false;
  if (objXMLShippers.load('order-data.aspx?list=shippers')) {

    // fill drop-down list of shipper names and values
    // get collection of Shippers nodes
    var strXPath = '//Shippers';
    var objNodeSet = objXMLShippers.selectNodes(strXPath);

    // get a reference to the ShipName drop-down list
    var objViaList = document.all('selShipName');

    // add an <option> element for each shipper
    for (var intLoop = 0; intLoop < objNodeSet.length; intLoop++) {
      var strShipID = objNodeSet[intLoop].childNodes[0].text;
      var strShipName = objNodeSet[intLoop].childNodes[1].text;
      objViaList.options.length += 1;
      objViaList.options[objViaList.options.length - 1].value = strShipID;
      objViaList.options[objViaList.options.length - 1].text = strShipName;
    }
    return true;
  }
}
```

Loading the Products Data

When the user adds a new line to an existing order (a new row for the Order Details table), they must specify the product. As you saw in the version of this application for down-level HTML clients (as described in Chapter 8), you need the ProductID value to create a new Order Details row because it forms part of the primary key for that table. In the HTML section of the page, you declare a drop-down list named selProducts and provide a single default <option> element. Figure 11-4 shows the fully populated drop-down list.

```
<select size="1" id="selProducts" accesskey="P" tabindex="25"
        onchange="selectProduct(this)" />
  <option value="-1">Select product...</option>
</select>
```

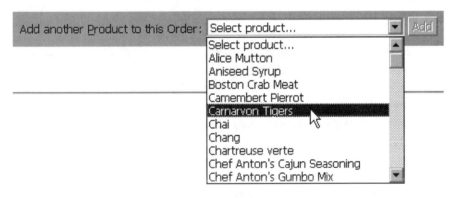

Figure 11-4. The drop-down list for the product values

The loadProducts function loads the diffgram that's exposed by the middle tier and that contains the list of products extracted from the database. It does this in the same way as the previous example where you loaded the list of shipping companies, and the function uses the data in the diffgram to populate the selProducts list using the <ProductID> and <ProductName> elements:

```
function loadProductsList() {

  objXMLProducts = new ActiveXObject('MSXML2.FreeThreadedDOMDocument');
  objXMLProducts.async = false;
  if (objXMLProducts.load('order-data.aspx?list=products')) {
    var strXPath = '//Products';
    var objNodeSet = objXMLProducts.selectNodes(strXPath);
```

```
        var objViaList = document.all('selProducts');
        for (var intLoop = 0; intLoop < objNodeSet.length; intLoop++) {
          var strProductID = objNodeSet[intLoop].childNodes[0].text;
          var strProductName = objNodeSet[intLoop].childNodes[1].text;
          objViaList.options.length += 1;
          objViaList.options[objViaList.options.length - 1].value
                                            = strProductID;
          objViaList.options[objViaList.options.length - 1].text
                                            = strProductName;
        }
        return true;
      }
    }
```

Having seen how you load the data, you've now finished looking at the middle tier of the application and can move on to see how the remainder of the page works. As you probably guessed from Figure 11-1, much of it is similar to the page you used in previous chapters to view the order data.

However, a major feature of the code in this page is the ability to manipulate a diffgram to properly reflect the changes the user makes to the data while it's cached in the MSXML parser instance on the client. So, before you look at the interface itself, you'll see how you go about editing a diffgram to get what you want in the DataSet that you'll create from it when the user submits the edits to the server for processing.

Editing a .NET DataSet Diffgram

You looked at the format of a diffgram in Chapter 9, where you used one to fill a DataSet with data. We briefly discussed the way that it preserves both the current and original values of each row and how it stores row error information. You can use the example application in this chapter to experiment with the diffgram format if you want. After editing the details of an order for a selected customer, click the View Updated Diffgram link at the top right of the page, as shown in Figure 11-5.

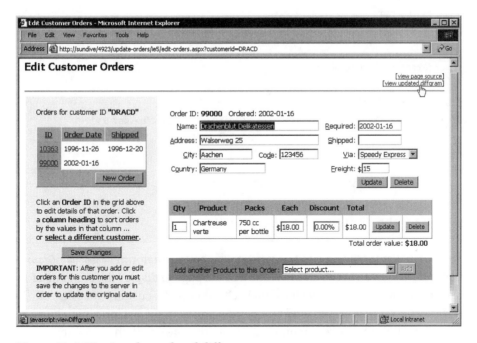

Figure 11-5. Viewing the updated diffgram

Viewing the Updated Diffgram

This opens a page that, rather than updating the database, just displays the edited values. It first loads the appropriate schema into the DataSet from a file on the server's disk and then loads the diffgram posted from the edit-orders.aspx page into this DataSet:

```
'create a new DataSet object
Dim objDataSet As New DataSet()

Try

    'create an XmlTextReader to read data sent from client
    'specifying that string fragment is an XML Document
    Dim objReader As New XmlTextReader(Request.Form("hidPostXML"), _
                                    XmlNodeType.Document, Nothing)

    'read the schema into the DataSet from file on disk
    'must use the Physical path to the file not the Virtual path
    objDataSet.ReadXmlSchema(Request.MapPath("orders-schema.xsd"))
```

```
'read in the DiffGram posted from the client
objDataSet.ReadXml(objReader)


Catch objError As Exception

  'display error details
  outError.InnerHTML = "<b>* Error while reading disk file</b>.<br />" _
                  & objError.Message & " " & objError.Source


End Try
```

Displaying the Contents of the DataSet

Now you can display the data in the DataSet. You first use a normal <asp:DataGrid> server control located in the HTML section of the page to display the contents of the Tables collection. To display the data itself, you use the custom user control show-dataset.ascx that was created and demonstrated in the two previous chapters. You insert two instances of this control into the page (with the id values ctlShow1 and ctlShow2) and then use these to display the contents of the two tables in the DataSet:

```
Try

  'bind DataGrid control to DataSet Tables collection
  dgr1.DataSource = objDataSet.Tables
  dgr1.DataBind()

  'display Orders current and original values after loading
  Dim objTable As DataTable = objDataSet.Tables("Orders")
  ctlShow1.ShowValues(objTable, _
              "Orders row values after loading DiffGram")

  'display Order Details current and original values
  objTable = objDataSet.Tables("Order Details")
  ctlShow2.ShowValues(objTable, _
              "Order Details row values after loading DiffGram")

Catch
End Try
```

Figure 11-6 shows the result from this section of code. You can see that there's a Modified, a Deleted, and an Added (new) row in the Orders table and an

Unchanged and an Added row in the Order Details table. You can also see the Current and Original values for each column.

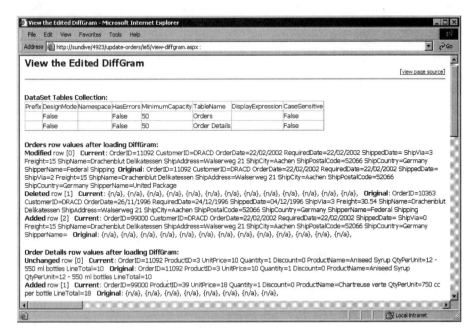

Figure 11-6. The table and row details visible when viewing the updated diffgram

Displaying the Diffgram Contents

Further down this page is the "raw" content of the diffgram that was posted from the edit-orders.aspx page. You simply insert it into a `<div>` element declared within the HTML section of the page, enclosing it in an `<xmp>` element so that the XML elements themselves are visible (rather than being treated as HTML elements by the page-rendering engine):

```
'display the XML DiffGram itself
outXML.InnerHtml = "<xmp>" & Request.Form("hidPostXML") & "</xmp>"
```

Figure 11-7 shows part of the raw diffgram displayed in the page. There's too much to be able to see it all in one figure, but you'll investigate the actual changes that the edit-orders.aspx page has made to it shortly. Notice that the edit process does not "wrap" the new elements you insert into the diffgram, so the indentation becomes a little ragged (for example, the closing `</NewDataSet>` element has disappeared off to the right at the end of the line before the `<diffgr:before>` section).

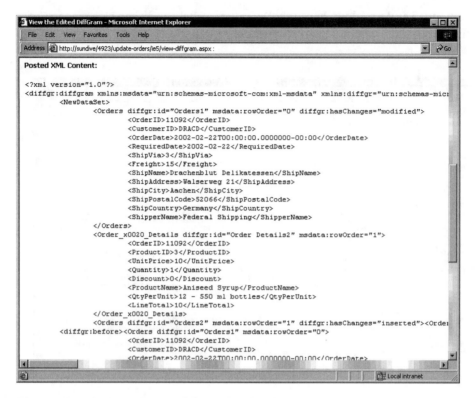

Figure 11-7. The raw content of the updated diffgram

The Updated Diffgram Format

To help you understand more clearly what's going on when you edit a diffgram, the following listing shows an abridged version of the diffgram in Figure 11-7, with several elements (including the Order Details rows) removed for clarity and the indentation sorted out. We've also added some blank rows and comments (using <<-----) to make it easier to see the format and content:

```
<?xml version="1.0"?>
<diffgr:diffgram xmlns:msdata="... etc ...">

  <NewDataSet>        <<----- contains current versions of all existing rows

    <Orders diffgr:id="Orders1" msdata:rowOrder="0"
                          diffgr:hasChanges="modified">
      <OrderID>11092</OrderID>
      <CustomerID>DRACD</CustomerID>
      <OrderDate>2002-02-22</OrderDate>
      ... elements removed for clarity ...
```

```
      <ShipVia>3</ShipVia>                               <<----- modified value
      ... elements removed for clarity ...
      <ShipCountry>Germany</ShipCountry>
      <ShipperName>Federal Shipping</ShipperName>    <<----- modified value
   </Orders>


    ...


   <Orders diffgr:id="Orders3" msdata:rowOrder="2"   <<----- inserted row
                             diffgr:hasChanges="inserted">
      <OrderID>99000</OrderID>
      <CustomerID>DRACD</CustomerID>
      <OrderDate>2002-02-22</OrderDate>
      ... elements removed for clarity ...
      <ShipCountry>Germany</ShipCountry>
      <ShipperName>Speedy Express</ShipperName>
   </Orders>
</NewDataSet>

<diffgr:before>        <<----- contains original versions of edited rows

   <Orders diffgr:id="Orders1" msdata:rowOrder="0">

      <OrderID>11092</OrderID>
      <CustomerID>DRACD</CustomerID>
      <OrderDate>2002-02-22</OrderDate>
      ... elements removed for clarity ...
      <ShipVia>2</ShipVia>                               <<----- original value
      ... elements removed for clarity ...
      <ShipCountry>Germany</ShipCountry>
      <ShipperName>United Package</ShipperName>      <<----- original value

   </Orders>

   <Orders diffgr:id="Orders2" msdata:rowOrder="1">   <<----- deleted row
      <OrderID>10363</OrderID>
      <CustomerID>DRACD</CustomerID>
      <OrderDate>1996-11-26</OrderDate>
      ... elements removed for clarity ...
      <ShipCountry>Germany</ShipCountry>
      <ShipperName>Federal Shipping</ShipperName>
   </Orders>

   </diffgr:before>
</diffgr:diffgram>
```

One point to note (you can see this in Figure 11-7) is that table names containing spaces change when the diffgram is created from a DataSet. The space is replaced by the series of characters _x0020_ (the code for a space character in hexadecimal is 20). However, the diffgr:id attribute does contain the original table name. So, the Order Details table rows are represented as follows:

```
<Order_x0020_Details diffgr:id="Order Details1" msdata:rowOrder="0">
  ...
</Order_x0020_Details>
```

The Update Rules for a DataSet Diffgram

To create this diffgram, you would have needed to do the following:

Edited (modified) the order with the OrderID value 11092. This is identified with the attributes diffgr:id="Orders1" and msdata:rowOrder="0", so it was the first row in the Orders table of the DataSet when you loaded the data. The complete <Orders> element is copied to the <diffgr:before> section (which specifies the original values when you load the diffgram back into a DataSet). Then the edited values (taken from the controls in the page) are placed in the <Orders> element within the <NewDataSet> section (which specifies the current values for the row in the DataSet). Finally, the attribute msdata:hasChanges="modified" is added to this element.

Deleted the order with the OrderID value 10363. This is identified with the attributes diffgr:id="Orders2" and msdata:rowOrder="1", so it was the second row in the Orders t\able of the DataSet when you loaded the data. The complete <Orders> element is copied to the <diffgr:before> section to set the original values, and the element is removed from the <NewDataSet> section altogether. (If the order you deleted had any related child rows, they would also appear as deleted rows).

Added (inserted) a new order with the temporary OrderID value 99000. This is identified with the attributes diffgr:id="Orders3" and msdata:rowOrder="2". Notice that there's no corresponding element within the <diffgr:before> section because there are no original values for an inserted row. The edited values (taken from the controls in the page) are placed in the <Orders> element within the <NewDataSet> section so as to set the current values for the new row in the DataSet. This time the attribute msdata:hasChanges="inserted" is added to the element.

If you look back at Figure 11-6 of the DataSet contents, you'll see how these modifications to the diffgram do in fact create the expected values within the DataSet. So it looks like it'll be easy to build the rich client application—you just need to manipulate the diffgram in line with the "rules" listed previously.

Custom Functions for Manipulating the Diffgram

Obviously, some of the tasks involved in updating the diffgram involve common and repetitive actions. We created a couple of functions that you can reuse for these tasks when manipulating the diffgram. You use the first function to get a reference to a node in the diffgram given an OrderID value and (in the case of the Order Details rows) a ProductID value.

You first create a suitable XPath query string, depending on the table name passed into the function as the first parameter, the OrderID value, and (for an Order Details element) the ProductID value as well. Then you can get a reference to the node using the selectSingleNode function and return it:

```
function getNodeReference(strTableName, intThisOrder, strThisProduct) {
  // get node in <NewDataSet> from named table
  // optionally with specified OrderID and ProductID

  // create appropriate XPath
  var strXPath = '//NewDataSet/' + strTableName
               + '[OrderID="' + intThisOrder.toString() + '"'
  if (strTableName != 'Orders')
    strXPath += ' and ProductID="' + strThisProduct + '"';
  strXPath += ']';

  // select and return the matching node
  return objXMLData.selectSingleNode(strXPath);
}
```

Copying Nodes to the *<diffgr:before>* Section

The second function you create is quite generic and could be used in almost any application that manipulates DataSet diffgrams. Given a reference to a node in the <NewDataSet> section of the diffgram, it copies that node and all its child nodes into the <diffgr:before> section.

There are some issues you have to be aware of for this process. First, if the row you're modifying was inserted during the current session, you don't want to copy it to the <diffgr:before> section—even if you subsequently modify the values in it. Because it isn't already in the database (until you send the updates to the server), there can be no original values.

Second, you only want to copy the node to the `<diffgr:before>` section once—the first time it's modified (or when it is deleted). So, in the function, you check that the element *doesn't* have an `msdata:hasChanges` attribute. If it does, you simply return from the function:

```
function copyToDiffgrBefore(objNode) {
  // copy node to <diffgr:before> section if not already there

  // see if it has already been modified or inserted
  if (objNode.getAttribute('diffgr:hasChanges') != null) return;
  ...
```

If it *isn't* an inserted or modified node, you need to make sure it doesn't already exist in the `<diffgr:before>` section. In theory, the previous check on the `hasChanges` attribute should prevent this happening, but it does no harm to be sure. You get the value of the `msdata:rowOrder` attribute from the existing element and create an XPath that'll search for it in the `<diffgr:before>` section. However, before you perform the search, you need to make sure that there actually is a `<diffgr:before>` section. When first load the diffgram, it won't contain this section. You execute an XPath query to check, and if it isn't there, you create it:

```
...
// get node name and "rowOrder" attribute value
var strElemName = objNode.nodeName;
var strRowOrder = objNode.getAttribute('msdata:rowOrder');

// create appropriate XPath
var strXPath = '//diffgr:before/' + strElemName
             + '[@msdata:rowOrder="' + strRowOrder + '"]';

// see if node is already in <diffgr:before> section
var colNodeSet = objXMLData.selectNodes(strXPath);
if (colNodeSet.length == 0) {

  // copy node to <diffgr:before> section
  // see if there actually is a <diffgr:before> section
  var colBeforeNodes = objXMLData.selectNodes('//diffgr:before');
  if (colBeforeNodes.length == 0) {

    // create <diffgr:before> section and get reference to it
    var objNewNode = objXMLData.createElement('diffgr:before');
    objXMLData.documentElement.appendChild(objNewNode);
    colBeforeNodes = objXMLData.selectNodes('//diffgr:before');
  }
  ...
```

Using the appendChild and cloneNode Methods

Now you can copy the original node into the `<diffgr:before>` section. You use the `appendChild` method to insert the node at the end of the list of child nodes in the `<diffgr:before>` section (the order of nodes here doesn't actually matter—the `rowOrder` attribute is used to insert them into the correct rows of the `DataSet` when you load the diffgram into it).

One point to bear in mind when using the XML DOM methods (such as you're doing with the MSXML parser) is that the `appendChild` method actually *moves* a node to the new position. It doesn't copy it. So, to maintain the original node in the `<NewDataSet>` section, you have to use the `cloneNode` method to create a copy of the node, specifying `true` for the second parameter to indicate that you want to clone all the descendant nodes of this node as well. Then you can pass this copy of the node to the `appendChild` method:

```
    ...
    // make copy of node and put into <diffgr:before> section
    colBeforeNodes[0].appendChild(objNode.cloneNode(true));
  }
}
```

The edit-orders.aspx Page Code and HTML

Before you go on to see how you use the functions described previously to manipulate the diffgram, you'll look in more detail at some other parts of the `edit-orders.aspx` page. In particular, you'll examine how it differs from the version of the application that just displays customer order data, and how the visual interface for editing the data is created by the HTML section of the page and the XSLT stylesheets that create the tables.

When you compare the `edit-orders.aspx` page to the page you used for just viewing customer's orders, you can see that quite a lot of the HTML and code is reused. Much of the display is created by two XSLT stylesheets that transform the data to create the list of orders in the left side of the page and the list of order lines (the `Order Detail` rows) in the right side of the page.

Creating the List of Orders

In the read-only version of the customer orders application for Internet Explorer 5 and higher, you obtained the data via a middle tier component, in much the same way as you do in this version. However, the XML document you extracted from the

DataSet for the previous version was purely a representation of the current values in the DataSet. You created it using the WriteXml method, but you didn't specify the optional parameter that creates a diffgram. In this version of the application, you do use this parameter, forcing a diffgram to be output instead.

However, this makes only a minor difference to the way you extract values from the XML document on this client. Recall that the format of a diffgram simply wraps the existing root element (by default named <NewDataSet>) with a new root element named <diffgr:diffgram>. When rows are edited, a <diffgr:before> element is added as a child of the new root element. And, if there are any rows with the RowError property set, there will also be a <diffgr:errors> element as a child of the <diffgr:diffgram> root element. The "normal" (nondiffgram) format XML document is as follows:

```
<?xml version="1.0"?>
<NewDataSet>
   ... "normal" XML data goes here ...
</NewDataSet>
```

The diffgram from the same DataSet is as follows:

```
<?xml version="1.0"?>
<diffgr:diffgram xmlns:msdata="...etc...">
  <NewDataSet>
     ... "normal" XML data goes here ...
  </NewDataSet>
  <diffgr:before>
     ... original values after editing data ...
  </diffgr:before>
  <diffgr:errors>
     ... values from RowError property ...
  </diffgr:errors>
</diffgr:diffgram>
```

So, if you use XPath to select nodes, you have to be aware of the new hierarchy within the document. In most cases, you use syntax that selects a node irrespective of its parent or position in the hierarchy, such as "//Orders/OrderID". When you use a diffgram, however, you'll usually want to include the "normal format" root element name in the XPath as well so that you don't get any matching nodes from the <diffgr:before> section returned. In other words, you would use something such as "//NewDataSet/Orders/OrderID".

In other situations in the page, you use the more verbose XSLT syntax for the XPaths. For example, in the Chapter 6 version of the application, you selected the <Orders> element with a specific OrderID value using this:

```
descendant::Orders[descendant::OrderID=$orderid]
```

In this version of the application, to be sure you don't get a match in the <diffgr:before> section, you use this:

```
descendant::NewDataSet/Orders[descendant::OrderID=$orderid]
```

Other than the changes to the XPaths, the stylesheet you use to create the list of orders, and the code that executes the transformation, is almost identical to the view orders version of the application. One difference is that you add an extra row to the foot of the table and put into it a button that the user can click to add a new order for this customer.

You create the stylesheets in the page as strings, as you'll recall from Chapter 6. Effectively, the stylesheet content to create the new button is as follows:

```
<tr style="background-color:silver;">
  <td colspan="3" align="right">
    <input type="button" id="btnNewOrder" value="New Order"
           tabindex="21" onclick="newOrder()" />
  </td>
</tr>
```

This creates a normal <input type="button"> element with the caption New Order. You can see that you take advantage of Internet Explorer 5's ability to set the tab order of controls in a page and specify that the client-side function in the page named newOrder will execute when the button is clicked.

Posting the Updated Diffgram to the Server

When you looked at the method in the data access tier that you use to update the database (in the previous chapter), you saw that it can return the same set of rows that were originally loaded from the server, but with the underlying database values and error details included for rows where the update failed. However, this is really only useful where you can display the underlying values and the error details in the same page you use to edit the data.

In the case of the example page, you don't provide this feature. Although you could build it in, you actually gain little extra performance or functionality with this approach. Reconciling the changes mainly involves the user making a few simple choices about which values to keep and which to overwrite—followed by another attempt at updating the database. So, you can choose to perform this part of the process using server-side code only, rather than remoting the DataSet containing the errors back to the client again.

The result is that you post the updated diffgram to a separate page named reconcile-changes.aspx. The easiest way to do this is to insert it into a <hidden> HTML control on a <form> that has the action attribute set to the name of the target page. The following listing shows the HTML form you use. You also include a <hidden> control for the customer ID because you need this to perform the update and reconciliation process:

```
<!-- form to submit updated DiffGram to server -->
<form id="frmPostXml" action="reconcile-changes.aspx" method="post">
  <input type="hidden" id="hidCustID" name="hidCustID" />
  <input type="hidden" id="hidPostXML" name="hidPostXML" />
</form>
```

The Button to Save Changes to the Server

Below the list of orders in the left part of the page is an <input type="button"> element with the caption Save Changes, as shown in Figure 11-8. Initially the button is disabled, but you enable it whenever a value in one of the edit controls on the page changes so that the changes can be saved back to the server:

```
<div id="divSaveChanges" align="center" style="padding=10">
  <input type="button" id="btnSaveChanges" disabled="true"
         value="Save Changes" onclick="postToServer()" />
</div>
```

When this button is clicked, it executes a client-side function named postToServer that sends the updated diffgram to the reconcile-changes.aspx page, where the updates are persisted into the database. The code to do this is simple enough—you insert the complete diffgram, extracted from the xml property of the MSXML parser instance, into the hidden control and submit the form:

```
function postToServer() {
  // send XML DiffGram to server to update database
```

```
// disable "Save Changes" button
document.all('btnSaveChanges').disabled = true;

// clear "dirty" flag to allow new page to load
blnIsDirty = false;

// insert XML and CustomerID into hidden controls and submit form
document.all('hidCustID').value = strCustID;
document.all('hidPostXML').value = objXMLData.xml;
document.all('frmPostXML').submit();
}
```

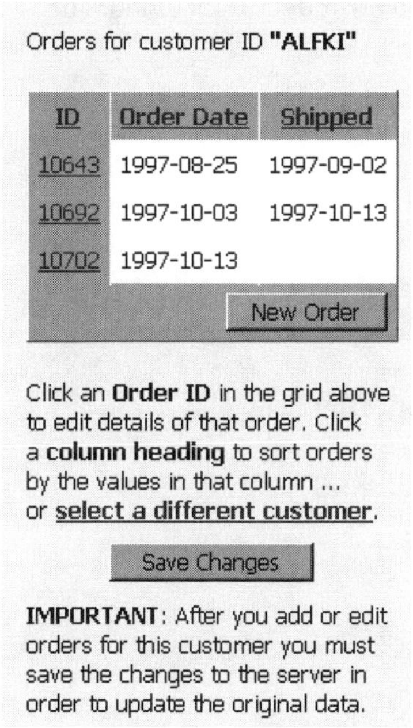

Orders for customer ID **"ALFKI"**

ID	Order Date	Shipped
10643	1997-08-25	1997-09-02
10692	1997-10-03	1997-10-13
10702	1997-10-13	

New Order

Click an **Order ID** in the grid above to edit details of that order. Click a **column heading** to sort orders by the values in that column ... or **select a different customer**.

Save Changes

IMPORTANT: After you add or edit orders for this customer you must save the changes to the server in order to update the original data.

Figure 11-8. The list of orders and the button to save changes back to the server

> **NOTE** *A similar routine, named* viewDiffgram, *is used to post the diffgram to the page you saw earlier where the values in the diffgram are displayed. The code just changes the action attribute of the form to* "view-diffgram.aspx" *before submitting the form.*

Sending the Diffgram via XMLHTTP

If you were handling the display and reconciliation in the same page, you wouldn't have to post it to the server using a <form>, as you do the example. Instead, you could take advantage of a component that can execute an HTTP request while the page is still displayed. There are custom components that can do this, but you already have a free one included within the MSXML parser itself that you can use. You can instantiate an XMLHTTP object and use it to make a request to the server. The methods and properties of this object allow you to specify the HTTP headers you require, so you can add the customer ID and diffgram to the request and "catch" them in the Request.Form collection within an ASP.NET page. That page would perform the update process and then return the DataSet containing the same set of rows, but with the underlying values and error details included. The following code shows how you can use the XMLHTTP object:

```
// create instance of XMLHTTP component
var objHttpRequest = new ActiveXObject('MSXML2.XMLHTTP');

// specify URL to POST request and HTTP headers to
// specify false for synchronous loading, true for async loading
objHttpRequest.open('POST', 'http://servername/updateorders.aspx', false);

// add HTTP headers that will appear in ASP.NET Form collection
objHttpRequest.setRequestHeader('CustID', strCustID);
objHttpRequest.setRequestHeader('postedXML', objXMLData.xml);

// send request and check if returned status is 200 (OK)
objHttpRequest.send();
if (objHttpRequest.status == 200) {

  // create a new XML parser and load the returned XML into it
  var objReturnedXML = new ActiveXObject('MSXML2.DOMDocument');
  objReturnedXML.loadXML(objHttpRequest.responseXML.xml);
  alert(objReturnedXML.xml);   // display the returned XML
}
```

Marshaling Changed Rows

One other point worth mentioning here is whether you should marshal just the changed rows in the diffgram before you post it back to the server. This would probably reduce its size quite considerably—depending on how many edits the user has made to the orders for the current customer.

Unfortunately, the task of marshaling changes in a diffgram is much more difficult than doing the same in a .NET environment. When you have a `DataSet` object, you can, as described in previous chapters, marshal the changed rows into another `DataSet` object using this:

```
objMarshaledDataSet = objOriginalDataSet.GetChanges()
```

However, when you're working in an environment where there's no concept of a `DataSet` object, as is the case in the Internet Explorer 5 client application, you can achieve the same result only by editing the diffgram directly using XML DOM methods. The process required is to check each `<Orders>` and `<Order Details>` element to see if it has an `msdata:hasChanges` attribute. If not, you can remove it from the diffgram.

However, you then have to go through the remaining nodes changing all the `diffgr:id` and `msdata:rowOrder` attribute values to be contiguous. At the same time, you have to find the corresponding elements in the `<diffgr:before>` section and update their `diffgr:id` and `msdata:rowOrder` attribute values to match the elements in the "current" section.

Displaying Details of the Selected Order

The page allows the user to edit most of the values for the order selected in the list on the left side of the page. Some values, such as the order ID (the primary key for the row) and the order date, can't be edited—they're shown as text rather than within an `<input type="text">` control, as shown in Figure 11-9.

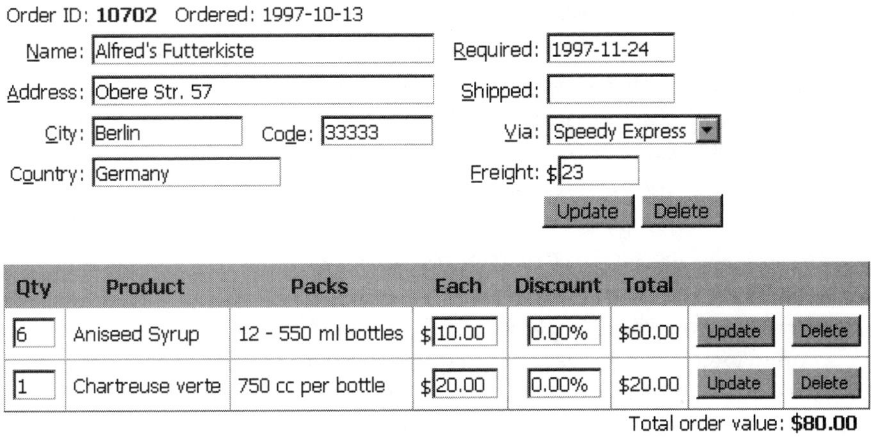

Figure 11-9. The edit controls for the order and order details rows

Notice that, rather than using a text box to display the name of the shipper for this order, it's displayed in the Via drop-down list. The selection for this order can be changed here if required. You saw earlier in this chapter how you fill this list from the database Shippers table via the data access and middle tiers. You'll see how you set the values of all these controls shortly.

Below the order details is the list of order lines; you'll come back to this later. Below the order lines table is the total value of the order as it stands now. This is automatically updated when the order is edited, as you'll see in the next section.

The HTML Controls to Display the Order Details

The HTML section at the end of the page contains the declarations of all the controls on the page. Within it is the following section that creates the text boxes and drop-down list, plus the two buttons to update and delete this order:

```
<!-- controls to display order details -->
<table id="tblOrderDetail" border="0" style="display:none">
  <tr>
   <td colspan="4"><span id="lblOrderID"></span></td>
  </tr><tr>
    <td align="right" nowrap="nowrap"><u>N</u>ame:</td>
    <td align="left" nowrap="nowrap"><input type="text" id="txtShipName"
        size="40" accesskey="N" tabindex="10" />  </td>
    <td align="right" nowrap="nowrap"><u>R</u>equired:</td>
    <td align="left" nowrap="nowrap"><input type="text" id="txtRequiredDate"
        size="12" accesskey="R" tabindex="15" /></td>
  </tr><tr>
    <td align="right" nowrap="nowrap"><u>A</u>ddress:</td>
    <td align="left" nowrap="nowrap"><input type="text" id="txtShipAddress"
        size="40" accesskey="A" tabindex="11" />  </td>
    <td align="right" nowrap="nowrap"><u>S</u>hipped:</td>
    <td align="left" nowrap="nowrap"><input type="text" id="txtShippedDate"
        size="12" accesskey="S" tabindex="16" /></td>
  </tr><tr>
    <td align="right" nowrap="nowrap"><u>C</u>ity:</td>
    <td align="left" nowrap="nowrap"><input type="text" id="txtShipCity"
        size="15" accesskey="C" tabindex="12" />  
        Co<u>d</u>e: <input type="text" id="txtShipPostCode" size="10"
                          accesskey="D" tabindex="13" />  </td>
    <td align="right" nowrap="nowrap"><u>V</u>ia:</td>
    <td align="left" nowrap="nowrap">
      <select size="1" id="selShipName" accesskey="V" tabindex="17">
```

```
          <option value="0">Select...</option>
        </select>
      </td>
    </tr><tr>
      <td align="right" nowrap="nowrap">C<u>o</u>untry:</td>
      <td align="left" nowrap="nowrap"><input type="text" id="txtShipCountry"
          size="20" accesskey="O" tabindex="14" /></td>
      <td align="right" nowrap="nowrap"><u>F</u>reight:</td>
      <td align="left" nowrap="nowrap">$<input type="text" id="txtFreight"
          size="6" accesskey="F" tabindex="18" /></td>
    </tr><tr>
      <td colspan="4" align="right">
        <input type="button" id="btnUpdateOrder" value="Update"
              tabindex="19" onclick="updateOrder()" />
        <input type="button" id="btnDeleteOrder" value="Delete"
              tabindex="20" onclick="deleteOrder()" />
      </td>
    </tr>
</table>
```

Specifying the Tab Index and Shortcut Keys

You can again see how the `tabindex` attribute is used to specify the tab order for
each control, making it possible for the user to tab through the controls in the
expected order rather than the order they appear in the page (for example, you
can tab directly through the address text boxes and then across to the date and
shipping details text boxes).

You also used the `accesskey` attribute to specify shortcut keys for most of the
controls, and you indicate the corresponding key by underlining one character in
the captions for the controls. You can see this if you look back at Figure 11-9.

At the end of the listing are the two buttons to update or delete the currently
selected order (you can see these buttons in Figure 11-9). They execute two functions in the page, named `updateOrder` and `deleteOrder`. Following on from the previous table are the `<div>` elements that you use to display the order lines for this
order, the total value of this order, and the controls to add a new order line. All are
hidden when the page first loads because they have their `display` style attribute set
to "none":

```
<div id="divOrderLines" tabindex="22" style="display:none"></div>
<div align="right" id="lblOrderTotal"></div><p />
<div id="divAddLine" style="background-color:#fff0f5;display:none">
  Add another <u>P</u>roduct to this Order:
```

```
<select size="1" id="selProducts" accesskey="P" tabindex="25"
       onchange="selectProduct(this)" />
  <option value="-1">Select product...</option>
</select>
<input type="button" id="btnAddLine" value="Add" tabindex="25"
       disabled="true" onclick="addOrderLine()" />
</div>
```

The "Add Another Product..." section shown in the previous listing (and in Figure 11-10) contains the drop-down list selProducts that you saw being filled with a list of products earlier in this chapter, when you loaded the data for the page.

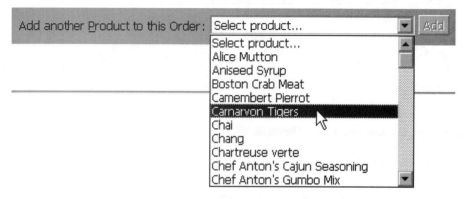

Figure 11-10. The controls to add a new order line to an existing order

The Add button next to the drop-down list executes a function named addOrderLine when clicked, which you'll investigate later. Notice that this button is disabled by default—you enable it by reacting to the onchange event when the selection in the list changes. You execute a simple function named selectProduct and pass it a reference to the list box:

```
function selectProduct(objList) {
  // enable or disable "Add" button
  document.all('btnAddLine').disabled = (objList.selectedIndex == 0);
}
```

Hence, the Add button will only be enabled when the selection in the list *isn't* the first entry, which has the value zero and text *Select product*.

The Code to Display the Order Details

When the user makes a selection in the list of orders in the left part of the page, the function named showOrderDetail executes. It receives the selected order ID as a parameter. Inside this function, you first build an XPath expression that'll select the correct <Orders> node from the diffgram in the MSXML parser instance. Then you can get a reference to this node and start accessing the child nodes to get the values into local variables ready for display:

```
function showOrderDetail(strOrderID) {

  // get the details of the order to display above table
  // from the current XML parser object using DOM methods
  var strXPath = '//NewDataSet/Orders[OrderID="' + strOrderID + '"]'
  var objOrderNode = objXMLData.selectSingleNode(strXPath);
  var strThisOrderID = objOrderNode.childNodes[0].text;
  intOrderID = parseInt(strThisOrderID);
  var strThisOrdered = objOrderNode.childNodes[2].text;
  var strThisRequired = objOrderNode.childNodes[3].text;
  ...
```

The intOrderID variable is a page-level variable, declared outside of all the functions in the <script> section of the page. In the previous code, you can see that you set this to the ID of the current order so that you can access it in any function later.

Detecting Null ShippedDate Values

One problem you met in the view orders version of the application also arises here. The value for the ShippedDate column of an order may not be specified if it hasn't yet shipped, and the database will contain <NULL> in this case. When you fill the DataSet from the database and then export it as XML or a diffgram, the <ShippedDate> element won't appear in the document. So you need to take the same action as before to get the correct values into each variable depending on the name of the fifth node (at index 4)—which is where the <ShippedDate> node will be if it exists:

```
// if ShippedDate is null in database, node will not
// appear in XML so check next node name
if (objOrderNode.childNodes[4].nodeName == 'ShippedDate') {
  var strThisShipped = objOrderNode.childNodes[4].text;
  var strThisVia = objOrderNode.childNodes[5].text;
```

```
      var strThisFreight = formatDecimal(objOrderNode.childNodes[6].text);
      var strThisCustName = objOrderNode.childNodes[7].text;
      var strThisAddress = objOrderNode.childNodes[8].text;
      var strThisCity = objOrderNode.childNodes[9].text;
      var strThisPostCode = objOrderNode.childNodes[10].text;
      var strThisCountry = objOrderNode.childNodes[11].text;
  }
  else {
    var strThisShipped = '';
    var strThisVia = objOrderNode.childNodes[4].text;
    var strThisFreight = formatDecimal(objOrderNode.childNodes[5].text);
    var strThisCustName = objOrderNode.childNodes[6].text;
    var strThisAddress = objOrderNode.childNodes[7].text;
    var strThisCity = objOrderNode.childNodes[8].text;
    var strThisPostCode = objOrderNode.childNodes[9].text;
    var strThisCountry = objOrderNode.childNodes[10].text;
  }
  ...
```

You need to format numbers to two decimal places in several places in the page, so you create a simple function that does this given a string containing the value. This function is named formatDecimal, and you can see it used in the previous code to format the value from the <Freight> node (at index 5 or 6 in the previous code, depending on whether there's a <ShippedDate> node present). The function itself is just three lines of code:

```
function formatDecimal(strValue) {
  // format a value to two decimal places for display
  if (strValue.indexOf('.') < 0) strValue += '.';
  strValue += '00';
  return strValue.substring(0, strValue.indexOf('.') + 3);
}
```

Populating the Controls on the Page

Having extracted the values for the current order from the XML diffgram, you can now use them to populate the controls in the page. The order ID and order date display in the <span> element in the first row of the table shown earlier, and the other values are used to set the value attributes (properties) of the appropriate text box controls. There's one "nontextbox" control in this part of the page, the selShipName drop-down list, but you can select the appropriate item in the list simply by setting the value property to the current ShipVia value you placed in the strThisVia variable:

```
...
// fill in order details on page
document.all('lblOrderID').innerHTML = 'Order ID: <b>'
    + strThisOrderID + '</b>   '
    + 'Ordered: ' + strThisOrdered.substring(0, 10);
document.all('txtShipName').value = strThisCustName;
document.all('txtShipAddress').value = strThisAddress;
document.all('txtShipCity').value = strThisCity;
document.all('txtShipPostCode').value = strThisPostCode;
document.all('txtShipCountry').value = strThisCountry;
document.all('txtRequiredDate').value = strThisRequired.substring(0, 10);
document.all('txtShippedDate').value = strThisShipped.substring(0, 10);
document.all('txtFreight').value = strThisFreight;
document.all('selShipName').value = strThisVia;

// show table containing order details and select Name
document.all('tblOrderDetail').style.display = '';
document.all('txtShipName').select();
...
```

You end the previous code section by clearing the display style property—by default it is set to "none" when the page first loads so that the controls aren't visible until an order has been selected. You also move the input focus to the Name text box ready for the user to start tabbing through and editing the values in the text boxes.

Getting and Displaying a List of Order Lines

The next step is to get the result of transforming the related <Order Details> elements for this order. You'll come back and look at the stylesheet itself later. You display the list of order lines in a <div> element located below the order details section you just looked at and make it and the section where the user can add a new order line visible by clearing their display style properties:

```
...
// get result of transforming Order Details XML into
// a string and display it, and show update buttons
var strResult = getStyledResult(true, strOrderID, '');
document.all('divOrderLines').innerHTML = strResult;
document.all('divOrderLines').style.display = '';
document.all('divAddline').style.display = '';
...
```

Calculating and Displaying the Order Total

Finally, you can calculate the order total in the same way as you did in the view orders version of this application. The difference is that you include the `<NewDataSet>` element in the XPath so that you only get rows from the "current values" section of the diffgram and not from the `<diffgr:before>` section. After formatting the result using the `formatDecimal` function you saw earlier, you display it in the `<span>` element with the `id` of `"lblOrderTotal"`:

```
...
// get the order total by iterating the OrderLines nodes
strXPath = '//NewDataSet/Order_x0020_Details[OrderID="' + strOrderID + '"]'
var objOrderLines = objOrderNode.selectNodes(strXPath);
var dblTotal = new Number(0);
for (i = 0; i < objOrderLines.length; i++) {
  dblTotal += parseFloat(objOrderLines[i].childNodes[7].text);
}

// format it with two decimal places and display it
var strTotal = formatDecimal(dblTotal.toString());
var msg = 'Total order value: <b>$' + strTotal + '</b>  ';
document.all('lblOrderTotal').innerHTML = msg;
}
```

Creating the List of Order Lines

The table containing the list of order lines for the currently selected order is created by an XSLT transformation on the diffgram. Most of the stylesheet is the same as in the previous version of the application (the view orders version), but now you need to create text boxes for the three columns that contain values that can be edited, rather than just inserting the values into the table cells, as shown in Figure 11-11.

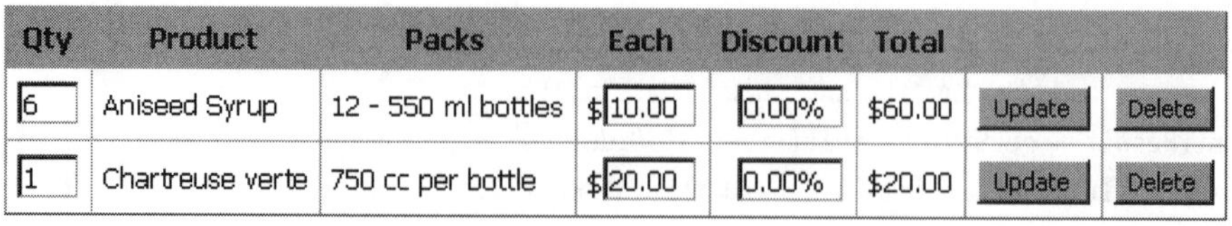

Qty	Product	Packs	Each	Discount	Total		
6	Aniseed Syrup	12 - 550 ml bottles	$10.00	0.00%	$60.00	Update	Delete
1	Chartreuse verte	750 cc per bottle	$20.00	0.00%	$20.00	Update	Delete

Figure 11-11. The editing controls for the order details rows

You also need to include the two buttons in each row to allow the user to update or delete individual lines on this order.

The following listing shows the parts of the stylesheet that differ in this version of the application. For example, to create the text boxes for the Qty column in the table, you use this XSLT code:

```
<td align="center">
  <input type="text" size="1">
    <xsl:attribute name="id">
      txtQuantity-<xsl:value-of select="ProductID" />
    </xsl:attribute>
    <xsl:attribute name="value">
      <xsl:value-of select="Quantity" />
    </xsl:attribute>
  </input>
</td>
```

Notice how it sets the id attribute of the text box to txtQuantity- followed by the product ID from this row. This allows you to differentiate between the text boxes in each row when you come to apply the user's edited values. You use the same techniques to create the text boxes for editing the unit price and the discount for each order line, as shown next. Here you also format the value before setting the value attribute:

```
<td align="right" nowrap="nowrap">
  $<input type="text" size="4">
    <xsl:attribute name="id">
      txtPrice-<xsl:value-of select="ProductID" />
    </xsl:attribute>
    <xsl:attribute name="value">
      <xsl:value-of select="format-number(UnitPrice,\'#,##0.00\')" />
    </xsl:attribute>
  </input>
</td>
...
<td align="right" nowrap="nowrap">
  <input type="text" size="5">
    <xsl:attribute name="id">
      txtDiscount-<xsl:value-of select="ProductID" /></xsl:attribute>
    <xsl:attribute name="value">
      <xsl:value-of select="format-number(Discount,\'#0.00%\')" />
    </xsl:attribute>
  </input>
</td>
```

Creating the Update Line and Delete Line Buttons

The final section of the stylesheet creates the two buttons in each row of the table. You set the `onclick` attribute for each button to the name of the appropriate function (either `updateOrderLine` or `deleteOrderLine`) and add the product ID for this row as the value of a parameter for these functions:

```
<td align="center" nowrap="nowrap">
  <input type="button" value="Update" style="font-size:11px">
    <xsl:attribute name="onclick">
      updateOrderLine(<xsl:value-of select="ProductID" />)
    </xsl:attribute>\n'
  </input>
</td>
<td align="center" nowrap="nowrap">
  <input type="button" value="Delete" style="font-size:11px">
    <xsl:attribute name="onclick">
        deleteOrderLine(<xsl:value-of select="ProductID" />)
     </xsl:attribute>
  </input>
</td>
```

That just about covers the way that the page displays existing orders ready for editing. The next step is to consider how you manage the editing process and update the diffgram you're storing in the MSXML parser instance. Before you do that, however, you'll just see how the Save Changes button gets to be enabled when rows are edited and how you try and prevent a user from forgetting to save their edited values.

It's Time to Talk Dirty

One of the quaintest terms to be adopted by the IT industry is the concept of "dirty" data. Though it fits in nicely with the detective novel scenario (remember the film *Dirty Harry*?), what we really mean, of course, is data that has been edited but not yet saved. The page implements a "dirty flag" using a page-level variable that's set to `false` when the page is first loaded:

```
// flag to indicate if updates have not been saved to server
var blnIsDirty = false;
```

As the user updates, deletes, or inserts rows, you set this flag to `true` to indicate that the locally cached data contains changes that haven't yet been applied to the back-end database. You could also use the value of this variable to set the `disabled` property of the Save Changes button each time. However, in the page, you simply set it to the appropriate value in each routine that changes the dirty flag:

```
// this occurs in all routines that update the diffgram
blnIsDirty = true;  // set "dirty" flag

// enable "Save Changes" button
document.all('btnSaveChanges').disabled = false;
```

If the user navigates to another page, you want to prompt them to submit any unsaved changes they made to the data. You add the `onunload` attribute to the opening <body> tag in the page, so the function you specify (`checkIfDirty`) will execute whenever the user navigates to another page:

```
<body ... onunload="checkIfDirty()">
```

In this function you can check the value of the dirty flag and pop up a `confirm` dialog box if there are changes that need to be saved. If they click OK, you call the `postToServer` function to update the database:

```
function checkIfDirty() {
  // see if data has been changed before page is unloaded
  if (blnIsDirty) {

    // prompt user to save changes to server
    var strConfirm = 'The order details for this customer have changed.\n'
                + 'Do you want to save these changes to the server?';
    if (confirm(strConfirm)) postToServer();
  }
}
```

Updating the Orders Diffgram

The final tasks you need to perform in the edit-orders.aspx page are to update the diffgram stored in the MSXML parser instance in response to the various buttons on the page, as shown in Figure 11-12. There are six different tasks to perform:

- **Adding a new order**: This is accomplished by clicking the New Order button below the list of orders in the left section of the page.

- **Deleting an existing order**: This is accomplished by selecting the order and clicking the Delete button below the text boxes that show the order details.

- **Updating an existing order**: This is accomplished by selecting the order, editing the values in the text boxes in the right section of the page, and clicking the Update button just below these text boxes.

- **Adding a new line to an existing order**: This is accomplished by selecting a product in the drop-down list at the bottom-right side of the page and clicking the Add button next to it.

- **Deleting a line from an existing order**: This is accomplished by clicking the Delete button in that order line row of the table in the right side of the page.

- **Updating a line for an existing order**: This is accomplished by editing the values in the text boxes of that order line row and clicking the Update button in the row.

Each of these actions updates the diffgram to reflect the changes to the data, preserving the original values so that the appropriate DataSet can be constructed from it and used to perform the updates in the database. You'll look at each of these six tasks in turn.

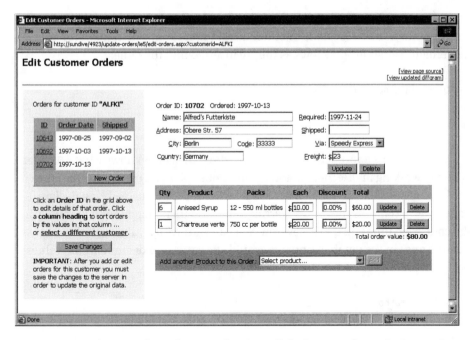

Figure 11-12. The complete edit page showing all the buttons for updating and adding orders

Adding a New Order

One thing you discovered in the previous chapter is that inserting a row into a table when working with data that's cached on a remote client can cause problems if the table contains an auto-increment (IDENTITY or AutoNumber) column. The data access component manages this by inserting the row and then retrieving the new value for the auto-increment column from the database and updating the DataSet during the process.

All you have to do is ensure that you use a value for this column on the client that's unique within the remotely cached data (the DataSet or the diffgram used to fill the DataSet). One approach with int-type auto-increment columns is to start at -1 and work backward (assuming the values in the existing rows of the DataSet extracted from the database use positive values for the auto-increment column).

In fact, the `DataSet` supports this approach directly. You can set the properties for a column in a `DataSet` table to automatically create auto-increment (or auto-decrement) values for new rows as they're inserted into the table:

```
objColumn.AutoIncrement = True
objColumn.AutoIncrementSeed = -1
objColumn.AutoIncrementStep = -1
```

However, this approach will only work where the client knows what a `DataSet` is. You're working in Internet Explorer 5 and not depending on the .NET Framework being installed, so you can't use this technique here. Instead, you declare a page-level variable as the "seed" starting value and then increment it manually in the code each time you add a new row. You can start with a value well above any existing ones in the database, but you could start at -1 and decrement the values instead if preferred:

```
// variable to hold ID of last inserted order row
var intLastNewID = 99000;
```

Setting Default Values for New Order Rows

In the down-level client examples, you set all the columns of a new order row to default values when you insert it into the database (this is done immediately in that case because you're not caching the data remotely). Although you don't have to set default values for all columns in the current example, it still makes sense to do so. Users will expect the application to set the order date and the default shipping address automatically. Of course, you also have to set the temporary value for the `OrderID` primary key column.

One other point is that the `RequiredDate` column can't be null or else it'll upset the code that extracts the values of the nodes. You can cope with a null value for the `ShippedDate` column (you built this feature into the code earlier in this chapter), but you need all the other columns to contain values. You include a simple routine in the page that creates a string for the current date in the correct format for the diffgram, and you'll use this later on to prefill the `OrderDate` and `RequiredDate` columns in new rows:

```
function getCurrentDateString() {
  // creates a string in format yyyy-mm-dd for current date

  var objToday = new Date();
  var strMonth = '0' + (objToday.getMonth() + 1).toString();
  var strDay = '0' + objToday.getDate().toString();
```

```
    return objToday.getYear().toString() + '-'
      + strMonth.substring(strMonth.length - 2, strMonth.length)
      + '-' + strDay.substring(strDay.length - 2, strDay.length);
}
```

Validating the Values for New Order Rows

In a real application, validation of the values that users enter is extremely important. To some extent, the process of filling a diffgram and loading the data into a DataSet will catch most errors, as will the update process if the values conflict with rules and constraints in the database itself. To keep the example relatively simple, we've avoided including complex validation code, other than validating a few values for order line rows.

One thing we've done is establish a rule that the RequiredDate must be filled in, and if empty, it's automatically filled with the current date. This happens when a new row is inserted but also when an order row is updated after editing. You'll see how later.

The example page allows you to cause an update error when submitting changes to the database so that you can experiment and see the consequences in the reconcile-changes.aspx page. For this reason, it allows a row to be submitted when the shipper (in the Via drop-down list) isn't specified. This will cause a foreign-key exception when the update is performed. When you build your applications for release, you'll obviously want to check for situations such as this and prevent the user from submitting the changes if they haven't selected a valid value.

Creating a New Orders Node

You include a function in the page that creates an XML node representing a new order, ready to insert into the diffgram. You start by creating a new element node with the name Orders and set the values for the id, rowOrder, and hasChanges attributes. The function expects to receive an integer value that's the rowOrder to use for the new row:

```
function createOrdersNode(intRowOrder) {
  // create a new empty Orders node with default values

  // create <Orders> element node
  var objNode = objXMLData.createElement('Orders');

  // set "id", "rowOrder" and "hasChanges" attributes for new node
  var strRowOrder = intRowOrder.toString();
  intRowOrder++;
```

```
    var strID = 'Orders' + intRowOrder.toString();
    objNode.setAttribute('diffgr:id', strID);
    objNode.setAttribute('msdata:rowOrder', strRowOrder);
    objNode.setAttribute('diffgr:hasChanges', 'inserted');
    ...
```

Adding the Child Nodes

Now you can add the child elements that represent the columns in the new row. You can get the OrderID for the new order from the page-level variable that indicates the currently selected order (you set this to the next free "dummy" or temporary order number before calling this function). The customer ID is also available from a page-level variable that you set when the page is first loaded. After these two child nodes come the OrderDate and RequiredDate, both of which you set to the current date using the getCurrentDateString function you saw earlier:

```
...
// add child node for current OrderID
var objChildNode = objXMLData.createElement('OrderID');
objChildNode.text = intOrderID.toString();
objNode.appendChild(objChildNode);

// add child node for current CustomerID
objChildNode = objXMLData.createElement('CustomerID');
objChildNode.text = strCustID;
objNode.appendChild(objChildNode);

// add child node for OrderDate (default is today)
objChildNode = objXMLData.createElement('OrderDate');
objChildNode.text = getCurrentDateString();
objNode.appendChild(objChildNode);

// add child node for RequiredDate (default is today)
objChildNode = objXMLData.createElement('RequiredDate');
objChildNode.text = getCurrentDateString();
objNode.appendChild(objChildNode);
...
```

Next come the ShipVia and Freight child nodes, for which you use generic default values. A ShipVia value of zero corresponds to the default Select... entry in the drop-down list of shippers, and you specify a default freight charge of $15.00:

```
...
// add child node for ShipVia (default is 0)
objChildNode = objXMLData.createElement('ShipVia');
objChildNode.text = '0';
objNode.appendChild(objChildNode);

// add child node for Freight (default is $15.00)
objChildNode = objXMLData.createElement('Freight');
objChildNode.text = '15';
objNode.appendChild(objChildNode);
...
```

The Name and Address Details

You know you need to avoid having null values for anything other than the ShippedDate column. In the down-level clients, you prefilled the name and address of a new order by querying the Customers table in the database during the postback where you inserted the new row. However, in the remote environment, you don't have access to the Customers table in the database, so you'll prefill the name and address details from the first existing <Orders> node in the current diffgram as the default. You could, of course, remote the complete list of customers to the client as well as all the other data you're using, but this is probably overkill unless the main purpose of the application is to add new orders.

So, you set up some default values for the name and address in case there's no existing <Orders> node in the diffgram (no orders for this customer), then get a reference to the first <Orders> node if one exists. From this node, you can copy the values you want—though again you have to cope with the situation where there may not be a ShippedDate node in the existing order!

```
...
// get name and address from existing order if possible
var strShipName = '[name]';          // default values
var strShipAddress = '[address]';
var strShipCity = '[city]';
var strShipPostCode = '[post code]';
var strShipCountry = '[country]';
```

```
// get reference to first existing order
var colAnyOrders = objXMLData.selectNodes('//NewDataSet/Orders');
if (colAnyOrders.length != 0) {

  // got at least one order node, see where name and address
  // are depending on whether ShippedDate node exists
  if (colAnyOrders[0].childNodes[4].nodeName == 'ShippedDate') {
    strShipName = colAnyOrders[0].childNodes[7].text;
    strShipAddress = colAnyOrders[0].childNodes[8].text;
    strShipCity = colAnyOrders[0].childNodes[9].text;
    strShipPostCode = colAnyOrders[0].childNodes[10].text;
    strShipCountry = colAnyOrders[0].childNodes[11].text;
  }
  else {
    strShipName = colAnyOrders[0].childNodes[6].text;
    strShipAddress = colAnyOrders[0].childNodes[7].text;
    strShipCity = colAnyOrders[0].childNodes[8].text;
    strShipPostCode = colAnyOrders[0].childNodes[9].text;
    strShipCountry = colAnyOrders[0].childNodes[10].text;
  }
}

// add child node for ShipName (use existing order details)
objChildNode = objXMLData.createElement('ShipName');
objChildNode.text = strShipName;
objNode.appendChild(objChildNode);

// add child node for ShipAddress
objChildNode = objXMLData.createElement('ShipAddress');
objChildNode.text = strShipAddress;
objNode.appendChild(objChildNode);

// add child node for ShipCity
objChildNode = objXMLData.createElement('ShipCity');
objChildNode.text = strShipCity;
objNode.appendChild(objChildNode);

// add child node for ShipPostalCode
objChildNode = objXMLData.createElement('ShipPostalCode');
objChildNode.text = strShipPostCode;
objNode.appendChild(objChildNode);
```

```
// add child node for ShipCountry
objChildNode = objXMLData.createElement('ShipCountry');
objChildNode.text = strShipCountry;
objNode.appendChild(objChildNode);

// add empty child node for ShipperName
objChildNode = objXMLData.createElement('ShipperName');
objNode.appendChild(objChildNode);

return objNode;
}
```

Right at the end of the previous listing, just before you return the new node to the calling routine, you add the node for the name of the shipping company. As the default value for the <ShipVia> node is zero, you don't need to provide a value for this node—the page will display Select... in the drop-down list until the user selects a shipping company.

Adding the New Node to the Diffgram

As shown in the last line of the previous code, you return the new node from the createOrdersNode function, ready to insert into the diffgram. You do this in the newOrder function, which runs when the New Order button is clicked. You get the temporary order ID from the page-level variable (as discussed earlier) and increment it ready for the next new order.

Next, you need to figure out what the rowOrder attribute of the new row should be so that you can pass it to the createOrdersNode function. You do this by getting a NodeList of the existing <Orders> elements and from this a reference to the last one in the diffgram. You can't just use the length of the NodeList because the user may previously have deleted one or more orders, so the number of existing nodes provides no guide to the actual rowOrder attribute value required. Instead, you get the value from the last existing node and increment it:

```
function newOrder() {
  // runs when the "New Order" button is clicked

  // get temporary new order ID and increment ready for next one
  intOrderID = intLastNewID;
  intLastNewID++;

  // need row order number, or zero if no existing Orders node
  var intRowOrder = 0;  // assume no existing Orders nodes
```

```
// get NodeList of <Orders> nodes
var objOrdersList = objXMLData.selectNodes('//NewDataSet/Orders');
if (objOrdersList.length > 0) {
  var objLastOrder = objOrdersList[objOrdersList.length - 1];
  intRowOrder =
    parseInt(objLastOrder.getAttribute('msdata:rowOrder')) + 1;
}
...
```

Now you can call the createOrdersNode function to create the new node and then append it to the list of existing nodes in the diffgram. It'll appear after any existing <Order Details> nodes, but that doesn't affect the way the data is loaded into the DataSet from the diffgram. However, if there are no existing orders for this customer, the diffgram won't actually contain a <NewDatSet> node, so you check for this first and insert one if it's not there:

```
...
// create the new Order node
var objNode = createOrdersNode(intRowOrder);

// get reference to <NewDataSet> node in diffgram
var objParentNode = objXMLData.selectSingleNode('//NewDataSet');

// make sure that <NewDataSet> element exists
if (objParentNode == null) {

    // does not exist, so create <NewDataSet> element node
    var objParentNode = objXMLData.createElement('NewDataSet');

    // get reference to diffgram root node and append it
    var objDGNode = objXMLData.selectSingleNode('//diffgr:diffgram');
    objDGNode.appendChild(objParentNode);
}

// append new <Orders> node as child of <NewDataSet> node
objParentNode.appendChild(objNode);

// refresh list of orders in left-hand table
showOrderList('OrderID');

// show new order in right-hand section of page
showOrderDetail(intOrderID);

blnIsDirty = true;  // set "dirty" flag
```

```
  // enable "Save Changes" button
  document.all('btnSaveChanges').disabled = false;
}
```

After inserting the new <Orders> node, you refresh the list of orders in the left side of the page to show the new order and display the order details in the right side of the page. Finally, you set the "dirty" flag and enable the Save Changes button.

Deleting an Existing Order

When the user selects an existing order and clicks the Delete button, a function in the page named deleteOrder executes. This function first gets a reference to the <Orders> node in the diffgram for this order and copies it to the <diffgr:before> section of the diffgram using the generic copyToDiffgrBefore function. Then it can delete this node from the "current values" section (the <NewDataSet> element) of the diffgram:

```
function deleteOrder() {
  // runs when the "Delete" (Order) button is clicked

  // get reference to existing node
  var objNode = getNodeReference('Orders', intOrderID);

  // copy to <diffgr:before> if not already there
  copyToDiffgrBefore(objNode);

  // delete this node from XML
  objNode.parentNode.removeChild(objNode);
  ...
```

However, if there are any existing <Order Details> nodes (order lines) for this order, you must also mark these as deleted within the diffgram. If not, the update process will fail when processing the data. So you also iterate through the nodes that represent the related <Order Details> rows, copying them to the <diffgr:before> section of the diffgram and then removing them from the <NewDataSet> section:

```
...
// delete all related Order Details nodes from XML
// required to "cascade deletes" as would happen if
// we were using a DataSet that has a relation set up
```

```
// create XPath and get NodeList of related Order Details nodes
var strXPath = '//NewDataSet/Order_x0020_Details[OrderID="'
              + intOrderID + '"]';
var colNodeList = objXMLData.selectNodes(strXPath);

// iterate through NodeList deleting nodes
// and adding them to <diffgr:before> section
for (var intLoop = colNodeList.length - 1; intLoop >= 0; intLoop--) {
  var objChildNode = colNodeList[intLoop];
  copyToDiffgrBefore(objChildNode);
  objChildNode.parentNode.removeChild(objChildNode);
}
...
```

Next you can refresh the list of orders in the left part of the page and then hide all the controls in the right part of the page to indicate that the order has been deleted. You then finish off by setting the "dirty" flag and enabling the Save Changes button:

```
...
// refresh list of orders in left-hand table
// in case ShippedDate has been changed
showOrderList('OrderID');

// hide order details section of page
document.all('divAddLine').style.display = 'none';
document.all('lblOrderTotal').innerHTML = '';
document.all('divOrderLines').style.display = 'none';
document.all('tblOrderDetail').style.display = 'none';

blnIsDirty = true;  // set "dirty" flag

// enable "Save Changes" button
document.all('btnSaveChanges').disabled = false;
}
```

Modifying an Existing Order

To modify an existing order, you need to be able to extract the values from the text boxes and the drop-down list in the page. You create a separate function for this, which can be used with either an <Orders> node or an <Order Details> node. The function expects to receive three parameters. The first is a reference to the node object you're modifying, the second is the name of the table you're performing updates for, and the third is the product ID if you're updating an <Order Details> node:

```
function getEditedValuesNode(objNode, strTableName, strProductID) {
  // gets values in page controls and puts into
  // supplied node, depending on table name
  ...
```

Setting the Updated RequiredDate Value

If the table name provided in the second parameter is Orders, you start by getting the value for the RequiredDate from the appropriate text box in the page. Recall that you don't want this to be null, so if there's no value in the text box, you use the current date instead—obtained from the getCurrentDateString function you described earlier in this chapter when you looked at inserting a new <Orders> node. Once you've got the value, you insert it into the third child node of the <Orders> node that's passed in the first parameter of the function:

```
...
if (strTableName == 'Orders') {

  // set RequiredDate - use today if no value provided
  var strRequired = document.all('txtRequiredDate').value;
  if (strRequired == '') {
    strRequired = getCurrentDateString();
    document.all('txtRequiredDate').value = strRequired;
  }
  objNode.childNodes[3].text = strRequired;
  ...
```

Setting the Updated ShippedDate Value

The optional <ShippedDate> node that caused problems in earlier functions gets
in the way again here. If there's no value set for the Shipped text box, you have to
remove the child node named <ShippedDate> from the current <Orders> node in the
diffgram if it exists. However, if the user entered a value in the text box when it was
previously empty, you have to add the <ShippedDate> node into the current <Orders>
element. Finally, when there's a value in the text box, you set the value of this child
node:

```
...
// set ShippedDate if provided
// create or remove node in XML as appropriate
var strShipped = document.all('txtShippedDate').value;
if (strShipped == '') {

  // remove ShippedDate child node if it exists
  if (objNode.childNodes[4].nodeName == 'ShippedDate')
    objNode.removeChild(objNode.childNodes[4]);
}
else {

  // add ShippedDate child node if not already there
  if (objNode.childNodes[4].nodeName != 'ShippedDate') {
    objNewNode = objXMLData.createElement('ShippedDate');
    objNode.insertBefore(objNewNode, objNode.childNodes[4]);
  }
  objNode.childNodes[4].text = strShipped;
}
...
```

Setting the Rest of the Node Values

The remainder of the process is much simpler. You extract the numeric key value
and the text name of the selected shipping company from the value and text
attributes of the selected <option> in the selShipName drop-down list into two variables named strShipVia and strShipper. Then, taking account of the fact that the
<ShippedDate> node might or might not exist, you can copy the values of the other
controls straight into the corresponding child nodes:

```
  ...
  // get Shipper values from drop-down list
  var objViaList = document.all('selShipName');
  var strShipVia = objViaList.options[objViaList.selectedIndex].value;
  var strShipper = objViaList.options[objViaList.selectedIndex].text;

  // now set following nodes in XML
  if (objNode.childNodes[4].nodeName == 'ShippedDate') {
    objNode.childNodes[5].text = strShipVia;
    objNode.childNodes[6].text = document.all('txtFreight').value;
    objNode.childNodes[7].text = document.all('txtShipName').value;
    objNode.childNodes[8].text = document.all('txtShipAddress').value;
    objNode.childNodes[9].text = document.all('txtShipCity').value;
    objNode.childNodes[10].text = document.all('txtShipPostCode').value;
    objNode.childNodes[11].text = document.all('txtShipCountry').value;
    objNode.childNodes[12].text = strShipper;
  }
  else {
    objNode.childNodes[4].text = strShipVia;
    objNode.childNodes[5].text = document.all('txtFreight').value;
    objNode.childNodes[6].text = document.all('txtShipName').value;
    objNode.childNodes[7].text = document.all('txtShipAddress').value;
    objNode.childNodes[8].text = document.all('txtShipCity').value;
    objNode.childNodes[9].text = document.all('txtShipPostCode').value;
    objNode.childNodes[10].text = document.all('txtShipCountry').value;
    objNode.childNodes[11].text = strShipper;
  }
}
...
```

Updating an Order Details Node

If the getEditedValuesNode function is called with the value Order Details for the
table name parameter, you need to extract the values from the controls in the current row of the table that displays the list of order lines. In this case, you'll get the
ProductID value passed to the function as the third parameter, and you use this to
locate the appropriate controls on the page.

Each text box within the rows of the order lines table has an `id` attribute that ends with the `ProductID` value for that row. So you can get the three values into variables by appending the value from the third function parameter to the fixed part of each text box `id`:

```
...
else {    // -- processing Order Details table

  // get values from current order line into strings and validate
  // text box IDs include the product ID allowing direct access
  strQuantity = document.all('txtQuantity-' + strProductID).value;
  strUnitPrice = document.all('txtPrice-' + strProductID).value;
  strDiscount = document.all('txtDiscount-' + strProductID).value;
  ...
```

Validating the User's Input

In an attempt to prevent too many update errors, we've included some rudimentary validation code in this function for the three numeric values that can be edited in each order line. You parse each value to ensure that it's numeric and check that it's greater than zero. For the quantity, you display an error message in an `alert` dialog box, and for the other two values, you just set them to zero. You might decide to include something more robust here in a real-world application:

```
...
// validate input values as numbers
try {
  var intQty = parseInt(strQuantity);
  var sngPrice = parseFloat(strUnitPrice);
  var sngDisc = parseFloat(strDiscount);
}
catch(e) {
}

// if Quantity is NaN or less than zero show error message
if (! intQty > 0) {
  alert('The value you entered for\n"Qty" is not a valid number.');
  return;
}
```

```
// if UnitPrice is NaN or less than zero assume zero
if (! sngPrice > 0) sngPrice = 0;

// if Discount is NaN or less than zero assume zero
if (sngDisc > 0)
  sngDisc = sngDisc / 100
else
  sngDisc = 0;
...
```

Figure 11-13 shows the alert dialog box that's displayed when an invalid value is detected.

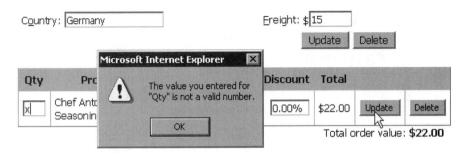

Figure 11-13. The alert dialog box that's displayed when an invalid value is entered

Calculating the Line Total

Finally, you can recalculate the line total (this is one of the reasons you added the primitive validation code) and then update the child nodes of this node:

```
...
//calculate LineTotal value
var dblTotal = intQty * (sngPrice - (sngPrice * sngDisc));

// update nodes in XML Order Details node
objNode.childNodes[2].text = sngPrice.toString();
objNode.childNodes[3].text = intQty.toString();
objNode.childNodes[4].text = sngDisc.toString();
objNode.childNodes[7].text = dblTotal.toString();
  }
}
```

The updateOrder Function

In theory, the getEditedValuesNode function does all the hard work for you, so updating an existing <Orders> node is just a matter of calling the functions you've already created. You use the getNodeReference function to get a reference to the node you're updating and copy it to the <diffgr:before> section of the diffgram. Then you can call the getEditedValuesNode function you've just been describing to fill in the values of the original node (in the <NewDataSet> section of the diffgram) with the current values in the controls on the page:

```
function updateOrder() {
  // runs when the "Update" (Order) button is clicked

  // get reference to existing node
  var objNode = getNodeReference('Orders', intOrderID, 0);

  // copy to <diffgr:before> if not already there
  copyToDiffgrBefore(objNode);

  // update values of existing node from page controls
  getEditedValuesNode(objNode, 'Orders')
  ...
```

Now you add the diffgr:hasChanges="modified" attribute to the node, but only if it *isn't* a node that was inserted during the current session (otherwise, when you post the diffgram back to the data access tier, the new DataSet won't know it's a new node that wasn't in the original DataSet). Then you refresh both the list of orders in the left part of the page (in case the ShippedDate has changed) and the details of the order—which includes the table containing the list of order lines. The final tasks are setting the dirty flag and enabling the Save Changes button:

```
  ...
  // add 'modified' attribute to node but not if it
  // is a node that was inserted in this session
  if (objNode.getAttribute('diffgr:hasChanges') != 'inserted')
    objNode.setAttribute('diffgr:hasChanges', 'modified');

  // refresh list of orders in left-hand table
  // in case ShippedDate has been changed
  showOrderList('OrderID');

  // refresh order details in right-hand section of page
  // to show formatted values
  showOrderDetail(intOrderID);
```

```
blnIsDirty = true;   // set "dirty" flag

  // enable "Save Changes" button
  document.all('btnSaveChanges').disabled = false;
}
```

Adding a New Order Line

When the user selects a product to add to an existing order and clicks the Add button, you must add a new <Order Details> node to the diffgram. As when adding a new order, a separate function that creates a new <Order Details> node with appropriate default values is used. Although there's a lot of code here, it's mainly repetitive.

You start by building an XPath that'll retrieve the correct <Products> node from the list of products stored in the MSXML parser instance named objXMLProducts, using the product ID passed as a parameter to this function. From this node, you can collect the product name, the "quantity per unit" string, and the unit price:

```
function createOrderLinesNode(strProductID, intRowOrder) {
  // create a new empty Order Details node with default values

  // get details of selected product
  var strXPath = '//Products[ProductID="' + strProductID + '"]'
  var objProductNode = objXMLProducts.selectSingleNode(strXPath);
  var strProductName = objProductNode.childNodes[1].text;
  var strQtyPerUnit = objProductNode.childNodes[2].text;
  var strUnitPrice = objProductNode.childNodes[3].text;
  ...
```

Now you create a new element named <Order_x0020_Details> (the encoded table name) and set the rowOrder and id attributes using the value for the row order passed into the function. You also add the hasChanges attribute, setting it to inserted:

```
...
// create <Order_x0020_Details> element node
var objNode = objXMLData.createElement('Order_x0020_Details');

// set "id", "rowOrder" and "hasChanges" attributes for new node
var strRowOrder = intRowOrder.toString();
intRowOrder++;
var strID = 'Order Details' + intRowOrder.toString();
```

```
objNode.setAttribute('diffgr:id', strID);
objNode.setAttribute('msdata:rowOrder', strRowOrder);
objNode.setAttribute('diffgr:hasChanges', 'inserted');
...
```

Setting the Child Node Values

The remainder of the process just involves creating each child node in turn (in the correct order that matches the schema for the DataSet), setting their values, and adding them to the new <Order Details> node. Afterward you can return the new node to the calling routine:

```
...
// add child node for current OrderID
var objChildNode = objXMLData.createElement('OrderID');
objChildNode.text = intOrderID.toString();
objNode.appendChild(objChildNode);

// add child node for current ProductID
var objChildNode = objXMLData.createElement('ProductID');
objChildNode.text = strProductID;
objNode.appendChild(objChildNode);

// add child node for current UnitPrice
var objChildNode = objXMLData.createElement('UnitPrice');
objChildNode.text = strUnitPrice;
objNode.appendChild(objChildNode);

// add child node for current Quantity (default is 1)
var objChildNode = objXMLData.createElement('Quantity');
objChildNode.text = '1';
objNode.appendChild(objChildNode);

// add child node for current Discount (default is 0)
var objChildNode = objXMLData.createElement('Discount');
objChildNode.text = '0';
objNode.appendChild(objChildNode);

// add child node for current ProductName
var objChildNode = objXMLData.createElement('ProductName');
objChildNode.text = strProductName;
objNode.appendChild(objChildNode);
```

```
// add child node for current QtyPerUnit
var objChildNode = objXMLData.createElement('QtyPerUnit');
objChildNode.text = strQtyPerUnit;
objNode.appendChild(objChildNode);

// add child node for current LineTotal
var objChildNode = objXMLData.createElement('LineTotal');
objChildNode.text = strUnitPrice;
objNode.appendChild(objChildNode);

return objNode;
}
```

The addOrderLine Function

Even though you've now got a function that creates the new <Order Details> node for you, there's still quite a bit to do in adding a new line to an existing order. First you get the product ID from the value attribute of the currently selected <option> element in the selProducts drop-down list. Then you change the list back to the default entry of Select Product and disable the Add button again.

Each <Order Details> row has a primary key made up of the combination of the OrderID and ProductID columns. As you discovered in the down-level client versions of the application, this means you have to check if the selected product is already on the current order because it can only appear once. You do this by searching for an existing <Order Details> element with the same OrderID and ProductID child node values and display a message and exit from the function if you find one:

```
function addOrderLine() {
  // runs when the "Add (Order line) button is clicked

  // get selected ProductID from drop-down list
  var objList = document.all('selProducts');
  var strProductID = objList.options[objList.selectedIndex].value;

  // change list back to "Select product..."
  // and disable "Add" button
  document.all('selProducts').selectedIndex = 0;
  document.all('btnAddLine').disabled = true;

  // see if selected product already exists in this order
  var strXPath = '//NewDataSet/Order_x0020_Details[OrderID="'
```

```
            + intOrderID.toString() + '" and ProductID="'
            + strProductID + '"]';
var objLinesNodes = objXMLData.selectNodes(strXPath);
if (objLinesNodes.length > 0) {
  var strMsg = 'This product is already on the order.\n'
            + 'Edit the quantity to add more items.'
  alert(strMsg);
  return;
}
```

Figure 11-14 shows the alert dialog box that's displayed when the user tries to add a product to an order that already contains this product.

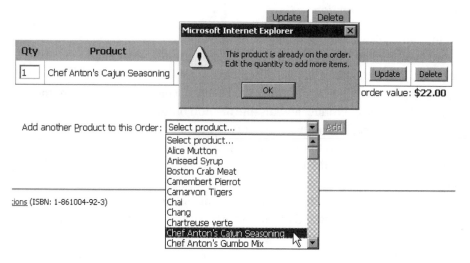

Figure 11-14. The dialog box that prevents the same product from being added more than once

Creating the New Order Details Node

To add a new order line, you need to get the appropriate value for the row order that the `createOrderLinesNode` function will use to add the correct `id` and `rowOrder` attributes to the new node. You do this in the same way you did when adding a new order—you get a `NodeList` of all `<Order Details>` nodes, get the `rowOrder` of the last one, and increment it:

```
// need row order number, or zero if no existing Order Lines node
// get NodeList of <Order Lines> nodes if there are any
var objOrdersList =
```

```
      objXMLData.selectNodes('//NewDataSet/Order_x0020_Details');
if (objOrdersList.length > 0) {
  var objLastOrder = objOrdersList[objOrdersList.length - 1];
  var intRowOrder =
      parseInt(objLastOrder.getAttribute('msdata:rowOrder')) + 1;
}
else      // no existing order lines for this customer
  var intRowOrder = 0;
...
```

Now you can call the createOrderLinesNode function with the current product ID and row order values. The new node that this function returns is then appended to the end of the list of child nodes within the <NewDataSet> element. Then you finish up by refreshing the right section of the page to show the updated order line, set the input focus to the Qty text box ready for the user to change it if required, set the dirty flag, and enable the Save Changes button:

```
  ...
  // create the new Order Details node
  var objNode = createOrderLinesNode(strProductID, intRowOrder);

  // append new node as child of <NewDataSet> element in diffgram
  objOrdersList = objXMLData.selectNodes('//NewDataSet');
  objOrdersList[0].appendChild(objNode);

  // refresh list of order lines in right-hand section of page
  showOrderDetail(intOrderID);

  // select Quantity text box for order added
  document.all('txtQuantity-' + strProductID).select();

  blnIsDirty = true;  // set "dirty" flag

  // enable "Save Changes" button
  document.all('btnSaveChanges').disabled = false;
}
```

Chapter 11

Deleting an Existing Order Line

The last two functions in the page we need to cover here are relatively simple. The first of these executes when the Delete button in an existing row within the list of order lines is clicked. Both the Delete and the Update buttons in the list of order lines pass the product ID of the row in which they're located as a parameter to the functions because you declared them (via the transformation of the XSLT stylesheet) like this:

```
<input type="button" value="Update" style="font-size:11px">
  <xsl:attribute name="onclick">
    updateOrderLine(<xsl:value-of select="ProductID" />)
  </xsl:attribute>
</input>
...
<input type="button" value="Delete" style="font-size:11px">
  <xsl:attribute name="onclick">
    deleteOrderLine(<xsl:value-of select="ProductID" />)
  </xsl:attribute>'
</input>
```

So, in the deleteOrderLine function, you can get a reference to the corresponding node in the diffgram by supplying the product ID that's passed to the function, as well as the table name and order ID. Then you copy this node to the `<diffgr:before>` section of the diffgram and delete if from the "current values" `<NewDataSet>` section:

```
function deleteOrderLine(strProductID) {
  // runs when the "Delete" (Order Lines) button is clicked

  // get reference to existing node
  var objNode = getNodeReference('Order_x0020_Details', intOrderID,
                                 strProductID);

  // copy to <diffgr:before> if not already there
  copyToDiffgrBefore(objNode);

  // delete this node from XML
  objNode.parentNode.removeChild(objNode);

  // refresh list of order lines in right-hand section of page
  showOrderDetail(intOrderID);
```

```
blnIsDirty = true;   // set "dirty" flag

  // enable "Save Changes" button
  document.all('btnSaveChanges').disabled = false;
}
```

As in the other similar functions, you finish by refreshing the list of order lines, setting the dirty flag, and enabling the Save Changes button.

Modifying an Existing Order Line

To modify an existing order line, you do much the same as you just saw when deleting an order line. You use the product ID passed to the function to get a reference to the node in the diffgram and copy it to the <diffgr:before> section. Next, however, you call the getEditedValuesNode function you saw earlier (when looking at the updateOrder function), which directly updates the values in the diffgram for you using the current values in the controls for this order line row in the table on the page:

```
function updateOrderLine(strProductID) {
  // runs when the "Update" (Order Lines) button is clicked

  // get reference to existing node
  var objNode = getNodeReference('Order_x0020_Details', intOrderID, strProductID);

  // copy to <diffgr:before> if not already there
  copyToDiffgrBefore(objNode);

  // update values of existing node from page controls
  getEditedValuesNode(objNode, 'Order_x0020_Details', strProductID);
  ...
```

Then you can add the hasChanges node to the <Order Details> element in the diffgram if it isn't a node you inserted during the current session and perform all the same "finishing off stuff" you did in the previous functions:

```
  ...
  // add 'modified' attribute to node but not if it
  // is a node that was inserted in this session
  if (objNode.getAttribute('diffgr:hasChanges') != 'inserted')
    objNode.setAttribute('diffgr:hasChanges', 'modified');
```

```
// refresh list of order lines to get actual values used
showOrderDetail(intOrderID);

// select Quantity text box for order modified
document.all('txtQuantity-' + strProductID).select();

blnIsDirty = true;   // set "dirty" flag

// enable "Save Changes" button
document.all('btnSaveChanges').disabled = false;
}
```

That's it—you've built a rich client interface for Internet Explorer 5.0 and higher that allows you to display and edit orders and the related order lines for any of the customers. The edits are saved in the remotely cached diffgram on the client, ready to be posted back to the server and used to update the back-end database.

Summary

As you can see, building rich client applications that can cache and edit data remote from the server isn't a trivial task. As well as getting your head around the way diffgrams work and the code you need to manipulate them, you also have to write a lot of client-side code to create the interface, display the data, and manage user input. In fact, the page you've been using in this chapter, edit-orders.aspx, contains some 350 lines of JavaScript code after all the comments and blank lines have been taken into account.

The point is, however, that this application is generally much more pleasant to use than the down-level version you examined in earlier chapters. This is especially true if you're at the other end of a slow (and perhaps recalcitrant) Internet connection. OK, so there's some delay while the data loads when the page is first displayed, but after that it's smooth, fast, and as sweet as a kitten to use. You can see from the metaphors that we've really impressed ourselves!

The topics you concentrated on in this chapter were as follows:

- Understanding what's required from the rich client application

- Building routines that manipulate a diffgram to reflect updates to the data

- Building a remote data update client interface for Internet Explorer 5 and higher

However, this is only half the battle. OK, so you've got an edited diffgram to send back to the server. You also have, as you saw in the previous chapter, a data access component that can apply the changes to the database. What you haven't got is the magic ingredient to connect them together and handle the reconciliation process for any error that might arise.

We did discuss this issue early in this chapter and mentioned the middle tier reconcile-changes.aspx page, but then we got too involved in the client application to take it any further. So, the topic for the next chapter is to investigate the reconciliation process in more detail and see an example at work.

CHAPTER 12

Reconciling Update Errors

THE PREVIOUS CHAPTER considered the ramifications of, and techniques for, updating remotely cached data and then applying these updates to a back-end data store. You also built an application that can perform the updates on the client and send them back to the server as a diffgram from which you can reconstruct a suitable DataSet object.

Later in this chapter, you'll consider some other rich client applications and how they might be able to perform the remote updates in the same way as the Internet Explorer 5.0 version demonstrated in the previous chapter. However, first, you need to expand that example by catching the diffgram it sends to the server and applying the updates it contains to the data store.

You also, of course, need to consider what happens when any update errors occur at this point. The data access component you built in Chapter 10 will form the basis for the updates, and it automatically checks for concurrency and other types of errors. However, you need to find a way to communicate these errors to the user and allow them (where possible) to decide how to reconcile them.

So, in this chapter, we'll cover the following:

- Handling a posted diffgram in the middle tier on the server

- Using the data access tier component to update the data source

- Handling any errors that arise from the updates and reconciling them

- Using a Web Service to communicate data updates to and from a client

- Examining other rich client techniques for updating remotely cached data

One thing that you won't be looking at in this chapter is how you can accomplish the whole process when the client has the .NET Framework installed. This is the topic of the next chapter. Here, you'll start by handling data posted as a diffgram from the client.

Reconciling Update Errors in Overview

Before you look at the code that performs the error reporting and reconciliation, we'll briefly summarize where you are with the application as a whole. We'll also overview the process, showing the steps that are required. Then you'll look at the implementation in the example application.

A Summary of the Process

Currently, you have a rich client page named edit-orders.aspx (designed for Internet Explorer 5.0 and higher) that updates a diffgram and posts it to an ASP.NET page named reconcile-changes.aspx on the server. You also have a data access component, UpdateDataSet.dll, that exposes several methods used in the previous chapter to provide the data for the edit-order.aspx page.

You examined the contents of this component in Chapter 10 and saw that it also exposes a method named UpdateAllOrderDetails that takes a DataSet object and uses this to update the data source. It returns a DataSet object that contains the same set of rows as the original DataSet. Update errors are reported within this DataSet using the RowError property of each row, and the original values of each column are updated to reflect the underlying values that were in the data store when the update was attempted.

Therefore, all you need to do is create a middle tier component (in this case, an ASP.NET page named reconcile-changes.aspx) that receives the diffgram, converts it to a DataSet, and calls the UpdateAllOrderDetails method. It can then take the DataSet returned from this method, display the errors, and allow the user to decide what to do about them. As a reminder of the whole process, Figure 12-1 shows the process used in the previous chapter.

In this chapter, you'll concentrate on the bottom half of this figure—how the reconcile-changes.aspx page works, and how it accesses the data access component.

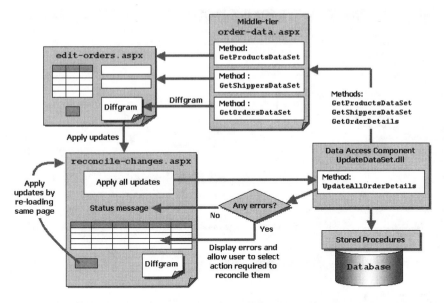

Figure 12-1. An overview of the process for Internet Explorer 5.0 and higher

The Error Reporting and Reconciliation Process

So that you can see the error reporting and reconciliation process in outline, and associate it with Figure 12-1, we've included figures of the result as well as a description of the various stages of the process. They show editing some orders for a customer using the rich client application described in the previous chapter. Figure 12-2 shows adding a new order with the temporary order ID of 99000, and changing the freight charge for order 10609 from $19.54 to $25.75. Clicking the Save Changes button posts the updated diffgram and the customer ID to the reconcile-changes.aspx page.

The figure you'll see next describes the processing steps within the reconcile-changes.aspx middle tier page. As well as the diffgram, you collect the customer ID that's sent from the client (you need this to be able to update the original data store and get back the underlying values in case of an error). You also save this in a hidden-type input control on the page so that you can access it when the page is reloaded during the reconciliation process.

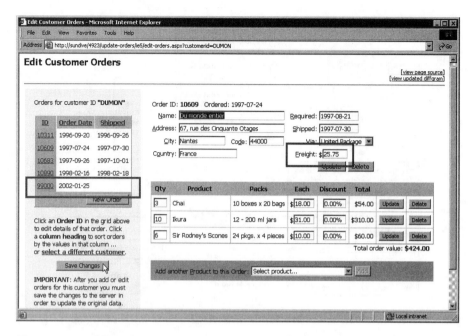

Figure 12-2. Adding a new order and editing details of an existing order

Editing the DataSet After Update Errors Have Occurred

Next, you check if this is a postback or if this is the first time that the page has been loaded during the current update session. If it's a postback, the user will have set the values of HTML <form> controls on the page to specify what actions they want to take to reconcile any update errors. So, in this case, you apply these settings to the DataSet (by editing the contents of the appropriate rows and columns) so that it can be resubmitted to the data access tier.

Note that the ADO.NET Update method you'll shortly be calling from within the data access tier UpdateAllOrderDetails method doesn't replace existing RowError values. It concatenates new error messages with existing ones so that you can see if more than one error has arisen. However, you only want to display the most recent error. After editing the rows, you remove any existing RowError values that may have been placed in them during the last iteration of this page (see Figure 12-3).

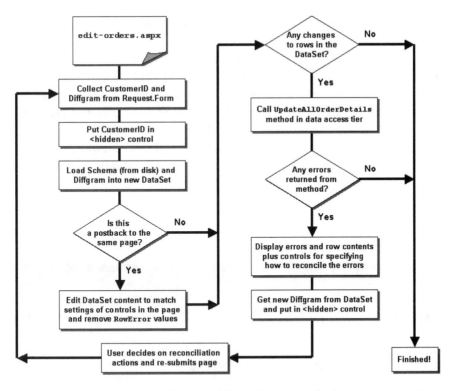

Figure 12-3. The steps taken for reconciling changes to the data

Next you can check if there are any changed rows in the DataSet (rows that are marked as "deleted," "added," or "modified")—if the user decides to abandon all their changes during the reconciliation stage, the code will have set the RowState property of all the rows to "unchanged." If you do have some rows to update, you can now call the UpdateAllOrderDetails method.

After the update has been carried out, you check if there were any errors by examining the returned DataSet. If there are errors, you display them in the page, with the appropriate HTML <form> controls that allow the user to specify the reconciliation action they want to take. You also need to access the DataSet again when the page is reloaded, so you extract the data as a diffgram and store this in another hidden-type control.

Displaying the Update Errors for Reconciliation

At this point, the user can see any errors and choose which values to keep and which to discard. Figure 12-4 shows what this page looks like for the updates carried out in Figure 12-3, assuming that some other user concurrently updated the same order (10609) as you did. You can see the concurrency error in the first table of values, where this "other user" changed the address details while you changed the Freight column value. You've selected the check box for the Freight column because you want to replace the existing value in the database with the new value, but you'll allow the Address value entered by the other user to remain (in other words, you don't replace it with the old Address value that's still in your updated row).

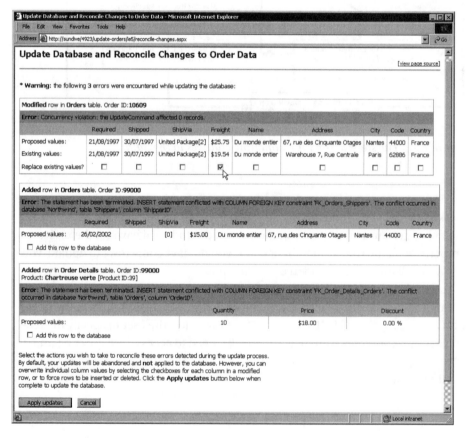

Figure 12-4. The resulting page for reconciling conflicting changes to the data

The new order you added for this customer couldn't be inserted into the database, as shown by the other two tables of values in Figure 12-4. This is because you forgot to select the shipping company, so this column in the Orders row contains the default value 0 (zero). Because there's no shipping company with this value as the primary key (the ShipperID), the foreign key constraint in the database rejected the new row. Furthermore, because this row couldn't be inserted into the Orders table, the order line (Order Details) row was also rejected. There's no Orders row in the database with the matching OrderID primary key value.

For rows that couldn't be added or deleted, the user only has the option to retry the process or abandon it for the complete row. In the case of the foreign key constraint errors, the insert will never succeed until they go back and change the values. However, if a delete process fails because the row has been changed concurrently, the user can set the check box and try the delete again. Because the DataSet now contains the correct underlying values, the process should succeed when attempted again.

Following a Successful Update

Once the user has made their selections, they click the Apply updates button to resubmit this page for processing—and the process starts all over again. If all the updates succeed, or they abandon their changes, the page displays a couple of links where they can go back and edit more orders for this customer or select another customer, as shown in Figure 12-5.

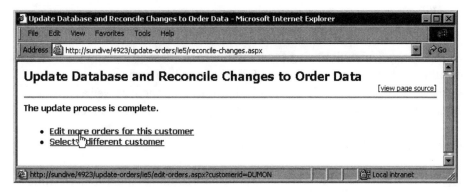

Figure 12-5. The result when the update process is successful

If you select the first of these links, you can see the order (10609) that you just updated. The address is the one that the other concurrent user entered, and the freight is the one you entered, as shown in Figure 12-6. Successful reconciliation!

Of course, the order you tried to insert isn't shown, but you can try adding a new order (or deleting an existing one) to prove that it does work. When you insert a new order, remember to select a shipping company from the drop-down list and then click the Update button to update the locally cached diffgram before saving the changes to the server.

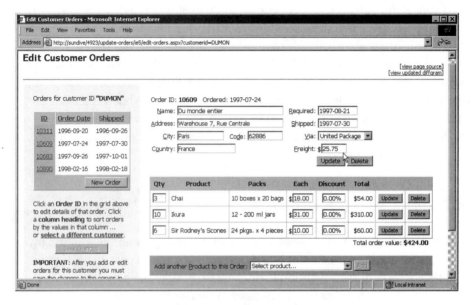

Figure 12-6. The updated order shown in the browser

Displaying Trace Information

Remember that you built tracing capabilities into the data access component? So one other option in the reconcile-changes.aspx page is to turn on tracing so you can see the number of rows being handled by the component as well as the reconciliation details. Simply add the attribute Trace="True" to the Page directive:

```
<%@Page Language="VB" EnableViewState="False" Trace="True" %>
```

For example, Figure 12-7 shows the trace information being displayed while you attempt to update two orders (one that succeeds and one that fails) and add a new order and order line (which succeeds)

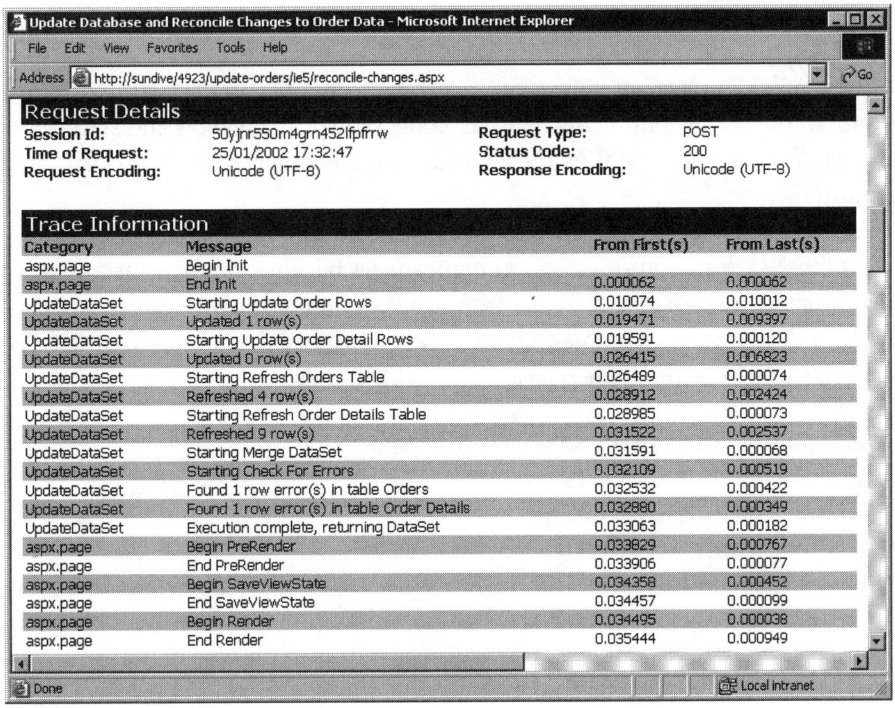

Figure 12-7. The trace information created by the data access component when updating the database

The Reconciliation Process in Detail

You'll now see the code you use to implement the reconciliation page you just saw in action. You'll recall from the previous chapter that the client application posts the updated diffgram and the customer ID to the reconcile-changes.aspx page when the user clicks the Save Changes button. The following listing shows the client-side code in the client application that performs this post:

```
function postToServer() {
  // send XML DiffGram to server to update database
  ...
  ...
  // insert XML and CustomerID into hidden controls and submit form
  document.all('hidCustID').value = strCustID;
  document.all('hidPostXML').value = objXMLData.xml;
  document.all('frmPostXML').submit();
}
```

The `reconcile-changes.aspx` Page

So, in the ASP.NET page, after declaring a few namespaces and the custom user control for the connection string, you can collect the posted values and start the processing involved in updating the data store and reconciling any errors that are encountered.

As well as the namespace of the data access component (UpdateDataSet), you import the System.Data and System.Xml namespaces because you'll be instantiating objects that are declared in these namespaces throughout the code. You also need the System.IO namespace in this page to allow you to read the contents of a DataSet object into a string—you'll see how and why a little later:

```
<%@Page Language="VB" EnableViewState="False" %>
<%@Import Namespace="System.Data" %>
<%@Import Namespace="System.Xml" %>
<%@Import Namespace="System.IO" %>
<%@Import Namespace="DataSetUpdate" %>
```

You also add the EnableViewState="False" attribute to the Page directive, as you can see in the previous listing. You don't want to preserve the values for any controls on this page between postbacks (in fact, you specifically want to avoid doing so), and as a by-product this will also save both processing and memory resources when the page executes.

The HTML Form and Hyperlinks

There's very little declarative HTML in the reconcile-changes.aspx page. The tables containing the controls where the user specifies the actions to take to reconcile update errors are created dynamically as the page executes. So, all you need is the <form> section to allow the page to be reloaded (posted back to itself) when an error does occur and the user specifies the reconciliation actions required and some hyperlinks to allow them to go off and edit some more orders once the current updates are completed.

The <form> section is next—note that by default it's not actually included in the page output because the visible attribute (property) is set to false. You only want to show the <form> and the controls it contains when an update error is detected. The <form> contains a <div> element where you display the update errors and reconciliation controls, some explanatory text, a couple of buttons, and two hidden-type controls:

```
<form id="frmSubmit" visible="false" runat="server">
  <div id="outResult" runat="server"></div>
  Select the actions you wish to take to reconcile these errors detected
  during the update process.<br />By default, your updates ...etc...<p />
  <input type="submit" id="btnSubmit" value="Apply updates"
         runat="server" />
  <input type="submit" id="btnCancel" value="Cancel" runat="server" />
  <input type="hidden" id="hidCustID" runat="server" />
  <input type="hidden" id="hidPostXML" runat="server" />
</form>
```

The Apply updates button allows the user to apply their reconciliation actions, and they can use the Cancel button to quickly and easily abandon all the updates that resulted in an error if they prefer. The two hidden-type controls are used to pass the customer ID and the edited diffgram back to this page when it's reloaded.

If all the updates succeed—either the first time they're attempted or after the user has taken the requisite reconciliation actions to allow rows with errors to be persisted into the data store—two hyperlinks are displayed. These allow the user to go back and edit more orders for this customer or select a different customer. As with the <form> you just looked at, the <div> containing these hyperlinks isn't output by default because the visible attribute is set to false:

```
<div id="divLinks" visible="false" runat="server">
<b>The update process is complete.</b>
<ul>
<li><b><a href="edit-orders.aspx?customerid=<% = strCustID %>">
        Edit more orders for this customer</a></b></li>
<li><b><a href="../../customer-orders/ie5/default.aspx">
        Select a different customer</a></b></li>
</ul>
</div>
```

Notice that you use a page-level variable named strCustID to insert the current customer ID into the href attribute of the first hyperlink, allowing the edit-orders.aspx page to be opened showing the orders for the current customer.

Collecting the Posted Values

The code in the page declares the page-level variable you just saw and then defines the Page_Load event handler where most of the work of applying the updates and displaying errors takes place. You can see that you collect the customer ID and the diffgram from the Request.Form collection members named hidCustID and hidPostXML. You also put the customer ID into the hidden-type control named hidCustID on this page. Controls with matching names exist in the edit-orders.aspx page as well as in this page, so the values will be collected when this page is first loaded and then passed on each time it's reloaded.

Because the page also contains a Cancel button, which the user can click to abandon all their updates at any point in the process, you next check if they did just that. If so, you simply redirect them to the edit-orders.aspx page, adding the current customer ID to the query string so that orders for this customer are shown:

```
<script language="VB" runat="server">

Dim strCustID As String

Sub Page_Load()

   '-------------- load Diffgram from client into DataSet ----------------
   'get CustomerID from posted Form collection values
   strCustID = Request.Form("hidCustID")

   'see if user clicked the "Cancel" button
   If Request.Form("btnCancel") > "" Then
     Response.Redirect("edit-orders.aspx?customerid=" & strCustID)
   End If

   'put into hidden control to post back to this page
   hidCustID.Value = strCustID

   'get DiffGram from posted Form collection values
   Dim strDiffGram As String = Request.Form("hidPostXML")
```

The hidden-type controls that contain the customer ID and the diffgram are server controls, meaning that you can easily insert values into them in the server-side code. However, because you've turned off viewstate support for the page, their values won't be automatically persisted across postbacks. Therefore, you have to set these in the Page_Load event every time.

This also provides a bonus by reducing the size of the page you send to the client. If viewstate support were enabled, the page would contain not only the values in the two hidden-type controls but also the viewstate content that's required to persist these values for the next postback.

Loading the Edited Diffgram

Next, you need to load the diffgram into a DataSet. You create a shiny new DataSet object and declare some variables you'll need later:

```
'create a new DataSet object
Dim objDataSet As New DataSet()

'variables to hold references to tables, rows, and columns in DataSets
Dim objTable As DataTable
Dim objRow As DataRow
```

However, this is one issue that requires a kludge to get around a bug in the ReadXml method of the DataSet object. Diffgram support was a relatively late addition to the DataSet, and the format changed regularly during development of the .NET Framework. The result is that there are a couple of "holes" in the release version.

DataSet Issues in Versions 1.0 and 1.1 of the .NET Framework

If you're running your applications on version 1.0 of the .NET Framework, there are two issues with the way the DataSet works that you need to be aware of when loading a diffgram. These don't affect version 1.1, where these bugs have been fixed. However, because this application works on both version 1.0 and 1.1, you have to include a work-around for these two issues:

- The DataSet in version 1.0 doesn't correctly parse a diffgram that contains only deleted rows and no current rows.

- The DataSet in version 1.0 doesn't correctly assign internal GUID values to the rows it imports, preventing the Merge process from working properly because the DataSet then appears to contain "extra" rows.

You'll look at the second of these two issues in the section "Working Round the Extra Rows Issue." However, you'll explore the first one now.

Working Round the "Empty Diffgram" Issue in Version 1.0

In version 1.0, the DataSet doesn't correctly recognize a legal diffgram, exported from MSXML, that contains only deleted rows. For example, the following diffgram is perfectly legal and describes the situation where the only existing order for a customer has been deleted:

```
<diffgr:diffgram xmlns:msdata="urn:schemas-microsoft-com:xml-msdata"
                 xmlns:diffgr="urn:schemas-microsoft-com:xml-diffgram-v1">
  <NewDataSet>
  </NewDataSet>
  <diffgr:before><Orders diffgr:id="Orders1" msdata:rowOrder="0">
    <OrderID>11144</OrderID>
      <CustomerID>DUMON</CustomerID>
      <OrderDate>2002-01-29T00:00:00.0000000-00:00</OrderDate>
      <RequiredDate>2002-01-29T00:00:00.0000000-00:00</RequiredDate>
      <ShipVia>2</ShipVia>
      <Freight>15</Freight>
      <ShipName>Du monde entier</ShipName>
      <ShipAddress>67, rue des Cinquante Otages</ShipAddress>
      <ShipCity>Nantes</ShipCity>
      <ShipPostalCode>44000</ShipPostalCode>
      <ShipCountry>France</ShipCountry>
      <ShipperName>United Package</ShipperName>
    </Orders>
  </diffgr:before>
</diffgr:diffgram>
```

The DataSet object's ReadXml method in version 1.0 of the .NET Framework insists that such an XML diffgram must contain <NewDataSet /> rather than <NewDataSet></NewDataSet>. If not, it doesn't parse the following <diffgr:before> section, and hence the DataSet remains empty. Therefore, you have to replace the offending combination of tags with the required single tag. The actual combination of characters exported from MSXML is as follows:

```
"<NewDataSet>" & vbCrlf & vbTab & "</NewDataSet>"
```

So, the code you use is as follows:

```
Dim strOldElement = "<NewDataSet>" & vbCrlf & vbTab & "</NewDataSet>"
strDiffGram = strDiffGram.Replace(strOldElement, "<NewDataSet />")
```

This isn't required in version 1.1, where the DataSet will correctly parse the diffgram shown earlier.

Loading the Schema into the DataSet

At last, you can get on and load the diffgram. As you saw in earlier chapters, you have to load the appropriate schema first. This is held as a disk file on the server, so you can read it directly using the physical path obtained from the MapPath method of the Request object:

```
Try

   'read the schema into the DataSet from file on disk
   objDataSet.ReadXmlSchema(Request.MapPath("orders-schema.xsd"))

Catch objError As Exception

   'display error details
   outError.InnerHTML = "<b>* Error while reading schema</b>.<br />" _
                     & objError.Message & "<br />" _
                     & "No updates were applied to the database."
   Exit Sub  ' and stop execution

End Try
```

Remember that you have to set the primary keys in the DataSet, and specify the relationship between the two tables, before you use the DataSet to update the original database tables. Without the primary keys, the Merge method used after the update will fail to match the original and refreshed rows in the DataSet. And without the proper relationship between the tables, the automatic cascade of deleted rows and updated row key values won't take place within the Update method. We discussed all these issues in detail in Chapters 9 and 10.

So that the DataSet has the correct format for its tables and includes the correct primary keys and relationship you need, you include these details in the schema that you load into it. The relevant sections of the schema are shown in the next two listings. In the first, you can see the two `<xs:unique>` elements that define the constraints for the two tables (Orders and Order Details) and how they specify that these are the primary key columns using an `msdata:PrimaryKey` attribute. The nested `<xs:selector>` and `<xs:field>` elements then identify the column(s) in the table that these constraints apply to:

```
...
<xs:unique name="Constraint1" msdata:PrimaryKey="true">
  <xs:selector xpath=".//Orders" />
  <xs:field xpath="OrderID" />
</xs:unique>
<xs:unique name="Order_x0020_Details_Constraint1"
          msdata:ConstraintName="Constraint1"
          msdata:PrimaryKey="true">
  <xs:selector xpath=".//Order_x0020_Details" />
  <xs:field xpath="OrderID" />
  <xs:field xpath="ProductID" />
</xs:unique>
...
```

The schema can now specify the relationship between the tables using an `<xs:keyref>` element, which refers to the first of the two constraints shown previously, and specifies that the column the constraint applies to is related to the column selected by the nested `<xs:selector>` and `<xs:field>` elements within this `<keyref>` section:

```
...
<xs:keyref name="CustOrders" refer="Constraint1">
  <xs:selector xpath=".//Order_x0020_Details" />
  <xs:field xpath="OrderID" />
</xs:keyref>
...
```

Loading the Data into the DataSet

Although reading a schema into a `DataSet` is a simple enough task, reading the diff-gram into the `DataSet` isn't so easy. The `ReadXml` method doesn't have an overload that accepts a `String`, so you have to use the version that takes an `XmlTextReader` instead (which is why you needed to import the `System.Xml` namespace into the page). You create a new `XmlTextReader` object, specifying the `String` containing the diffgram as the source. You set the second parameter of the constructor to the value `XmlNodeType.Document` to indicate that you're reading a complete XML document. The third parameter specifies an `XmlContext` object that defines the namespace, encoding, language, and so on of the XML document, but you can use the value `Nothing` to indicate that you'll accept the default settings:

```
Try

    'create an XmlTextReader to read data sent from client
    'specifying that string fragment is an XML Document
    Dim objReader As New XmlTextReader(strDiffGram, _
                        XmlNodeType.Document, Nothing)

    'read in the DiffGram posted from the client
    objDataSet.ReadXml(objReader, XmlReadMode.DiffGram)

Catch objError As Exception

    'display error details
    outError.InnerHTML = "Error while reading the DiffGram<br />" _
                    & objError.Message & "<br />" _
                    & "No updates were applied to the database."
    Exit Sub   ' and stop execution

End Try
```

If you encounter an error reading the XML document or the schema, you simply display a message and stop execution of the page. Obviously, if this happens, you can't go any further because the `DataSet` will be empty.

Removing the Extra Calculated Column

This DataSet contains a calculated column in the Order Details table, which contains the total value of each order line for the customer's orders. You could leave this in the DataSet if you wanted because the stored procedures don't reference it during the update process. However, you'll remove it before processing the DataSet to see how to do it if this is an issue in your own applications:

```
'get a reference to the Columns collection and remove column
'we added in the middle tier for total value of each order line
Dim colDataCols As DataColumnCollection
colDataCols = objDataSet.Tables("Order Details").Columns
colDataCols.Remove("LineTotal")
```

Working Around the "Extra Rows" Issue in Version 1.0 of the DataSet

Earlier we discussed a couple of issues with the DataSet in version 1.0 of the .NET Framework. The second of these issues comes into play with the diffgram-parsing process of the DataSet object's ReadXml method. If a diffgram contains the definition of a Modified row, it doesn't always get parsed correctly by the ReadXml method. When a new DataSet is created from an existing DataSet using the GetChanges method, both contain GUIDs for each row, and these assist in identifying matching rows when the Merge method of the DataSet is called (as it will be as part of the FEGURM process described in detail in previous chapters).

However, these GUIDs aren't persisted in a diffgram, and reading a diffgram into the DataSet object appears to cause incorrect row GUIDs to be created instead. This isn't visible in the DataSet itself, where everything looks fine. However, the "refresh" (Fill method) step of the process sometimes results in two copies of the row occurring in the DataSet—one marked as Modified and one marked as Unchanged. The subsequent Merge method then fails to match the rows with those in the original DataSet, and it can't re-establish the primary key constraint afterward—resulting in a runtime error.

You can get around this by simply calling the GetChanges method on the DataSet first—before you do anything else with it. This appears to correct the errant RowState value for the modified row and has no other effect on the process:

```
objDataSet = objDataSet.GetChanges()
```

> **NOTE** *This isn't required in version 1.1, where the* DataSet *appears to correctly match the two versions of the row.*

Editing the DataSet Contents for a Postback

Next, you need to see if this is a postback. If the page is currently being loaded directly from the edit-orders.aspx page, you just need to apply the updates defined in the diffgram and check for any update errors. However, if one or more errors do occur, you'll display the controls for the user to reconcile the errors and then reload (post back) this page. At this point, you'll edit the contents of the DataSet after loading it to carry out the reconciliation actions that the user specified.

You therefore query the IsPostBack property of the Page object to see if this is a postback, and if so, you call a routine named EditTable (declared later in the page) twice—once for each table in the DataSet. This routine edits the contents of the tables to perform the reconciliation actions specified by the user. You enclose each method call in a Try...Catch construct because the process will fail if you're trying to edit a row that has been concurrently deleted by another user:

```
'-------------- if it's a postback, edit the DataSet ----------------

If Page.IsPostBack() Then

  'call routines in page to apply user's reconciliation choices
  'do in Try...Catch in case row has been deleted by another user
  Try
    EditTable(objDataSet.Tables("Orders"))
  Catch
  End Try
  Try
    EditTable(objDataSet.Tables("Order Details"))
  Catch
  End Try

End If
```

You'll come back and look at the EditTable routine in detail later.

Updating the Database from the DataSet

Now you can check to see if there are any changed rows in the DataSet tables. If there aren't (either because the diffgram was empty or because you've abandoned all the changes when editing the tables during a postback), you've finished. The code that follows the If...Then construct you see in the next section of the listing will display the links to edit some more orders.

However, if there are changed rows in the DataSet, you execute the UpdateAllOrderDetails method of the data access component next. You get the connection string from the user control, instantiate the component, and pass the current customer ID and the DataSet to this method:

```
'--------- use data access component to update database ---------------

If objDataSet.HasChanges Then    'there are edited rows in DataSet

  'get connection string from web.config
  Dim strConnect As String
  strConnect = ConfigurationSettings.AppSettings("NorthwindConnectString")

  'create an instance of the data access component
  Dim objOrderUpdate As New UpdateDataSet(strConnect)

  Try

    'call function in data access component to do the updates
    objDataSet = objOrderUpdate.UpdateAllOrderDetails(strCustID, objDataSet)

  Catch objError As Exception

    'get error message string
    Dim strError As String = objError.Message

    'see if it was a "constraints" violation within the component, if so a
    'concurrent user probaby inserted same product in Order Details table
    If strError.IndexOf("Failed to enable constraints") >= 0 Then
      strError = "This product was added to the order by another user."
    End If

    'display error details and links to edit more rows
    outError.InnerHtml = "* Error during updates to original data.<br />" _
      & strError & " Source: " & objError.Source & "<p />"
    divLinks.Visible = True

    Exit Sub  ' and stop execution

  End Try
```

If the component itself fails for any reason—for example, an internal error such as not being able to connect to the data source—you display a message and stop. Sensibly, you can go no further should this happen. However, there's one situation that can cause an error, but that's related to the results of concurrent changes to the data rather than failure of the component. This is where the current user is trying to insert a new row in the Order Details table when another user has inserted a row for the same product concurrently.

The design of the Northwind sample database you're using is such that an order can only contain one order line for any individual product. The primary key of the Order Details table is the combination of the OrderID and ProductID columns. Attempting to add a row with the same combination of OrderID and ProductID values results in the component producing the error message "Failed to enable constraints..." (plus some more descriptive text). You trap this error separately and display a more informative message instead, before displaying the links to go back to the edit-orders.aspx page and terminating processing in the current page.

Checking for Errors After the Update Process

The UpdateAllOrderDetails method returns a DataSet containing the same set of rows as you started with, but with the RowError property set for rows where update errors occurred and with the original value in each row updated to match that currently in the database. So now you can check if any errors were encountered during the update process.

You create two arrays of DataRow objects and use the GetErrors method to fill these arrays with references to the rows in the DataSet where an error occurred. Then you can check how many errors there were in each table, and in total, by examining the length of each array:

```
'-------- check for any update errors and display these -------------

'get two arrays of the rows with errors from original DataSet
Dim arrOrdersErrors() As DataRow = objDataSet.Tables("Orders").GetErrors()
Dim arrDetailsErrors() As DataRow = _
                        objDataSet.Tables("Order Details").GetErrors()

'get number of errors in each table and total number
Dim intOrdersErrors As Integer = arrOrdersErrors.GetLength(0)
Dim intDetailsErrors As Integer = arrDetailsErrors.GetLength(0)
Dim intTotalErrors As Integer = intOrdersErrors + intDetailsErrors
```

If there were update errors, you now have to construct the page where the user will specify the reconciliation actions to take. You display a warning message and then iterate through the two arrays of error rows, passing each row in turn to a function named GetDisplayString. This is located elsewhere in the page and creates the HTML tables containing the error details and the check box controls you saw in the page earlier in this chapter:

```
If intTotalErrors > 0 Then    'there were update errors detected

  'display a warning message
  outResult.InnerHtml = "<b>* Warning:</b> the following"
  If intTotalErrors = 1 Then
    outResult.InnerHtml &= " error was encountered while " _
                        & "updating the database:<p />"
  Else
    outResult.InnerHtml &= " <b>" & intTotalErrors.ToString() _
    & "</b> errors were encountered while updating the database:<p />"
  End If

  'iterate through the Orders rows with errors
  For Each objRow In arrOrdersErrors

    'call function elsewhere in page to display error details
    outResult.InnerHtml &= GetDisplayString(objRow) & "<p />"

  Next

  'iterate through the Order Details rows with errors
  For Each objRow In arrDetailsErrors

    'call function elsewhere in page to display error details
    outResult.InnerHtml &= GetDisplayString(objRow) & "<p />"

  Next
```

You'll come back and look at the GetDisplayString function later to see how it works.

Getting a Diffgram As a String from a DataSet

Having displayed the error details, you can now finish the page by putting the current diffgram into the hidden-type control named hidPostXML. Remember that, if this is a postback, the user will have specified the reconciliation actions required and the code will have edited the DataSet contents to reflect these changes. You therefore need to extract the new diffgram from the DataSet.

Of course, as you should be getting used to by now, nothing is ever as simple as it seems once you introduce technology into the equation. How do you get a diffgram out of a DataSet as a String? You can't use the GetXml method (which does return a String) because it can't return a diffgram. It only returns an "XML representation" of the current values.

The WriteXml method used in the middle tier in several places throughout this book can export a diffgram but not as a String. It can only export to a Stream, a disk file, a TextWriter, or an XmlWriter. Another workaround is required. You instantiate a new MemoryStream object (which is why you needed to import the System.IO namespace into the page) and write the diffgram to this using the WriteXml method and specifying the value XmlWriteMode.DiffGram for the second parameter as before:

```
'get XML diffgram from DataSet after applying updates
'create a MemoryStream for writing XML from DataSet into
Dim objStream As New MemoryStream()
objDataSet.WriteXml(objStream, XmlWriteMode.DiffGram)
```

Now you can call the GetBuffer method of the stream to get an array of characters that represent the diffgram and close the MemoryStream. Then you create a System.Text.Encoding.UTF8 object. This has a useful method that converts an array of characters into a String. At last, you can fill in the hidPostXML control:

```
'get contents of Stream as an array of bytes
Dim arrXML() As Byte = objStream.GetBuffer()
objStream.Close()    'remember to close the Stream

'use the Encoding class to convert the array to a String
Dim objEncoding As System.Text.Encoding = System.Text.Encoding.UTF8
strDiffGram = objEncoding.GetString(arrXML)

'put into hidden control to post back to this page
hidPostXML.Value = strDiffGram
```

Finally, you make the `<form>` containing the reconciliation instructions visible in the page by setting its `visible` property to `True`. On the other hand, if you didn't find any errors after updating the database, you can display the `<div>` element that contains the message "The update process is complete" and the links to edit more orders for this customer or to search for another customer:

```
'display the SUBMIT button to post changes back to this page
'and hide list of links to edit more orders
frmSubmit.Visible = True

Else  'no errors after updating

'no errors during update, show message and links to edit more rows
divLinks.Visible = True

End If
```

Finally, if there were no changed rows in the `DataSet`, you do the same thing:

```
...
Else   'no changed rows found in DataSet

'no updates performed, show message and links to edit more rows
divLinks.Visible = True

End If

End Sub
```

You can use Figure 12-3 to follow the steps that the code performs and see more easily how they relate to the whole process. What you haven't yet looked at in detail are the two routines that you skipped over in this description of the page code. The `EditTable` routine is responsible for performing the edits on the `DataSet` in line with the user's reconciliation actions. The other, the `GetDisplayString` function, is used to generate the HTML tables containing the error details and the controls where the user specifies the reconciliation actions they require.

In the code you just looked at, the `EditTable` routine is actually called first. However, you'll look at the `GetDisplayString` function first, which will make it easier to see how the actions specified by the user are applied to the tables in the `DataSet` afterward.

Displaying the Errors and Reconciliation Options

The GetDisplayString function you used in the main Page_Load event handler shown previously is responsible for creating the visual output in the page that indicates an update error. It's called for a row that failed the update process (for whatever reason) and displays details of the row, the error that occurred, the values for that row, and one or more HTML check box controls that specify the actions required to reconcile the error if possible.

The Design Decisions

You'll notice when you look at the code in this part of the page that it doesn't use ASP.NET server controls (there's no runat="server" attribute). There are many different ways you can build the visual section of the page that shows the reconciliation information. What you're looking for is this:

- Details of the row that caused the error—the RowState (such as Modified or Added), the table name, and the primary key value(s)

- Details of the error that occurred—why it failed to update the data source and how to reconcile the error

- A list of the proposed values—the values that the user entered or edited on the client

- A list of the existing values in the database when the update was attempted

- Controls that enable the user to decide how to solve the problem if possible, for example, by selecting which column values to overwrite or abandoning the update for the row

The obvious layout for all this is a table, with each column containing the proposed and original values. For example, if the user's changes to an existing Orders row can't be applied to the database, a table like that in Figure 12-8 displays.

Modified row in **Orders** table. Order ID:**10890**									
Error: Concurrency violation: the UpdateCommand affected 0 records.									
	Required	Shipped	ShipVia	Freight	Name	Address	City	Code	Country
Proposed values:	16/03/1998	18/02/1998	Speedy Express[1]	$10.00	Du monde entier	67, rue des Cinquante Otages	Nantes	44000	France
Existing values:	16/03/1998	18/02/1998	Speedy Express[1]	$20.00	Du monde entier	67, rue des Cinquante Otages	Nantes	442222	France
Replace existing values?	☐	☐	☐	☐	☐	☐	☐	☐	☐

Figure 12-8. The reconciliation table for a modified row

So, how could you create this table dynamically each time you detect an error? Some of the techniques that spring to mind are the following:

Build a user control that you can insert into the page. You could build one that automatically detects which table the row comes from (Orders or Order Details) or build two different user controls.

Build one or more server controls that work like the built-in ASP.NET controls. This isn't a simple task and is well beyond the scope of this book, but it might well be a useful approach if you need to create this kind of display on a regular basis. Again, you could build one that automatically detects which table the row comes from (Orders or Order Details) or build two different ones. You could also, of course, build a generic one that will work with any table.

Use ASP.NET techniques to create the table dynamically. You could use the ASP.NET Table, TableRow, and TableCell server controls or the HtmlTable, HtmlTableRow, and HtmlTableCell versions. In fact, this provides a useful way to build generic routines that could handle any table row.

Use traditional ASP techniques to build the table as a string and then insert it into a control on the page. Although this might be frowned on, it's actually the most efficient way when you don't need to build generic routines. You can directly specify exactly the output you want, with minimum server processing required.

Building Tables Dynamically with ASP.NET

As an example of the third option mentioned previously, you can easily build routines that display the information identified in the previous section for any row from a DataSet table. The following code shows how you can display the column names in a table row:

```
'create a new Table control
Dim ctlTable As New Table()

'declare variables to hold a TableRow and TableCell
Dim ctlRow As TableRow
Dim ctlCell As TableCell

'set properties (attributes) of table
With ctlTable
  .BorderWidth = Unit.Pixel(1)
```

```
  .CellSpacing = 0
  .CellPadding = 5
  .GridLines = GridLines.Vertical
End With

'create a new table row and set the background color to silver
ctlRow = New TableRow()
ctlRow.BackColor = System.Drawing.Color.FromName("silver")

'iterate through the columns in the DataTable referenced by objTable
Dim objColumn As DataColumn
For Each objColumn In objTable.Columns

  'create a new table cell
  ctlCell = New TableCell()

  'create the text content of the cell using a LiteralControl
  ctlCell.Controls.Add(New LiteralControl(objColumn.ColumnName))

  'add the cell to the table row
  ctlRow.Cells.Add(ctlCell)

Next

'add the completed row to the table
ctlTable.Rows.Add(ctlRow)
```

Obviously, as you iterate through the columns, you can create cells for more than one row within the For Each...Next construct—one for the proposed values, one for the existing values, and one for the check boxes you display in the final row of each table. You'd add each cell to its target row as you go and then, once you've assembled the complete table, insert it into the page. The easiest way is to do this is to declare an <asp.PlaceHolder> server control at the point in the page you want the table to appear:

```
<asp:PlaceHolder id="ctlOutput" runat="server" />
```

Then you can insert the table into it, so that it's displayed, using this:

```
ctlOutput.Controls.Add(ctlTable)
```

Building Tables As a String

The dynamic technique with ASP.NET server controls is elegant, but unfortunately there are a few issues why the alternative "low-tech" route was taken in the example page. It's easy to get carried away and use ASP.NET server controls everywhere on every page, but bear in mind that they introduce a performance hit. Although this is unlikely to bring your server to its knees with the few instances of update errors that will arise in your applications, it's worth keeping in mind.

ASP.NET server controls are best used in specific situations. For example, the following scenarios *don't* require the use of server controls:

- When the element is only used to run some client-side script, for example, a button that opens a new browser window, interacts with a client-side ActiveX control or Java applet, or calculates some value for display in the page using DHTML or in an alert dialog.

- When the element is a Submit button that's only used to submit a form to the server. In this case, the code in the Page_Load event handler can still extract the values from the other controls.

- When the element is a hyperlink that opens a different page or URL and there's no need to process the values for the hyperlink on the server.

- Any other times when access to the element's properties, methods, or events in server-side code isn't required.

Notice the last of these. The bulk of the controls you'll use are check boxes that will be accessed through the Request.Form collection when the page loads, not through their intrinsic "server control" properties. You also want each one to be unchecked by default, even when the page is reloaded from a postback, which means you don't need them to persist their values automatically as server controls would (although you can disable this with the EnableViewState="False" attribute).

You also want to control the output for the table quite strictly. For example, you only want to display specific columns from each row, not all of them, so the technique of iterating through the columns you saw in the previous section will be of no help here.

You'll briefly look at the output that the page displays for the three different row states (Modified, Deleted, or Added) next and then see how the code you use generates this output.

The Display for Modified Rows

When an error occurs while attempting to update a modified row, the page displays the new values that the user entered or changed for the row and the values currently in the database, as shown in Figure 12-9. From the discussions of the FEGURM update process in previous chapters, you'll realize that these two sets of values are those stored in the DataSet after this process has completed.

Modified row in **Orders** table. Order ID:**10890**									
Error: Concurrency violation: the UpdateCommand affected 0 records.									
	Required	Shipped	ShipVia	Freight	Name	Address	City	Code	Country
Proposed values:	16/03/1998	18/02/1998	Speedy Express[1]	$10.00	Du monde entier	67, rue des Cinquante Otages	Nantes	44000	France
Existing values:	16/03/1998	18/02/1998	Speedy Express[1]	$20.00	Du monde entier	67, rue des Cinquante Otages	Nantes	442222	France
Replace existing values?	☐	☐	☐	☐	☐	☐	☐	☐	☐

Figure 12-9. The two sets of values displayed for a modified row during the reconciliation process

If the error occurred because another user has changed the row since this user loaded the data (into the remote cache in their browser—an MSXML parser instance), the existing values shown will be different from the values they saw when editing the data. This is the case in Figure 12-9 (for the Freight and Code columns), where a concurrency error has occurred.

For each column, the user can opt to overwrite the current value in the database with their edited value by setting the appropriate check box. If they don't set the check box, their edited value for that column will be abandoned.

Notice that you display the "raw" error message returned by the database. Often this isn't very informative and certainly wouldn't help inexperienced users decide how to reconcile the error. One approach you'd probably decide to take in your real-world applications would be to map this to a more informative message—perhaps using a lookup table in the database that contains plain-English error descriptions and hints for reconciling the error. Alternatively, you could use a simple code function to add some more useful text to the message.

The Display for Added Rows

If a row that the user added can't be persisted into the database, a table like that shown in Figure 12-10 displays. Obviously, you can't display the existing values because the row doesn't exist in the database. However, you can display the values that the user entered for the new row. You can also only offer them the option to try the insert again or abandon it completely.

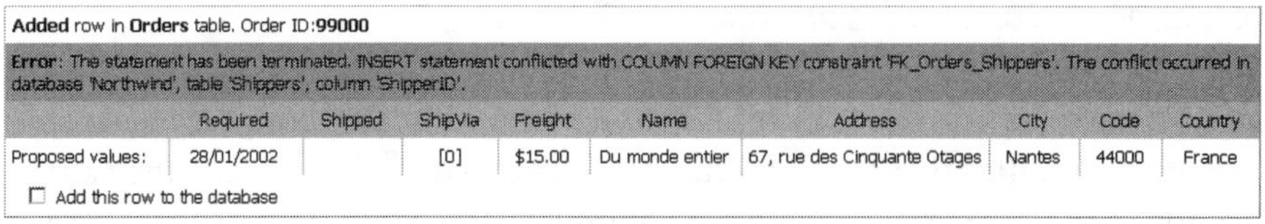

Added row in **Orders** table. Order ID:**99000**									
Error: The statement has been terminated. INSERT statement conflicted with COLUMN FOREIGN KEY constraint 'FK_Orders_Shippers'. The conflict occurred in database 'Northwind', table 'Shippers', column 'ShipperID'.									
	Required	Shipped	ShipVia	Freight	Name	Address	City	Code	Country
Proposed values:	28/01/2002		[0]	$15.00	Du monde entier	67, rue des Cinquante Otages	Nantes	44000	France
☐ Add this row to the database									

Figure 12-10. The reconciliation output for a row that has been added to the DataSet

> **NOTE** *As you saw in the previous chapter, this kind of error should be trapped by the user interface. However, we allow it to "get through" in the example application simply so that you can see what happens when such an update is attempted—and so you can experiment with the reconciliation process as a whole.*

The Display for Deleted Rows

For a deleted row, you obviously can't show any proposed values—there won't be any. Nevertheless, you can show the values currently in the database, allowing the user to see what's there. In Figure 12-11, the error has occurred through a concurrency violation, where another user has changed the values. The "current" user can see these updated values and make a reasoned decision before they actually delete the row.

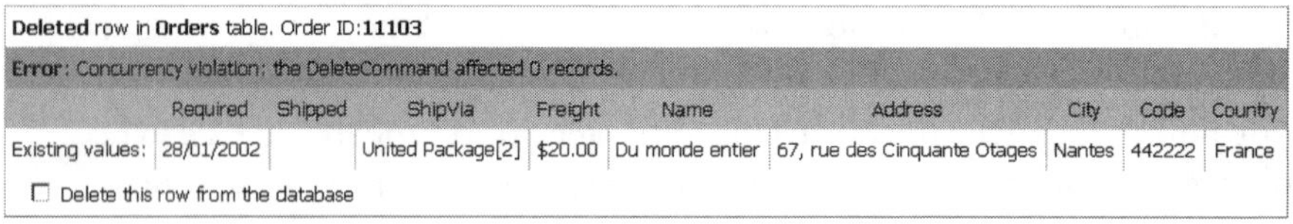

Deleted row in **Orders** table. Order ID:**11103**									
Error: Concurrency violation; the DeleteCommand affected 0 records.									
	Required	Shipped	ShipVia	Freight	Name	Address	City	Code	Country
Existing values:	28/01/2002		United Package[2]	$20.00	Du monde entier	67, rue des Cinquante Otages	Nantes	442222	France
☐ Delete this row from the database									

Figure 12-11. The reconciliation output for a row that has been deleted from the DataSet

The occurrence of errors should be few and far between in most cases, and the facilities offered here will usually be sufficient for reconciling errors. However, one possible development of the reconciliation page would be to display the "proposed" values in text boxes and allow the user to directly edit the values they want to persist in the database. You may want to go down this route in your own applications or in specific circumstances. All it involves is replacing the current value(s) in the table row within the DataSet with the value(s) entered into the text boxes, ready for the next update attempt.

The Code for the GetDisplayString Function

Having seen what you want to create as output, you can now examine the code. Although there seems to be a lot of it, most is taken up by the need to handle both the Orders table and the Order Details table—which means lots of If...Then constructs. You also have to check what type of update action is being performed (an INSERT, UPDATE, or DELETE) each time you reference the column values to ensure that you use the correct version of the row. Remember that there are no current values for a deleted row and no original values for an added row.

So, after declaring the variables you'll need, you start by using the reference to the row passed to the function to get a reference to the table that contains this row and the name of the table as a String:

```
Private Function GetDisplayString(objRow As DataRow) As String
'creates string containing HTML table with values and controls
'to be used to reconcile the error if possible

  'declare variables we'll need
  Dim objTable As DataTable
  Dim strTableName, strKey, strDisplay As String
  Dim intColCount As Integer
  Dim decFreight, decPrice As Decimal
  Dim sngDiscount As Single

  'get reference to table for this row and table name as a String
  objTable = objRow.Table
  strTableName = objTable.TableName
```

Now that you know which table the row comes from, you can decide how many columns there will be in the HTML table you'll be creating and construct a String that contains the value of the primary key for this row. If it's an Order Details row, you need both the OrderID and the ProductID, but you only need the OrderID for an Orders row:

```
'get number of columns and key value for row depending on table name
intColCount = 10
If objRow.RowState = DataRowState.Deleted Then
  strKey = objRow("OrderID", DataRowVersion.Original)
Else
  strKey = objRow("OrderID", DataRowVersion.Current)
End If
If strTableName = "Order Details" Then
```

```
    intColCount = 4
  If objRow.RowState = DataRowState.Deleted Then
    strKey &= "_" & objRow("ProductID", DataRowVersion.Original)
  Else
    strKey &= "_" & objRow("ProductID", DataRowVersion.Current)
  End If
End If
```

Building the HTML Table

Next you can start to build the HTML table in a String variable named strDisplay. The first row contains the type of action being performed and the row key value(s). Notice how you use the original value(s) where this is a deleted row because there are no current values in this case. You also have to use a Try...Catch construct for the Order Details table because (depending on the client application you use) there may not be a product name for new rows that were added to the DataSet:

```
'build output <table> as a String
strDisplay = "<table cellspacing='0' cellpadding='5' " _
  & "rules='cols' border='1' style='border-collapse:collapse;'>"

'first row, containing row details and order ID, etc.
strDisplay &= "<tr><td colspan='" & intColCount & "'><b>" _
            & objRow.RowState.ToString() & "</b> row in <b>" _
            & strTableName & "</b> table. Order ID:<b>"
If objRow.RowState = DataRowState.Deleted Then
  strDisplay &= objRow("OrderID", DataRowVersion.Original) & "</b>"
  If strTableName = "Order Details" Then
    strDisplay &= "<br />Product: "
    Try
      strDisplay &= "<b>" _
        & objRow("ProductName", DataRowVersion.Original) _
        & "</b> [Product ID:" _
        & objRow("ProductID", DataRowVersion.Original) & "]"
    Catch
      strDisplay &= "{details not available}"
    End Try
  End If
Else
  strDisplay &= objRow("OrderID", DataRowVersion.Current) & "</b>"
  If strTableName = "Order Details" Then
    strDisplay &= "<br />Product: "
```

```
     Try
       strDisplay &= "<b>" _
         & objRow("ProductName", DataRowVersion.Current) _
         & "</b> [Product ID:" _
         & objRow("ProductID", DataRowVersion.Current) & "]"
     Catch
       strDisplay &= "{details not available}"
     End Try
   End If
 End If
 strDisplay &= "</td></tr>"
```

In the second row of the table, you place the error message. Then, in the third row, you place the column names for the row—depending on which table the row comes from:

```
'second row, containing error message from RowError property
strDisplay &= "<tr bgcolor='#ffeeee'><td colspan='" & intColCount _
            & "'><b>Error</b>: " & objRow.RowError & "</td></tr>"


'third row, containing column names from row depending on table name
If strTableName = "Orders" Then
   strDisplay &= "<tr bgcolor='#c0c0c0'><td></td><td>Required</td>" _
              & "<td>Shipped</td><td>ShipVia</td><td>Freight</td>" _
              & "<td>Name</td><td>Address</td><td>City</td><td>Code</td>" _
              & "<td>Country</td></tr>"
Else
   strDisplay &= "<tr bgcolor='#c0c0c0'><td></td><td>Quantity</td>" _
              & "<td>Price</td><td>Discount</td></tr>"
End If
```

Displaying the Proposed and Existing Values

In the next row, you place the proposed values—the current values of each column in this row. You can only do this for modified or added rows, of course, so you first check the RowState property of the row. Notice how you extract and format the currency and percentage values for the Freight column (if this is a row from the Orders table) or for the Price and Discount columns in an Order Details row:

```
'next row, add Proposed value if applicable depending on table name
If (objRow.RowState = DataRowState.Modified) _
Or (objRow.RowState = DataRowState.Added) Then
```

```
    strDisplay &= "<tr><td>Proposed values:</td>"
  If strTableName = "Orders" Then
    decFreight = objRow("Freight", DataRowVersion.Current)
    strDisplay &= "<td>" _
      & objRow("RequiredDate", DataRowVersion.Current) & "</td><td>" _
      & objRow("ShippedDate", DataRowVersion.Current) & "</td><td>" _
      & objRow("ShipperName", DataRowVersion.Current) & "[" _
      & objRow("ShipVia", DataRowVersion.Current) & "]</td><td>$" _
      & decFreight.ToString("#0.00") & "</td><td>" _
      & objRow("ShipName", DataRowVersion.Current) & "</td><td>" _
      & objRow("ShipAddress", DataRowVersion.Current) & "</td><td>" _
      & objRow("ShipCity", DataRowVersion.Current) & "</td><td>" _
      & objRow("ShipPostalCode", DataRowVersion.Current) & "</td><td>" _
      & objRow("ShipCountry", DataRowVersion.Current) & "</td></tr>"
  Else
    decPrice = objRow("UnitPrice", DataRowVersion.Current)
    sngDiscount = objRow("Discount", DataRowVersion.Current)
    strDisplay &= "<td>" & objRow("Quantity", DataRowVersion.Current) _
      & "</td><td>$" & decPrice.ToString("#0.00") & "</td><td>" _
      & sngDiscount.ToString("P") & "</td></tr>"
  End If
End If
```

For a modified or deleted row, you can now add the existing values, taking these from the original version of the row. Again, you format the currency and percentage column values:

```
'next row, add Existing value if applicable depending on table name
If (objRow.RowState = DataRowState.Modified) _
Or (objRow.RowState = DataRowState.Deleted) Then
  strDisplay &= "<tr><td>Existing values:</td>"
  If strTableName = "Orders" Then
    decFreight = objRow("Freight", DataRowVersion.Original)
    strDisplay &= "<td>" _
      & objRow("RequiredDate", DataRowVersion.Original) & "</td><td>" _
      & objRow("ShippedDate", DataRowVersion.Original) & "</td><td>" _
      & objRow("ShipperName", DataRowVersion.Original) & "[" _
      & objRow("ShipVia", DataRowVersion.Original) & "]</td><td>$" _
      & decFreight.ToString("#0.00") & "</td><td>" _
      & objRow("ShipName", DataRowVersion.Original) & "</td><td>" _
      & objRow("ShipAddress", DataRowVersion.Original) & "</td><td>" _
      & objRow("ShipCity", DataRowVersion.Original) & "</td><td>" _
      & objRow("ShipPostalCode", DataRowVersion.Original) & "</td><td>" _
```

```
          & objRow("ShipCountry", DataRowVersion.Original) & "</td></tr>"
  Else
    decPrice = objRow("UnitPrice", DataRowVersion.Original)
    sngDiscount = objRow("Discount", DataRowVersion.Original)
    strDisplay &= "<td>" & objRow("Quantity", DataRowVersion.Original) _
        & "</td><td>$" & decPrice.ToString("#0.00") & "</td><td>" _
        & sngDiscount.ToString("P") & "</td></tr>"
  End If
End If
```

Displaying the HTML Check Box Controls

The next row in the HTML table contains the check boxes where the user specifies
the reconciliation actions to be taken by the code. For an added row or a deleted
row, you just need one check box—but you have a different caption. To keep the
code as easy to follow as possible, you process each type of row separately in
the following code. Notice that the name attribute of the check box is made up
of the characters "chk_" followed by the row key you created earlier:

```
'now add table row containing HTML controls, depending on update type
'user can only try again to insert complete row for failed Inserts
If objRow.RowState = DataRowState.Added Then
  strDisplay &= "<tr><td colspan='" & intColCount _
            & "'>  <input type='checkbox' name='chk_" & strKey _
            & "'> Add this row to the database</td></tr>"
End If
```

```
'user can only try again to delete complete row for failed Deletes
If objRow.RowState = DataRowState.Deleted Then
  strDisplay &= "<tr><td colspan='" & intColCount _
            & "'>  <input type='checkbox' name='chk_" & strKey _
            & "'> Delete this row from the database</td></tr>"
End If
```

For a modified row, you have to provide a check box for each column. Again,
you use a name attribute made up of the characters "chk_" followed by the row key.
However, to be able to identify which column the check box refers to, you also add
the name of the column to the value of the name attribute:

```
'user can select which columns to keep for Modified rows
If objRow.RowState = DataRowState.Modified Then
  strDisplay &= "<tr><td>Replace existing values?</td>"
```

```
    If strTableName = "Orders" Then
      strDisplay &= "<td><input type='checkbox' " _
                  & "name='chk_" & strKey & "_RequiredDate'></td>" _
                  & "<td><input type='checkbox' " _
                  & "name='chk_" & strKey & "_ShippedDate'></td>" _
                  & "<td><input type='checkbox' " _
                  & "name='chk_" & strKey & "_ShipVia'></td>" _
                  & "<td><input type='checkbox' " _
                  & "name='chk_" & strKey & "_Freight'></td>" _
                  & "<td><input type='checkbox' " _
                  & "name='chk_" & strKey & "_ShipName'></td>" _
                  & "<td><input type='checkbox' " _
                  & "name='chk_" & strKey & "_ShipAddress'></td>" _
                  & "<td><input type='checkbox' " _
                  & "name='chk_" & strKey & "_ShipCity'></td>" _
                  & "<td><input type='checkbox' " _
                  & "name='chk_" & strKey & "_ShipPostalCode'></td>" _
                  & "<td><input type='checkbox' " _
                  & "name='chk_" & strKey & "_ShipCountry'></td></tr>"
    Else
      strDisplay &= "<td><input type='checkbox' " _
                  & "name='chk_" & strKey & "_Quantity'></td>" _
                  & "<td><input type='checkbox' " _
                  & "name='chk_" & strKey & "_UnitPrice'></td>" _
                  & "<td><input type='checkbox' " _
                  & "name='chk_" & strKey & "_Discount'></td></tr>"
    End If
  End If
```

You can see that you add a check box to every column here, irrespective of whether this column caused the error. When resolving concurrency errors, it might prove useful to display the check box for only the columns where the proposed and existing values are different or to disable ("gray out") the check boxes where the values are the same (and therefore didn't cause a concurrency violation). Either of these approaches could easily be accomplished by comparing the current and original values for the columns.

Finally, you can add the closing `</table>` tag and return the "result" String value to the calling routine (our Page_Load event handler):

```
  strDisplay &= "</table>"

  Return strDisplay

End Function
```

Editing the Values in the DataSet Tables

When the user specifies the actions required to reconcile an update error, you need to apply these to the DataSet you'll be using to perform the next update attempt. When there's an update error, the page will contain an HTML table showing the proposed and the existing values for that row—as you've just seen. Depending on the type of update being performed (an INSERT, DELETE, or UPDATE), there will be one or more check boxes displayed for the row.

The EditTable routine is called when the page is reloaded (posted back), before you have another attempt at applying the user's updates to the database. This routine is passed a reference to one of the tables in the DataSet as a parameter, and in it you edit the values in this table in line with the settings made in the check boxes when the page was submitted.

The Process in Outline

The process in outline is to iterate through the rows in the table building up the String value that's the name attribute of the matching check box for that row or column. Then you see if the user set (checked) this matching check box. If they did, this indicates they want to overwrite the existing values for that column or force an insert or delete of that row.

If they didn't set the matching check box, you need to abandon their changes. If it's an added or a deleted row, you can do this simply by calling the AcceptChanges method of this row, which sets the RowState back to DataRowState.Unchanged. The Update method used in the data access component's UpdateAllOrderDetails method will then ignore this row, and when GetChanges is subsequently called, it'll be removed from the DataSet.

> **NOTE** *We use* AcceptChanges, *rather than removing it directly with the* Remove *method, because it may be the parent row for related child rows that are still in the* DataSet. *If this is this case and you remove the parent row, you'll cause a foreign key constraint violation and an error will occur during the subsequent update process. The* GetChanges *method, as discussed in the previous chapter, doesn't remove parent rows where it'd break referential integrity, simply leaving them in the* DataSet *marked as "unchanged."*

If it's a modified row, however, you have to manipulate the values in the row. For each column where the check box *wasn't* set, you replace the user's edited value (the current value of that column) with the existing value in the database (the original value of that column). This will also leave the RowState for this row as DataRowState.Modified, as you require.

You might be waving your hands wildly in the air right now to question the approach because it doesn't seem the most obvious way to go about things. It'd be a lot more efficient to iterate through the Request.Form collection and just see which check boxes were set. However, bear in mind that an HTML check box only produces a value in the Form collection if it's set (checked), whereupon you get the name/value pair "[control-name]=on". If it's not checked, it doesn't appear in the Form collection at all.

This means that the check boxes would have to work "the other way around." They'd have to be set by default, and the user would then have to uncheck them to force an edited value to be persisted (because the table editing process needs to know which rows and columns it should abandon, not which ones it should keep). This isn't an intuitive approach and is why we chose the alternative described previously. Another approach, of course, would be to use server controls for the check boxes—which would mean that you could access their current setting (via their Checked property) even if they weren't set.

The Code for the EditTable Routine

So, after all that, let's look at the code itself. After declaring the variables you need in this routine, you can get the name of the table (so that you know what the row key string should look like) and then start to iterate through the rows in the table. If the RowError property of the row is empty, you know that the previous update succeeded, so you can call AcceptChanges for the row. This sets the RowState to DataRowState.Unchanged, so the Update process will ignore it this time:

```
Private Sub EditTable(objTable As DataTable)
  'updates rows to reflect reconciliation choices made by user

  'declare variables we'll need
  Dim objRow As DataRow
  Dim objColumn As DataColumn
  Dim intLoop As Integer
  Dim strKey, strColName As String

  'get name of table for display in page
  Dim strTableName As String = objTable.TableName
```

```
'iterate through each row in table
For Each objRow In objTable.Rows

   'see if this row resulted in an error during previous
   'update process - if so, RowError will not be empty

  If objRow.RowError = "" Then    'no error

    'the previous update succeeded, so prevent another
    'update this time by setting RowState to "Unchanged"
    objRow.AcceptChanges()
    ...
```

If there's a row error, you know that the details of this row and the error details will have been presented to the user the last time the page was displayed, so you can edit this row in line with their reconciliation selections. Before you do that, however, you need to remove the row error so that any subsequent error message won't be added to the existing one:

```
  ...
Else    'error occurred

  'first remove the error message in RowError property
  objRow.ClearErrors()
```

You also need to build up a string that will match the check boxes where the user specified their reconciliation selections. If you're processing the Orders table, you know that the name attribute of the matching HTML check box controls will have the characters "chk_" followed by the value of the OrderID for this row. However, as in the GetDisplayString function you just saw, you have to check what kind of row it is to decide where to get the value from.

If you're processing an Order Details row, the name attribute of the check box will be of the form "chk_" followed by the OrderID, another underscore, and the value of the ProductID for this row. Again, you have to make sure you access the correct row version:

```
'get primary key value(s)
If objRow.RowState = DataRowState.Deleted Then
   strKey = objRow("OrderID", DataRowVersion.Original)
Else
   strKey = objRow("OrderID", DataRowVersion.Current)
End If
If strTableName = "Order Details" Then
```

```
    If objRow.RowState = DataRowState.Deleted Then
      strKey &= "_" & objRow("ProductID", DataRowVersion.Original)
    Else
      strKey &= "_" & objRow("ProductID", DataRowVersion.Current)
    End If
  End If
End If
```

Editing Modified Rows

At last, you can perform the edits to the row. If this is a modified row, you need to iterate through the columns in the row creating a name attribute value that includes the column name as well, based on the row key value you created in the previous section of code. Then, if the matching check box for each column *isn't* set, you copy the original value for this column into the current value:

```
'see if it's a modified row
If objRow.RowState = DataRowState.Modified Then

  'iterate through each column in this row
  For Each objColumn In objTable.Columns

    'get the name of the column as a String
    strColName = objColumn.ColumnName

    'see if the check box to keep this value is *not* set
    If Request.Form("chk_" & strKey & "_" & strColName) = Nothing Then

      'set Current value to same as existing (Original) value
      'so that Original values are persisted in database
      objRow(strColName) = objRow(strColName, DataRowVersion.Original)

    End If

  Next 'column

End If
```

You can read the original value of a column by specifying the DataRowVersion. When you set the value of a column (using the value from the original version), it automatically sets the value of the current version. This means the subsequent update process will still attempt to update the row, but this time it'll have the existing database value in that column.

One minor point here is that, even if the user leaves all the check boxes unchecked to abandon all their edited values, you still execute the update process for the row. However, because the current and underlying values are the same, the data itself isn't changed.

In fact, technically, this is the correct approach because it means you perform another concurrency check at this point. If another user has changed the values in the database while the user was deciding what to do, there will be (another) concurrency error. If you didn't re-attempt the update, the values that will be in the database after the reconciliation process is complete could be different from those displayed and upon which the user made their reconciliation decision.

However, if you decide you don't want to perform this extra update, you could check if any existing values are being retained for this row—and if not, call AcceptChanges to prevent the update being occurring.

Removing Added and Deleted Rows

If the current row was an added or a deleted row, you simply test if the matching check box was set (checked) when the page was posted back to the server. If it *wasn't* set, you call AcceptChanges on this row. This has the effect of preventing the update being applied, as well as removing it from the DataSet when GetChanges is subsequently called:

```
'see if it's an added or deleted row
If (objRow.RowState = DataRowState.Added) _
Or (objRow.RowState = DataRowState.Deleted) Then

  'see if the check box to keep this row is *not* set
  If Request.Form("chk_" & strKey) = Nothing Then

    'call AcceptChanges to set RowState to Unchanged
    'so that the update is not applied to the database
    objRow.AcceptChanges()

  End If

End If

End If

Next   'process next error row

End Sub
```

And Around You Go Again

After this routine executes for each table in the DataSet, the rows that remain will then be used to update the database—as you saw when you looked at the Page_Load event. Only this time, the original values in the DataSet have been updated to reflect the underlying values in the database—so errors that occurred through concurrency violations should succeed this time (unless another user edits the row again while the user is viewing the reconcile-changes.aspx page).

If all the updates succeed this time, the user will be presented with the links to edit more orders for this or another customer. However, if any of the updates fail, they'll see these errors displayed in HTML tables all over again. The process continues until either they abandon all their changes or the changes they do decide to keep are successfully applied to the database.

Rich Client Updates via a Web Service

Having seen how you can perform server-based error reconciliation using an ASP.NET page, we really should look at another obvious and possibly advantageous approach. When we discussed the Internet Explorer 5 application in the previous chapter, we mentioned you could send the updated diffgram back to the server using the XMLHTTP (or some other similar) component, rather than posting it from a client-side <form> on the page. This would allow the results to be shown in the same page as was used to perform the edits, without reloading it from the server. It would produce a "smoother" result, but it's more difficult to implement.

When you depend on a Web Service to communicate the data between client and server, you don't have the automatic "posting" feature of the HTML <form> available. You could use client-side code to load a different page that communicates with the Web Service, but this rather defeats the object of using background server interaction techniques. In the Web Service example in this chapter, you'll produce a "single-page" version that interacts with the Web Service in the background. The user edits the data and performs error reconciliation all in the same page, without requiring a postback to the server or a page reload at any point.

In fact, this is an interesting scenario in many ways. It provides the "smooth" interfacementioned earlier, acting much more like a traditional executable application rather than a Web page. It also makes it more likely that the user will push their edits back to the server more regularly, minimizing the chances of concurrency errors arising as they're working with "fresher" data. Of course, this does mean increased loading on the server and back-end data tier, but you can't have it all ways—there will always be a downside.

Notice that we're not talking about the advantages or disadvantages of a Web Service compared to any other data transport mechanism here. We're talking about whether you use postbacks that load a new page (or reload the same page) compared to sending and receiving data in the background while the page is loaded in the client browser. Sending data from the XMLHTTP object in a Web page to an ASP.NET page that returns only data is no different in principle to using a Web Service. It's really just the format of the data during transport that differs. With XMLHTTP you'd tend to use a simple XML document, such as a diffgram, whereas a Web Service wraps the data (whatever format it is in) inside a SOAP envelope for delivery.

The Issues and Work-Arounds

Unfortunately, the issues you encountered with the ReadXml method in the 1.0 version of the DataSet object, and the fact that you're using the Internet Explorer 5 Web Service behavior for the communication path, prevent you from achieving the complete aims you might have for such an application.

The Internet Explorer 5 Web Service behavior doesn't support .NET objects such as the DataSet directly, so you have to add some kludges to successfully send the diffgram back to the server. When you build .NET clients (Windows Forms applications) that use Web Services natively, this problem doesn't arise.

The version you'll build does work well, however, with a couple of minor exceptions. It can't correctly recognize database errors (such as a failure on the part of SQL Server or loss of connectivity), and it can't handle values that contain an ampersand character. You can solve the first with some extra server-based processing to create some recognized form of diffgram that indicates a database server error. The second issue seems to be because of problems or incompatibilities between the output from MSXML and the (currently beta release) Internet Explorer 5 Web Service behavior.

Still, all said, the techniques are worth examining. You'll only look at the differences between this version of the application and the Internet Explorer 5 version covered in the previous chapter. Much of the code is identical because you're still using MSXML to cache a diffgram on the client that represents the DataSet. It's how you interact with the Web Service that's the main difference.

The Middle Tier Web Service Component

To handle communication between the Internet Explorer 5 Web Service behavior on the client and the data access component on the server, you use an ASP.NET Web Service component. It exposes three methods that provide the list of products

(GetProductsDataSet), the list of shippers (GetShippersDataSet), and the orders data that the user will be editing (GetOrdersDataSet). Other than the addition of the <WebMethod> attribute, these are fundamentally the same as the middle tier methods you used for the Internet Explorer 5 version of the application, so we won't list them again here. The main difference is that the Web Service methods expose the data as DataSet objects directly, not as diffgrams.

The order-data.asmx page that implements these three methods also exposes a method that accepts the updated diffgram and returns an "errors" DataSet following the application of the updates to the database. As you're dealing with a client that doesn't understand the .NET architecture, you have to receive the DataSet from the client as a String (the diffgram itself). You also, of course, need the ID of the customer for which you're updating orders because this is required by the data access component:

```
<WebMethod> Public Function UpdateAllOrders(strCustID As String, _
                                       strDiffGram As String) As DataSet
'uses data access component to update all edits to orders

  'while Web Services support DataSet objects directly, the IE5
  'Web Service Behavior (Beta) does not, so data is sent to the
  'server as an HTMLEncoded string you have to decode
  strDiffGram = HttpUtility.HtmlDecode(strDiffGram)
```

Notice that you have to decode the HTML-encoded representation of the diffgram string—as you'll see later, you have to perform the HTML-encoding on the client to prevent the Internet Explorer 5 Web Service behavior from trying to send it back as an XML document object.

Loading the Diffgram into a DataSet

Once you've got the diffgram from the client, you can create a new DataSet object and read in the schema from a disk file. To get the physical path of this file (located in the same folder as the rest of the application files), you use the MapPath method of the Request object. However, because this is a Web Service, the Request object isn't available by default. Instead, you have to import the appropriate namespace using this statement at the top of the page:

```
Imports System.Web
```

Then you get a reference to the current HttpContext and from it the Request object. Notice that you do nothing if there's an error. In reality, depending on the way you decide to address database server errors in your applications, you might decide to create some specific format of DataSet here and return it to the client to indicate that an error occurred:

```
'create new DataSet to load diffgram
Dim objDataSet As New DataSet()

Try

    'read the schema into the DataSet from file on disk
    'must use the Physical path to the file not the Virtual path
    'need reference to a Request object to use MapPath method
    Dim m_Context As HttpContext = HttpContext.Current

    objDataSet.ReadXmlSchema(m_Context.Request.MapPath("orders-schema.xsd"))

Catch
End Try
```

Next you can load the diffgram. You do this in the same way as you did it in the reconcile-changes.aspx page discussed earlier in this chapter. Afterward you perform the kludge used in the previous example to correct any inconsistent updated row values in version 1.0 of the DataSet:

```
Try

    'create an XmlTextReader to read data sent from client
    'specifying that string fragment is an XML Document
    Dim objReader As New XmlTextReader(strDiffGram, _
                        XmlNodeType.Document, Nothing)

    'read in the DiffGram posted from the client
    objDataSet.ReadXml(objReader, XmlReadMode.DiffGram)

Catch
End Try

'kludge required to get correct RowState values in DataSet
objDataSet = objDataSet.GetChanges()
```

Updating the Database

Now you collect the connection string from the local web.config file (as in Chapter 6), and instantiate the data access component. Then you can call the UpdateAllOrderDetails method, passing in the customer ID and the new DataSet and specifying that you only want rows with errors returned. The "errors" DataSet returned from the method is then sent back to the client:

```
Try

    'get connection string from web.config <appSettings> section
    Dim strConnect As String
    strConnect = ConfigurationSettings.AppSettings("NorthwindConnectString")

    'create an instance of the data access component
    Dim objOrderUpdate As New UpdateDataSet(strConnect)

    'call function to do updates and return all rows
    Return objOrderUpdate.UpdateAllOrderDetails(strCustID, objDataSet)

    Return objDataSet

  Catch objErr As Exception
  End Try

End Function
```

The Web Service Client Application

The page that uses the order-data.asmx Web Service is similar to the Internet Explorer 5 version used in the previous chapter. However, now that the data comes from a Web Service via the Internet Explorer 5 Web Service behavior, you have to use different techniques for loading it. We discussed the workings of the Web Service behavior in Chapter 6, so we'll just show you how to apply the same techniques here.

You need to load three DataSet objects as diffgrams into instances of the MSXML parser when the page is first loaded—the products list, the shipping company list, and the customer's orders. You also need to load the "errors" DataSet from the Web Method you've just been examining in the previous section when the user applies the changes to the server.

Loading the Data via the Web Service

To provide some code reuse, a generic set of functions that can load a diffgram from a Web Service are used. The first of these, openWebService, is shown next. As in the example in Chapter 6, you first call the useService method of the behavior to fetch the WSDL service description document and establish a "friendly" reference to the Web Service:

```
function openWebService() {
// runs when the page is first loaded to open the Web Service

  // establish the "friendly name" for the Web Service
  htcWService.useService("order-data.asmx?WSDL", "UpdateOrders");

  // get the customer ID from the query string
  strID = new String(window.location.search);
  strCustID = strID.substring(strID.indexOf('=') + 1, strID.length);
  if (strCustID == '') {

    // display error message
    strURL = '../../customer-orders/webservices/customer-list.aspx';
    document.all('lblStatus').innerHTML =
      '* ERROR: no Customer ID provided.<br />You must '
      + '<a href="' + strURL + '"><b>select a customer</b></a> first.';
  }
  else {
    ...
```

Next, you create instances of the three parsers you'll need. You also have three variables—strMethodName, strDataName and objXMLInstance—declared at page-level. You use these to reference the shippers details first and then call a function on the page named loadServiceData:

```
    ...
    // create the XML parser instances we'll need
    objXMLData = new ActiveXObject('MSXML2.FreeThreadedDOMDocument');
    objXMLProducts = new ActiveXObject('MSXML2.FreeThreadedDOMDocument');
    objXMLShippers = new ActiveXObject('MSXML2.FreeThreadedDOMDocument');

    // set current parser instance to load shippers data first
    // and set method name and data set name
    strMethodName = 'GetShippersDataSet';
    strDataName = 'Shippers';
```

693

```
   objXMLInstance = objXMLShippers;

   // call function to load orders data
   loadServiceData();
  }
}
```

The `loadServiceData` function simply calls the Web Service behavior's `callService` method, specifying the `dataLoaded` event handler (also declared in the page) to handle the callback once the data has been fetched:

```
function loadServiceData() {
// loads data from Web Service using current page-level method name

  document.all('lblStatus').innerHTML = 'Accessing ' + strDataName
     + ' data via<br />Web Service - please wait ...';

  // call the Web Service to get the data
  var iCallID = htcWService.UpdateOrders.callService(dataLoaded,
                                          strMethodName, strCustID);

}
```

Handling the Web Service Behavior's DataLoaded Event

Once the Web Service has returned the data, the callback function named `dataLoaded` executes. In it, you can collect the results or display any error message that might be returned. If there's no error, you pass the diffgram that's exposed by the `raw.xml` property of the `result` object to the instance of MSXML created earlier in the code. You specify that the event handler named `changeFunction` will execute in response to the `onreadystatechange` event of the parser:

```
function dataLoaded(objResult) {
// runs once the Web Service has loaded the data from the server

  // see if there was an error
  if (objResult.error) {

    // get error details from errorDetail properties
    // of the objResult object passed to the function
    var strErrorCode = objResult.errorDetail.code;
    var strErrorMsg = objResult.errorDetail.string;
    var strErrorRaw = objResult.errorDetail.raw;
```

```
  // and display it
  document.all('lblStatus').innerHTML = '<b>* ERROR:</b> '
    + 'could not load ' + strDataName + ' data.<br />' + strErrorMsg;
}
else {

  document.all('lblStatus').innerHTML = 'Loading ' + strDataName
    + ' data from<br />Web Service - please wait ...';

  // there was no error so ready to use XML to fill MSXML parser
  // connect event with function to check when loading completes
  objXMLInstance.onreadystatechange = changeFunction;

  //set properties to load asynchronously
  objXMLInstance.validateOnParse = true;
  objXMLInstance.async = true;

  // load SOAP document (the results) from the Web Service
  objXMLInstance.loadXML(objResult.raw.xml);
  }
}
```

Handling the MSXML onreadystatechange Event

The function named changeFunction is called repeatedly while the MSXML
parser is loading the XML diffgram. Once loading is complete (the point when
the readyState property value is 4), you can decide what to do next. You've only
loaded the shipper data so far, and you still need to load the products list and
the selected customer's order data. Depending on the values of the page-level
variable strDataName, you can update the three page-level variables and call the
loadServiceData function again to load the next diffgram. Note that you only need
to open the Web Service once in the page (using the openWebService function you
called at the start), not every time you access it:

```
function changeFunction() {
// check value of readyState property of XML parser

  // value 4 indicates loading complete
  if (objXMLInstance.readyState == 4) {

    if (objXMLInstance.parseError.errorCode != 0) {

      // there was an error while loading
```

```
        document.all('lblStatus').innerHTML =
          '<b>* ERROR</b> - could not load ' + strDataName + ' list.';
      }
      else {

        // get ready to load next set of data from server
        if (strDataName == 'Shippers') {
          // load products data
          strDataName = 'Products';
          strMethodName = 'GetProductsDataSet';
          objXMLInstance = objXMLProducts;
          loadServiceData();
        }
        else {
          if (strDataName == 'Products') {
            // load orders data
            strDataName = 'Orders';
            strMethodName = 'GetOrdersDataSet';
            objXMLInstance = objXMLData;
            loadServiceData();
          }
          else {
            ...
```

Filling the Shippers and Products Drop-Down Lists

After you've loaded the data required for this page, you must add the values from the shipper and product list diffgrams to the two drop-down lists in the page—as you did in the Internet Explorer 5 version in the previous chapter. There are two functions named fillShippersList and fillProductsList that do just this, using the two diffgrams now loaded into two instances of the MSXML parser. We haven't listed the code for these functions here because they use the same techniques as the Internet Explorer 5 version:

```
...
// finished with current parser variable
objXMLInstance = null;

// fill Shippers and Products drop-down lists
fillShippersList();
fillProductsList();
...
```

Extracting the Diffgram

The Internet Explorer 5 Web Service behavior can't cope with variables such as a
.NET DataSet, so you have to work with the orders data as a diffgram, in the same
way as the Internet Explorer 5 version. However, when a DataSet is serialized via a
Web Service, the XML document that's sent to the client is a SOAP message containing a diffgram. You want to be able to manipulate the diffgram on the client
and send it back as a String via the Web Service behavior, so you use the XPath
//diffgr:diffgram in the selectSingleNode method of the parser object to extract
just the diffgram from the SOAP message. You saw the use of XPaths with the
selectSingleNode method in many places in previous chapters:

```
...
// extract diffgram section from SOAP document
var objDGNode = objXMLData.selectSingleNode('//diffgr:diffgram');
var strDiffGram = objDGNode.xml;
var objTempXML =
    new ActiveXObject('MSXML2.FreeThreadedDOMDocument');
objTempXML.validateOnParse = false;
objTempXML.async = false;
objTempXML.loadXML(strDiffGram);
objXMLData = objTempXML;

// replace "Loading" message with customer ID
document.all('lblStatus').innerHTML =
  'Orders for customer ID <b>"' + strCustID + '"</b>';

// display list of matching orders in left-hand table
showOrderList('OrderID');
      }
    }
  }
 }
}
```

Finally, as shown, you can display the appropriate message to indicate that
you've loaded all the data you need and display a list of orders for this customer. At
this point, as shown in Figure 12-12, the page looks and works just the same as the
Internet Explorer 5 version—as it should because the majority of the page and the
client-side JavaScript code is the same.

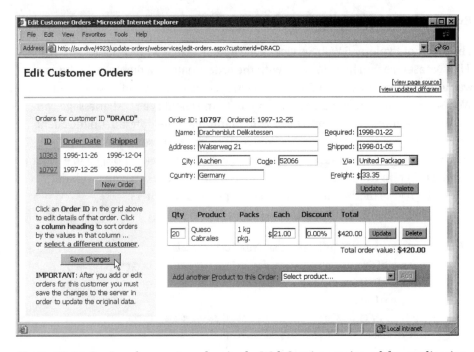

Figure 12-12. Saving changes to orders in the Web Service version of the application

The process for updating the cached diffgram is also the same as in the Internet Explorer 5 version from the previous chapter. However, it's once you submit the changes to the server—when the user clicks the Save Changes button—that things are very different.

Sending Data Back to the Server via the Web Service

In the Internet Explorer 5 version of the application, you posted the updated diffgram back to the server for processing using an HTML <form> and hidden-type controls. Just because you used a Web Service to load the data for this version of the application doesn't mean you can't do the same here, using the same reconcile-changes.aspx page to display the update errors.

However, as you saw earlier, the Web Service you're using exposes a method that can perform the updates, and you can send the diffgram to it without using a <form>. It's just a shame that, at least at the time of writing, you have to jump through hoops to do so—you'll see why shortly. The Web Service described earlier exposes this method:

```
<WebMethod> Public Function UpdateAllOrders(strCustID As String, _
                           strDiffGram As String) As DataSet
```

So, all you need to do is extract the updated diffgram from the MSXML parser and pass it (along with the current customer ID) to this method using the Internet Explorer 5 Web Service behavior. You'll get back a DataSet that the Web Service behavior will expose to the code as a diffgram. You can just load this back into the same MSXML parser and display the contents using the same code as you did when displaying it for editing originally.

Unfortunately, things aren't quite that simple. You need to manipulate the diffgram first before the Web Service behavior will accept it.

Modifying the Diffgram

After the user has finished editing the data cached locally in the MSXML parser, they click the Save Changes button to submit the changes to the server. In theory, all you have to do is collect the diffgram from the parser's xml property and pass it to the Web Service as a String. However, the Internet Explorer 5 Web Service behavior lives in an environment that's very different to what you've gotten used to in ASP.NET pages.

In client-side script, there's no variable typing—you can't declare variables of a specific data type (as is the situation with JScript and VBScript in ASP 3.0). So, the Web Service behavior can't tell what type of variable you're providing—it can only use the service description provided by the Web Service itself (the WSDL document it downloads when you execute the useService method to initialize the Web Service connection), which does specify the data type that the Web Service exposes. This also means that a type conversion is required from the object (in JavaScript) or Variant (in VBScript) to the data type specified in the WSDL document.

Generally, with standard types such as integers, strings, and so on, there's no problem. However, when you provide a string that contains XML as a parameter to the callService method of the Web Service behavior, it tries to send it as an XML document object. This causes an error in the .asmx Web Service page on the server. To prevent this, you have to HTML-encode the string to disguise it. Then the Web Service behavior simply passes it to the Web Service on the server as a String.

HTML-Encoding the String

JScript provides an encode method, but this encodes a string into URL-equivalent form rather than HTML-equivalent form. Instead, a basic HTML-encode method (named htmlEncode) is included in the client-side code within the edit-orders.aspx page. You can see it if you click the View Source link in this page, and we haven't listed it here. In essence, all you need to do is convert the XML tag delimiters < and >, plus the nonlegal characters such as single and double quotes, to their HTML equivalents < > ' and ". The MSXML parser automatically converts the ampersand & to its HTML equivalent. You also convert any characters with an ANSI code greater than 128 to the equivalent numeric form &#*xxx*, where *xxx* is the ANSI value of the character.

> **NOTE** *This solution isn't the ideal way of handling the diffgram, but it does solve the problem temporarily until the Web Service behavior reaches a state of maturity—remember that it's still a beta product at the time of writing.*

Calling the Web Service UpdateAllOrders Method

So, now you're in a position to send the diffgram to the server. The appropriately named sendToServer function in the page first disables the Save Changes button and displays some status information to the user:

```
function sendToServer() {
  // send XML DiffGram to server via Web Service

  // disable "Save Changes" button
  document.all('btnSaveChanges').disabled = true;

  // show message in status label and clear "Errors" label
  document.all('lblStatus').innerHTML = 'Sending order updates...'
  document.all('lblUpdateStatus').innerHTML = '';
```

If you've previously performed updates for this customer, the diffgram you're using may contain details of update errors that occurred when that update was attempted. If you leave these in the diffgram, they'll be persisted within the DataSet you create on the server and appear as errors when you get the results back again. So, the next step is to remove the entire <diffgr:errors> element from the diffgram:

```
// remove any row errors that might be in diffgram
// will be there if reconciling a previous error
var strXPath = '//diffgr:errors';
var objErrorsNode = objXMLData.selectSingleNode(strXPath);
if (objErrorsNode != null) {
  objErrorsNode.parentNode.removeChild(objErrorsNode);
}
```

Now you can HTML-encode the contents of the XML parser that contains the diffgram and pass it, along with the current customer ID, to the UpdateAllOrders method of the Web Service. You also specify the client-side function named dataSent as the event handler for the Web Service behavior to call once the UpdateAllOrders method returns:

```
// get XML string to send to server as method parameter
// cannot send an XML document directly, so HTMLEncode it
// using custom function defined below in this page
var strDiffGram = htmlEncode(objXMLData.xml);

// call the Web Service to send the data. At the same time set up
// the callback handler named "dataSent" to handle the results
var iCallID = htcWService.UpdateOrders.callService(dataSent, "UpdateAllOrders",
                                          strCustID, strDiffGram);
}
```

Handling the Returned Errors DataSet

The Web Service UpdateAllOrders method performs the update to the database and returns a DataSet containing the same set of rows you started with (unless there's a database server error). The dataSent event handler function executes when the response from the Web Service containing the result has been received. In this function, you first check for an error in the same way as earlier examples. Note that the code shows how to retrieve several error property values here, even though you only use one of them in the example:

```
function dataSent(objResult) {
// runs once the Web Service has sent the data to the server

  // see if there was an error
  if (objResult.error) {

    // get error details from errorDetail properties
    // of the objResult object passed to the function
    var strErrorCode = objResult.errorDetail.code;
    var strErrorMsg = objResult.errorDetail.string;
    var strErrorRaw = objResult.errorDetail.raw;

    // and display it
    document.all('lblStatus').innerHTML = '<b>* ERROR:</b> '
      + 'could not send data.<br />' + strErrorMsg;
  }
  else {
```

If there's no error, you can do the housekeeping required by the application—clearing the "dirty" flag and displaying status information. Then you load the SOAP document containing the diffgram that's returned by the `UpdateAllOrders` method into a temporary instance of MSXML and extract just the `<diffgr:diffgram>` section into the original parser instance you use to store the orders data:

```
// clear "dirty" flag and update status
blnIsDirty = false;
document.all('lblStatus').innerHTML =
            'Orders for customer ID <b>"' + strCustID + '"</b>';

// load returned diffgram into temporary XML parser
var objTempXML = new ActiveXObject('MSXML2.FreeThreadedDOMDocument');
objTempXML.validateOnParse = false;
objTempXML.async = false;
objTempXML.loadXML(objResult.raw.xml);

// extract diffgram section from SOAP document
var objDGNode = objTempXML.selectSingleNode('//diffgr:diffgram');
var strDiffGram = objDGNode.xml;
objXMLData.loadXML(strDiffGram);
objTempXML = null;    // destroy temporary parser
```

A Diffgram with Row Errors

You want to count how many rows have update errors and display the error details to the user. From the earlier discussion of the format of the diffgram that's exposed by a `DataSet`, you'll remember that the `<diffgr:errors>` section is where any row errors are located. If there's an error, the row in the `<NewDataSet>` section also carries the attribute `diffgr:hasErrors="true"`. As a refresher, the following extract shows the outline structure of a diffgram that contains row errors:

```
<diffgr:diffgram ...>
  <NewDataSet>
    <Orders diffgr:id="Orders1" msdata:rowOrder="0"
            diffgr:hasChanges="modified" diffgr:hasErrors="true">
      <OrderID>11036</OrderID>
      <CustomerID>DRACD</CustomerID>
      <OrderDate>1998-04-20</OrderDate>
      <RequiredDate>1998-05-18</RequiredDate>
      ... etc ...
    </Orders>
```

```
    ... more current row values here ...
  </NewDataSet>
  <diffgr:before>
    ... original row values here ...
  </diffgr:before>
  <diffgr:errors>
    <Orders diffgr:id="Orders1" diffgr:Error="The statement has been
            terminated. UPDATE statement conflicted ...etc..." xmlns=""/>
    <Orders diffgr:id="Orders2" diffgr:Error="Concurrency violation:
            the UpdateCommand affected O records." xmlns=""/>
  </diffgr:errors>
</diffgr:diffgram>
```

You can see that the <diffgr:errors> section contains elements that each indicate a row error. They specify as attributes the id of the row to which the error applies and the error message text. Looking at the row in the <NewDataSet> section you can see the row with the id value of "Orders1" and the diffgr:hasErrors="true" attribute that it contains.

So, you can count the total number of errors easily by seeing how many rows are in the <diffgr:errors> section. However, to get details of each one, specifically the order number, you have to look up the row in the <NewDataSet> or <diffgr:before> section using the ID value from the diffgr:id attribute in the <diffgr:errors> section.

Counting and Displaying the Row Errors

So, first, you create an XPath query that references all the child nodes of the <diffgr:errors> node in the diffgram. After applying this XPath with the selectNodes method, you can see how many error rows there are by querying the length of the collection within a try...catch construct:

```
// count number of rows with errors
// create XPath for <diffgr:errors> section
var strXPath = '//diffgr:errors/*';
var strResult = '';    // to hold update message

//see how many rows with errors were returned
var colErrorNodes = objXMLData.selectNodes(strXPath);
var intErrors;
try {
  intErrors = colErrorNodes.length;
}
```

```
catch(e) {
  intErrors = 0;
}
```

If all the updates succeeded, there won't be any nodes (error row details) here. However, if you have at least one error, you create a string to hold the message for the page to display and a couple of other variables you'll need in the code:

```
if (intErrors != 0) {

  strResult = '<b>Update errors occurred in '
            + intErrors.toString() + ' row(s)</b>:<p />';

  var strErrorID;        // to hold diffgr:id value from node
  var objOriginalNode;   // to hold <NewDataSet> node
```

Now you can iterate through the rows you found in the <diffgr:errors> section, extracting the value of the diffgr:id attribute. You then create an XPath that'll locate the first row with a matching id attribute in either the <NewDataSet> or <diffgr:before> section—it doesn't matter where because the OrderID (and ProductName in the case of an Order Details row) can't be changed by the application:

```
// iterate through all the <diffgr:errors> nodes
for (var intLoop = 0; intLoop < intErrors; intLoop++) {

  // get the diffgr:id attribute value
  strErrorID = colErrorNodes[intLoop].getAttribute('diffgr:id');

  // create XPath to find this node anywhere in the
  // <NewDataSet> or <diffgr:before> sections of diffgram
  if (strErrorID.indexOf('Order Details') == -1)
    strXPath = '//Orders[@diffgr:id="' + strErrorID + '"]'
  else
    strXPath = '//Order_x0020_Details[@diffgr:id="' + strErrorID + '"]';
```

You can now use this XPath to get a reference to a suitable node, and from it extract the value of the OrderID column. If you're dealing with an Order Details row, you also extract the value from the ProductName column. Then you extract the text of the error message from the current node in the <diffgr:errors> section. You use all the values in turn to build the string you want to display:

```
  // get reference to matching node
  objOriginalNode = objXMLData.selectSingleNode(strXPath);
```

```
    // extract the OrderID value
    strResult += 'Order ID: ' + objOriginalNode.childNodes[0].text;

    // if it's an order line, extract the product name as well
    if (strErrorID.indexOf('Order Details') != -1) {
      strResult += ', Product: ' + objOriginalNode.childNodes[5].text;
    }

    // extract the error message from node in the diffgr:errors section
    strResult += ' - '
      + colErrorNodes[intLoop].getAttribute('diffgr:Error') + '<p />';
  }
}
```

However, if there were no errors in the returned DataSet (the <diffgr:errors> section is empty or doesn't exist), you just display a message to this effect:

```
else {

  strResult = '<b>All your updates were successfully applied.</b>';
```

Updating the Display

Then, irrespective of whether there were errors, you hide the display of the order details in the right section of the page and refresh the list of orders in the left section. This will show the current values for this customer's orders as retrieved from the database during the update process, including the "real" order ID for any orders you inserted. Lastly, you display the string just created (the list of errors or the "success" message) in the status label at the top of the right section of the page:

```
    // hide order details section
    document.all('divAddLine').style.display = 'none';
    document.all('lblOrderTotal').innerHTML = '';
    document.all('divOrderLines').style.display = 'none';
    document.all('tblOrderDetail').style.display = 'none';

    // show list of orders and result message
    showOrderList('OrderID');
    document.all('lblUpdateStatus').innerHTML = strResult + '<p />';
  }
}
```

Viewing the Application

Try the application yourself (remember that it's online at http://www.daveandal.net/ books/4923/) to see just how smooth and seamless the operation of this version is when compared to loading a separate reconciliation page. For example, Figure 12-13 shows the page after submitting four updates that failed. There was a concurrency error detected for orders 10290 and 10494, and you were unable to insert the new order row and related product row (which are still shown with the temporary "dummy" order ID value of 99000).

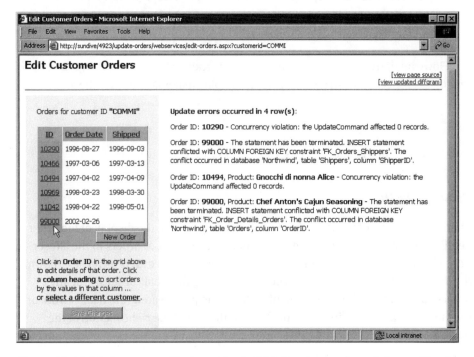

Figure 12-13. Update errors displayed in the Web Service version of the application

At this point, you can select the orders for which errors occurred. You can edit the value for these rows again, or just leave them set as they were, and save the changes to the database. Because the original row values have been updated to reflect the values that are in the database (the underlying values), the next update attempt should succeed if the original error was because of a concurrency violation.

In Figure 12-14, you can see the two inserted rows that caused errors. These are still marked with the temporary order ID that you assigned to them in the code on the client. The insert process failed when you submitted them to the server only because you forgot to select a shipping company.

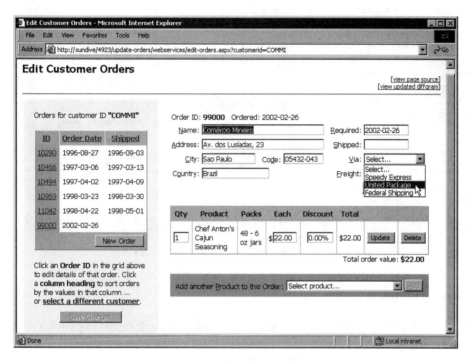

Figure 12-14. The rows added to the DataSet *that failed during the insert operation*

However, you can see that both the parent Orders row and the related Order Details child row are still here in the data. So you can select a shipping company now, click Update to save the row locally, and then click Save Changes to send the update back to the server via the Web Service. This time the order and the order line rows are successfully inserted into the database, and—on return—you see the "real" order ID that was generated by the IDENTITY column within the database, as shown in Figure 12-15.

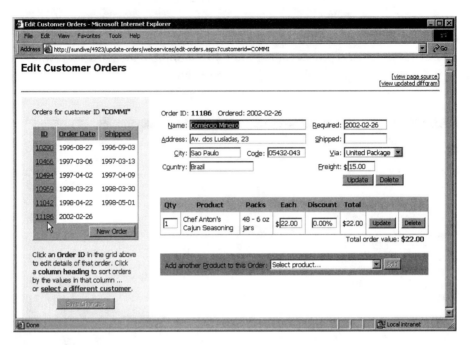

Figure 12-15. The new rows after the update process succeeds

Showing the Original Row Values

As with the `reconcile-changes.aspx` page you used with the Internet Explorer 5 version of the application earlier in this chapter, it's important to remember that the `DataSet` you're now displaying (via a diffgram, of course) contains the user's edited values as the current values for the rows, but the original row values have been updated to reflect the values that are in the database (the underlying values).

Where the update succeeded, these two values are the same. However, for rows where the update failed, the user can simply resubmit the updates using the Save Changes button, and this time they'll be applied to the database (unless another user has changed them again). Notice that, in this case, you aren't showing the original (underlying) values in the page. It's not impossible to do so—an easy way would be to add them to each control as the HTML `title` attribute in which case they would pop up as a "tool tip" when the mouse hovers over the control. Alternatively, you could add extra controls and show the original values below the text boxes holding the current values. Either approach just involves some extra code in the `showOrderDetail` routine that creates and displays the table in the right part of the page.

A Few Other Differences

There are a few other differences between this page and the one in Internet Explorer 5 earlier in this chapter. The Internet Explorer 5 example uses the reconcile-changes.aspx page to display the update errors (and hence is reloaded when all the updates are complete), but the Web Services example doesn't get reloaded each time you save the edits to the server. The changes required to the code for this are mainly concerned with showing, hiding, and refreshing the various parts of the display at appropriate times.

If you implement this kind of client application, you need to keep checking for updated versions of the Framework (especially System.Data) and the Internet Explorer 5 Web Service behavior. Updates and new releases of these will allow you to get around the problems discovered when working with diffgrams. In fact, there's no doubt that the issues *will* be resolved in the near future because Web Services have already been recognized as providing an ideal platform for the kind of distributed application you've been looking at here.

Other Rich Client Update Techniques

In previous chapters, you saw two versions of the application for displaying (rather than editing) customers' order data where the equivalent update process isn't implemented in our example:

- The version designed for Internet Explorer 4 and higher, which uses the Tabular Data Control (TDC) to cache tab-delimited data on the client

- The Hypertext Application version that caches the data as an XML format file on the client's disk.

The reasons have more to do with practicality and usefulness rather than idleness (it's true, honest!). Neither is likely to provide a solution that has a long-term future, and they aren't particularly efficient either. However, for completeness, the final sections of this chapter look at some of the ways you might extend the techniques introduced in these two versions of the application to allow updating of the data if required.

Rich Client Updates Using Delimited Data

The Internet Explorer 4 version of the customer orders application demonstrates how you can use the TDC (sometimes called the Text Data Control) to cache data on the client. This is easy to program and quite efficient in displaying the data using client-side data binding. The data cached by the TDC can also be edited and updated within the control itself, so you could build code into the page to allow the values of each order to be edited.

However, there's no obvious way to manage concurrent updates and errors in this situation. You can get the data out of the TDC easily by iterating through the rows exposed by its recordset property. However, there's no concept of current and original values—the TDC can only hold one set of values (one value per column for each row).

Because it's unlikely that you have many users running Internet Explorer 4 now, the more efficient Internet Explorer 5 and higher version is far more likely to be the sensible choice. However, if you do decide to have a go at building a TDC version to update the orders, you might decide to do so by having two TDC objects for each table. There would be one to hold the current values for the Orders table and one to hold the original values. There would also be a pair to hold the current and original values for the Order Details table.

Then, when ready to perform an update, you could do one of two things:

- You could use the two sets of values for each row to build a diffgram as a String and post it to the same reconcile-changes.aspx page you used at the start of this chapter.

- You could simply post the two sets of rows as delimited text strings to a middle tier component (perhaps an ASP.NET page) and assemble a DataSet object using their values.

We briefly discussed how you might fill a DataSet from a delimited string in Chapter 9. It just involves creating the DataSet and tables in code and then parsing the data String into separate values. Each column value is inserted into the row directly using code by simply setting the value.

Setting the Current and Original Row Values

You can set the appropriate mix of current and original values by setting the values of each column from the String containing the original values and then calling the AcceptChanges method for the row or the table to copy these into the original row values. Then process the String containing the current values and set the column values in each row again to give the correct current values in each row (and *don't* call AcceptChanges afterward).

Marshaling the Changed Rows

The other issue is that it really does make sense here to marshal just the changed rows before sending the values back to the server for processing. This would save considerable processing on the server while parsing the values from each String to build the DataSet content. Perhaps a good approach would be to add a column to one of the TDC rowsets to contain a "flag" value, similar to the hasChanges attribute of the diffgrams you saw in earlier chapters. This could be set when a row is updated and then used to detect the changed rows when marshaling the data before posting it to the server.

Caching the Original Rows on the Server

To save sending the original values to the client and back to the server again, another approach might be to cache them on the server instead. After all, the client never gets to change the original values (this would break the concurrency error protection feature). You could test if the client supports ASP.NET sessions, and if so, store the delimited text string in their Session object while they're editing the data remotely. Then only one TDC per data table would be required.

In fact, following on the same theme, you might even decide to cache the DataSet exposed by the data access tier in the user's Session and then just update it using the values they post back after editing the data. This way the structure of the DataSet is preserved, and the code required is much simpler. But it's at the expense of extra server resource requirements.

You also need to consider the possibility that the user's Session might end before they post their updates. This might require extending the session timeout setting or storing the data in some other way—such as in the ASP.NET cache or as a disk file using their user name or some other user-specific value as the key or filename.

Hypertext Application Updates

The other application version where we demonstrated remote data caching for displaying orders was the one that used an Internet Explorer 5 (and higher) Hypertext Application (HTA). This version provides an ideal platform for a completely disconnected data display application because it downloads the data and stores it as two XML files on the client's own hard disk. They can refresh the data when connected to the server, but the application will work fully using only the disk files if required.

Here, the way you might approach updating the data needs some serious contemplation. If the client is likely to be disconnected for long periods, the risk of concurrency errors increases dramatically. The one scenario where it's most appropriate is when the remote user is mainly adding new rows (orders and so on) to the data, to be applied to the data store afterward. We discussed at some length in previous chapters how you might allow this to take place using temporary values for the new row primary key columns.

The HTA version uses the MSXML parser, with almost identical code to the Internet Explorer 5 version. The main difference is that you'd have to persist the data as a diffgram on the client's disk. So, you could easily add the code to perform updates in the HTA version or convert the Internet Explorer 5 version into an HTA like you did in Chapter 6. After performing their remote updates to the disk-based XML files, the user would connect to the server and post these files to the server as strings. You could catch them in the same `reconcile-changes.aspx` page and apply the changes.

Of course, the current `reconcile-changes.aspx` page is designed to work with orders for one customer only, so another task will be to modify it to handle multiple customers. In the main, this will only involve reading the customer ID dynamically from the posted diffgram for each update, rather than sending it via a `hidden`-type control.

Marshaling the Changed Rows

The one major issue with the HTA version is the amount of data that's likely to be sent to and from the client. Remember that the version you saw in Chapter 6 cached details of all the customers in the database and all the orders and order lines for all the customers. Posting this back to the server would be highly inefficient, especially if only a couple of orders have been modified.

So marshaling only the changed rows will be a definite requirement in this version of the application. However, the data is held as a diffgram, and you already considered in previous chapters how difficult it might be to marshal the changes using just client-side JavaScript code.

Install the .NET Framework Instead

For a client-based application that persists data locally, as the HTA version does, the best plan for building an "update" version is to do it using .NET. The data could then be cached in memory and on disk as a DataSet object. Edits to the data are easy, as is displaying it using the intrinsic Windows Forms controls. Marshaling the changes is then just a matter of calling the GetChanges method.

By a sheer noncoincidence, this leads you nicely into the next chapter, which discusses how you can build a version of the customer orders application for updating data using .NET on the client and .NET Remoting to transport the data from server to client and back again.

Summary

In this chapter, you looked at the "other part" of the Internet Explorer 5 rich client application you built in the previous chapter. You post an updated diffgram back to the server from the client-side application, and you use this to apply the updates to the server-side data store. The FEGURM process described in earlier chapters also allows you to detect update errors and obtain the underlying (database) values at the same time. Using these, you can report back to the user details of any updates that failed and allow them to reconcile the updates through an ASP.NET page.

The Internet Explorer 5 version demonstrated in this chapter works well, but we also discussed other approaches to passing the data back to the server (via XMLHTTP rather than posting it from a form). That way, the page becomes almost seamless because there's no separate display for reconciling changes. However, this introduces other issues, such as how the application might display the errors and the original values.

We resolved these issues to some extent in the Web Services example in this chapter. You sent the errors DataSet back to the client, where it uses the RowError property of each row to display the errors and allows the user to attempt the update again after reconciling the errors. Although not perfect, it does show how you might approach such a task if this is a suitable approach for your applications.

Finally, you considered the two versions of the application that don't include an update feature. You looked at why these are more difficult to implement, and generally less efficient, and how you can get round some of the problems if you do need to go down this route.

In summary, the chapter covered the following:

- Handling a posted diffgram in the middle tier on the server

- Using the data access tier component to update the data source

- Handling any errors that arise from the updates and reconciling them

- Using a Web Service to communicate data updates to and from a client

- Other rich client techniques for updating remotely cached data

In the next chapter, you go back to .NET Remoting again and see how much easier all this stuff gets when you have .NET running on the client.

CHAPTER 13

Updating Data from Remote .NET Applications

IN THE PREVIOUS FEW CHAPTERS you've been looking at the process of updating data, and you've seen that although this is relatively straightforward in theory, there's more to it in reality. When dealing with different clients, you have to consider the problems the clients might have in processing data, as well as how to actually update the data. Add to this the possibility of other people changing the same data, and there's a lot to consider. Because we've covered all of this for Web clients, it's now time for you to look at .NET clients.

In this chapter, you'll revisit the Windows Forms application, not only adding update capability but also revisiting the design to make it easier to use. In its previous incarnations, you allowed the viewing of orders and order details, both shown in a hierarchical fashion in the standard Windows DataGrid. Although this modelling of data is quite cool, it's not actually the best interface in terms of usability because once you drill down into order lines, you lose most of the details of the order itself.

In particular, this chapter covers the following topics:

- Windows Forms data binding

- Managing edits on Windows Forms

- Updating the data source

- Handling concurrency errors

The topics are similar to those you've already seen in other chapters, but unlike the Web clients where there's a common theme, the Windows Forms application has plenty of differences.

The Windows Forms Application

The Windows application is similar in overall structure to the Web-based applications but differs in two major ways:

- It can use the .NET Framework's data handling techniques.

- It's stateful and can therefore be highly intelligent.

Figure 13-1 should refresh your memory of the architecture.

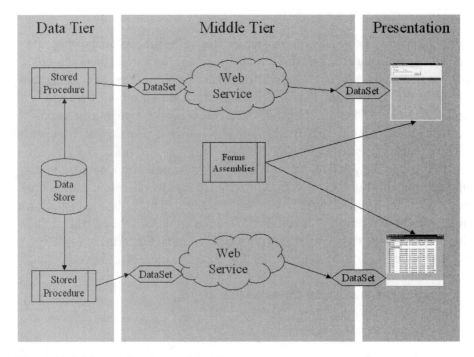

Figure 13-1. The application architecture

You have the presentation tier consisting of Windows Forms, either loaded remotely via a Web page or locally from the hard disk. The Web Service provides the data, extracting it from the data tier using the same components as the Web applications. To modify your application to allow updates, there are several things you need to consider:

- Is the existing architecture valid?

- Do you need to modify any components or Web Services?

- Do you need to add components or Web Services?

Saying no to all of these is one of the key things you've been aiming for throughout the book. You could say no to all of them and use exactly what you've previously used, but the client has different capabilities to the Web applications, so is it sensible to do so? That really depends on what sort of changes you'd need. Because you're building a Windows application, you can rely upon the .NET Framework, and that means you have DataSets available for use. In the Web applications, this isn't possible, so there are a variety of ways in which data is processed. Being able to use DataSets means that you can pass these to and from the Web Services without the use of diffgrams and the problems they provide.

In practice, you've actually had to do very little to the middle tier. You've used a separate Web Service purely to abstract out the Windows Forms requirements, but you could have just as easily added methods to cater for the new functionality, or modified the existing ones, perhaps by addition of a flag to indicate the target application. You'll now look at the methods in the Web Service and see what changes have been made.

The Orders Method

The Orders method retrieves orders and order details for a selected customer:

```
<WebMethod> _
Public Function Orders(strCustID As String) As DataSet

  Dim objDataSet As DataSet

  Try
    Dim strConnect As String = _
      ConfigurationSettings.AppSettings("NorthwindConnectString")

    Dim objOrderUpdate As New UpdateDataSet(strConnect)

    ' call component to get DataSet containing order details for customer
    objDataSet = objOrderUpdate.GetOrderDetails(strCustID)

    ' add column containing total value of each line in OrderLines table
    Dim objLinesTable As DataTable = objDataSet.Tables("Order Details")
    Dim objColumn As DataColumn = _
              objLinesTable.Columns.Add("LineTotal", _
                             System.Type.GetType("System.Double"))
    objColumn.Expression = "[Quantity] * " _
                       & "([UnitPrice] - ([UnitPrice] * [Discount]))"
```

```
        ' set the Nested property of the relationship between the tables so they
        ' are appropriately linked (OrderLines nested within each Order)
        objDataSet.Relations(0).Nested = True

        ' add autoincrement details, so the DataSet handles
        ' new values correctly. Using 0 & -1 ensures that new order IDs
        ' don't clash with existing ones. The database will generate correct IDs
        ' during update, and these are flushed back to the DataSet
        With objDataSet.Tables("Orders").Columns("OrderID")
            .AutoIncrement = True
            .AutoIncrementStep = -1
            .AutoIncrementSeed = 0
            .AllowDBNull = False
            .Unique = True
        End With

        ' return the DataSet to the calling routine
        Return objDataSet

    Catch objErr As Exception

        ' there was an error so no data is returned

    End Try

End Function
```

As you can see, this is similar to ones you've used earlier. The crucial point is
that you set the AutoIncrement details. Because you're dealing with a DataSet on
the client, you can use the Add methods of the rows to add new rows, and setting
AutoIncrement to True ensures that ID values automatically increment. You also set
the seed and step properties to ensure that any IDs you generate won't clash with
other people, so you start at zero and work downward.

The Lookups Method

The Lookups method is used to retrieve a DataSet of lookup values, such as the Shippers and Products:

```
<WebMethod> _
Public Function Lookups() As DataSet

   Try

      ' get connection string from web.config <appSettings> section
      Dim strConnect As String = _
         ConfigurationSettings.AppSettings("NorthwindConnectString")

      ' create an instance of the data access component
      Dim objOrderUpdate As New UpdateDataSet(strConnect)

      ' call component to get DataSet containing shipper details
      Dim dsLookups As DataSet = objOrderUpdate.GetShippersDataSet()

      ' now add more data for other lookups
      dsLookups.Merge (objOrderUpdate.GetProductsDataSet())


      Return dsLookups

   Catch objErr As Exception

      ' there was an error so no data is returned
      Return Nothing

   End Try

End Function
```

For the Web application, you used two methods to extract the two sets of data, but because you can easily deal with multiple tables, you create a DataSet containing two tables. Unlike the Orders and Order Details situation, you don't create a relationship because you're using two unconnected tables. Adding them into the same DataSet means that you can return them to the client in one hit instead of two. It's the same amount of data but uses one less call to the Web service.

The UpdateOrders Method

The UpdateOrders method takes a DataSet and updates the data source. This differs quite a lot from the versions used by the Web applications as it accepts a DataSet, so it only has to pass this through to the component that does the actual update:

```
<WebMethod> _
Public Function UpdateOrders(ByVal strCustID As String, _
                             ByVal objDataSet As DataSet) As DataSet

  ' kludge required to get correct RowState values in DataSet
  ' only required for .NET 1.0
  objDataSet = objDataSet.GetChanges()

  ' get connection string from web.config <appSettings> section
  Dim strConnect As String = _
    ConfigurationSettings.AppSettings("NorthwindConnectString")

  ' create an instance of the data access component
  Dim objOrderUpdate As New UpdateDataSet(strConnect)

  ' call function to do updates and return error rows only
  Return objOrderUpdate.UpdateAllOrderDetails(strCustID, objDataSet)

End Function
```

One interesting thing to note is that you still have the kludge to get around the RowState problem, which was discussed in Chapter 12. Although this isn't required for .NET 1.1 because the problem has been fixed, it's good to leave this code in place for backward compatibility reasons—it allows the Web Service to reside on a 1.0 server if required.

What this shows is that the problem encountered in .NET 1.0 is a problem with serializing the DataSet into XML because this is the format that you also use. Even though you have DataSets at both the server and the client, you're still using Hypertext Transfer Protocol (HTTP) and Simple Object Access Protocol (SOAP) as the transport protocol, and SOAP uses XML. One way around this would be to not use a Web service for this method and create a component using remoting and the binary formatter. However, this reduces the simplicity and ease of maintenance that the current architecture has brought, and because the problem is easily fixed (or "kludged"), you'll stick with this Web service method.

The New Editable Orders Form

In Chapter 7, we provided the hierarchical form of orders and order details. Although this was (barely) acceptable for read-only purposes, it certainly isn't suitable for editing data. The grid is fine, but using it for two sets of data invariably means that functionality is compromised. There are several Visual Studio .NET Windows grids from third-party vendors that provide enhanced flexibility (and look extremely cool), but they all mean buying extra software. For this purpose, that isn't necessary, so we've decided to use a combination of grids and data entry fields. The Orders form (in the UpdatableRemoteFormsApplication\Orders directory in the samples) now looks like Figure 13-2.

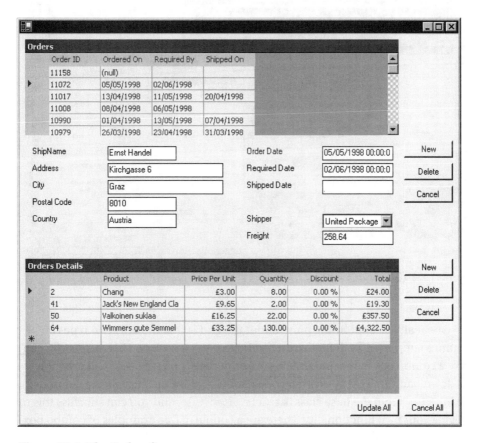

Figure 13-2. The Orders form

Here you have a grid at the top showing the outline of the order details. This just aids navigation. Underneath that are the data entry fields for the order details, and below them is a grid for the order lines. There are buttons to perform various functions on the data, and you'll examine those as you go through the chapter.

DataGrids and TableStyles

By default, when you bind data to a DataGrid, all columns are shown. To change this, you can use the TableStyles collection, which contains a list of styles to be used. Each grid can have multiple styles to cater for different sets and looks of data, and each style can contain a list of column styles to indicate the columns to be displayed.

You can set these styles in code or using the collections editors provided by Visual Studio .NET, as shown in Figure 13-3.

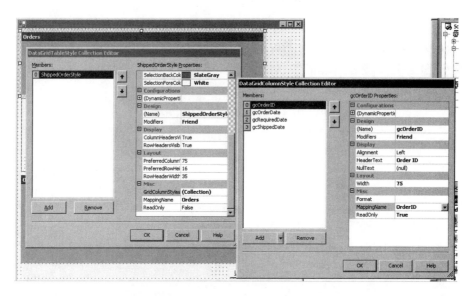

Figure 13-3. Collections editors

One really disappointing point about the grid is that the only two types of columns supported by default are a text box and a check box. This means you can't have a combo box in the grid unless you write code, or as the case will probably be, download some ready-written code. This is achievable because the columns are inherited from the base class DataGridColumnStyle, and you can subclass this to provide your own functionality. There are a couple of free examples of combo box styles available on http://www.gotdotnet.com, as well as some commercial ones. We haven't used any of these in the application just to keep things simple and concentrate on the data handling side of things.

Windows Forms Data Binding

Like Web Forms, Windows Forms provide the ability to bind controls to source of data. However, unlike Web Forms, which are stateless, Windows Forms are stateful and therefore have the ability to manage the data more efficiently. The binding revolves around the CurrencyManager and BindingContext objects.

The CurrencyManager Object

The CurrencyManager object manages the binding to a single source of data. Multiple controls bound to the same data source share the same CurrencyManager, and controls bound to different data sources will have different CurrenyManagers. The CurrencyManager keeps all of the controls it manages synchronized, ensuring that they all show data from the same record. It is, in a loose way, similar to the Data control in previous versions of Visual Basic, but you don't have to implicitly create a CurrencyManager. When a control is bound to a set of data, a CurrencyManager is created if one doesn't already exist for the data source or reused if it does. In practical use, the CurrencyManager effectively provides a "cursor" on the data, allowing editing, positioning, and so on.

The CurrencyManager provides, amongst others, the members listed in Table 13-1.

Table 13-1. CurrencyManager *Members*

Member	Type	Description
Count	Property	The number of rows in the underlying data source
Current	Property	A DataRowView object representing the current row
Position	Property	The current row number
AddNew()	Method	Adds a new row to the underlying data
CancelCurrentEdit()	Method	Cancels any edits currently in progress
EndCurrentEdit()	Method	Commits any errors currently in progress
RemoveAt()	Method	Removes a row at the given position

(Continued)

Table 13-1. CurrencyManager *Members (Continued)*

Member	Type	Description
CurrentChanged()	Event	Raised when the bound value changes
ItemChanged()	Event	Raised when the current item has been changed
PositionChanged()	Event	Raised when the position has been changed

The *BindingContext* Object

Because there can be multiple sets of data and multiple controls bound to them, the BindingContext object manages the CurrencyManager objects. Like the CurrencyManager, it doesn't need to be implicitly created because each form automatically contains a BindingContext.

For this form, you'll have a structure like that shown in Figure 13-4.

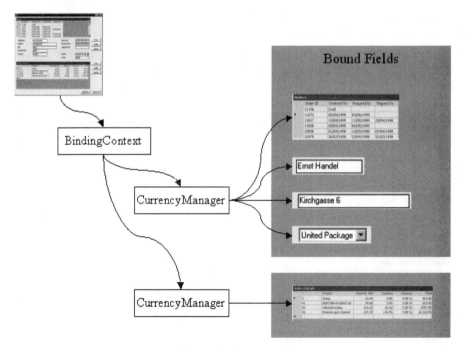

Figure 13-4. BindingContext *and* CurrencyManagers

The form contains one BindingContext object, which in turn contains two CurrencyManager objects. These bind to the Orders and Order Details tables.

Binding the DataGrid Control

Binding to a DataGrid on a form is similar to that in Web Forms. You can use either the properties or a single method. So if your grid is named dgOrders and your DataSet is named _dsOrders, you can do this:

```
dgOrders.DataSource = _dsOrders
dgOrders.DataMember = "Orders"
```

or this:

```
dgOrders.SetDataBinding(_dsOrders, "Orders")
```

The arguments of the SetDataBinding call correspond to the DataSource and the DataMember.

If your DataSet only has one table or if you want to have a hierarchical DataSet, then you can omit the DataMember.

On the form, you have two grids—one for the orders and one for the details. Because the source of these grids is the same DataSet, you can bind in such a way that the two grids remain synchronized. The DataSet has two tables (Orders and Order Details) and a relationship between them (CustOrders). To bind the second grid to the order details, you bind to the relation name rather than the table name:

```
dgOrderDetails.SetDataBinding(_dsOrders, "Orders.CustOrders")
```

This ensures the synchronization so that when you select an order, the order details grid automatically shows the correct details. Binding to just the table name would show all order details and have no relationship with the parent grid.

Binding TextBox Controls

For TextBox controls (and other controls that provide binding to a single item), you use the DataBindings collection. For example:

```
ShipPostalCode.DataBindings.Add("Text", _dsOrders, _
                                "Orders.ShipPostalCode")
ShipCountry.DataBindings.Add("Text", _dsOrders, "Orders.ShipCountry")
```

The three arguments are as follows:

- **Property name**: This is the property of the text box to which the data will be
  bound. In this case, it is the Text property, so the bound data shows in the
  text portion of the control. Although you don't use it in this application,
  being able to bind properties to the underlying data is extremely flexible
  and allows controls to change appearance based upon the underlying data.

- **Data source**: This is the source of the data.

- **Data member**: This is the member, or column in the data source, to which
  the control should be bound.

Like the order details grid, these text boxes are bound to the same data source
as the order grid and therefore share the same CurrencyManager, meaning they stay
synchronized with the Orders grid.

Binding ComboBox Controls

The data binding for a combo box is the same as for text boxes, except that you
need to populate the combo box with its data first:

```
ShipperID.DataSource = _dsLookups.Tables("Shippers")
ShipperID.DisplayMember = "ShipperName"
ShipperID.ValueMember = "ShipperID"
```

In this example, you have a combo box called ShipperID, the data source of
which is a different set of data. Remember that the Web Service provides a DataSet
containing two sets of lookup information—the Shipppers and Products. Here the
source of this combo box is the Shippers. The DisplayMember and ValueMember properties of the combo identify which columns hold the descriptive text and which
the ID value.

Finally, you use the same data binding addition as for the text box:

```
ShipperID.DataBindings.Add("SelectedValue", _dsOrders, "Orders.ShipVia")
```

Notice that this time you don't bind the data to the Text property but to the
SelectedValue property of the combo box. You're still binding to the same data
source as the rest of the data, so you still get synchronization. In the Orders table,
the foreign key to the shipper information is the ShipVia column, so you bind this
to the SelectedValue. When the underlying row changes, and there's a new value in
the ShipVia column, this value is matched to the ValueMember property of the
combo.

The DataBindings Collection

The DataBindings collection allows the binding of more than one property on a
control to multiple sources of data. At runtime you can use this collection to see
which controls are bound to which data source and data member, allowing a great
deal of generic programming. Each item in the DataBindings collection is a Binding
object, which contains properties such as DataSource and PropertyName to identity
the source of the data and the bound property. What it also contains is another
property called BindingMemberInfo, which contains three further properties. These
are as follows:

- BindingPath, which is the path to the data source

- BindingField, which is the field in the data source being bound to

- BindingMember, which is the fill path to the bound member

For example, for the binding on the form, some of the controls have the binding details listed in Table 13-2.

Table 13-2. The Binding Properties for the Orders Form

Control	BindingPath	BindingField	BindingMember
Quantity	Orders.CustOrders	Quantity	Orders.CustOrders.Quantity
UnitPrice	Orders.CustOrders	UnitPrice	Orders.CustOrders.UnitPrice
Freight	Orders	Freight	Orders.Freight
ShipperName	Orders	ShipperName	Orders.ShipperName

This means that given a bound form control, you can extract the details to
where it is bound. You'll see this used in the code later in the chapter.

Maintaining the Current Row

One of the rules you've decided to add to this application is that you can only edit
orders that haven't yet been shipped. To enforce this, you disable the text boxes
and certain buttons depending upon whether ShippedDate field has been filled.
Because you're using a grid to display the orders, there are no navigation buttons,
so you need some way to determine when the row current row has changed. To do
that, you use the PositionChanged event of the CurrencyManager object.

In Figure 13-4 for the binding of the form, you can see you have two CurrencyManager objects, so how do you determine which one to use? Well, they are members of the BindingContext object, so you can just index into that, using the DataSource and DataMember as arguments. For example:

```
Dim ourManager As CurrencyManager = Me.BindingContext(_dsOrders, "Orders")
```

You can now use the AddHandler method to add an event handler:

```
AddHandler ourManager.PositionChanged, AddressOf OrdersRowPositionChanged
```

As an alternative, you can perform this on one line:

```
AddHandler Me.BindingContext(_dsOrders, "Orders").PositionChanged, _
                    AddressOf OrdersRowPosition_Changed
```

Handling the PositionChanged Event

The rule you want to enforce is quite simple, but there are a couple of steps you have to go through in the event handler. This event is fired each time the row is changed, so you need to extract the row. You'll first look at the declaration of the event handler, which should be familiar:

```
Private Sub OrdersRowPosition_Changed(ByVal sender As Object, _
                            ByVal e As EventArgs)
```

The two arguments are the sender and any subsidiary arguments. You're only interested in the former because this is the CurrencyManager that raised the event. You can't use this directly because it's supplied as an object, so you have to cast it to the correct type first. For example:

```
Dim ourManager As CurrencyManager = CType(sender, CurrencyManager)
```

In fact, you don't explicitly need the currency manager itself, just the reference to the current row. So, what you can do is this:

```
Dim CurrentRowView As DataRowView = CType(sender, CurrencyManager).Current
```

Now that you have the current row, you can see if the ShippedDate column is blank and set a flag accordingly:

```
Dim AllowEdit = CurrentRow.Item("ShippedDate").ToString() = ""
```

You now know whether to enable or disable the fields and buttons, so you pass this value into the procedure that does this. You use a separate procedure because it's called elsewhere:

```
SetButtonUsability(AllowEdit)

End Sub
```

The routine that sets the usability of controls just sets the `Enabled` property:

```
Private Sub SetButtonUsability(ByVal Allowed As Boolean)

    btnDelete.Enabled = Allowed
    btnDeleteOrderDetails.Enabled = Allowed
    btnNewOrderDetails.Enabled = Allowed
    btnCancelOrderDetails.Enabled = Allowed
    btnCancel.Enabled = Allowed
    panDates.Enabled = Allowed
    panShipAddress.Enabled = Allowed
    panShipper.Enabled = Allowed
    dgOrderDetails.Enabled = Allowed

End Sub
```

The Code So Far...

Because you've only looked at fragments, it's best if you look at the code so far in one chunk. This will give you a greater understanding of how the application is constructed and will make the later sections of the book easier to read.

First, you have some global variables:

```
Private _CustID As String
Private _dsOrders As DataSet
Private _dsLookups As DataSet
```

These hold the customer number, which was passed from the calling form (the one that showed a list of customer), a `DataSet` containing the orders and order details, and a `DataSet` containing the lookup information. These are global because they're used in several applications.

Now you have the form constructor:

```
Public Sub New(ByVal CustID As String)

  Me.New()

  _CustID = CustID

  ' create an instance of the orders Web Service and fetch the data
  Dim wsOrders As New OrdersService.RemotingOrders()
  _dsOrders = wsOrders.Orders(CustID)
  _dsLookups = wsOrders.Lookups()

  BindData()

  ' set some default values for new rows
  _dsOrders.Tables("Orders").Columns("CustomerID").DefaultValue = _CustID
  _dsOrders.Tables("Orders").Columns("ShipVia").DefaultValue = _
                       _dsLookups.Tables("Shippers").Rows(0)("ShipperID")

  ' set the position for the first row
  ' this ensures that the buttons/textboxes are enabled
  ' or disabled according to the data
  OrdersRowPosition_Changed(Me.BindingContext(_dsOrders, "Orders"), _
                       CType(Nothing, EventArgs))

End Sub
```

First, you call the base constructor to ensure the controls are initialized, and then you load the data from the Web Service. Second, you call the BindData routine (shown next) to bind the loaded data to the controls. Then you set some default values, ready for the addition of new orders. The first is the customer ID, and the second is the shipper ID, which you default to the first value in the lookup table. The alternative to this would be to validate the data before submitting it back to the server, but this means a potentially distracting (and annoying) dialog box. It's just as valid as setting a default, but you don't want to annoy the users (unless you really want to!).

The BindData procedure contains the following:

```
Private Sub BindData()

  ' Add the delegate for the PositionChanged event.
  AddHandler Me.BindingContext(_dsOrders, "Orders").PositionChanged, _
                       AddressOf OrdersRowPosition_Changed
```

```
' bind the orders grid to the orders for that customer
dgOrders.SetDataBinding(_dsOrders, "Orders")

' and bind the order details grid to the relation in the DataSet
' this keeps them in sync
dgOrderDetails.SetDataBinding(_dsOrders, "Orders.CustOrders")

' and bind the textboxes
ShipPostalCode.DataBindings.Add("Text", _dsOrders,"Orders.ShipPostalCode")
ShipCountry.DataBindings.Add("Text", _dsOrders, "Orders.ShipCountry")
ShipCity.DataBindings.Add("Text", _dsOrders, "Orders.ShipCity")
ShipAddress.DataBindings.Add("Text", _dsOrders, "Orders.ShipAddress")
ShipName.DataBindings.Add("Text", _dsOrders, "Orders.ShipName")
Freight.DataBindings.Add("Text", _dsOrders, "Orders.Freight")
ShippedDate.DataBindings.Add("Text", _dsOrders, "Orders.ShippedDate")
RequiredDate.DataBindings.Add("Text", _dsOrders, "Orders.RequiredDate")
OrderDate.DataBindings.Add("Text", _dsOrders, "Orders.OrderDate")

' load and bind shipper details
ShipperID.DataSource = _dsLookups.Tables("Shippers")
ShipperID.DisplayMember = "ShipperName"
ShipperID.ValueMember = "ShipperID"
ShipperID.DataBindings.Add("SelectedValue", _dsOrders, "Orders.ShipVia")
```

End Sub

This uses the binding techniques you saw earlier. It adds the event handler for the PositionChanged event and then binds the two grids. Following that, it binds the text boxes and then fills and binds the combo box for the shipper details.

At this stage, you have a functional form that allows navigation. You now need to add the editing capability.

Handling Data Changes

Both the bound text boxes and the order details grid naturally support the editing of data, so there's nothing you need to do to allow users to start editing data. However, you need to provide ways for users to add and delete rows, as well as cancel any editing changes.

Adding Rows

Adding rows is handled by the currency manager, where you use the AddNew method. Before you add the new row, though, you first call EndCurrentEdit, which ensures that the data currently being edited is flushed into the underlying data source. The procedures to add rows to the Orders and Order Details only differ in the currency manager that they use:

```
Private Sub btnNew_Click(ByVal sender As System.Object, _
                        ByVal e As System.EventArgs) Handles btnNew.Click

   Me.BindingContext(_dsOrders, "Orders").EndCurrentEdit()
   Me.BindingContext(_dsOrders, "Orders").AddNew()

   SetButtonUsability(True)

End Sub

Private Sub btnNewOrderDetails_Click(ByVal sender As System.Object, _
            ByVal e As System.EventArgs) Handles btnNewOrderDetails.Click

   Me.BindingContext(_dsOrders, "Orders.CustOrders").EndCurrentEdit()
   Me.BindingContext(_dsOrders, "Orders.CustOrders").AddNew()

End Sub
```

Deleting Rows

For deleting orders, you don't have to worry about flushing any changes back to the data source because the row will be deleted. However, you do add want to check that the user is sure about deleting the row, so you put up a warning message first. Then you use the RemoveAt method of the currency manager, which removes rows at a given position. For this position, you use the current position of the currency manager, which indicates the current row:

```
Private Sub btnDelete_Click(ByVal sender As System.Object, _
            ByVal e As System.EventArgs) Handles btnDelete.Click

   Dim cmgr As CurrencyManager = Me.BindingContext(_dsOrders, "Orders")

   If MessageBox.Show("Are you sure you wish to delete this order?", _
```

```
         "Delete Order", MessageBoxButtons.YesNo, _
      MessageBoxIcon.Question) = DialogResult.Yes Then

      ' now we can delete the parent row
      cmgr.RemoveAt(cmgr.Position)

   End If
End Sub
```

Deleting order details differs slightly in that you first check that there are some rows to delete before displaying the warning message:

```
Private Sub btnDeleteOrderDetails_Click(ByVal sender As System.Object, _
            ByVal e As System.EventArgs) _
                    Handles btnDeleteOrderDetails.Click

   Dim cmgr As CurrencyManager = _
                    Me.BindingContext(_dsOrders, "Orders.CustOrders")

   If (cmgr.Count > 0) Then

      If MessageBox.Show("Are you sure you wish to delete this line?", _
         "Delete Order Line", MessageBoxButtons.YesNo, _
         MessageBoxIcon.Question) = DialogResult.Yes Then

         ' now we can delete the row
         cmgr.RemoveAt(cmgr.Position)

      End If
   End If

End Sub
```

Cancelling Edits

To cancel the changes made to a row, you use the CancelCurrentEdit method of the currency manager, which replaces the edited values with the underlying values:

```
Private Sub btnCancel_Click(ByVal sender As System.Object, _
            ByVal e As System.EventArgs) Handles btnCancel.Click
```

```
        Me.BindingContext(_dsOrders, "Orders").CancelCurrentEdit()

End Sub

Private Sub btnCancelOrderDetails_Click(ByVal sender As System.Object, _
            ByVal e As System.EventArgs) _
            Handles btnCancelOrderDetails.Click

    Me.BindingContext(_dsOrders, "Orders.CustOrders").CancelCurrentEdit()

End Sub
```

There's not much more to this process if you want to cancel all changes that you've made so far:

```
Private Sub btnCancelAll_Click(ByVal sender As System.Object, _
            ByVal e As System.EventArgs) Handles btnCancelAll.Click

    ' cancel any current edits
    Me.BindingContext(_dsOrders, "Orders.CustOrders").CancelCurrentEdit()
    Me.BindingContext(_dsOrders, "Orders").CancelCurrentEdit()

    ' reject all changes
    Me._dsOrders.RejectChanges()

    ' clear the errors
    ClearAllErrors()

End Sub
```

Here you first cancel the current edits, and then you call the RejectChanges method of the DataSet. This reverts all changed data back to the state it was when the DataSet was loaded.

Finally, you clear all the errors from the DataSet so that future updates won't be affected by any outstanding errors. This procedure just loops through the tables and rows calling the ClearErrors method on each row:

```
Private Sub ClearAllErrors()

    Dim dt As DataTable
    Dim dr As DataRow

    For Each dt In _dsOrders.Tables
```

```
   For Each dr In dt.Rows
     dr.ClearErrors()
   Next
 Next

End Sub
```

Flushing Changes to the Database

At this stage, the application is fully functioning, with the exception that any data changes can't yet be sent back to the data store. You've covered much of this technique earlier in the book, but it's worth reiterating for a couple of reasons. First, it reinforces the steps you need to go through to perform updates, and second, you're using it in a different context, so there are minor variations.

The first thing you do is declare a variable to be used as a reference to the Web Service:

```
Private Sub btnUpdate_Click(ByVal sender As System.Object, _
            ByVal e As System.EventArgs) Handles btnUpdate.Click

  Dim OrdersService As OrdersService.RemotingOrders
```

Next, you end any edits currently in progress:

```
  Me.BindingContext(_dsOrders, "Orders").EndCurrentEdit()
  Me.BindingContext(_dsOrders, "Orders.CustOrders").EndCurrentEdit()
```

You then check to see if there are any changes. The HasChanges method of a DataSet will be true if any changes have been made to any of the tables within it. If there are no changes, then the procedure just exits:

```
If _dsOrders.HasChanges Then
```

If there are changes to be processed, you'll need to extract these and send them back to the Web Service, which in turn will pass them to the data layer. For this you have two DataSets—one to hold the changes and one to hold the updated data:

```
Dim dsUpdate As DataSet
Dim dsChanges As DataSet
```

Before you get the changes, you clear any existing row errors, ensuring that any errors generated during the update aren't confused with any previous errors:

```
ClearAllErrors()
```

Next, you call GetChanges to return a DataSet containing just the changed data. This saves having to pass the entire DataSet back to the Web Service if only a few rows have changed. Also, because the two tables in the DataSet have a relationship, GetChanges ensures that if any Order Details rows that are changed, then their associated Order rows are included, even if the order wasn't changed. This stops orphaned Order Detail rows being included in the DataSet:

```
dsChanges = _dsOrders.GetChanges()
```

If the changes DataSet contains data, you can start the process of updates:

```
If Not (dsChanges Is Nothing) Then
```

The actual update involves passing the changes data to the Web Services. This calls the data layer component to perform the actual update and returns a DataSet containing all of the rows. You return the entire set of records again to ensure that the client has the latest data from the server. If you don't do this, the client gradually becomes more and more out-of-date with the server data, and this increases the risk of concurrency errors. The more up-to-date the client is, the less chance of changing data that someone else is changing:

```
OrdersService = New OrdersService.RemotingOrders()
dsUpdate = OrdersService.UpdateOrders(_CustID, dsChanges)
```

At this stage, the changes have been processed, and you have a DataSet with the current server data. This may be different from the current data you have, so you clear the current data and merge the new data into the main DataSet. The reason for this is that you have controls bound to the main DataSet, and this stops you from having to re-create the bindings:

```
_dsOrders.Clear()
_dsOrders.Merge(dsUpdate, False)
```

Now you need to check the DataSet to see if any errors occurred during the update:

```
If _dsOrders.HasErrors Then
```

If there are errors, then you load a separate form to process them. You pass any data into this form that it requires—the current customer ID, the DataSet of the changes, and the DataSet containing the lookup details. Once the form is shown, you add an event handler for the Closed event of the form so that you can be notified when the error form is closed:

```
Dim f As New ErrorsForm(_CustID, dsUpdate, _dsLookups)
Me.AddOwnedForm(f)
f.Show()


AddHandler f.Closed, AddressOf ErrorFormClosed
```

If there are no errors, then you can just call AcceptChanges to set the state of each row in the DataSet to Unchanged:

```
      Else
          ' no errors, so just accept the changes
          _dsOrders.AcceptChanges()
      End If
    End If
  End If

End Sub
```

During the processing of errors (shown next), you may have updated the server data, correcting errors or perhaps cancelling changes. In either case, you reload the data from the server and merge it into the current DataSet, accepting any changes. This means that once you have processed errors, the current data is correct and up-to-date:

```
Private Sub ErrorFormClosed(ByVal sender As Object, ByVal e As EventArgs)

  Dim wsOrders As New OrdersService.RemotingOrders()
  Dim dsOrders As DataSet = wsOrders.Orders(_CustID)

  _dsOrders.Merge(dsOrders, False)
  _dsOrders.AcceptChanges()

End Sub
```

Handling Concurrency Conflicts

As explained in previous chapters, handling concurrency conflicts isn't a simple task. You're dealing with the problem of two people changing the same row (or rows) of data at the same time, and although this shouldn't happen very often, you have to cater for the situation. There's no way to automate this process because the requirements could be different for each application. In the Web application, you saw how each set of changes had to be processed on the server. For the Windows application, you have data handling capabilities locally, so you can do the error correction before sending the changes back to the server.

There are two ways you could have handled errors in this application. The first is to highlight the errors in the existing window, as shown in Figure 13-5.

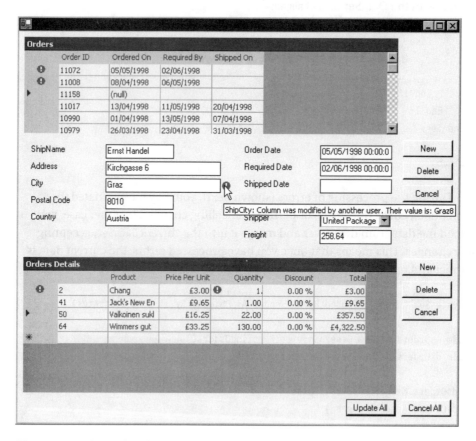

Figure 13-5. The Orders form with concurrency conflicts

Here you use the native error handling details of the grids, plus the ErrorProvider object, to automatically highlight errors. There's nothing wrong with this approach but when concurrency errors occur, they really need to be dealt with in a more authoritative manner. Using the same form for errors as for editing allows the user to make more changes as well as correcting errors, and this can lead to confusion. The user could be unsure as to why there are errors—was it something they just did or something that happened earlier?

The ErrorProvider Object

The ErrorProvider object is what provides the little exclamation marks identifying errors in the underlying form data. You either drop the ErrorProvider onto your form from the Toolbox at design time or create one at runtime. Whichever method you use, you need to set its binding details:

```
ErrorProvider1.DataSource = _dsOrders
ErrorProvider1.DataMember = "Orders"
ErrorProvider1.ContainerControl = Me

ErrorProvider2.DataSource = _dsOrders
ErrorProvider2.DataMember = "Orders.CustOrders"
ErrorProvider2.ContainerControl = Me
```

Here you set the DataSource and DataMember properties to point to the data. You have two ErrorProvider objects, as you have two currency managers, one for the Orders and one for the Order Details. You also set the ContainerControl property, which identifies the object that contains the error provider. In this code, it's the current form.

Once this is done, any controls that are managed by the same currency manager automatically show an icon next to them if they're in error. The icon can be changed, as can how the icon blinks and how often. Books don't yet have blinking ink, so you'll have to run the application to see this working!

The DataGrid objects provide their own ErrorProvider objects, so any rows and columns with errors in a grid automatically get the icons without further coding.

The Error Handling Form

The preferred approach is to use a separate form to handle resolution of concurrency errors, as shown in Figure 13-6.

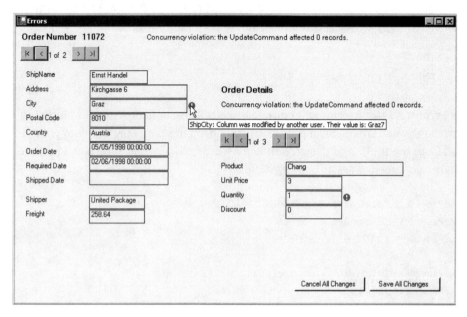

Figure 13-6. Identifying a concurrency error

Here you have a simpler approach, dedicated to the handling of errors. On the left you have the orders, and on the right you have the order details, with navigation for each. Errors are highlighted, with a ToolTip describing the error, and clicking the field in error shows buttons that allow the correction of the error, as shown in Figure 13-7.

Here you have the option of keeping the user value or keeping the database value. You can also save all changes or cancel all changes.

The approach is similar for rows that you delete but that another user modifies, where buttons appear allowing you to reinsert the row (keeping the database values) or to leave the row as deleted. You'll look at how this form works.

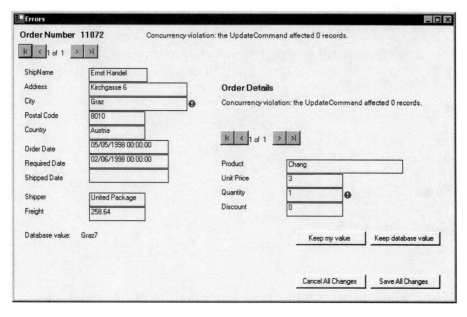

Figure 13-7. Correcting a concurrency error

First, you have some global variables to hold the customer ID, orders, and
lookup details:

```
Private _CustID As String
Private _dsOrders As DataSet
Private _dsLookups As DataSet
```

Second, you have an Enum, which is used for the navigation controls:

```
Private Enum MovePosition
   FirstRow
   PreviousRow
   NextRow
   LastRow
End Enum
```

Now you come to the form constructor:

```
Public Sub New(ByVal CustID As String, ByVal dsChanges As DataSet, _
                                ByVal dsLookups As DataSet)

  Me.New()

  _CustID = CustID
  _dsLookups = dsLookups

  _dsOrders = dsChanges.Clone()

  ShowData(dsChanges)

End Sub
```

Here you call the base constructor to ensure the components are initialized. Then you set the global customer ID and lookups. Then, rather than setting the global DataSet to reference the orders DataSet passed in (dsChanges), you use the Clone method. This copies the DataSet but doesn't copy any of the data; so you have a DataSet with the correct schema, but no data. This is done because you only want a DataSet with the errors in, rather than all of the data (where the user would have to hunt for the rows with errors). The ShowData procedure extracts the errors and binds the data to the controls.

Identifying Errors

It is extremely simple to extract the error rows from a DataSet because the DataTable object contains a GetErrors method, which returns an array of rows with errors. Before doing that, though, you have to consider the nature of the data—you have nested tables, so what happens if there's an error in a child table, but no error in the parent table? For example:

```
drOrders = dsChanges.Tables("Orders").GetErrors()
drOrderDetail = dsChanges.Tables("Orders Details").GetErrors()
```

This would give you two arrays of DataRow objects, but the drOrders array would be empty because there aren't errors in this table. Why is this a problem? Because you want to use the hierarchical binding features that keep parent and child in synchronization. So, what you have to do is force an error for a parent row if any of the children for that parent have errors. This involves looping through the child rows searching for errors. Because you're doing that, you'll also take the opportunity to set errors on individual columns.

Setting Column Errors

In the previous chapters, we discussed that the RowState property of a row indicates that the row has been changed, and you can examine the current value and the original value (if present) to identify the error. This is fairly straightforward, but you also want to use the fancy error display capabilities of the form, and unfortunately these aren't clever enough to look at the data. However, they do look at the error details for rows and columns. You know the rows have errors set because the update process automatically sets them, but there are no errors on the columns. So, while looping through the rows, you might as well loop through the columns at the same time. Setting the error messages isn't only useful from the user interface perspective (users can easily see the columns in error), but it also makes the task of identifying columns in error simple. This is because the DataRow has a method called GetColumnError, which returns the error string for a selected column. You can then use that to determine whether the error is active or has been cleared by the user. You'll see how that's achieved later, but for now, you'll look at how you set the column errors:

```
Private Sub SetColumnErrors(ByRef dsChanges As DataSet)

    Dim dt As DataTable
    Dim dr As DataRow
    Dim dc As DataColumn
    Dim parentRow As DataRow
```

Here you start to loop through the tables and the rows in each table, and it's only if the row has errors that you want to deal with them:

```
For Each dt In dsChanges.Tables
    For Each dr In dt.Rows

        If dr.HasErrors Then
```

Now you want to ensure that the parent row has an error, so you use the GetParentRow method to get a reference to the parent of the current row. The argument to this method is the relationship name used between the two tables.

```
parentRow = dr.GetParentRow("CustOrders")
```

Because this routine is generic and loops through both tables, there won't be a parent row if you're already on the parent (in other words, the Orders table). In this case the parentRow variable will be Nothing. However, if you're on a child row, parentRow will contain a reference (and it won't be Nothing), so you also need to see if the parent row already has an error. If so, the HasErrors property of the row will be True, and you don't need to do anything:

```
If Not (parentRow Is Nothing) AndAlso _
    Not parentRow.HasErrors Then
```

If there's no error, you set the RowError property to the error message you want displayed. You don't want to overwrite the error message if it already exists so you only do this if it's already empty:

```
    If parentRow.RowError = "" Then
      parentRow.RowError = "Error occured in Order Details"
    End If
End If
```

You've set the parent row error, so ensuring that the parent row will be returned as an error row when you extract the errors. There may not be any columns in error in that parent row, so it's safe to do this.

Now you need to loop through the columns, but only those columns that aren't derived. Remember that the Order Details table has a LineTotal total column, added as part of the business logic in the Web service. If the columns that this column derive from have errors, then this column is also in error, but because it's a derived column, there's no correction that needs to be done. So, you ignore derived columns and only process columns where the Expression is empty:

```
For Each dc In dr.Table.Columns

    If dc.Expression = "" Then
```

Now you can determine what sort of conflict occurred. This is all that happens within the inner loop, so we've removed some of the indenting to make it easier to read. What this does is determine what the state of the row is and set an error message on the column accordingly:

```
Select Case dr.RowState
```

So, for modified records, you know that there's been a conflict with two people changing the same column. To provide a decent error message, you want to show the value that the other user updated this column to. The value you changed is the Current version, and the value that the other user changed is the Original version. When extracting columns form a row, you normally only need the column name (or index), which retrieves the Current value. However, you can also pass in a member of the DataRowVersion enumeration to specify which value you want. You check both values to ensure that they aren't null and then compare them. If they're the same, then there was no change, but if they're different, then you've found an error, so you set the error message, using the SetColumnError method of the row:

```
Case DataRowState.Modified
  If Not ((dr.IsNull(dc,DataRowVersion.Current) _
        OrElse dr.IsNull(dc,DataRowVersion.Original)) _
      OrElse (dr(dc, DataRowVersion.Current) = _
            dr(dc, DataRowVersion.Original))) Then

    Dim val As String = dr(dc,DataRowVersion.Original).ToString()
    dr.SetColumnError(dc, "Column was modified by another user. " _
                  & "Their value is: " & val)
  End If
```

For deleted or added rows, there's no comparison to be made, so you just set an appropriate error message.

```
    Case DataRowState.Added
        dr.SetColumnError(dc, "Row has been added")

    Case DataRowState.Deleted
        dr.SetColumnError(dc, "This row has been deleted by another user")
End Select
```

Extracting the Errors

Once the error details have been set, you can extract the rows in error and show the data. This routine is called from the form constructor:

```
Private Sub ShowData(ByVal dsChanges As DataSet)
```

First, you have two arrays to hold the rows in error.

```
Dim drOrders As DataRow()
Dim drOrderDetails As DataRow()
```

Second, you call the SetColumnErrors procedure, which is the one just discussed:

```
SetColumnErrors(dsChanges)
```

At this point, you have still only have a DataSet (dsChanges) with errors. Before you extract the errors, though, you clear any rows out of the global DataSet. It's this to which you'll bind the data. In the form constructor, you created the DataSet using the Clone method, which doesn't copy any data. The reason you clear rows is that once you've rectified any errors and updated the original data again, there may be more errors. If that's the case, you don't close the error form—you just rerun through this routine, so you need to ensure that the data you're going to show doesn't contain any rows from previous corrections:

```
_dsOrders.Clear()
```

Now you can get the rows in error. You start with the Orders table, and you merge these row errors into the global DataSet:

```
drOrders = dsChanges.Tables("Orders").GetErrors()
_dsOrders.Merge(drOrders)
```

Now you merge in any child rows, first checking that there are rows in error in the Order Details table:

```
If dsChanges.Tables("Order Details").HasErrors Then
    drOrderDetails = dsChanges.Tables("Order Details").GetErrors()
    _dsOrders.Merge(drOrderDetails)
```

Because you've now merged in the order details, you create the relationship between the two tables. You only do this if it doesn't already exist (which will be the first time through):

```
    If _dsOrders.Relations.Count = 0 Then
        Dim ParentCol, ChildCol As DataColumn
        ParentCol = _dsOrders.Tables("Orders").Columns("OrderID")
        ChildCol = _dsOrders.Tables("Order Details").Columns("OrderID")
        Dim objRelation As New DataRelation("CustOrders", _
                                        ParentCol, ChildCol)
        _dsOrders.Relations.Add(objRelation)
    End If
End If
```

At this stage, the global DataSet (_dsOrders) contains only the rows in error, so you can bind the form controls and the error providers:

```
' bind the textboxes for the orders
lblOrderNumber.DataBindings.Add("Text", _dsOrders, "Orders.OrderID")
ShipPostalCode.DataBindings.Add("Text", _dsOrders, _
                                    "Orders.ShipPostalCode")
ShipCountry.DataBindings.Add("Text", _dsOrders, "Orders.ShipCountry")
ShipCity.DataBindings.Add("Text", _dsOrders, "Orders.ShipCity")
ShipAddress.DataBindings.Add("Text", _dsOrders, "Orders.ShipAddress")
ShipName.DataBindings.Add("Text", _dsOrders, "Orders.ShipName")
Freight.DataBindings.Add("Text", _dsOrders, "Orders.Freight")
ShippedDate.DataBindings.Add("Text", _dsOrders, "Orders.ShippedDate")
RequiredDate.DataBindings.Add("Text", _dsOrders, "Orders.RequiredDate")
OrderDate.DataBindings.Add("Text", _dsOrders, "Orders.OrderDate")
ShipperName.DataBindings.Add("Text", _dsOrders, "Orders.ShipperName")


' bind error provider
ErrorProvider1.DataSource = _dsOrders
ErrorProvider1.DataMember = "Orders"
ErrorProvider1.ContainerControl = Me
```

In the editing form, you saw the order details in a grid, but here we're showing them in single controls, so you use the same binding method as the other controls. Notice that the field you bind to contains the full name for the child column—this is the parent table, the relationship name, and the column name:

```
' only bind to order details if there are errors in the order details
If Not (drOrderDetails Is Nothing) Then
    ' bind the textboxes for the order details
    ProductID.DataBindings.Add("Text", _dsOrders, _
                            "Orders.CustOrders.ProductID")
    ProductName.DataBindings.Add("Text", _dsOrders, _
                                "Orders.CustOrders.ProductName")
    UnitPrice.DataBindings.Add("Text", _dsOrders, _
                            "Orders.CustOrders.UnitPrice")
    Quantity.DataBindings.Add("Text", _dsOrders, _
                            "Orders.CustOrders.Quantity")
    Discount.DataBindings.Add("Text", _dsOrders, _
                            "Orders.CustOrders.Discount")
```

```
    ' bind error provider
    ' this gives us automatic notification of errors on the text boxes
    ErrorProvider2.DataSource = _dsOrders
    ErrorProvider2.DataMember = "Orders.CustOrders"
    ErrorProvider2.ContainerControl = Me
End If
```

Finally, you add an event handler to manage the `PositionChanged` event of the currency manager for the Orders table. This will be raised every time the row is changed:

```
AddHandler Me.BindingContext(_dsOrders, "Orders").PositionChanged, _
                        AddressOf OrdersRowPosition_Changed
```

You then call a procedure to update the current view, such as enabling and disabling buttons and so on, before finally calling a routine to check for deleted rows. These are a special case, and you'll look at them in detail later:

```
    UpdateParentView()

    CheckForDeleted()

End Sub
```

Changing the View

Like the editing form, you want to control what's shown on the form as each row is being navigated to. As shown previously, you call a method called `UpdateParent` after you've bound the data, and you also call it when the row position changes from the event handler you added previously.

```
Private Sub OrdersRowPosition_Changed(ByVal sender As Object, _
                                    ByVal e As EventArgs)

    UpdateParentView()

End Sub
```

Changing the Parent View

Although what you're doing when the row changes is fairly simple, it needs explaining so you understand the reasoning behind it. The first thing you do is get references to the current row number and the current row using the currency manager for the Orders table:

```
Private Sub UpdateParentView()

  Dim CurrentRowNumber As Integer = _
      Me.BindingContext(_dsOrders, "Orders").Position
  Dim CurrentRow As DataRow = _
      CType(Me.BindingContext(_dsOrders, "Orders").Current, DataRowView).Row
```

Next, you set a label to show the RowError for this row. You also show the current and maximum row numbers, so users can see where they are and how may rows in total there are:

```
lblOrderError.Text = CurrentRow.RowError
lblOrderNav.Text = (CurrentRowNumber + 1).ToString _
    & " of " & _dsOrders.Tables("Orders").Rows.Count.ToString()
```

If the row has been deleted, you show a set of buttons to allow the user to resolve the errors on the deleted row. As mentioned earlier, you have to process deleted rows differently. These buttons are contained within a Panel control, so you can just make the panel visible (or not):

```
If CurrentRow.RowError = "Deleted" Then
  panDeleted.Visible = True
Else
  panDeleted.Visible = False
End If
```

Next, you enable or disable the controls for Order Details, depending on whether there are any for this particular order:

```
Dim EnableChild As Boolean = _
                  (CurrentRow.GetChildRows("CustOrders").Length > 0)
btnMoveFirstDetail.Enabled = EnableChild
btnMoveLastDetail.Enabled = EnableChild
btnMoveNextDetail.Enabled = EnableChild
btnMovePrevDetail.Enabled = EnableChild
```

```
ProductName.Enabled = EnableChild
UnitPrice.Enabled = EnableChild
Quantity.Enabled = EnableChild
Discount.Enabled = EnableChild
```

If there are Order Details, you call a routine to update the child view (this is shown a little later):

```
If EnableChild Then
  UpdateChildView()
End If
```

You then make sure that the panel allowing edits to be corrected isn't shown. This will be shown when users click a control with an error:

```
panOriginal.Visible = False
```

And finally, you set the error message for each control on the form. You might wonder about this because you've already said that these controls are bound, and the ErrorProvider manages the displaying of errors. That's correct, but there's one big feature missing from the ADO.NET, and that's the ability to clear an error for a single column. You can clear all errors for a row but not for a column. You can also set the error text for a column to an empty string, but that doesn't actually clear the error—it just leaves the column with an error and no description. So you have a set of data, with errors, and you allow the user to correct those errors, but you have no way to clear the errors as they're corrected. This means that a user can correct the error, but the form still shows an error—very confusing. Luckily, the ErrorProvider gives you the ability to overcome this because setting the error for a given control to an empty string removes the icon from display. What you do, therefore, is when correcting the errors, set the error for the underlying column to an empty string, signifying that it has been corrected. When the navigation for this row is run, you loop through the columns for this row and set the error for the ErrorProvider to be the same as the error on the column. Thus, any cleared errors will have an empty errors message, and this will clear the error icon from the screen:

```
Dim ctl As Control
For Each ctl In Me.Controls
  If CurrentRow.Table.Columns.Contains(ctl.Name) Then
    ErrorProvider1.SetError(ctl, CurrentRow.GetColumnError(ctl.Name))
  End If
Next

End Sub
```

The method of this loop also deserves some explanation. There are two ways you could provide this functionality—either by looping through the Controls collection of the form or by looping through the Columns collection of the table. Whichever you choose, there will be some controls on the form that don't exist in the table as columns (such as buttons, labels, and so on) and some columns in the table that don't exist as controls (such as ID fields and derived columns). If you loop through the columns, you still need access to the control, and there's no way to index into the Controls collection of a Form by name. You can only index by the index number of the control. So rather than looping through the column, you loop through the controls, and you only set the error for controls that exist within the Columns collection of the table. The SetError method of the ErrorProvider takes two arguments. The first is the control to set the error for, and the second is the error message. This is retrieved from the underlying data using the GetColumnError, specifying the name of the column. These controls have the same name as their columns. Remember that the underlying data will either have an error message or have an empty string, so this loop has the effect of showing error icons for columns with errors but not showing them where you've cleared the error message.

Changing the Child View

You have a similar routine for Order Details, which just uses a different currency manager because you're dealing with the child table:

```
Private Sub UpdateChildView()

  Dim CurrentRowNumber As Integer = _
      Me.BindingContext(_dsOrders, "Orders.CustOrders").Position
  Dim CurrentRow As DataRow = _
      CType(Me.BindingContext(_dsOrders, "Orders.CustOrders").Current, _
          DataRowView).Row

  ' set the error label
  lblOrderDetailsError.Text = CurrentRow.RowError
  lblOrderDetailsNav.Text = (CurrentRowNumber + 1).ToString _
      & " of " & _dsOrders.Tables("Order Details").Rows.Count.ToString()

  ' if deleted show different buttons
  If CurrentRow.RowError = "Deleted" Then
    panDeletedDetails.Visible = True
```

```
    Else
      panDeletedDetails.Visible = False
    End If


    panOriginal.Visible = False


    Dim ctl As Control
    For Each ctl In Me.Controls
      If CurrentRow.Table.Columns.Contains(ctl.Name) Then
        ErrorProvider2.SetError(ctl, CurrentRow.GetColumnError(ctl.Name))
      End If
    Next


End Sub
```

Correcting Errors

There are several stages to correcting errors. The first is to handle what happens when a user clicks one of the controls in error. On this form, these controls are Labels because you don't want the user editing the data. You only want to them to pick from one of two choices—their data or the underlying database data. You can make this routine generic because it's the same for all columns, as the Handles clause of event procedure shows:

```
Private Sub Item_Click(ByVal sender As Object, _
                       ByVal e As System.EventArgs) _
     Handles ShipperName.Click, ShipAddress.Click, ShipCity.Click, _
             ShipPostalCode.Click, ShipCountry.Click, _
             OrderDate.Click, RequiredDate.Click, ShippedDate.Click, _
             ProductName.Click, UnitPrice.Click, Quantity.Click, _
             Discount.Click
```

First, you define a Label variable to point to the control on which the user is working. Because this event procedure handles the Click event for all the labels, you know that the sender (in other words, the control that raised the event) is a Label, so you cast the sender to a label:

```
Dim ctl As Label = CType(sender, Label)
```

Second, you extract the table name to which the control belongs. Earlier in the chapter, we talked about the DataBindings collection, showing how you can bind properties of controls. Each of these bindings is represented by a Binding object, and one of whose properties a `BindingMemberInfo` class. You use the `BindingPath` property to give you the table name to which this control is bound:

```
Dim TableName As String = _
                ctl.DataBindings("Text").BindingMemberInfo.BindingPath
```

Next, you extract the current row and the original row value for the current field. `GetOriginalRowValue` is a procedure that just returns the `Original` value of a current column. It checks for the row state and then performs some validity checking on the data before returning the correct value:

```
Dim CurrentRow As DataRow = _
                CType(Me.BindingContext(_dsOrders, TableName).Current, _
                    DataRowView).Row
Dim value As String = GetOriginalRowValue(CurrentRow, ctl.Name)
```

You now have the original value for the row, so you need to see if this matches the current value:

```
If Not (value Is Nothing) AndAlso (value <> CurrentRow(ctl.Name)) Then
```

The values are different, so you then extract the error message for this column:

```
Dim err As String = CurrentRow.GetColumnError(ctl.Name)
```

If the error message is empty, then you've already cleared this error (you'll see how you do this in a little while), so you just make the editing panel invisible. If you haven't cleared the error, make the panel visible and set the display text to show the original value. You also store the current control on the `Tag` property of the label—this will be used later when the user makes the decision of which value to keep. You're using the `Tag` property because it's not used on this control for any other purpose and saves on having to create a global variable just to identify which control you're correcting the value for:

```
    If err <> "" Then
        panOriginal.Visible = True
        lblOriginalValue.Text = value
        lblOriginalValue.Tag = ctl
    End If
  Else
        panOriginal.Visible = False
  End If

End Sub
```

The user can now see their value, the original value currently stored in the database, and two buttons allowing them to pick one or the other.

The event procedures for these buttons are simple, just calling another routine, indicating which version of the data is to be kept:

```
Private Sub btnKeepMine_Click(ByVal sender As System.Object, _
                            ByVal e As System.EventArgs) _
          Handles btnKeepMine.Click


  CorrectValue(DataRowVersion.Current)


End Sub


Private Sub btnKeepTheirs_Click(ByVal sender As System.Object, _
                            ByVal e As System.EventArgs) _
          Handles btnKeepTheirs.Click


  CorrectValue(DataRowVersion.Original)


End Sub
```

The procedure for correcting the error is fairly simple, but there are a couple of points to watch out for. In short, you decide which version the user is keeping and do one of two things:

- Overwrite the current version with the original if they want to keep the original database version.

- Do nothing if they want to keep their version.

To start with, you extract the details of the control being corrected. Remember, earlier you stored the control into the Tag property of this label—here's where it gets used:

```
Private Sub CorrectValue(ByVal Version As DataRowVersion)

  Dim ctl As Control = CType(lblOriginalValue.Tag, Label)
```

Next, you get the table and row details using the bindings and the currency manager:

```
Dim TableName As String = _
        ctl.DataBindings("Text").BindingMemberInfo.BindingPath
```

```
Dim Manager As CurrencyManager = _
            CType(Me.BindingContext(_dsOrders, TableName), CurrencyManager)
Dim CurrentRow As DataRow = CType(Manager.Current, DataRowView).Row
Dim ControlName As String = ctl.Name
```

Now you need to decide what to do, and it's only if the Original value is being kept that you have to do anything:

```
If Version = DataRowVersion.Original Then
    CurrentRow(ControlName) = lblOriginalValue.Text
End If
```

Handling Lookup Values

At this point, you might think you're done, but you have to take into account lookup fields. For values such as the ProductName or ShipperName, you show them as text values, but they are stored as foreign key fields in the underlying data. So, how do you know where to get the value from and which column to overwrite? The simple answer is that you don't—there's no automatic way to derive this information. However, you can provide this information and still retain the flexibility of this routine. The way you do this is to store these lookup details in the Tag property of the display fields. For example, on the form, you have ShipperName and ProductName controls, as shown in Table 13-3.

Table 13-3. The Tag Property Values for the Lookup Fields

Control	Tag Property
ShipperName	Shippers;ShipperID;ShipperName;ShipVia
ProductName	Products;ProductID;ProductName;ProductID

These semicolon-separated values correspond to the following:

- The lookup table name

- The value (ID) column in the lookup table

- The descriptive column in the lookup table

- The foreign key field in the current table

Using this information, you can look up the ID value and use that to correct the error. So the correction routine is now as follows:

```
If Version = DataRowVersion.Original Then
  If ctl.Tag <> "" Then
    Dim LookupDetails As String() = CType(ctl.Tag, String).Split(";")
    Dim dr As DataRow()
    dr = _dsLookups.Tables(LookupDetails(0)).Select(LookupDetails(2) _
                         & "='" & lblOriginalValue.Text & "'")
    CurrentRow(LookupDetails(3)) = dr(0).Item(LookupDetails(1))
  Else
    CurrentRow(ControlName) = lblOriginalValue.Text
  End If
End If
```

Here you check the Tag property of the control. If it's empty, you can just copy the value over the current value, but if it's not empty, then this is a lookup field. You therefore take the value that's stored in the Tag and split it into an array. You have the lookup tables in a global DataSet so you can use these array values to find the required ID value.

Clearing the Current Error

Once you've corrected the error, you need to clear the error details. Remember that earlier we said there's no way to actually clear the error for a single column, so what you do is clear the error message, as well as clearing the message for the appropriate ErrorProvider. This immediately clears the icon from view:

```
CurrentRow.SetColumnError(ControlName, "")
If TableName = "Orders" Then
  ErrorProvider1.SetError(ctl, "")
Else
  ErrorProvider2.SetError(ctl, "")
End If
```

Finally, you hide the editing panel and update the parent view:

```
panOriginal.Visible = False

UpdateParentView()

End Sub
```

Navigation

On the editing form you didn't need to worry about navigation because the grid handled it for you, but on this form you're using single field binding, so you need to provide a way for the user to move between rows. You use the usual VCR-type display of four buttons, one set for the Orders and one set for the Order Details. You don't need to see the event procedure for each of these buttons because each just calls another routing, passing in the appropriate table name and the direction to move in:

```
Private Sub MoveToRow(ByVal BindingTable As String, _
                    ByVal MoveTo As MovePosition)
```

You first get a reference to the currency manager and the maximum number of records:

```
Dim CcyManager As BindingManagerBase = _
                    Me.BindingContext(_dsOrders, BindingTable)
Dim MaxRows As Integer = CcyManager.Count
```

Then you perform the movement, setting the Position to the required row number:

```
  Select Case MoveTo
    Case MovePosition.FirstRow
      CcyManager.Position = 0

    Case MovePosition.LastRow
      CcyManager.Position = MaxRows - 1

    Case MovePosition.NextRow
      If CcyManager.Position < MaxRows - 1 Then
        CcyManager.Position += 1
      End If

    Case MovePosition.PreviousRow
      If CcyManager.Position > 0 Then
        CcyManager.Position -= 1
      End If
  End Select

  UpdateParentView()

End Sub
```

Handling Deleted Rows

Handling deleted rows is a little tricky because they've been deleted. How then do you deal with them if they don't exist? Well, they do exist; it just depends on how you look for them (a bit like Schroedinger's cat). The problem is that you can't bind to rows that are deleted—they just don't show up. This is fairly logical if you think about it (they've been deleted, so why do you need to see them?), but it makes your job of resolving conflicts a little harder. Luckily, the deleted rows still exist in the DataTable, but with a RowState of Deleted.

To check for deleted rows, you compare the number of rows in the currency manager with the number of rows in the table. If they're different, then you know there are some deleted rows:

```
Private Sub CheckForDeleted()

  If _dsOrders.Tables("Orders").Rows.Count <> _
              Me.BindingContext(_dsOrders, "Orders").Count _
    Or _dsOrders.Tables("Order Details").Rows.Count <> _
              Me.BindingContext(_dsOrders, "Order Details").Count Then
```

For any deleted rows, your loop will mark them as undeleted by simply rejecting any changes made to the row. The RejectChanges method of the DataRow resets all of the values of a row back to their original values, so the row suddenly becomes live again. You also set the RowError so you can identify this as a deleted row:

```
    Dim dt As DataTable
    Dim dr As DataRow
    Dim i As Integer

    For Each dt In _dsOrders.Tables
      For i = 0 To dt.Rows.Count - 1
        dr = dt.Rows(i)
        If dr.RowState = DataRowState.Deleted Then
          dr.RejectChanges()
          dr.RowError = "Deleted"
        End If
      Next
    Next

  End If

End Sub
```

The UpdateParentView and UpdateChildView procedures check for this RowError and enable or disable the set of buttons to allow this row error to be corrected.

Correcting Errors in Deleted Rows

For correcting deleted rows, you have for buttons—two four the Orders and two for the Order Details. Each of these pairs follows a similar principle to the normal error correction buttons, allowing either the current or original value to be kept. Also like the other errors, these call a single routine to handle the correction:

```
Private Sub btnDeletedDelete_Click(ByVal sender As System.Object, _
                                   ByVal e As System.EventArgs) _
        Handles btnDeletedDelete.Click

  ProcessDeleted("Orders", DataRowVersion.Current)

End Sub


Private Sub btnDeletedLeaveIn_Click(ByVal sender As System.Object, _
                                    ByVal e As System.EventArgs) _
        Handles btnDeletedLeaveIn.Click

  ProcessDeleted("Orders", DataRowVersion.Original)

End Sub


Private Sub btnDeletedDetailsDelete_Click(ByVal sender As System.Object, _
                                          ByVal e As System.EventArgs) _
        Handles btnDeletedDetailsDelete.Click

  ProcessDeleted("Order Details", DataRowVersion.Current)

End Sub


Private Sub btnDeletedDetailsLeave_Click(ByVal sender As System.Object, _
                                         ByVal e As System.EventArgs) _
        Handles btnDeletedDetailsLeave.Click

  ProcessDeleted("Order Details", DataRowVersion.Original)

End Sub
```

The routine to correct a deleted row is quite simple because all you have to do is keep the row or delete it again:

```
Private Sub ProcessDeleted(ByVal TableName As String, _
                            ByVal Version As DataRowVersion)

  Dim Manager As CurrencyManager = _
      CType(Me.BindingContext(_dsOrders, TableName), CurrencyManager)
  Dim CurrentRow As DataRow = CType(Manager.Current, DataRowView).Row

  If Version = DataRowVersion.Original Then
```

If the user decides to keep the database version, then you just accept the changes (which sets the correct current values) and clear any errors. This row is now part of the data once again. Notice that you don't have to clear any error messages because you use ClearErrors on the row. This clears the errors in the underlying row, and the ErrorProvider picks this up. It's only for column corrections you can't use this method:

```
CurrentRow.AcceptChanges()
CurrentRow.ClearErrors()
```

If you decide to keep this version (in other words, still delete the row), then you just delete it again. This marks the rows as deleted, and this deletion will be enforced once you push the changes back to the server again:

```
  Else
    ' to keep the row as deleted just re-delete it
    CurrentRow.Delete()
  End If

  panDeleted.Visible = False

End Sub
```

Saving the Corrected Data

Having been through the rigmarole of correcting errors, you now need to send the data back to the server again. This follows a similar principle to the routine in the editing form:

```
Private Sub btnSave_Click(ByVal sender As System.Object, _
                          ByVal e As System.EventArgs) Handles btnSave.Click
```

The first thing to do is clear any existing errors. You may have corrected them, but the columns and rows are still marked as having errors:

```
ClearAllErrors()
```

Next, you get a DataSet containing the changes:

```
Dim dsChanges As DataSet = _dsOrders.GetChanges()

If Not (dsChanges Is Nothing) Then
```

If there are changes, you push those changes back to the server using the Web service:

```
Dim OrdersService As New Orders.OrdersService.RemotingOrders()
Dim dsUpdate As DataSet = OrdersService.UpdateOrders(_CustID, dsChanges)
```

The Web service returns a complete set of data, so you need to check again for errors:

```
If dsUpdate.HasErrors Then
```

If there are errors, then you clear the data bindings and reshow the data, calling the routine that ran first when the form was loaded:

```
lblStatus.Text = "There are still errors with the data."
ClearBindings()
ShowData(dsUpdate)
```

This process will be repeated until there are no more errors or until the user cancels from this form. In this case, you just close the form:

```
Else
    Me.Close()
    End If
  Else
    Me.Close()
  End If

End Sub
```

At this point, you've resolved all of the concurrency errors, and the `FormClosed` event procedure is run in the opening form.

The Application in Practice

There's been an awful lot of code here, so how do you go about testing this sort of thing? After all, you only get these problems when other people change data at the same time as you. The simple way is you either have two copies of this application open and change the same data or you use SQL Query Analyzer to change the data directly. And, no, it's not cheating—it's just the simplest way of modifying data and guarantees that the data on the server is changed.

The procedure you need to go through is to first load the editing form. You can either run the main customers form and from that load this one or use a text project to load this directly. The latter is the simplest way, and building a test harness such as this makes the job of developing and testing these sorts of forms a lot easier. In the downloadable code, this editable form is in the `UpdatableRemoteFormsApplication`, under the directory `Orders`. Loading the order solution (`Orders.sln`) not only loads the `Orders` form but a test form, too. When run, this test form simply loads the orders form directly, passing in the customer ID of `ERNSH`.

When the form is loaded, you must remember that you're dealing with disconnected data. Even though you have a Windows client and can use ADO.NET in your client application, you're still disconnected from the data store. At this stage, you can go ahead and make changes to the data (remembering that you can only change rows that aren't shipped). At the same time as you modify the data in this client, switch to SQL Query Analyzer and connect to the database. Open the SQL script `ServerChanges.sql` and run it—this will modify an order row and order details for order number 11072 and some order details for order number 11008. You can now save your changes from the orders form, and if you've updated the same details, you'll see the errors form displayed. Here you can click the fields with errors and resolve them.

If you want to repeat this, you'll need to keep modifying the data in the SQL Script, so that each time it's different from the version that the orders form has loaded.

Summary

In this chapter, you've covered a huge amount of ground, essentially building a fully functional editable form, allowing the complete manipulation of Orders and Order Details. The architecture of this form builds on the work of previous chapters and works either running from a local machine or running remotely from a Web server. The essentials of updating data have been similar to those you saw in the data tier components that actually update the data for the Web applications and actually form a minor part of this application.

What you've concentrated on in this chapter is providing rich editing capabilities with as little change to the existing functionality as possible. You've seen that most of the coding has gone toward managing the data on the client, binding controls, resolving conflicts, and so on.

You've come a long way since the humble beginnings in Chapter 1, where we defined the problems of using data across multiple platforms and applications. And although we haven't written that detective story, there's been lots of investigative work going on, analyzing the best way to architect applications to handle data. Right from the outset you've seen that you can build applications with a great deal of reusability, even if the target clients are different. And different they can be because the feature set of a phone is vastly inferior to that of a Windows application. Despite this vast gap in features, the Windows application has been built with little change to the middle tier and no change to the data tier. In fact, you could have actually managed with just a single additional method in our Web services to allow the Web-based application tier to be used by the Windows application. You didn't because it just gives you a little more flexibility for enhancing the application in the future.

We hope this book has given you the confidence to tackle similar projects. Even if you only ever target one client, the techniques you've learned should cover what you need. The application is running live at http://daveandal.net/books/4923, where you can also download all of the source code in both Visual Basic .NET and C#.

Epilogue

It was on a fine evening that Cressey found himself in the park and wondered if he'd even been there before when he wasn't following someone. He'd never really noticed the lake before, except as a means of keeping a distance from someone. Now he had time to take in its size, the way the reeds kept rustling in the light breeze and the ducks making a beeline straight for him. The ducklings were struggling to keep up with their parents. He liked ducks and often fed them during his tails. It gave him an excuse to look inconspicuous.

He smiled and sat down to watch, feeling peaceful for the first time since that rain soaked night seven months ago. He'd been watching the grubby apartment, hugging the shadows around a large tree when it happened. He shuddered and tried to forget about the roller coaster his life had been since then. He closed his eyes and let the rays of the dimming sun warm his face and accepted what had happened. He couldn't change that. He had learned a lot and wondered whether he really wanted to go through it all again. The offer was tempting, but he just wasn't sure. Maybe he'd make the decision tomorrow....

Index

ASP Today

ASPToday is a unique solutions library for professional ASP Developers, giving quick and convenient access to a constantly growing library of **over 1000 practical and relevant articles and case studies**. We aim to publish a completely original professionally written and reviewed article every working day of the year. Consequently our resource is completely without parallel in the industry. Thousands of web developers use and recommend this site for real solutions, keeping up to date with new technologies, or simply increasing their knowledge.

Exciting Site Features!

Find it FAST!
Powerful full-text search engine so you can find exactly the solution you need.

Printer-friendly!
Print articles for a bound archive and quick desk reference.

Working Sample Code Solutions!
Many articles include complete downloadable sample code ready to adapt for your own projects.

ASPToday covers a broad range of topics including:

- ▶ ASP.NET 1.x and 2.0
- ▶ ADO.NET and SQL
- ▶ XML
- ▶ Web Services
- ▶ E-Commerce

- ▶ Security
- ▶ Site Design
- ▶ Site Admin
- ▶ SMTP and Mail
- ▶ Classic ASP and ADO

and much, much more…

To receive a FREE two-month subscription to ASPToday, visit **www.asptoday.com/subscribe.aspx** and answer the question about this book!

forums.apress.com

JOIN THE APRESS FORUMS AND BE PART OF OUR COMMUNITY. You'll find discussions that cover topics of interest to IT professionals, programmers, and enthusiasts just like you. If you post a query to one of our forums, you can expect that some of the best minds in the business—especially Apress authors, who all write with *The Expert's Voice™*—will chime in to help you. Why not aim to become one of our most valuable participants (MVPs) and win cool stuff? Here's a sampling of what you'll find:

DATABASES
Data drives everything.
Share information, exchange ideas, and discuss any database programming or administration issues.

INTERNET TECHNOLOGIES AND NETWORKING
Try living without plumbing (and eventually IPv6).
Talk about networking topics including protocols, design, administration, wireless, wired, storage, backup, certifications, trends, and new technologies.

JAVA
We've come a long way from the old Oak tree.
Hang out and discuss Java in whatever flavor you choose: J2SE, J2EE, J2ME, Jakarta, and so on.

MAC OS X
All about the Zen of OS X.
OS X is both the present and the future for Mac apps. Make suggestions, offer up ideas, or boast about your new hardware.

OPEN SOURCE
Source code is good; understanding (open) source is better.
Discuss open source technologies and related topics such as PHP, MySQL, Linux, Perl, Apache, Python, and more.

PROGRAMMING/BUSINESS
Unfortunately, it is.
Talk about the Apress line of books that cover software methodology, best practices, and how programmers interact with the "suits."

WEB DEVELOPMENT/DESIGN
Ugly doesn't cut it anymore, and CGI is absurd.
Help is in sight for your site. Find design solutions for your projects and get ideas for building an interactive Web site.

SECURITY
Lots of bad guys out there—the good guys need help.
Discuss computer and network security issues here. Just don't let anyone else know the answers!

TECHNOLOGY IN ACTION
Cool things. Fun things.
It's after hours. It's time to play. Whether you're into LEGO® MINDSTORMS™ or turning an old PC into a DVR, this is where technology turns into fun.

WINDOWS
No defenestration here.
Ask questions about all aspects of Windows programming, get help on Microsoft technologies covered in Apress books, or provide feedback on any Apress Windows book.

HOW TO PARTICIPATE:
Go to the Apress Forums site at **http://forums.apress.com/**.
Click the New User link.